Table of Contents

BETA ESTIMATES FOR VALUATION AND COST OF CAPITAL

CAPM, Down-market, and Up-market Betas by Industry

Data for Common Stocks,
Preferred Stocks, and Mutual Funds
As of the End of the 1st Quarter, 2017

G. Michael Phillips

William P. Jennings

James Chong

George Arzumanyan

WALNUT OAK PRESS

ISBN: 978-0-9989077-9-6

Suggested Citation
Phillips, G. M., Jennings, W., Chong, J. & Arzumanyan, G. (2017). *Beta Estimates for Valuation & Cost of Capital: CAPM, Down-market, & Up-market Betas by Industry: Data for Common Stocks, Preferred Stocks, and Mutual Funds, As of the End of the 1st Quarter, 2017*. Pasadena, CA: Walnut Oak Press.

Business Director: Robert Neff, CPA, ABV
Art Director: Austin Fuentes

A Note from the Authors

Valuation analysts are concerned with estimating the present value of future benefit streams (usually earnings or cash flows), using some risk-adjusted discount rate.

This may be computed using a "build-up" method, a "weighted average cost of capital" approach (when capital structure is assumed to be fixed), or it might be done using a statistical equation relating a discount rate to various external or market factors.

Perhaps the most common way to estimate a discount rate is to use a variation of the Capital Asset Pricing Model (CAPM), which relates expected returns of an asset to the expected returns of a broad stock market index. The original CAPM approach assumed that the expected responses by an asset to changes in the benchmark index were symmetrical in that a 1 unit increase in the index would be expected to generate the same absolute response as a 1 unit decrease.

Research has shown that such an assumption of strict symmetry is rarely maintained. Rather, the up-market response (when the benchmark goes up in value) might be larger or smaller than the associated down-market response (when the benchmark falls in value).

Two papers, attached as appendices in the main volumes of this series, explain in detail the use and computation of these different up-market and down-market beta statistics, their relationship to traditional CAPM Beta, and their use in estimating discount rates and cost of capital estimates. These papers in part discuss the use of a down-market beta rather than a traditional CAPM beta, which may give more accurate statements of an asset's expected loss when markets fall. Such "downside measures" might be better interpreted as what risk premia in discount rates are intended to capture in the sense that risk is usually associated with losses, and unexpected gains aren't usually considered as "risk".

The tables in this book provide up-market, down-market, and CAPM beta estimates by two-, three-, and four-digit SIC codes, using data for common stocks and preferred stocks in separate tables. In addition, tables are provided using Net Asset Value data (akin to prices) for mutual funds organized by fund type. For a given asset type and SIC code or fund category, the tables provide the mean, median, and various percentile values as well as a count of how many assets were in the analysis population.

This presentation of the up-market and down-market betas is among the most complete available. The use of common stock data provides a tool for general equity valuation. The use of preferred stocks provides a measure that can be used for somewhat more senior holdings and might be used by valuation analysts as a proxy for a wide range of private ownership structures.

The use of mutual fund-based beta estimates derived from mutual fund data provides a new resource for valuation analysts. There are many mutual fund categories, with descriptions based on the size of companies being targeted for investment, the geographical locations of the investments, and even other asset types, such as various types of bond funds, international holdings funds, and other more specific strategies, including "narrowness" and "broadness" of holdings. The sophisticated valuation analyst may find a reasonable proxy for a current exercise by selecting beta data for an appropriate corresponding mutual fund which may represent specific industry or holding company composition.

The data in this book are estimated using approximately one year of daily data, culminating on the date given for the table. These volumes are intended to be updated quarterly. Some beta estimations are performed using monthly data and a three- to five-year look-back period. However, the quality of estimates using the longer term monthly data are not as good as those obtained using a year of daily data. First, even five years of monthly data provides just 60 observations compared to the over 200 observations when using daily trading data. Second, the observed CAPM beta is essentially a weighted average of the up-market and down-market betas, where the proportions for weighting are based on the proportion of "up" versus "down" days (or months) for the benchmark. Consequently, even when there an equal number of up and down months, the five years of monthly estimates would tend to have only 30 observations for estimating up-market or down-market betas compared to over 100 expected observations using daily data. Third, the mix of up and down days or months is not the same year to year, so there is a tendency to blur the up-market and down-market betas in the estimation process. The bottom line is that research indicates greater forecasting accuracy for future betas, whether CAPM, up-market, or down-market, when using daily rather than monthly data.

Finally, the valuation analyst should take careful note of the percentile values provided. As part of a valuation exercise, one might simply choose to use the midpoint (median) or perhaps the average. However, as the valuation proceeds, a better sense of how the target company compares to its industry may develop. For superior (or more financially stable, longer established, or better diversified) companies, it may be desirable to use a lower beta than just the midpoint; for relatively inferior (or smaller, newer, or otherwise riskier) companies, it may be desirable to use a higher beta than just the midpoint. We have provided a range of estimates facilitating the computation of 95% confidence intervals for valuation.

Each new volume will be available from www.WalnutOakPress.com and from select distributors soon after the new quarter. Several of the tables are also separately available for purchase in an e-book format. The data are generated using the www.MacroRisk.com online research platform and are used with permission.

Table of Contents for SIC Codes

Sorted by description

Disclaimer: some SIC codes may not appear in this book.

Table of Contents for SIC Codes

Sorted by description

Table of Contents for SIC Codes

Sorted by description

Table of Contents for SIC Codes

Sorted by description

Table of Contents for SIC Codes

Sorted by description

Table of Contents for SIC Codes

Sorted by description

SIC Code	Description	Dvision Description
3576	Computer Communications Equipment	Manufacturing
7376	Computer Facilities Management Services	Services
7373	Computer Integrated Systems Design	Services
7378	Computer Maintenance And Repair	Services
3577	Computer Peripheral Equipment, Nec	Manufacturing
3577	Computer Peripheral Equipment, Not Elsewhere Classified	Manufacturing
7374	Computer Processing And Data Preparation And Processing Services	Services
7371	Computer Programming Services	Services
737	Computer Programming, Data Processing, And Other Computer Related	Services
7379	Computer Related Services, Not Elsewhere Classified	Services
7377	Computer Rental And Leasing	Services
3572	Computer Storage Devices	Manufacturing
3572	Computer Storage Devices	Manufacturing
3575	Computer Terminals	Manufacturing
3575	Computer Terminals	Manufacturing
5045	Computers And Computer Peripheral Equipment And Software	Wholesale Trade
3271	Concrete Block And Brick	Manufacturing
3272	Concrete Products, Except Block & Brick	Manufacturing
3272	Concrete Products, Except Block And Brick	Manufacturing
177	Concrete Work	Construction
1771	Concrete Work	Construction
3270	Concrete, Gypsum & Plaster Products	Manufacturing
327	Concrete, Gypsum, And Plaster Products	Manufacturing
5145	Confectionery	Wholesale Trade
15	Construction	Construction
1700	Construction - Special Trade Contractors	Construction
5082	Construction And Mining (Except Petroleum) Machinery And Equipment	Wholesale Trade
3531	Construction Machinery & Equip	Manufacturing
3531	Construction Machinery And Equipment	Manufacturing
5039	Construction Materials, Not Elsewhere Classified	Wholesale Trade
1442	Construction Sand And Gravel	Mining
3530	Construction, Mining & Materials Handling Machinery & Equip	Manufacturing
353	Construction, Mining, And Materials Handling Machinery And Equipment	Manufacturing
17	Construction-Special Trade Contractors	Construction
732	Consumer Credit Reporting Agencies, Mercantile Reporting Agencies	Services
2670	Converted Paper & Paperboard Prods (No Contaners/Boxes)	Manufacturing
267	Converted Paper And Paperboard Products, Except Containers And Boxes	Manufacturing
2679	Converted Paper And Paperboard Products, Not Elsewhere Classified	Manufacturing
3535	Conveyors And Conveying Equipment	Manufacturing
2052	Cookies & Crackers	Manufacturing
2052	Cookies And Crackers	Manufacturing
3366	Copper Foundries	Manufacturing
102	Copper Ores	Mining
1021	Copper Ores	Mining
2298	Cordage And Twine	Manufacturing
0115	Corn	Agriculture, Forestry, And Fishing
9223	Correctional Institutions	Public Adminstration
2653	Corrugated And Solid Fiber Boxes	Manufacturing
3960	Costume Jewelry & Novelties	Manufacturing
3961	Costume Jewelry And Costume Novelties, Except Precious Metal	Manufacturing
396	Costume Jewelry, Costume Novelties, Buttons, And Miscellaneous	Manufacturing
0131	Cotton	Agriculture, Forestry, And Fishing
0724	Cotton Ginning	Agriculture, Forestry, And Fishing
2074	Cottonseed Oil Mills	Manufacturing
4215	Courier Services, Except By Air	Transportation, Communications, Electric, Gas, And Sanitary Service
921	Courts	Public Adminstration
9211	Courts	Public Adminstration
2021	Creamery Butter	Manufacturing
7323	Credit Reporting Services	Services
606	Credit Unions	Finance, Insurance, And Real Estate
6061	Credit Unions, Federally Chartered	Finance, Insurance, And Real Estate
6062	Credit Unions, Not Federally Chartered	Finance, Insurance, And Real Estate
0722	Crop Harvesting, Primarily By Machine	Agriculture, Forestry, And Fishing
0721	Crop Planting, Cultivating, And Protecting	Agriculture, Forestry, And Fishing

Table of Contents for SIC Codes

Sorted by description

Table of Contents for SIC Codes

Sorted by description

Table of Contents for SIC Codes

Sorted by description

SIC Code	Description	Dvision Description
821	Elementary And Secondary Schools	Services
8211	Elementary And Secondary Schools	Services
3534	Elevators And Moving Stairways	Manufacturing
7361	Employment Agencies	Services
3431	Enameled Iron And Metal Sanitary Ware	Manufacturing
8711	Engineering Services	Services
87	Engineering, Accounting, Research, Management, And Related Services	Services
871	Engineering, Architectural, And Surveying Services	Services
3510	Engines & Turbines	Manufacturing
351	Engines And Turbines	Manufacturing
2677	Envelopes	Manufacturing
7359	Equipment Rental And Leasing, Not Elsewhere Classified	Services
1794	Excavation Work	Construction
913	Executive And Legislative Offices Combined	Public Adminstration
9131	Executive And Legislative Offices Combined	Public Adminstration
911	Executive Offices	Public Adminstration
9111	Executive Offices	Public Adminstration
91	Executive, Legislative, And General Government, Except Finance	Public Adminstration
2892	Explosives	Manufacturing
34	Fabricated Metal Products, Except Machinery And Transportation Equipment	Manufacturing
3499	Fabricated Metal Products, Not Elsewhere Classified	Manufacturing
3498	Fabricated Pipe And Pipe Fittings	Manufacturing
3443	Fabricated Plate Work (Boiler Shops)	Manufacturing
3443	Fabricated Plate Work (Boiler Shops)	Manufacturing
3060	Fabricated Rubber Products, Nec	Manufacturing
306	Fabricated Rubber Products, Not Elsewhere Classified	Manufacturing
3069	Fabricated Rubber Products, Not Elsewhere Classified	Manufacturing
3441	Fabricated Structural Metal	Manufacturing
344	Fabricated Structural Metal Products	Manufacturing
3440	Fabricated Structural Metal Products	Manufacturing
2399	Fabricated Textile Products, Not Elsewhere Classified	Manufacturing
8744	Facilities Support Management Services	Services
565	Family Clothing Stores	Retail Trade
5651	Family Clothing Stores	Retail Trade
352	Farm And Garden Machinery And Equipment	Manufacturing
5083	Farm And Garden Machinery And Equipment	Wholesale Trade
076	Farm Labor And Management Services	Agriculture, Forestry, And Fishing
0761	Farm Labor Contractors And Crew Leaders	Agriculture, Forestry, And Fishing
3523	Farm Machinery & Equipment	Manufacturing
3523	Farm Machinery And Equipment	Manufacturing
0762	Farm Management Services	Agriculture, Forestry, And Fishing
4221	Farm Product Warehousing And Storage	Transportation, Communications, Electric, Gas, And Sanitary Service
5191	Farm Supplies	Wholesale Trade
515	Farm-Product Raw Materials	Wholesale Trade
5159	Farm-Product Raw Materials, Not Elsewhere Classified	Wholesale Trade
3965	Fasteners, Buttons, Needles, And Pins	Manufacturing
2070	Fats & Oils	Manufacturing
207	Fats And Oils	Manufacturing
6111	Federal & Federally-Sponsored Credit Agencies	Finance, Insurance, And Real Estate
611	Federal And Federally-Sponsored Credit Agencies	Finance, Insurance, And Real Estate
6111	Federal And Federally-Sponsored Credit Agencies	Finance, Insurance, And Real Estate
6011	Federal Reserve Banks	Finance, Insurance, And Real Estate
4482	Ferries	Transportation, Communications, Electric, Gas, And Sanitary Service
106	Ferroalloy Ores, Except Vanadium	Mining
1061	Ferroalloy Ores, Except Vanadium	Mining
2875	Fertilizers, Mixing Only	Manufacturing
2655	Fiber Cans, Tubes, Drums, And Similar Products	Manufacturing
013	Field Crops, Except Cash Grains	Agriculture, Forestry, And Fishing
0139	Field Crops, Except Cash Grains, Not Elsewhere Classified	Agriculture, Forestry, And Fishing
6172	Finance Lessors	Finance, Insurance, And Real Estate
6199	Finance Services	Finance, Insurance, And Real Estate
3263	Fine Earthenware (Whiteware) Table And Kitchen Articles	Manufacturing
0912	Finfish	Agriculture, Forestry, And Fishing
2261	Finishers Of Broadwoven Fabrics Of Cotton	Manufacturing

Table of Contents for SIC Codes

Sorted by description

Table of Contents for SIC Codes

Sorted by description

SIC Code	Description	Dvision Description
5021	Furniture	Wholesale Trade
25	Furniture And Fixtures	Manufacturing
2599	Furniture And Fixtures, Not Elsewhere Classified	Manufacturing
502	Furniture And Homefurnishings	Wholesale Trade
5712	Furniture Stores	Retail Trade
3944	Games, Toys & Children's Vehicles (No Dolls & Bicycles)	Manufacturing
3944	Games, Toys, And Children's Vehicles, Except Dolls And Bicycles	Manufacturing
7212	Garment Pressing, And Agents For Laundries And Drycleaners	Services
4932	Gas & Other Services Combined	Transportation, Communications, Electric, Gas, And Sanitary Service
4932	Gas And Other Services Combined	Transportation, Communications, Electric, Gas, And Sanitary Service
492	Gas Production And Distribution	Transportation, Communications, Electric, Gas, And Sanitary Service
3050	Gaskets, Packg & Sealg Devices & Rubber & Plastics Hose	Manufacturing
3053	Gaskets, Packing, And Sealing Devices	Manufacturing
305	Gaskets, Packing, And Sealing Devices And Rubber And Plastics Hose	Manufacturing
554	Gasoline Service Stations	Retail Trade
5541	Gasoline Service Stations	Retail Trade
7538	General Automotive Repair Shops	Services
1540	General Bldg Contractors - Nonresidential Bldgs	Construction
1520	General Bldg Contractors - Residential Bldgs	Construction
154	General Building Contractors-Nonresidential Buildings	Construction
152	General Building Contractors-Residential Buildings	Construction
1541	General Contractors-Industrial Buildings And Warehouses	Construction
1542	General Contractors-Nonresidential Buildings, Other Than Industrial	Construction
1522	General Contractors-Residential Buildings, Other Than Single-Family	Construction
1521	General Contractors-Single-Family Houses	Construction
019	General Farms, Primarily Crop	Agriculture, Forestry, And Fishing
0191	General Farms, Primarily Crop	Agriculture, Forestry, And Fishing
029	General Farms, Primarily Livestock And Animal Specialties	Agriculture, Forestry, And Fishing
0291	General Farms, Primarily Livestock And Animal Specialties	Agriculture, Forestry, And Fishing
919	General Government, Not Elsewhere Classified	Public Adminstration
9199	General Government, Not Elsewhere Classified	Public Adminstration
3560	General Industrial Machinery & Equipment	Manufacturing
3569	General Industrial Machinery & Equipment, Nec	Manufacturing
356	General Industrial Machinery And Equipment	Manufacturing
3569	General Industrial Machinery And Equipment, Not Elsewhere Classified	Manufacturing
0219	General Livestock, Except Dairy And Poultry	Agriculture, Forestry, And Fishing
8062	General Medical And Surgical Hospitals	Services
53	General Merchandise Stores	Retail Trade
4225	General Warehousing And Storage	Transportation, Communications, Electric, Gas, And Sanitary Service
5947	Gift, Novelty, And Souvenir Shops	Retail Trade
2361	Girls', Children's, And Infants' Dresses, Blouses, And Shirts	Manufacturing
236	Girls', Children's, And Infants' Outerwear	Manufacturing
2369	Girls', Children's, And Infants' Outerwear, Not Elsewhere Classified	Manufacturing
3220	Glass & Glassware, Pressed Or Blown	Manufacturing
322	Glass And Glassware, Pressed Or Blown	Manufacturing
1793	Glass And Glazing Work	Construction
3221	Glass Containers	Manufacturing
3221	Glass Containers	Manufacturing
1793	Glass Installation, Except Automotive-Contractors	Construction
323	Glass Products, Made Of Purchased Glass	Manufacturing
3231	Glass Products, Made Of Purchased Glass	Manufacturing
3231	Glass Products, Made Of Purchased Glass	Manufacturing
104	Gold And Silver Ores	Mining
1040	Gold And Silver Ores	Mining
1041	Gold Ores	Mining
5153	Grain And Field Beans	Wholesale Trade
204	Grain Mill Products	Manufacturing
2040	Grain Mill Products	Manufacturing
0172	Grapes	Agriculture, Forestry, And Fishing
3321	Gray And Ductile Iron Foundries	Manufacturing
277	Greeting Cards	Manufacturing
2771	Greeting Cards	Manufacturing
2771	Greeting Cards	Manufacturing
514	Groceries And Related Products	Wholesale Trade

Table of Contents for SIC Codes

Sorted by description

Table of Contents for SIC Codes

Sorted by description

Table of Contents for SIC Codes

Sorted by description

SIC Code	Description	Dvision Description
6282	Investment Advice	Finance, Insurance, And Real Estate
672	Investment Offices	Finance, Insurance, And Real Estate
6799	Investors, Nec	Finance, Insurance, And Real Estate
6799	Investors, Not Elsewhere Classified	Finance, Insurance, And Real Estate
0134	Irish Potatoes	Agriculture, Forestry, And Fishing
3320	Iron & Steel Foundries	Manufacturing
3462	Iron And Steel Forgings	Manufacturing
332	Iron And Steel Foundries	Manufacturing
101	Iron Ores	Mining
1011	Iron Ores	Mining
497	Irrigation Systems	Transportation, Communications, Electric, Gas, And Sanitary Service
4971	Irrigation Systems	Transportation, Communications, Electric, Gas, And Sanitary Service
3915	Jewelers' Findings And Materials, And Lapidary Work	Manufacturing
5944	Jewelry Stores	Retail Trade
3911	Jewelry, Precious Metal	Manufacturing
3911	Jewelry, Precious Metal	Manufacturing
3910	Jewelry, Silverware & Plated Ware	Manufacturing
391	Jewelry, Silverware, And Plated Ware	Manufacturing
5094	Jewelry, Watches, Precious Stones, And Precious Metals	Wholesale Trade
833	Job Training And Vocational Rehabilitation Services	Services
8331	Job Training And Vocational Rehabilitation Services	Services
8222	Junior Colleges And Technical Institutes	Services
92	Justice, Public Order, And Safety	Public Adminstration
1455	Kaolin And Ball Clay	Mining
8092	Kidney Dialysis Centers	Services
2253	Knit Outerwear Mills	Manufacturing
2253	Knit Outerwear Mills	Manufacturing
2254	Knit Underwear And Nightwear Mills	Manufacturing
225	Knitting Mills	Manufacturing
2250	Knitting Mills	Manufacturing
2259	Knitting Mills, Not Elsewhere Classified	Manufacturing
863	Labor Unions And Similar Labor Organizations	Services
8631	Labor Unions And Similar Labor Organizations	Services
3826	Laboratory Analytical Instruments	Manufacturing
3826	Laboratory Analytical Instruments	Manufacturing
3821	Laboratory Apparatus & Furniture	Manufacturing
382	Laboratory Apparatus And Analytical, Optical, Measuring, And Control	Manufacturing
3821	Laboratory Apparatus And Furniture	Manufacturing
2258	Lace And Warp Knit Fabric Mills	Manufacturing
3083	Laminated Plastics Plate, Sheet, And Profile Shapes	Manufacturing
6552	Land Subdividers & Developers (No Cemeteries)	Finance, Insurance, And Real Estate
655	Land Subdividers And Developers	Finance, Insurance, And Real Estate
6552	Land Subdividers And Developers, Except Cemeteries	Finance, Insurance, And Real Estate
9512	Land, Mineral, Wildlife, And Forest Conservation	Public Adminstration
078	Landscape And Horticultural Services	Agriculture, Forestry, And Fishing
0781	Landscape Counseling And Planning	Agriculture, Forestry, And Fishing
7219	Laundry And Garment Services, Not Elsewhere Classified	Services
721	Laundry, Cleaning, And Garment Services	Services
3524	Lawn & Garden Tractors & Home Lawn & Gardens Equip	Manufacturing
0782	Lawn And Garden Services	Agriculture, Forestry, And Fishing
3524	Lawn And Garden Tractors And Home Lawn And Garden Equipment	Manufacturing
103	Lead And Zinc Ores	Mining
1031	Lead And Zinc Ores	Mining
3952	Lead Pencils, Crayons, And Artists' Materials	Manufacturing
3100	Leather & Leather Products	Manufacturing
31	Leather And Leather Products	Manufacturing
2386	Leather And Sheep-Lined Clothing	Manufacturing
315	Leather Gloves And Mittens	Manufacturing
3151	Leather Gloves And Mittens	Manufacturing
319	Leather Goods, Not Elsewhere Classified	Manufacturing
3199	Leather Goods, Not Elsewhere Classified	Manufacturing
311	Leather Tanning And Finishing	Manufacturing
3111	Leather Tanning And Finishing	Manufacturing
9222	Legal Counsel And Prosecution	Public Adminstration

Table of Contents for SIC Codes

Sorted by description

Table of Contents for SIC Codes

Sorted by description

Table of Contents for SIC Codes

Sorted by description

Table of Contents for SIC Codes

Sorted by description

Table of Contents for SIC Codes

Sorted by description

Table of Contents for SIC Codes

Sorted by description

SIC Code	Description	Dvision Description
1382	Oil And Gas Field Exploration Services	Mining
3533	Oil And Gas Field Machinery And Equipment	Manufacturing
138	Oil And Gas Field Services	Mining
1389	Oil And Gas Field Services, Not Elsewhere Classified	Mining
6792	Oil Royalty Traders	Finance, Insurance, And Real Estate
6792	Oil Royalty Traders	Finance, Insurance, And Real Estate
153	Operative Builders	Construction
1531	Operative Builders	Construction
1531	Operative Builders	Construction
6513	Operators Of Apartment Buildings	Finance, Insurance, And Real Estate
6513	Operators Of Apartment Buildings	Finance, Insurance, And Real Estate
6514	Operators Of Dwellings Other Than Apartment Buildings	Finance, Insurance, And Real Estate
6512	Operators Of Nonresidential Buildings	Finance, Insurance, And Real Estate
6512	Operators Of Nonresidential Buildings	Finance, Insurance, And Real Estate
6515	Operators Of Residential Mobile Home Sites	Finance, Insurance, And Real Estate
385	Ophthalmic Goods	Manufacturing
3851	Ophthalmic Goods	Manufacturing
3851	Ophthalmic Goods	Manufacturing
5048	Ophthalmic Goods	Wholesale Trade
5995	Optical Goods Stores	Retail Trade
3827	Optical Instruments & Lenses	Manufacturing
3827	Optical Instruments And Lenses	Manufacturing
3480	Ordnance & Accessories, (No Vehicles/Guided Missiles)	Manufacturing
348	Ordnance And Accessories, Except Vehicles And Guided Missiles	Manufacturing
3489	Ordnance And Accessories, Not Elsewhere Classified	Manufacturing
704	Organization Hotels And Lodging Houses, On Membership Basis	Services
7041	Organization Hotels And Lodging Houses, On Membership Basis	Services
0181	Ornamental Floriculture And Nursery Products	Agriculture, Forestry, And Fishing
0783	Ornamental Shrub And Tree Services	Agriculture, Forestry, And Fishing
3842	Orthopedic, Prosthetic & Surgical Appliances & Supplies	Manufacturing
3842	Orthopedic, Prosthetic, And Surgical Appliances And Supplies	Manufacturing
7312	Outdoor Advertising Services	Services
3536	Overhead Traveling Cranes, Hoists, And Monorail Systems	Manufacturing
5142	Packaged Frozen Foods	Wholesale Trade
3565	Packaging Machinery	Manufacturing
2671	Packaging Paper And Plastics Film, Coated And Laminated	Manufacturing
4783	Packing And Crating	Transportation, Communications, Electric, Gas, And Sanitary Service
523	Paint, Glass, And Wallpaper Stores	Retail Trade
5231	Paint, Glass, And Wallpaper Stores	Retail Trade
172	Painting And Paper Hanging	Construction
1721	Painting And Paper Hanging	Construction
5198	Paints, Varnishes, And Supplies	Wholesale Trade
2851	Paints, Varnishes, Lacquers, Enamels & Allied Prods	Manufacturing
285	Paints, Varnishes, Lacquers, Enamels, And Allied Products	Manufacturing
2851	Paints, Varnishes, Lacquers, Enamels, And Allied Products	Manufacturing
26	Paper And Allied Products	Manufacturing
511	Paper And Paper Products	Wholesale Trade
3554	Paper Industries Machinery	Manufacturing
262	Paper Mills	Manufacturing
2621	Paper Mills	Manufacturing
2621	Paper Mills	Manufacturing
2650	Paperboard Containers & Boxes	Manufacturing
265	Paperboard Containers And Boxes	Manufacturing
263	Paperboard Mills	Manufacturing
2631	Paperboard Mills	Manufacturing
2631	Paperboard Mills	Manufacturing
2600	Papers & Allied Products	Manufacturing
2540	Partitions, Shelvg, Lockers, & Office & Store Fixtures	Manufacturing
254	Partitions, Shelving, Lockers, And Office And Store Fixtures	Manufacturing
7515	Passenger Car Leasing	Services
7514	Passenger Car Rental	Services
6794	Patent Owners & Lessors	Finance, Insurance, And Real Estate
6794	Patent Owners And Lessors	Finance, Insurance, And Real Estate
3951	Pens, Mechanical Pencils, And Parts	Manufacturing

Table of Contents for SIC Codes

Sorted by description

SIC Code	Description	Dvision Description
3950	Pens, Pencils & Other Artists' Materials	Manufacturing
395	Pens, Pencils, And Other Artists' Materials	Manufacturing
637	Pension, Health, And Welfare Funds	Finance, Insurance, And Real Estate
6371	Pension, Health, And Welfare Funds	Finance, Insurance, And Real Estate
2844	Perfumes, Cosmetics & Other Toilet Preparations	Manufacturing
2844	Perfumes, Cosmetics, And Other Toilet Preparations	Manufacturing
2721	Periodicals: Publishing Or Publishing & Printing	Manufacturing
272	Periodicals: Publishing, Or Publishing And Printing	Manufacturing
2721	Periodicals: Publishing, Or Publishing And Printing	Manufacturing
614	Personal Credit Institutions	Finance, Insurance, And Real Estate
6141	Personal Credit Institutions	Finance, Insurance, And Real Estate
6141	Personal Credit Institutions	Finance, Insurance, And Real Estate
3172	Personal Leather Goods, Except Women's Handbags And Purses	Manufacturing
72	Personal Services	Services
736	Personnel Supply Services	Services
2879	Pesticides And Agricultural Chemicals, Not Elsewhere Classified	Manufacturing
517	Petroleum And Petroleum Products	Wholesale Trade
5172	Petroleum And Petroleum Products Wholesalers, Except Bulk Station	Wholesale Trade
5171	Petroleum Bulk Stations And Terminals	Wholesale Trade
291	Petroleum Refining	Manufacturing
2911	Petroleum Refining	Manufacturing
2911	Petroleum Refining	Manufacturing
29	Petroleum Refining And Related Industries	Manufacturing
2834	Pharmaceutical Preparations	Manufacturing
2834	Pharmaceutical Preparations	Manufacturing
3652	Phonograph Records & Prerecorded Audio Tapes & Disks	Manufacturing
3652	Phonograph Records And Prerecorded Audio Tapes And Disks	Manufacturing
1475	Phosphate Rock	Mining
2874	Phosphatic Fertilizers	Manufacturing
7334	Photocopying And Duplicating Services	Services
7384	Photofinishing Laboratories	Services
3861	Photographic Equipment & Supplies	Manufacturing
386	Photographic Equipment And Supplies	Manufacturing
3861	Photographic Equipment And Supplies	Manufacturing
5043	Photographic Equipment And Supplies	Wholesale Trade
722	Photographic Studios, Portrait	Services
7221	Photographic Studios, Portrait	Services
7991	Physical Fitness Facilities	Services
2035	Pickled Fruits And Vegetables, Vegetable Sauces And Seasonings	Manufacturing
5131	Piece Goods, Notions, And Other Dry Goods	Wholesale Trade
4610	Pipe Lines (No Natural Gas)	Transportation, Communications, Electric, Gas, And Sanitary Service
46	Pipelines, Except Natural Gas	Transportation, Communications, Electric, Gas, And Sanitary Service
461	Pipelines, Except Natural Gas	Transportation, Communications, Electric, Gas, And Sanitary Service
4619	Pipelines, Not Elsewhere Classified	Transportation, Communications, Electric, Gas, And Sanitary Service
1742	Plastering, Drywall, Acoustical, And Insulation Work	Construction
2820	Plastic Material, Synth Resin/Rubber, Cellulos (No Glass)	Manufacturing
2821	Plastic Materials, Synth Resins & Nonvulcan Elastomers	Manufacturing
3085	Plastics Bottles	Manufacturing
3086	Plastics Foam Products	Manufacturing
3086	Plastics Foam Products	Manufacturing
5162	Plastics Materials And Basic Forms And Shapes	Wholesale Trade
282	Plastics Materials And Synthetic Resins, Synthetic Rubber, Cellulosic Manmade Fibers	Manufacturing
2821	Plastics Materials, Synthetic Resins, And Nonvulcanizable Elastomers	Manufacturing
3084	Plastics Pipe	Manufacturing
3088	Plastics Plumbing Fixtures	Manufacturing
3089	Plastics Products, Nec	Manufacturing
3089	Plastics Products, Not Elsewhere Classified	Manufacturing
2673	Plastics, Foil & Coated Paper Bags	Manufacturing
2673	Plastics, Foil, And Coated Paper Bags	Manufacturing
2796	Platemaking And Related Services	Manufacturing
2395	Pleating, Decorative And Novelty Stitching, And Tucking	Manufacturing
5074	Plumbing And Heating Equipment And Supplies (Hydronics)	Wholesale Trade
3432	Plumbing Fixture Fittings And Trim	Manufacturing

Table of Contents for SIC Codes

Sorted by description

SIC Code	Description	Dvision Description
171	Plumbing, Heating And Air-Conditioning	Construction
1711	Plumbing, Heating And Air-Conditioning	Construction
9221	Police Protection	Public Adminstration
865	Political Organizations	Services
8651	Political Organizations	Services
3264	Porcelain Electrical Supplies	Manufacturing
1474	Potash, Soda, And Borate Minerals	Mining
2096	Potato Chips, Corn Chips, And Similar Snacks	Manufacturing
3260	Pottery & Related Products	Manufacturing
326	Pottery And Related Products	Manufacturing
3269	Pottery Products, Not Elsewhere Classified	Manufacturing
025	Poultry And Eggs	Agriculture, Forestry, And Fishing
0259	Poultry And Eggs, Not Elsewhere Classified	Agriculture, Forestry, And Fishing
5144	Poultry And Poultry Products	Wholesale Trade
0254	Poultry Hatcheries	Agriculture, Forestry, And Fishing
2015	Poultry Slaughtering And Processing	Manufacturing
2015	Poultry Slaughtering And Processing	Manufacturing
7211	Power Laundries, Family And Commercial	Services
3612	Power, Distribution & Specialty Transformers	Manufacturing
3612	Power, Distribution, And Specialty Transformers	Manufacturing
3546	Power-Driven Handtools	Manufacturing
3448	Prefabricated Metal Buildings & Components	Manufacturing
3448	Prefabricated Metal Buildings And Components	Manufacturing
2452	Prefabricated Wood Bldgs & Components	Manufacturing
2452	Prefabricated Wood Buildings And Components	Manufacturing
7372	Prepackaged Software	Services
2048	Prepared Feeds And Feed Ingredients For Animals And Fowls, Except Dog And Cat	Manufacturing
2045	Prepared Flour Mixes And Doughs	Manufacturing
2092	Prepared Fresh Or Frozen Fish & Seafoods	Manufacturing
2092	Prepared Fresh Or Frozen Fish And Seafoods	Manufacturing
3229	Pressed And Blown Glass And Glassware, Not Elsewhere Classified	Manufacturing
3692	Primary Batteries, Dry And Wet	Manufacturing
33	Primary Metal Industries	Manufacturing
3399	Primary Metal Products, Not Elsewhere Classified	Manufacturing
3334	Primary Production Of Aluminum	Manufacturing
3334	Primary Production Of Aluminum	Manufacturing
3330	Primary Smelting & Refining Of Nonferrous Metals	Manufacturing
3331	Primary Smelting And Refining Of Copper	Manufacturing
333	Primary Smelting And Refining Of Nonferrous Metals	Manufacturing
3339	Primary Smelting And Refining Of Nonferrous Metals, Except Copper	Manufacturing
3672	Printed Circuit Boards	Manufacturing
3672	Printed Circuit Boards	Manufacturing
5111	Printing And Writing Paper	Wholesale Trade
2893	Printing Ink	Manufacturing
3555	Printing Trades Machinery & Equipment	Manufacturing
3555	Printing Trades Machinery And Equipment	Manufacturing
27	Printing, Publishing, And Allied Industries	Manufacturing
88	Private Households	Services
881	Private Households	Services
8811	Private Households	Services
2999	Products Of Petroleum And Coal, Not Elsewhere Classified	Manufacturing
504	Professional And Commercial Equipment And Supplies	Wholesale Trade
5049	Professional Equipment And Supplies, Not Elsewhere Classified	Wholesale Trade
862	Professional Membership Organizations	Services
8621	Professional Membership Organizations	Services
7941	Professional Sports Clubs And Promoters	Services
8063	Psychiatric Hospitals	Services
2531	Public Bldg & Related Furniture	Manufacturing
253	Public Building And Related Furniture	Manufacturing
2531	Public Building And Related Furniture	Manufacturing
93	Public Finance, Taxation, And Monetary Policy	Public Adminstration
931	Public Finance, Taxation, And Monetary Policy	Public Adminstration
9311	Public Finance, Taxation, And Monetary Policy	Public Adminstration

Table of Contents for SIC Codes

Sorted by description

SIC Code	Description	Dvision Description
7992	Public Golf Courses	Services
922	Public Order And Safety	Public Adminstration
9229	Public Order And Safety, Not Elsewhere Classified	Public Adminstration
8743	Public Relations Services	Services
4220	Public Warehousing & Storage	Transportation, Communications, Electric, Gas, And Sanitary Service
422	Public Warehousing And Storage	Transportation, Communications, Electric, Gas, And Sanitary Service
261	Pulp Mills	Manufacturing
2611	Pulp Mills	Manufacturing
2611	Pulp Mills	Manufacturing
3561	Pumps & Pumping Equipment	Manufacturing
3561	Pumps And Pumping Equipment	Manufacturing
7948	Racing, Including Track Operation	Services
3663	Radio & Tv Broadcasting & Communications Equipment	Manufacturing
3663	Radio And Television Broadcasting And Communications Equipment	Manufacturing
483	Radio And Television Broadcasting Stations	Transportation, Communications, Electric, Gas, And Sanitary Service
7622	Radio And Television Repair Shops	Services
4832	Radio Broadcasting Stations	Transportation, Communications, Electric, Gas, And Sanitary Service
4832	Radio Broadcasting Stations	Transportation, Communications, Electric, Gas, And Sanitary Service
5731	Radio, Television, And Consumer Electronics Stores	Retail Trade
7313	Radio, Television, And Publishers' Advertising Representatives	Services
573	Radio, Television, Consumer Electronics, And Music Stores	Retail Trade
4812	Radiotelephone Communications	Transportation, Communications, Electric, Gas, And Sanitary Service
4812	Radiotelephone Communications	Transportation, Communications, Electric, Gas, And Sanitary Service
374	Railroad Equipment	Manufacturing
3743	Railroad Equipment	Manufacturing
3743	Railroad Equipment	Manufacturing
4013	Railroad Switching & Terminal Establishments	Transportation, Communications, Electric, Gas, And Sanitary Service
4013	Railroad Switching And Terminal Establishments	Transportation, Communications, Electric, Gas, And Sanitary Service
40	Railroad Transportation	Transportation, Communications, Electric, Gas, And Sanitary Service
401	Railroads	Transportation, Communications, Electric, Gas, And Sanitary Service
4011	Railroads, Line-Haul Operating	Transportation, Communications, Electric, Gas, And Sanitary Service
4011	Railroads, Line-Haul Operating	Transportation, Communications, Electric, Gas, And Sanitary Service
3273	Ready-Mixed Concrete	Manufacturing
65	Real Estate	Finance, Insurance, And Real Estate
6500	Real Estate	Finance, Insurance, And Real Estate
6531	Real Estate Agents & Managers (For Others)	Finance, Insurance, And Real Estate
653	Real Estate Agents And Managers	Finance, Insurance, And Real Estate
6531	Real Estate Agents And Managers	Finance, Insurance, And Real Estate
6532	Real Estate Dealers (For Their Own Account)	Finance, Insurance, And Real Estate
6798	Real Estate Investment Trusts	Finance, Insurance, And Real Estate
6798	Real Estate Investment Trusts	Finance, Insurance, And Real Estate
651	Real Estate Operators (Except Developers) And Lessors	Finance, Insurance, And Real Estate
6510	Real Estate Operators (No Developers) & Lessors	Finance, Insurance, And Real Estate
2493	Reconstituted Wood Products	Manufacturing
5735	Record And Prerecorded Tape Stores	Retail Trade
556	Recreational Vehicle Dealers	Retail Trade
5561	Recreational Vehicle Dealers	Retail Trade
7033	Recreational Vehicle Parks And Campsites	Services
4613	Refined Petroleum Pipelines	Transportation, Communications, Electric, Gas, And Sanitary Service
4222	Refrigerated Warehousing And Storage	Transportation, Communications, Electric, Gas, And Sanitary Service
3580	Refrigeration & Service Industry Machinery	Manufacturing
7623	Refrigeration And Air-Conditioning Service And Repair Shops	Services
358	Refrigeration And Service Industry Machinery	Manufacturing
5078	Refrigeration Equipment And Supplies	Wholesale Trade
4953	Refuse Systems	Transportation, Communications, Electric, Gas, And Sanitary Service
4953	Refuse Systems	Transportation, Communications, Electric, Gas, And Sanitary Service
963	Regulation And Administration Of Communications, Electric, Gas	Public Adminstration
9631	Regulation And Administration Of Communications, Electric, Gas	Public Adminstration
962	Regulation And Administration Of Transportation Programs	Public Adminstration
9621	Regulation And Administration Of Transportation Programs	Public Adminstration
964	Regulation Of Agricultural Marketing And Commodities	Public Adminstration
9641	Regulation Of Agricultural Marketing And Commodities	Public Adminstration
965	Regulation, Licensing, And Inspection Of Miscellaneous Commercial	Public Adminstration
9651	Regulation, Licensing, And Inspection Of Miscellaneous Commercial	Public Adminstration

Table of Contents for SIC Codes

Sorted by description

SIC Code	Description	Dvision Description
3625	Relays And Industrial Controls	Manufacturing
866	Religious Organizations	Services
8661	Religious Organizations	Services
474	Rental Of Railroad Cars	Transportation, Communications, Electric, Gas, And Sanitary Service
4741	Rental Of Railroad Cars	Transportation, Communications, Electric, Gas, And Sanitary Service
7699	Repair Shops And Related Services, Not Elsewhere Classified	Services
873	Research, Development, And Testing Services	Services
836	Residential Care	Services
8361	Residential Care	Services
3645	Residential Electric Lighting Fixtures	Manufacturing
546	Retail Bakeries	Retail Trade
5461	Retail Bakeries	Retail Trade
526	Retail Nurseries, Lawn And Garden Supply Stores	Retail Trade
5261	Retail Nurseries, Lawn And Garden Supply Stores	Retail Trade
599	Retail Stores, Not Elsewhere Classified	Retail Trade
52	Retail Trade	Retail Trade
5600	Retail-Apparel & Accessory Stores	Retail Trade
5531	Retail-Auto & Home Supply Stores	Retail Trade
5500	Retail-Auto Dealers & Gasoline Stations	Retail Trade
5200	Retail-Building Materials, Hardware, Garden Supply	Retail Trade
5961	Retail-Catalog & Mail-Order Houses	Retail Trade
5734	Retail-Computer & Computer Software Stores	Retail Trade
5412	Retail-Convenience Stores	Retail Trade
5311	Retail-Department Stores	Retail Trade
5912	Retail-Drug Stores And Proprietary Stores	Retail Trade
5810	Retail-Eating & Drinking Places	Retail Trade
5812	Retail-Eating Places	Retail Trade
5651	Retail-Family Clothing Stores	Retail Trade
5400	Retail-Food Stores	Retail Trade
5712	Retail-Furniture Stores	Retail Trade
5411	Retail-Grocery Stores	Retail Trade
5945	Retail-Hobby, Toy & Game Shops	Retail Trade
5700	Retail-Home Furniture, Furnishings & Equipment Stores	Retail Trade
5944	Retail-Jewelry Stores	Retail Trade
5211	Retail-Lumber & Other Building Materials Dealers	Retail Trade
5399	Retail-Misc General Merchandise Stores	Retail Trade
5900	Retail-Miscellaneous Retail	Retail Trade
5940	Retail-Miscellaneous Shopping Goods Stores	Retail Trade
5271	Retail-Mobile Home Dealers	Retail Trade
5960	Retail-Nonstore Retailers	Retail Trade
5731	Retail-Radio, Tv & Consumer Electronics Stores	Retail Trade
5735	Retail-Record & Prerecorded Tape Stores	Retail Trade
5990	Retail-Retail Stores, Nec	Retail Trade
5661	Retail-Shoe Stores	Retail Trade
5331	Retail-Variety Stores	Retail Trade
5621	Retail-Women's Clothing Stores	Retail Trade
764	Reupholstery And Furniture Repair	Services
7641	Reupholstery And Furniture Repair	Services
0112	Rice	Agriculture, Forestry, And Fishing
2044	Rice Milling	Manufacturing
2095	Roasted Coffee	Manufacturing
2384	Robes And Dressing Gowns	Manufacturing
3350	Rolling Drawing & Extruding Of Nonferrous Metals	Manufacturing
3547	Rolling Mill Machinery And Equipment	Manufacturing
3351	Rolling, Drawing, And Extruding Of Copper	Manufacturing
335	Rolling, Drawing, And Extruding Of Nonferrous Metals	Manufacturing
3356	Rolling, Drawing, And Extruding Of Nonferrous Metals, Except Copper	Manufacturing
5033	Roofing, Siding, And Insulation Materials	Wholesale Trade
176	Roofing, Siding, And Sheet Metal Work	Construction
1761	Roofing, Siding, And Sheet Metal Work	Construction
702	Rooming And Boarding Houses	Services
7021	Rooming And Boarding Houses	Services
3021	Rubber & Plastics Footwear	Manufacturing
30	Rubber And Miscellaneous Plastics Products	Manufacturing

Table of Contents for SIC Codes

Sorted by description

SIC Code	Description	Dvision Description
302	Rubber And Plastics Footwear	Manufacturing
3021	Rubber And Plastics Footwear	Manufacturing
3052	Rubber And Plastics Hose And Belting	Manufacturing
2068	Salted And Roasted Nuts And Seeds	Manufacturing
144	Sand And Gravel	Mining
2656	Sanitary Food Containers, Except Folding	Manufacturing
2676	Sanitary Paper Products	Manufacturing
495	Sanitary Services	Transportation, Communications, Electric, Gas, And Sanitary Service
4950	Sanitary Services	Transportation, Communications, Electric, Gas, And Sanitary Service
4959	Sanitary Services, Not Elsewhere Classified	Transportation, Communications, Electric, Gas, And Sanitary Service
2013	Sausages & Other Prepared Meat Products	Manufacturing
2013	Sausages And Other Prepared Meat Products	Manufacturing
6035	Savings Institution, Federally Chartered	Finance, Insurance, And Real Estate
603	Savings Institutions	Finance, Insurance, And Real Estate
6035	Savings Institutions, Federally Chartered	Finance, Insurance, And Real Estate
6036	Savings Institutions, Not Federally Chartered	Finance, Insurance, And Real Estate
6036	Savings Institutions, Not Federally Chartered	Finance, Insurance, And Real Estate
3425	Saw Blades And Handsaws	Manufacturing
2421	Sawmills & Planting Mills, General	Manufacturing
242	Sawmills And Planing Mills	Manufacturing
2421	Sawmills And Planing Mills, General	Manufacturing
3596	Scales And Balances, Except Laboratory	Manufacturing
2397	Schiffli Machine Embroideries	Manufacturing
415	School Buses	Transportation, Communications, Electric, Gas, And Sanitary Service
4151	School Buses	Transportation, Communications, Electric, Gas, And Sanitary Service
829	Schools And Educational Services, Not Elsewhere Classified	Services
8299	Schools And Educational Services, Not Elsewhere Classified	Services
5093	Scrap And Waste Materials	Wholesale Trade
3451	Screw Machine Products	Manufacturing
3451	Screw Machine Products	Manufacturing
345	Screw Machine Products, And Bolts, Nuts, Screws, Rivets, And Washers	Manufacturing
3812	Search, Detection, Navagation, Guidance, Aeronautical Sys	Manufacturing
381	Search, Detection, Navigation, Guidance, Aeronautical, And Nautical	Manufacturing
3812	Search, Detection, Navigation, Guidance, Aeronautical, And Nautical	Manufacturing
3341	Secondary Smelting & Refining Of Nonferrous Metals	Manufacturing
334	Secondary Smelting And Refining Of Nonferrous Metals	Manufacturing
3341	Secondary Smelting And Refining Of Nonferrous Metals	Manufacturing
7338	Secretarial And Court Reporting Services	Services
6200	Security & Commodity Brokers, Dealers, Exchanges & Services	Finance, Insurance, And Real Estate
62	Security And Commodity Brokers, Dealers, Exchanges, And Services	Finance, Insurance, And Real Estate
623	Security And Commodity Exchanges	Finance, Insurance, And Real Estate
6231	Security And Commodity Exchanges	Finance, Insurance, And Real Estate
6211	Security Brokers, Dealers & Flotation Companies	Finance, Insurance, And Real Estate
621	Security Brokers, Dealers, And Flotation Companies	Finance, Insurance, And Real Estate
6211	Security Brokers, Dealers, And Flotation Companies	Finance, Insurance, And Real Estate
7382	Security Systems Services	Services
3674	Semiconductors & Related Devices	Manufacturing
3674	Semiconductors And Related Devices	Manufacturing
5087	Service Establishment Equipment And Supplies	Wholesale Trade
279	Service Industries For The Printing Trade	Manufacturing
2790	Service Industries For The Printing Trade	Manufacturing
3589	Service Industry Machinery, Not Elsewhere Classified	Manufacturing
7829	Services Allied To Motion Picture Distribution	Services
7819	Services Allied To Motion Picture Production	Services
628	Services Allied With The Exchange Of Securities Or Commodities	Finance, Insurance, And Real Estate
6289	Services Allied With The Exchange Of Securities Or Commodities	Finance, Insurance, And Real Estate
449	Services Incidental To Water Transportation	Transportation, Communications, Electric, Gas, And Sanitary Service
734	Services To Dwellings And Other Buildings	Services
89	Services, Not Elsewhere Classified	Services
899	Services, Not Elsewhere Classified	Services
8999	Services, Not Elsewhere Classified	Services
7310	Services-Advertising	Services
7311	Services-Advertising Agencies	Services
7829	Services-Allied To Motion Picture Distribution	Services

Table of Contents for SIC Codes

Sorted by description

SIC Code	Description	Dvision Description
7819	Services-Allied To Motion Picture Production	Services
7900	Services-Amusement & Recreation Services	Services
7510	Services-Auto Rental & Leasing (No Drivers)	Services
7500	Services-Automotive Repair, Services & Parking	Services
7389	Services-Business Services, Nec	Services
8351	Services-Child Day Care Services	Services
8731	Services-Commercial Physical & Biological Research	Services
7373	Services-Computer Integrated Systems Design	Services
7374	Services-Computer Processing & Data Preparation	Services
7371	Services-Computer Programming Services	Services
7370	Services-Computer Programming, Data Processing, Etc.	Services
7377	Services-Computer Rental & Leasing	Services
7320	Services-Consumer Credit Reporting, Collection Agencies	Services
7381	Services-Detective, Guard & Armored Car Services	Services
7331	Services-Direct Mail Advertising Services	Services
8200	Services-Educational Services	Services
7361	Services-Employment Agencies	Services
8711	Services-Engineering Services	Services
8700	Services-Engineering, Accounting, Research, Management	Services
7359	Services-Equipment Rental & Leasing, Nec	Services
8744	Services-Facilities Support Management Services	Services
8062	Services-General Medical & Surgical Hospitals, Nec	Services
8000	Services-Health Services	Services
7363	Services-Help Supply Services	Services
8082	Services-Home Health Care Services	Services
8060	Services-Hospitals	Services
8111	Services-Legal Services	Services
7330	Services-Mailing, Reproduction, Commercial Art & Photography	Services
8742	Services-Management Consulting Services	Services
8741	Services-Management Services	Services
8071	Services-Medical Laboratories	Services
8600	Services-Membership Organizations	Services
7997	Services-Membership Sports & Recreation Clubs	Services
8090	Services-Misc Health & Allied Services, Nec	Services
7990	Services-Miscellaneous Amusement & Recreation	Services
7380	Services-Miscellaneous Business Services	Services
7350	Services-Miscellaneous Equipment Rental & Leasing	Services
7600	Services-Miscellaneous Repair Services	Services
7822	Services-Motion Picture & Video Tape Distribution	Services
7812	Services-Motion Picture & Video Tape Production	Services
7830	Services-Motion Picture Theaters	Services
8050	Services-Nursing & Personal Care Facilities	Services
8011	Services-Offices & Clinics Of Doctors Of Medicine	Services
7200	Services-Personal Services	Services
7384	Services-Photofinishing Laboratories	Services
7372	Services-Prepackaged Software	Services
7948	Services-Racing, Including Track Operation	Services
8900	Services-Services, Nec	Services
8051	Services-Skilled Nursing Care Facilities	Services
8300	Services-Social Services	Services
8093	Services-Specialty Outpatient Facilities, Nec	Services
7385	Services-Telephone Interconnect Systems	Services
8734	Services-Testing Laboratories	Services
7340	Services-To Dwellings & Other Buildings	Services
7841	Services-Video Tape Rental	Services
2652	Setup Paperboard Boxes	Manufacturing
4952	Sewerage Systems	Transportation, Communications, Electric, Gas, And Sanitary Service
5949	Sewing, Needlework, And Piece Goods Stores	Retail Trade
0214	Sheep And Goats	Agriculture, Forestry, And Fishing
3444	Sheet Metal Work	Manufacturing
3444	Sheet Metalwork	Manufacturing
0913	Shellfish	Agriculture, Forestry, And Fishing
3730	Ship & Boat Building & Repairing	Manufacturing
373	Ship And Boat Building And Repairing	Manufacturing

Table of Contents for SIC Codes

Sorted by description

SIC Code	Description	Dvision Description
3731	Ship Building And Repairing	Manufacturing
725	Shoe Repair Shops And Shoeshine Parlors	Services
7251	Shoe Repair Shops And Shoeshine Parlors	Services
566	Shoe Stores	Retail Trade
5661	Shoe Stores	Retail Trade
2079	Shortening, Table Oils, Margarine, And Other Edible Fats And Oils	Manufacturing
6153	Short-Term Business Credit Institutions	Finance, Insurance, And Real Estate
6153	Short-Term Business Credit Institutions, Except Agricultural	Finance, Insurance, And Real Estate
3993	Signs And Advertising Specialties	Manufacturing
1044	Silver Ores	Mining
3914	Silverware, Plated Ware, And Stainless Steel Ware	Manufacturing
8051	Skilled Nursing Care Facilities	Services
3484	Small Arms	Manufacturing
3482	Small Arms Ammunition	Manufacturing
2841	Soap And Other Detergents, Except Specialty Cleaners	Manufacturing
284	Soap, Detergents, And Cleaning Preparations; Perfumes, Cosmetics	Manufacturing
2840	Soap, Detergents, Cleang Preparations, Perfumes, Cosmetics	Manufacturing
83	Social Services	Services
839	Social Services, Not Elsewhere Classified	Services
8399	Social Services, Not Elsewhere Classified	Services
2436	Softwood Veneer And Plywood	Manufacturing
071	Soil Preparation Services	Agriculture, Forestry, And Fishing
0711	Soil Preparation Services	Agriculture, Forestry, And Fishing
2075	Soybean Oil Mills	Manufacturing
0116	Soybeans	Agriculture, Forestry, And Fishing
966	Space Research And Technology	Public Adminstration
9661	Space Research And Technology	Public Adminstration
3544	Special Dies And Tools, Die Sets, Jigs And Fixtures, And Industrial Tools	Manufacturing
3550	Special Industry Machinery (No Metalworking Machinery)	Manufacturing
355	Special Industry Machinery, Except Metalworking Machinery	Manufacturing
3559	Special Industry Machinery, Nec	Manufacturing
3559	Special Industry Machinery, Not Elsewhere Classified	Manufacturing
2429	Special Product Sawmills, Not Elsewhere Classified	Manufacturing
1799	Special Trade Contractors, Not Elsewhere Classified	Construction
4226	Special Warehousing And Storage, Not Elsewhere Classified	Transportation, Communications, Electric, Gas, And Sanitary Service
2842	Specialty Cleaning, Polishing And Sanitation Preparations	Manufacturing
2842	Specialty Cleaning, Polishing, And Sanitation Preparations	Manufacturing
8069	Specialty Hospitals, Except Psychiatric	Services
8093	Specialty Outpatient Facilities, Not Elsewhere Classified	Services
3566	Speed Changers, Industrial High-Speed Drives, And Gears	Manufacturing
3949	Sporting & Athletic Goods, Nec	Manufacturing
3949	Sporting And Athletic Goods, Not Elsewhere Classified	Manufacturing
7032	Sporting And Recreational Camps	Services
5091	Sporting And Recreational Goods And Supplies	Wholesale Trade
5941	Sporting Goods Stores And Bicycle Shops	Retail Trade
6022	State Commercial Banks	Finance, Insurance, And Real Estate
6022	State Commercial Banks	Finance, Insurance, And Real Estate
5112	Stationery And Office Supplies	Wholesale Trade
5943	Stationery Stores	Retail Trade
2678	Stationery, Tablets, And Related Products	Manufacturing
4961	Steam & Air-Conditioning Supply	Transportation, Communications, Electric, Gas, And Sanitary Service
496	Steam And Air-Conditioning Supply	Transportation, Communications, Electric, Gas, And Sanitary Service
4961	Steam And Air-Conditioning Supply	Transportation, Communications, Electric, Gas, And Sanitary Service
3511	Steam, Gas, And Hydraulic Turbines, And Turbine Generator Set Units	Manufacturing
3325	Steel Foundries, Not Elsewhere Classified	Manufacturing
3324	Steel Investment Foundries	Manufacturing
3317	Steel Pipe & Tubes	Manufacturing
3317	Steel Pipe And Tubes	Manufacturing
3493	Steel Springs, Except Wire	Manufacturing
3315	Steel Wiredrawing And Steel Nails And Spikes	Manufacturing
3310	Steel Works, Blast Furnaces & Rolling & Finishing Mills	Manufacturing
3312	Steel Works, Blast Furnaces & Rolling Mills (Coke Ovens)	Manufacturing
3312	Steel Works, Blast Furnaces (Including Coke Ovens), And Rolling Mills	Manufacturing
331	Steel Works, Blast Furnaces, And Rolling And Finishing Mills	Manufacturing

Table of Contents for SIC Codes

Sorted by description

SIC Code	Description	Dvision Description
32	Stone, Clay, Glass, And Concrete Products	Manufacturing
3691	Storage Batteries	Manufacturing
325	Structural Clay Products	Manufacturing
3250	Structural Clay Products	Manufacturing
3259	Structural Clay Products, Not Elsewhere Classified	Manufacturing
1791	Structural Steel Erection	Construction
2439	Structural Wood Members, Not Elsewhere Classified	Manufacturing
2060	Sugar & Confectionery Products	Manufacturing
206	Sugar And Confectionery Products	Manufacturing
0133	Sugarcane And Sugar Beets	Agriculture, Forestry, And Fishing
635	Surety Insurance	Finance, Insurance, And Real Estate
6351	Surety Insurance	Finance, Insurance, And Real Estate
6351	Surety Insurance	Finance, Insurance, And Real Estate
2843	Surface Active Agents, Finishing Agents, Sulfonated Oils	Manufacturing
3841	Surgical & Medical Instruments & Apparatus	Manufacturing
3841	Surgical And Medical Instruments And Apparatus	Manufacturing
384	Surgical, Medical, And Dental Instruments And Supplies	Manufacturing
8713	Surveying Services	Services
3613	Switchgear & Switchboard Apparatus	Manufacturing
3613	Switchgear And Switchboard Apparatus	Manufacturing
2822	Synthetic Rubber (Vulcanizable Elastomers)	Manufacturing
3795	Tanks And Tank Components	Manufacturing
7291	Tax Return Preparation Services	Services
412	Taxicabs	Transportation, Communications, Electric, Gas, And Sanitary Service
4121	Taxicabs	Transportation, Communications, Electric, Gas, And Sanitary Service
4822	Telegraph & Other Message Communications	Transportation, Communications, Electric, Gas, And Sanitary Service
482	Telegraph And Other Message Communications	Transportation, Communications, Electric, Gas, And Sanitary Service
4822	Telegraph And Other Message Communications	Transportation, Communications, Electric, Gas, And Sanitary Service
3661	Telephone & Telegraph Apparatus	Manufacturing
3661	Telephone And Telegraph Apparatus	Manufacturing
481	Telephone Communications	Transportation, Communications, Electric, Gas, And Sanitary Service
4813	Telephone Communications (No Radiotelephone)	Transportation, Communications, Electric, Gas, And Sanitary Service
4813	Telephone Communications, Except Radiotelephone	Transportation, Communications, Electric, Gas, And Sanitary Service
4833	Television Broadcasting Stations	Transportation, Communications, Electric, Gas, And Sanitary Service
4833	Television Broadcasting Stations	Transportation, Communications, Electric, Gas, And Sanitary Service
423	Terminal And Joint Terminal Maintenance Facilities For Motor Freight	Transportation, Communications, Electric, Gas, And Sanitary Service
4231	Terminal And Joint Terminal Maintenance Facilities For Motor Freight	Transportation, Communications, Electric, Gas, And Sanitary Service
417	Terminal And Service Facilities For Motor Vehicle Passenger Transportation	Transportation, Communications, Electric, Gas, And Sanitary Service
4173	Terminal And Service Facilities For Motor Vehicle Passenger Transportation	Transportation, Communications, Electric, Gas, And Sanitary Service
4231	Terminal Maintenance Facilities For Motor Freight Transport	Transportation, Communications, Electric, Gas, And Sanitary Service
1743	Terrazzo, Tile, Marble, And Mosaic Work	Construction
8734	Testing Laboratories	Services
2393	Textile Bags	Manufacturing
2299	Textile Goods, Not Elsewhere Classified	Manufacturing
3552	Textile Machinery	Manufacturing
22	Textile Mill Products	Manufacturing
2200	Textile Mill Products	Manufacturing
7922	Theatrical Producers (Except Motion Picture) And Miscellaneous Theater	Services
792	Theatrical Producers (Except Motion Picture), Bands, Orchestras	Services
2284	Thread Mills	Manufacturing
081	Timber Tracts	Agriculture, Forestry, And Fishing
0811	Timber Tracts	Agriculture, Forestry, And Fishing
2296	Tire Cord And Fabrics	Manufacturing
7534	Tire Retreading And Repair Shops	Services
3011	Tires & Inner Tubes	Manufacturing
301	Tires And Inner Tubes	Manufacturing
3011	Tires And Inner Tubes	Manufacturing
5014	Tires And Tubes	Wholesale Trade
654	Title Abstract Offices	Finance, Insurance, And Real Estate
6541	Title Abstract Offices	Finance, Insurance, And Real Estate
636	Title Insurance	Finance, Insurance, And Real Estate
6361	Title Insurance	Finance, Insurance, And Real Estate
6361	Title Insurance	Finance, Insurance, And Real Estate
0132	Tobacco	Agriculture, Forestry, And Fishing

Table of Contents for SIC Codes

Sorted by description

SIC Code	Description	Dvision Description
5194	Tobacco And Tobacco Products	Wholesale Trade
21	Tobacco Products	Manufacturing
2100	Tobacco Products	Manufacturing
214	Tobacco Stemming And Redrying	Manufacturing
2141	Tobacco Stemming And Redrying	Manufacturing
5993	Tobacco Stores And Stands	Retail Trade
7532	Top, Body, And Upholstery Repair Shops And Paint Shops	Services
3824	Totalizing Fluid Meters & Counting Devices	Manufacturing
3824	Totalizing Fluid Meters And Counting Devices	Manufacturing
4725	Tour Operators	Transportation, Communications, Electric, Gas, And Sanitary Service
4492	Towing And Tugboat Services	Transportation, Communications, Electric, Gas, And Sanitary Service
5092	Toys And Hobby Goods And Supplies	Wholesale Trade
45	Transportation By Air	Transportation, Communications, Electric, Gas, And Sanitary Service
37	Transportation Equipment	Manufacturing
5088	Transportation Equipment And Supplies, Except Motor Vehicles	Wholesale Trade
3799	Transportation Equipment, Not Elsewhere Classified	Manufacturing
47	Transportation Services	Transportation, Communications, Electric, Gas, And Sanitary Service
4700	Transportation Services	Transportation, Communications, Electric, Gas, And Sanitary Service
4789	Transportation Services, Not Elsewhere Classified	Transportation, Communications, Electric, Gas, And Sanitary Service
4724	Travel Agencies	Transportation, Communications, Electric, Gas, And Sanitary Service
3792	Travel Trailers And Campers	Manufacturing
0173	Tree Nuts	Agriculture, Forestry, And Fishing
3713	Truck & Bus Bodies	Manufacturing
3713	Truck And Bus Bodies	Manufacturing
7513	Truck Rental And Leasing, Without Drivers	Services
3715	Truck Trailers	Manufacturing
3715	Truck Trailers	Manufacturing
4210	Trucking & Courier Services (No Air)	Transportation, Communications, Electric, Gas, And Sanitary Service
4213	Trucking (No Local)	Transportation, Communications, Electric, Gas, And Sanitary Service
421	Trucking And Courier Services, Except Air	Transportation, Communications, Electric, Gas, And Sanitary Service
4213	Trucking, Except Local	Transportation, Communications, Electric, Gas, And Sanitary Service
673	Trusts	Finance, Insurance, And Real Estate
6733	Trusts, Except Educational, Religious, And Charitable	Finance, Insurance, And Real Estate
0253	Turkeys And Turkey Eggs	Agriculture, Forestry, And Fishing
2791	Typesetting	Manufacturing
2674	Uncoated Paper And Multiwall Bags	Manufacturing
6726	Unit Investment Trusts, Face-Amount Certificate Offices	Finance, Insurance, And Real Estate
43	United States Postal Service	Transportation, Communications, Electric, Gas, And Sanitary Service
431	United States Postal Service	Transportation, Communications, Electric, Gas, And Sanitary Service
4311	United States Postal Service	Transportation, Communications, Electric, Gas, And Sanitary Service
3081	Unsupported Plastics Film & Sheet	Manufacturing
3081	Unsupported Plastics Film And Sheet	Manufacturing
3082	Unsupported Plastics Profile Shapes	Manufacturing
1094	Uranium-Radium-Vanadium Ores	Mining
593	Used Merchandise Stores	Retail Trade
5932	Used Merchandise Stores	Retail Trade
7519	Utility Trailer And Recreational Vehicle Rental	Services
3494	Valves And Pipe Fittings, Not Elsewhere Classified	Manufacturing
533	Variety Stores	Retail Trade
5331	Variety Stores	Retail Trade
2076	Vegetable Oil Mills, Except Corn, Cottonseed, And Soybean	Manufacturing
016	Vegetables And Melons	Agriculture, Forestry, And Fishing
0161	Vegetables And Melons	Agriculture, Forestry, And Fishing
3647	Vehicular Lighting Equipment	Manufacturing
074	Veterinary Services	Agriculture, Forestry, And Fishing
0742	Veterinary Services For Animal Specialties	Agriculture, Forestry, And Fishing
0741	Veterinary Services For Livestock	Agriculture, Forestry, And Fishing
784	Video Tape Rental	Services
7841	Video Tape Rental	Services
3261	Vitreous China Plumbing Fixtures And China And Earthenware Fittings	Manufacturing
3262	Vitreous China Table And Kitchen Articles	Manufacturing
824	Vocational Schools	Services
8249	Vocational Schools, Not Elsewhere Classified	Services
5075	Warm Air Heating And Air-Conditioning Equipment And Supplies	Wholesale Trade

Table of Contents for SIC Codes

Sorted by description

SIC Code	Description	Dvision Description
763	Watch, Clock, And Jewelry Repair	Services
7631	Watch, Clock, And Jewelry Repair	Services
387	Watches, Clocks, Clockwork Operated Devices, And Parts	Manufacturing
3873	Watches, Clocks, Clockwork Operated Devices, And Parts	Manufacturing
3873	Watches, Clocks, Clockwork Operated Devices/Parts	Manufacturing
494	Water Supply	Transportation, Communications, Electric, Gas, And Sanitary Service
4941	Water Supply	Transportation, Communications, Electric, Gas, And Sanitary Service
4941	Water Supply	Transportation, Communications, Electric, Gas, And Sanitary Service
44	Water Transportation	Transportation, Communications, Electric, Gas, And Sanitary Service
4400	Water Transportation	Transportation, Communications, Electric, Gas, And Sanitary Service
444	Water Transportation Of Freight, Not Elsewhere Classified	Transportation, Communications, Electric, Gas, And Sanitary Service
4449	Water Transportation Of Freight, Not Elsewhere Classified	Transportation, Communications, Electric, Gas, And Sanitary Service
448	Water Transportation Of Passengers	Transportation, Communications, Electric, Gas, And Sanitary Service
4489	Water Transportation Of Passengers, Not Elsewhere Classified	Transportation, Communications, Electric, Gas, And Sanitary Service
4499	Water Transportation Services, Not Elsewhere Classified	Transportation, Communications, Electric, Gas, And Sanitary Service
178	Water Well Drilling	Construction
1781	Water Well Drilling	Construction
1623	Water, Sewer, Pipeline, And Communications And Power Line Construction	Construction
1623	Water, Sewer, Pipeline, Comm & Power Line Construction	Construction
2385	Waterproof Outerwear	Manufacturing
2257	Weft Knit Fabric Mills	Manufacturing
7692	Welding Repair	Services
2046	Wet Corn Milling	Manufacturing
0111	Wheat	Agriculture, Forestry, And Fishing
50	Wholesale Trade¨Durable Goods	Wholesale Trade
51	Wholesale Trade¨Nondurable Goods	Wholesale Trade
5130	Wholesale-Apparel, Piece Goods & Notions	Wholesale Trade
5180	Wholesale-Beer, Wine & Distilled Alcoholic Beverages	Wholesale Trade
5160	Wholesale-Chemicals & Allied Products	Wholesale Trade
5045	Wholesale-Computers & Peripheral Equipment & Software	Wholesale Trade
5082	Wholesale-Construction & Mining (No Petro) Machinery & Equip	Wholesale Trade
5122	Wholesale-Drugs, Proprietaries & Druggists' Sundries	Wholesale Trade
5000	Wholesale-Durable Goods	Wholesale Trade
5099	Wholesale-Durable Goods, Nec	Wholesale Trade
5063	Wholesale-Electrical Apparatus & Equipment, Wiring Supplies	Wholesale Trade
5064	Wholesale-Electrical Appliances, Tv & Radio Sets	Wholesale Trade
5065	Wholesale-Electronic Parts & Equipment, Nec	Wholesale Trade
5150	Wholesale-Farm Product Raw Materials	Wholesale Trade
5020	Wholesale-Furniture & Home Furnishings	Wholesale Trade
5140	Wholesale-Groceries & Related Products	Wholesale Trade
5141	Wholesale-Groceries, General Line	Wholesale Trade
5072	Wholesale-Hardware	Wholesale Trade
5070	Wholesale-Hardware & Plumbing & Heating Equipment & Supplies	Wholesale Trade
5084	Wholesale-Industrial Machinery & Equipment	Wholesale Trade
5094	Wholesale-Jewelry, Watches, Precious Stones & Metals	Wholesale Trade
5030	Wholesale-Lumber & Other Construction Materials	Wholesale Trade
5031	Wholesale-Lumber, Plywood, Millwork & Wood Panels	Wholesale Trade
5080	Wholesale-Machinery, Equipment & Supplies	Wholesale Trade
5047	Wholesale-Medical, Dental & Hospital Equipment & Supplies	Wholesale Trade
5050	Wholesale-Metals & Minerals (No Petroleum)	Wholesale Trade
5051	Wholesale-Metals Service Centers & Offices	Wholesale Trade
5090	Wholesale-Misc Durable Goods	Wholesale Trade
5190	Wholesale-Miscellaneous Nondurable Goods	Wholesale Trade
5013	Wholesale-Motor Vehicle Supplies & New Parts	Wholesale Trade
5010	Wholesale-Motor Vehicles & Motor Vehicle Parts & Supplies	Wholesale Trade
5110	Wholesale-Paper & Paper Products	Wholesale Trade
5172	Wholesale-Petroleum & Petroleum Products (No Bulk Stations)	Wholesale Trade
5171	Wholesale-Petroleum Bulk Stations & Terminals	Wholesale Trade
5040	Wholesale-Professional & Commercial Equipment & Supplies	Wholesale Trade
5182	Wine And Distilled Alcoholic Beverages	Wholesale Trade
2084	Wines, Brandy, And Brandy Spirits	Manufacturing
3495	Wire Springs	Manufacturing
563	Women's Accessory And Specialty Stores	Retail Trade
5632	Women's Accessory And Specialty Stores	Retail Trade

Table of Contents for SIC Codes

Sorted by description

SIC Code	Description	Dvision Description
562	Women's Clothing Stores	Retail Trade
5621	Women's Clothing Stores	Retail Trade
3144	Women's Footwear, Except Athletic	Manufacturing
2251	Women's Full-Length And Knee-Length Hosiery, Except Socks	Manufacturing
3171	Women's Handbags And Purses	Manufacturing
5137	Women's, Children's, And Infants' Clothing And Accessories	Wholesale Trade
2331	Women's, Misses', And Juniors' Blouses And Shirts	Manufacturing
2335	Women's, Misses', And Juniors' Dresses	Manufacturing
2330	Women's, Misses', And Juniors Outerwear	Manufacturing
233	Women's, Misses', And Juniors' Outerwear	Manufacturing
2339	Women's, Misses', And Juniors' Outerwear, Not Elsewhere Classified	Manufacturing
2337	Women's, Misses', And Juniors' Suits, Skirts, And Coats	Manufacturing
2340	Women's, Misses', Children's & Infants' Undergarments	Manufacturing
234	Women's, Misses', Children's, And Infants' Undergarments	Manufacturing
2341	Women's, Misses', Children's, And Infants' Underwear And Nightwear	Manufacturing
245	Wood Buildings And Mobile Homes	Manufacturing
244	Wood Containers	Manufacturing
2449	Wood Containers, Not Elsewhere Classified	Manufacturing
2511	Wood Household Furniture, (No Upholstered)	Manufacturing
2511	Wood Household Furniture, Except Upholstered	Manufacturing
2512	Wood Household Furniture, Upholstered	Manufacturing
2434	Wood Kitchen Cabinets	Manufacturing
2541	Wood Office And Store Fixtures, Partitions, Shelving, And Lockers	Manufacturing
2521	Wood Office Furniture	Manufacturing
2448	Wood Pallets And Skids	Manufacturing
2491	Wood Preserving	Manufacturing
2499	Wood Products, Not Elsewhere Classified	Manufacturing
2517	Wood Television, Radio, Phonograph, And Sewing Machine Cabinets	Manufacturing
3553	Woodworking Machinery	Manufacturing
1795	Wrecking And Demolition Work	Construction
3844	X-Ray Apparatus & Tubes & Related Irradiation Apparatus	Manufacturing
3844	X-Ray Apparatus And Tubes And Related Irradiation Apparatus	Manufacturing
228	Yarn And Thread Mills	Manufacturing
2281	Yarn Spinning Mills	Manufacturing
2282	Yarn Texturizing, Throwing, Twisting, And Winding Mills	Manufacturing

Common Stocks by SIC Codes

Betas of Common Stocks by SIC Codes as of March 31, 2017

Details:
Benchmark: S&P 500 Index
Returns period and frequency: 1 year of daily returns
Risk-free rate: Federal Funds Rate

SIC Code	Description	Number of Companies	Mean	Median	1st Percentile	2.5th Percentile	5th Percentile	40th Percentile	50th Percentile	60th Percentile	95th Percentile	97.5th Percentile	99th Percentile
	AGRICULTURE, FORESTRY, AND FISHING												
01	AGRICULTURAL PRODUCTION-CROPS	7	0.773005	0.740322	0.062989	0.065153	0.068758	0.638665	0.740322	0.857139	1.662085	1.777023	1.845985
011	CASH GRAINS	2	0.593628	0.593628	0.072188	0.088151	0.114755	0.487212	0.593628	0.700045	1.072502	1.099106	1.115068
0115	Corn	1	0.061547	0.061547	0.061547	0.061547	0.061547	0.061547	0.061547	0.061547	0.061547	0.061547	0.061547
0116	Soybeans	1	1.125710	1.125710	1.125710	1.125710	1.125710	1.125710	1.125710	1.125710	1.125710	1.125710	1.125710
013	FIELD CROPS, EXCEPT CASH GRAINS	1	0.085586	0.085586	0.085586	0.085586	0.085586	0.085586	0.085586	0.085586	0.085586	0.085586	0.085586
0131	Cotton	1	0.085586	0.085586	0.085586	0.085586	0.085586	0.085586	0.085586	0.085586	0.085586	0.085586	0.085586
016	VEGETABLES AND MELONS	1	1.891960	1.891960	1.891960	1.891960	1.891960	1.891960	1.891960	1.891960	1.891960	1.891960	1.891960
0161	Vegetables And Melons	1	1.891960	1.891960	1.891960	1.891960	1.891960	1.891960	1.891960	1.891960	1.891960	1.891960	1.891960
017	FRUITS AND TREE NUTS	2	0.837670	0.837670	0.742269	0.745189	0.750057	0.818200	0.837670	0.857139	0.925282	0.930150	0.933070
0174	Citrus Fruits	2	0.837670	0.837670	0.742269	0.745189	0.750057	0.818200	0.837670	0.857139	0.925282	0.930150	0.933070
019	GENERAL FARMS, PRIMARILY CROP	1	0.570894	0.570894	0.570894	0.570894	0.570894	0.570894	0.570894	0.570894	0.570894	0.570894	0.570894
0191	General Farms, Primarily Crop	1	0.570894	0.570894	0.570894	0.570894	0.570894	0.570894	0.570894	0.570894	0.570894	0.570894	0.570894
02	AGRICULTURAL PRODUCTION-LIVESTOCK AND ANIMAL SPECIALTIES	2	0.683066	0.683066	0.573300	0.576660	0.582261	0.660664	0.683066	0.705467	0.783870	0.789471	0.792831
021	LIVESTOCK, EXCEPT DAIRY AND POULTRY	1	0.795071	0.795071	0.795071	0.795071	0.795071	0.795071	0.795071	0.795071	0.795071	0.795071	0.795071
0213	Hogs	1	0.795071	0.795071	0.795071	0.795071	0.795071	0.795071	0.795071	0.795071	0.795071	0.795071	0.795071
025	POULTRY AND EGGS	1	0.571060	0.571060	0.571060	0.571060	0.571060	0.571060	0.571060	0.571060	0.571060	0.571060	0.571060
0252	Chicken Eggs	1	0.571060	0.571060	0.571060	0.571060	0.571060	0.571060	0.571060	0.571060	0.571060	0.571060	0.571060
07	AGRICULTURAL SERVICES	6	1.536922	1.596557	0.174154	0.209768	0.269126	0.883964	1.596557	2.309150	2.760390	2.827400	2.867606
074	VETERINARY SERVICES	2	1.621147	1.621147	0.898708	0.920823	0.957682	1.473710	1.621147	1.768584	2.284612	2.321471	2.343586
0741	Veterinary Services For Livestock	1	0.883964	0.883964	0.883964	0.883964	0.883964	0.883964	0.883964	0.883964	0.883964	0.883964	0.883964
0742	Veterinary Services For Animal Specialties	1	2.358330	2.358330	2.358330	2.358330	2.358330	2.358330	2.358330	2.358330	2.358330	2.358330	2.358330
075	ANIMAL SERVICES, EXCEPT VETERINARY	2	1.522411	1.522411	0.177851	0.219011	0.287611	1.248011	1.522411	1.796810	2.757210	2.825810	2.866970
0752	Animal Specialty Services, Except Veterinary	2	1.522411	1.522411	0.177851	0.219011	0.287611	1.248011	1.522411	1.796810	2.757210	2.825810	2.866970
076	FARM LABOR AND MANAGEMENT SERVICES	1	2.309150	2.309150	2.309150	2.309150	2.309150	2.309150	2.309150	2.309150	2.309150	2.309150	2.309150
0762	Farm Management Services	1	2.309150	2.309150	2.309150	2.309150	2.309150	2.309150	2.309150	2.309150	2.309150	2.309150	2.309150
078	LANDSCAPE AND HORTICULTURAL SERVICES	1	0.625269	0.625269	0.625269	0.625269	0.625269	0.625269	0.625269	0.625269	0.625269	0.625269	0.625269
0782	Lawn And Garden Services	1	0.625269	0.625269	0.625269	0.625269	0.625269	0.625269	0.625269	0.625269	0.625269	0.625269	0.625269
09	FISHING, HUNTING, AND TRAPPING	1	-0.023275	-0.023275	-0.023275	-0.023275	-0.023275	-0.023275	-0.023275	-0.023275	-0.023275	-0.023275	-0.023275
	MINING												
10	METAL MINING	205	0.530409	0.401570	-1.399521	-1.123113	-0.583235	0.272528	0.401570	0.619594	2.244194	2.363948	2.971379
1000	METAL MINING	2	1.251078	1.251078	0.205465	0.237474	0.290821	1.037688	1.251078	1.464468	2.211335	2.264682	2.296691
101	IRON ORES	6	0.925286	1.121540	-0.249559	-0.160616	-0.012377	1.106440	1.121540	1.136640	1.389468	1.399094	1.404870
1011	Iron Ores	6	0.925286	1.121540	-0.249559	-0.160616	-0.012377	1.106440	1.121540	1.136640	1.389468	1.399094	1.404870
102	COPPER ORES	15	1.256297	1.189620	-0.050689	-0.041641	-0.026562	0.697644	1.189620	1.382412	2.987487	2.992279	2.995153
1021	Copper Ores	15	1.256297	1.189620	-0.050689	-0.041641	-0.026562	0.697644	1.189620	1.382412	2.987487	2.992279	2.995153

Betas of Common Stocks by SIC Codes as of March 31, 2017

SIC Code	Description	Number of Companies	Mean	Median	1st Percentile	2.5th Percentile	5th Percentile	40th Percentile	50th Percentile	60th Percentile	95th Percentile	97.5th Percentile	99th Percentile
103	LEAD AND ZINC ORES	2	1.468647	1.468647	0.894383	0.911962	0.941261	1.351450	1.468647	1.585843	1.996032	2.025331	2.042910
1031	Lead And Zinc Ores	2	1.468647	1.468647	0.894383	0.911962	0.941261	1.351450	1.468647	1.585843	1.996032	2.025331	2.042910
104	GOLD AND SILVER ORES	126	0.332246	0.285530	-1.395640	-1.121889	-0.732834	0.156299	0.285530	0.400423	1.445115	1.654948	2.280255
1041	Gold Ores	116	0.311905	0.261782	-1.397488	-1.159731	-0.839471	0.120619	0.261782	0.356390	1.463395	1.746226	2.280417
1044	Silver Ores	10	0.568202	0.748671	-0.387271	-0.341829	-0.266093	0.615456	0.748671	0.831846	0.990502	1.013781	1.027748
106	FERROALLOY ORES, EXCEPT VANADIUM	4	0.806268	1.003222	-0.412371	-0.375754	-0.314726	0.627443	1.003222	1.379001	1.651527	1.653468	1.654633
1061	Ferroalloy Ores, Except Vanadium	4	0.806268	1.003222	-0.412371	-0.375754	-0.314726	0.627443	1.003222	1.379001	1.651527	1.653468	1.654633
108	METAL MINING SERVICES	26	0.391584	0.382772	-1.380840	-1.344330	-1.215549	0.224103	0.382772	0.537059	2.057848	2.358938	2.553585
1081	Metal Mining Services	26	0.391584	0.382772	-1.380840	-1.344330	-1.215549	0.224103	0.382772	0.537059	2.057848	2.358938	2.553585
109	MISCELLANEOUS METAL ORES	24	0.984541	1.089615	-0.427180	-0.416045	-0.382320	0.983053	1.089615	1.213296	2.220402	2.308744	2.344928
1094	Uranium-Radium-Vanadium Ores	13	1.317557	1.297120	-0.321657	-0.152238	0.130129	1.242648	1.297120	1.509450	2.306122	2.337586	2.356464
1099	Miscellaneous Metal Ores, Not Elsewhere Classified	11	0.590976	0.589738	-0.388989	-0.368982	-0.335638	0.359986	0.589738	0.969784	1.325075	1.397333	1.440687
12	COAL MINING	5	0.988941	1.669510	-0.953095	-0.867304	-0.724317	1.169536	1.669510	1.698262	2.047894	2.086207	2.109195
122	BITUMINOUS COAL AND LIGNITE MINING	4	1.131283	1.705450	-0.929896	-0.809305	-0.608320	1.683886	1.705450	1.727014	2.067051	2.095785	2.113026
1221	Bituminous Coal And Lignite Surface Mining	4	1.131283	1.705450	-0.929896	-0.809305	-0.608320	1.683886	1.705450	1.727014	2.067051	2.095785	2.113026
124	COAL MINING SERVICES	1	0.419574	0.419574	0.419574	0.419574	0.419574	0.419574	0.419574	0.419574	0.419574	0.419574	0.419574
1241	Coal Mining Services	1	0.419574	0.419574	0.419574	0.419574	0.419574	0.419574	0.419574	0.419574	0.419574	0.419574	0.419574
13	OIL AND GAS EXTRACTION	201	3.205081	1.513650	-1.976980	-0.794336	-0.353258	1.342370	1.513650	1.721690	3.044860	3.628580	8.045820
131	CRUDE PETROLEUM AND NATURAL GAS	131	1.935090	1.459190	-1.622187	-0.659047	-0.269573	1.302990	1.459190	1.622250	3.207705	4.108385	6.961863
1311	Crude Petroleum And Natural Gas	131	1.935090	1.459190	-1.622187	-0.659047	-0.269573	1.302990	1.459190	1.622250	3.207705	4.108385	6.961863
132	NATURAL GAS LIQUIDS	5	1.850740	2.007470	1.080002	1.105626	1.148332	1.800474	2.007470	2.091050	2.424812	2.450861	2.466490
1321	Natural Gas Liquids	5	1.850740	2.007470	1.080002	1.105626	1.148332	1.800474	2.007470	2.091050	2.424812	2.450861	2.466490
138	OIL AND GAS FIELD SERVICES	65	5.868780	1.647460	-1.529613	-1.047128	-0.420834	1.456888	1.647460	1.911816	2.987976	3.118528	104.623739
1381	Drilling Oil And Gas Wells	23	2.058537	2.241140	0.622035	0.644820	0.684047	2.192374	2.241140	2.308244	3.033402	3.127737	3.188513
1382	Oil And Gas Field Exploration Services	20	15.125854	1.293310	-1.986354	-1.697085	-1.214969	1.093614	1.293310	1.461756	16.595984	150.738492	231.223997
1389	Oil And Gas Field Services, Not Elsewhere Classified	22	1.436692	1.487910	-0.857681	-0.690602	-0.424481	1.409170	1.487910	1.685032	2.710509	2.852460	2.942424
14	MINING AND QUARRYING OF NONMETALLIC MINERALS, EXCEPT FUELS	26	0.769734	0.693966	-0.646646	-0.446444	-0.169299	0.458312	0.693966	0.908400	2.286418	2.509508	2.682765
1400	MINING & QUARRYING OF NONMETALLIC MINERALS (NO FUELS)	1	0.908400	0.908400	0.908400	0.908400	0.908400	0.908400	0.908400	0.908400	0.908400	0.908400	0.908400
141	DIMENSION STONE	3	0.404486	0.458312	0.069469	0.081373	0.101212	0.378956	0.458312	0.505372	0.670082	0.681847	0.688906
1411	Dimension Stone	3	0.404486	0.458312	0.069469	0.081373	0.101212	0.378956	0.458312	0.505372	0.670082	0.681847	0.688906
142	CRUSHED AND BROKEN STONE, INCLUDING RIPRAP	2	1.680025	1.680025	1.232268	1.245975	1.268820	1.588646	1.680025	1.771404	2.091231	2.114075	2.127782
1422	Crushed And Broken Limestone	1	2.136920	2.136920	2.136920	2.136920	2.136920	2.136920	2.136920	2.136920	2.136920	2.136920	2.136920
1423	Crushed And Broken Granite	1	1.223130	1.223130	1.223130	1.223130	1.223130	1.223130	1.223130	1.223130	1.223130	1.223130	1.223130
144	SAND AND GRAVEL	3	1.482715	1.173630	0.942972	0.950033	0.961802	1.126557	1.173630	1.406154	2.219988	2.278119	2.312998

Betas of Common Stocks by SIC Codes as of March 31, 2017

SIC Code	Description	Number of Companies	Mean	Median	1st Percentile	2.5th Percentile	5th Percentile	40th Percentile	50th Percentile	60th Percentile	95th Percentile	97.5th Percentile	99th Percentile
1442	Construction Sand And Gravel	1	1.173630	1.173630	1.173630	1.173630	1.173630	1.173630	1.173630	1.173630	1.173630	1.173630	1.173630
1446	Industrial Sand	2	1.637258	1.637258	0.952245	0.973215	1.008164	1.497459	1.637258	1.777056	2.266351	2.301300	2.322270
147	CHEMICAL AND FERTILIZER MINERAL MINING	8	0.493819	0.478943	-0.714067	-0.614998	-0.449884	0.339969	0.478943	0.651183	1.266811	1.295081	1.312042
1474	Potash, Soda, And Borate Minerals	5	0.417567	0.581920	-0.741069	-0.682503	-0.584893	0.427547	0.581920	0.720445	1.115095	1.138452	1.152467
1479	Chemical And Fertilizer Mineral Mining, Not Elsewhere Classified	3	0.620905	0.375965	0.167650	0.174027	0.184656	0.333452	0.375965	0.565442	1.228612	1.275981	1.304402
148	NONMETALLIC MINERALS SERVICES, EXCEPT FUELS	3	1.368217	0.940957	0.376935	0.394201	0.422977	0.825850	0.940957	1.312420	2.612539	2.705404	2.761124
1481	Nonmetallic Minerals Services, Except Fuels	3	1.368217	0.940957	0.376935	0.394201	0.422977	0.825850	0.940957	1.312420	2.612539	2.705404	2.761124
149	MISCELLANEOUS NONMETALLIC MINERALS, EXCEPT FUELS	6	0.337973	0.283397	-0.227931	-0.200462	-0.154682	0.197762	0.283397	0.369031	0.843306	0.868137	0.883036
1499	Miscellaneous Nonmetallic Minerals, Except Fuels	6	0.337973	0.283397	-0.227931	-0.200462	-0.154682	0.197762	0.283397	0.369031	0.843306	0.868137	0.883036
	CONSTRUCTION												
15	CONSTRUCTION	27	1.403051	1.323290	-0.709404	-0.289972	0.098934	1.250548	1.323290	1.447490	2.460161	3.770537	5.222905
152	GENERAL BUILDING CONTRACTORS-RESIDENTIAL BUILDINGS	3	2.912440	1.536460	1.020245	1.036048	1.062385	1.431110	1.536460	2.467398	5.725681	5.958416	6.098056
1521	General Contractors-Single-Family Houses	2	1.273085	1.273085	1.014978	1.022879	1.036048	1.220410	1.273085	1.325760	1.510123	1.523291	1.531193
1522	General Contractors-Residential Buildings, Other Than Single-Family	1	6.191150	6.191150	6.191150	6.191150	6.191150	6.191150	6.191150	6.191150	6.191150	6.191150	6.191150
153	OPERATIVE BUILDERS	19	1.311541	1.323290	0.138636	0.154468	0.180854	1.291954	1.323290	1.430646	2.187437	2.327284	2.411191
1531	Operative Builders	19	1.311541	1.323290	0.138636	0.154468	0.180854	1.291954	1.323290	1.430646	2.187437	2.327284	2.411191
154	GENERAL BUILDING CONTRACTORS-NONRESIDENTIAL BUILDINGS	5	0.845157	0.770160	-0.946006	-0.881478	-0.773932	0.496673	0.770160	1.227820	2.337982	2.390941	2.422716
1541	General Contractors-Industrial Buildings And Warehouses	3	0.741678	0.770160	-0.953841	-0.901066	-0.813107	0.418323	0.770160	1.104908	2.276526	2.360213	2.410425
1542	General Contractors-Nonresidential Buildings, Other Than Industrial	2	1.000376	1.000376	0.104720	0.132138	0.177835	0.817589	1.000376	1.183163	1.822917	1.868613	1.896031
16	HEAVY CONSTRUCTION OTHER THAN BUILDING CONSTRUCTION-CONTRACTORS	20	1.331948	1.592505	-0.717166	-0.518439	-0.187226	1.417594	1.592505	1.777186	2.260659	2.497194	2.639116
161	HIGHWAY AND STREET CONSTRUCTION, EXCEPT ELEVATED HIGHWAYS	3	0.058306	0.113124	-0.830396	-0.801512	-0.753374	-0.079431	0.113124	0.272788	0.831612	0.871528	0.895478
1611	Highway And Street Construction, Except Elevated Highways	3	0.058306	0.113124	-0.830396	-0.801512	-0.753374	-0.079431	0.113124	0.272788	0.831612	0.871528	0.895478
162	HEAVY CONSTRUCTION, EXCEPT HIGHWAY AND STREET CONSTRUCTION	17	1.556708	1.765770	-0.026455	0.162406	0.477174	1.589488	1.765770	1.796614	2.335354	2.534542	2.654055
1622	Bridge, Tunnel, And Elevated Highway Construction	1	1.794310	1.794310	1.794310	1.794310	1.794310	1.794310	1.794310	1.794310	1.794310	1.794310	1.794310

Betas of Common Stocks by SIC Codes as of March 31, 2017

SIC Code	Description	Number of Companies	Mean	Median	1st Percentile	2.5th Percentile	5th Percentile	40th Percentile	50th Percentile	60th Percentile	95th Percentile	97.5th Percentile	99th Percentile
1623	Water, Sewer, Pipeline, And Communications And Power Line Construction	9	1.281715	1.577420	-0.089408	0.005022	0.162406	1.303980	1.577420	1.601556	2.094704	2.142582	2.171309
1629	Heavy Construction, Not Elsewhere Classified	7	1.876328	1.996880	0.790271	0.861949	0.981413	1.877642	1.996880	2.051780	2.584339	2.659035	2.703852
17	CONSTRUCTION-SPECIAL TRADE CONTRACTORS	10	1.360172	1.343920	0.643824	0.692546	0.773751	1.183560	1.343920	1.442940	2.055092	2.088871	2.109138
171	PLUMBING, HEATING AND AIR-CONDITIONING	1	1.085940	1.085940	1.085940	1.085940	1.085940	1.085940	1.085940	1.085940	1.085940	1.085940	1.085940
1711	Plumbing, Heating And Air-Conditioning	1	1.085940	1.085940	1.085940	1.085940	1.085940	1.085940	1.085940	1.085940	1.085940	1.085940	1.085940
173	ELECTRICAL WORK	5	1.346608	1.448550	0.630318	0.658783	0.706224	1.303430	1.448550	1.515082	1.900992	1.936756	1.958214
1731	Electrical Work	5	1.346608	1.448550	0.630318	0.658783	0.706224	1.303430	1.448550	1.515082	1.900992	1.936756	1.958214
174	MASONRY, STONEWORK, TILE SETTING, AND PLASTERING	2	1.343920	1.343920	1.250546	1.253404	1.258168	1.324864	1.343920	1.362976	1.429672	1.434436	1.437294
1742	Plastering, Drywall, Acoustical, And Insulation Work	2	1.343920	1.343920	1.250546	1.253404	1.258168	1.324864	1.343920	1.362976	1.429672	1.434436	1.437294
177	CONCRETE WORK	1	0.972250	0.972250	0.972250	0.972250	0.972250	0.972250	0.972250	0.972250	0.972250	0.972250	0.972250
1771	Concrete Work	1	0.972250	0.972250	0.972250	0.972250	0.972250	0.972250	0.972250	0.972250	0.972250	0.972250	0.972250
178	WATER WELL DRILLING	1	2.122650	2.122650	2.122650	2.122650	2.122650	2.122650	2.122650	2.122650	2.122650	2.122650	2.122650
1781	Water Well Drilling	1	2.122650	2.122650	2.122650	2.122650	2.122650	2.122650	2.122650	2.122650	2.122650	2.122650	2.122650
	MANUFACTURING												
20	FOOD AND KINDRED PRODUCTS	98	0.711510	0.727181	-0.288229	-0.253054	-0.143449	0.629105	0.727181	0.811994	1.508573	1.713138	1.801039
201	MEAT PRODUCTS	7	0.598915	0.500710	0.072959	0.093685	0.128229	0.466132	0.500710	0.532236	1.330524	1.448372	1.519081
2011	Meat Packing Plants	2	1.059737	1.059737	0.563383	0.578577	0.603901	0.958440	1.059737	1.161033	1.515572	1.540896	1.556090
2013	Sausages And Other Prepared Meat Products	2	0.174287	0.174287	0.061445	0.064899	0.070656	0.151258	0.174287	0.197316	0.277917	0.283675	0.287129
2015	Poultry Slaughtering And Processing	3	0.574785	0.500710	0.444233	0.445962	0.448843	0.489184	0.500710	0.556681	0.752580	0.766572	0.774968
202	DAIRY PRODUCTS	10	0.751210	0.737632	0.437546	0.446509	0.461447	0.690381	0.737632	0.774538	1.126405	1.223687	1.282057
2022	Natural, Processed, And Imitation Cheese	2	1.094919	1.094919	0.873388	0.880170	0.891472	1.049708	1.094919	1.140129	1.298365	1.309667	1.316449
2023	Dry, Condensed, And Evaporated Dairy Products	3	0.750053	0.728796	0.634680	0.637561	0.642363	0.709589	0.728796	0.760757	0.872622	0.880613	0.885407
2024	Ice Cream And Frozen Desserts	1	0.579460	0.579460	0.579460	0.579460	0.579460	0.579460	0.579460	0.579460	0.579460	0.579460	0.579460
2026	Fluid Milk	4	0.623161	0.622215	0.433563	0.436550	0.441530	0.547662	0.622215	0.696767	0.806116	0.811379	0.814537
203	CANNED, FROZEN, AND PRESERVED FRUITS, VEGETABLES, AND FOOD SPECIAL	9	0.899983	0.974154	0.415736	0.429678	0.452913	0.927145	0.974154	1.061271	1.246864	1.283802	1.305965
2030	CANNED, FROZEN & PRESERVD FRUIT, VEG & FOOD SPECIALTIES	1	1.320740	1.320740	1.320740	1.320740	1.320740	1.320740	1.320740	1.320740	1.320740	1.320740	1.320740
2032	Canned Specialties	2	0.802835	0.802835	0.528224	0.536631	0.550642	0.746792	0.802835	0.858878	1.055029	1.069039	1.077446
2033	Canned Fruits, Vegetables, Preserves, Jams, And Jellies	4	0.765809	0.764941	0.412683	0.422046	0.437649	0.674670	0.764941	0.855212	1.095182	1.111046	1.120564
2034	Dried And Dehydrated Fruits, Vegetables, And Soup Mixes	1	1.136050	1.136050	1.136050	1.136050	1.136050	1.136050	1.136050	1.136050	1.136050	1.136050	1.136050
2037	Frozen Fruits, Fruit Juices, And Vegetables	1	0.974154	0.974154	0.974154	0.974154	0.974154	0.974154	0.974154	0.974154	0.974154	0.974154	0.974154

Betas of Common Stocks by SIC Codes as of March 31, 2017

SIC Code	Description	Number of Companies	Mean	Median	1st Percentile	2.5th Percentile	5th Percentile	40th Percentile	50th Percentile	60th Percentile	95th Percentile	97.5th Percentile	99th Percentile
204	GRAIN MILL PRODUCTS	8	0.692864	0.699436	-0.204473	-0.112072	0.041928	0.667917	0.699436	0.782188	1.079954	1.090902	1.097471
2041	Flour And Other Grain Mill Products	2	0.857029	0.857029	0.678413	0.683881	0.692994	0.820577	0.857029	0.893481	1.021064	1.030177	1.035645
2043	Cereal Breakfast Foods	1	0.640512	0.640512	0.640512	0.640512	0.640512	0.640512	0.640512	0.640512	0.640512	0.640512	0.640512
2044	Rice Milling	1	-0.266073	-0.266073	-0.266073	-0.266073	-0.266073	-0.266073	-0.266073	-0.266073	-0.266073	-0.266073	-0.266073
2046	Wet Corn Milling	2	0.857891	0.857891	0.618810	0.626129	0.638327	0.809099	0.857891	0.906682	1.077454	1.089652	1.096971
2047	Dog And Cat Food	1	0.724103	0.724103	0.724103	0.724103	0.724103	0.724103	0.724103	0.724103	0.724103	0.724103	0.724103
2048	Prepared Feeds And Feed Ingredients For Animals And Fowls, Except Dog And Cat	1	1.014530	1.014530	1.014530	1.014530	1.014530	1.014530	1.014530	1.014530	1.014530	1.014530	1.014530
205	BAKERY PRODUCTS	7	0.689584	0.672424	0.137188	0.164236	0.209315	0.614678	0.672424	0.788537	1.148336	1.194453	1.222123
2051	Bread And Other Bakery Products, Except Cookies And Crackers	3	0.556097	0.576180	0.422817	0.427512	0.435336	0.544881	0.576180	0.595429	0.662800	0.667612	0.670499
2052	Cookies And Crackers	4	0.789699	0.899535	0.141560	0.175165	0.231175	0.879382	0.899535	0.919688	1.194453	1.217512	1.231347
206	SUGAR AND CONFECTIONERY PRODUCTS	4	0.763441	0.681297	0.205051	0.223471	0.254173	0.633793	0.681297	0.728801	1.387711	1.443055	1.476262
2061	Cane Sugar, Except Refining	1	1.498400	1.498400	1.498400	1.498400	1.498400	1.498400	1.498400	1.498400	1.498400	1.498400	1.498400
2066	Chocolate And Cocoa Products	2	0.397447	0.397447	0.196864	0.203004	0.213238	0.356511	0.397447	0.438382	0.581655	0.591889	0.598029
2068	Salted And Roasted Nuts And Seeds	1	0.760471	0.760471	0.760471	0.760471	0.760471	0.760471	0.760471	0.760471	0.760471	0.760471	0.760471
207	FATS AND OILS	4	1.050541	0.961503	0.560284	0.574827	0.599066	0.908866	0.961503	1.014139	1.626669	1.677620	1.708190
2075	Soybean Oil Mills	1	0.873775	0.873775	0.873775	0.873775	0.873775	0.873775	0.873775	0.873775	0.873775	0.873775	0.873775
2077	Animal And Marine Fats And Oils	2	1.388900	1.388900	1.056023	1.066214	1.083197	1.320966	1.388900	1.456834	1.694603	1.711587	1.721777
2079	Shortening, Table Oils, Margarine, And Other Edible Fats And Oils	1	0.550588	0.550588	0.550588	0.550588	0.550588	0.550588	0.550588	0.550588	0.550588	0.550588	0.550588
208	BEVERAGES	32	0.670353	0.741270	-0.218355	-0.192730	-0.156466	0.637638	0.741270	0.800285	1.467585	1.715903	1.764765
2082	Malt Beverages	4	1.059230	0.880062	0.682850	0.687941	0.696428	0.827588	0.880062	0.932536	1.672867	1.735103	1.772445
2084	Wines, Brandy, And Brandy Spirits	5	0.349813	0.167146	-0.127706	-0.113855	-0.090771	0.137850	0.167146	0.424957	0.812957	0.813118	0.813214
2085	Distilled And Blended Liquors	5	0.774903	0.776577	0.548532	0.558371	0.574770	0.748331	0.776577	0.785324	1.000937	1.026248	1.041435
2086	Bottled And Canned Soft Drinks And Carbonated Waters	17	0.582266	0.633940	-0.226622	-0.213395	-0.191352	0.552045	0.633940	0.738182	1.256448	1.270104	1.278298
2087	Flavoring Extracts And Flavoring Syrups, Not Elsewhere Classified	1	1.692260	1.692260	1.692260	1.692260	1.692260	1.692260	1.692260	1.692260	1.692260	1.692260	1.692260
209	MISCELLANEOUS FOOD PREPARATIONS AND KINDRED PRODUCTS	17	0.638025	0.725565	-0.714631	-0.588290	-0.377721	0.582757	0.725565	0.804975	1.342430	1.631530	1.804990
2095	Roasted Coffee	4	0.266700	0.357120	-0.778301	-0.747463	-0.696068	0.074697	0.357120	0.639542	1.102880	1.127150	1.141712
2096	Potato Chips, Corn Chips, And Similar Snacks	1	1.197880	1.197880	1.197880	1.197880	1.197880	1.197880	1.197880	1.197880	1.197880	1.197880	1.197880
2097	Manufactured Ice	1	1.124350	1.124350	1.124350	1.124350	1.124350	1.124350	1.124350	1.124350	1.124350	1.124350	1.124350
2099	Food Preparations, Not Elsewhere Classified	11	0.677945	0.584394	-0.247094	-0.209081	-0.145725	0.581665	0.584394	0.725565	1.550705	1.735668	1.846645
21	TOBACCO PRODUCTS	9	0.496204	0.415094	0.268596	0.280358	0.299962	0.379388	0.415094	0.545823	0.757664	0.766866	0.772387
211	CIGARETTES	9	0.496204	0.415094	0.268596	0.280358	0.299962	0.379388	0.415094	0.545823	0.757664	0.766866	0.772387
2111	Cigarettes	9	0.496204	0.415094	0.268596	0.280358	0.299962	0.379388	0.415094	0.545823	0.757664	0.766866	0.772387

Betas of Common Stocks by SIC Codes as of March 31, 2017

SIC Code	Description	Number of Companies	Mean	Median	1st Percentile	2.5th Percentile	5th Percentile	40th Percentile	50th Percentile	60th Percentile	95th Percentile	97.5th Percentile	99th Percentile
22	TEXTILE MILL PRODUCTS	11	1.322688	1.387540	0.109897	0.282897	0.571232	1.341230	1.387540	1.402340	1.935440	2.075940	2.160240
221	BROADWOVEN FABRIC MILLS, COTTON	2	0.617837	0.617837	0.007029	0.025727	0.056891	0.493182	0.617837	0.742491	1.178783	1.209946	1.228645
2211	Broadwoven Fabric Mills, Cotton	2	0.617837	0.617837	0.007029	0.025727	0.056891	0.493182	0.617837	0.742491	1.178783	1.209946	1.228645
222	BROADWOVEN FABRIC MILLS, MANMADE FIBER AND SILK	2	1.935440	1.935440	1.660060	1.668490	1.682540	1.879240	1.935440	1.991640	2.188340	2.202390	2.210820
2221	Broadwoven Fabric Mills, Manmade Fiber And Silk	2	1.935440	1.935440	1.660060	1.668490	1.682540	1.879240	1.935440	1.991640	2.188340	2.202390	2.210820
225	KNITTING MILLS	3	1.294180	1.201960	1.148981	1.150603	1.153306	1.191148	1.201960	1.268104	1.499608	1.516144	1.526066
2252	Hosiery, Not Elsewhere Classified	1	1.201960	1.201960	1.201960	1.201960	1.201960	1.201960	1.201960	1.201960	1.201960	1.201960	1.201960
2253	Knit Outerwear Mills	2	1.340290	1.340290	1.151748	1.157520	1.167139	1.301812	1.340290	1.378768	1.513441	1.523061	1.528832
227	CARPETS AND RUGS	3	1.386043	1.387540	1.342156	1.343546	1.345861	1.378278	1.387540	1.395904	1.425178	1.427269	1.428524
2273	Carpets And Rugs	3	1.386043	1.387540	1.342156	1.343546	1.345861	1.378278	1.387540	1.395904	1.425178	1.427269	1.428524
228	YARN AND THREAD MILLS	1	1.402340	1.402340	1.402340	1.402340	1.402340	1.402340	1.402340	1.402340	1.402340	1.402340	1.402340
2282	Yarn Texturizing, Throwing, Twisting, And Winding Mills	1	1.402340	1.402340	1.402340	1.402340	1.402340	1.402340	1.402340	1.402340	1.402340	1.402340	1.402340
23	APPAREL AND OTHER FINISHED PRODUCTS MADE FROM FABRICS AND SIMILAR MATERIAL	19	1.177982	1.161670	0.290974	0.361648	0.479438	1.125284	1.161670	1.282544	1.615328	1.877669	2.035074
2300	APPAREL & OTHER FINISHD PRODS OF FABRICS & SIMILAR MATL	1	1.530320	1.530320	1.530320	1.530320	1.530320	1.530320	1.530320	1.530320	1.530320	1.530320	1.530320
232	MEN'S AND BOYS' FURNISHINGS, WORK CLOTHING, AND ALLIED GARMENTS	7	1.178878	1.150620	0.903202	0.909235	0.919290	1.131618	1.150620	1.157250	1.489577	1.498444	1.503763
2321	Men's And Boys' Shirts, Except Work Shirts	2	1.477755	1.477755	1.448791	1.449678	1.451156	1.471844	1.477755	1.483666	1.504355	1.505832	1.506719
2325	Men's And Boys' Separate Trousers And Slacks	1	1.118950	1.118950	1.118950	1.118950	1.118950	1.118950	1.118950	1.118950	1.118950	1.118950	1.118950
2326	Men's And Boys' Work Clothing	2	0.932697	0.932697	0.899850	0.900856	0.902532	0.925994	0.932697	0.939400	0.962862	0.964538	0.965544
2329	Men's And Boys' Clothing, Not Elsewhere Classified	2	1.156145	1.156145	1.150731	1.150896	1.151173	1.155040	1.156145	1.157250	1.161118	1.161394	1.161560
233	WOMEN'S, MISSES', AND JUNIORS' OUTERWEAR	7	1.238530	1.260680	0.530183	0.567038	0.628463	1.106222	1.260680	1.277078	1.965116	2.052563	2.105031
2337	Women's, Misses', And Juniors' Suits, Skirts, And Coats	1	1.260680	1.260680	1.260680	1.260680	1.260680	1.260680	1.260680	1.260680	1.260680	1.260680	1.260680
2339	Women's, Misses', And Juniors' Outerwear, Not Elsewhere Classified	6	1.234838	1.145630	0.526088	0.556801	0.607988	1.003250	1.145630	1.288010	1.994265	2.067138	2.110861
234	WOMEN'S, MISSES', CHILDREN'S, AND INFANTS' UNDERGARMENTS	1	0.873227	0.873227	0.873227	0.873227	0.873227	0.873227	0.873227	0.873227	0.873227	0.873227	0.873227
2341	Women's, Misses', Children's, And Infants' Underwear And Nightwear	1	0.873227	0.873227	0.873227	0.873227	0.873227	0.873227	0.873227	0.873227	0.873227	0.873227	0.873227
238	MISCELLANEOUS APPAREL AND ACCESSORIES	3	1.018753	1.390970	0.266800	0.301214	0.358569	1.161548	1.390970	1.397062	1.418384	1.419907	1.420821
2385	Waterproof Outerwear	2	0.817414	0.817414	0.255329	0.272536	0.301214	0.702703	0.817414	0.932125	1.333614	1.362292	1.379499

Betas of Common Stocks by SIC Codes as of March 31, 2017

SIC Code	Description	Number of Companies	Mean	Median	1st Percentile	2.5th Percentile	5th Percentile	40th Percentile	50th Percentile	60th Percentile	95th Percentile	97.5th Percentile	99th Percentile
2389	Apparel And Accessories, Not Elsewhere Classified	1	1.421430	1.421430	1.421430	1.421430	1.421430	1.421430	1.421430	1.421430	1.421430	1.421430	1.421430
24	LUMBER AND WOOD PRODUCTS, EXCEPT FURNITURE	13	1.494501	1.506650	0.703012	0.790045	0.935102	1.439832	1.506650	1.554288	2.032874	2.074547	2.099551
2400	LUMBER & WOOD PRODUCTS (NO FURNITURE)	1	1.576920	1.576920	1.576920	1.576920	1.576920	1.576920	1.576920	1.576920	1.576920	1.576920	1.576920
241	LOGGING	1	1.977310	1.977310	1.977310	1.977310	1.977310	1.977310	1.977310	1.977310	1.977310	1.977310	1.977310
2411	Logging	1	1.977310	1.977310	1.977310	1.977310	1.977310	1.977310	1.977310	1.977310	1.977310	1.977310	1.977310
242	SAWMILLS AND PLANING MILLS	3	1.259556	1.265820	0.657406	0.676031	0.707072	1.141654	1.265820	1.386228	1.807656	1.837758	1.855819
2421	Sawmills And Planing Mills, General	3	1.259556	1.265820	0.657406	0.676031	0.707072	1.141654	1.265820	1.386228	1.807656	1.837758	1.855819
243	MILLWORK, VENEER, PLYWOOD, AND STRUCTURAL WOOD MEMBERS	3	1.503567	1.506650	1.456445	1.457982	1.460543	1.496404	1.506650	1.515046	1.544432	1.546531	1.547790
2431	Millwork	1	1.548630	1.548630	1.548630	1.548630	1.548630	1.548630	1.548630	1.548630	1.548630	1.548630	1.548630
2434	Wood Kitchen Cabinets	1	1.506650	1.506650	1.506650	1.506650	1.506650	1.506650	1.506650	1.506650	1.506650	1.506650	1.506650
2439	Structural Wood Members, Not Elsewhere Classified	1	1.455420	1.455420	1.455420	1.455420	1.455420	1.455420	1.455420	1.455420	1.455420	1.455420	1.455420
245	WOOD BUILDINGS AND MOBILE HOMES	2	1.232455	1.232455	1.130589	1.133707	1.138905	1.211666	1.232455	1.253244	1.326006	1.331203	1.334321
2451	Mobile Homes	2	1.232455	1.232455	1.130589	1.133707	1.138905	1.211666	1.232455	1.253244	1.326006	1.331203	1.334321
249	MISCELLANEOUS WOOD PRODUCTS	3	1.706667	1.626300	1.382456	1.389921	1.402362	1.576536	1.626300	1.724284	2.067228	2.091724	2.106422
2491	Wood Preserving	1	2.116220	2.116220	2.116220	2.116220	2.116220	2.116220	2.116220	2.116220	2.116220	2.116220	2.116220
2493	Reconstituted Wood Products	1	1.626300	1.626300	1.626300	1.626300	1.626300	1.626300	1.626300	1.626300	1.626300	1.626300	1.626300
2499	Wood Products, Not Elsewhere Classified	1	1.377480	1.377480	1.377480	1.377480	1.377480	1.377480	1.377480	1.377480	1.377480	1.377480	1.377480
25	FURNITURE AND FIXTURES	20	1.102773	1.248670	-0.259977	-0.089924	0.193496	1.133318	1.248670	1.286134	1.679645	1.835588	1.929153
251	HOUSEHOLD FURNITURE	12	1.045492	1.162595	-0.297707	-0.184249	0.004847	1.079798	1.162595	1.292828	1.793041	1.892285	1.951832
2511	Wood Household Furniture, Except Upholstered	7	0.984690	1.089080	0.324512	0.339865	0.365453	1.057592	1.089080	1.177298	1.377342	1.385886	1.391012
2512	Wood Household Furniture, Upholstered	1	-0.373345	-0.373345	-0.373345	-0.373345	-0.373345	-0.373345	-0.373345	-0.373345	-0.373345	-0.373345	-0.373345
2515	Mattresses, Foundations, And Convertible Beds	3	1.344963	1.330640	1.078751	1.086462	1.099313	1.279234	1.330640	1.390640	1.600640	1.615640	1.624640
2519	Household Furniture, Not Elsewhere Classified	1	1.991530	1.991530	1.991530	1.991530	1.991530	1.991530	1.991530	1.991530	1.991530	1.991530	1.991530
252	OFFICE FURNITURE	6	1.353903	1.287075	1.048516	1.065309	1.093298	1.282370	1.287075	1.291780	1.644295	1.653763	1.659443
2521	Wood Office Furniture	3	1.305530	1.291780	1.042409	1.050043	1.062766	1.240888	1.291780	1.350922	1.557919	1.572705	1.581576
2522	Office Furniture, Except Wood	3	1.402277	1.282370	1.261653	1.262287	1.263344	1.278142	1.282370	1.358542	1.625144	1.644187	1.655613
253	PUBLIC BUILDING AND RELATED FURNITURE	2	0.693070	0.693070	0.232725	0.246817	0.270304	0.599122	0.693070	0.787018	1.115836	1.139323	1.153415
2531	Public Building And Related Furniture	2	0.693070	0.693070	0.232725	0.246817	0.270304	0.599122	0.693070	0.787018	1.115836	1.139323	1.153415
26	PAPER AND ALLIED PRODUCTS	25	1.198447	1.163580	0.079938	0.143958	0.256463	1.104168	1.163580	1.306322	2.082004	2.165906	2.203720
261	PULP MILLS	3	0.690678	0.941905	0.055352	0.082491	0.127723	0.760976	0.941905	0.972098	1.077774	1.085322	1.089851
2611	Pulp Mills	3	0.690678	0.941905	0.055352	0.082491	0.127723	0.760976	0.941905	0.972098	1.077774	1.085322	1.089851
262	PAPER MILLS	9	1.279248	1.284820	0.441929	0.471898	0.521847	1.146324	1.284820	1.322028	2.103142	2.166036	2.203772

Betas of Common Stocks by SIC Codes as of March 31, 2017

SIC Code	Description	Number of Companies	Mean	Median	1st Percentile	2.5th Percentile	5th Percentile	40th Percentile	50th Percentile	60th Percentile	95th Percentile	97.5th Percentile	99th Percentile
2621	Paper Mills	9	1.279248	1.284820	0.441929	0.471898	0.521847	1.146324	1.284820	1.322028	2.103142	2.166036	2.203772
263	PAPERBOARD MILLS	4	1.150085	1.154085	1.006782	1.013175	1.023831	1.148388	1.154085	1.159782	1.270740	1.280195	1.285868
2631	Paperboard Mills	4	1.150085	1.154085	1.006782	1.013175	1.023831	1.148388	1.154085	1.159782	1.270740	1.280195	1.285868
265	PAPERBOARD CONTAINERS AND BOXES	3	1.549690	1.480900	1.350158	1.354161	1.360831	1.454218	1.480900	1.548856	1.786702	1.803691	1.813884
2655	Fiber Cans, Tubes, Drums, And Similar Products	2	1.650790	1.650790	1.484298	1.489395	1.497889	1.616812	1.650790	1.684768	1.803691	1.812186	1.817282
2657	Folding Paperboard Boxes, Including Sanitary	1	1.347490	1.347490	1.347490	1.347490	1.347490	1.347490	1.347490	1.347490	1.347490	1.347490	1.347490
267	CONVERTED PAPER AND PAPERBOARD PRODUCTS, EXCEPT CONTAINERS AND BOXES	6	1.187750	1.238551	0.231122	0.255169	0.295248	0.955321	1.238551	1.521780	2.036593	2.080241	2.106431
2671	Packaging Paper And Plastics Film, Coated And Laminated	3	0.897397	0.955321	0.229896	0.252103	0.289114	0.807275	0.955321	1.068613	1.465134	1.493457	1.510451
2673	Plastics, Foil, And Coated Paper Bags	1	2.123890	2.123890	2.123890	2.123890	2.123890	2.123890	2.123890	2.123890	2.123890	2.123890	2.123890
2679	Converted Paper And Paperboard Products, Not Elsewhere Classified	2	1.155209	1.155209	0.548108	0.566693	0.597667	1.031311	1.155209	1.279107	1.712751	1.743725	1.762310
27	PRINTING, PUBLISHING, AND ALLIED INDUSTRIES	41	1.005681	1.106610	-0.190149	-0.138617	-0.013929	0.968178	1.106610	1.197900	1.567490	1.636270	1.683640
271	NEWSPAPERS: PUBLISHING, OR PUBLISHING AND PRINTING	18	0.991342	1.136415	-0.117420	-0.085625	-0.032633	1.100302	1.136415	1.221696	1.534179	1.550834	1.560828
2711	Newspapers: Publishing, Or Publishing And Printing	18	0.991342	1.136415	-0.117420	-0.085625	-0.032633	1.100302	1.136415	1.221696	1.534179	1.550834	1.560828
272	PERIODICALS: PUBLISHING, OR PUBLISHING AND PRINTING	3	1.064385	1.136480	0.844023	0.852975	0.867897	1.076795	1.136480	1.152908	1.210406	1.214513	1.216977
2721	Periodicals: Publishing, Or Publishing And Printing	3	1.064385	1.136480	0.844023	0.852975	0.867897	1.076795	1.136480	1.152908	1.210406	1.214513	1.216977
273	BOOKS	4	1.073802	1.081282	0.658981	0.671712	0.692931	0.992560	1.081282	1.170003	1.444200	1.463175	1.474560
2731	Books: Publishing, Or Publishing And Printing	4	1.073802	1.081282	0.658981	0.671712	0.692931	0.992560	1.081282	1.170003	1.444200	1.463175	1.474560
274	MISCELLANEOUS PUBLISHING	4	0.824703	0.914315	0.512901	0.529247	0.556489	0.884870	0.914315	0.943760	0.967460	0.967819	0.968034
2741	Miscellaneous Publishing	4	0.824703	0.914315	0.512901	0.529247	0.556489	0.884870	0.914315	0.943760	0.967460	0.967819	0.968034
275	COMMERCIAL PRINTING	8	1.035316	1.148995	-0.169549	-0.087117	0.050269	1.020581	1.148995	1.277208	1.687588	1.701404	1.709694
2752	Commercial Printing, Lithographic	3	1.087296	0.986107	0.569072	0.581838	0.603116	0.900998	0.986107	1.131930	1.642309	1.678764	1.700638
2754	Commercial Printing, Gravure	3	0.813656	1.029200	-0.199429	-0.161818	-0.099133	0.778459	1.029200	1.150614	1.575563	1.605917	1.624129
2759	Commercial Printing, Not Elsewhere Classified	2	1.289835	1.289835	1.269211	1.269842	1.270895	1.285626	1.289835	1.294044	1.308776	1.309828	1.310459
276	MANIFOLD BUSINESS FORMS	1	1.269250	1.269250	1.269250	1.269250	1.269250	1.269250	1.269250	1.269250	1.269250	1.269250	1.269250
2761	Manifold Business Forms	1	1.269250	1.269250	1.269250	1.269250	1.269250	1.269250	1.269250	1.269250	1.269250	1.269250	1.269250
277	GREETING CARDS	1	0.876891	0.876891	0.876891	0.876891	0.876891	0.876891	0.876891	0.876891	0.876891	0.876891	0.876891
2771	Greeting Cards	1	0.876891	0.876891	0.876891	0.876891	0.876891	0.876891	0.876891	0.876891	0.876891	0.876891	0.876891
278	BLANKBOOKS, LOOSELEAF BINDERS, AND BOOKBINDING AND RELATED WORK	2	1.086464	1.086464	0.744379	0.754851	0.772305	1.016651	1.086464	1.156277	1.400623	1.418077	1.428549

Betas of Common Stocks by SIC Codes as of March 31, 2017

SIC Code	Description	Number of Companies	Mean	Median	1st Percentile	2.5th Percentile	5th Percentile	40th Percentile	50th Percentile	60th Percentile	95th Percentile	97.5th Percentile	99th Percentile
2782	Blankbooks, Looseleaf Binders And Devices	2	1.086464	1.086464	0.744379	0.754851	0.772305	1.016651	1.086464	1.156277	1.400623	1.418077	1.428549
28	CHEMICALS AND ALLIED PRODUCTS	479	1.269932	1.262450	-1.046172	-0.265537	-0.029115	1.050830	1.262450	1.455032	2.699830	2.919498	3.138062
281	INDUSTRIAL INORGANIC CHEMICALS	15	1.847721	1.845110	0.402039	0.507095	0.682189	1.188842	1.845110	2.105690	3.214135	3.235188	3.247819
2812	Alkalies And Chlorine	1	1.845110	1.845110	1.845110	1.845110	1.845110	1.845110	1.845110	1.845110	1.845110	1.845110	1.845110
2813	Industrial Gases	3	1.066633	1.019360	0.995231	0.995970	0.997201	1.014436	1.019360	1.052648	1.169156	1.177478	1.182471
2816	Inorganic Pigments	4	2.717558	2.728290	2.224660	2.235310	2.253059	2.563848	2.728290	2.892732	3.167031	3.181560	3.190278
2819	Industrial Inorganic Chemicals, Not Elsewhere Classified	7	1.685796	1.190870	0.362017	0.407041	0.482082	1.084802	1.190870	1.695014	3.222565	3.239403	3.249505
282	PLASTICS MATERIALS AND SYNTHETIC RESINS, SYNTHETIC RUBBER, CELLULOSIC MANMADE FIBERS	14	1.506620	1.604645	0.845681	0.846543	0.847980	1.372092	1.604645	1.714014	2.076583	2.220162	2.306309
2821	Plastics Materials, Synthetic Resins, And Nonvulcanizable Elastomers	14	1.506620	1.604645	0.845681	0.846543	0.847980	1.372092	1.604645	1.714014	2.076583	2.220162	2.306309
283	DRUGS	378	1.287674	1.282540	-1.068061	-0.248239	-0.017550	1.067636	1.282540	1.518234	2.714137	2.831435	3.074743
2833	Medicinal Chemicals And Botanical Products	15	0.947538	1.039860	0.037179	0.057036	0.090130	0.829369	1.039860	1.154604	1.743633	1.824487	1.872999
2834	Pharmaceutical Preparations	281	1.280839	1.292570	-1.045870	-0.261642	0.041561	1.055950	1.292570	1.523370	2.697000	2.830170	3.100766
2835	In Vitro And In Vivo Diagnostic Substances	21	1.006636	1.031770	-0.927549	-0.666008	-0.230105	0.864857	1.031770	1.226540	2.416120	2.688595	2.852080
2836	Biological Products, Except Diagnostic Substances	61	1.499552	1.508210	-1.051785	0.026734	0.456294	1.262450	1.508210	1.723330	2.777610	2.888765	3.009984
284	SOAP, DETERGENTS, AND CLEANING PREPARATIONS; PERFUMES, COSMETICS	19	0.708752	0.585277	-0.286070	-0.205858	-0.072173	0.515578	0.585277	0.755307	1.530174	1.893882	2.112107
2841	Soap And Other Detergents, Except Specialty Cleaners	5	0.796829	0.585277	0.514956	0.515189	0.515578	0.558642	0.585277	0.717578	1.342686	1.396018	1.428017
2842	Specialty Cleaning, Polishing, And Sanitation Preparations	3	0.239695	0.213337	0.141436	0.143637	0.147306	0.198663	0.213337	0.243826	0.350536	0.358158	0.362731
2844	Perfumes, Cosmetics, And Other Toilet Preparations	11	0.796642	0.777138	-0.309836	-0.265274	-0.191004	0.667984	0.777138	1.026420	1.750655	2.004123	2.156203
285	PAINTS, VARNISHES, LACQUERS, ENAMELS, AND ALLIED PRODUCTS	6	0.891223	1.407940	-0.807728	-0.727734	-0.594410	1.354400	1.407940	1.461480	1.653750	1.683880	1.701958
2851	Paints, Varnishes, Lacquers, Enamels, And Allied Products	6	0.891223	1.407940	-0.807728	-0.727734	-0.594410	1.354400	1.407940	1.461480	1.653750	1.683880	1.701958
286	INDUSTRIAL ORGANIC CHEMICALS	21	1.304355	1.353490	-0.371499	-0.325805	-0.249649	1.267670	1.353490	1.416240	2.509160	2.533790	2.548568
2861	Gum And Wood Chemicals	2	0.986476	0.986476	0.565306	0.578199	0.599687	0.900523	0.986476	1.072428	1.373264	1.394752	1.407645
2865	Cyclic Organic Crudes And Intermediates, And Organic Dyes And Pigments	1	1.045530	1.045530	1.045530	1.045530	1.045530	1.045530	1.045530	1.045530	1.045530	1.045530	1.045530
2869	Industrial Organic Chemicals, Not Elsewhere Classified	18	1.354054	1.378490	-0.376068	-0.337228	-0.272496	1.269990	1.378490	1.483168	2.516549	2.537485	2.550046
287	AGRICULTURAL CHEMICALS	13	1.122410	1.029280	-0.006438	0.107191	0.296573	0.971787	1.029280	1.123300	2.132094	2.230632	2.289755
2873	Nitrogenous Fertilizers	6	1.063431	1.101070	-0.048183	0.002829	0.087849	1.029280	1.101070	1.172860	1.916023	1.958366	1.983773
2874	Phosphatic Fertilizers	2	1.343920	1.343920	1.115570	1.122561	1.134211	1.297318	1.343920	1.390522	1.553629	1.565280	1.572270

Betas of Common Stocks by SIC Codes as of March 31, 2017

SIC Code	Description	Number of Companies	Mean	Median	1st Percentile	2.5th Percentile	5th Percentile	40th Percentile	50th Percentile	60th Percentile	95th Percentile	97.5th Percentile	99th Percentile
2879	Pesticides And Agricultural Chemicals, Not Elsewhere Classified	5	1.104581	0.949018	0.555845	0.565990	0.582897	0.856674	0.949018	0.960402	2.058832	2.194001	2.275102
289	MISCELLANEOUS CHEMICAL PRODUCTS	13	0.919362	1.035140	-0.137171	-0.097747	-0.032041	0.937191	1.035140	1.315238	1.562544	1.583322	1.595789
2890	MISCELLANEOUS CHEMICAL PRODUCTS	1	0.055568	0.055568	0.055568	0.055568	0.055568	0.055568	0.055568	0.055568	0.055568	0.055568	0.055568
2891	Adhesives And Sealants	2	0.746757	0.746757	0.110528	0.130005	0.162465	0.616914	0.746757	0.876600	1.331049	1.363509	1.382986
2893	Printing Ink	1	1.321510	1.321510	1.321510	1.321510	1.321510	1.321510	1.321510	1.321510	1.321510	1.321510	1.321510
2895	Carbon Black	1	1.604100	1.604100	1.604100	1.604100	1.604100	1.604100	1.604100	1.604100	1.604100	1.604100	1.604100
2899	Chemicals And Chemical Preparations, Not Elsewhere Classified	8	0.934626	1.014649	-0.104010	-0.014844	0.133767	0.937191	1.014649	1.090846	1.476299	1.505570	1.523132
29	PETROLEUM REFINING AND RELATED INDUSTRIES	22	1.485533	1.492720	0.508506	0.605551	0.757274	1.302350	1.492720	1.657322	2.240511	2.350014	2.419828
291	PETROLEUM REFINING	20	1.558602	1.566885	0.772353	0.803050	0.854211	1.404716	1.566885	1.712946	2.255822	2.361096	2.424260
2911	Petroleum Refining	20	1.558602	1.566885	0.772353	0.803050	0.854211	1.404716	1.566885	1.712946	2.255822	2.361096	2.424260
295	ASPHALT PAVING AND ROOFING MATERIALS	1	1.065870	1.065870	1.065870	1.065870	1.065870	1.065870	1.065870	1.065870	1.065870	1.065870	1.065870
2951	Asphalt Paving Mixtures And Blocks	1	1.065870	1.065870	1.065870	1.065870	1.065870	1.065870	1.065870	1.065870	1.065870	1.065870	1.065870
299	MISCELLANEOUS PRODUCTS OF PETROLEUM AND COAL	1	0.443809	0.443809	0.443809	0.443809	0.443809	0.443809	0.443809	0.443809	0.443809	0.443809	0.443809
2999	Products Of Petroleum And Coal, Not Elsewhere Classified	1	0.443809	0.443809	0.443809	0.443809	0.443809	0.443809	0.443809	0.443809	0.443809	0.443809	0.443809
30	RUBBER AND MISCELLANEOUS PLASTICS PRODUCTS	36	0.770269	1.128925	-3.922699	-2.362473	-0.983820	0.999062	1.128925	1.167940	1.793255	1.827716	1.832657
301	TIRES AND INNER TUBES	2	1.367125	1.367125	1.171924	1.177899	1.187859	1.327288	1.367125	1.406962	1.546392	1.556351	1.562326
3011	Tires And Inner Tubes	2	1.367125	1.367125	1.171924	1.177899	1.187859	1.327288	1.367125	1.406962	1.546392	1.556351	1.562326
302	RUBBER AND PLASTICS FOOTWEAR	4	1.279422	1.223545	0.853494	0.867649	0.891239	1.184578	1.223545	1.262512	1.745833	1.786186	1.810399
3021	Rubber And Plastics Footwear	4	1.279422	1.223545	0.853494	0.867649	0.891239	1.184578	1.223545	1.262512	1.745833	1.786186	1.810399
305	GASKETS, PACKING, AND SEALING DEVICES AND RUBBER AND PLASTICS HOSE	3	-0.906659	0.658882	-4.850415	-4.681763	-4.400677	-0.465464	0.658882	0.843904	1.491479	1.537735	1.565488
3052	Rubber And Plastics Hose And Belting	1	-4.962850	-4.962850	-4.962850	-4.962850	-4.962850	-4.962850	-4.962850	-4.962850	-4.962850	-4.962850	-4.962850
3053	Gaskets, Packing, And Sealing Devices	2	1.121436	1.121436	0.668133	0.682010	0.705137	1.028925	1.121436	1.213947	1.537735	1.560862	1.574739
306	FABRICATED RUBBER PRODUCTS, NOT ELSEWHERE CLASSIFIED	3	0.578491	0.584254	0.127815	0.141788	0.165075	0.491103	0.584254	0.673947	0.987873	1.010297	1.023751
3069	Fabricated Rubber Products, Not Elsewhere Classified	3	0.578491	0.584254	0.127815	0.141788	0.165075	0.491103	0.584254	0.673947	0.987873	1.010297	1.023751
308	MISCELLANEOUS PLASTICS PRODUCTS	24	0.869260	1.128925	-1.682124	-1.218826	-0.543026	1.003550	1.128925	1.198588	1.766002	1.805021	1.823578
3081	Unsupported Plastics Film And Sheet	3	0.701870	0.255577	0.177194	0.179593	0.183592	0.239580	0.255577	0.539350	1.532554	1.603497	1.646063
3084	Plastics Pipe	1	1.471550	1.471550	1.471550	1.471550	1.471550	1.471550	1.471550	1.471550	1.471550	1.471550	1.471550
3086	Plastics Foam Products	3	0.981544	1.021500	0.775991	0.783507	0.796033	0.971396	1.021500	1.047630	1.139085	1.145618	1.149537

Betas of Common Stocks by SIC Codes as of March 31, 2017

SIC Code	Description	Number of Companies	Mean	Median	1st Percentile	2.5th Percentile	5th Percentile	40th Percentile	50th Percentile	60th Percentile	95th Percentile	97.5th Percentile	99th Percentile
3089	Plastics Products, Not Elsewhere Classified	17	0.843556	1.159420	-1.776127	-1.453832	-0.916675	1.041717	1.159420	1.241398	1.792918	1.814434	1.827344
31	LEATHER AND LEATHER PRODUCTS	7	0.993418	1.142920	0.205655	0.217069	0.236093	1.048491	1.142920	1.207120	1.622653	1.694907	1.738259
314	FOOTWEAR, EXCEPT RUBBER	4	1.090760	1.135504	0.344691	0.374421	0.423971	1.045524	1.135504	1.225484	1.694907	1.731033	1.752709
3142	House Slippers	1	0.985538	0.985538	0.985538	0.985538	0.985538	0.985538	0.985538	0.985538	0.985538	0.985538	0.985538
3143	Men's Footwear, Except Athletic	1	1.285470	1.285470	1.285470	1.285470	1.285470	1.285470	1.285470	1.285470	1.285470	1.285470	1.285470
3149	Footwear, Except Rubber, Not Elsewhere Classified	2	1.046016	1.046016	0.339294	0.360928	0.396985	0.901787	1.046016	1.190244	1.695046	1.731103	1.752737
317	HANDBAGS AND OTHER PERSONAL LEATHER GOODS	1	1.142920	1.142920	1.142920	1.142920	1.142920	1.142920	1.142920	1.142920	1.142920	1.142920	1.142920
3171	Women's Handbags And Purses	1	1.142920	1.142920	1.142920	1.142920	1.142920	1.142920	1.142920	1.142920	1.142920	1.142920	1.142920
319	LEATHER GOODS, NOT ELSEWHERE CLASSIFIED	2	0.723983	0.723983	0.208564	0.224342	0.250639	0.618795	0.723983	0.829170	1.197326	1.223623	1.239401
3199	Leather Goods, Not Elsewhere Classified	2	0.723983	0.723983	0.208564	0.224342	0.250639	0.618795	0.723983	0.829170	1.197326	1.223623	1.239401
32	STONE, CLAY, GLASS, AND CONCRETE PRODUCTS	14	0.917246	1.061017	-0.686666	-0.540366	-0.296532	0.747409	1.061017	1.376480	1.754374	1.871192	1.941283
322	GLASS AND GLASSWARE, PRESSED OR BLOWN	2	1.600945	1.600945	1.221621	1.233233	1.252587	1.523532	1.600945	1.678358	1.949304	1.968657	1.980269
3221	Glass Containers	1	1.988010	1.988010	1.988010	1.988010	1.988010	1.988010	1.988010	1.988010	1.988010	1.988010	1.988010
3229	Pressed And Blown Glass And Glassware, Not Elsewhere Classified	1	1.213880	1.213880	1.213880	1.213880	1.213880	1.213880	1.213880	1.213880	1.213880	1.213880	1.213880
323	GLASS PRODUCTS, MADE OF PURCHASED GLASS	1	1.468660	1.468660	1.468660	1.468660	1.468660	1.468660	1.468660	1.468660	1.468660	1.468660	1.468660
3231	Glass Products, Made Of Purchased Glass	1	1.468660	1.468660	1.468660	1.468660	1.468660	1.468660	1.468660	1.468660	1.468660	1.468660	1.468660
324	CEMENT, HYDRAULIC	3	0.924758	0.908153	0.250963	0.271081	0.304611	0.774033	0.908153	1.052236	1.556528	1.592549	1.614162
3241	Cement, Hydraulic	3	0.924758	0.908153	0.250963	0.271081	0.304611	0.774033	0.908153	1.052236	1.556528	1.592549	1.614162
325	STRUCTURAL CLAY PRODUCTS	1	-0.033942	-0.033942	-0.033942	-0.033942	-0.033942	-0.033942	-0.033942	-0.033942	-0.033942	-0.033942	-0.033942
3253	Ceramic Wall And Floor Tile	1	-0.033942	-0.033942	-0.033942	-0.033942	-0.033942	-0.033942	-0.033942	-0.033942	-0.033942	-0.033942	-0.033942
326	POTTERY AND RELATED PRODUCTS	1	-0.784200	-0.784200	-0.784200	-0.784200	-0.784200	-0.784200	-0.784200	-0.784200	-0.784200	-0.784200	-0.784200
3264	Porcelain Electrical Supplies	1	-0.784200	-0.784200	-0.784200	-0.784200	-0.784200	-0.784200	-0.784200	-0.784200	-0.784200	-0.784200	-0.784200
327	CONCRETE, GYPSUM, AND PLASTER PRODUCTS	6	1.035793	1.062177	0.390632	0.400763	0.417647	0.707223	1.062177	1.417130	1.608113	1.615276	1.619575
3272	Concrete Products, Except Block And Brick	3	1.190483	1.565130	0.407503	0.442941	0.502003	1.328880	1.565130	1.576592	1.616709	1.619575	1.621294
3273	Ready-Mixed Concrete	1	0.707223	0.707223	0.707223	0.707223	0.707223	0.707223	0.707223	0.707223	0.707223	0.707223	0.707223
3274	Lime	1	0.518955	0.518955	0.518955	0.518955	0.518955	0.518955	0.518955	0.518955	0.518955	0.518955	0.518955
3275	Gypsum Products	1	1.417130	1.417130	1.417130	1.417130	1.417130	1.417130	1.417130	1.417130	1.417130	1.417130	1.417130
33	PRIMARY METAL INDUSTRIES	39	1.674315	1.739100	0.254522	0.284881	0.353843	1.442742	1.739100	1.874964	3.017410	3.057156	3.069074
331	STEEL WORKS, BLAST FURNACES, AND ROLLING AND FINISHING MILLS	21	1.808681	1.741780	0.259668	0.297747	0.361210	1.673220	1.741780	1.948520	3.056110	3.066565	3.072838
3312	Steel Works, Blast Furnaces (Including Coke Ovens), And Rolling Mills	15	1.916153	1.849780	0.437496	0.551925	0.742641	1.740708	1.849780	2.120084	3.032283	3.054652	3.068073

Betas of Common Stocks by SIC Codes as of March 31, 2017

SIC Code	Description	Number of Companies	Mean	Median	1st Percentile	2.5th Percentile	5th Percentile	40th Percentile	50th Percentile	60th Percentile	95th Percentile	97.5th Percentile	99th Percentile
3313	Electrometallurgical Products, Except Steel	1	1.948520	1.948520	1.948520	1.948520	1.948520	1.948520	1.948520	1.948520	1.948520	1.948520	1.948520
3315	Steel Wiredrawing And Steel Nails And Spikes	1	1.480750	1.480750	1.480750	1.480750	1.480750	1.480750	1.480750	1.480750	1.480750	1.480750	1.480750
3316	Cold-Rolled Steel Sheet, Strip, And Bars	1	1.673220	1.673220	1.673220	1.673220	1.673220	1.673220	1.673220	1.673220	1.673220	1.673220	1.673220
3317	Steel Pipe And Tubes	3	1.379167	0.847108	0.246540	0.264924	0.295566	0.724543	0.847108	1.288908	2.835210	2.945660	3.011930
332	IRON AND STEEL FOUNDRIES	1	0.933281	0.933281	0.933281	0.933281	0.933281	0.933281	0.933281	0.933281	0.933281	0.933281	0.933281
3324	Steel Investment Foundries	1	0.933281	0.933281	0.933281	0.933281	0.933281	0.933281	0.933281	0.933281	0.933281	0.933281	0.933281
333	PRIMARY SMELTING AND REFINING OF NONFERROUS METALS	5	1.572253	1.784780	0.317387	0.362153	0.436761	1.484320	1.784780	1.827112	2.669882	2.767291	2.825736
3334	Primary Production Of Aluminum	2	2.377655	2.377655	1.900351	1.914962	1.939315	2.280246	2.377655	2.475064	2.815996	2.840348	2.854959
3339	Primary Smelting And Refining Of Nonferrous Metals, Except Copper	3	1.035318	1.033630	0.302466	0.324848	0.362153	0.884413	1.033630	1.183860	1.709665	1.747223	1.769757
335	ROLLING, DRAWING, AND EXTRUDING OF NONFERROUS METALS	12	1.543454	1.371950	0.689230	0.695939	0.707119	1.294772	1.371950	1.702052	2.301815	2.315347	2.323467
3351	Rolling, Drawing, And Extruding Of Copper	3	1.342693	1.310660	1.284710	1.285504	1.286828	1.305364	1.310660	1.335176	1.420982	1.427111	1.430788
3353	Aluminum Sheet, Plate, And Foil	1	2.106420	2.106420	2.106420	2.106420	2.106420	2.106420	2.106420	2.106420	2.106420	2.106420	2.106420
3356	Rolling, Drawing, And Extruding Of Nonferrous Metals, Except Copper	1	2.254680	2.254680	2.254680	2.254680	2.254680	2.254680	2.254680	2.254680	2.254680	2.254680	2.254680
3357	Drawing And Insulating Of Nonferrous Wire	7	1.447467	1.250070	0.687197	0.690857	0.696955	1.089358	1.250070	1.628784	2.314117	2.321499	2.325927
34	FABRICATED METAL PRODUCTS, EXCEPT MACHINERY AND TRANSPORTATION EQUIPMENT	42	1.019255	1.170425	-0.205795	-0.098881	0.073090	1.059716	1.170425	1.297976	1.862405	1.957588	2.380796
341	METAL CANS AND SHIPPING CONTAINERS	5	1.058656	1.107410	0.366689	0.408016	0.476894	1.075614	1.107410	1.117574	1.575356	1.630673	1.663863
3411	Metal Cans	4	1.238535	1.120115	1.030305	1.033882	1.039844	1.112492	1.120115	1.127738	1.603015	1.644502	1.669395
3412	Metal Shipping Barrels, Drums, Kegs, And Pails	1	0.339138	0.339138	0.339138	0.339138	0.339138	0.339138	0.339138	0.339138	0.339138	0.339138	0.339138
342	CUTLERY, HANDTOOLS, AND GENERAL HARDWARE	7	0.621075	0.395138	0.086170	0.092438	0.102885	0.291691	0.395138	0.850569	1.171632	1.172166	1.172486
3421	Cutlery	2	0.238565	0.238565	0.085123	0.089820	0.097649	0.207250	0.238565	0.269879	0.379481	0.387309	0.392007
3423	Hand And Edge Tools, Except Machine Tools And Handsaws	1	1.154190	1.154190	1.154190	1.154190	1.154190	1.154190	1.154190	1.154190	1.154190	1.154190	1.154190
3429	Hardware, Not Elsewhere Classified	4	0.679051	0.695933	0.153771	0.156970	0.162301	0.412009	0.695933	0.979857	1.172166	1.172433	1.172593
343	HEATING EQUIPMENT, EXCEPT ELECTRIC AND WARM AIR; AND PLUMBING FIXTURES	3	0.762104	0.582268	0.250925	0.261068	0.277974	0.514647	0.582268	0.757790	1.372119	1.415999	1.442328
3433	Heating Equipment, Except Electric And Warm Air Furnaces	3	0.762104	0.582268	0.250925	0.261068	0.277974	0.514647	0.582268	0.757790	1.372119	1.415999	1.442328
344	FABRICATED STRUCTURAL METAL PRODUCTS	9	1.510659	1.339760	0.979961	1.020013	1.086767	1.311248	1.339760	1.356400	2.387932	2.530646	2.616274

Betas of Common Stocks by SIC Codes as of March 31, 2017

SIC Code	Description	Number of Companies	Mean	Median	1st Percentile	2.5th Percentile	5th Percentile	40th Percentile	50th Percentile	60th Percentile	95th Percentile	97.5th Percentile	99th Percentile
3441	Fabricated Structural Metal	2	1.631955	1.631955	1.310677	1.320512	1.336904	1.566388	1.631955	1.697522	1.927007	1.943398	1.953233
3442	Metal Doors, Sash, Frames, Molding, And Trim	3	1.352603	1.339760	1.289780	1.291310	1.293860	1.329560	1.339760	1.357666	1.420337	1.424814	1.427499
3443	Fabricated Plate Work (Boiler Shops)	2	1.813310	1.813310	0.970460	0.996262	1.039264	1.641299	1.813310	1.985320	2.587355	2.630357	2.656159
3448	Prefabricated Metal Buildings And Components	2	1.323795	1.323795	1.287765	1.288868	1.290707	1.316442	1.323795	1.331148	1.356884	1.358722	1.359825
345	SCREW MACHINE PRODUCTS, AND BOLTS, NUTS, SCREWS, RIVETS, AND WASHERS	4	0.197603	0.249271	-0.266545	-0.250811	-0.224587	0.143281	0.249271	0.355260	0.547458	0.558182	0.564616
3451	Screw Machine Products	1	0.425920	0.425920	0.425920	0.425920	0.425920	0.425920	0.425920	0.425920	0.425920	0.425920	0.425920
3452	Bolts, Nuts, Screws, Rivets, And Washers	3	0.121497	0.072621	-0.270042	-0.259552	-0.242069	0.002690	0.072621	0.171878	0.519278	0.544092	0.558980
346	METAL FORGINGS AND STAMPINGS	4	1.448720	1.473980	0.987521	1.005961	1.036694	1.420592	1.473980	1.527368	1.825381	1.848535	1.862428
3463	Nonferrous Forgings	1	1.871690	1.871690	1.871690	1.871690	1.871690	1.871690	1.871690	1.871690	1.871690	1.871690	1.871690
3465	Automotive Stampings	2	1.473980	1.473980	1.386780	1.389449	1.393898	1.456184	1.473980	1.491776	1.554062	1.558511	1.561180
3469	Metal Stampings, Not Elsewhere Classified	1	0.975228	0.975228	0.975228	0.975228	0.975228	0.975228	0.975228	0.975228	0.975228	0.975228	0.975228
347	COATING, ENGRAVING, AND ALLIED SERVICES	1	1.171710	1.171710	1.171710	1.171710	1.171710	1.171710	1.171710	1.171710	1.171710	1.171710	1.171710
3479	Coating, Engraving, And Allied Services, Not Elsewhere Classified	1	1.171710	1.171710	1.171710	1.171710	1.171710	1.171710	1.171710	1.171710	1.171710	1.171710	1.171710
348	ORDNANCE AND ACCESSORIES, EXCEPT VEHICLES AND GUIDED MISSILES	2	0.489715	0.489715	0.323466	0.328555	0.337037	0.455787	0.489715	0.523643	0.642393	0.650875	0.655964
3484	Small Arms	2	0.489715	0.489715	0.323466	0.328555	0.337037	0.455787	0.489715	0.523643	0.642393	0.650875	0.655964
349	MISCELLANEOUS FABRICATED METAL PRODUCTS	7	1.221317	1.423570	-0.017583	0.110961	0.325199	1.405540	1.423570	1.453690	1.534378	1.546414	1.553636
3491	Industrial Valves	3	1.475247	1.473770	1.395125	1.397533	1.401545	1.457720	1.473770	1.490706	1.549982	1.554216	1.556756
3495	Wire Springs	1	1.423570	1.423570	1.423570	1.423570	1.423570	1.423570	1.423570	1.423570	1.423570	1.423570	1.423570
3499	Fabricated Metal Products, Not Elsewhere Classified	3	0.899971	1.324980	-0.074713	-0.031865	0.039548	1.039328	1.324980	1.355626	1.462887	1.470549	1.475145
35	INDUSTRIAL AND COMMERCIAL MACHINERY AND COMPUTER EQUIPMENT	176	1.217468	1.297785	-0.422106	0.027319	0.126228	1.128510	1.297785	1.419400	2.174760	2.240468	2.333983
351	ENGINES AND TURBINES	9	1.256929	1.117820	0.686293	0.701172	0.725970	1.093412	1.117820	1.418132	1.798068	1.799724	1.800718
3511	Steam, Gas, And Hydraulic Turbines, And Turbine Generator Set Units	5	1.126826	1.087310	0.687700	0.704689	0.733004	1.036196	1.087310	1.099514	1.658044	1.725572	1.766089
3519	Internal Combustion Engines, Not Elsewhere Classified	4	1.419558	1.538245	0.821148	0.852327	0.904290	1.511224	1.538245	1.565266	1.768665	1.785023	1.794837
352	FARM AND GARDEN MACHINERY AND EQUIPMENT	10	1.030242	1.106465	0.106635	0.170756	0.277623	1.033813	1.106465	1.158730	1.572263	1.625216	1.656989
3523	Farm Machinery And Equipment	8	1.032512	1.166285	0.097136	0.147007	0.230126	1.062520	1.166285	1.244294	1.595798	1.636984	1.661696
3524	Lawn And Garden Tractors And Home Lawn And Garden Equipment	2	1.021161	1.021161	0.959167	0.961065	0.964228	1.008509	1.021161	1.033813	1.078094	1.081257	1.083155

Betas of Common Stocks by SIC Codes as of March 31, 2017

SIC Code	Description	Number of Companies	Mean	Median	1st Percentile	2.5th Percentile	5th Percentile	40th Percentile	50th Percentile	60th Percentile	95th Percentile	97.5th Percentile	99th Percentile
353	CONSTRUCTION, MINING, AND MATERIALS HANDLING MACHINERY AND EQUIPMENT	25	1.428664	1.445460	-0.014880	0.129963	0.331905	1.403800	1.445460	1.637970	2.171708	2.194722	2.212787
3531	Construction Machinery And Equipment	6	0.928943	1.285085	-0.091326	-0.061150	-0.010857	1.275790	1.285085	1.294380	1.428738	1.437099	1.442116
3532	Mining Machinery And Equipment, Except Oil And Gas Field Machinery	4	1.547632	1.582325	0.907855	0.933500	0.976242	1.509320	1.582325	1.655330	2.070452	2.102786	2.122186
3533	Oil And Gas Field Machinery And Equipment	9	1.673217	1.792090	0.561309	0.659393	0.822867	1.633578	1.792090	1.865346	2.204758	2.214794	2.220816
3535	Conveyors And Conveying Equipment	1	1.421610	1.421610	1.421610	1.421610	1.421610	1.421610	1.421610	1.421610	1.421610	1.421610	1.421610
3536	Overhead Traveling Cranes, Hoists, And Monorail Systems	1	1.913500	1.913500	1.913500	1.913500	1.913500	1.913500	1.913500	1.913500	1.913500	1.913500	1.913500
3537	Industrial Trucks, Tractors, Trailers, And Stackers	4	1.389591	1.299427	0.803597	0.804912	0.807103	1.018931	1.299427	1.579923	2.098310	2.127550	2.145094
354	METALWORKING MACHINERY AND EQUIPMENT	9	1.377850	1.290460	0.165272	0.252228	0.397155	1.267460	1.290460	1.732092	2.165656	2.231888	2.271627
3541	Machine Tools, Metal Cutting Types	4	1.492277	1.585105	0.845692	0.866325	0.900715	1.408318	1.585105	1.761892	1.953879	1.960419	1.964344
3542	Machine Tools, Metal Forming Types	2	1.091811	1.091811	0.925309	0.930406	0.938901	1.057831	1.091811	1.125790	1.244720	1.253215	1.258312
3545	Cutting Tools, Machine Tool Accessories, And Machinists' Precision Tools	1	1.842500	1.842500	1.842500	1.842500	1.842500	1.842500	1.842500	1.842500	1.842500	1.842500	1.842500
3546	Power-Driven Handtools	1	0.107301	0.107301	0.107301	0.107301	0.107301	0.107301	0.107301	0.107301	0.107301	0.107301	0.107301
3549	Metalworking Machinery, Not Elsewhere Classified	1	2.298120	2.298120	2.298120	2.298120	2.298120	2.298120	2.298120	2.298120	2.298120	2.298120	2.298120
355	SPECIAL INDUSTRY MACHINERY, EXCEPT METALWORKING MACHINERY	21	1.218877	1.233410	0.258969	0.286754	0.333063	1.103750	1.233410	1.396830	2.222670	2.332120	2.397790
3554	Paper Industries Machinery	1	1.103750	1.103750	1.103750	1.103750	1.103750	1.103750	1.103750	1.103750	1.103750	1.103750	1.103750
3555	Printing Trades Machinery And Equipment	2	1.387317	1.387317	0.354148	0.385776	0.438488	1.176466	1.387317	1.598167	2.336145	2.388857	2.420485
3556	Food Products Machinery	1	0.339279	0.339279	0.339279	0.339279	0.339279	0.339279	0.339279	0.339279	0.339279	0.339279	0.339279
3559	Special Industry Machinery, Not Elsewhere Classified	17	1.257574	1.297950	0.291583	0.368289	0.496133	1.226774	1.297950	1.410372	2.201790	2.212230	2.218494
356	GENERAL INDUSTRIAL MACHINERY AND EQUIPMENT	29	1.309028	1.351940	0.216747	0.249556	0.321385	1.246284	1.351940	1.368178	2.228754	2.341978	2.450405
3561	Pumps And Pumping Equipment	9	1.670238	1.750900	1.222129	1.222712	1.223684	1.445468	1.750900	1.753500	2.228754	2.246642	2.257375
3562	Ball And Roller Bearings	4	1.654296	1.608385	0.891950	0.913290	0.948856	1.454518	1.608385	1.762252	2.424011	2.473351	2.502954
3564	Industrial And Commercial Fans And Blowers And Air Purification Equipment	5	0.940204	1.094000	0.399162	0.406937	0.419897	0.865828	1.094000	1.186408	1.356564	1.360507	1.362873
3566	Speed Changers, Industrial High-Speed Drives, And Gears	1	1.518270	1.518270	1.518270	1.518270	1.518270	1.518270	1.518270	1.518270	1.518270	1.518270	1.518270

Betas of Common Stocks by SIC Codes as of March 31, 2017

SIC Code	Description	Number of Companies	Mean	Median	1st Percentile	2.5th Percentile	5th Percentile	40th Percentile	50th Percentile	60th Percentile	95th Percentile	97.5th Percentile	99th Percentile
3568	Mechanical Power Transmission Equipment, Not Elsewhere Classified	1	1.956510	1.956510	1.956510	1.956510	1.956510	1.956510	1.956510	1.956510	1.956510	1.956510	1.956510
3569	General Industrial Machinery And Equipment, Not Elsewhere Classified	9	0.904077	0.835503	0.201124	0.210498	0.226121	0.713205	0.835503	0.974477	1.645142	1.664836	1.676652
357	COMPUTER AND OFFICE EQUIPMENT	58	1.120439	1.232730	-0.579700	-0.260691	0.094840	0.932335	1.232730	1.457396	2.023466	2.090361	2.167343
3571	Electronic Computers	12	1.084162	1.049288	0.215125	0.267034	0.353550	0.862438	1.049288	1.355898	1.787109	1.799160	1.806390
3572	Computer Storage Devices	8	1.282471	1.541440	-0.679245	-0.587707	-0.435142	1.513108	1.541440	1.646268	2.187050	2.218450	2.237290
3576	COMPUTER COMMUNICATIONS EQUIPMENT	9	0.883281	0.744295	0.037707	0.083731	0.160438	0.624330	0.744295	0.888778	1.822460	1.918820	1.976636
3577	Computer Peripheral Equipment, Not Elsewhere Classified	21	1.008343	1.090170	-0.344787	-0.174116	0.110337	0.934194	1.090170	1.256520	1.847530	1.907355	1.943250
3578	Calculating And Accounting Machines, Except Electronic Computers	6	1.516598	1.666450	0.760173	0.789834	0.839269	1.550960	1.666450	1.781940	2.025153	2.065126	2.089111
3579	Office Machines, Not Elsewhere Classified	2	1.745720	1.745720	1.720681	1.721448	1.722725	1.740610	1.745720	1.750830	1.768715	1.769993	1.770759
358	REFRIGERATION AND SERVICE INDUSTRY MACHINERY	11	0.927977	1.233870	-0.362842	-0.292178	-0.174404	1.095940	1.233870	1.275370	1.336560	1.339640	1.341488
3580	REFRIGERATION & SERVICE INDUSTRY MACHINERY	2	0.578542	0.578542	0.071492	0.087014	0.112884	0.475063	0.578542	0.682022	1.044200	1.070070	1.085592
3585	Air-Conditioning And Warm Air Heating Equipment	3	1.160476	1.275370	0.871578	0.883939	0.904540	1.192963	1.275370	1.288840	1.335985	1.339353	1.341373
3589	Service Industry Machinery, Not Elsewhere Classified	6	0.928206	1.266705	-0.349016	-0.257612	-0.105272	1.233870	1.266705	1.299540	1.324453	1.327426	1.329211
359	MISCELLANEOUS INDUSTRIAL AND COMMERCIAL MACHINERY AND EQUIPMENT	4	1.447706	1.467730	0.851798	0.879603	0.925944	1.457776	1.467730	1.477684	1.941433	1.981767	2.005967
3592	Carburetors, Pistons, Piston Rings, And Valves	1	1.451140	1.451140	1.451140	1.451140	1.451140	1.451140	1.451140	1.451140	1.451140	1.451140	1.451140
3594	Fluid Power Pumps And Motors	1	1.484320	1.484320	1.484320	1.484320	1.484320	1.484320	1.484320	1.484320	1.484320	1.484320	1.484320
3596	Scales And Balances, Except Laboratory	1	0.833262	0.833262	0.833262	0.833262	0.833262	0.833262	0.833262	0.833262	0.833262	0.833262	0.833262
3599	Industrial And Commercial Machinery And Equipment, Not Elsewhere Classified	1	2.022100	2.022100	2.022100	2.022100	2.022100	2.022100	2.022100	2.022100	2.022100	2.022100	2.022100
36	ELECTRONIC AND OTHER ELECTRICAL EQUIPMENT AND COMPONENTS, EXCEPT COMPUTER	266	1.105136	1.201335	-0.423505	-0.152843	0.113859	1.058160	1.201335	1.313490	2.009878	2.125778	2.444841
361	ELECTRIC TRANSMISSION AND DISTRIBUTION EQUIPMENT	5	0.948111	1.129280	0.405669	0.413379	0.426227	0.889174	1.129280	1.202952	1.357308	1.362789	1.366078
3612	Power, Distribution, And Specialty Transformers	3	0.686275	0.529015	0.403100	0.406954	0.413379	0.503318	0.529015	0.649068	1.069254	1.099267	1.117275
3613	Switchgear And Switchboard Apparatus	2	1.340865	1.340865	1.314008	1.314830	1.316201	1.335384	1.340865	1.346346	1.365530	1.366900	1.367722

Betas of Common Stocks by SIC Codes as of March 31, 2017

SIC Code	Description	Number of Companies	Mean	Median	1st Percentile	2.5th Percentile	5th Percentile	40th Percentile	50th Percentile	60th Percentile	95th Percentile	97.5th Percentile	99th Percentile
362	ELECTRICAL INDUSTRIAL APPARATUS	18	1.061698	1.075895	0.178644	0.238888	0.339294	0.941199	1.075895	1.179478	1.625070	1.798895	1.903190
3621	Motors And Generators	11	1.095171	1.247590	0.162106	0.197544	0.256607	1.087700	1.247590	1.359500	1.768220	1.870470	1.931820
3625	Relays And Industrial Controls	3	0.872626	0.810254	0.744867	0.746869	0.750205	0.796910	0.810254	0.861021	1.038706	1.051398	1.059013
3629	Electrical Industrial Apparatus, Not Elsewhere Classified	4	1.111454	1.056210	0.907430	0.909403	0.912692	0.992466	1.056210	1.119954	1.387556	1.407418	1.419335
363	HOUSEHOLD APPLIANCES	5	0.969406	1.047000	-0.106898	-0.043253	0.062821	0.992767	1.047000	1.214252	1.551274	1.562042	1.568503
3632	Household Refrigerators And Home And Farm Freezers	1	1.572810	1.572810	1.572810	1.572810	1.572810	1.572810	1.572810	1.572810	1.572810	1.572810	1.572810
3633	Household Laundry Equipment	2	0.657901	0.657901	-0.133183	-0.108967	-0.068605	0.496455	0.657901	0.819347	1.384407	1.424769	1.448985
3634	Electric Housewares And Fans	2	0.979209	0.979209	0.912774	0.914808	0.918197	0.965651	0.979209	0.992767	1.040221	1.043610	1.045644
364	ELECTRIC LIGHTING AND WIRING EQUIPMENT	9	1.070124	0.877448	0.736963	0.746167	0.761507	0.843394	0.877448	1.061818	1.556618	1.557814	1.558532
3640	ELECTRIC LIGHTING & WIRING EQUIPMENT	1	0.877448	0.877448	0.877448	0.877448	0.877448	0.877448	0.877448	0.877448	0.877448	0.877448	0.877448
3641	Electric Lamp Bulbs And Tubes	3	1.231293	1.333320	0.818044	0.833818	0.860107	1.228162	1.333320	1.377262	1.531059	1.542045	1.548636
3643	Current-Carrying Wiring Devices	1	1.107910	1.107910	1.107910	1.107910	1.107910	1.107910	1.107910	1.107910	1.107910	1.107910	1.107910
3645	Residential Electric Lighting Fixtures	2	0.778997	0.778997	0.731790	0.733235	0.735644	0.769363	0.778997	0.788630	0.822349	0.824758	0.826203
3646	Commercial, Industrial, And Institutional Electric Lighting Fixtures	2	1.196945	1.196945	0.842121	0.852983	0.871087	1.124532	1.196945	1.269358	1.522804	1.540907	1.551769
365	HOUSEHOLD AUDIO AND VIDEO EQUIPMENT, AND AUDIO RECORDINGS	7	0.837503	0.620010	-0.174010	-0.117236	-0.022612	0.591292	0.620010	0.755140	1.954185	2.063063	2.128389
3651	Household Audio And Video Equipment	7	0.837503	0.620010	-0.174010	-0.117236	-0.022612	0.591292	0.620010	0.755140	1.954185	2.063063	2.128389
366	COMMUNICATIONS EQUIPMENT	72	0.987208	1.051345	-0.197509	-0.062081	0.082972	0.778293	1.051345	1.162860	2.007377	2.134582	2.288687
3661	Telephone And Telegraph Apparatus	19	1.075532	1.194630	-0.022592	0.001107	0.040605	1.125234	1.194630	1.311462	1.765287	1.931684	2.031521
3663	Radio And Television Broadcasting And Communications Equipment	37	1.026347	1.100710	-0.052190	0.085041	0.196406	0.778293	1.100710	1.160300	1.974834	2.106889	2.257652
3669	Communications Equipment, Not Elsewhere Classified	16	0.791814	0.644888	-0.262894	-0.163282	0.002739	0.449782	0.644888	0.860901	1.772743	2.016526	2.162797
367	ELECTRONIC COMPONENTS AND ACCESSORIES	130	1.199166	1.268200	-0.499484	-0.118793	0.127732	1.195268	1.268200	1.376026	2.039538	2.357474	2.586475
3671	Electron Tubes	1	0.402526	0.402526	0.402526	0.402526	0.402526	0.402526	0.402526	0.402526	0.402526	0.402526	0.402526
3672	Printed Circuit Boards	14	1.019597	1.226870	-0.101172	-0.014878	0.128945	1.104032	1.226870	1.262812	1.450264	1.463527	1.471485
3674	Semiconductors And Related Devices	94	1.292322	1.313545	-0.561693	0.050034	0.178609	1.239654	1.313545	1.461814	2.038585	2.319427	2.727376
3675	Electronic Capacitors	1	0.833094	0.833094	0.833094	0.833094	0.833094	0.833094	0.833094	0.833094	0.833094	0.833094	0.833094
3676	Electronic Resistors	1	0.937137	0.937137	0.937137	0.937137	0.937137	0.937137	0.937137	0.937137	0.937137	0.937137	0.937137
3677	Electronic Coils, Transformers, And Other Inductors	2	1.062496	1.062496	0.803497	0.811425	0.824639	1.009639	1.062496	1.115352	1.300352	1.313566	1.321494
3678	Electronic Connectors	4	1.080106	1.197657	0.478934	0.501802	0.539916	1.062187	1.197657	1.333127	1.455723	1.458572	1.460281
3679	Electronic Components, Not Elsewhere Classified	13	0.886215	0.404731	-0.293137	-0.208387	-0.067138	0.279373	0.404731	0.975804	2.206922	2.327516	2.399872

Betas of Common Stocks by SIC Codes as of March 31, 2017

SIC Code	Description	Number of Companies	Mean	Median	1st Percentile	2.5th Percentile	5th Percentile	40th Percentile	50th Percentile	60th Percentile	95th Percentile	97.5th Percentile	99th Percentile
369	MISCELLANEOUS ELECTRICAL MACHINERY, EQUIPMENT, AND SUPPLIES	20	1.140192	1.320455	-0.692262	-0.345857	0.231483	1.260142	1.320455	1.380446	1.719757	1.722003	1.723351
3691	Storage Batteries	9	1.301999	1.355990	0.864695	0.871850	0.883775	1.305062	1.355990	1.404902	1.664366	1.694308	1.712273
3692	Primary Batteries, Dry And Wet	2	0.752058	0.752058	0.301452	0.315246	0.338236	0.660098	0.752058	0.844018	1.165880	1.188870	1.202664
3694	Electrical Equipment For Internal Combustion Engines	1	1.057290	1.057290	1.057290	1.057290	1.057290	1.057290	1.057290	1.057290	1.057290	1.057290	1.057290
3695	Magnetic And Optical Recording Media	4	1.457040	1.397550	1.313955	1.314577	1.315615	1.355442	1.397550	1.439658	1.681752	1.700636	1.711966
3699	Electrical Machinery, Equipment, And Supplies, Not Elsewhere Classified	4	0.674071	1.087722	-0.873534	-0.799039	-0.674880	0.874440	1.087722	1.301003	1.443913	1.443976	1.444015
37	TRANSPORTATION EQUIPMENT	100	1.279501	1.345115	-0.237494	0.142650	0.244481	1.227436	1.345115	1.405958	2.041406	2.175874	2.502020
371	MOTOR VEHICLES AND MOTOR VEHICLE EQUIPMENT	56	1.422260	1.379500	0.218993	0.262006	0.398740	1.310440	1.379500	1.555490	2.144833	2.393741	2.737869
3711	Motor Vehicles And Passenger Car Bodies	19	1.194865	1.271820	0.196225	0.212839	0.240530	1.021070	1.271820	1.332282	1.873552	2.453116	2.800854
3713	Truck And Bus Bodies	2	1.598750	1.598750	1.380308	1.386995	1.398140	1.554170	1.598750	1.643330	1.799360	1.810505	1.817192
3714	Motor Vehicle Parts And Accessories	32	1.524052	1.532005	0.415877	0.608376	0.813843	1.371744	1.532005	1.713682	2.165467	2.283961	2.411581
3715	Truck Trailers	1	1.838640	1.838640	1.838640	1.838640	1.838640	1.838640	1.838640	1.838640	1.838640	1.838640	1.838640
3716	Motor Homes	2	1.569170	1.569170	1.474874	1.477761	1.482572	1.549926	1.569170	1.588414	1.655768	1.660579	1.663466
372	AIRCRAFT AND PARTS	28	1.061920	1.060530	-0.142563	-0.005661	0.138652	0.954310	1.060530	1.214076	1.901467	2.020359	2.082940
3721	Aircraft	9	1.189040	1.232900	0.850659	0.851269	0.852285	1.161316	1.232900	1.241780	1.453356	1.464388	1.471007
3724	Aircraft Engines And Engine Parts	7	0.836573	0.903854	0.110104	0.118964	0.133730	0.747232	0.903854	0.935616	1.535753	1.545427	1.551231
3728	Aircraft Parts And Auxiliary Equipment, Not Elsewhere Classified	12	1.098034	0.997673	-0.161620	-0.053304	0.127224	0.953411	0.997673	1.136982	2.039674	2.082167	2.107663
373	SHIP AND BOAT BUILDING AND REPAIRING	4	0.948222	0.887727	0.327503	0.352295	0.393615	0.872235	0.887727	0.903219	1.587523	1.646992	1.682673
3731	Ship Building And Repairing	2	0.586441	0.586441	0.316484	0.324748	0.338522	0.531348	0.586441	0.641534	0.834360	0.848134	0.856398
3732	Boat Building And Repairing	2	1.310004	1.310004	0.921476	0.933370	0.953193	1.230712	1.310004	1.389295	1.666814	1.686637	1.698531
374	RAILROAD EQUIPMENT	5	1.739878	1.810630	1.361828	1.382255	1.416300	1.761842	1.810630	1.812206	1.992770	2.015045	2.028410
3743	Railroad Equipment	5	1.739878	1.810630	1.361828	1.382255	1.416300	1.761842	1.810630	1.812206	1.992770	2.015045	2.028410
375	MOTORCYCLES, BICYCLES, AND PARTS	2	1.476795	1.476795	1.411855	1.413843	1.417157	1.463542	1.476795	1.490048	1.536434	1.539747	1.541735
3751	Motorcycles, Bicycles, And Parts	2	1.476795	1.476795	1.411855	1.413843	1.417157	1.463542	1.476795	1.490048	1.536434	1.539747	1.541735
376	GUIDED MISSILES AND SPACE VEHICLES AND PARTS	3	0.224657	0.475496	-0.578579	-0.546312	-0.492532	0.260379	0.475496	0.540110	0.766260	0.782413	0.792106
3761	Guided Missiles And Space Vehicles	1	0.475496	0.475496	0.475496	0.475496	0.475496	0.475496	0.475496	0.475496	0.475496	0.475496	0.475496
3764	Guided Missile And Space Vehicle Propulsion Units And Propulsion	1	0.798567	0.798567	0.798567	0.798567	0.798567	0.798567	0.798567	0.798567	0.798567	0.798567	0.798567
3769	Guided Missile And Space Vehicle Parts And Auxiliary Equipment, Not Elsewhere Classified	1	-0.600091	-0.600091	-0.600091	-0.600091	-0.600091	-0.600091	-0.600091	-0.600091	-0.600091	-0.600091	-0.600091
379	MISCELLANEOUS TRANSPORTATION EQUIPMENT	2	1.224930	1.224930	1.071589	1.076284	1.084107	1.193636	1.224930	1.256224	1.365753	1.373577	1.378271

Betas of Common Stocks by SIC Codes as of March 31, 2017

SIC Code	Description	Number of Companies	Mean	Median	1st Percentile	2.5th Percentile	5th Percentile	40th Percentile	50th Percentile	60th Percentile	95th Percentile	97.5th Percentile	99th Percentile
3795	Tanks And Tank Components	1	1.068460	1.068460	1.068460	1.068460	1.068460	1.068460	1.068460	1.068460	1.068460	1.068460	1.068460
3799	Transportation Equipment, Not Elsewhere Classified	1	1.381400	1.381400	1.381400	1.381400	1.381400	1.381400	1.381400	1.381400	1.381400	1.381400	1.381400
38	MEASURING, ANALYZING, AND CONTROLLING INSTRUMENTS; PHOTOGRAPHIC, MEDICAL	259	0.984995	1.108240	-0.735581	-0.426906	-0.137020	0.933598	1.108240	1.223132	2.073545	2.317024	2.456135
381	SEARCH, DETECTION, NAVIGATION, GUIDANCE, AERONAUTICAL, AND NAUTICAL	14	1.057081	1.094145	0.135644	0.223417	0.369704	1.012808	1.094145	1.235050	1.536408	1.584469	1.613306
3812	Search, Detection, Navigation, Guidance, Aeronautical, And Nautical	14	1.057081	1.094145	0.135644	0.223417	0.369704	1.012808	1.094145	1.235050	1.536408	1.584469	1.613306
382	LABORATORY APPARATUS AND ANALYTICAL, OPTICAL, MEASURING, AND CONTROL	92	0.936568	1.085010	-0.510197	-0.395684	-0.246571	0.874487	1.085010	1.245894	1.931728	2.073218	2.434797
3821	Laboratory Apparatus And Furniture	3	0.379533	0.281807	-0.421064	-0.399547	-0.363687	0.138364	0.281807	0.483886	1.191161	1.241680	1.271992
3822	Automatic Controls For Regulating Residential And Commercial Environment	3	1.519828	1.515500	0.572048	0.600929	0.649065	1.322959	1.515500	1.710638	2.393621	2.442406	2.471676
3823	Industrial Instruments For Measurement, Display, And Control Of Processes	16	1.095029	1.160735	-0.017360	0.075671	0.230721	1.048360	1.160735	1.270850	1.866515	1.981798	2.050967
3824	Totalizing Fluid Meters And Counting Devices	1	1.199040	1.199040	1.199040	1.199040	1.199040	1.199040	1.199040	1.199040	1.199040	1.199040	1.199040
3825	Instruments For Measuring And Testing Of Electricity And Electric	22	0.781046	0.900028	-0.280098	-0.263811	-0.234009	0.394995	0.900028	1.068370	1.693877	1.726138	1.744313
3826	Laboratory Analytical Instruments	19	1.062023	1.242240	-0.190448	-0.092847	0.069822	1.116364	1.242240	1.250578	1.981780	1.996045	2.004604
3827	Optical Instruments And Lenses	8	1.052455	1.074770	0.719375	0.737691	0.768216	1.024408	1.074770	1.107150	1.343869	1.382384	1.405494
3829	Measuring And Controlling Devices, Not Elsewhere Classified	20	0.798277	0.867427	-0.983564	-0.796189	-0.483899	0.499693	0.867427	1.213450	1.920163	2.174691	2.327409
384	SURGICAL, MEDICAL, AND DENTAL INSTRUMENTS AND SUPPLIES	143	0.992009	1.086810	-0.776738	-0.510684	-0.067722	0.935375	1.086810	1.210926	2.220600	2.373121	2.547724
3841	Surgical And Medical Instruments And Apparatus	84	0.974518	1.097525	-1.351939	-0.627414	-0.146908	0.967353	1.097525	1.207866	2.054231	2.352154	2.431346
3842	Orthopedic, Prosthetic, And Surgical Appliances And Supplies	20	1.061698	1.070110	-0.040820	-0.032310	-0.018128	0.870317	1.070110	1.292026	2.191065	2.480768	2.654589
3843	Dental Equipment And Supplies	5	1.240650	1.207730	1.009038	1.018336	1.033832	1.187758	1.207730	1.214258	1.533474	1.572152	1.595359
3844	X-Ray Apparatus And Tubes And Related Irradiation Apparatus	2	1.707745	1.707745	1.196847	1.212486	1.238553	1.603480	1.707745	1.812010	2.176938	2.203004	2.218644
3845	Electromedical And Electrotherapeutic Apparatus	32	0.910784	0.933461	-0.356465	-0.266390	-0.130978	0.773810	0.933461	1.186780	1.993636	2.273053	2.367671
385	OPHTHALMIC GOODS	2	1.041369	1.041369	0.807676	0.814830	0.826753	0.993676	1.041369	1.089061	1.255984	1.267907	1.275061
3851	Ophthalmic Goods	2	1.041369	1.041369	0.807676	0.814830	0.826753	0.993676	1.041369	1.089061	1.255984	1.267907	1.275061
386	PHOTOGRAPHIC EQUIPMENT AND SUPPLIES	6	1.055587	1.145195	0.107152	0.132641	0.175123	1.133830	1.145195	1.156560	1.770295	1.774703	1.777347

Betas of Common Stocks by SIC Codes as of March 31, 2017

SIC Code	Description	Number of Companies	Mean	Median	1st Percentile	2.5th Percentile	5th Percentile	40th Percentile	50th Percentile	60th Percentile	95th Percentile	97.5th Percentile	99th Percentile
3861	Photographic Equipment And Supplies	6	1.055587	1.145195	0.107152	0.132641	0.175123	1.133830	1.145195	1.156560	1.770295	1.774703	1.777347
387	WATCHES, CLOCKS, CLOCKWORK OPERATED DEVICES, AND PARTS	2	1.938335	1.938335	1.653346	1.662070	1.676611	1.880174	1.938335	1.996496	2.200060	2.214600	2.223324
3873	Watches, Clocks, Clockwork Operated Devices, And Parts	2	1.938335	1.938335	1.653346	1.662070	1.676611	1.880174	1.938335	1.996496	2.200060	2.214600	2.223324
39	MISCELLANEOUS MANUFACTURING INDUSTRIES	30	0.731098	0.936008	-0.808826	-0.705472	-0.476781	0.674048	0.936008	0.963386	1.707213	1.735525	1.773940
391	JEWELRY, SILVERWARE, AND PLATED WARE	2	0.299500	0.299500	-0.065350	-0.054181	-0.035566	0.225040	0.299500	0.373959	0.634565	0.653180	0.664349
3911	Jewelry, Precious Metal	2	0.299500	0.299500	-0.065350	-0.054181	-0.035566	0.225040	0.299500	0.373959	0.634565	0.653180	0.664349
394	DOLLS, TOYS, GAMES AND SPORTING AND ATHLETIC GOODS	21	0.711885	0.929648	-0.830209	-0.758931	-0.640134	0.674722	0.929648	0.952196	1.702290	1.706765	1.709450
3942	Dolls And Stuffed Toys	2	1.282355	1.282355	1.274589	1.274826	1.275223	1.280770	1.282355	1.283940	1.289488	1.289884	1.290122
3944	Games, Toys, And Children's Vehicles, Except Dolls And Bicycles	11	0.397696	0.611517	-0.853969	-0.818330	-0.758931	0.584767	0.611517	0.673038	1.322329	1.512309	1.626298
3949	Sporting And Athletic Goods, Not Elsewhere Classified	8	1.001278	1.068001	-0.137565	-0.045855	0.106994	0.952352	1.068001	1.205140	1.617535	1.664387	1.692499
399	MISCELLANEOUS MANUFACTURING INDUSTRIES	7	0.912052	1.054700	-0.236053	-0.174441	-0.071754	1.009807	1.054700	1.075670	1.658763	1.729157	1.771393
3990	MISCELLANEOUS MANUFACTURING INDUSTRIES	1	-0.277128	-0.277128	-0.277128	-0.277128	-0.277128	-0.277128	-0.277128	-0.277128	-0.277128	-0.277128	-0.277128
3993	Signs And Advertising Specialties	1	0.407452	0.407452	0.407452	0.407452	0.407452	0.407452	0.407452	0.407452	0.407452	0.407452	0.407452
3996	Linoleum, Asphalted-Felt-Base, And Other Hard Surface Floor Cover	1	1.330260	1.330260	1.330260	1.330260	1.330260	1.330260	1.330260	1.330260	1.330260	1.330260	1.330260
3999	Manufacturing Industries, Not Elsewhere Classified	4	1.230945	1.072175	0.982124	0.985491	0.991102	1.061690	1.072175	1.082660	1.693065	1.746308	1.778253
	TRANSPORTATION, COMMUNICATIONS, ELECTRIC, GAS, AND SANITARY SERVICE												
40	RAILROAD TRANSPORTATION	7	1.306924	1.222920	1.030177	1.037793	1.050486	1.175904	1.222920	1.224702	1.855092	1.963806	2.029034
401	RAILROADS	7	1.306924	1.222920	1.030177	1.037793	1.050486	1.175904	1.222920	1.224702	1.855092	1.963806	2.029034
4011	Railroads, Line-Haul Operating	7	1.306924	1.222920	1.030177	1.037793	1.050486	1.175904	1.222920	1.224702	1.855092	1.963806	2.029034
41	LOCAL AND SUBURBAN TRANSIT AND INTERURBAN HIGHWAY PASSENGER TRANSPORTATION	1	0.460598	0.460598	0.460598	0.460598	0.460598	0.460598	0.460598	0.460598	0.460598	0.460598	0.460598
415	SCHOOL BUSES	1	0.460598	0.460598	0.460598	0.460598	0.460598	0.460598	0.460598	0.460598	0.460598	0.460598	0.460598
4151	School Buses	1	0.460598	0.460598	0.460598	0.460598	0.460598	0.460598	0.460598	0.460598	0.460598	0.460598	0.460598
42	MOTOR FREIGHT TRANSPORTATION AND WAREHOUSING	22	1.593950	1.534120	0.391991	0.560429	0.823430	1.300326	1.534120	1.702438	2.515198	2.594755	2.647174
421	TRUCKING AND COURIER SERVICES, EXCEPT AIR	21	1.587855	1.413090	0.386644	0.547061	0.814422	1.288350	1.413090	1.673170	2.515710	2.598915	2.648838
4213	Trucking, Except Local	21	1.587855	1.413090	0.386644	0.547061	0.814422	1.288350	1.413090	1.673170	2.515710	2.598915	2.648838
422	PUBLIC WAREHOUSING AND STORAGE	1	1.721950	1.721950	1.721950	1.721950	1.721950	1.721950	1.721950	1.721950	1.721950	1.721950	1.721950
4225	General Warehousing And Storage	1	1.721950	1.721950	1.721950	1.721950	1.721950	1.721950	1.721950	1.721950	1.721950	1.721950	1.721950
44	WATER TRANSPORTATION	46	1.336578	1.438880	-3.888137	-1.440683	-0.417976	1.260970	1.438880	1.806200	2.777525	2.887565	3.064387

Betas of Common Stocks by SIC Codes as of March 31, 2017

SIC Code	Description	Number of Companies	Mean	Median	1st Percentile	2.5th Percentile	5th Percentile	40th Percentile	50th Percentile	60th Percentile	95th Percentile	97.5th Percentile	99th Percentile
4400	WATER TRANSPORTATION	1	0.990361	0.990361	0.990361	0.990361	0.990361	0.990361	0.990361	0.990361	0.990361	0.990361	0.990361
441	DEEP SEA FOREIGN TRANSPORTATION OF FREIGHT	34	1.190581	1.406905	-4.397314	-2.296960	-0.963031	1.228730	1.406905	1.796296	2.654422	2.690503	2.696789
4412	Deep Sea Foreign Transportation Of Freight	34	1.190581	1.406905	-4.397314	-2.296960	-0.963031	1.228730	1.406905	1.796296	2.654422	2.690503	2.696789
442	DEEP SEA DOMESTIC TRANSPORTATION OF FREIGHT	1	1.571410	1.571410	1.571410	1.571410	1.571410	1.571410	1.571410	1.571410	1.571410	1.571410	1.571410
4424	Deep Sea Domestic Transportation Of Freight	1	1.571410	1.571410	1.571410	1.571410	1.571410	1.571410	1.571410	1.571410	1.571410	1.571410	1.571410
443	FREIGHT TRANSPORTATION ON THE GREAT LAKES¨ST. LAWRENCE SEAWAY	1	0.261884	0.261884	0.261884	0.261884	0.261884	0.261884	0.261884	0.261884	0.261884	0.261884	0.261884
4432	Freight Transportation On The Great Lakes¨St. Lawrence Seaway	1	0.261884	0.261884	0.261884	0.261884	0.261884	0.261884	0.261884	0.261884	0.261884	0.261884	0.261884
444	WATER TRANSPORTATION OF FREIGHT, NOT ELSEWHERE CLASSIFIED	1	1.445500	1.445500	1.445500	1.445500	1.445500	1.445500	1.445500	1.445500	1.445500	1.445500	1.445500
4449	Water Transportation Of Freight, Not Elsewhere Classified	1	1.445500	1.445500	1.445500	1.445500	1.445500	1.445500	1.445500	1.445500	1.445500	1.445500	1.445500
448	WATER TRANSPORTATION OF PASSENGERS	3	1.665340	1.302170	1.084326	1.090995	1.102109	1.257712	1.302170	1.564530	2.482790	2.548380	2.587734
4481	Deep Sea Transportation Of Passengers, Except By Ferry	3	1.665340	1.302170	1.084326	1.090995	1.102109	1.257712	1.302170	1.564530	2.482790	2.548380	2.587734
449	SERVICES INCIDENTAL TO WATER TRANSPORTATION	5	2.347527	2.803040	0.986506	1.042774	1.136552	2.436536	2.803040	2.841680	3.139272	3.169226	3.187198
4491	Marine Cargo Handling	1	3.199180	3.199180	3.199180	3.199180	3.199180	3.199180	3.199180	3.199180	3.199180	3.199180	3.199180
4492	Towing And Tugboat Services	1	2.899640	2.899640	2.899640	2.899640	2.899640	2.899640	2.899640	2.899640	2.899640	2.899640	2.899640
4499	Water Transportation Services, Not Elsewhere Classified	3	1.879605	1.886780	0.967751	0.995884	1.042774	1.699223	1.886780	2.070032	2.711414	2.757227	2.784715
45	TRANSPORTATION BY AIR	22	1.409575	1.378065	0.186209	0.340889	0.586058	1.298294	1.378065	1.516852	1.982837	2.415078	2.699737
451	AIR TRANSPORTATION, SCHEDULED, AND AIR COURIER SERVICES	17	1.376105	1.379170	0.199805	0.374878	0.666667	1.372892	1.379170	1.516852	1.937942	1.961886	1.976252
4512	Air Transportation, Scheduled	13	1.516604	1.386160	1.107988	1.128459	1.162578	1.378728	1.386160	1.616390	1.949914	1.967872	1.978647
4513	Air Courier Services	4	0.919483	0.984606	0.104973	0.137800	0.192510	0.881380	0.984606	1.087832	1.555283	1.590457	1.611561
452	AIR TRANSPORTATION, NONSCHEDULED	5	1.523375	1.212190	0.599014	0.636328	0.698520	1.205734	1.212190	1.425310	2.660606	2.775058	2.843729
4522	Air Transportation, Nonscheduled	5	1.523375	1.212190	0.599014	0.636328	0.698520	1.205734	1.212190	1.425310	2.660606	2.775058	2.843729
46	PIPELINES, EXCEPT NATURAL GAS	11	1.313505	1.390350	0.876877	0.890068	0.912051	1.209790	1.390350	1.413220	1.724450	1.791290	1.831394
461	PIPELINES, EXCEPT NATURAL GAS	11	1.313505	1.390350	0.876877	0.890068	0.912051	1.209790	1.390350	1.413220	1.724450	1.791290	1.831394
4612	Crude Petroleum Pipelines	6	1.221333	1.152745	0.958690	0.962697	0.969376	1.095700	1.152745	1.209790	1.551320	1.562720	1.569560
4613	Refined Petroleum Pipelines	1	1.858130	1.858130	1.858130	1.858130	1.858130	1.858130	1.858130	1.858130	1.858130	1.858130	1.858130
4619	Pipelines, Not Elsewhere Classified	4	1.315606	1.401785	0.883752	0.907254	0.946424	1.394924	1.401785	1.408646	1.564138	1.577454	1.585444
47	TRANSPORTATION SERVICES	16	1.255689	1.348490	-0.004965	0.014347	0.046533	1.204840	1.348490	1.393830	2.257370	2.563940	2.747882

Betas of Common Stocks by SIC Codes as of March 31, 2017

SIC Code	Description	Number of Companies	Mean	Median	1st Percentile	2.5th Percentile	5th Percentile	40th Percentile	50th Percentile	60th Percentile	95th Percentile	97.5th Percentile	99th Percentile
472	ARRANGEMENT OF PASSENGER TRANSPORTATION	4	0.925778	1.150850	0.016708	0.068530	0.154900	1.140596	1.150850	1.161104	1.381554	1.400402	1.411711
4724	Travel Agencies	1	1.419250	1.419250	1.419250	1.419250	1.419250	1.419250	1.419250	1.419250	1.419250	1.419250	1.419250
4725	Tour Operators	3	0.761287	1.133760	0.005192	0.039740	0.097320	0.903440	1.133760	1.140596	1.164522	1.166231	1.167256
473	ARRANGEMENT OF TRANSPORTATION OF FREIGHT AND CARGO	10	1.345887	1.371425	0.108321	0.168815	0.269639	1.348596	1.371425	1.403614	2.502626	2.686568	2.796933
4731	Arrangement Of Transportation Of Freight And Cargo	10	1.345887	1.371425	0.108321	0.168815	0.269639	1.348596	1.371425	1.403614	2.502626	2.686568	2.796933
478	MISCELLANEOUS SERVICES INCIDENTAL TO TRANSPORTATION	2	1.464525	1.464525	1.210034	1.217824	1.230809	1.412588	1.464525	1.516462	1.698242	1.711226	1.719016
4789	Transportation Services, Not Elsewhere Classified	2	1.464525	1.464525	1.210034	1.217824	1.230809	1.412588	1.464525	1.516462	1.698242	1.711226	1.719016
48	COMMUNICATIONS	137	1.033593	1.020100	-0.497013	-0.226073	0.076265	0.927380	1.020100	1.171464	1.965622	2.278546	2.543072
481	TELEPHONE COMMUNICATIONS	61	1.030162	1.061980	-0.467946	-0.182115	0.075643	0.968476	1.061980	1.117620	1.970730	2.328870	2.551612
4812	Radiotelephone Communications	18	0.907891	0.927435	0.083530	0.095361	0.115080	0.880300	0.927435	0.987177	2.043593	2.250036	2.373903
4813	Telephone Communications, Except Radiotelephone	43	1.081345	1.116800	-0.529179	-0.316895	0.004544	1.042828	1.116800	1.200430	1.897084	2.186083	2.487229
482	TELEGRAPH AND OTHER MESSAGE COMMUNICATIONS	4	0.569383	0.500574	-0.051925	-0.028747	0.009882	0.468837	0.500574	0.532311	1.225216	1.284488	1.320051
4822	Telegraph And Other Message Communications	4	0.569383	0.500574	-0.051925	-0.028747	0.009882	0.468837	0.500574	0.532311	1.225216	1.284488	1.320051
483	RADIO AND TELEVISION BROADCASTING STATIONS	27	0.934001	0.935447	-0.502487	-0.481138	-0.228608	0.723346	0.935447	1.129162	1.632034	1.762631	1.884478
4832	Radio Broadcasting Stations	13	0.868997	1.004800	-0.510151	-0.500297	-0.483875	0.847150	1.004800	1.063462	1.778252	1.871981	1.928218
4833	Television Broadcasting Stations	14	0.994362	0.840328	0.415123	0.435184	0.468620	0.716059	0.840328	1.149305	1.564325	1.573393	1.578833
484	CABLE AND OTHER PAY TELEVISION SERVICES	24	1.033760	0.939107	0.549890	0.555457	0.569604	0.857624	0.939107	0.975471	1.770141	1.883530	1.932772
4841	Cable And Other Pay Television Services	24	1.033760	0.939107	0.549890	0.555457	0.569604	0.857624	0.939107	0.975471	1.770141	1.883530	1.932772
489	COMMUNICATIONS SERVICES, NOT ELSEWHERE CLASSIFIED	21	1.259836	1.345270	0.130677	0.212063	0.347706	1.186350	1.345270	1.381910	2.330070	2.460925	2.539438
4899	Communications Services, Not Elsewhere Classified	21	1.259836	1.345270	0.130677	0.212063	0.347706	1.186350	1.345270	1.381910	2.330070	2.460925	2.539438
49	ELECTRIC, GAS, AND SANITARY SERVICES	138	0.718345	0.640899	-0.585477	-0.226172	0.076032	0.510321	0.640899	0.749038	1.807128	1.993776	2.198643
491	ELECTRIC SERVICES	53	0.714813	0.487085	-0.296011	0.065085	0.101609	0.426632	0.487085	0.667392	1.974710	2.127657	2.240363
4911	Electric Services	53	0.714813	0.487085	-0.296011	0.065085	0.101609	0.426632	0.487085	0.667392	1.974710	2.127657	2.240363
492	GAS PRODUCTION AND DISTRIBUTION	27	0.864602	0.816429	0.106004	0.170198	0.265112	0.734035	0.816429	0.955008	1.465827	1.617634	1.782607
4922	Natural Gas Transmission	8	1.111671	0.991110	0.508682	0.539349	0.590462	0.975279	0.991110	1.066582	1.744537	1.818563	1.862979
4923	Natural Gas Transmission And Distribution	9	0.853191	0.837169	0.086323	0.120997	0.178787	0.820577	0.837169	0.999370	1.399562	1.428316	1.445568
4924	Natural Gas Distribution	9	0.727152	0.654339	0.572755	0.573090	0.573649	0.640665	0.654339	0.655240	1.064943	1.098261	1.118253
4925	Mixed, Manufactured, Or Liquefied Petroleum Gas Production	1	0.227808	0.227808	0.227808	0.227808	0.227808	0.227808	0.227808	0.227808	0.227808	0.227808	0.227808

Betas of Common Stocks by SIC Codes as of March 31, 2017

SIC Code	Description	Number of Companies	Mean	Median	1st Percentile	2.5th Percentile	5th Percentile	40th Percentile	50th Percentile	60th Percentile	95th Percentile	97.5th Percentile	99th Percentile
493	COMBINATION ELECTRIC AND GAS, AND OTHER UTILITY SERVICES	23	0.592547	0.505797	-0.057083	0.018472	0.126693	0.475328	0.505797	0.513732	1.708411	1.987373	2.125923
4931	Electric And Other Services Combined	17	0.479442	0.395830	-0.070821	-0.015871	0.075712	0.378288	0.395830	0.501559	0.957117	1.377778	1.630175
4932	Gas And Other Services Combined	5	0.966702	0.703446	0.502570	0.503123	0.504046	0.626638	0.703446	0.781328	1.954262	2.086276	2.165484
4939	Combination Utilities, Not Elsewhere Classified	1	0.644550	0.644550	0.644550	0.644550	0.644550	0.644550	0.644550	0.644550	0.644550	0.644550	0.644550
494	WATER SUPPLY	13	0.746234	0.708589	0.335428	0.360360	0.401914	0.651223	0.708589	0.779539	1.180786	1.271263	1.325549
4941	Water Supply	13	0.746234	0.708589	0.335428	0.360360	0.401914	0.651223	0.708589	0.779539	1.180786	1.271263	1.325549
495	SANITARY SERVICES	22	0.662394	0.775449	-0.656190	-0.569065	-0.431499	0.485986	0.775449	0.908130	1.409653	1.513708	1.578371
4952	Sewerage Systems	1	0.426766	0.426766	0.426766	0.426766	0.426766	0.426766	0.426766	0.426766	0.426766	0.426766	0.426766
4953	Refuse Systems	18	0.633418	0.849544	-0.667253	-0.596724	-0.479175	0.540729	0.849544	0.945940	1.304893	1.360546	1.393939
4955	HAZARDOUS WASTE MANAGEMENT	2	1.167819	1.167819	0.723230	0.736840	0.759523	1.077086	1.167819	1.258551	1.576114	1.598797	1.612407
4959	Sanitary Services, Not Elsewhere Classified	1	0.408722	0.408722	0.408722	0.408722	0.408722	0.408722	0.408722	0.408722	0.408722	0.408722	0.408722
	WHOLESALE TRADE												
50	WHOLESALE TRADE¨DURABLE GOODS	75	1.079665	1.149900	-1.091865	-0.286466	-0.027371	0.991842	1.149900	1.334788	2.148980	2.367179	2.592024
501	MOTOR VEHICLES AND MOTOR VEHICLE PARTS AND SUPPLIES	10	0.968053	1.080755	-0.895627	-0.669993	-0.293936	1.052584	1.080755	1.230822	1.598103	1.600521	1.601973
5012	Automobiles And Other Motor Vehicles	2	1.139190	1.139190	0.788595	0.799328	0.817215	1.067640	1.139190	1.210740	1.461165	1.479053	1.489785
5013	Motor Vehicle Supplies And New Parts	7	0.905145	1.095370	-0.945768	-0.795345	-0.544641	1.057498	1.095370	1.298548	1.599715	1.601328	1.602295
5015	Motor Vehicle Parts, Used	1	1.066140	1.066140	1.066140	1.066140	1.066140	1.066140	1.066140	1.066140	1.066140	1.066140	1.066140
503	LUMBER AND OTHER CONSTRUCTION MATERIALS	6	1.157047	1.285790	0.753529	0.755205	0.757997	1.260360	1.285790	1.311220	1.425825	1.427853	1.429069
5031	Lumber, Plywood, Millwork, And Wood Panels	4	1.092676	1.094206	0.753082	0.754088	0.755763	0.902534	1.094206	1.285878	1.427447	1.428664	1.429393
5033	Roofing, Siding, And Insulation Materials	1	1.311220	1.311220	1.311220	1.311220	1.311220	1.311220	1.311220	1.311220	1.311220	1.311220	1.311220
5039	Construction Materials, Not Elsewhere Classified	1	1.260360	1.260360	1.260360	1.260360	1.260360	1.260360	1.260360	1.260360	1.260360	1.260360	1.260360
504	PROFESSIONAL AND COMMERCIAL EQUIPMENT AND SUPPLIES	18	1.027618	1.011625	-0.016135	0.024122	0.091217	0.877317	1.011625	1.172212	1.770989	1.863804	1.919494
5044	Office Equipment	1	0.114897	0.114897	0.114897	0.114897	0.114897	0.114897	0.114897	0.114897	0.114897	0.114897	0.114897
5045	Computers And Computer Peripheral Equipment And Software	8	1.562896	1.651960	1.157709	1.169423	1.188946	1.577174	1.651960	1.684570	1.880184	1.918402	1.941333
5047	Medical, Dental, And Hospital Equipment And Supplies	9	0.653229	0.826237	-0.015734	0.025124	0.093220	0.662271	0.826237	0.858292	1.013484	1.017202	1.019433
505	METALS AND MINERALS, EXCEPT PETROLEUM	6	1.835113	1.900220	0.550427	0.599683	0.681775	1.547160	1.900220	2.253280	2.957510	3.056685	3.116190
5051	Metals Service Centers And Offices	6	1.835113	1.900220	0.550427	0.599683	0.681775	1.547160	1.900220	2.253280	2.957510	3.056685	3.116190
506	ELECTRICAL GOODS	17	0.986846	1.028770	-0.127809	-0.090889	-0.029356	0.899807	1.028770	1.413172	1.786896	1.896808	1.962755

Betas of Common Stocks by SIC Codes as of March 31, 2017

SIC Code	Description	Number of Companies	Mean	Median	1st Percentile	2.5th Percentile	5th Percentile	40th Percentile	50th Percentile	60th Percentile	95th Percentile	97.5th Percentile	99th Percentile
5063	Electrical Apparatus And Equipment, Wiring Supplies, And Construction	5	1.437614	1.624360	0.854026	0.861656	0.874373	1.365060	1.624360	1.667392	1.951764	1.979242	1.995729
5065	Electronic Parts And Equipment, Not Elsewhere Classified	12	0.799026	0.710854	-0.135500	-0.110118	-0.067814	0.366115	0.710854	1.233592	1.592729	1.619879	1.636170
507	HARDWARE, AND PLUMBING AND HEATING EQUIPMENT AND SUPPLIES	3	1.543153	1.565610	0.971690	0.989871	1.020173	1.444402	1.565610	1.673344	2.050413	2.077347	2.093507
5074	Plumbing And Heating Equipment And Supplies (Hydronics)	2	1.834945	1.834945	1.570997	1.579077	1.592544	1.781078	1.834945	1.888812	2.077347	2.090813	2.098893
5075	Warm Air Heating And Air-Conditioning Equipment And Supplies	1	0.959569	0.959569	0.959569	0.959569	0.959569	0.959569	0.959569	0.959569	0.959569	0.959569	0.959569
508	MACHINERY, EQUIPMENT, AND SUPPLIES	8	1.276055	1.244665	0.041158	0.133923	0.288532	1.140153	1.244665	1.331460	2.284867	2.339394	2.372109
5084	Industrial Machinery And Equipment	6	1.286518	1.200372	0.023489	0.089749	0.200184	0.951043	1.200372	1.449700	2.316025	2.354973	2.378341
5085	Industrial Supplies	1	1.187430	1.187430	1.187430	1.187430	1.187430	1.187430	1.187430	1.187430	1.187430	1.187430	1.187430
5087	Service Establishment Equipment And Supplies	1	1.301900	1.301900	1.301900	1.301900	1.301900	1.301900	1.301900	1.301900	1.301900	1.301900	1.301900
509	MISCELLANEOUS DURABLE GOODS	7	0.461418	0.205450	-1.145528	-1.030430	-0.838601	0.168505	0.205450	0.711886	1.632709	1.733460	1.793910
5091	Sporting And Recreational Goods And Supplies	3	1.009198	1.049510	0.161988	0.189157	0.234439	0.868383	1.049510	1.206450	1.755740	1.794975	1.818516
5094	Jewelry, Watches, Precious Stones, And Precious Metals	3	0.474865	0.205450	0.059581	0.064047	0.071489	0.175681	0.205450	0.396868	1.066831	1.114686	1.143398
5099	Durable Goods, Not Elsewhere Classified	1	-1.222260	-1.222260	-1.222260	-1.222260	-1.222260	-1.222260	-1.222260	-1.222260	-1.222260	-1.222260	-1.222260
51	WHOLESALE TRADE¨NONDURABLE GOODS	60	1.066095	1.075445	-0.816814	-0.250271	-0.086870	0.974771	1.075445	1.224904	2.094030	2.272733	2.544347
511	PAPER AND PAPER PRODUCTS	1	1.024710	1.024710	1.024710	1.024710	1.024710	1.024710	1.024710	1.024710	1.024710	1.024710	1.024710
5111	Printing And Writing Paper	1	1.024710	1.024710	1.024710	1.024710	1.024710	1.024710	1.024710	1.024710	1.024710	1.024710	1.024710
512	DRUGS, DRUG PROPRIETARIES, AND DRUGGISTS' SUNDRIES	22	1.359314	1.395985	-0.131065	-0.112252	-0.053707	1.203858	1.395985	1.479872	2.361265	2.571722	2.704381
5122	Drugs, Drug Proprietaries, And Druggists' Sundries	22	1.359314	1.395985	-0.131065	-0.112252	-0.053707	1.203858	1.395985	1.479872	2.361265	2.571722	2.704381
513	APPAREL, PIECE GOODS, AND NOTIONS	2	0.947261	0.947261	0.926315	0.926957	0.928025	0.942986	0.947261	0.951536	0.966497	0.967565	0.968207
5136	Men's And Boys' Clothing And Furnishings	1	0.968634	0.968634	0.968634	0.968634	0.968634	0.968634	0.968634	0.968634	0.968634	0.968634	0.968634
5139	Footwear	1	0.925888	0.925888	0.925888	0.925888	0.925888	0.925888	0.925888	0.925888	0.925888	0.925888	0.925888
514	GROCERIES AND RELATED PRODUCTS	15	0.597083	0.759120	-1.332709	-1.091958	-0.690706	0.728450	0.759120	0.847321	1.376644	1.501622	1.576609
5141	Groceries, General Line	10	0.620282	0.721599	-0.310686	-0.256550	-0.166324	0.647504	0.721599	0.806438	1.245112	1.257316	1.264638
5145	Confectionery	1	1.034750	1.034750	1.034750	1.034750	1.034750	1.034750	1.034750	1.034750	1.034750	1.034750	1.034750
5148	Fresh Fruits And Vegetables	1	0.758032	0.758032	0.758032	0.758032	0.758032	0.758032	0.758032	0.758032	0.758032	0.758032	0.758032
5149	Groceries And Related Products, Not Elsewhere Classified	3	0.320216	0.827258	-1.446801	-1.377187	-1.261163	0.363164	0.827258	0.987126	1.546666	1.586633	1.610613

Betas of Common Stocks by SIC Codes as of March 31, 2017

SIC Code	Description	Number of Companies	Mean	Median	1st Percentile	2.5th Percentile	5th Percentile	40th Percentile	50th Percentile	60th Percentile	95th Percentile	97.5th Percentile	99th Percentile
515	FARM-PRODUCT RAW MATERIALS	4	1.060151	1.064869	0.511834	0.529533	0.559032	0.961956	1.064869	1.167782	1.554664	1.582747	1.599597
5153	Grain And Field Beans	2	0.868213	0.868213	0.507399	0.518444	0.536853	0.794577	0.868213	0.941848	1.199572	1.217981	1.229026
5159	Farm-Product Raw Materials, Not Elsewhere Classified	2	1.252089	1.252089	0.900523	0.911285	0.929222	1.180341	1.252089	1.323837	1.574956	1.592893	1.603655
516	CHEMICALS AND ALLIED PRODUCTS	5	1.457614	1.502980	1.183482	1.195019	1.214248	1.449020	1.502980	1.516924	1.670272	1.686826	1.696758
5162	Plastics Materials And Basic Forms And Shapes	1	1.703380	1.703380	1.703380	1.703380	1.703380	1.703380	1.703380	1.703380	1.703380	1.703380	1.703380
5169	Chemicals And Allied Products, Not Elsewhere Classified	4	1.396173	1.435530	1.181559	1.190212	1.204634	1.395060	1.435530	1.476000	1.532611	1.535226	1.536794
517	PETROLEUM AND PETROLEUM PRODUCTS	5	1.063680	1.169820	0.514181	0.532894	0.564081	1.027325	1.169820	1.200560	1.518630	1.552625	1.573022
5172	Petroleum And Petroleum Products Wholesalers, Except Bulk Station	5	1.063680	1.169820	0.514181	0.532894	0.564081	1.027325	1.169820	1.200560	1.518630	1.552625	1.573022
519	MISCELLANEOUS NONDURABLE GOODS	6	0.889703	1.061750	0.020609	0.066561	0.143147	1.049700	1.061750	1.073800	1.351585	1.371858	1.384021
5191	Farm Supplies	2	1.139825	1.139825	1.051503	1.054206	1.058713	1.121800	1.139825	1.157850	1.220938	1.225444	1.228148
5192	Books, Periodicals, And Newspapers	1	0.602664	0.602664	0.602664	0.602664	0.602664	0.602664	0.602664	0.602664	0.602664	0.602664	0.602664
5199	Nondurable Goods, Not Elsewhere Classified	3	0.818635	1.073800	0.011652	0.044166	0.098358	0.857035	1.073800	1.137466	1.360297	1.376214	1.385763
	RETAIL TRADE												
52	RETAIL TRADE	13	1.005471	0.980902	-0.471248	-0.247480	0.125466	0.936568	0.980902	1.073446	1.861476	2.064123	2.185711
521	LUMBER AND OTHER BUILDING MATERIALS DEALERS	11	1.040038	1.064070	-0.496111	-0.309638	0.001150	0.980902	1.064070	1.110950	1.929025	2.097898	2.199221
5211	Lumber And Other Building Materials Dealers	11	1.040038	1.064070	-0.496111	-0.309638	0.001150	0.980902	1.064070	1.110950	1.929025	2.097898	2.199221
523	PAINT, GLASS, AND WALLPAPER STORES	1	0.941392	0.941392	0.941392	0.941392	0.941392	0.941392	0.941392	0.941392	0.941392	0.941392	0.941392
5231	Paint, Glass, And Wallpaper Stores	1	0.941392	0.941392	0.941392	0.941392	0.941392	0.941392	0.941392	0.941392	0.941392	0.941392	0.941392
526	RETAIL NURSERIES, LAWN AND GARDEN SUPPLY STORES	1	0.689309	0.689309	0.689309	0.689309	0.689309	0.689309	0.689309	0.689309	0.689309	0.689309	0.689309
5261	Retail Nurseries, Lawn And Garden Supply Stores	1	0.689309	0.689309	0.689309	0.689309	0.689309	0.689309	0.689309	0.689309	0.689309	0.689309	0.689309
53	GENERAL MERCHANDISE STORES	20	1.080707	1.032200	0.536293	0.553859	0.583136	0.883689	1.032200	1.126764	1.905774	1.932127	1.947939
531	DEPARTMENT STORES	10	1.179668	1.137150	0.699078	0.722098	0.760465	1.086896	1.137150	1.181940	1.769435	1.863958	1.920671
5311	Department Stores	10	1.179668	1.137150	0.699078	0.722098	0.760465	1.086896	1.137150	1.181940	1.769435	1.863958	1.920671
533	VARIETY STORES	8	1.010365	0.812710	0.531489	0.541849	0.559115	0.749962	0.812710	0.888994	1.836700	1.869850	1.889740
5331	Variety Stores	8	1.010365	0.812710	0.531489	0.541849	0.559115	0.749962	0.812710	0.888994	1.836700	1.869850	1.889740
539	MISCELLANEOUS GENERAL MERCHANDISE STORES	2	0.867264	0.867264	0.591839	0.600270	0.614323	0.811055	0.867264	0.923473	1.120205	1.134258	1.142689
5399	Miscellaneous General Merchandise Stores	2	0.867264	0.867264	0.591839	0.600270	0.614323	0.811055	0.867264	0.923473	1.120205	1.134258	1.142689
54	FOOD STORES	22	0.621059	0.829396	-3.857658	-2.240805	0.211179	0.659493	0.829396	0.868344	1.499925	1.654865	1.754912
541	GROCERY STORES	16	0.862473	0.829396	0.244498	0.315284	0.433262	0.698608	0.829396	0.854596	1.583403	1.702506	1.773969
5411	Grocery Stores	16	0.862473	0.829396	0.244498	0.315284	0.433262	0.698608	0.829396	0.854596	1.583403	1.702506	1.773969

Betas of Common Stocks by SIC Codes as of March 31, 2017

SIC Code	Description	Number of Companies	Mean	Median	1st Percentile	2.5th Percentile	5th Percentile	40th Percentile	50th Percentile	60th Percentile	95th Percentile	97.5th Percentile	99th Percentile
544	CANDY, NUT, AND CONFECTIONERY STORES	1	0.963423	0.963423	0.963423	0.963423	0.963423	0.963423	0.963423	0.963423	0.963423	0.963423	0.963423
5441	Candy, Nut, And Confectionery Stores	1	0.963423	0.963423	0.963423	0.963423	0.963423	0.963423	0.963423	0.963423	0.963423	0.963423	0.963423
549	MISCELLANEOUS FOOD STORES	5	-0.219939	0.547217	-4.719148	-4.394529	-3.853498	0.518230	0.547217	0.884890	1.416280	1.419390	1.421256
5499	Miscellaneous Food Stores	5	-0.219939	0.547217	-4.719148	-4.394529	-3.853498	0.518230	0.547217	0.884890	1.416280	1.419390	1.421256
55	AUTOMOTIVE DEALERS AND GASOLINE SERVICE STATIONS	20	0.997085	1.566970	-2.960470	-2.673641	-2.195591	1.325036	1.566970	1.620866	1.978624	2.005452	2.021549
551	MOTOR VEHICLE DEALERS (NEW AND USED)	9	1.634619	1.645920	1.383121	1.404662	1.440564	1.635640	1.645920	1.646304	1.775056	1.785458	1.791699
5511	Motor Vehicle Dealers (New And Used)	9	1.634619	1.645920	1.383121	1.404662	1.440564	1.635640	1.645920	1.646304	1.775056	1.785458	1.791699
552	MOTOR VEHICLE DEALERS (USED ONLY)	2	-0.783010	-0.783010	-3.104316	-3.033256	-2.914822	-1.256746	-0.783010	-0.309274	1.348802	1.467236	1.538296
5521	Motor Vehicle Dealers (Used Only)	2	-0.783010	-0.783010	-3.104316	-3.033256	-2.914822	-1.256746	-0.783010	-0.309274	1.348802	1.467236	1.538296
553	AUTO AND HOME SUPPLY STORES	3	0.159575	0.591715	-2.090530	-2.008421	-1.871572	0.044318	0.591715	0.879828	1.888224	1.960252	2.003469
5531	Auto And Home Supply Stores	3	0.159575	0.591715	-2.090530	-2.008421	-1.871572	0.044318	0.591715	0.879828	1.888224	1.960252	2.003469
554	GASOLINE SERVICE STATIONS	4	1.044370	0.921691	0.365068	0.375221	0.392144	0.719036	0.921691	1.124346	1.868348	1.922074	1.954310
5541	Gasoline Service Stations	4	1.044370	0.921691	0.365068	0.375221	0.392144	0.719036	0.921691	1.124346	1.868348	1.922074	1.954310
555	BOAT DEALERS	2	1.069971	1.069971	0.942641	0.946538	0.953035	1.043985	1.069971	1.095957	1.186907	1.193404	1.197301
5551	Boat Dealers	2	1.069971	1.069971	0.942641	0.946538	0.953035	1.043985	1.069971	1.095957	1.186907	1.193404	1.197301
56	APPAREL AND ACCESSORY STORES	35	1.176975	1.187490	0.451095	0.457813	0.540537	1.087790	1.187490	1.248372	1.903182	2.138199	2.250291
5600	RETAIL-APPAREL & ACCESSORY STORES	1	1.814430	1.814430	1.814430	1.814430	1.814430	1.814430	1.814430	1.814430	1.814430	1.814430	1.814430
561	MEN'S AND BOYS' CLOTHING AND ACCESSORY STORES	1	1.519290	1.519290	1.519290	1.519290	1.519290	1.519290	1.519290	1.519290	1.519290	1.519290	1.519290
5611	Men's And Boys' Clothing And Accessory Stores	1	1.519290	1.519290	1.519290	1.519290	1.519290	1.519290	1.519290	1.519290	1.519290	1.519290	1.519290
562	WOMEN'S CLOTHING STORES	8	1.205403	1.224135	0.588595	0.608772	0.642401	1.075376	1.224135	1.369994	1.741533	1.779061	1.801579
5621	Women's Clothing Stores	8	1.205403	1.224135	0.588595	0.608772	0.642401	1.075376	1.224135	1.369994	1.741533	1.779061	1.801579
563	WOMEN'S ACCESSORY AND SPECIALTY STORES	1	1.215880	1.215880	1.215880	1.215880	1.215880	1.215880	1.215880	1.215880	1.215880	1.215880	1.215880
5632	Women's Accessory And Specialty Stores	1	1.215880	1.215880	1.215880	1.215880	1.215880	1.215880	1.215880	1.215880	1.215880	1.215880	1.215880
565	FAMILY CLOTHING STORES	15	1.216793	1.199560	0.641208	0.667624	0.711650	1.192668	1.199560	1.313430	1.729512	1.917371	2.030086
5651	Family Clothing Stores	15	1.216793	1.199560	0.641208	0.667624	0.711650	1.192668	1.199560	1.313430	1.729512	1.917371	2.030086
566	SHOE STORES	7	1.086369	1.083380	0.459742	0.479429	0.512241	0.931473	1.083380	1.090490	1.975145	2.150083	2.255045
5661	Shoe Stores	7	1.086369	1.083380	0.459742	0.479429	0.512241	0.931473	1.083380	1.090490	1.975145	2.150083	2.255045
569	MISCELLANEOUS APPAREL AND ACCESSORY STORES	2	0.572407	0.572407	0.462041	0.465420	0.471051	0.549883	0.572407	0.594930	0.673762	0.679393	0.682772
5699	Miscellaneous Apparel And Accessory Stores	2	0.572407	0.572407	0.462041	0.465420	0.471051	0.549883	0.572407	0.594930	0.673762	0.679393	0.682772
57	HOME FURNITURE, FURNISHINGS, AND EQUIPMENT STORES	13	1.248621	1.109810	-0.030348	0.135791	0.412688	1.069328	1.109810	1.310294	2.113700	2.267675	2.360060
571	HOME FURNITURE AND FURNISHINGS STORES	6	1.408708	1.372970	1.094639	1.095836	1.097833	1.268510	1.372970	1.477430	1.828035	1.866388	1.889399
5712	Furniture Stores	3	1.532167	1.597920	1.103922	1.119044	1.144248	1.497104	1.597920	1.659284	1.874058	1.889399	1.898604

Betas of Common Stocks by SIC Codes as of March 31, 2017

SIC Code	Description	Number of Companies	Mean	Median	1st Percentile	2.5th Percentile	5th Percentile	40th Percentile	50th Percentile	60th Percentile	95th Percentile	97.5th Percentile	99th Percentile
5713	Floor Covering Stores	1	1.109810	1.109810	1.109810	1.109810	1.109810	1.109810	1.109810	1.109810	1.109810	1.109810	1.109810
5719	Miscellaneous Homefurnishings Stores	2	1.372970	1.372970	1.270599	1.273733	1.278956	1.352078	1.372970	1.393862	1.466984	1.472207	1.475341
572	HOUSEHOLD APPLIANCE STORES	1	0.968499	0.968499	0.968499	0.968499	0.968499	0.968499	0.968499	0.968499	0.968499	0.968499	0.968499
5722	Household Appliance Stores	1	0.968499	0.968499	0.968499	0.968499	0.968499	0.968499	0.968499	0.968499	0.968499	0.968499	0.968499
573	RADIO, TELEVISION, CONSUMER ELECTRONICS, AND MUSIC STORES	6	1.135221	0.920248	-0.094957	-0.025733	0.089641	0.869216	0.920248	0.971280	2.293338	2.357494	2.395988
5731	Radio, Television, And Consumer Electronics Stores	4	1.542637	1.439840	0.872278	0.876871	0.884526	1.158704	1.439840	1.720976	2.344663	2.383156	2.406253
5734	Computer And Computer Software Stores	1	0.781885	0.781885	0.781885	0.781885	0.781885	0.781885	0.781885	0.781885	0.781885	0.781885	0.781885
5735	Record And Prerecorded Tape Stores	1	-0.141107	-0.141107	-0.141107	-0.141107	-0.141107	-0.141107	-0.141107	-0.141107	-0.141107	-0.141107	-0.141107
58	EATING AND DRINKING PLACES	66	0.781944	0.836243	-0.923240	-0.413139	-0.033829	0.800514	0.836243	0.904728	1.282845	1.327448	1.398604
581	EATING AND DRINKING PLACES	66	0.781944	0.836243	-0.923240	-0.413139	-0.033829	0.800514	0.836243	0.904728	1.282845	1.327448	1.398604
5810	RETAIL-EATING & DRINKING PLACES	1	1.129040	1.129040	1.129040	1.129040	1.129040	1.129040	1.129040	1.129040	1.129040	1.129040	1.129040
5812	Eating Places	64	0.780406	0.836243	-0.941697	-0.428107	-0.055015	0.800758	0.836243	0.904302	1.282967	1.333005	1.398701
5813	Drinking Places (Alcoholic Beverages)	1	0.533308	0.533308	0.533308	0.533308	0.533308	0.533308	0.533308	0.533308	0.533308	0.533308	0.533308
59	MISCELLANEOUS RETAIL	72	0.817375	1.000962	-4.279697	-1.735112	-0.342392	0.888748	1.000962	1.148952	1.885001	2.174989	2.634004
591	DRUG STORES AND PROPRIETARY STORES	10	0.752784	0.644019	-0.147999	-0.119929	-0.073146	0.551060	0.644019	0.761424	1.808043	1.950842	2.036521
5912	Drug Stores And Proprietary Stores	10	0.752784	0.644019	-0.147999	-0.119929	-0.073146	0.551060	0.644019	0.761424	1.808043	1.950842	2.036521
592	LIQUOR STORES	1	0.072107	0.072107	0.072107	0.072107	0.072107	0.072107	0.072107	0.072107	0.072107	0.072107	0.072107
5921	Liquor Stores	1	0.072107	0.072107	0.072107	0.072107	0.072107	0.072107	0.072107	0.072107	0.072107	0.072107	0.072107
593	USED MERCHANDISE STORES	3	0.999919	1.153280	0.482732	0.503259	0.537470	1.016433	1.153280	1.198110	1.355015	1.366223	1.372947
5932	Used Merchandise Stores	3	0.999919	1.153280	0.482732	0.503259	0.537470	1.016433	1.153280	1.198110	1.355015	1.366223	1.372947
594	MISCELLANEOUS SHOPPING GOODS STORES	16	1.028815	1.359750	-2.452636	-1.653310	-0.321100	1.259650	1.359750	1.440620	1.871463	1.889886	1.900941
5941	Sporting Goods Stores And Bicycle Shops	4	0.953327	0.905206	0.743687	0.744351	0.745457	0.816878	0.905206	0.993534	1.228566	1.244108	1.253433
5942	Book Stores	2	1.797365	1.797365	1.688639	1.691967	1.697515	1.775176	1.797365	1.819554	1.897216	1.902763	1.906091
5943	Stationery Stores	2	1.795360	1.795360	1.732816	1.734731	1.737922	1.782596	1.795360	1.808124	1.852798	1.855989	1.857904
5944	Jewelry Stores	3	-0.081620	1.300040	-2.899809	-2.771242	-2.556964	0.442928	1.300040	1.328156	1.426562	1.433591	1.437808
5945	Hobby, Toy, And Game Shops	3	0.875418	0.639753	0.568494	0.570676	0.574311	0.625210	0.639753	0.795694	1.341489	1.380475	1.403866
5947	Gift, Novelty, And Souvenir Shops	2	1.540445	1.540445	1.534266	1.534455	1.534771	1.539184	1.540445	1.541706	1.546120	1.546435	1.546624
596	NONSTORE RETAILERS	25	0.792739	1.013060	-5.794339	-3.313548	-0.412133	0.983391	1.013060	1.061184	2.337338	2.701830	2.923806
5960	RETAIL-NONSTORE RETAILERS	1	0.333523	0.333523	0.333523	0.333523	0.333523	0.333523	0.333523	0.333523	0.333523	0.333523	0.333523
5961	Catalog And Mail-Order Houses	24	0.811873	1.015685	-5.863250	-3.485825	-0.448378	0.984956	1.015685	1.088028	2.366801	2.717245	2.929972
598	FUEL DEALERS	4	0.206737	0.213850	0.083081	0.087791	0.095641	0.196302	0.213850	0.231397	0.307874	0.313590	0.317020
5983	Fuel Oil Dealers	4	0.206737	0.213850	0.083081	0.087791	0.095641	0.196302	0.213850	0.231397	0.307874	0.313590	0.317020
599	RETAIL STORES, NOT ELSEWHERE CLASSIFIED	13	0.857294	1.142460	-1.192625	-0.923428	-0.474767	0.847868	1.142460	1.178614	1.656282	1.659801	1.661912
5992	Florists	1	1.142460	1.142460	1.142460	1.142460	1.142460	1.142460	1.142460	1.142460	1.142460	1.142460	1.142460
5995	Optical Goods Stores	1	0.750521	0.750521	0.750521	0.750521	0.750521	0.750521	0.750521	0.750521	0.750521	0.750521	0.750521

Betas of Common Stocks by SIC Codes as of March 31, 2017

SIC Code	Description	Number of Companies	Mean	Median	1st Percentile	2.5th Percentile	5th Percentile	40th Percentile	50th Percentile	60th Percentile	95th Percentile	97.5th Percentile	99th Percentile
5999	Miscellaneous Retail Stores, Not Elsewhere Classified	11	0.841076	1.172780	-1.222536	-0.998205	-0.624321	0.872205	1.172780	1.201950	1.657455	1.660388	1.662147
	FINANCE, INSURANCE, AND REAL ESTATE												
60	DEPOSITORY INSTITUTIONS	397	0.957318	1.009830	-0.128878	-0.076529	-0.020182	0.798936	1.009830	1.208846	1.913554	2.080833	2.451024
602	COMMERCIAL BANKS	305	1.040126	1.140050	-0.121805	-0.028529	0.002440	0.918025	1.140050	1.342642	1.963248	2.185072	2.674216
6021	National Commercial Banks	112	1.082156	1.211220	-0.114752	-0.037885	0.000958	1.015454	1.211220	1.459176	1.928457	1.998421	2.135481
6022	State Commercial Banks	166	0.975184	1.052015	-0.167687	-0.029854	-0.007350	0.783747	1.052015	1.318780	1.906773	2.067310	2.408671
6029	Commercial Banks, Not Elsewhere Classified	27	1.265058	1.199330	0.078878	0.126907	0.182624	1.026180	1.199330	1.230936	2.807863	2.983312	3.147459
603	SAVINGS INSTITUTIONS	83	0.664074	0.597675	-0.153446	-0.084092	-0.043089	0.440435	0.597675	0.813032	1.578634	1.684324	1.933549
6035	Savings Institutions, Federally Chartered	61	0.710712	0.650849	-0.160307	-0.065100	-0.031164	0.538001	0.650849	0.888922	1.583730	1.802320	1.952834
6036	Savings Institutions, Not Federally Chartered	22	0.534759	0.372812	-0.111546	-0.087762	-0.050634	0.224613	0.372812	0.559192	1.479330	1.557012	1.604369
606	CREDIT UNIONS	1	0.383797	0.383797	0.383797	0.383797	0.383797	0.383797	0.383797	0.383797	0.383797	0.383797	0.383797
6061	Credit Unions, Federally Chartered	1	0.383797	0.383797	0.383797	0.383797	0.383797	0.383797	0.383797	0.383797	0.383797	0.383797	0.383797
609	FUNCTIONS RELATED TO DEPOSITORY BANKING	8	0.914335	1.090125	-0.022088	0.058031	0.191562	1.002517	1.090125	1.135678	1.289101	1.304141	1.313164
6099	Functions Related To Depository Banking, Not Elsewhere Classified	8	0.914335	1.090125	-0.022088	0.058031	0.191562	1.002517	1.090125	1.135678	1.289101	1.304141	1.313164
61	NONDEPOSITORY CREDIT INSTITUTIONS	44	1.248438	1.297345	0.016229	0.126225	0.171434	1.209014	1.297345	1.514604	2.190324	2.360457	2.397893
611	FEDERAL AND FEDERALLY-SPONSORED CREDIT AGENCIES	5	1.212285	1.268490	0.168486	0.237174	0.351653	1.268090	1.268490	1.401770	1.761186	1.781123	1.793085
6111	Federal And Federally-Sponsored Credit Agencies	5	1.212285	1.268490	0.168486	0.237174	0.351653	1.268090	1.268490	1.401770	1.761186	1.781123	1.793085
614	PERSONAL CREDIT INSTITUTIONS	13	1.362994	1.536790	0.181784	0.199805	0.229842	1.374886	1.536790	1.563078	2.112300	2.141490	2.159004
6141	Personal Credit Institutions	13	1.362994	1.536790	0.181784	0.199805	0.229842	1.374886	1.536790	1.563078	2.112300	2.141490	2.159004
615	BUSINESS CREDIT INSTITUTIONS	11	0.742455	0.550528	-0.039591	-0.002847	0.058392	0.473871	0.550528	0.761612	1.552320	1.650265	1.709032
6153	Short-Term Business Credit Institutions, Except Agricultural	7	0.623548	0.473871	0.187262	0.196848	0.212825	0.438171	0.473871	0.519865	1.238243	1.245247	1.249449
6159	Miscellaneous Business Credit Institutions	4	0.950541	1.059021	-0.039315	-0.002159	0.059768	0.880576	1.059021	1.237466	1.689443	1.718827	1.736457
616	MORTGAGE BANKERS AND BROKERS	12	1.408928	1.376030	0.637682	0.649596	0.669453	1.225712	1.376030	1.534358	2.293758	2.354849	2.391504
6162	Mortgage Bankers And Loan Correspondents	9	1.436098	1.425860	0.713722	0.731385	0.760823	1.346132	1.425860	1.570524	2.202404	2.309172	2.373233
6163	Loan Brokers	3	1.327416	1.158720	0.640319	0.656188	0.682637	1.052924	1.158720	1.365734	2.090283	2.142037	2.173089
6172	FINANCE LESSORS	1	2.373970	2.373970	2.373970	2.373970	2.373970	2.373970	2.373970	2.373970	2.373970	2.373970	2.373970
6199	FINANCE SERVICES	2	1.851420	1.851420	1.564652	1.573431	1.588062	1.792896	1.851420	1.909944	2.114778	2.129409	2.138188
62	SECURITY AND COMMODITY BROKERS, DEALERS, EXCHANGES, AND SERVICES	96	1.142119	1.237060	-0.429107	-0.132247	0.032440	0.925563	1.237060	1.418250	2.319625	2.480755	2.599760
621	SECURITY BROKERS, DEALERS, AND FLOTATION COMPANIES	35	1.261294	1.465200	-1.105663	-0.540018	-0.199258	1.280590	1.465200	1.664918	2.442418	2.535699	2.572107
6211	Security Brokers, Dealers, And Flotation Companies	35	1.261294	1.465200	-1.105663	-0.540018	-0.199258	1.280590	1.465200	1.664918	2.442418	2.535699	2.572107

Betas of Common Stocks by SIC Codes as of March 31, 2017

SIC Code	Description	Number of Companies	Mean	Median	1st Percentile	2.5th Percentile	5th Percentile	40th Percentile	50th Percentile	60th Percentile	95th Percentile	97.5th Percentile	99th Percentile
622	COMMODITY CONTRACTS BROKERS AND DEALERS	2	1.833305	1.833305	1.019253	1.044173	1.085707	1.667172	1.833305	1.999438	2.580904	2.622437	2.647357
6221	Commodity Contracts Brokers And Dealers	2	1.833305	1.833305	1.019253	1.044173	1.085707	1.667172	1.833305	1.999438	2.580904	2.622437	2.647357
623	SECURITY AND COMMODITY EXCHANGES	6	0.778639	0.816534	0.465506	0.477025	0.496224	0.814209	0.816534	0.818858	1.041167	1.069368	1.086289
6231	Security And Commodity Exchanges	6	0.778639	0.816534	0.465506	0.477025	0.496224	0.814209	0.816534	0.818858	1.041167	1.069368	1.086289
628	SERVICES ALLIED WITH THE EXCHANGE OF SECURITIES OR COMMODITIES	53	1.078486	1.221440	-0.033350	0.079277	0.125473	0.851820	1.221440	1.368902	2.073374	2.112444	2.180832
6282	Investment Advice	52	1.098029	1.237060	-0.006342	0.122010	0.149483	0.879208	1.237060	1.378406	2.075480	2.112937	2.182134
6289	Services Allied With The Exchange Of Securities Or Commodities	1	0.062219	0.062219	0.062219	0.062219	0.062219	0.062219	0.062219	0.062219	0.062219	0.062219	0.062219
63	INSURANCE CARRIERS	145	0.893717	0.885179	-0.337923	-0.067299	0.057797	0.814532	0.885179	1.003518	1.827938	2.124286	2.226225
631	LIFE INSURANCE	37	1.052256	1.039620	-0.339552	-0.328560	0.011022	0.745529	1.039620	1.492312	2.216926	2.241302	2.261347
6311	Life Insurance	37	1.052256	1.039620	-0.339552	-0.328560	0.011022	0.745529	1.039620	1.492312	2.216926	2.241302	2.261347
632	ACCIDENT AND HEALTH INSURANCE AND MEDICAL SERVICE PLANS	21	0.992685	0.986020	0.202389	0.202706	0.203235	0.948343	0.986020	0.994220	1.583500	1.687700	1.750220
6321	Accident And Health Insurance	11	1.046616	0.983437	0.202283	0.202442	0.202706	0.948343	0.983437	1.031970	1.687700	1.739800	1.771060
6324	Hospital And Medical Service Plans	10	0.933361	0.986944	0.680825	0.682904	0.686371	0.967473	0.986944	0.990408	1.139442	1.163211	1.177472
633	FIRE, MARINE, AND CASUALTY INSURANCE	69	0.740932	0.830903	-0.163393	-0.045870	0.008732	0.779303	0.830903	0.891207	1.281748	1.316742	1.396172
6331	Fire, Marine, And Casualty Insurance	69	0.740932	0.830903	-0.163393	-0.045870	0.008732	0.779303	0.830903	0.891207	1.281748	1.316742	1.396172
635	SURETY INSURANCE	8	1.278822	1.183530	0.763365	0.777118	0.800040	1.084358	1.183530	1.341404	1.788219	1.795724	1.800228
6351	Surety Insurance	8	1.278822	1.183530	0.763365	0.777118	0.800040	1.084358	1.183530	1.341404	1.788219	1.795724	1.800228
636	TITLE INSURANCE	7	0.859711	0.818407	0.676567	0.683011	0.693749	0.799152	0.818407	0.831840	1.150289	1.204384	1.236842
6361	Title Insurance	7	0.859711	0.818407	0.676567	0.683011	0.693749	0.799152	0.818407	0.831840	1.150289	1.204384	1.236842
637	PENSION, HEALTH, AND WELFARE FUNDS	1	1.441660	1.441660	1.441660	1.441660	1.441660	1.441660	1.441660	1.441660	1.441660	1.441660	1.441660
6371	Pension, Health, And Welfare Funds	1	1.441660	1.441660	1.441660	1.441660	1.441660	1.441660	1.441660	1.441660	1.441660	1.441660	1.441660
639	INSURANCE CARRIERS, NOT ELSEWHERE CLASSIFIED	2	0.497274	0.497274	-0.081128	-0.063422	-0.033911	0.379233	0.497274	0.615315	1.028459	1.057970	1.075676
6399	Insurance Carriers, Not Elsewhere Classified	2	0.497274	0.497274	-0.081128	-0.063422	-0.033911	0.379233	0.497274	0.615315	1.028459	1.057970	1.075676
64	INSURANCE AGENTS, BROKERS, AND SERVICE	15	1.071236	1.077160	0.403833	0.464427	0.565415	1.037708	1.077160	1.153338	1.448077	1.612819	1.711663
641	INSURANCE AGENTS, BROKERS, AND SERVICE	15	1.071236	1.077160	0.403833	0.464427	0.565415	1.037708	1.077160	1.153338	1.448077	1.612819	1.711663
6411	Insurance Agents, Brokers, And Service	15	1.071236	1.077160	0.403833	0.464427	0.565415	1.037708	1.077160	1.153338	1.448077	1.612819	1.711663
65	REAL ESTATE	42	1.041261	0.982164	-0.192555	-0.135804	0.131481	0.835474	0.982164	1.232006	1.894927	2.051465	2.234895
6500	REAL ESTATE	2	0.312744	0.312744	0.212694	0.215757	0.220861	0.292326	0.312744	0.333162	0.404627	0.409731	0.412794

Betas of Common Stocks by SIC Codes as of March 31, 2017

SIC Code	Description	Number of Companies	Mean	Median	1st Percentile	2.5th Percentile	5th Percentile	40th Percentile	50th Percentile	60th Percentile	95th Percentile	97.5th Percentile	99th Percentile
651	REAL ESTATE OPERATORS (EXCEPT DEVELOPERS) AND LESSORS	16	0.846782	0.732971	-0.214590	-0.195521	-0.163739	0.539335	0.732971	0.871611	1.822343	1.860761	1.883813
6512	Operators Of Nonresidential Buildings	11	0.990289	0.871611	-0.158795	-0.056033	0.115237	0.811383	0.871611	1.131950	1.847955	1.873568	1.888935
6513	Operators Of Apartment Buildings	3	0.165969	0.127314	-0.137154	-0.129058	-0.115565	0.073341	0.127314	0.204480	0.474560	0.493852	0.505426
6519	Lessors Of Real Property, Not Elsewhere Classified	2	1.078713	1.078713	0.550123	0.566304	0.593273	0.970837	1.078713	1.186588	1.564152	1.591121	1.607302
653	REAL ESTATE AGENTS AND MANAGERS	20	1.289837	1.333040	0.522357	0.530863	0.545040	1.120146	1.333040	1.388438	2.070584	2.215117	2.301837
6531	Real Estate Agents And Managers	20	1.289837	1.333040	0.522357	0.530863	0.545040	1.120146	1.333040	1.388438	2.070584	2.215117	2.301837
655	LAND SUBDIVIDERS AND DEVELOPERS	4	0.940562	1.020695	0.336384	0.361295	0.402813	0.932288	1.020695	1.109102	1.366124	1.383602	1.394089
6552	Land Subdividers And Developers, Except Cemeteries	4	0.940562	1.020695	0.336384	0.361295	0.402813	0.932288	1.020695	1.109102	1.366124	1.383602	1.394089
67	HOLDING AND OTHER INVESTMENT OFFICES	228	0.763623	0.718488	-0.863372	-0.173660	-0.042222	0.592049	0.718488	0.886826	1.761192	1.911017	1.983536
671	HOLDING OFFICES	56	0.843772	0.838918	-0.159133	-0.120703	0.017487	0.732922	0.838918	0.989835	1.787983	1.904890	1.911112
6712	Offices Of Bank Holding Companies	46	0.873756	0.919647	-0.161961	-0.137838	-0.046081	0.750921	0.919647	1.072770	1.827833	1.908810	1.911188
6719	Offices Of Holding Companies, Not Elsewhere Classified	10	0.705849	0.641258	0.149079	0.153625	0.161201	0.409845	0.641258	0.736930	1.686877	1.719579	1.739199
672	INVESTMENT OFFICES	28	0.645421	0.557097	-0.003588	0.120485	0.248591	0.465278	0.557097	0.599782	1.581618	1.760818	1.877567
6722	Management Investment Offices, Open-End	3	1.594190	1.667130	1.170182	1.185395	1.210749	1.565712	1.667130	1.724784	1.926573	1.940987	1.949635
6726	Unit Investment Trusts, Face-Amount Certificate Offices	25	0.531569	0.547922	-0.012778	0.097509	0.236359	0.449525	0.547922	0.571660	0.966384	1.177188	1.324561
673	TRUSTS	7	0.293634	0.135584	-0.863560	-0.776743	-0.632049	0.114174	0.135584	0.186970	1.330127	1.398859	1.440097
6733	Trusts, Except Educational, Religious, And Charitable	7	0.293634	0.135584	-0.863560	-0.776743	-0.632049	0.114174	0.135584	0.186970	1.330127	1.398859	1.440097
679	MISCELLANEOUS INVESTING	137	0.779034	0.731086	-0.968357	-0.402697	-0.029461	0.640094	0.731086	0.909145	1.768448	1.943388	2.184084
6794	Patent Owners And Lessors	12	1.047751	1.252315	-0.935149	-0.664292	-0.212864	1.167392	1.252315	1.341126	1.846208	1.918189	1.961378
6798	Real Estate Investment Trusts	51	0.737441	0.703393	-0.054693	-0.045058	0.019717	0.592768	0.703393	0.781922	1.690730	1.918770	2.129380
6799	Investors, Not Elsewhere Classified	74	0.764123	0.768133	-0.921312	-0.582084	-0.065506	0.646712	0.768133	1.032197	1.727705	1.878374	2.049568
	SERVICES												
70	HOTELS, ROOMING HOUSES, CAMPS, AND OTHER LODGING PLACES	29	1.175610	1.184880	0.305323	0.330098	0.500304	1.122414	1.184880	1.245688	1.743632	1.988402	2.210053
701	HOTELS AND MOTELS	29	1.175610	1.184880	0.305323	0.330098	0.500304	1.122414	1.184880	1.245688	1.743632	1.988402	2.210053
7011	Hotels And Motels	29	1.175610	1.184880	0.305323	0.330098	0.500304	1.122414	1.184880	1.245688	1.743632	1.988402	2.210053
72	PERSONAL SERVICES	13	0.766256	0.869257	-0.258620	-0.216777	-0.147038	0.755912	0.869257	0.944051	1.557104	1.955297	2.194213
721	LAUNDRY, CLEANING, AND GARMENT SERVICES	3	0.722351	0.811578	0.368669	0.382227	0.404825	0.721188	0.811578	0.848432	0.977419	0.986633	0.992161
7211	Power Laundries, Family And Commercial	1	0.359630	0.359630	0.359630	0.359630	0.359630	0.359630	0.359630	0.359630	0.359630	0.359630	0.359630
7215	Coin-Operated Laundries And Drycleaning	1	0.811578	0.811578	0.811578	0.811578	0.811578	0.811578	0.811578	0.811578	0.811578	0.811578	0.811578
7218	Industrial Launderers	1	0.995846	0.995846	0.995846	0.995846	0.995846	0.995846	0.995846	0.995846	0.995846	0.995846	0.995846

Betas of Common Stocks by SIC Codes as of March 31, 2017

SIC Code	Description	Number of Companies	Mean	Median	1st Percentile	2.5th Percentile	5th Percentile	40th Percentile	50th Percentile	60th Percentile	95th Percentile	97.5th Percentile	99th Percentile
723	BEAUTY SHOPS	2	0.369832	0.369832	-0.273389	-0.253699	-0.220881	0.238562	0.369832	0.501102	0.960545	0.993363	1.013053
7231	Beauty Shops	2	0.369832	0.369832	-0.273389	-0.253699	-0.220881	0.238562	0.369832	0.501102	0.960545	0.993363	1.013053
726	FUNERAL SERVICE AND CREMATORIES	2	0.903777	0.903777	0.869947	0.870983	0.872709	0.896873	0.903777	0.910680	0.934844	0.936570	0.937606
7261	Funeral Service And Crematories	2	0.903777	0.903777	0.869947	0.870983	0.872709	0.896873	0.903777	0.910680	0.934844	0.936570	0.937606
729	MISCELLANEOUS PERSONAL SERVICES	6	0.874510	0.750159	-0.029269	0.007906	0.069865	0.533248	0.750159	0.967070	2.016540	2.185015	2.286100
7291	Tax Return Preparation Services	1	0.967070	0.967070	0.967070	0.967070	0.967070	0.967070	0.967070	0.967070	0.967070	0.967070	0.967070
7299	Miscellaneous Personal Services, Not Elsewhere Classified	5	0.855998	0.533248	-0.034226	-0.004486	0.045081	0.496595	0.533248	0.722225	2.083930	2.218710	2.299578
73	BUSINESS SERVICES	431	0.978363	1.057130	-1.350578	-0.833650	-0.322607	0.934815	1.057130	1.184020	2.001420	2.200540	2.645441
731	ADVERTISING	20	0.643235	0.868480	-1.283735	-1.214384	-1.098797	0.606561	0.868480	0.899453	1.848017	1.905369	1.939779
7310	SERVICES-ADVERTISING	1	0.865402	0.865402	0.865402	0.865402	0.865402	0.865402	0.865402	0.865402	0.865402	0.865402	0.865402
7311	Advertising Agencies	12	0.722583	0.929584	-1.230726	-1.081861	-0.833752	0.688197	0.929584	1.007521	1.896313	1.929517	1.949439
7312	Outdoor Advertising Services	2	0.892844	0.892844	0.871983	0.872621	0.873686	0.888586	0.892844	0.897101	0.912001	0.913066	0.913704
7313	Radio, Television, And Publishers' Advertising Representatives	3	0.343993	0.342225	0.053959	0.062783	0.077491	0.283395	0.342225	0.402116	0.611734	0.626706	0.635690
7319	Advertising, Not Elsewhere Classified	2	0.255315	0.255315	-1.059791	-1.019533	-0.952436	-0.013074	0.255315	0.523704	1.463066	1.530163	1.570421
732	CONSUMER CREDIT REPORTING AGENCIES, MERCANTILE REPORTING AGENCIES	10	1.183118	1.218640	0.577377	0.650252	0.771711	1.133552	1.218640	1.301112	1.485413	1.506641	1.519379
7320	SERVICES-CONSUMER CREDIT REPORTING, COLLECTION AGENCIES	1	1.300300	1.300300	1.300300	1.300300	1.300300	1.300300	1.300300	1.300300	1.300300	1.300300	1.300300
7322	Adjustment And Collection Services	3	1.302067	1.335700	1.140954	1.146916	1.156852	1.295956	1.335700	1.355264	1.423738	1.428629	1.431564
7323	Credit Reporting Services	6	1.104114	1.098540	0.555784	0.596270	0.663747	1.068670	1.098540	1.128410	1.471485	1.499678	1.516593
733	MAILING, REPRODUCTION, COMMERCIAL ART AND PHOTOGRAPHY, AND STENOGRAPHY	3	1.101733	1.588210	-0.045874	0.004149	0.087521	1.254724	1.588210	1.629810	1.775410	1.785810	1.792050
7331	Direct Mail Advertising Services	2	0.754494	0.754494	-0.062548	-0.037536	0.004149	0.587751	0.754494	0.921237	1.504838	1.546524	1.571536
7338	Secretarial And Court Reporting Services	1	1.796210	1.796210	1.796210	1.796210	1.796210	1.796210	1.796210	1.796210	1.796210	1.796210	1.796210
734	SERVICES TO DWELLINGS AND OTHER BUILDINGS	3	0.717930	0.783499	0.457559	0.467537	0.484166	0.716981	0.783499	0.810676	0.905796	0.912590	0.916666
7342	Disinfecting And Pest Control Services	1	0.783499	0.783499	0.783499	0.783499	0.783499	0.783499	0.783499	0.783499	0.783499	0.783499	0.783499
7349	Building Cleaning And Maintenance Services, Not Elsewhere Classified	2	0.685146	0.685146	0.455592	0.462619	0.474331	0.638298	0.685146	0.731993	0.895960	0.907672	0.914699
735	MISCELLANEOUS EQUIPMENT RENTAL AND LEASING	20	1.348340	1.583250	-1.509532	-1.008924	-0.174579	1.406666	1.583250	1.811636	2.426967	2.565069	2.647929
7350	SERVICES-MISCELLANEOUS EQUIPMENT RENTAL & LEASING	1	-1.843270	-1.843270	-1.843270	-1.843270	-1.843270	-1.843270	-1.843270	-1.843270	-1.843270	-1.843270	-1.843270
7353	Heavy Construction Equipment Rental And Leasing	1	2.031870	2.031870	2.031870	2.031870	2.031870	2.031870	2.031870	2.031870	2.031870	2.031870	2.031870

Betas of Common Stocks by SIC Codes as of March 31, 2017

SIC Code	Description	Number of Companies	Mean	Median	1st Percentile	2.5th Percentile	5th Percentile	40th Percentile	50th Percentile	60th Percentile	95th Percentile	97.5th Percentile	99th Percentile
7359	Equipment Rental And Leasing, Not Elsewhere Classified	18	1.487678	1.583250	-0.084137	-0.080214	-0.073676	1.428568	1.583250	1.801568	2.456041	2.579606	2.653744
736	PERSONNEL SUPPLY SERVICES	24	1.037622	1.099130	-0.011962	0.072460	0.179900	0.772000	1.099130	1.215086	1.902280	1.921237	1.935765
7361	Employment Agencies	4	1.041016	0.946357	0.336016	0.351188	0.376475	0.776380	0.946357	1.116333	1.838080	1.891765	1.923976
7363	Help Supply Services	20	1.036944	1.099130	-0.021750	0.047990	0.164223	0.914065	1.099130	1.200606	1.896624	1.899982	1.901997
737	COMPUTER PROGRAMMING, DATA PROCESSING, AND OTHER COMPUTER RELATED	265	0.971618	1.067520	-1.425474	-0.766602	-0.295690	0.946357	1.067520	1.176998	1.872224	2.036956	2.232954
7370	SERVICES-COMPUTER PROGRAMMING, DATA PROCESSING, ETC.	1	0.162958	0.162958	0.162958	0.162958	0.162958	0.162958	0.162958	0.162958	0.162958	0.162958	0.162958
7371	Computer Programming Services	58	1.082672	1.248450	-0.941925	-0.492837	0.046177	1.065104	1.248450	1.340434	1.968220	2.041916	2.080267
7372	Prepackaged Software	118	0.926279	1.082365	-1.473815	-0.837926	-0.347733	0.968694	1.082365	1.201956	1.853709	1.998628	2.288144
7373	Computer Integrated Systems Design	35	1.020424	1.132700	-1.131917	-0.434592	0.030737	1.061076	1.132700	1.165144	1.796318	1.862384	2.050211
7374	Computer Processing And Data Preparation And Processing Services	37	0.897220	0.934815	-0.856727	-0.196302	-0.052008	0.894167	0.934815	0.979499	1.616316	1.688447	1.819921
7375	Information Retrieval Services	10	1.058538	1.003785	0.806271	0.814905	0.829293	0.982204	1.003785	1.006958	1.475810	1.482355	1.486282
7376	Computer Facilities Management Services	1	3.885030	3.885030	3.885030	3.885030	3.885030	3.885030	3.885030	3.885030	3.885030	3.885030	3.885030
7379	Computer Related Services, Not Elsewhere Classified	5	0.367516	0.631337	-0.706587	-0.663686	-0.592186	0.370730	0.631337	0.746615	1.017570	1.029825	1.037178
738	MISCELLANEOUS BUSINESS SERVICES	86	0.955476	1.033490	-0.929503	-0.635236	-0.336784	0.890722	1.033490	1.184020	2.146955	2.596246	2.945855
7381	Detective, Guard, And Armored Car Services	1	0.173595	0.173595	0.173595	0.173595	0.173595	0.173595	0.173595	0.173595	0.173595	0.173595	0.173595
7382	Security Systems Services	3	1.450093	1.270320	1.263009	1.263233	1.263606	1.268828	1.270320	1.379676	1.762422	1.789761	1.806164
7384	Photofinishing Laboratories	1	0.670566	0.670566	0.670566	0.670566	0.670566	0.670566	0.670566	0.670566	0.670566	0.670566	0.670566
7389	Business Services, Not Elsewhere Classified	81	0.950327	1.033330	-0.941528	-0.667613	-0.341217	0.890722	1.033330	1.183940	2.177660	2.642970	2.977820
75	AUTOMOTIVE REPAIR, SERVICES, AND PARKING	6	0.556374	0.894959	-2.115515	-1.962043	-1.706257	0.814067	0.894959	0.975851	2.055618	2.099004	2.125036
751	AUTOMOTIVE RENTAL AND LEASING, WITHOUT DRIVERS	3	1.637847	1.795300	0.992240	1.016823	1.057796	1.631410	1.795300	1.864718	2.107681	2.125036	2.135448
7513	Truck Rental And Leasing, Without Drivers	2	1.385576	1.385576	0.984045	0.996337	1.016823	1.303631	1.385576	1.467520	1.754328	1.774814	1.787106
7514	Passenger Car Rental	1	2.142390	2.142390	2.142390	2.142390	2.142390	2.142390	2.142390	2.142390	2.142390	2.142390	2.142390
753	AUTOMOTIVE REPAIR SHOPS	3	-0.525100	-0.171536	-2.176904	-2.115515	-2.013201	-0.580795	-0.171536	0.025585	0.715507	0.764787	0.794355
7538	General Automotive Repair Shops	3	-0.525100	-0.171536	-2.176904	-2.115515	-2.013201	-0.580795	-0.171536	0.025585	0.715507	0.764787	0.794355
76	MISCELLANEOUS REPAIR SERVICES	3	0.353938	0.257884	-0.132911	-0.120948	-0.101009	0.178130	0.257884	0.395270	0.876122	0.910468	0.931076
762	ELECTRICAL REPAIR SHOPS	2	0.401965	0.401965	-0.130029	-0.113743	-0.086601	0.293394	0.401965	0.510535	0.890530	0.917672	0.933958
7623	Refrigeration And Air-Conditioning Service And Repair Shops	2	0.401965	0.401965	-0.130029	-0.113743	-0.086601	0.293394	0.401965	0.510535	0.890530	0.917672	0.933958
769	MISCELLANEOUS REPAIR SHOPS AND RELATED SERVICES	1	0.257884	0.257884	0.257884	0.257884	0.257884	0.257884	0.257884	0.257884	0.257884	0.257884	0.257884

Betas of Common Stocks by SIC Codes as of March 31, 2017

SIC Code	Description	Number of Companies	Mean	Median	1st Percentile	2.5th Percentile	5th Percentile	40th Percentile	50th Percentile	60th Percentile	95th Percentile	97.5th Percentile	99th Percentile
7699	Repair Shops And Related Services, Not Elsewhere Classified	1	0.257884	0.257884	0.257884	0.257884	0.257884	0.257884	0.257884	0.257884	0.257884	0.257884	0.257884
78	MOTION PICTURES	17	0.569590	0.653834	-1.149965	-0.963343	-0.652306	0.525097	0.653834	0.783512	1.483754	1.799442	1.988855
781	MOTION PICTURE PRODUCTION AND ALLIED SERVICES	11	0.493256	0.448949	-1.196621	-1.079982	-0.885584	0.290038	0.448949	0.738018	1.720520	1.917825	2.036208
7812	Motion Picture And Video Tape Production	9	0.730942	0.738018	-0.437661	-0.348972	-0.201158	0.506763	0.738018	0.798677	1.799442	1.957286	2.051992
7819	Services Allied To Motion Picture Production	2	-0.576330	-0.576330	-1.260419	-1.239478	-1.204575	-0.715940	-0.576330	-0.436720	0.051915	0.086818	0.107759
782	MOTION PICTURE DISTRIBUTION AND ALLIED SERVICES	1	-0.194062	-0.194062	-0.194062	-0.194062	-0.194062	-0.194062	-0.194062	-0.194062	-0.194062	-0.194062	-0.194062
7822	Motion Picture And Video Tape Distribution	1	-0.194062	-0.194062	-0.194062	-0.194062	-0.194062	-0.194062	-0.194062	-0.194062	-0.194062	-0.194062	-0.194062
783	MOTION PICTURE THEATERS	4	0.798414	0.767434	0.639753	0.640407	0.641495	0.699274	0.767434	0.835594	0.998705	1.009087	1.015317
7832	Motion Picture Theaters, Except Drive-In	4	0.798414	0.767434	0.639753	0.640407	0.641495	0.699274	0.767434	0.835594	0.998705	1.009087	1.015317
784	VIDEO TAPE RENTAL	1	1.257620	1.257620	1.257620	1.257620	1.257620	1.257620	1.257620	1.257620	1.257620	1.257620	1.257620
7841	Video Tape Rental	1	1.257620	1.257620	1.257620	1.257620	1.257620	1.257620	1.257620	1.257620	1.257620	1.257620	1.257620
79	AMUSEMENT AND RECREATION SERVICES	31	0.180853	0.469749	-4.502659	-3.676968	-2.649540	0.231907	0.469749	0.795206	1.553120	1.814895	2.054772
7900	SERVICES-AMUSEMENT & RECREATION SERVICES	1	-0.576879	-0.576879	-0.576879	-0.576879	-0.576879	-0.576879	-0.576879	-0.576879	-0.576879	-0.576879	-0.576879
792	THEATRICAL PRODUCERS (EXCEPT MOTION PICTURE), BANDS, ORCHESTRAS	2	0.477487	0.477487	-0.209860	-0.188818	-0.153750	0.337212	0.477487	0.617761	1.108723	1.143791	1.164833
7922	Theatrical Producers (Except Motion Picture) And Miscellaneous Theater	1	1.178860	1.178860	1.178860	1.178860	1.178860	1.178860	1.178860	1.178860	1.178860	1.178860	1.178860
7929	Bands, Orchestras, Actors, And Other Entertainers And Entertainment	1	-0.223887	-0.223887	-0.223887	-0.223887	-0.223887	-0.223887	-0.223887	-0.223887	-0.223887	-0.223887	-0.223887
793	BOWLING CENTERS	1	0.071477	0.071477	0.071477	0.071477	0.071477	0.071477	0.071477	0.071477	0.071477	0.071477	0.071477
7933	Bowling Centers	1	0.071477	0.071477	0.071477	0.071477	0.071477	0.071477	0.071477	0.071477	0.071477	0.071477	0.071477
794	COMMERCIAL SPORTS	9	0.110018	0.798609	-3.127256	-2.990766	-2.763282	0.418063	0.798609	0.891519	1.505822	1.593726	1.646468
7941	Professional Sports Clubs And Promoters	3	-0.246004	0.798609	-3.137913	-3.017407	-2.816564	-0.004763	0.798609	0.975213	1.593328	1.637479	1.663970
7948	Racing, Including Track Operation	6	0.288029	0.618837	-1.970075	-1.803941	-1.527053	0.322926	0.618837	0.914747	1.230318	1.236214	1.239752
799	MISCELLANEOUS AMUSEMENT AND RECREATION SERVICES	18	0.231484	0.519104	-4.484932	-3.632651	-2.212182	0.318917	0.519104	0.659015	1.543122	1.878906	2.080376
7993	Coin-Operated Amusement Devices	1	0.094361	0.094361	0.094361	0.094361	0.094361	0.094361	0.094361	0.094361	0.094361	0.094361	0.094361
7996	Amusement Parks	3	0.675575	0.624967	0.346355	0.354884	0.369099	0.568107	0.624967	0.712192	1.017478	1.039284	1.052368
7997	Membership Sports And Recreation Clubs	4	-0.477466	0.951748	-4.877670	-4.614496	-4.175871	0.857823	0.951748	1.045673	1.220040	1.229900	1.235816
7999	Amusement And Recreation Services, Not Elsewhere Classified	10	0.395549	0.350828	-1.573649	-1.367861	-1.024883	0.175844	0.350828	0.509233	1.859154	2.036922	2.143583
80	HEALTH SERVICES	81	1.087467	1.117090	-1.163519	-0.397859	-0.202834	0.922495	1.117090	1.290640	2.250350	2.369140	2.493858

Betas of Common Stocks by SIC Codes as of March 31, 2017

SIC Code	Description	Number of Companies	Mean	Median	1st Percentile	2.5th Percentile	5th Percentile	40th Percentile	50th Percentile	60th Percentile	95th Percentile	97.5th Percentile	99th Percentile
801	OFFICES AND CLINICS OF DOCTORS OF MEDICINE	15	1.190764	1.374680	-2.410022	-1.700870	-0.518951	1.021551	1.374680	1.708206	2.325168	2.385879	2.422306
8011	Offices And Clinics Of Doctors Of Medicine	15	1.190764	1.374680	-2.410022	-1.700870	-0.518951	1.021551	1.374680	1.708206	2.325168	2.385879	2.422306
804	OFFICES AND CLINICS OF OTHER HEALTH PRACTITIONERS	1	1.145710	1.145710	1.145710	1.145710	1.145710	1.145710	1.145710	1.145710	1.145710	1.145710	1.145710
8041	Offices And Clinics Of Chiropractors	1	1.145710	1.145710	1.145710	1.145710	1.145710	1.145710	1.145710	1.145710	1.145710	1.145710	1.145710
805	NURSING AND PERSONAL CARE FACILITIES	10	1.120280	1.286035	-0.107593	-0.025388	0.111619	1.002455	1.286035	1.486128	1.773653	1.789346	1.798763
8051	Skilled Nursing Care Facilities	10	1.120280	1.286035	-0.107593	-0.025388	0.111619	1.002455	1.286035	1.486128	1.773653	1.789346	1.798763
806	HOSPITALS	15	1.127868	1.147100	-0.246021	-0.232253	-0.209305	0.892373	1.147100	1.479016	2.123860	2.246500	2.320084
8062	General Medical And Surgical Hospitals	10	0.892063	0.880809	-0.181057	-0.168187	-0.146739	0.811881	0.880809	1.022017	1.822537	1.847473	1.862435
8069	Specialty Hospitals, Except Psychiatric	5	1.599476	1.947110	-0.168288	-0.037921	0.179358	1.935302	1.947110	1.975762	2.299060	2.334100	2.355124
807	MEDICAL AND DENTAL LABORATORIES	17	0.870610	0.922495	-0.648762	-0.521354	-0.309007	0.688250	0.922495	1.118742	2.159614	2.164842	2.167979
8071	Medical Laboratories	17	0.870610	0.922495	-0.648762	-0.521354	-0.309007	0.688250	0.922495	1.118742	2.159614	2.164842	2.167979
808	HOME HEALTH CARE SERVICES	9	1.298103	1.219140	0.676034	0.694355	0.724890	1.113212	1.219140	1.311084	2.054644	2.057072	2.058529
8082	Home Health Care Services	9	1.298103	1.219140	0.676034	0.694355	0.724890	1.113212	1.219140	1.311084	2.054644	2.057072	2.058529
809	MISCELLANEOUS HEALTH AND ALLIED SERVICES, NOT ELSEWHERE CLASSIFIED	14	1.033822	0.910760	-0.321016	-0.205752	-0.013645	0.818470	0.910760	1.146553	2.090644	2.386787	2.564473
8093	Specialty Outpatient Facilities, Not Elsewhere Classified	6	1.131482	0.910760	0.200974	0.212575	0.231910	0.866235	0.910760	0.955285	2.448018	2.565474	2.635948
8099	Health And Allied Services, Not Elsewhere Classified	8	0.960577	1.000450	-0.328472	-0.224393	-0.050926	0.796505	1.000450	1.244128	1.682537	1.727128	1.753883
81	LEGAL SERVICES	1	0.994620	0.994620	0.994620	0.994620	0.994620	0.994620	0.994620	0.994620	0.994620	0.994620	0.994620
811	LEGAL SERVICES	1	0.994620	0.994620	0.994620	0.994620	0.994620	0.994620	0.994620	0.994620	0.994620	0.994620	0.994620
8111	Legal Services	1	0.994620	0.994620	0.994620	0.994620	0.994620	0.994620	0.994620	0.994620	0.994620	0.994620	0.994620
82	EDUCATIONAL SERVICES	18	1.006826	1.056440	-0.073232	-0.070582	-0.066167	0.947243	1.056440	1.149334	1.919981	2.018100	2.076972
8200	SERVICES-EDUCATIONAL SERVICES	2	0.466040	0.466040	-0.053996	-0.038076	-0.011544	0.359910	0.466040	0.572170	0.943624	0.970157	0.986076
821	ELEMENTARY AND SECONDARY SCHOOLS	6	1.193736	1.222505	0.344443	0.376418	0.429710	1.097870	1.222505	1.347140	1.853880	1.869615	1.879056
8211	Elementary And Secondary Schools	6	1.193736	1.222505	0.344443	0.376418	0.429710	1.097870	1.222505	1.347140	1.853880	1.869615	1.879056
822	COLLEGES, UNIVERSITIES, PROFESSIONAL SCHOOLS, AND JUNIOR COLLEGES	3	0.868364	1.015010	-0.053198	-0.020497	0.034003	0.797008	1.015010	1.145024	1.600073	1.632577	1.652079
8221	Colleges, Universities, And Professional Schools	3	0.868364	1.015010	-0.053198	-0.020497	0.034003	0.797008	1.015010	1.145024	1.600073	1.632577	1.652079
823	LIBRARIES	1	1.486720	1.486720	1.486720	1.486720	1.486720	1.486720	1.486720	1.486720	1.486720	1.486720	1.486720
8231	Libraries	1	1.486720	1.486720	1.486720	1.486720	1.486720	1.486720	1.486720	1.486720	1.486720	1.486720	1.486720
824	VOCATIONAL SCHOOLS	3	1.155273	1.255870	0.116973	0.151837	0.209944	1.023442	1.255870	1.427940	2.030185	2.073203	2.099013
8249	Vocational Schools, Not Elsewhere Classified	3	1.155273	1.255870	0.116973	0.151837	0.209944	1.023442	1.255870	1.427940	2.030185	2.073203	2.099013

Betas of Common Stocks by SIC Codes as of March 31, 2017

SIC Code	Description	Number of Companies	Mean	Median	1st Percentile	2.5th Percentile	5th Percentile	40th Percentile	50th Percentile	60th Percentile	95th Percentile	97.5th Percentile	99th Percentile
829	SCHOOLS AND EDUCATIONAL SERVICES, NOT ELSEWHERE CLASSIFIED	3	0.823581	0.682175	0.666195	0.666684	0.667500	0.678914	0.682175	0.770280	1.078648	1.100674	1.113890
8299	Schools And Educational Services, Not Elsewhere Classified	3	0.823581	0.682175	0.666195	0.666684	0.667500	0.678914	0.682175	0.770280	1.078648	1.100674	1.113890
83	SOCIAL SERVICES	3	1.455059	1.786450	0.757339	0.788843	0.841348	1.576427	1.786450	1.797638	1.836796	1.839593	1.841271
832	INDIVIDUAL AND FAMILY SOCIAL SERVICES	1	1.842390	1.842390	1.842390	1.842390	1.842390	1.842390	1.842390	1.842390	1.842390	1.842390	1.842390
8322	Individual And Family Social Services	1	1.842390	1.842390	1.842390	1.842390	1.842390	1.842390	1.842390	1.842390	1.842390	1.842390	1.842390
833	JOB TRAINING AND VOCATIONAL REHABILITATION SERVICES	1	1.786450	1.786450	1.786450	1.786450	1.786450	1.786450	1.786450	1.786450	1.786450	1.786450	1.786450
8331	Job Training And Vocational Rehabilitation Services	1	1.786450	1.786450	1.786450	1.786450	1.786450	1.786450	1.786450	1.786450	1.786450	1.786450	1.786450
835	CHILD DAY CARE SERVICES	1	0.736337	0.736337	0.736337	0.736337	0.736337	0.736337	0.736337	0.736337	0.736337	0.736337	0.736337
8351	Child Day Care Services	1	0.736337	0.736337	0.736337	0.736337	0.736337	0.736337	0.736337	0.736337	0.736337	0.736337	0.736337
86	MEMBERSHIP ORGANIZATIONS	1	1.289150	1.289150	1.289150	1.289150	1.289150	1.289150	1.289150	1.289150	1.289150	1.289150	1.289150
869	MEMBERSHIP ORGANIZATIONS, NOT ELSEWHERE CLASSIFIED	1	1.289150	1.289150	1.289150	1.289150	1.289150	1.289150	1.289150	1.289150	1.289150	1.289150	1.289150
8699	Membership Organizations, Not Elsewhere Classified	1	1.289150	1.289150	1.289150	1.289150	1.289150	1.289150	1.289150	1.289150	1.289150	1.289150	1.289150
87	ENGINEERING, ACCOUNTING, RESEARCH, MANAGEMENT, AND RELATED SERVICES	172	1.129080	1.149665	-1.170396	-0.395601	-0.176417	0.960549	1.149665	1.287792	2.533694	2.672533	2.724557
871	ENGINEERING, ARCHITECTURAL, AND SURVEYING SERVICES	20	1.407519	1.493370	0.467599	0.513471	0.589923	1.382236	1.493370	1.547528	1.957348	1.992474	2.013550
8711	Engineering Services	19	1.398819	1.460620	0.465990	0.509447	0.581876	1.347392	1.460620	1.540664	1.961045	1.994323	2.014289
8712	Architectural Services	1	1.572820	1.572820	1.572820	1.572820	1.572820	1.572820	1.572820	1.572820	1.572820	1.572820	1.572820
872	ACCOUNTING, AUDITING, AND BOOKKEEPING SERVICES	2	1.136986	1.136986	0.475638	0.495883	0.529625	1.002017	1.136986	1.271954	1.744346	1.778088	1.798333
8721	Accounting, Auditing, And Bookkeeping Services	2	1.136986	1.136986	0.475638	0.495883	0.529625	1.002017	1.136986	1.271954	1.744346	1.778088	1.798333
873	RESEARCH, DEVELOPMENT, AND TESTING SERVICES	96	1.256068	1.246440	-0.698255	-0.291564	-0.202744	1.086460	1.246440	1.444750	2.622503	2.686896	2.716085
8731	Commercial Physical And Biological Research	83	1.235719	1.256990	-0.934932	-0.303272	-0.216972	1.029820	1.256990	1.457054	2.608426	2.686184	2.720674
8732	Commercial Economic, Sociological, And Educational Research	6	1.420087	1.258305	0.473765	0.509728	0.569668	1.041270	1.258305	1.475340	2.498300	2.591245	2.647012
8733	Noncommercial Research Organizations	5	1.451922	1.404540	0.876507	0.889629	0.911499	1.277308	1.404540	1.618480	1.957046	1.959253	1.960577
8734	Testing Laboratories	2	1.118860	1.118860	1.089940	1.090826	1.092301	1.112958	1.118860	1.124762	1.145419	1.146895	1.147780
874	MANAGEMENT AND PUBLIC RELATIONS SERVICES	54	0.799905	0.895499	-1.581614	-0.583070	-0.254059	0.769500	0.895499	0.960385	1.878759	2.086113	3.599672
8741	Management Services	14	0.879644	0.676599	-0.156037	-0.151059	-0.142763	0.515402	0.676599	0.919539	2.668922	3.959266	4.733472
8742	Management Consulting Services	34	0.799293	0.902213	-0.581936	-0.469640	-0.168605	0.842485	0.902213	0.958342	1.667688	1.878262	2.033217
8743	Public Relations Services	1	1.981420	1.981420	1.981420	1.981420	1.981420	1.981420	1.981420	1.981420	1.981420	1.981420	1.981420

Betas of Common Stocks by SIC Codes as of March 31, 2017

SIC Code	Description	Number of Companies	Mean	Median	1st Percentile	2.5th Percentile	5th Percentile	40th Percentile	50th Percentile	60th Percentile	95th Percentile	97.5th Percentile	99th Percentile
8744	Facilities Support Management Services	1	0.823894	0.823894	0.823894	0.823894	0.823894	0.823894	0.823894	0.823894	0.823894	0.823894	0.823894
8748	Business Consulting Services, Not Elsewhere Classified	4	0.224650	0.886551	-2.527956	-2.383155	-2.141820	0.710607	0.886551	1.062494	1.664460	1.707225	1.732884
88	PRIVATE HOUSEHOLDS	1	1.002350	1.002350	1.002350	1.002350	1.002350	1.002350	1.002350	1.002350	1.002350	1.002350	1.002350
8880	AMERICAN DEPOSITARY RECEIPTS	1	1.002350	1.002350	1.002350	1.002350	1.002350	1.002350	1.002350	1.002350	1.002350	1.002350	1.002350
89	SERVICES, NOT ELSEWHERE CLASSIFIED	14	0.761276	0.907743	-0.678221	-0.656402	-0.620037	0.665267	0.907743	1.281000	1.692614	1.741497	1.770827
899	SERVICES, NOT ELSEWHERE CLASSIFIED	14	0.761276	0.907743	-0.678221	-0.656402	-0.620037	0.665267	0.907743	1.281000	1.692614	1.741497	1.770827
8999	Services, Not Elsewhere Classified	14	0.761276	0.907743	-0.678221	-0.656402	-0.620037	0.665267	0.907743	1.281000	1.692614	1.741497	1.770827
	PUBLIC ADMINISTRATION												
94	ADMINISTRATION OF HUMAN RESOURCE PROGRAMS	1	1.079140	1.079140	1.079140	1.079140	1.079140	1.079140	1.079140	1.079140	1.079140	1.079140	1.079140
943	ADMINISTRATION OF PUBLIC HEALTH PROGRAMS	1	1.079140	1.079140	1.079140	1.079140	1.079140	1.079140	1.079140	1.079140	1.079140	1.079140	1.079140
9431	Administration Of Public Health Programs	1	1.079140	1.079140	1.079140	1.079140	1.079140	1.079140	1.079140	1.079140	1.079140	1.079140	1.079140
95	ADMINISTRATION OF ENVIRONMENTAL QUALITY AND HOUSING PROGRAMS	2	1.580946	1.580946	0.434195	0.469300	0.527807	1.346915	1.580946	1.814977	2.634085	2.692592	2.727697
951	ADMINISTRATION OF ENVIRONMENTAL QUALITY PROGRAMS	2	1.580946	1.580946	0.434195	0.469300	0.527807	1.346915	1.580946	1.814977	2.634085	2.692592	2.727697
9511	Air And Water Resource And Solid Waste Management	2	1.580946	1.580946	0.434195	0.469300	0.527807	1.346915	1.580946	1.814977	2.634085	2.692592	2.727697
96	ADMINISTRATION OF ECONOMIC PROGRAMS	2	-0.733965	-0.733965	-3.010010	-2.940335	-2.824211	-1.198464	-0.733965	-0.269466	1.356281	1.472405	1.542080
961	ADMINISTRATION OF GENERAL ECONOMIC PROGRAMS	1	1.588530	1.588530	1.588530	1.588530	1.588530	1.588530	1.588530	1.588530	1.588530	1.588530	1.588530
9611	Administration Of General Economic Programs	1	1.588530	1.588530	1.588530	1.588530	1.588530	1.588530	1.588530	1.588530	1.588530	1.588530	1.588530
963	REGULATION AND ADMINISTRATION OF COMMUNICATIONS, ELECTRIC, GAS	1	-3.056460	-3.056460	-3.056460	-3.056460	-3.056460	-3.056460	-3.056460	-3.056460	-3.056460	-3.056460	-3.056460
9631	Regulation And Administration Of Communications, Electric, Gas	1	-3.056460	-3.056460	-3.056460	-3.056460	-3.056460	-3.056460	-3.056460	-3.056460	-3.056460	-3.056460	-3.056460
	NONCLASSIFIABLE ESTABLISHMENTS												
99	NONCLASSIFIABLE ESTABLISHMENTS	61	0.760725	0.675865	-1.344210	-1.124565	-1.080350	0.536651	0.675865	0.901375	2.851750	3.143315	3.481018
999	NONCLASSIFIABLE ESTABLISHMENTS	61	0.760725	0.675865	-1.344210	-1.124565	-1.080350	0.536651	0.675865	0.901375	2.851750	3.143315	3.481018
9995	NON-OPERATING ESTABLISHMENTS	1	0.640356	0.640356	0.640356	0.640356	0.640356	0.640356	0.640356	0.640356	0.640356	0.640356	0.640356
9999	Nonclassifiable Establishments	60	0.762731	0.685258	-1.349676	-1.124615	-1.082511	0.519848	0.685258	0.917016	2.856016	3.153628	3.484304

Down-market Betas of Common Stocks by SIC Codes as of March 31, 2017

Details:
Benchmark: S&P 500 Index
Returns period and frequency: 1 year of daily returns
Risk-free rate: Federal Funds Rate

SIC Code	Description	Number of Companies	Mean	Median	1st Percentile	2.5th Percentile	5th Percentile	40th Percentile	50th Percentile	60th Percentile	95th Percentile	97.5th Percentile	99th Percentile
	AGRICULTURE, FORESTRY, AND FISHING												
01	AGRICULTURAL PRODUCTION-CROPS	7	0.246157	0.151979	-0.866114	-0.812182	-0.722294	0.078920	0.151979	0.293814	1.342887	1.466018	1.539897
011	CASH GRAINS	2	0.343541	0.343541	-0.877157	-0.839789	-0.777508	0.094419	0.343541	0.592662	1.464589	1.526870	1.564238
0115	Corn	1	-0.902069	-0.902069	-0.902069	-0.902069	-0.902069	-0.902069	-0.902069	-0.902069	-0.902069	-0.902069	-0.902069
0116	Soybeans	1	1.589150	1.589150	1.589150	1.589150	1.589150	1.589150	1.589150	1.589150	1.589150	1.589150	1.589150
013	FIELD CROPS, EXCEPT CASH GRAINS	1	0.030214	0.030214	0.030214	0.030214	0.030214	0.030214	0.030214	0.030214	0.030214	0.030214	0.030214
0131	Cotton	1	0.030214	0.030214	0.030214	0.030214	0.030214	0.030214	0.030214	0.030214	0.030214	0.030214	0.030214
016	VEGETABLES AND MELONS	1	-0.302819	-0.302819	-0.302819	-0.302819	-0.302819	-0.302819	-0.302819	-0.302819	-0.302819	-0.302819	-0.302819
0161	Vegetables And Melons	1	-0.302819	-0.302819	-0.302819	-0.302819	-0.302819	-0.302819	-0.302819	-0.302819	-0.302819	-0.302819	-0.302819
017	FRUITS AND TREE NUTS	2	0.578321	0.578321	0.392169	0.397868	0.407365	0.540331	0.578321	0.616311	0.749277	0.758774	0.764473
0174	Citrus Fruits	2	0.578321	0.578321	0.392169	0.397868	0.407365	0.540331	0.578321	0.616311	0.749277	0.758774	0.764473
019	GENERAL FARMS, PRIMARILY CROP	1	0.151979	0.151979	0.151979	0.151979	0.151979	0.151979	0.151979	0.151979	0.151979	0.151979	0.151979
0191	General Farms, Primarily Crop	1	0.151979	0.151979	0.151979	0.151979	0.151979	0.151979	0.151979	0.151979	0.151979	0.151979	0.151979
02	AGRICULTURAL PRODUCTION-LIVESTOCK AND ANIMAL SPECIALTIES	2	1.536833	1.536833	0.467166	0.499911	0.554486	1.318534	1.536833	1.755132	2.519180	2.573755	2.606500
021	LIVESTOCK, EXCEPT DAIRY AND POULTRY	1	2.628330	2.628330	2.628330	2.628330	2.628330	2.628330	2.628330	2.628330	2.628330	2.628330	2.628330
0213	Hogs	1	2.628330	2.628330	2.628330	2.628330	2.628330	2.628330	2.628330	2.628330	2.628330	2.628330	2.628330
025	POULTRY AND EGGS	1	0.445336	0.445336	0.445336	0.445336	0.445336	0.445336	0.445336	0.445336	0.445336	0.445336	0.445336
0252	Chicken Eggs	1	0.445336	0.445336	0.445336	0.445336	0.445336	0.445336	0.445336	0.445336	0.445336	0.445336	0.445336
07	AGRICULTURAL SERVICES	6	1.764105	1.588110	0.649715	0.688719	0.753727	1.554980	1.588110	1.621240	3.059963	3.179711	3.251561
074	VETERINARY SERVICES	2	1.349375	1.349375	1.147882	1.154050	1.164331	1.308254	1.349375	1.390496	1.534420	1.544700	1.550868
0741	Veterinary Services For Livestock	1	1.143770	1.143770	1.143770	1.143770	1.143770	1.143770	1.143770	1.143770	1.143770	1.143770	1.143770
0742	Veterinary Services For Animal Specialties	1	1.554980	1.554980	1.554980	1.554980	1.554980	1.554980	1.554980	1.554980	1.554980	1.554980	1.554980
075	ANIMAL SERVICES, EXCEPT VETERINARY	2	2.820465	2.820465	2.351050	2.365420	2.389370	2.724666	2.820465	2.916264	3.251561	3.275510	3.289880
0752	Animal Specialty Services, Except Veterinary	2	2.820465	2.820465	2.351050	2.365420	2.389370	2.724666	2.820465	2.916264	3.251561	3.275510	3.289880
076	FARM LABOR AND MANAGEMENT SERVICES	1	1.621240	1.621240	1.621240	1.621240	1.621240	1.621240	1.621240	1.621240	1.621240	1.621240	1.621240
0762	Farm Management Services	1	1.621240	1.621240	1.621240	1.621240	1.621240	1.621240	1.621240	1.621240	1.621240	1.621240	1.621240
078	LANDSCAPE AND HORTICULTURAL SERVICES	1	0.623712	0.623712	0.623712	0.623712	0.623712	0.623712	0.623712	0.623712	0.623712	0.623712	0.623712
0782	Lawn And Garden Services	1	0.623712	0.623712	0.623712	0.623712	0.623712	0.623712	0.623712	0.623712	0.623712	0.623712	0.623712
09	FISHING, HUNTING, AND TRAPPING	1	0.142601	0.142601	0.142601	0.142601	0.142601	0.142601	0.142601	0.142601	0.142601	0.142601	0.142601
	MINING												
10	METAL MINING	205	0.475449	0.414386	-2.920234	-1.607229	-1.116938	0.182718	0.414386	0.613335	2.223972	2.675616	2.807278
1000	METAL MINING	2	1.802315	1.802315	1.034451	1.057957	1.097134	1.645608	1.802315	1.959022	2.507497	2.546673	2.570179
101	IRON ORES	6	0.489600	0.506111	-1.079683	-0.996558	-0.858015	0.387939	0.506111	0.624282	1.880320	2.048670	2.149680
1011	Iron Ores	6	0.489600	0.506111	-1.079683	-0.996558	-0.858015	0.387939	0.506111	0.624282	1.880320	2.048670	2.149680
102	COPPER ORES	15	1.142494	0.705427	-0.216982	-0.185899	-0.134094	0.591707	0.705427	1.460640	2.866283	2.934152	2.974873
1021	Copper Ores	15	1.142494	0.705427	-0.216982	-0.185899	-0.134094	0.591707	0.705427	1.460640	2.866283	2.934152	2.974873

Down-market Betas of Common Stocks by SIC Codes as of March 31, 2017

SIC Code	Description	Number of Companies	Mean	Median	1st Percentile	2.5th Percentile	5th Percentile	40th Percentile	50th Percentile	60th Percentile	95th Percentile	97.5th Percentile	99th Percentile
103	LEAD AND ZINC ORES	2	2.111460	2.111460	1.940891	1.946113	1.954815	2.076650	2.111460	2.146270	2.268105	2.276808	2.282029
1031	Lead And Zinc Ores	2	2.111460	2.111460	1.940891	1.946113	1.954815	2.076650	2.111460	2.146270	2.268105	2.276808	2.282029
104	GOLD AND SILVER ORES	126	0.178404	0.263402	-2.960155	-2.143299	-1.501190	0.044863	0.263402	0.417661	1.486450	1.878631	2.497225
1041	Gold Ores	116	0.161588	0.234343	-2.961325	-2.270053	-1.550673	0.017668	0.234343	0.393822	1.518565	1.892764	2.572571
1044	Silver Ores	10	0.373472	0.662778	-1.359795	-1.272489	-1.126977	0.371469	0.662778	0.922732	1.250751	1.256201	1.259470
106	FERROALLOY ORES, EXCEPT VANADIUM	4	0.698605	0.966505	-0.310872	-0.256682	-0.166365	0.900940	0.966505	1.032070	1.188516	1.198463	1.204431
1061	Ferroalloy Ores, Except Vanadium	4	0.698605	0.966505	-0.310872	-0.256682	-0.166365	0.900940	0.966505	1.032070	1.188516	1.198463	1.204431
108	METAL MINING SERVICES	26	0.922065	0.491845	-1.238097	-0.991583	-0.737464	0.098537	0.491845	0.756721	2.051070	5.086794	8.121958
1081	Metal Mining Services	26	0.922065	0.491845	-1.238097	-0.991583	-0.737464	0.098537	0.491845	0.756721	2.051070	5.086794	8.121958
109	MISCELLANEOUS METAL ORES	24	0.846557	0.730636	-0.548933	-0.540795	-0.490763	0.621395	0.730636	1.167798	2.458015	2.631855	2.675418
1094	Uranium-Radium-Vanadium Ores	13	1.091274	0.842429	-0.501054	-0.421097	-0.287836	0.766494	0.842429	1.325518	2.628698	2.666579	2.689308
1099	Miscellaneous Metal Ores, Not Elsewhere Classified	11	0.557346	0.567487	-0.504099	-0.464091	-0.397411	0.347151	0.567487	0.613129	1.501055	1.513643	1.521195
12	COAL MINING	5	1.118241	1.396590	-0.325037	-0.264726	-0.164208	1.093929	1.396590	1.593162	2.003124	2.017512	2.026145
122	BITUMINOUS COAL AND LIGNITE MINING	4	1.237817	1.642305	-0.312389	-0.233106	-0.100969	1.494876	1.642305	1.789734	2.010318	2.021109	2.027584
1221	Bituminous Coal And Lignite Surface Mining	4	1.237817	1.642305	-0.312389	-0.233106	-0.100969	1.494876	1.642305	1.789734	2.010318	2.021109	2.027584
124	COAL MINING SERVICES	1	0.639938	0.639938	0.639938	0.639938	0.639938	0.639938	0.639938	0.639938	0.639938	0.639938	0.639938
1241	Coal Mining Services	1	0.639938	0.639938	0.639938	0.639938	0.639938	0.639938	0.639938	0.639938	0.639938	0.639938	0.639938
13	OIL AND GAS EXTRACTION	201	1.429422	1.282590	-3.248590	-1.793120	-0.733761	1.117870	1.282590	1.490270	3.097500	3.382060	4.174280
131	CRUDE PETROLEUM AND NATURAL GAS	131	1.438216	1.242050	-3.168595	-1.856570	-1.321230	1.073430	1.242050	1.374940	3.070250	3.304978	6.542434
1311	Crude Petroleum And Natural Gas	131	1.438216	1.242050	-3.168595	-1.856570	-1.321230	1.073430	1.242050	1.374940	3.070250	3.304978	6.542434
132	NATURAL GAS LIQUIDS	5	1.999321	1.903660	0.784208	0.852511	0.966348	1.893016	1.903660	2.154504	2.863314	2.904882	2.929823
1321	Natural Gas Liquids	5	1.999321	1.903660	0.784208	0.852511	0.966348	1.893016	1.903660	2.154504	2.863314	2.904882	2.929823
138	OIL AND GAS FIELD SERVICES	65	1.367861	1.330520	-1.849722	-0.707166	-0.516866	1.219918	1.330520	1.590238	3.201452	3.597036	3.865723
1381	Drilling Oil And Gas Wells	23	1.594471	1.620520	0.301101	0.346892	0.414470	1.432354	1.620520	1.850038	2.578261	3.015344	3.326310
1382	Oil And Gas Field Exploration Services	20	0.805260	1.121045	-3.183260	-2.297869	-0.822219	0.824220	1.121045	1.281162	2.145419	2.686429	3.011036
1389	Oil And Gas Field Services, Not Elsewhere Classified	22	1.642406	1.386085	-0.483065	-0.056286	0.598163	1.195474	1.386085	1.599250	3.662427	3.921167	4.073035
14	MINING AND QUARRYING OF NONMETALLIC MINERALS, EXCEPT FUELS	26	0.842552	0.932016	-1.170605	-0.956892	-0.724532	0.694690	0.932016	1.015270	2.008055	2.166160	2.318020
1400	MINING & QUARRYING OF NONMETALLIC MINERALS (NO FUELS)	1	1.307780	1.307780	1.307780	1.307780	1.307780	1.307780	1.307780	1.307780	1.307780	1.307780	1.307780
141	DIMENSION STONE	3	0.988324	0.909792	0.703206	0.709530	0.720070	0.867632	0.909792	0.999072	1.311550	1.333870	1.347262
1411	Dimension Stone	3	0.988324	0.909792	0.703206	0.709530	0.720070	0.867632	0.909792	0.999072	1.311550	1.333870	1.347262
142	CRUSHED AND BROKEN STONE, INCLUDING RIPRAP	2	1.276572	1.276572	0.586977	0.608087	0.643271	1.135838	1.276572	1.417306	1.909873	1.945057	1.966167
1422	Crushed And Broken Limestone	1	1.980240	1.980240	1.980240	1.980240	1.980240	1.980240	1.980240	1.980240	1.980240	1.980240	1.980240
1423	Crushed And Broken Granite	1	0.572904	0.572904	0.572904	0.572904	0.572904	0.572904	0.572904	0.572904	0.572904	0.572904	0.572904
144	SAND AND GRAVEL	3	1.239999	1.254180	0.492051	0.515381	0.554265	1.098643	1.254180	1.401208	1.915806	1.952563	1.974617

Down-market Betas of Common Stocks by SIC Codes as of March 31, 2017

SIC Code	Description	Number of Companies	Mean	Median	1st Percentile	2.5th Percentile	5th Percentile	40th Percentile	50th Percentile	60th Percentile	95th Percentile	97.5th Percentile	99th Percentile
1442	Construction Sand And Gravel	1	0.476497	0.476497	0.476497	0.476497	0.476497	0.476497	0.476497	0.476497	0.476497	0.476497	0.476497
1446	Industrial Sand	2	1.621750	1.621750	1.261531	1.272559	1.290937	1.548236	1.621750	1.695264	1.952563	1.970942	1.981969
147	CHEMICAL AND FERTILIZER MINERAL MINING	8	0.686171	0.984755	-1.273187	-1.213347	-1.113615	0.863822	0.984755	1.056064	1.953442	1.983871	2.002128
1474	Potash, Soda, And Borate Minerals	5	0.475565	0.954239	-1.240471	-1.131557	-0.950033	0.773405	0.954239	0.978651	1.178446	1.198843	1.211081
1479	Chemical And Fertilizer Mineral Mining, Not Elsewhere Classified	3	1.037180	1.840420	-0.691507	-0.613999	-0.484819	1.323700	1.840420	1.875196	1.996912	2.005606	2.010822
148	NONMETALLIC MINERALS SERVICES, EXCEPT FUELS	3	0.921116	0.202023	0.143263	0.145062	0.148060	0.190031	0.202023	0.645470	2.197536	2.308398	2.374915
1481	Nonmetallic Minerals Services, Except Fuels	3	0.921116	0.202023	0.143263	0.145062	0.148060	0.190031	0.202023	0.645470	2.197536	2.308398	2.374915
149	MISCELLANEOUS NONMETALLIC MINERALS, EXCEPT FUELS	6	0.517959	0.671437	-0.619168	-0.545034	-0.421478	0.648184	0.671437	0.694690	1.085912	1.100466	1.109198
1499	Miscellaneous Nonmetallic Minerals, Except Fuels	6	0.517959	0.671437	-0.619168	-0.545034	-0.421478	0.648184	0.671437	0.694690	1.085912	1.100466	1.109198
	CONSTRUCTION												
15	CONSTRUCTION	27	1.320554	1.355850	-2.231813	-1.392538	-0.384712	1.304970	1.355850	1.438570	2.773895	3.340851	3.838436
152	GENERAL BUILDING CONTRACTORS-RESIDENTIAL BUILDINGS	3	2.215962	1.571020	0.919991	0.939921	0.973137	1.438157	1.571020	2.090848	3.910246	4.040203	4.118177
1521	General Contractors-Single-Family Houses	2	1.238863	1.238863	0.913348	0.923313	0.939921	1.172431	1.238863	1.305294	1.537804	1.554412	1.564377
1522	General Contractors-Residential Buildings, Other Than Single-Family	1	4.170160	4.170160	4.170160	4.170160	4.170160	4.170160	4.170160	4.170160	4.170160	4.170160	4.170160
153	OPERATIVE BUILDERS	19	1.453446	1.355850	0.675189	0.772529	0.934761	1.315448	1.355850	1.429744	2.425387	2.459169	2.479437
1531	Operative Builders	19	1.453446	1.355850	0.675189	0.772529	0.934761	1.315448	1.355850	1.429744	2.425387	2.459169	2.479437
154	GENERAL BUILDING CONTRACTORS-NONRESIDENTIAL BUILDINGS	5	0.278319	0.209428	-2.705251	-2.576131	-2.360933	-0.130080	0.209428	0.813073	2.659148	2.776724	2.847270
1541	General Contractors-Industrial Buildings And Warehouses	3	-0.178791	-0.639343	-2.748290	-2.683731	-2.576131	-1.069740	-0.639343	0.067386	2.540936	2.717618	2.823627
1542	General Contractors-Nonresidential Buildings, Other Than Industrial	2	0.963984	0.963984	0.224519	0.247156	0.284884	0.813073	0.963984	1.114895	1.643084	1.680812	1.703449
16	HEAVY CONSTRUCTION OTHER THAN BUILDING CONSTRUCTION-CONTRACTORS	20	1.276253	1.531935	-0.559303	-0.351959	-0.006385	1.429094	1.531935	1.584012	2.037666	2.166448	2.243717
161	HIGHWAY AND STREET CONSTRUCTION, EXCEPT ELEVATED HIGHWAYS	3	0.840324	0.993321	0.049258	0.078158	0.126324	0.800655	0.993321	1.094189	1.447226	1.472443	1.487573
1611	Highway And Street Construction, Except Elevated Highways	3	0.840324	0.993321	0.049258	0.078158	0.126324	0.800655	0.993321	1.094189	1.447226	1.472443	1.487573
162	HEAVY CONSTRUCTION, EXCEPT HIGHWAY AND STREET CONSTRUCTION	17	1.353182	1.574620	-0.549765	-0.328113	0.041308	1.485774	1.574620	1.646262	2.078334	2.186782	2.251851
1622	Bridge, Tunnel, And Elevated Highway Construction	1	1.781760	1.781760	1.781760	1.781760	1.781760	1.781760	1.781760	1.781760	1.781760	1.781760	1.781760

Down-market Betas of Common Stocks by SIC Codes as of March 31, 2017

SIC Code	Description	Number of Companies	Mean	Median	1st Percentile	2.5th Percentile	5th Percentile	40th Percentile	50th Percentile	60th Percentile	95th Percentile	97.5th Percentile	99th Percentile
1623	Water, Sewer, Pipeline, And Communications And Power Line Construction	9	1.103883	1.432150	-0.623649	-0.512823	-0.328113	1.073798	1.432150	1.539398	2.048486	2.171858	2.245881
1629	Heavy Construction, Not Elsewhere Classified	7	1.612484	1.679090	1.010503	1.050142	1.116207	1.616408	1.679090	1.698128	1.983925	2.004018	2.016073
17	CONSTRUCTION-SPECIAL TRADE CONTRACTORS	10	1.569350	1.603770	0.842786	0.897858	0.989644	1.470980	1.603770	1.702436	2.085218	2.185579	2.245796
171	PLUMBING, HEATING AND AIR-CONDITIONING	1	1.214010	1.214010	1.214010	1.214010	1.214010	1.214010	1.214010	1.214010	1.214010	1.214010	1.214010
1711	Plumbing, Heating And Air-Conditioning	1	1.214010	1.214010	1.214010	1.214010	1.214010	1.214010	1.214010	1.214010	1.214010	1.214010	1.214010
173	ELECTRICAL WORK	5	1.627048	1.698600	1.384793	1.392552	1.405484	1.622736	1.698600	1.702436	1.813550	1.826720	1.834622
1731	Electrical Work	5	1.627048	1.698600	1.384793	1.392552	1.405484	1.622736	1.698600	1.702436	1.813550	1.826720	1.834622
174	MASONRY, STONEWORK, TILE SETTING, AND PLASTERING	2	1.626120	1.626120	1.418282	1.424644	1.435248	1.583704	1.626120	1.668536	1.816992	1.827596	1.833958
1742	Plastering, Drywall, Acoustical, And Insulation Work	2	1.626120	1.626120	1.418282	1.424644	1.435248	1.583704	1.626120	1.668536	1.816992	1.827596	1.833958
177	CONCRETE WORK	1	0.806072	0.806072	0.806072	0.806072	0.806072	0.806072	0.806072	0.806072	0.806072	0.806072	0.806072
1771	Concrete Work	1	0.806072	0.806072	0.806072	0.806072	0.806072	0.806072	0.806072	0.806072	0.806072	0.806072	0.806072
178	WATER WELL DRILLING	1	2.285940	2.285940	2.285940	2.285940	2.285940	2.285940	2.285940	2.285940	2.285940	2.285940	2.285940
1781	Water Well Drilling	1	2.285940	2.285940	2.285940	2.285940	2.285940	2.285940	2.285940	2.285940	2.285940	2.285940	2.285940
	MANUFACTURING												
20	FOOD AND KINDRED PRODUCTS	98	0.658512	0.671548	-1.680855	-1.467342	-0.579819	0.598907	0.671548	0.812360	1.596976	1.746019	1.877302
201	MEAT PRODUCTS	7	0.511078	0.325501	0.121260	0.129568	0.143414	0.310025	0.325501	0.353050	1.220276	1.289043	1.330303
2011	Meat Packing Plants	2	0.864613	0.864613	0.381280	0.396076	0.420736	0.765974	0.864613	0.963252	1.308490	1.333150	1.347946
2013	Sausages And Other Prepared Meat Products	2	0.161875	0.161875	0.116645	0.118030	0.120337	0.152644	0.161875	0.171106	0.203413	0.205720	0.207105
2015	Poultry Slaughtering And Processing	3	0.508191	0.325501	0.300224	0.300998	0.302287	0.320342	0.325501	0.440273	0.841977	0.870670	0.887886
202	DAIRY PRODUCTS	10	0.882581	0.773427	0.356877	0.388674	0.441671	0.642239	0.773427	0.902213	1.557656	1.641088	1.691147
2022	Natural, Processed, And Imitation Cheese	2	1.132266	1.132266	0.915250	0.921893	0.932965	1.087977	1.132266	1.176554	1.331566	1.342638	1.349281
2023	Dry, Condensed, And Evaporated Dairy Products	3	0.601941	0.584227	0.571477	0.571868	0.572518	0.581625	0.584227	0.597457	0.643764	0.647071	0.649056
2024	Ice Cream And Frozen Desserts	1	1.724520	1.724520	1.724520	1.724520	1.724520	1.724520	1.724520	1.724520	1.724520	1.724520	1.724520
2026	Fluid Milk	4	0.757735	0.763251	0.344509	0.357754	0.379831	0.683317	0.763251	0.843185	1.127917	1.148339	1.160591
203	CANNED, FROZEN, AND PRESERVED FRUITS, VEGETABLES, AND FOOD SPECIAL	9	0.902206	0.719999	0.419032	0.421701	0.426149	0.635378	0.719999	0.848542	1.645998	1.703954	1.738728
2030	CANNED, FROZEN & PRESERVD FRUIT, VEG & FOOD SPECIALTIES	1	1.761910	1.761910	1.761910	1.761910	1.761910	1.761910	1.761910	1.761910	1.761910	1.761910	1.761910
2032	Canned Specialties	2	0.660086	0.660086	0.443905	0.450523	0.461552	0.615967	0.660086	0.704204	0.858619	0.869648	0.876266
2033	Canned Fruits, Vegetables, Preserves, Jams, And Jellies	4	0.737855	0.641538	0.421628	0.428190	0.439126	0.594461	0.641538	0.688614	1.171426	1.211258	1.235157
2034	Dried And Dehydrated Fruits, Vegetables, And Soup Mixes	1	1.472130	1.472130	1.472130	1.472130	1.472130	1.472130	1.472130	1.472130	1.472130	1.472130	1.472130
2037	Frozen Fruits, Fruit Juices, And Vegetables	1	0.614223	0.614223	0.614223	0.614223	0.614223	0.614223	0.614223	0.614223	0.614223	0.614223	0.614223

Down-market Betas of Common Stocks by SIC Codes as of March 31, 2017

SIC Code	Description	Number of Companies	Mean	Median	1st Percentile	2.5th Percentile	5th Percentile	40th Percentile	50th Percentile	60th Percentile	95th Percentile	97.5th Percentile	99th Percentile
204	GRAIN MILL PRODUCTS	8	0.656650	0.633485	-0.406004	-0.322662	-0.183759	0.594955	0.633485	0.725158	1.312038	1.336034	1.350432
2041	Flour And Other Grain Mill Products	2	0.785399	0.785399	0.606233	0.611718	0.620859	0.748834	0.785399	0.821963	0.949938	0.959079	0.964564
2043	Cereal Breakfast Foods	1	0.664393	0.664393	0.664393	0.664393	0.664393	0.664393	0.664393	0.664393	0.664393	0.664393	0.664393
2044	Rice Milling	1	-0.461565	-0.461565	-0.461565	-0.461565	-0.461565	-0.461565	-0.461565	-0.461565	-0.461565	-0.461565	-0.461565
2046	Wet Corn Milling	2	0.962248	0.962248	0.572421	0.584354	0.604243	0.882691	0.962248	1.041804	1.320252	1.340141	1.352074
2047	Dog And Cat Food	1	0.332166	0.332166	0.332166	0.332166	0.332166	0.332166	0.332166	0.332166	0.332166	0.332166	0.332166
2048	Prepared Feeds And Feed Ingredients For Animals And Fowls, Except Dog And Cat	1	1.222910	1.222910	1.222910	1.222910	1.222910	1.222910	1.222910	1.222910	1.222910	1.222910	1.222910
205	BAKERY PRODUCTS	7	0.671019	0.716686	0.210195	0.210743	0.211656	0.431324	0.716686	0.765600	1.350167	1.419514	1.461121
2051	Bread And Other Bakery Products, Except Cookies And Crackers	3	0.416374	0.241083	0.210455	0.211393	0.212955	0.234832	0.241083	0.352508	0.742496	0.770353	0.787066
2052	Cookies And Crackers	4	0.862004	0.871618	0.230941	0.253476	0.291033	0.778659	0.871618	0.964577	1.419514	1.454187	1.474991
206	SUGAR AND CONFECTIONERY PRODUCTS	4	0.891791	0.622613	0.446707	0.448412	0.451254	0.539122	0.622613	0.706103	1.709179	1.792774	1.842932
2061	Cane Sugar, Except Refining	1	1.876370	1.876370	1.876370	1.876370	1.876370	1.876370	1.876370	1.876370	1.876370	1.876370	1.876370
2066	Chocolate And Cocoa Products	2	0.464516	0.464516	0.445949	0.446517	0.447465	0.460727	0.464516	0.468305	0.481567	0.482515	0.483083
2068	Salted And Roasted Nuts And Seeds	1	0.761763	0.761763	0.761763	0.761763	0.761763	0.761763	0.761763	0.761763	0.761763	0.761763	0.761763
207	FATS AND OILS	4	1.173251	1.043450	0.707939	0.721852	0.745041	1.022090	1.043450	1.064810	1.783182	1.845311	1.882588
2075	Soybean Oil Mills	1	1.079050	1.079050	1.079050	1.079050	1.079050	1.079050	1.079050	1.079050	1.079050	1.079050	1.079050
2077	Animal And Marine Fats And Oils	2	1.303052	1.303052	0.710751	0.728882	0.759102	1.182174	1.303052	1.423929	1.847001	1.877221	1.895352
2079	Shortening, Table Oils, Margarine, And Other Edible Fats And Oils	1	1.007850	1.007850	1.007850	1.007850	1.007850	1.007850	1.007850	1.007850	1.007850	1.007850	1.007850
208	BEVERAGES	32	0.546185	0.737163	-1.664538	-1.643850	-1.418372	0.622940	0.737163	0.834075	1.580434	1.598173	1.605599
2082	Malt Beverages	4	0.782730	0.889724	0.375188	0.399043	0.438800	0.889521	0.889724	0.889927	0.976867	0.984527	0.989122
2084	Wines, Brandy, And Brandy Spirits	5	0.470887	0.420509	-0.135835	-0.110317	-0.067789	0.361281	0.420509	0.558851	0.991649	1.019809	1.036706
2085	Distilled And Blended Liquors	5	0.955637	0.855791	0.630458	0.641148	0.658965	0.834075	0.855791	0.868279	1.465842	1.538196	1.581608
2086	Bottled And Canned Soft Drinks And Carbonated Waters	17	0.332090	0.622679	-1.671212	-1.660534	-1.642738	0.488465	0.622679	0.702041	1.511324	1.552952	1.577929
2087	Flavoring Extracts And Flavoring Syrups, Not Elsewhere Classified	1	1.568860	1.568860	1.568860	1.568860	1.568860	1.568860	1.568860	1.568860	1.568860	1.568860	1.568860
209	MISCELLANEOUS FOOD PREPARATIONS AND KINDRED PRODUCTS	17	0.489561	0.623489	-1.673974	-1.541216	-1.319952	0.507128	0.623489	0.659684	1.535668	1.546684	1.553294
2095	Roasted Coffee	4	0.608761	0.472590	-0.029436	-0.013147	0.014002	0.382050	0.472590	0.563129	1.394159	1.462160	1.502960
2096	Potato Chips, Corn Chips, And Similar Snacks	1	1.196780	1.196780	1.196780	1.196780	1.196780	1.196780	1.196780	1.196780	1.196780	1.196780	1.196780
2097	Manufactured Ice	1	1.080220	1.080220	1.080220	1.080220	1.080220	1.080220	1.080220	1.080220	1.080220	1.080220	1.080220
2099	Food Preparations, Not Elsewhere Classified	11	0.328227	0.558658	-1.707164	-1.624190	-1.485900	0.472775	0.558658	0.639877	1.453035	1.505368	1.536767
21	TOBACCO PRODUCTS	9	0.484235	0.637764	-0.917507	-0.776053	-0.540296	0.609191	0.637764	0.744319	1.053499	1.085205	1.104228
211	CIGARETTES	9	0.484235	0.637764	-0.917507	-0.776053	-0.540296	0.609191	0.637764	0.744319	1.053499	1.085205	1.104228
2111	Cigarettes	9	0.484235	0.637764	-0.917507	-0.776053	-0.540296	0.609191	0.637764	0.744319	1.053499	1.085205	1.104228

Down-market Betas of Common Stocks by SIC Codes as of March 31, 2017

SIC Code	Description	Number of Companies	Mean	Median	1st Percentile	2.5th Percentile	5th Percentile	40th Percentile	50th Percentile	60th Percentile	95th Percentile	97.5th Percentile	99th Percentile
22	TEXTILE MILL PRODUCTS	11	1.315888	1.305980	0.063054	0.188352	0.397181	1.281220	1.305980	1.370630	2.096570	2.169805	2.213746
221	BROADWOVEN FABRIC MILLS, COTTON	2	0.630371	0.630371	-0.007460	0.012065	0.044607	0.500202	0.630371	0.760541	1.216135	1.248678	1.268203
2211	Broadwoven Fabric Mills, Cotton	2	0.630371	0.630371	-0.007460	0.012065	0.044607	0.500202	0.630371	0.760541	1.216135	1.248678	1.268203
222	BROADWOVEN FABRIC MILLS, MANMADE FIBER AND SILK	2	1.912275	1.912275	1.588125	1.598048	1.614587	1.846122	1.912275	1.978428	2.209964	2.226502	2.236425
2221	Broadwoven Fabric Mills, Manmade Fiber And Silk	2	1.912275	1.912275	1.588125	1.598048	1.614587	1.846122	1.912275	1.978428	2.209964	2.226502	2.236425
225	KNITTING MILLS	3	1.163817	1.305980	0.824663	0.839397	0.863954	1.207752	1.305980	1.318910	1.364165	1.367398	1.369337
2252	Hosiery, Not Elsewhere Classified	1	1.370630	1.370630	1.370630	1.370630	1.370630	1.370630	1.370630	1.370630	1.370630	1.370630	1.370630
2253	Knit Outerwear Mills	2	1.060410	1.060410	0.819751	0.827119	0.839397	1.011296	1.060410	1.109524	1.281423	1.293702	1.301069
227	CARPETS AND RUGS	3	1.614720	1.724120	1.181024	1.197649	1.225358	1.613284	1.724120	1.769316	1.927502	1.938801	1.945580
2273	Carpets And Rugs	3	1.614720	1.724120	1.181024	1.197649	1.225358	1.613284	1.724120	1.769316	1.927502	1.938801	1.945580
228	YARN AND THREAD MILLS	1	1.053860	1.053860	1.053860	1.053860	1.053860	1.053860	1.053860	1.053860	1.053860	1.053860	1.053860
2282	Yarn Texturizing, Throwing, Twisting, And Winding Mills	1	1.053860	1.053860	1.053860	1.053860	1.053860	1.053860	1.053860	1.053860	1.053860	1.053860	1.053860
23	APPAREL AND OTHER FINISHED PRODUCTS MADE FROM FABRICS AND SIMILAR MATERIAL	19	1.316674	1.300720	0.288197	0.306444	0.336855	1.050738	1.300720	1.566152	2.291480	2.298320	2.302424
2300	APPAREL & OTHER FINISHD PRODS OF FABRICS & SIMILAR MATL	1	0.757619	0.757619	0.757619	0.757619	0.757619	0.757619	0.757619	0.757619	0.757619	0.757619	0.757619
232	MEN'S AND BOYS' FURNISHINGS, WORK CLOTHING, AND ALLIED GARMENTS	7	1.384962	1.522480	0.379999	0.434578	0.525542	1.389424	1.522480	1.555234	2.069655	2.121593	2.152755
2321	Men's And Boys' Shirts, Except Work Shirts	2	1.737125	1.737125	1.309448	1.322540	1.344361	1.649844	1.737125	1.824406	2.129890	2.151710	2.164802
2325	Men's And Boys' Separate Trousers And Slacks	1	1.522480	1.522480	1.522480	1.522480	1.522480	1.522480	1.522480	1.522480	1.522480	1.522480	1.522480
2326	Men's And Boys' Work Clothing	2	0.646829	0.646829	0.349677	0.358774	0.373935	0.586185	0.646829	0.707472	0.919722	0.934883	0.943980
2329	Men's And Boys' Clothing, Not Elsewhere Classified	2	1.702175	1.702175	1.579572	1.583325	1.589581	1.677154	1.702175	1.727196	1.814770	1.821025	1.824778
233	WOMEN'S, MISSES', AND JUNIORS' OUTERWEAR	7	1.418208	1.242610	0.459439	0.491090	0.543841	1.098706	1.242610	1.612204	2.300600	2.302880	2.304248
2337	Women's, Misses', And Juniors' Suits, Skirts, And Coats	1	1.858600	1.858600	1.858600	1.858600	1.858600	1.858600	1.858600	1.858600	1.858600	1.858600	1.858600
2339	Women's, Misses', And Juniors' Outerwear, Not Elsewhere Classified	6	1.344809	1.122690	0.455922	0.482298	0.526257	1.002770	1.122690	1.242610	2.301360	2.303260	2.304400
234	WOMEN'S, MISSES', CHILDREN'S, AND INFANTS' UNDERGARMENTS	1	0.765848	0.765848	0.765848	0.765848	0.765848	0.765848	0.765848	0.765848	0.765848	0.765848	0.765848
2341	Women's, Misses', Children's, And Infants' Underwear And Nightwear	1	0.765848	0.765848	0.765848	0.765848	0.765848	0.765848	0.765848	0.765848	0.765848	0.765848	0.765848
238	MISCELLANEOUS APPAREL AND ACCESSORIES	3	1.290384	1.646950	0.303451	0.344579	0.413125	1.372767	1.646950	1.707194	1.918048	1.933109	1.942146
2385	Waterproof Outerwear	2	1.112102	1.112102	0.292754	0.317836	0.359640	0.944888	1.112102	1.279315	1.864563	1.906367	1.931449

Down-market Betas of Common Stocks by SIC Codes as of March 31, 2017

SIC Code	Description	Number of Companies	Mean	Median	1st Percentile	2.5th Percentile	5th Percentile	40th Percentile	50th Percentile	60th Percentile	95th Percentile	97.5th Percentile	99th Percentile
2389	Apparel And Accessories, Not Elsewhere Classified	1	1.646950	1.646950	1.646950	1.646950	1.646950	1.646950	1.646950	1.646950	1.646950	1.646950	1.646950
24	LUMBER AND WOOD PRODUCTS, EXCEPT FURNITURE	13	1.589136	1.477740	0.962429	0.981323	1.012813	1.338798	1.477740	1.765358	2.245738	2.267329	2.280284
2400	LUMBER & WOOD PRODUCTS (NO FURNITURE)	1	1.841470	1.841470	1.841470	1.841470	1.841470	1.841470	1.841470	1.841470	1.841470	1.841470	1.841470
241	LOGGING	1	2.288920	2.288920	2.288920	2.288920	2.288920	2.288920	2.288920	2.288920	2.288920	2.288920	2.288920
2411	Logging	1	2.288920	2.288920	2.288920	2.288920	2.288920	2.288920	2.288920	2.288920	2.288920	2.288920	2.288920
242	SAWMILLS AND PLANING MILLS	3	1.386640	1.222240	1.058149	1.063172	1.071544	1.188752	1.222240	1.354368	1.816816	1.849848	1.869667
2421	Sawmills And Planing Mills, General	3	1.386640	1.222240	1.058149	1.063172	1.071544	1.188752	1.222240	1.354368	1.816816	1.849848	1.869667
243	MILLWORK, VENEER, PLYWOOD, AND STRUCTURAL WOOD MEMBERS	3	1.626683	1.477740	1.231378	1.238920	1.251489	1.427462	1.477740	1.617384	2.106138	2.141049	2.161996
2431	Millwork	1	2.175960	2.175960	2.175960	2.175960	2.175960	2.175960	2.175960	2.175960	2.175960	2.175960	2.175960
2434	Wood Kitchen Cabinets	1	1.226350	1.226350	1.226350	1.226350	1.226350	1.226350	1.226350	1.226350	1.226350	1.226350	1.226350
2439	Structural Wood Members, Not Elsewhere Classified	1	1.477740	1.477740	1.477740	1.477740	1.477740	1.477740	1.477740	1.477740	1.477740	1.477740	1.477740
245	WOOD BUILDINGS AND MOBILE HOMES	2	1.079107	1.079107	0.952418	0.956297	0.962760	1.053252	1.079107	1.104961	1.195453	1.201916	1.205795
2451	Mobile Homes	2	1.079107	1.079107	0.952418	0.956297	0.962760	1.053252	1.079107	1.104961	1.195453	1.201916	1.205795
249	MISCELLANEOUS WOOD PRODUCTS	3	1.776730	1.746330	1.374498	1.385881	1.404852	1.670446	1.746330	1.840454	2.169888	2.193419	2.207538
2491	Wood Preserving	1	2.216950	2.216950	2.216950	2.216950	2.216950	2.216950	2.216950	2.216950	2.216950	2.216950	2.216950
2493	Reconstituted Wood Products	1	1.746330	1.746330	1.746330	1.746330	1.746330	1.746330	1.746330	1.746330	1.746330	1.746330	1.746330
2499	Wood Products, Not Elsewhere Classified	1	1.366910	1.366910	1.366910	1.366910	1.366910	1.366910	1.366910	1.366910	1.366910	1.366910	1.366910
25	FURNITURE AND FIXTURES	20	1.121718	1.337570	-0.508333	-0.419284	-0.270871	1.273306	1.337570	1.422996	1.902235	1.992242	2.046247
251	HOUSEHOLD FURNITURE	12	1.048981	1.316990	-0.223544	-0.175988	-0.096727	1.264034	1.316990	1.377836	1.783816	1.838288	1.870971
2511	Wood Household Furniture, Except Upholstered	7	0.946632	1.245490	-0.224799	-0.179125	-0.103001	0.839045	1.245490	1.371214	1.686121	1.690401	1.692968
2512	Wood Household Furniture, Upholstered	1	0.032972	0.032972	0.032972	0.032972	0.032972	0.032972	0.032972	0.032972	0.032972	0.032972	0.032972
2515	Mattresses, Foundations, And Convertible Beds	3	1.528750	1.401640	1.294046	1.297340	1.302829	1.379682	1.401640	1.499864	1.843648	1.868204	1.882938
2519	Household Furniture, Not Elsewhere Classified	1	1.342130	1.342130	1.342130	1.342130	1.342130	1.342130	1.342130	1.342130	1.342130	1.342130	1.342130
252	OFFICE FURNITURE	6	1.440308	1.503950	0.830802	0.844350	0.866932	1.333010	1.503950	1.674890	1.993565	2.037908	2.064513
2521	Wood Office Furniture	3	1.302146	1.002420	0.825382	0.830802	0.839834	0.966290	1.002420	1.218386	1.974267	2.028259	2.060653
2522	Office Furniture, Except Wood	3	1.578470	1.674890	1.339848	1.350104	1.367198	1.606514	1.674890	1.685414	1.722248	1.724879	1.726458
253	PUBLIC BUILDING AND RELATED FURNITURE	2	0.602366	0.602366	-0.544297	-0.509195	-0.450692	0.368353	0.602366	0.836379	1.655424	1.713927	1.749029
2531	Public Building And Related Furniture	2	0.602366	0.602366	-0.544297	-0.509195	-0.450692	0.368353	0.602366	0.836379	1.655424	1.713927	1.749029
26	PAPER AND ALLIED PRODUCTS	25	1.572636	1.536660	0.427439	0.496560	0.576713	1.312060	1.536660	1.628524	2.684844	3.201826	3.605130
261	PULP MILLS	3	2.214203	1.536660	1.238044	1.247186	1.262421	1.475718	1.536660	2.004128	3.640266	3.757133	3.827253
2611	Pulp Mills	3	2.214203	1.536660	1.238044	1.247186	1.262421	1.475718	1.536660	2.004128	3.640266	3.757133	3.827253
262	PAPER MILLS	9	1.589968	1.477250	0.583364	0.598368	0.623376	1.381546	1.477250	1.661346	2.615978	2.684844	2.726164

Down-market Betas of Common Stocks by SIC Codes as of March 31, 2017

SIC Code	Description	Number of Companies	Mean	Median	1st Percentile	2.5th Percentile	5th Percentile	40th Percentile	50th Percentile	60th Percentile	95th Percentile	97.5th Percentile	99th Percentile
2621	Paper Mills	9	1.589968	1.477250	0.583364	0.598368	0.623376	1.381546	1.477250	1.661346	2.615978	2.684844	2.726164
263	PAPERBOARD MILLS	4	1.190410	1.202595	0.823966	0.839624	0.865719	1.177920	1.202595	1.227270	1.498040	1.520480	1.533944
2631	Paperboard Mills	4	1.190410	1.202595	0.823966	0.839624	0.865719	1.177920	1.202595	1.227270	1.498040	1.520480	1.533944
265	PAPERBOARD CONTAINERS AND BOXES	3	1.974857	1.960900	1.583659	1.595207	1.614454	1.883912	1.960900	2.046262	2.345029	2.366370	2.379174
2655	Fiber Cans, Tubes, Drums, And Similar Products	2	2.174305	2.174305	1.965168	1.971570	1.982241	2.131624	2.174305	2.216986	2.366370	2.377040	2.383442
2657	Folding Paperboard Boxes, Including Sanitary	1	1.575960	1.575960	1.575960	1.575960	1.575960	1.575960	1.575960	1.575960	1.575960	1.575960	1.575960
267	CONVERTED PAPER AND PAPERBOARD PRODUCTS, EXCEPT CONTAINERS AND BOXES	6	1.279561	1.425700	0.391796	0.407453	0.433548	1.041440	1.425700	1.809960	1.974538	1.998184	2.012372
2671	Packaging Paper And Plastics Film, Coated And Laminated	3	1.077586	1.041440	0.394560	0.414362	0.447366	0.909424	1.041440	1.195144	1.733108	1.771534	1.794590
2673	Plastics, Foil, And Coated Paper Bags	1	2.021830	2.021830	2.021830	2.021830	2.021830	2.021830	2.021830	2.021830	2.021830	2.021830	2.021830
2679	Converted Paper And Paperboard Products, Not Elsewhere Classified	2	1.211390	1.211390	0.602544	0.621183	0.652246	1.087135	1.211390	1.335644	1.770533	1.801596	1.820235
27	PRINTING, PUBLISHING, AND ALLIED INDUSTRIES	41	1.050605	1.119340	-0.290793	-0.219867	-0.068948	1.074130	1.119340	1.254100	1.667840	1.772560	1.789264
271	NEWSPAPERS: PUBLISHING, OR PUBLISHING AND PRINTING	18	1.087384	1.153985	-0.194211	-0.155727	-0.091586	1.110298	1.153985	1.335100	1.597891	1.612115	1.620650
2711	Newspapers: Publishing, Or Publishing And Printing	18	1.087384	1.153985	-0.194211	-0.155727	-0.091586	1.110298	1.153985	1.335100	1.597891	1.612115	1.620650
272	PERIODICALS: PUBLISHING, OR PUBLISHING AND PRINTING	3	1.412360	1.397760	1.046097	1.056862	1.074804	1.325992	1.397760	1.478288	1.760136	1.780268	1.792347
2721	Periodicals: Publishing, Or Publishing And Printing	3	1.412360	1.397760	1.046097	1.056862	1.074804	1.325992	1.397760	1.478288	1.760136	1.780268	1.792347
273	BOOKS	4	1.061765	1.146413	0.306245	0.336020	0.385646	1.027404	1.146413	1.265421	1.619378	1.643609	1.658148
2731	Books: Publishing, Or Publishing And Printing	4	1.061765	1.146413	0.306245	0.336020	0.385646	1.027404	1.146413	1.265421	1.619378	1.643609	1.658148
274	MISCELLANEOUS PUBLISHING	4	0.916659	0.921433	0.342075	0.357096	0.382130	0.768087	0.921433	1.074779	1.444505	1.468108	1.482269
2741	Miscellaneous Publishing	4	0.916659	0.921433	0.342075	0.357096	0.382130	0.768087	0.921433	1.074779	1.444505	1.468108	1.482269
275	COMMERCIAL PRINTING	8	0.906768	1.005124	-0.284503	-0.204142	-0.070208	0.908793	1.005124	1.120252	1.599433	1.685996	1.737935
2752	Commercial Printing, Lithographic	3	0.788064	0.850137	0.435721	0.448408	0.469551	0.765562	0.850137	0.897468	1.063125	1.074957	1.082057
2754	Commercial Printing, Gravure	3	0.904131	1.277910	-0.305757	-0.257278	-0.176478	0.954713	1.277910	1.376840	1.723095	1.747828	1.762667
2759	Commercial Printing, Not Elsewhere Classified	2	1.088779	1.088779	0.926763	0.931723	0.939989	1.055714	1.088779	1.121843	1.237568	1.245834	1.250794
276	MANIFOLD BUSINESS FORMS	1	1.105300	1.105300	1.105300	1.105300	1.105300	1.105300	1.105300	1.105300	1.105300	1.105300	1.105300
2761	Manifold Business Forms	1	1.105300	1.105300	1.105300	1.105300	1.105300	1.105300	1.105300	1.105300	1.105300	1.105300	1.105300
277	GREETING CARDS	1	0.467673	0.467673	0.467673	0.467673	0.467673	0.467673	0.467673	0.467673	0.467673	0.467673	0.467673
2771	Greeting Cards	1	0.467673	0.467673	0.467673	0.467673	0.467673	0.467673	0.467673	0.467673	0.467673	0.467673	0.467673
278	BLANKBOOKS, LOOSELEAF BINDERS, AND BOOKBINDING AND RELATED WORK	2	1.262005	1.262005	1.110923	1.115548	1.123257	1.231172	1.262005	1.292838	1.400754	1.408462	1.413087

Down-market Betas of Common Stocks by SIC Codes as of March 31, 2017

SIC Code	Description	Number of Companies	Mean	Median	1st Percentile	2.5th Percentile	5th Percentile	40th Percentile	50th Percentile	60th Percentile	95th Percentile	97.5th Percentile	99th Percentile
2782	Blankbooks, Looseleaf Binders And Devices	2	1.262005	1.262005	1.110923	1.115548	1.123257	1.231172	1.262005	1.292838	1.400754	1.408462	1.413087
28	CHEMICALS AND ALLIED PRODUCTS	479	1.290965	1.271860	-1.957488	-0.785543	-0.237886	1.037102	1.271860	1.503888	2.871015	3.076428	3.568911
281	INDUSTRIAL INORGANIC CHEMICALS	15	1.803682	1.838600	0.801375	0.830712	0.879608	1.594150	1.838600	2.090178	2.753113	2.796622	2.822727
2812	Alkalies And Chlorine	1	1.838600	1.838600	1.838600	1.838600	1.838600	1.838600	1.838600	1.838600	1.838600	1.838600	1.838600
2813	Industrial Gases	3	1.152137	1.123570	1.030068	1.032931	1.037701	1.104488	1.123570	1.159792	1.286569	1.295625	1.301058
2816	Inorganic Pigments	4	2.443288	2.572945	1.810189	1.844778	1.902426	2.562640	2.572945	2.583250	2.802629	2.821379	2.832630
2819	Industrial Inorganic Chemicals, Not Elsewhere Classified	7	1.712438	2.085050	0.790199	0.802772	0.823727	1.392490	2.085050	2.092742	2.637337	2.676579	2.700123
282	PLASTICS MATERIALS AND SYNTHETIC RESINS, SYNTHETIC RUBBER, CELLULOSIC MANMADE FIBERS	14	1.600677	1.522925	0.490067	0.597988	0.777858	1.503938	1.522925	1.672544	2.572165	2.804497	2.943897
2821	Plastics Materials, Synthetic Resins, And Nonvulcanizable Elastomers	14	1.600677	1.522925	0.490067	0.597988	0.777858	1.503938	1.522925	1.672544	2.572165	2.804497	2.943897
283	DRUGS	378	1.291395	1.261770	-2.062277	-1.034526	-0.239246	1.018496	1.261770	1.483498	2.934894	3.302813	3.691281
2833	Medicinal Chemicals And Botanical Products	15	1.041775	0.924599	-0.587532	-0.469698	-0.273306	0.832661	0.924599	1.304244	2.261367	2.558934	2.737473
2834	Pharmaceutical Preparations	281	1.249547	1.209030	-1.687576	-1.155440	-0.231918	0.981399	1.209030	1.444850	2.941940	3.361450	4.144852
2835	In Vitro And In Vivo Diagnostic Substances	21	1.229611	1.178720	-2.385342	-1.683674	-0.514228	1.120430	1.178720	1.439310	2.980940	3.197895	3.328068
2836	Biological Products, Except Diagnostic Substances	61	1.566820	1.669420	-1.205339	-0.465898	-0.091741	1.436800	1.669420	1.909360	2.834690	2.931995	3.194000
284	SOAP, DETERGENTS, AND CLEANING PREPARATIONS; PERFUMES, COSMETICS	19	0.845225	0.871774	-0.059442	-0.055468	-0.048844	0.687749	0.871774	0.994240	1.668141	2.112251	2.378716
2841	Soap And Other Detergents, Except Specialty Cleaners	5	0.923487	0.906159	0.615732	0.616991	0.619089	0.798044	0.906159	0.988003	1.301946	1.325843	1.340181
2842	Specialty Cleaning, Polishing, And Sanitation Preparations	3	0.492326	0.264013	0.198052	0.200071	0.203437	0.250552	0.264013	0.414462	0.941035	0.978648	1.001215
2844	Perfumes, Cosmetics, And Other Toilet Preparations	11	0.905896	0.871774	-0.060620	-0.058412	-0.054732	0.706737	0.871774	1.042110	2.062905	2.309633	2.457669
285	PAINTS, VARNISHES, LACQUERS, ENAMELS, AND ALLIED PRODUCTS	6	0.902784	1.724575	-1.845272	-1.681564	-1.408719	1.712620	1.724575	1.736530	1.884233	1.902946	1.914175
2851	Paints, Varnishes, Lacquers, Enamels, And Allied Products	6	0.902784	1.724575	-1.845272	-1.681564	-1.408719	1.712620	1.724575	1.736530	1.884233	1.902946	1.914175
286	INDUSTRIAL ORGANIC CHEMICALS	21	1.446132	1.428510	-0.379796	-0.347615	-0.293980	1.383560	1.428510	1.592890	2.644890	2.810435	2.909762
2861	Gum And Wood Chemicals	2	1.081175	1.081175	0.643785	0.657175	0.679491	0.991911	1.081175	1.170438	1.482858	1.505174	1.518564
2865	Cyclic Organic Crudes And Intermediates, And Organic Dyes And Pigments	1	1.110100	1.110100	1.110100	1.110100	1.110100	1.110100	1.110100	1.110100	1.110100	1.110100	1.110100
2869	Industrial Organic Chemicals, Not Elsewhere Classified	18	1.505351	1.510700	-0.383014	-0.355660	-0.310071	1.400120	1.510700	1.652068	2.694554	2.835267	2.919695
287	AGRICULTURAL CHEMICALS	13	1.077454	1.159930	-0.451126	-0.402056	-0.320272	1.083078	1.159930	1.241042	2.073350	2.145305	2.188478
2873	Nitrogenous Fertilizers	6	1.028899	1.054635	-0.439731	-0.373568	-0.263297	1.007230	1.054635	1.102040	2.146038	2.181649	2.203016
2874	Phosphatic Fertilizers	2	1.571485	1.571485	1.436799	1.440922	1.447794	1.543998	1.571485	1.598972	1.695177	1.702048	1.706171

Down-market Betas of Common Stocks by SIC Codes as of March 31, 2017

SIC Code	Description	Number of Companies	Mean	Median	1st Percentile	2.5th Percentile	5th Percentile	40th Percentile	50th Percentile	60th Percentile	95th Percentile	97.5th Percentile	99th Percentile
2879	Pesticides And Agricultural Chemicals, Not Elsewhere Classified	5	0.938106	1.159930	-0.179913	-0.132941	-0.054656	0.924610	1.159930	1.173074	1.820486	1.898948	1.946025
289	MISCELLANEOUS CHEMICAL PRODUCTS	13	1.146821	1.188980	-0.520282	-0.358529	-0.088941	1.154328	1.188980	1.517938	2.042804	2.135477	2.191081
2890	MISCELLANEOUS CHEMICAL PRODUCTS	1	0.701960	0.701960	0.701960	0.701960	0.701960	0.701960	0.701960	0.701960	0.701960	0.701960	0.701960
2891	Adhesives And Sealants	2	1.111021	1.111021	0.521110	0.539168	0.569266	0.990631	1.111021	1.231410	1.652775	1.682873	1.700931
2893	Printing Ink	1	1.504310	1.504310	1.504310	1.504310	1.504310	1.504310	1.504310	1.504310	1.504310	1.504310	1.504310
2895	Carbon Black	1	1.919240	1.919240	1.919240	1.919240	1.919240	1.919240	1.919240	1.919240	1.919240	1.919240	1.919240
2899	Chemicals And Chemical Preparations, Not Elsewhere Classified	8	1.070140	1.187640	-0.565213	-0.470857	-0.313598	1.154328	1.187640	1.265674	2.049041	2.138596	2.192328
29	PETROLEUM REFINING AND RELATED INDUSTRIES	22	1.134901	1.041867	0.405412	0.476367	0.583410	0.946756	1.041867	1.167268	1.875785	2.053718	2.167077
291	PETROLEUM REFINING	20	1.106476	0.979509	0.400907	0.465105	0.572101	0.913151	0.979509	1.154052	1.900774	2.071712	2.174275
2911	Petroleum Refining	20	1.106476	0.979509	0.400907	0.465105	0.572101	0.913151	0.979509	1.154052	1.900774	2.071712	2.174275
295	ASPHALT PAVING AND ROOFING MATERIALS	1	1.095430	1.095430	1.095430	1.095430	1.095430	1.095430	1.095430	1.095430	1.095430	1.095430	1.095430
2951	Asphalt Paving Mixtures And Blocks	1	1.095430	1.095430	1.095430	1.095430	1.095430	1.095430	1.095430	1.095430	1.095430	1.095430	1.095430
299	MISCELLANEOUS PRODUCTS OF PETROLEUM AND COAL	1	1.742870	1.742870	1.742870	1.742870	1.742870	1.742870	1.742870	1.742870	1.742870	1.742870	1.742870
2999	Products Of Petroleum And Coal, Not Elsewhere Classified	1	1.742870	1.742870	1.742870	1.742870	1.742870	1.742870	1.742870	1.742870	1.742870	1.742870	1.742870
30	RUBBER AND MISCELLANEOUS PLASTICS PRODUCTS	36	0.982311	1.217630	-1.948945	-1.659916	-0.484444	1.039560	1.217630	1.330720	2.084263	2.129816	2.186291
301	TIRES AND INNER TUBES	2	1.433755	1.433755	1.128853	1.138186	1.153743	1.371530	1.433755	1.495980	1.713768	1.729324	1.738658
3011	Tires And Inner Tubes	2	1.433755	1.433755	1.128853	1.138186	1.153743	1.371530	1.433755	1.495980	1.713768	1.729324	1.738658
302	RUBBER AND PLASTICS FOOTWEAR	4	1.273693	1.402120	0.736049	0.764394	0.811635	1.369072	1.402120	1.435168	1.555953	1.564667	1.569895
3021	Rubber And Plastics Footwear	4	1.273693	1.402120	0.736049	0.764394	0.811635	1.369072	1.402120	1.435168	1.555953	1.564667	1.569895
305	GASKETS, PACKING, AND SEALING DEVICES AND RUBBER AND PLASTICS HOSE	3	0.146765	0.630376	-1.546670	-1.480026	-1.368952	0.186081	0.630376	0.784505	1.323956	1.362488	1.385607
3052	Rubber And Plastics Hose And Belting	1	-1.591100	-1.591100	-1.591100	-1.591100	-1.591100	-1.591100	-1.591100	-1.591100	-1.591100	-1.591100	-1.591100
3053	Gaskets, Packing, And Sealing Devices	2	1.015698	1.015698	0.638082	0.649642	0.668908	0.938634	1.015698	1.092762	1.362488	1.381754	1.393314
306	FABRICATED RUBBER PRODUCTS, NOT ELSEWHERE CLASSIFIED	3	0.960129	1.129300	0.506841	0.525896	0.557654	1.002268	1.129300	1.154830	1.244185	1.250568	1.254397
3069	Fabricated Rubber Products, Not Elsewhere Classified	3	0.960129	1.129300	0.506841	0.525896	0.557654	1.002268	1.129300	1.154830	1.244185	1.250568	1.254397
308	MISCELLANEOUS PLASTICS PRODUCTS	24	1.003342	1.217630	-1.675634	-0.976639	-0.108747	0.957694	1.217630	1.312912	2.109949	2.162087	2.199199
3081	Unsupported Plastics Film And Sheet	3	1.115704	0.693576	0.582248	0.585656	0.591336	0.670856	0.693576	0.969573	1.935562	2.004561	2.045960
3084	Plastics Pipe	1	1.039560	1.039560	1.039560	1.039560	1.039560	1.039560	1.039560	1.039560	1.039560	1.039560	1.039560
3086	Plastics Foam Products	3	1.057005	0.937228	0.849381	0.852070	0.856552	0.919300	0.937228	1.027022	1.341303	1.363751	1.377221

Down-market Betas of Common Stocks by SIC Codes as of March 31, 2017

SIC Code	Description	Number of Companies	Mean	Median	1st Percentile	2.5th Percentile	5th Percentile	40th Percentile	50th Percentile	60th Percentile	95th Percentile	97.5th Percentile	99th Percentile
3089	Plastics Products, Not Elsewhere Classified	17	0.971913	1.241680	-1.817459	-1.331202	-0.520773	1.214028	1.241680	1.389478	2.137884	2.180912	2.206729
31	LEATHER AND LEATHER PRODUCTS	7	1.176537	1.249960	0.420219	0.434175	0.457433	1.068263	1.249960	1.336240	1.933286	2.007743	2.052417
314	FOOTWEAR, EXCEPT RUBBER	4	1.208502	1.170446	0.427002	0.451132	0.491348	1.036457	1.170446	1.304434	1.978934	2.030567	2.061547
3142	House Slippers	1	0.947131	0.947131	0.947131	0.947131	0.947131	0.947131	0.947131	0.947131	0.947131	0.947131	0.947131
3143	Men's Footwear, Except Athletic	1	1.393760	1.393760	1.393760	1.393760	1.393760	1.393760	1.393760	1.393760	1.393760	1.393760	1.393760
3149	Footwear, Except Rubber, Not Elsewhere Classified	2	1.246558	1.246558	0.427629	0.452698	0.494480	1.079430	1.246558	1.413686	1.998636	2.040418	2.065487
317	HANDBAGS AND OTHER PERSONAL LEATHER GOODS	1	1.585820	1.585820	1.585820	1.585820	1.585820	1.585820	1.585820	1.585820	1.585820	1.585820	1.585820
3171	Women's Handbags And Purses	1	1.585820	1.585820	1.585820	1.585820	1.585820	1.585820	1.585820	1.585820	1.585820	1.585820	1.585820
319	LEATHER GOODS, NOT ELSEWHERE CLASSIFIED	2	0.907967	0.907967	0.572813	0.583073	0.600172	0.839568	0.907967	0.976365	1.215761	1.232860	1.243120
3199	Leather Goods, Not Elsewhere Classified	2	0.907967	0.907967	0.572813	0.583073	0.600172	0.839568	0.907967	0.976365	1.215761	1.232860	1.243120
32	STONE, CLAY, GLASS, AND CONCRETE PRODUCTS	14	0.787767	1.139645	-1.555008	-1.299015	-0.872360	0.732602	1.139645	1.154650	1.832873	2.018182	2.129367
322	GLASS AND GLASSWARE, PRESSED OR BLOWN	2	1.670325	1.670325	1.147823	1.163818	1.190477	1.563692	1.670325	1.776958	2.150174	2.176832	2.192827
3221	Glass Containers	1	2.203490	2.203490	2.203490	2.203490	2.203490	2.203490	2.203490	2.203490	2.203490	2.203490	2.203490
3229	Pressed And Blown Glass And Glassware, Not Elsewhere Classified	1	1.137160	1.137160	1.137160	1.137160	1.137160	1.137160	1.137160	1.137160	1.137160	1.137160	1.137160
323	GLASS PRODUCTS, MADE OF PURCHASED GLASS	1	1.532020	1.532020	1.532020	1.532020	1.532020	1.532020	1.532020	1.532020	1.532020	1.532020	1.532020
3231	Glass Products, Made Of Purchased Glass	1	1.532020	1.532020	1.532020	1.532020	1.532020	1.532020	1.532020	1.532020	1.532020	1.532020	1.532020
324	CEMENT, HYDRAULIC	3	0.931545	1.157780	0.167800	0.198105	0.248614	0.955743	1.157780	1.224076	1.456112	1.472686	1.482630
3241	Cement, Hydraulic	3	0.931545	1.157780	0.167800	0.198105	0.248614	0.955743	1.157780	1.224076	1.456112	1.472686	1.482630
325	STRUCTURAL CLAY PRODUCTS	1	-0.412885	-0.412885	-0.412885	-0.412885	-0.412885	-0.412885	-0.412885	-0.412885	-0.412885	-0.412885	-0.412885
3253	Ceramic Wall And Floor Tile	1	-0.412885	-0.412885	-0.412885	-0.412885	-0.412885	-0.412885	-0.412885	-0.412885	-0.412885	-0.412885	-0.412885
326	POTTERY AND RELATED PRODUCTS	1	-1.725670	-1.725670	-1.725670	-1.725670	-1.725670	-1.725670	-1.725670	-1.725670	-1.725670	-1.725670	-1.725670
3264	Porcelain Electrical Supplies	1	-1.725670	-1.725670	-1.725670	-1.725670	-1.725670	-1.725670	-1.725670	-1.725670	-1.725670	-1.725670	-1.725670
327	CONCRETE, GYPSUM, AND PLASTER PRODUCTS	6	0.916665	0.886797	0.311477	0.328010	0.355567	0.631463	0.886797	1.142130	1.542915	1.588113	1.615231
3272	Concrete Products, Except Block And Brick	3	1.098781	1.142130	0.533329	0.551965	0.583027	1.017885	1.142130	1.240366	1.584192	1.608751	1.623486
3273	Ready-Mixed Concrete	1	0.300454	0.300454	0.300454	0.300454	0.300454	0.300454	0.300454	0.300454	0.300454	0.300454	0.300454
3274	Lime	1	0.631463	0.631463	0.631463	0.631463	0.631463	0.631463	0.631463	0.631463	0.631463	0.631463	0.631463
3275	Gypsum Products	1	1.271730	1.271730	1.271730	1.271730	1.271730	1.271730	1.271730	1.271730	1.271730	1.271730	1.271730
33	PRIMARY METAL INDUSTRIES	39	1.586444	1.604640	-0.477521	-0.130138	0.124417	1.467300	1.604640	1.790584	3.022016	3.200745	3.231804
331	STEEL WORKS, BLAST FURNACES, AND ROLLING AND FINISHING MILLS	21	1.642272	1.567670	-0.049870	0.024825	0.149315	1.471580	1.567670	1.791090	3.198020	3.225265	3.241612
3312	Steel Works, Blast Furnaces (Including Coke Ovens), And Rolling Mills	15	1.735201	1.768500	0.228228	0.346597	0.543880	1.559654	1.768500	1.822938	3.077475	3.164993	3.217503

Down-market Betas of Common Stocks by SIC Codes as of March 31, 2017

SIC Code	Description	Number of Companies	Mean	Median	1st Percentile	2.5th Percentile	5th Percentile	40th Percentile	50th Percentile	60th Percentile	95th Percentile	97.5th Percentile	99th Percentile
3313	Electrometallurgical Products, Except Steel	1	1.471580	1.471580	1.471580	1.471580	1.471580	1.471580	1.471580	1.471580	1.471580	1.471580	1.471580
3315	Steel Wiredrawing And Steel Nails And Spikes	1	0.851044	0.851044	0.851044	0.851044	0.851044	0.851044	0.851044	0.851044	0.851044	0.851044	0.851044
3316	Cold-Rolled Steel Sheet, Strip, And Bars	1	2.594040	2.594040	2.594040	2.594040	2.594040	2.594040	2.594040	2.594040	2.594040	2.594040	2.594040
3317	Steel Pipe And Tubes	3	1.181007	0.444667	-0.088779	-0.072449	-0.045232	0.335800	0.444667	0.995338	2.922685	3.060352	3.142953
332	IRON AND STEEL FOUNDRIES	1	1.005750	1.005750	1.005750	1.005750	1.005750	1.005750	1.005750	1.005750	1.005750	1.005750	1.005750
3324	Steel Investment Foundries	1	1.005750	1.005750	1.005750	1.005750	1.005750	1.005750	1.005750	1.005750	1.005750	1.005750	1.005750
333	PRIMARY SMELTING AND REFINING OF NONFERROUS METALS	5	1.630210	2.095090	0.277756	0.305125	0.350742	1.543323	2.095090	2.258306	2.562746	2.570198	2.574669
3334	Primary Production Of Aluminum	2	2.540390	2.540390	2.503875	2.504993	2.506856	2.532938	2.540390	2.547842	2.573924	2.575787	2.576905
3339	Primary Smelting And Refining Of Nonferrous Metals, Except Copper	3	1.023424	0.715673	0.268632	0.282317	0.305125	0.624440	0.715673	0.991556	1.957148	2.026119	2.067502
335	ROLLING, DRAWING, AND EXTRUDING OF NONFERROUS METALS	12	1.518901	1.673290	-0.590918	-0.413629	-0.118149	1.521594	1.673290	1.769912	2.525579	2.638309	2.705948
3351	Rolling, Drawing, And Extruding Of Copper	3	1.604270	1.604640	1.468998	1.473151	1.480071	1.576958	1.604640	1.632100	1.728210	1.735075	1.739194
3353	Aluminum Sheet, Plate, And Foil	1	2.341110	2.341110	2.341110	2.341110	2.341110	2.341110	2.341110	2.341110	2.341110	2.341110	2.341110
3356	Rolling, Drawing, And Extruding Of Nonferrous Metals, Except Copper	1	2.093070	2.093070	2.093070	2.093070	2.093070	2.093070	2.093070	2.093070	2.093070	2.093070	2.093070
3357	Drawing And Insulating Of Nonferrous Wire	7	1.282832	1.417720	-0.644642	-0.547939	-0.386768	1.357834	1.417720	1.640224	2.540230	2.645635	2.708878
34	FABRICATED METAL PRODUCTS, EXCEPT MACHINERY AND TRANSPORTATION EQUIPMENT	42	1.013755	1.212370	-1.173015	-0.990300	-0.277679	1.083084	1.212370	1.419042	1.875078	1.957638	2.118557
341	METAL CANS AND SHIPPING CONTAINERS	5	1.124078	1.238530	0.131645	0.189988	0.287226	1.169170	1.238530	1.316818	1.718634	1.754182	1.775511
3411	Metal Cans	4	1.381910	1.336390	1.070332	1.078135	1.091140	1.277674	1.336390	1.395106	1.736408	1.763069	1.779066
3412	Metal Shipping Barrels, Drums, Kegs, And Pails	1	0.092750	0.092750	0.092750	0.092750	0.092750	0.092750	0.092750	0.092750	0.092750	0.092750	0.092750
342	CUTLERY, HANDTOOLS, AND GENERAL HARDWARE	7	0.584386	0.399009	-0.255459	-0.210284	-0.134994	0.337591	0.399009	0.729575	1.314681	1.357826	1.383712
3421	Cutlery	2	0.056717	0.056717	-0.278729	-0.268460	-0.251346	-0.011741	0.056717	0.125175	0.364780	0.381894	0.392163
3423	Hand And Edge Tools, Except Machine Tools And Handsaws	1	0.949952	0.949952	0.949952	0.949952	0.949952	0.949952	0.949952	0.949952	0.949952	0.949952	0.949952
3429	Hardware, Not Elsewhere Classified	4	0.756829	0.704993	0.218770	0.222383	0.228404	0.459984	0.704993	0.950001	1.357826	1.379398	1.392341
343	HEATING EQUIPMENT, EXCEPT ELECTRIC AND WARM AIR; AND PLUMBING FIXTURES	3	0.613826	0.658427	0.113278	0.129966	0.157780	0.547172	0.658427	0.742922	1.038653	1.059776	1.072451
3433	Heating Equipment, Except Electric And Warm Air Furnaces	3	0.613826	0.658427	0.113278	0.129966	0.157780	0.547172	0.658427	0.742922	1.038653	1.059776	1.072451
344	FABRICATED STRUCTURAL METAL PRODUCTS	9	1.577654	1.571470	1.094348	1.106330	1.126300	1.480678	1.571470	1.587358	2.089222	2.159106	2.201036

Down-market Betas of Common Stocks by SIC Codes as of March 31, 2017

SIC Code	Description	Number of Companies	Mean	Median	1st Percentile	2.5th Percentile	5th Percentile	40th Percentile	50th Percentile	60th Percentile	95th Percentile	97.5th Percentile	99th Percentile
3441	Fabricated Structural Metal	2	1.611935	1.611935	1.461059	1.465678	1.473376	1.581144	1.611935	1.642726	1.750495	1.758192	1.762811
3442	Metal Doors, Sash, Frames, Molding, And Trim	3	1.633997	1.591330	1.434295	1.439102	1.447114	1.559282	1.591330	1.648978	1.850746	1.865158	1.873805
3443	Fabricated Plate Work (Boiler Shops)	2	1.657675	1.657675	1.097786	1.114926	1.143492	1.543412	1.657675	1.771938	2.171859	2.200424	2.217564
3448	Prefabricated Metal Buildings And Components	2	1.378840	1.378840	1.190063	1.195842	1.205473	1.340314	1.378840	1.417366	1.552207	1.561839	1.567617
345	SCREW MACHINE PRODUCTS, AND BOLTS, NUTS, SCREWS, RIVETS, AND WASHERS	4	0.299842	0.170315	-0.122565	-0.114920	-0.102180	0.093453	0.170315	0.247176	0.883202	0.934800	0.965760
3451	Screw Machine Products	1	0.986399	0.986399	0.986399	0.986399	0.986399	0.986399	0.986399	0.986399	0.986399	0.986399	0.986399
3452	Bolts, Nuts, Screws, Rivets, And Washers	3	0.070990	0.042213	-0.124264	-0.119167	-0.110674	0.008238	0.042213	0.093453	0.272797	0.285607	0.293293
346	METAL FORGINGS AND STAMPINGS	4	1.676768	1.628420	1.491710	1.493391	1.496191	1.568126	1.628420	1.688714	1.925031	1.942335	1.952718
3463	Nonferrous Forgings	1	1.959640	1.959640	1.959640	1.959640	1.959640	1.959640	1.959640	1.959640	1.959640	1.959640	1.959640
3465	Automotive Stampings	2	1.628420	1.628420	1.529940	1.532955	1.537979	1.608322	1.628420	1.648518	1.718861	1.723886	1.726900
3469	Metal Stampings, Not Elsewhere Classified	1	1.490590	1.490590	1.490590	1.490590	1.490590	1.490590	1.490590	1.490590	1.490590	1.490590	1.490590
347	COATING, ENGRAVING, AND ALLIED SERVICES	1	1.546070	1.546070	1.546070	1.546070	1.546070	1.546070	1.546070	1.546070	1.546070	1.546070	1.546070
3479	Coating, Engraving, And Allied Services, Not Elsewhere Classified	1	1.546070	1.546070	1.546070	1.546070	1.546070	1.546070	1.546070	1.546070	1.546070	1.546070	1.546070
348	ORDNANCE AND ACCESSORIES, EXCEPT VEHICLES AND GUIDED MISSILES	2	0.019370	0.019370	-0.987815	-0.956983	-0.905596	-0.186178	0.019370	0.224918	0.944336	0.995723	1.026555
3484	Small Arms	2	0.019370	0.019370	-0.987815	-0.956983	-0.905596	-0.186178	0.019370	0.224918	0.944336	0.995723	1.026555
349	MISCELLANEOUS FABRICATED METAL PRODUCTS	7	1.047860	1.372790	-1.142874	-0.926040	-0.564649	1.361786	1.372790	1.441508	1.664491	1.680591	1.690250
3491	Industrial Valves	3	1.435283	1.487320	1.129150	1.140114	1.158388	1.414224	1.487320	1.529194	1.675753	1.686222	1.692503
3495	Wire Springs	1	1.354450	1.354450	1.354450	1.354450	1.354450	1.354450	1.354450	1.354450	1.354450	1.354450	1.354450
3499	Fabricated Metal Products, Not Elsewhere Classified	3	0.558240	1.372790	-1.234226	-1.154419	-1.021408	0.840746	1.372790	1.416104	1.567703	1.578532	1.585029
35	INDUSTRIAL AND COMMERCIAL MACHINERY AND COMPUTER EQUIPMENT	176	1.448536	1.413510	-1.270630	-0.452194	0.192353	1.269310	1.413510	1.569680	2.418868	2.942174	3.307395
351	ENGINES AND TURBINES	9	1.606716	1.569990	0.993467	1.000852	1.013162	1.562014	1.569990	1.636222	2.301914	2.343452	2.368375
3511	Steam, Gas, And Hydraulic Turbines, And Turbine Generator Set Units	5	1.591380	1.652780	1.058350	1.070740	1.091390	1.494304	1.652780	1.719724	2.105868	2.141584	2.163014
3519	Internal Combustion Engines, Not Elsewhere Classified	4	1.625886	1.565005	1.005687	1.031404	1.074265	1.562014	1.565005	1.567996	2.262740	2.323865	2.360540
352	FARM AND GARDEN MACHINERY AND EQUIPMENT	10	1.230258	1.179890	0.492597	0.521441	0.569514	1.146914	1.179890	1.222094	1.986592	2.076531	2.130494
3523	Farm Machinery And Equipment	8	1.231618	1.146495	0.488324	0.510758	0.548148	1.094725	1.146495	1.232936	2.026565	2.096517	2.138489
3524	Lawn And Garden Tractors And Home Lawn And Garden Equipment	2	1.224820	1.224820	1.211463	1.211872	1.212553	1.222094	1.224820	1.227546	1.237087	1.237769	1.238177

Down-market Betas of Common Stocks by SIC Codes as of March 31, 2017

SIC Code	Description	Number of Companies	Mean	Median	1st Percentile	2.5th Percentile	5th Percentile	40th Percentile	50th Percentile	60th Percentile	95th Percentile	97.5th Percentile	99th Percentile
353	CONSTRUCTION, MINING, AND MATERIALS HANDLING MACHINERY AND EQUIPMENT	25	1.233534	1.443700	-0.315644	-0.084568	0.201032	1.211720	1.443700	1.557748	1.993520	2.044302	2.063555
3531	Construction Machinery And Equipment	6	0.742219	0.913392	-0.430388	-0.371428	-0.273163	0.781013	0.913392	1.045770	1.438833	1.463301	1.477983
3532	Mining Machinery And Equipment, Except Oil And Gas Field Machinery	4	1.593492	1.875895	0.581279	0.634518	0.723250	1.787686	1.875895	1.964104	2.068368	2.072379	2.074786
3533	Oil And Gas Field Machinery And Equipment	9	1.288450	1.443700	0.243739	0.351076	0.529969	1.440220	1.443700	1.537468	1.629146	1.639128	1.645117
3535	Conveyors And Conveying Equipment	1	1.587380	1.587380	1.587380	1.587380	1.587380	1.587380	1.587380	1.587380	1.587380	1.587380	1.587380
3536	Overhead Traveling Cranes, Hoists, And Monorail Systems	1	1.864800	1.864800	1.864800	1.864800	1.864800	1.864800	1.864800	1.864800	1.864800	1.864800	1.864800
3537	Industrial Trucks, Tractors, Trailers, And Stackers	4	1.240713	1.322255	0.461776	0.490868	0.539354	1.182224	1.322255	1.462286	1.827912	1.851936	1.866350
354	METALWORKING MACHINERY AND EQUIPMENT	9	1.557759	1.953710	0.089042	0.204336	0.396492	1.446694	1.953710	1.971358	2.305392	2.317376	2.324566
3541	Machine Tools, Metal Cutting Types	4	1.597340	1.647855	0.983369	0.998984	1.025007	1.451106	1.647855	1.844604	2.098952	2.109821	2.116342
3542	Machine Tools, Metal Forming Types	2	1.667610	1.667610	1.077817	1.095872	1.125963	1.547244	1.667610	1.787976	2.209257	2.239349	2.257403
3545	Cutting Tools, Machine Tool Accessories, And Machinists' Precision Tools	1	1.953710	1.953710	1.953710	1.953710	1.953710	1.953710	1.953710	1.953710	1.953710	1.953710	1.953710
3546	Power-Driven Handtools	1	0.012180	0.012180	0.012180	0.012180	0.012180	0.012180	0.012180	0.012180	0.012180	0.012180	0.012180
3549	Metalworking Machinery, Not Elsewhere Classified	1	2.329360	2.329360	2.329360	2.329360	2.329360	2.329360	2.329360	2.329360	2.329360	2.329360	2.329360
355	SPECIAL INDUSTRY MACHINERY, EXCEPT METALWORKING MACHINERY	21	1.311762	1.474890	-0.298606	-0.111975	0.199076	1.270120	1.474890	1.554530	2.081750	2.204495	2.278142
3554	Paper Industries Machinery	1	0.978182	0.978182	0.978182	0.978182	0.978182	0.978182	0.978182	0.978182	0.978182	0.978182	0.978182
3555	Printing Trades Machinery And Equipment	2	1.233232	1.233232	0.442402	0.466611	0.506960	1.071838	1.233232	1.394625	1.959503	1.999852	2.024061
3556	Food Products Machinery	1	0.199076	0.199076	0.199076	0.199076	0.199076	0.199076	0.199076	0.199076	0.199076	0.199076	0.199076
3559	Special Industry Machinery, Not Elsewhere Classified	17	1.406075	1.549870	-0.221526	0.080725	0.584476	1.433604	1.549870	1.560962	2.130848	2.229044	2.287962
356	GENERAL INDUSTRIAL MACHINERY AND EQUIPMENT	29	1.415297	1.382700	0.174971	0.288503	0.507865	1.317104	1.382700	1.452382	2.522678	2.928647	3.136711
3561	Pumps And Pumping Equipment	9	1.763554	1.576530	1.273731	1.279178	1.288256	1.427138	1.576530	1.889090	2.522678	2.651354	2.728560
3562	Ball And Roller Bearings	4	1.856686	1.687595	0.794509	0.822070	0.868005	1.508198	1.687595	1.866992	3.082096	3.178758	3.236755
3564	Industrial And Commercial Fans And Blowers And Air Purification Equipment	5	0.976071	0.754359	0.715890	0.716824	0.718382	0.744951	0.754359	0.883123	1.498150	1.550885	1.582526
3566	Speed Changers, Industrial High-Speed Drives, And Gears	1	1.468030	1.468030	1.468030	1.468030	1.468030	1.468030	1.468030	1.468030	1.468030	1.468030	1.468030

Down-market Betas of Common Stocks by SIC Codes as of March 31, 2017

SIC Code	Description	Number of Companies	Mean	Median	1st Percentile	2.5th Percentile	5th Percentile	40th Percentile	50th Percentile	60th Percentile	95th Percentile	97.5th Percentile	99th Percentile
3568	Mechanical Power Transmission Equipment, Not Elsewhere Classified	1	2.103070	2.103070	2.103070	2.103070	2.103070	2.103070	2.103070	2.103070	2.103070	2.103070	2.103070
3569	General Industrial Machinery And Equipment, Not Elsewhere Classified	9	1.032602	1.001430	0.120909	0.153346	0.207409	0.866094	1.001430	1.259134	1.836486	1.913408	1.959561
357	COMPUTER AND OFFICE EQUIPMENT	58	1.727193	1.587160	-1.493173	-0.620660	0.322276	1.327670	1.587160	1.740026	2.756644	3.268778	9.795648
3571	Electronic Computers	12	1.220599	1.199315	0.428388	0.471557	0.543507	1.040132	1.199315	1.287746	1.982216	2.048238	2.087851
3572	Computer Storage Devices	8	1.375313	1.574270	-1.164453	-1.003613	-0.735546	1.407818	1.574270	1.767652	2.879837	2.983294	3.045367
3576	COMPUTER COMMUNICATIONS EQUIPMENT	9	3.182921	1.550980	0.336921	0.342437	0.351631	0.900761	1.550980	1.893212	11.941832	15.105516	17.003726
3577	Computer Peripheral Equipment, Not Elsewhere Classified	21	1.491687	1.669710	-1.276161	-0.510232	0.766316	1.414300	1.669710	1.727010	2.344380	2.873850	3.191532
3578	Calculating And Accounting Machines, Except Electronic Computers	6	1.829893	1.775540	1.040347	1.060428	1.093895	1.739700	1.775540	1.811380	2.625850	2.662120	2.683882
3579	Office Machines, Not Elsewhere Classified	2	1.788220	1.788220	1.774853	1.775262	1.775944	1.785492	1.788220	1.790948	1.800496	1.801178	1.801587
358	REFRIGERATION AND SERVICE INDUSTRY MACHINERY	11	0.672835	1.045960	-1.240348	-1.195451	-1.120622	1.038610	1.045960	1.088650	1.370475	1.392863	1.406295
3580	REFRIGERATION & SERVICE INDUSTRY MACHINERY	2	-0.009957	-0.009957	-0.951744	-0.922914	-0.874863	-0.202158	-0.009957	0.182245	0.854950	0.903001	0.931831
3585	Air-Conditioning And Warm Air Heating Equipment	3	1.124557	1.088650	1.039611	1.041112	1.043614	1.078642	1.088650	1.120202	1.230634	1.238522	1.243255
3589	Service Industry Machinery, Not Elsewhere Classified	6	0.674571	1.178615	-1.195790	-1.084054	-0.897829	1.045960	1.178615	1.311270	1.392863	1.404056	1.410773
359	MISCELLANEOUS INDUSTRIAL AND COMMERCIAL MACHINERY AND EQUIPMENT	4	1.788009	1.575975	0.974899	0.996308	1.031991	1.492224	1.575975	1.659726	2.840875	2.940168	2.999743
3592	Carburetors, Pistons, Piston Rings, And Valves	1	1.436390	1.436390	1.436390	1.436390	1.436390	1.436390	1.436390	1.436390	1.436390	1.436390	1.436390
3594	Fluid Power Pumps And Motors	1	1.715560	1.715560	1.715560	1.715560	1.715560	1.715560	1.715560	1.715560	1.715560	1.715560	1.715560
3596	Scales And Balances, Except Laboratory	1	0.960626	0.960626	0.960626	0.960626	0.960626	0.960626	0.960626	0.960626	0.960626	0.960626	0.960626
3599	Industrial And Commercial Machinery And Equipment, Not Elsewhere Classified	1	3.039460	3.039460	3.039460	3.039460	3.039460	3.039460	3.039460	3.039460	3.039460	3.039460	3.039460
36	ELECTRONIC AND OTHER ELECTRICAL EQUIPMENT AND COMPONENTS, EXCEPT COMPUTER	266	1.282050	1.377960	-1.087803	-0.690381	-0.192356	1.217270	1.377960	1.505560	2.448325	2.686191	3.250014
361	ELECTRIC TRANSMISSION AND DISTRIBUTION EQUIPMENT	5	1.809552	1.460920	0.836243	0.857835	0.893821	1.349236	1.460920	1.742560	3.167612	3.292936	3.368130
3612	Power, Distribution, And Specialty Transformers	3	2.135043	2.165020	0.848712	0.889008	0.956166	1.896386	2.165020	2.415668	3.292936	3.355598	3.393195
3613	Switchgear And Switchboard Apparatus	2	1.321315	1.321315	1.184502	1.188690	1.195671	1.293394	1.321315	1.349236	1.446960	1.453940	1.458128

Down-market Betas of Common Stocks by SIC Codes as of March 31, 2017

SIC Code	Description	Number of Companies	Mean	Median	1st Percentile	2.5th Percentile	5th Percentile	40th Percentile	50th Percentile	60th Percentile	95th Percentile	97.5th Percentile	99th Percentile
362	ELECTRICAL INDUSTRIAL APPARATUS	18	1.260154	1.315355	0.503665	0.558181	0.649042	1.249006	1.315355	1.365572	1.840738	1.867364	1.883340
3621	Motors And Generators	11	1.286334	1.336020	0.681303	0.681593	0.682075	1.294690	1.336020	1.368420	1.862665	1.878328	1.887725
3625	Relays And Industrial Controls	3	0.951140	1.168830	0.481351	0.502396	0.537472	1.028528	1.168830	1.178518	1.212426	1.214848	1.216301
3629	Electrical Industrial Apparatus, Not Elsewhere Classified	4	1.419920	1.433790	1.260178	1.265034	1.273128	1.392432	1.433790	1.475148	1.547294	1.551227	1.553587
363	HOUSEHOLD APPLIANCES	5	1.260786	1.420150	0.728580	0.734286	0.743794	1.180036	1.420150	1.464874	1.752136	1.779658	1.796171
3632	Household Refrigerators And Home And Farm Freezers	1	1.531960	1.531960	1.531960	1.531960	1.531960	1.531960	1.531960	1.531960	1.531960	1.531960	1.531960
3633	Household Laundry Equipment	2	1.313522	1.313522	0.829737	0.844547	0.869230	1.214790	1.313522	1.412254	1.757814	1.782497	1.797307
3634	Electric Housewares And Fans	2	1.072464	1.072464	0.731731	0.742161	0.759546	1.002926	1.072464	1.142001	1.385381	1.402766	1.413196
364	ELECTRIC LIGHTING AND WIRING EQUIPMENT	9	1.041355	1.281410	-0.622543	-0.462398	-0.195489	1.054754	1.281410	1.372490	1.688290	1.696850	1.701986
3640	ELECTRIC LIGHTING & WIRING EQUIPMENT	1	1.662610	1.662610	1.662610	1.662610	1.662610	1.662610	1.662610	1.662610	1.662610	1.662610	1.662610
3641	Electric Lamp Bulbs And Tubes	3	1.282915	1.395260	0.995249	1.007495	1.027903	1.313625	1.395260	1.409488	1.459286	1.462843	1.464977
3643	Current-Carrying Wiring Devices	1	0.998090	0.998090	0.998090	0.998090	0.998090	0.998090	0.998090	0.998090	0.998090	0.998090	0.998090
3645	Residential Electric Lighting Fixtures	2	-0.062035	-0.062035	-0.715962	-0.695943	-0.662580	-0.195489	-0.062035	0.071420	0.538511	0.571874	0.591893
3646	Commercial, Industrial, And Institutional Electric Lighting Fixtures	2	1.493410	1.493410	1.285650	1.292010	1.302610	1.451010	1.493410	1.535810	1.684210	1.694810	1.701170
365	HOUSEHOLD AUDIO AND VIDEO EQUIPMENT, AND AUDIO RECORDINGS	7	0.822444	0.936664	-1.808163	-1.579687	-1.198895	0.834672	0.936664	1.063172	2.314728	2.442549	2.519242
3651	Household Audio And Video Equipment	7	0.822444	0.936664	-1.808163	-1.579687	-1.198895	0.834672	0.936664	1.063172	2.314728	2.442549	2.519242
366	COMMUNICATIONS EQUIPMENT	72	1.133729	1.187990	-1.087494	-0.866379	-0.308545	1.043718	1.187990	1.352328	2.438473	2.643406	3.444190
3661	Telephone And Telegraph Apparatus	19	1.344573	1.491040	-0.646863	-0.413232	-0.023845	1.357872	1.491040	1.562696	2.638682	3.630221	4.225144
3663	Radio And Television Broadcasting And Communications Equipment	37	1.172008	1.228170	-0.233221	0.079458	0.269649	1.078448	1.228170	1.352296	2.059854	2.294204	2.695608
3669	Communications Equipment, Not Elsewhere Classified	16	0.794832	0.932775	-1.090378	-1.089219	-1.087288	0.641996	0.932775	1.037030	2.484950	2.517755	2.537438
367	ELECTRONIC COMPONENTS AND ACCESSORIES	130	1.409332	1.504900	-0.602779	-0.401141	-0.128244	1.387344	1.504900	1.625608	2.418041	2.649830	3.093433
3671	Electron Tubes	1	1.480990	1.480990	1.480990	1.480990	1.480990	1.480990	1.480990	1.480990	1.480990	1.480990	1.480990
3672	Printed Circuit Boards	14	1.303614	1.577615	0.115164	0.123185	0.136554	1.537258	1.577615	1.631932	2.000181	2.072340	2.115636
3674	Semiconductors And Related Devices	94	1.508686	1.536760	-0.692345	-0.388225	-0.097645	1.428144	1.536760	1.706298	2.512413	2.843701	3.517086
3675	Electronic Capacitors	1	1.838720	1.838720	1.838720	1.838720	1.838720	1.838720	1.838720	1.838720	1.838720	1.838720	1.838720
3676	Electronic Resistors	1	0.747726	0.747726	0.747726	0.747726	0.747726	0.747726	0.747726	0.747726	0.747726	0.747726	0.747726
3677	Electronic Coils, Transformers, And Other Inductors	2	1.377960	1.377960	1.165045	1.171563	1.182426	1.334508	1.377960	1.421412	1.573494	1.584357	1.590875
3678	Electronic Connectors	4	0.882215	1.136455	-0.009241	0.041294	0.125519	1.102624	1.136455	1.170286	1.282974	1.290927	1.295699
3679	Electronic Components, Not Elsewhere Classified	13	0.984139	1.076800	-0.412493	-0.363006	-0.280527	0.959867	1.076800	1.359116	2.126596	2.313718	2.425991

Down-market Betas of Common Stocks by SIC Codes as of March 31, 2017

SIC Code	Description	Number of Companies	Mean	Median	1st Percentile	2.5th Percentile	5th Percentile	40th Percentile	50th Percentile	60th Percentile	95th Percentile	97.5th Percentile	99th Percentile
369	MISCELLANEOUS ELECTRICAL MACHINERY, EQUIPMENT, AND SUPPLIES	20	1.150996	1.353565	-2.815916	-1.946959	-0.498698	1.180330	1.353565	1.476046	2.243185	2.486047	2.631765
3691	Storage Batteries	9	1.375592	1.340890	0.792758	0.796340	0.802310	1.211242	1.340890	1.361170	2.162412	2.190016	2.206578
3692	Primary Batteries, Dry And Wet	2	1.191330	1.191330	-0.315498	-0.269371	-0.192492	0.883814	1.191330	1.498846	2.575152	2.652031	2.698158
3694	Electrical Equipment For Internal Combustion Engines	1	0.825376	0.825376	0.825376	0.825376	0.825376	0.825376	0.825376	0.825376	0.825376	0.825376	0.825376
3695	Magnetic And Optical Recording Media	4	1.529705	1.606915	1.193814	1.212540	1.243750	1.601242	1.606915	1.612588	1.707567	1.715613	1.720441
3699	Electrical Machinery, Equipment, And Supplies, Not Elsewhere Classified	4	0.328185	1.322980	-3.259214	-3.055204	-2.715188	1.212190	1.322980	1.433770	1.978845	2.020422	2.045369
37	TRANSPORTATION EQUIPMENT	100	1.420247	1.422730	-0.985644	0.090410	0.352617	1.266632	1.422730	1.634942	2.574801	2.735554	2.941867
371	MOTOR VEHICLES AND MOTOR VEHICLE EQUIPMENT	56	1.605286	1.697905	-0.258455	0.355104	0.389535	1.461420	1.697905	1.813080	2.628655	2.875978	2.958433
3711	Motor Vehicles And Passenger Car Bodies	19	1.274887	1.367640	-0.761349	-0.393067	0.220735	1.248404	1.367640	1.667700	2.238250	2.242885	2.245666
3713	Truck And Bus Bodies	2	1.699805	1.699805	1.676888	1.677589	1.678759	1.695128	1.699805	1.704482	1.720852	1.722021	1.722722
3714	Motor Vehicle Parts And Accessories	32	1.789319	1.926025	0.408079	0.489372	0.551096	1.592050	1.926025	2.068866	2.845405	2.949961	2.967469
3715	Truck Trailers	1	1.735490	1.735490	1.735490	1.735490	1.735490	1.735490	1.735490	1.735490	1.735490	1.735490	1.735490
3716	Motor Homes	2	1.639920	1.639920	1.604032	1.605131	1.606962	1.632596	1.639920	1.647244	1.672878	1.674709	1.675808
372	AIRCRAFT AND PARTS	28	1.217498	1.110900	0.013677	0.188361	0.442023	0.995451	1.110900	1.303486	2.099744	2.329746	2.552517
3721	Aircraft	9	1.454637	1.369160	0.883497	0.891348	0.904432	1.352256	1.369160	1.456512	2.338310	2.519670	2.628486
3724	Aircraft Engines And Engine Parts	7	0.947707	0.817728	0.353006	0.389707	0.450875	0.817614	0.817728	0.932149	1.610777	1.721839	1.788475
3728	Aircraft Parts And Auxiliary Equipment, Not Elsewhere Classified	12	1.197023	1.140940	-0.019668	0.104999	0.312778	1.029990	1.140940	1.236438	2.070466	2.110723	2.134877
373	SHIP AND BOAT BUILDING AND REPAIRING	4	1.102609	0.772411	0.317463	0.337755	0.371574	0.761882	0.772411	0.782940	2.295922	2.428801	2.508528
3731	Ship Building And Repairing	2	0.546948	0.546948	0.308795	0.316086	0.328236	0.498345	0.546948	0.595550	0.765659	0.777809	0.785100
3732	Boat Building And Repairing	2	1.658271	1.658271	0.772930	0.800032	0.845203	1.477589	1.658271	1.838953	2.471339	2.516510	2.543612
374	RAILROAD EQUIPMENT	5	1.453258	1.373250	1.349949	1.350652	1.351824	1.368430	1.373250	1.390498	1.696066	1.731028	1.752005
3743	Railroad Equipment	5	1.453258	1.373250	1.349949	1.350652	1.351824	1.368430	1.373250	1.390498	1.696066	1.731028	1.752005
375	MOTORCYCLES, BICYCLES, AND PARTS	2	1.905510	1.905510	1.768330	1.772529	1.779528	1.877514	1.905510	1.933506	2.031492	2.038491	2.042690
3751	Motorcycles, Bicycles, And Parts	2	1.905510	1.905510	1.768330	1.772529	1.779528	1.877514	1.905510	1.933506	2.031492	2.038491	2.042690
376	GUIDED MISSILES AND SPACE VEHICLES AND PARTS	3	0.088997	0.355624	-0.958609	-0.918377	-0.851325	0.087413	0.355624	0.463859	0.842680	0.869738	0.885974
3761	Guided Missiles And Space Vehicles	1	0.355624	0.355624	0.355624	0.355624	0.355624	0.355624	0.355624	0.355624	0.355624	0.355624	0.355624
3764	Guided Missile And Space Vehicle Propulsion Units And Propulsion	1	0.896797	0.896797	0.896797	0.896797	0.896797	0.896797	0.896797	0.896797	0.896797	0.896797	0.896797
3769	Guided Missile And Space Vehicle Parts And Auxiliary Equipment, Not Elsewhere Classified	1	-0.985430	-0.985430	-0.985430	-0.985430	-0.985430	-0.985430	-0.985430	-0.985430	-0.985430	-0.985430	-0.985430
379	MISCELLANEOUS TRANSPORTATION EQUIPMENT	2	1.142009	1.142009	0.833435	0.842882	0.858625	1.079035	1.142009	1.204983	1.425393	1.441136	1.450583

Down-market Betas of Common Stocks by SIC Codes as of March 31, 2017

SIC Code	Description	Number of Companies	Mean	Median	1st Percentile	2.5th Percentile	5th Percentile	40th Percentile	50th Percentile	60th Percentile	95th Percentile	97.5th Percentile	99th Percentile
3795	Tanks And Tank Components	1	0.827138	0.827138	0.827138	0.827138	0.827138	0.827138	0.827138	0.827138	0.827138	0.827138	0.827138
3799	Transportation Equipment, Not Elsewhere Classified	1	1.456880	1.456880	1.456880	1.456880	1.456880	1.456880	1.456880	1.456880	1.456880	1.456880	1.456880
38	MEASURING, ANALYZING, AND CONTROLLING INSTRUMENTS; PHOTOGRAPHIC, MEDICAL	259	1.085889	1.114430	-1.247353	-0.870685	-0.326319	0.913502	1.114430	1.291884	2.371081	2.854121	3.569149
381	SEARCH, DETECTION, NAVIGATION, GUIDANCE, AERONAUTICAL, AND NAUTICAL	14	1.262218	1.201410	0.316033	0.317246	0.319267	1.132414	1.201410	1.400838	2.266006	2.301538	2.322857
3812	Search, Detection, Navigation, Guidance, Aeronautical, And Nautical	14	1.262218	1.201410	0.316033	0.317246	0.319267	1.132414	1.201410	1.400838	2.266006	2.301538	2.322857
382	LABORATORY APPARATUS AND ANALYTICAL, OPTICAL, MEASURING, AND CONTROL	92	1.096322	1.140710	-0.982821	-0.326273	-0.220619	0.908833	1.140710	1.448102	2.200541	2.262944	2.661724
3821	Laboratory Apparatus And Furniture	3	0.784846	0.138630	-0.053737	-0.047848	-0.038034	0.099371	0.138630	0.565618	2.060076	2.166823	2.230871
3822	Automatic Controls For Regulating Residential And Commercial Environment	3	1.136260	1.670310	-0.035342	0.016872	0.103895	1.322218	1.670310	1.697972	1.794789	1.801705	1.805854
3823	Industrial Instruments For Measurement, Display, And Control Of Processes	16	0.994108	0.988136	-0.240302	-0.205200	-0.146696	0.918810	0.988136	1.131080	2.034083	2.134001	2.193953
3824	Totalizing Fluid Meters And Counting Devices	1	1.191040	1.191040	1.191040	1.191040	1.191040	1.191040	1.191040	1.191040	1.191040	1.191040	1.191040
3825	Instruments For Measuring And Testing Of Electricity And Electric	22	1.087134	1.129600	-0.222168	-0.220733	-0.200832	0.927592	1.129600	1.376754	1.948406	1.994004	2.022808
3826	Laboratory Analytical Instruments	19	1.330477	1.393310	0.166356	0.176532	0.193490	0.884093	1.393310	1.508338	2.392870	3.103600	3.530038
3827	Optical Instruments And Lenses	8	1.236266	1.212800	0.533074	0.563780	0.614956	1.113054	1.212800	1.309036	1.889901	1.913800	1.928140
3829	Measuring And Controlling Devices, Not Elsewhere Classified	20	0.945769	1.300660	-1.345091	-1.201692	-0.962695	0.852624	1.300660	1.476078	2.113200	2.330465	2.460824
384	SURGICAL, MEDICAL, AND DENTAL INSTRUMENTS AND SUPPLIES	143	1.058130	1.075000	-1.361106	-1.043598	-0.556621	0.908824	1.075000	1.212396	2.657867	3.294429	3.598371
3841	Surgical And Medical Instruments And Apparatus	84	1.047393	1.083750	-1.648429	-1.099729	-0.612950	0.911078	1.083750	1.201714	2.662884	3.289971	3.523489
3842	Orthopedic, Prosthetic, And Surgical Appliances And Supplies	20	1.047694	0.987786	-0.478277	-0.350730	-0.138151	0.894639	0.987786	1.155558	2.059348	2.272504	2.400398
3843	Dental Equipment And Supplies	5	1.267650	1.206650	-1.002852	-0.872311	-0.654742	1.158314	1.206650	1.258634	3.306570	3.552815	3.700562
3844	X-Ray Apparatus And Tubes And Related Irradiation Apparatus	2	1.955060	1.955060	1.559836	1.571935	1.592099	1.874402	1.955060	2.035718	2.318021	2.338186	2.350284
3845	Electromedical And Electrotherapeutic Apparatus	32	1.004042	0.972080	-0.606393	-0.384445	-0.062253	0.772081	0.972080	1.143236	2.376897	2.806051	3.085920
385	OPHTHALMIC GOODS	2	0.696554	0.696554	0.439593	0.447459	0.460569	0.644113	0.696554	0.748994	0.932538	0.945648	0.953514
3851	Ophthalmic Goods	2	0.696554	0.696554	0.439593	0.447459	0.460569	0.644113	0.696554	0.748994	0.932538	0.945648	0.953514
386	PHOTOGRAPHIC EQUIPMENT AND SUPPLIES	6	0.972544	1.031108	-0.718059	-0.611680	-0.434382	0.778445	1.031108	1.283770	2.040845	2.078113	2.100473

Down-market Betas of Common Stocks by SIC Codes as of March 31, 2017

SIC Code	Description	Number of Companies	Mean	Median	1st Percentile	2.5th Percentile	5th Percentile	40th Percentile	50th Percentile	60th Percentile	95th Percentile	97.5th Percentile	99th Percentile
3861	Photographic Equipment And Supplies	6	0.972544	1.031108	-0.718059	-0.611680	-0.434382	0.778445	1.031108	1.283770	2.040845	2.078113	2.100473
387	WATCHES, CLOCKS, CLOCKWORK OPERATED DEVICES, AND PARTS	2	2.085815	2.085815	1.393146	1.414350	1.449691	1.944454	2.085815	2.227176	2.721940	2.757280	2.778484
3873	Watches, Clocks, Clockwork Operated Devices, And Parts	2	2.085815	2.085815	1.393146	1.414350	1.449691	1.944454	2.085815	2.227176	2.721940	2.757280	2.778484
39	MISCELLANEOUS MANUFACTURING INDUSTRIES	30	0.905785	0.985212	-1.252823	-1.045123	-0.794238	0.843421	0.985212	1.083944	2.334721	3.348961	4.310029
391	JEWELRY, SILVERWARE, AND PLATED WARE	2	0.346661	0.346661	-0.888608	-0.850794	-0.787770	0.094565	0.346661	0.598757	1.481092	1.544116	1.581930
3911	Jewelry, Precious Metal	2	0.346661	0.346661	-0.888608	-0.850794	-0.787770	0.094565	0.346661	0.598757	1.481092	1.544116	1.581930
394	DOLLS, TOYS, GAMES AND SPORTING AND ATHLETIC GOODS	21	0.877827	0.970900	-1.242649	-1.019688	-0.648085	0.818543	0.970900	1.023350	1.837680	3.394210	4.328128
3942	Dolls And Stuffed Toys	2	1.580710	1.580710	1.328879	1.336589	1.349437	1.529316	1.580710	1.632104	1.811983	1.824832	1.832541
3944	Games, Toys, And Children's Vehicles, Except Dolls And Bicycles	11	0.834086	0.966458	-1.316970	-1.205489	-1.019688	0.622149	0.966458	0.970900	3.199120	4.074930	4.600416
3949	Sporting And Athletic Goods, Not Elsewhere Classified	8	0.762249	0.909033	-0.419704	-0.320530	-0.155239	0.770706	0.909033	1.012354	1.354186	1.380063	1.395589
399	MISCELLANEOUS MANUFACTURING INDUSTRIES	7	1.149409	1.155440	-0.096790	-0.024206	0.096768	0.978180	1.155440	1.260884	2.351486	2.546438	2.663409
3990	MISCELLANEOUS MANUFACTURING INDUSTRIES	1	1.331180	1.331180	1.331180	1.331180	1.331180	1.331180	1.331180	1.331180	1.331180	1.331180	1.331180
3993	Signs And Advertising Specialties	1	-0.145180	-0.145180	-0.145180	-0.145180	-0.145180	-0.145180	-0.145180	-0.145180	-0.145180	-0.145180	-0.145180
3996	Linoleum, Asphalted-Felt-Base, And Other Hard Surface Floor Cover	1	1.441710	1.441710	1.441710	1.441710	1.441710	1.441710	1.441710	1.441710	1.441710	1.441710	1.441710
3999	Manufacturing Industries, Not Elsewhere Classified	4	1.354538	1.007723	0.667275	0.676216	0.691118	0.919093	1.007723	1.096353	2.503498	2.622444	2.693812
	TRANSPORTATION, COMMUNICATIONS, ELECTRIC, GAS, AND SANITARY SERVICE												
40	RAILROAD TRANSPORTATION	7	1.371316	1.250730	0.967061	0.972125	0.980565	1.153404	1.250730	1.293264	2.216185	2.395308	2.502781
401	RAILROADS	7	1.371316	1.250730	0.967061	0.972125	0.980565	1.153404	1.250730	1.293264	2.216185	2.395308	2.502781
4011	Railroads, Line-Haul Operating	7	1.371316	1.250730	0.967061	0.972125	0.980565	1.153404	1.250730	1.293264	2.216185	2.395308	2.502781
41	LOCAL AND SUBURBAN TRANSIT AND INTERURBAN HIGHWAY PASSENGER TRANSPORTATION	1	0.966283	0.966283	0.966283	0.966283	0.966283	0.966283	0.966283	0.966283	0.966283	0.966283	0.966283
415	SCHOOL BUSES	1	0.966283	0.966283	0.966283	0.966283	0.966283	0.966283	0.966283	0.966283	0.966283	0.966283	0.966283
4151	School Buses	1	0.966283	0.966283	0.966283	0.966283	0.966283	0.966283	0.966283	0.966283	0.966283	0.966283	0.966283
42	MOTOR FREIGHT TRANSPORTATION AND WAREHOUSING	22	1.350616	1.297870	0.803500	0.816506	0.836602	1.071018	1.297870	1.497894	2.058000	2.093373	2.113561
421	TRUCKING AND COURIER SERVICES, EXCEPT AIR	21	1.344591	1.227270	0.803087	0.815474	0.836117	1.046270	1.227270	1.511730	2.062930	2.094975	2.114202
4213	Trucking, Except Local	21	1.344591	1.227270	0.803087	0.815474	0.836117	1.046270	1.227270	1.511730	2.062930	2.094975	2.114202
422	PUBLIC WAREHOUSING AND STORAGE	1	1.477140	1.477140	1.477140	1.477140	1.477140	1.477140	1.477140	1.477140	1.477140	1.477140	1.477140
4225	General Warehousing And Storage	1	1.477140	1.477140	1.477140	1.477140	1.477140	1.477140	1.477140	1.477140	1.477140	1.477140	1.477140
44	WATER TRANSPORTATION	46	1.833090	1.748680	-3.830797	0.009822	0.633092	1.602560	1.748680	2.029300	4.178640	4.677250	4.742153

Down-market Betas of Common Stocks by SIC Codes as of March 31, 2017

SIC Code	Description	Number of Companies	Mean	Median	1st Percentile	2.5th Percentile	5th Percentile	40th Percentile	50th Percentile	60th Percentile	95th Percentile	97.5th Percentile	99th Percentile
4400	WATER TRANSPORTATION	1	0.829687	0.829687	0.829687	0.829687	0.829687	0.829687	0.829687	0.829687	0.829687	0.829687	0.829687
441	DEEP SEA FOREIGN TRANSPORTATION OF FREIGHT	34	1.831011	1.797140	-4.650008	-1.270760	0.370595	1.622678	1.797140	2.153996	4.038416	4.350445	4.588510
4412	Deep Sea Foreign Transportation Of Freight	34	1.831011	1.797140	-4.650008	-1.270760	0.370595	1.622678	1.797140	2.153996	4.038416	4.350445	4.588510
442	DEEP SEA DOMESTIC TRANSPORTATION OF FREIGHT	1	1.402270	1.402270	1.402270	1.402270	1.402270	1.402270	1.402270	1.402270	1.402270	1.402270	1.402270
4424	Deep Sea Domestic Transportation Of Freight	1	1.402270	1.402270	1.402270	1.402270	1.402270	1.402270	1.402270	1.402270	1.402270	1.402270	1.402270
443	FREIGHT TRANSPORTATION ON THE GREAT LAKES¨ST. LAWRENCE SEAWAY	1	1.020310	1.020310	1.020310	1.020310	1.020310	1.020310	1.020310	1.020310	1.020310	1.020310	1.020310
4432	Freight Transportation On The Great Lakes¨St. Lawrence Seaway	1	1.020310	1.020310	1.020310	1.020310	1.020310	1.020310	1.020310	1.020310	1.020310	1.020310	1.020310
444	WATER TRANSPORTATION OF FREIGHT, NOT ELSEWHERE CLASSIFIED	1	1.407220	1.407220	1.407220	1.407220	1.407220	1.407220	1.407220	1.407220	1.407220	1.407220	1.407220
4449	Water Transportation Of Freight, Not Elsewhere Classified	1	1.407220	1.407220	1.407220	1.407220	1.407220	1.407220	1.407220	1.407220	1.407220	1.407220	1.407220
448	WATER TRANSPORTATION OF PASSENGERS	3	1.811190	1.691870	1.449389	1.456812	1.469183	1.642384	1.691870	1.812948	2.236721	2.266991	2.285152
4481	Deep Sea Transportation Of Passengers, Except By Ferry	3	1.811190	1.691870	1.449389	1.456812	1.469183	1.642384	1.691870	1.812948	2.236721	2.266991	2.285152
449	SERVICES INCIDENTAL TO WATER TRANSPORTATION	5	2.394942	2.148420	1.158796	1.196156	1.258422	1.991672	2.148420	2.169008	4.228746	4.482353	4.634517
4491	Marine Cargo Handling	1	4.735960	4.735960	4.735960	4.735960	4.735960	4.735960	4.735960	4.735960	4.735960	4.735960	4.735960
4492	Towing And Tugboat Services	1	1.756550	1.756550	1.756550	1.756550	1.756550	1.756550	1.756550	1.756550	1.756550	1.756550	1.756550
4499	Water Transportation Services, Not Elsewhere Classified	3	1.827400	2.148420	1.154181	1.184617	1.235343	1.945514	2.148420	2.158714	2.194743	2.197317	2.198861
45	TRANSPORTATION BY AIR	22	1.403164	1.268560	0.531837	0.547170	0.578805	1.167626	1.268560	1.512920	2.334499	2.368473	2.383741
451	AIR TRANSPORTATION, SCHEDULED, AND AIR COURIER SERVICES	17	1.369521	1.306320	0.529403	0.541085	0.560556	1.167626	1.306320	1.512920	2.179920	2.286920	2.351120
4512	Air Transportation, Scheduled	13	1.495457	1.321790	0.777745	0.833517	0.926471	1.286356	1.321790	1.660114	2.233420	2.313670	2.361820
4513	Air Courier Services	4	0.960229	0.795916	0.523075	0.525266	0.528916	0.660541	0.795916	0.931290	1.621581	1.674525	1.706292
452	AIR TRANSPORTATION, NONSCHEDULED	5	1.517549	1.230800	0.973322	0.979379	0.989472	1.166568	1.230800	1.527276	2.270758	2.308104	2.330512
4522	Air Transportation, Nonscheduled	5	1.517549	1.230800	0.973322	0.979379	0.989472	1.166568	1.230800	1.527276	2.270758	2.308104	2.330512
46	PIPELINES, EXCEPT NATURAL GAS	11	1.253932	1.162240	0.831889	0.853256	0.888867	1.079880	1.162240	1.163030	1.777770	1.868480	1.922906
461	PIPELINES, EXCEPT NATURAL GAS	11	1.253932	1.162240	0.831889	0.853256	0.888867	1.079880	1.162240	1.163030	1.777770	1.868480	1.922906
4612	Crude Petroleum Pipelines	6	1.277183	1.080548	0.961442	0.963474	0.966859	0.998065	1.080548	1.163030	1.868280	1.913735	1.941008
4613	Refined Petroleum Pipelines	1	1.079880	1.079880	1.079880	1.079880	1.079880	1.079880	1.079880	1.079880	1.079880	1.079880	1.079880
4619	Pipelines, Not Elsewhere Classified	4	1.262569	1.318140	0.827983	0.843490	0.869334	1.224600	1.318140	1.411680	1.578004	1.587177	1.592681
47	TRANSPORTATION SERVICES	16	1.159559	1.422715	-3.058196	-2.157800	-0.657141	1.308470	1.422715	1.536870	2.575853	2.721461	2.808827

Down-market Betas of Common Stocks by SIC Codes as of March 31, 2017

SIC Code	Description	Number of Companies	Mean	Median	1st Percentile	2.5th Percentile	5th Percentile	40th Percentile	50th Percentile	60th Percentile	95th Percentile	97.5th Percentile	99th Percentile
472	ARRANGEMENT OF PASSENGER TRANSPORTATION	4	0.085530	1.063900	-3.517551	-3.306188	-2.953916	1.048660	1.063900	1.079140	1.755258	1.814019	1.849276
4724	Travel Agencies	1	1.872780	1.872780	1.872780	1.872780	1.872780	1.872780	1.872780	1.872780	1.872780	1.872780	1.872780
4725	Tour Operators	3	-0.510220	1.038500	-3.564521	-3.423612	-3.188764	0.099108	1.038500	1.048660	1.084220	1.086760	1.088284
473	ARRANGEMENT OF TRANSPORTATION OF FREIGHT AND CARGO	10	1.498411	1.422715	0.393275	0.468238	0.593178	1.352834	1.422715	1.492560	2.692340	2.779705	2.832124
4731	Arrangement Of Transportation Of Freight And Cargo	10	1.498411	1.422715	0.393275	0.468238	0.593178	1.352834	1.422715	1.492560	2.692340	2.779705	2.832124
478	MISCELLANEOUS SERVICES INCIDENTAL TO TRANSPORTATION	2	1.613355	1.613355	1.613174	1.613179	1.613189	1.613318	1.613355	1.613392	1.613522	1.613531	1.613536
4789	Transportation Services, Not Elsewhere Classified	2	1.613355	1.613355	1.613174	1.613179	1.613189	1.613318	1.613355	1.613392	1.613522	1.613531	1.613536
48	COMMUNICATIONS	137	1.026069	1.136740	-1.637225	-1.086022	-0.507328	0.963620	1.136740	1.224666	2.220468	2.536312	3.238832
481	TELEPHONE COMMUNICATIONS	61	1.010406	1.091450	-1.447124	-0.434227	0.141177	0.914975	1.091450	1.191990	1.931930	2.154665	3.257956
4812	Radiotelephone Communications	18	0.961003	1.118355	0.149524	0.207270	0.303514	0.771274	1.118355	1.206564	1.653904	1.708342	1.741005
4813	Telephone Communications, Except Radiotelephone	43	1.031086	1.083110	-1.657564	-0.923447	0.152636	0.967222	1.083110	1.184102	1.986668	2.300389	3.681575
482	TELEGRAPH AND OTHER MESSAGE COMMUNICATIONS	4	0.127284	0.075954	-1.150853	-1.141557	-1.126065	-0.539908	0.075954	0.691815	1.452497	1.483388	1.501923
4822	Telegraph And Other Message Communications	4	0.127284	0.075954	-1.150853	-1.141557	-1.126065	-0.539908	0.075954	0.691815	1.452497	1.483388	1.501923
483	RADIO AND TELEVISION BROADCASTING STATIONS	27	0.826080	1.203530	-1.642507	-1.621907	-1.329726	1.064127	1.203530	1.256354	2.189805	2.259189	2.276716
4832	Radio Broadcasting Stations	13	0.635012	1.203530	-1.649902	-1.640394	-1.624548	0.940719	1.203530	1.280226	1.926160	1.995385	2.036920
4833	Television Broadcasting Stations	14	1.003499	1.200245	-0.615455	-0.501979	-0.312854	1.026753	1.200245	1.251896	2.259189	2.273795	2.282558
484	CABLE AND OTHER PAY TELEVISION SERVICES	24	1.365792	1.201495	0.388048	0.429914	0.511365	1.019208	1.201495	1.328788	2.887693	3.133018	3.302813
4841	Cable And Other Pay Television Services	24	1.365792	1.201495	0.388048	0.429914	0.511365	1.019208	1.201495	1.328788	2.887693	3.133018	3.302813
489	COMMUNICATIONS SERVICES, NOT ELSEWHERE CLASSIFIED	21	1.111635	1.016320	0.112881	0.183830	0.302078	0.954753	1.016320	1.141320	2.118950	2.166835	2.195566
4899	Communications Services, Not Elsewhere Classified	21	1.111635	1.016320	0.112881	0.183830	0.302078	0.954753	1.016320	1.141320	2.118950	2.166835	2.195566
49	ELECTRIC, GAS, AND SANITARY SERVICES	138	0.778430	0.644939	-0.457079	-0.244590	0.102187	0.531723	0.644939	0.770036	2.010370	2.348604	2.746928
491	ELECTRIC SERVICES	53	0.797772	0.576383	-0.277281	-0.000429	0.106624	0.503363	0.576383	0.704438	2.044820	2.616891	2.985961
4911	Electric Services	53	0.797772	0.576383	-0.277281	-0.000429	0.106624	0.503363	0.576383	0.704438	2.044820	2.616891	2.985961
492	GAS PRODUCTION AND DISTRIBUTION	27	0.775678	0.770310	-0.206492	-0.041084	0.108221	0.687547	0.770310	0.893510	1.433535	1.633868	1.768827
4922	Natural Gas Transmission	8	1.042492	0.967164	0.576427	0.598092	0.634200	0.939237	0.967164	1.001788	1.645265	1.752033	1.816093
4923	Natural Gas Transmission And Distribution	9	0.643254	0.770310	-0.282834	-0.231939	-0.147115	0.688006	0.770310	0.863243	1.199776	1.223098	1.237091
4924	Natural Gas Distribution	9	0.744873	0.640108	0.386043	0.404352	0.434867	0.630684	0.640108	0.702200	1.283268	1.398009	1.466854
4925	Mixed, Manufactured, Or Liquefied Petroleum Gas Production	1	0.110231	0.110231	0.110231	0.110231	0.110231	0.110231	0.110231	0.110231	0.110231	0.110231	0.110231

Down-market Betas of Common Stocks by SIC Codes as of March 31, 2017

SIC Code	Description	Number of Companies	Mean	Median	1st Percentile	2.5th Percentile	5th Percentile	40th Percentile	50th Percentile	60th Percentile	95th Percentile	97.5th Percentile	99th Percentile
493	COMBINATION ELECTRIC AND GAS, AND OTHER UTILITY SERVICES	23	0.625419	0.550729	0.199310	0.217768	0.244435	0.490078	0.550729	0.658134	1.372665	1.440809	1.476192
4931	Electric And Other Services Combined	17	0.511698	0.404258	0.195954	0.209378	0.231752	0.363506	0.404258	0.529446	0.989479	1.244630	1.397720
4932	Gas And Other Services Combined	5	0.898430	0.786459	0.651442	0.653951	0.658134	0.748512	0.786459	0.860584	1.308402	1.350481	1.375728
4939	Combination Utilities, Not Elsewhere Classified	1	1.193610	1.193610	1.193610	1.193610	1.193610	1.193610	1.193610	1.193610	1.193610	1.193610	1.193610
494	WATER SUPPLY	13	0.695928	0.492018	0.265495	0.275760	0.292868	0.484075	0.492018	0.654698	1.245802	1.260406	1.269168
4941	Water Supply	13	0.695928	0.492018	0.265495	0.275760	0.292868	0.484075	0.492018	0.654698	1.245802	1.260406	1.269168
495	SANITARY SERVICES	22	0.943926	0.900747	-0.481067	-0.393438	-0.259333	0.691366	0.900747	1.047732	2.362348	2.481524	2.559342
4952	Sewerage Systems	1	0.397226	0.397226	0.397226	0.397226	0.397226	0.397226	0.397226	0.397226	0.397226	0.397226	0.397226
4953	Refuse Systems	18	0.900193	0.873535	-0.492194	-0.421257	-0.303027	0.630803	0.873535	1.061942	2.370084	2.490652	2.562993
4955	HAZARDOUS WASTE MANAGEMENT	2	1.599120	1.599120	0.849361	0.872313	0.910566	1.446108	1.599120	1.752132	2.287674	2.325927	2.348879
4959	Sanitary Services, Not Elsewhere Classified	1	0.967433	0.967433	0.967433	0.967433	0.967433	0.967433	0.967433	0.967433	0.967433	0.967433	0.967433
	WHOLESALE TRADE												
50	WHOLESALE TRADE¨DURABLE GOODS	75	1.135354	1.193640	-1.695169	-1.543998	-0.575893	1.012845	1.193640	1.283042	2.395608	2.841251	3.839268
501	MOTOR VEHICLES AND MOTOR VEHICLE PARTS AND SUPPLIES	10	1.073618	1.010777	0.199814	0.246110	0.323269	0.944472	1.010777	1.111950	1.916299	1.981770	2.021052
5012	Automobiles And Other Motor Vehicles	2	0.846371	0.846371	0.518572	0.528606	0.545331	0.779473	0.846371	0.913269	1.147411	1.164136	1.174170
5013	Motor Vehicle Supplies And New Parts	7	1.168521	1.066010	0.214485	0.282787	0.396625	0.999730	1.066010	1.181072	1.959946	2.003593	2.029781
5015	Motor Vehicle Parts, Used	1	0.863785	0.863785	0.863785	0.863785	0.863785	0.863785	0.863785	0.863785	0.863785	0.863785	0.863785
503	LUMBER AND OTHER CONSTRUCTION MATERIALS	6	1.205191	1.219665	0.614558	0.623193	0.637584	1.193640	1.219665	1.245690	1.863805	1.930938	1.971217
5031	Lumber, Plywood, Millwork, And Wood Panels	4	1.144123	0.984811	0.612256	0.617437	0.626071	0.828283	0.984811	1.141338	1.885213	1.941642	1.975499
5033	Roofing, Siding, And Insulation Materials	1	1.193640	1.193640	1.193640	1.193640	1.193640	1.193640	1.193640	1.193640	1.193640	1.193640	1.193640
5039	Construction Materials, Not Elsewhere Classified	1	1.461010	1.461010	1.461010	1.461010	1.461010	1.461010	1.461010	1.461010	1.461010	1.461010	1.461010
504	PROFESSIONAL AND COMMERCIAL EQUIPMENT AND SUPPLIES	18	1.300883	1.253925	-1.529203	-1.235987	-0.747294	1.214986	1.253925	1.392192	2.875837	3.442864	3.783079
5044	Office Equipment	1	0.780326	0.780326	0.780326	0.780326	0.780326	0.780326	0.780326	0.780326	0.780326	0.780326	0.780326
5045	Computers And Computer Peripheral Equipment And Software	8	1.832883	1.777760	1.239361	1.255322	1.281924	1.680216	1.777760	1.851634	2.574035	2.624873	2.655375
5047	Medical, Dental, And Hospital Equipment And Supplies	9	0.885835	1.116770	-1.632691	-1.494707	-1.264734	0.961637	1.116770	1.181058	2.917586	3.463738	3.791429
505	METALS AND MINERALS, EXCEPT PETROLEUM	6	1.633136	1.686015	0.666019	0.715194	0.797154	1.438740	1.686015	1.933290	2.255930	2.257735	2.258818
5051	Metals Service Centers And Offices	6	1.633136	1.686015	0.666019	0.715194	0.797154	1.438740	1.686015	1.933290	2.255930	2.257735	2.258818
506	ELECTRICAL GOODS	17	1.036256	1.024330	-1.340752	-1.073154	-0.627158	0.674334	1.024330	1.771354	2.140798	2.280334	2.364056

Down-market Betas of Common Stocks by SIC Codes as of March 31, 2017

SIC Code	Description	Number of Companies	Mean	Median	1st Percentile	2.5th Percentile	5th Percentile	40th Percentile	50th Percentile	60th Percentile	95th Percentile	97.5th Percentile	99th Percentile
5063	Electrical Apparatus And Equipment, Wiring Supplies, And Construction	5	1.612167	1.897640	0.758665	0.775269	0.802943	1.548316	1.897640	1.927144	2.330176	2.375023	2.401931
5065	Electronic Parts And Equipment, Not Elsewhere Classified	12	0.796293	0.614878	-1.396501	-1.212528	-0.905906	0.426632	0.614878	1.245297	2.001609	2.036320	2.057146
507	HARDWARE, AND PLUMBING AND HEATING EQUIPMENT AND SUPPLIES	3	1.482327	1.526290	1.031821	1.046958	1.072186	1.425378	1.526290	1.600824	1.861693	1.880327	1.891507
5074	Plumbing And Heating Equipment And Supplies (Hydronics)	2	1.712625	1.712625	1.530017	1.535607	1.544924	1.675358	1.712625	1.749892	1.880327	1.889643	1.895233
5075	Warm Air Heating And Air-Conditioning Equipment And Supplies	1	1.021730	1.021730	1.021730	1.021730	1.021730	1.021730	1.021730	1.021730	1.021730	1.021730	1.021730
508	MACHINERY, EQUIPMENT, AND SUPPLIES	8	1.219433	1.130340	-1.503452	-1.231430	-0.778059	1.102768	1.130340	1.158496	3.237331	3.508326	3.670922
5084	Industrial Machinery And Equipment	6	1.271228	1.198090	-1.555266	-1.360964	-1.037128	1.132100	1.198090	1.264080	3.392185	3.585753	3.701893
5085	Industrial Supplies	1	1.128580	1.128580	1.128580	1.128580	1.128580	1.128580	1.128580	1.128580	1.128580	1.128580	1.128580
5087	Service Establishment Equipment And Supplies	1	0.999518	0.999518	0.999518	0.999518	0.999518	0.999518	0.999518	0.999518	0.999518	0.999518	0.999518
509	MISCELLANEOUS DURABLE GOODS	7	0.307250	0.163503	-0.552791	-0.514361	-0.450311	0.160708	0.163503	0.281310	1.324761	1.493941	1.595448
5091	Sporting And Recreational Goods And Supplies	3	0.787294	0.535258	0.170938	0.182091	0.200679	0.460907	0.535258	0.760830	1.550334	1.606727	1.640563
5094	Jewelry, Watches, Precious Stones, And Precious Metals	3	-0.123325	-0.151412	-0.569871	-0.557061	-0.535711	-0.236812	-0.151412	-0.049160	0.308722	0.334285	0.349623
5099	Durable Goods, Not Elsewhere Classified	1	0.158844	0.158844	0.158844	0.158844	0.158844	0.158844	0.158844	0.158844	0.158844	0.158844	0.158844
51	WHOLESALE TRADE¨NONDURABLE GOODS	60	1.155103	1.044575	-0.982506	-0.263224	-0.001699	0.934828	1.044575	1.205150	2.745750	3.082767	3.364128
511	PAPER AND PAPER PRODUCTS	1	0.947900	0.947900	0.947900	0.947900	0.947900	0.947900	0.947900	0.947900	0.947900	0.947900	0.947900
5111	Printing And Writing Paper	1	0.947900	0.947900	0.947900	0.947900	0.947900	0.947900	0.947900	0.947900	0.947900	0.947900	0.947900
512	DRUGS, DRUG PROPRIETARIES, AND DRUGGISTS' SUNDRIES	22	1.648426	1.626460	-0.278825	-0.099318	0.173216	1.393666	1.626460	1.846874	3.137796	3.398984	3.567900
5122	Drugs, Drug Proprietaries, And Druggists' Sundries	22	1.648426	1.626460	-0.278825	-0.099318	0.173216	1.393666	1.626460	1.846874	3.137796	3.398984	3.567900
513	APPAREL, PIECE GOODS, AND NOTIONS	2	1.055196	1.055196	0.682948	0.694343	0.713335	0.979227	1.055196	1.131164	1.397056	1.416048	1.427443
5136	Men's And Boys' Clothing And Furnishings	1	1.435040	1.435040	1.435040	1.435040	1.435040	1.435040	1.435040	1.435040	1.435040	1.435040	1.435040
5139	Footwear	1	0.675351	0.675351	0.675351	0.675351	0.675351	0.675351	0.675351	0.675351	0.675351	0.675351	0.675351
514	GROCERIES AND RELATED PRODUCTS	15	0.622152	0.802773	-1.583622	-1.224691	-0.626472	0.743273	0.802773	0.852575	1.325631	1.488371	1.586014
5141	Groceries, General Line	10	0.737090	0.811017	-0.095704	-0.068690	-0.023667	0.781348	0.811017	0.857645	1.182450	1.184295	1.185402
5145	Confectionery	1	0.902546	0.902546	0.902546	0.902546	0.902546	0.902546	0.902546	0.902546	0.902546	0.902546	0.902546
5148	Fresh Fruits And Vegetables	1	0.522449	0.522449	0.522449	0.522449	0.522449	0.522449	0.522449	0.522449	0.522449	0.522449	0.522449
5149	Groceries And Related Products, Not Elsewhere Classified	3	0.178798	0.708193	-1.772288	-1.696355	-1.569800	0.201972	0.708193	0.896776	1.556818	1.603964	1.632252

Down-market Betas of Common Stocks by SIC Codes as of March 31, 2017

SIC Code	Description	Number of Companies	Mean	Median	1st Percentile	2.5th Percentile	5th Percentile	40th Percentile	50th Percentile	60th Percentile	95th Percentile	97.5th Percentile	99th Percentile
515	FARM-PRODUCT RAW MATERIALS	4	0.661987	0.585604	0.267313	0.280832	0.303365	0.569481	0.585604	0.601727	1.127545	1.172993	1.200261
5153	Grain And Field Beans	2	0.738370	0.738370	0.267901	0.282304	0.306307	0.642356	0.738370	0.834384	1.170433	1.194437	1.208839
5159	Farm-Product Raw Materials, Not Elsewhere Classified	2	0.585604	0.585604	0.559270	0.560077	0.561420	0.580230	0.585604	0.590978	0.609788	0.611131	0.611938
516	CHEMICALS AND ALLIED PRODUCTS	5	1.190622	1.288580	0.914575	0.920359	0.929999	1.175996	1.288580	1.296940	1.411664	1.424437	1.432101
5162	Plastics Materials And Basic Forms And Shapes	1	1.309480	1.309480	1.309480	1.309480	1.309480	1.309480	1.309480	1.309480	1.309480	1.309480	1.309480
5169	Chemicals And Allied Products, Not Elsewhere Classified	4	1.160907	1.147850	0.913611	0.917949	0.925179	1.063412	1.147850	1.232288	1.414916	1.426063	1.432751
517	PETROLEUM AND PETROLEUM PRODUCTS	5	0.949850	0.976188	0.639888	0.650946	0.669378	0.912444	0.976188	1.025793	1.198856	1.211188	1.218587
5172	Petroleum And Petroleum Products Wholesalers, Except Bulk Station	5	0.949850	0.976188	0.639888	0.650946	0.669378	0.912444	0.976188	1.025793	1.198856	1.211188	1.218587
519	MISCELLANEOUS NONDURABLE GOODS	6	1.216654	1.312981	0.043406	0.102220	0.200243	0.992372	1.312981	1.633590	2.088300	2.162105	2.206388
5191	Farm Supplies	2	1.318921	1.318921	0.998903	1.008699	1.025027	1.253611	1.318921	1.384231	1.612815	1.629143	1.638939
5192	Books, Periodicals, And Newspapers	1	0.004197	0.004197	0.004197	0.004197	0.004197	0.004197	0.004197	0.004197	0.004197	0.004197	0.004197
5199	Nondurable Goods, Not Elsewhere Classified	3	1.552628	1.633590	0.805287	0.830643	0.872904	1.464549	1.633590	1.754054	2.175678	2.205794	2.223864
	RETAIL TRADE												
52	RETAIL TRADE	13	1.153775	1.135040	-0.378491	-0.216078	0.054610	0.950333	1.135040	1.195540	2.292804	2.298327	2.301641
521	LUMBER AND OTHER BUILDING MATERIALS DEALERS	11	1.242999	1.182340	-0.363572	-0.178780	0.129206	1.135040	1.182340	1.248340	2.294645	2.299248	2.302009
5211	Lumber And Other Building Materials Dealers	11	1.242999	1.182340	-0.363572	-0.178780	0.129206	1.135040	1.182340	1.248340	2.294645	2.299248	2.302009
523	PAINT, GLASS, AND WALLPAPER STORES	1	0.910558	0.910558	0.910558	0.910558	0.910558	0.910558	0.910558	0.910558	0.910558	0.910558	0.910558
5231	Paint, Glass, And Wallpaper Stores	1	0.910558	0.910558	0.910558	0.910558	0.910558	0.910558	0.910558	0.910558	0.910558	0.910558	0.910558
526	RETAIL NURSERIES, LAWN AND GARDEN SUPPLY STORES	1	0.415527	0.415527	0.415527	0.415527	0.415527	0.415527	0.415527	0.415527	0.415527	0.415527	0.415527
5261	Retail Nurseries, Lawn And Garden Supply Stores	1	0.415527	0.415527	0.415527	0.415527	0.415527	0.415527	0.415527	0.415527	0.415527	0.415527	0.415527
53	GENERAL MERCHANDISE STORES	20	0.676330	0.533825	-0.402174	-0.270646	-0.051432	0.499637	0.533825	0.788330	1.471881	1.528600	1.562632
531	DEPARTMENT STORES	10	0.635302	0.594637	-0.448325	-0.386022	-0.282184	0.491482	0.594637	0.788330	1.396950	1.491135	1.547646
5311	Department Stores	10	0.635302	0.594637	-0.448325	-0.386022	-0.282184	0.491482	0.594637	0.788330	1.396950	1.491135	1.547646
533	VARIETY STORES	8	0.712075	0.515006	0.021559	0.064125	0.135068	0.490063	0.515006	0.625733	1.425338	1.445624	1.457796
5331	Variety Stores	8	0.712075	0.515006	0.021559	0.064125	0.135068	0.490063	0.515006	0.625733	1.425338	1.445624	1.457796
539	MISCELLANEOUS GENERAL MERCHANDISE STORES	2	0.738490	0.738490	0.539375	0.545470	0.555629	0.697854	0.738490	0.779126	0.921351	0.931510	0.937605
5399	Miscellaneous General Merchandise Stores	2	0.738490	0.738490	0.539375	0.545470	0.555629	0.697854	0.738490	0.779126	0.921351	0.931510	0.937605
54	FOOD STORES	22	1.304228	0.580815	-0.404011	-0.370808	-0.313778	0.418819	0.580815	1.057178	2.641946	7.494725	10.692290
541	GROCERY STORES	16	0.766902	0.476866	-0.410335	-0.386619	-0.347092	0.396918	0.476866	0.606756	2.207183	2.440091	2.579837
5411	Grocery Stores	16	0.766902	0.476866	-0.410335	-0.386619	-0.347092	0.396918	0.476866	0.606756	2.207183	2.440091	2.579837

Down-market Betas of Common Stocks by SIC Codes as of March 31, 2017

SIC Code	Description	Number of Companies	Mean	Median	1st Percentile	2.5th Percentile	5th Percentile	40th Percentile	50th Percentile	60th Percentile	95th Percentile	97.5th Percentile	99th Percentile
544	CANDY, NUT, AND CONFECTIONERY STORES	1	1.094970	1.094970	1.094970	1.094970	1.094970	1.094970	1.094970	1.094970	1.094970	1.094970	1.094970
5441	Candy, Nut, And Confectionery Stores	1	1.094970	1.094970	1.094970	1.094970	1.094970	1.094970	1.094970	1.094970	1.094970	1.094970	1.094970
549	MISCELLANEOUS FOOD STORES	5	3.065525	1.000490	-0.156269	-0.118455	-0.055431	0.779799	1.000490	1.094634	10.506370	11.665185	12.360474
5499	Miscellaneous Food Stores	5	3.065525	1.000490	-0.156269	-0.118455	-0.055431	0.779799	1.000490	1.094634	10.506370	11.665185	12.360474
55	AUTOMOTIVE DEALERS AND GASOLINE SERVICE STATIONS	20	1.036265	1.394095	-4.934877	-3.193387	-0.290904	1.166676	1.394095	1.509304	2.184924	3.039582	3.552377
551	MOTOR VEHICLE DEALERS (NEW AND USED)	9	1.526594	1.659740	1.011920	1.025914	1.049238	1.386564	1.659740	1.664940	1.998392	2.046676	2.075646
5511	Motor Vehicle Dealers (New And Used)	9	1.526594	1.659740	1.011920	1.025914	1.049238	1.386564	1.659740	1.664940	1.998392	2.046676	2.075646
552	MOTOR VEHICLE DEALERS (USED ONLY)	2	-2.306815	-2.306815	-6.020089	-5.906417	-5.716965	-3.064626	-2.306815	-1.549004	1.103335	1.292787	1.406459
5521	Motor Vehicle Dealers (Used Only)	2	-2.306815	-2.306815	-6.020089	-5.906417	-5.716965	-3.064626	-2.306815	-1.549004	1.103335	1.292787	1.406459
553	AUTO AND HOME SUPPLY STORES	3	1.994367	2.074240	0.055813	0.117602	0.220583	1.662316	2.074240	2.438240	3.712240	3.803240	3.857840
5531	Auto And Home Supply Stores	3	1.994367	2.074240	0.055813	0.117602	0.220583	1.662316	2.074240	2.438240	3.712240	3.803240	3.857840
554	GASOLINE SERVICE STATIONS	4	0.788048	0.635177	0.418521	0.428429	0.444941	0.633321	0.635177	0.637033	1.345173	1.407546	1.444971
5541	Gasoline Service Stations	4	0.788048	0.635177	0.418521	0.428429	0.444941	0.633321	0.635177	0.637033	1.345173	1.407546	1.444971
555	BOAT DEALERS	2	1.232149	1.232149	0.920752	0.930285	0.946172	1.168598	1.232149	1.295699	1.518125	1.534012	1.543545
5551	Boat Dealers	2	1.232149	1.232149	0.920752	0.930285	0.946172	1.168598	1.232149	1.295699	1.518125	1.534012	1.543545
56	APPAREL AND ACCESSORY STORES	35	1.022832	0.883406	-0.937101	0.036968	0.361815	0.755749	0.883406	1.027698	2.489817	2.891058	2.959153
5600	RETAIL-APPAREL & ACCESSORY STORES	1	1.482180	1.482180	1.482180	1.482180	1.482180	1.482180	1.482180	1.482180	1.482180	1.482180	1.482180
561	MEN'S AND BOYS' CLOTHING AND ACCESSORY STORES	1	0.632073	0.632073	0.632073	0.632073	0.632073	0.632073	0.632073	0.632073	0.632073	0.632073	0.632073
5611	Men's And Boys' Clothing And Accessory Stores	1	0.632073	0.632073	0.632073	0.632073	0.632073	0.632073	0.632073	0.632073	0.632073	0.632073	0.632073
562	WOMEN'S CLOTHING STORES	8	1.340464	1.299400	0.809085	0.821625	0.842526	1.160595	1.299400	1.401246	2.084620	2.189165	2.251892
5621	Women's Clothing Stores	8	1.340464	1.299400	0.809085	0.821625	0.842526	1.160595	1.299400	1.401246	2.084620	2.189165	2.251892
563	WOMEN'S ACCESSORY AND SPECIALTY STORES	1	0.803694	0.803694	0.803694	0.803694	0.803694	0.803694	0.803694	0.803694	0.803694	0.803694	0.803694
5632	Women's Accessory And Specialty Stores	1	0.803694	0.803694	0.803694	0.803694	0.803694	0.803694	0.803694	0.803694	0.803694	0.803694	0.803694
565	FAMILY CLOTHING STORES	15	1.130212	1.012390	0.367703	0.434069	0.544679	0.837053	1.012390	1.080392	2.529873	2.767212	2.909615
5651	Family Clothing Stores	15	1.130212	1.012390	0.367703	0.434069	0.544679	0.837053	1.012390	1.080392	2.529873	2.767212	2.909615
566	SHOE STORES	7	0.561603	0.501308	-1.468596	-1.291770	-0.997060	0.491713	0.501308	0.551022	2.219009	2.545019	2.740626
5661	Shoe Stores	7	0.561603	0.501308	-1.468596	-1.291770	-0.997060	0.491713	0.501308	0.551022	2.219009	2.545019	2.740626
569	MISCELLANEOUS APPAREL AND ACCESSORY STORES	2	0.636535	0.636535	0.558668	0.561052	0.565025	0.620644	0.636535	0.652426	0.708045	0.712018	0.714402
5699	Miscellaneous Apparel And Accessory Stores	2	0.636535	0.636535	0.558668	0.561052	0.565025	0.620644	0.636535	0.652426	0.708045	0.712018	0.714402
57	HOME FURNITURE, FURNISHINGS, AND EQUIPMENT STORES	13	1.218576	0.951241	-0.580004	-0.563102	-0.534930	0.899021	0.951241	1.154932	3.411290	4.235225	4.729586
571	HOME FURNITURE AND FURNISHINGS STORES	6	1.032386	1.038651	0.599536	0.620189	0.654610	0.951241	1.038651	1.126060	1.367373	1.383531	1.393227
5712	Furniture Stores	3	1.085872	1.126060	0.866434	0.874381	0.887628	1.073075	1.126060	1.154932	1.255984	1.263202	1.267533

Down-market Betas of Common Stocks by SIC Codes as of March 31, 2017

SIC Code	Description	Number of Companies	Mean	Median	1st Percentile	2.5th Percentile	5th Percentile	40th Percentile	50th Percentile	60th Percentile	95th Percentile	97.5th Percentile	99th Percentile
5713	Floor Covering Stores	1	0.585768	0.585768	0.585768	0.585768	0.585768	0.585768	0.585768	0.585768	0.585768	0.585768	0.585768
5719	Miscellaneous Homefurnishings Stores	2	1.175466	1.175466	0.955725	0.962452	0.973663	1.130621	1.175466	1.220310	1.377268	1.388479	1.395206
572	HOUSEHOLD APPLIANCE STORES	1	0.823922	0.823922	0.823922	0.823922	0.823922	0.823922	0.823922	0.823922	0.823922	0.823922	0.823922
5722	Household Appliance Stores	1	0.823922	0.823922	0.823922	0.823922	0.823922	0.823922	0.823922	0.823922	0.823922	0.823922	0.823922
573	RADIO, TELEVISION, CONSUMER ELECTRONICS, AND MUSIC STORES	6	1.470542	1.270011	-0.586578	-0.579535	-0.567797	0.908492	1.270011	1.631530	4.372548	4.715854	4.921838
5731	Radio, Television, And Consumer Electronics Stores	4	1.065365	1.270011	-0.546280	-0.478791	-0.366308	1.053100	1.270011	1.486922	2.210533	2.261622	2.292275
5734	Computer And Computer Software Stores	1	5.059160	5.059160	5.059160	5.059160	5.059160	5.059160	5.059160	5.059160	5.059160	5.059160	5.059160
5735	Record And Prerecorded Tape Stores	1	-0.497368	-0.497368	-0.497368	-0.497368	-0.497368	-0.497368	-0.497368	-0.497368	-0.497368	-0.497368	-0.497368
58	EATING AND DRINKING PLACES	66	0.808858	0.824046	-0.488707	-0.062579	-0.040799	0.695243	0.824046	0.906190	1.573590	1.662346	1.867710
581	EATING AND DRINKING PLACES	66	0.808858	0.824046	-0.488707	-0.062579	-0.040799	0.695243	0.824046	0.906190	1.573590	1.662346	1.867710
5810	RETAIL-EATING & DRINKING PLACES	1	1.436680	1.436680	1.436680	1.436680	1.436680	1.436680	1.436680	1.436680	1.436680	1.436680	1.436680
5812	Eating Places	64	0.801051	0.824046	-0.512158	-0.063838	-0.043616	0.702544	0.824046	0.904617	1.577618	1.672510	1.872185
5813	Drinking Places (Alcoholic Beverages)	1	0.680685	0.680685	0.680685	0.680685	0.680685	0.680685	0.680685	0.680685	0.680685	0.680685	0.680685
59	MISCELLANEOUS RETAIL	72	0.554849	0.860592	-6.576271	-4.153453	-0.989122	0.678572	0.860592	1.045818	1.808020	2.069347	2.717099
591	DRUG STORES AND PROPRIETARY STORES	10	0.511065	0.607669	-0.618535	-0.554907	-0.448861	0.561222	0.607669	0.674214	1.121139	1.148874	1.165516
5912	Drug Stores And Proprietary Stores	10	0.511065	0.607669	-0.618535	-0.554907	-0.448861	0.561222	0.607669	0.674214	1.121139	1.148874	1.165516
592	LIQUOR STORES	1	0.382037	0.382037	0.382037	0.382037	0.382037	0.382037	0.382037	0.382037	0.382037	0.382037	0.382037
5921	Liquor Stores	1	0.382037	0.382037	0.382037	0.382037	0.382037	0.382037	0.382037	0.382037	0.382037	0.382037	0.382037
593	USED MERCHANDISE STORES	3	0.474134	0.230229	0.222002	0.222254	0.222674	0.228550	0.230229	0.378251	0.896328	0.933334	0.955537
5932	Used Merchandise Stores	3	0.474134	0.230229	0.222002	0.222254	0.222674	0.228550	0.230229	0.378251	0.896328	0.933334	0.955537
594	MISCELLANEOUS SHOPPING GOODS STORES	16	0.677484	0.952889	-4.004074	-2.902899	-1.067608	0.778991	0.952889	1.126290	1.983370	2.143930	2.240266
5941	Sporting Goods Stores And Bicycle Shops	4	0.480617	0.414706	0.385592	0.386785	0.388774	0.412668	0.414706	0.416744	0.664735	0.686497	0.699554
5942	Book Stores	2	1.127459	1.127459	0.865885	0.873893	0.887238	1.074076	1.127459	1.180841	1.367679	1.381024	1.389032
5943	Stationery Stores	2	1.763860	1.763860	1.653639	1.657014	1.662637	1.741366	1.763860	1.786354	1.865083	1.870707	1.874081
5944	Jewelry Stores	3	-0.820337	1.045230	-4.622522	-4.449019	-4.159848	-0.111454	1.045230	1.082574	1.213278	1.222614	1.228216
5945	Hobby, Toy, And Game Shops	3	0.687067	0.778991	0.168381	0.187074	0.218227	0.654377	0.778991	0.848451	1.091560	1.108925	1.119344
5947	Gift, Novelty, And Souvenir Shops	2	1.767225	1.767225	1.240705	1.256823	1.283687	1.659772	1.767225	1.874678	2.250764	2.277627	2.293745
596	NONSTORE RETAILERS	25	0.356134	1.046210	-9.374150	-6.820774	-3.402120	0.921110	1.046210	1.180216	1.951290	2.691560	3.312992
5960	RETAIL-NONSTORE RETAILERS	1	0.222312	0.222312	0.222312	0.222312	0.222312	0.222312	0.222312	0.222312	0.222312	0.222312	0.222312
5961	Catalog And Mail-Order Houses	24	0.361710	1.063035	-9.445077	-6.998092	-3.547513	0.972631	1.063035	1.194472	1.963738	2.734715	3.330254
598	FUEL DEALERS	4	0.234983	0.203510	0.051259	0.055834	0.063458	0.171328	0.203510	0.235692	0.450570	0.467637	0.477877
5983	Fuel Oil Dealers	4	0.234983	0.203510	0.051259	0.055834	0.063458	0.171328	0.203510	0.235692	0.450570	0.467637	0.477877
599	RETAIL STORES, NOT ELSEWHERE CLASSIFIED	13	0.950077	1.067830	-0.740516	-0.474033	-0.029896	0.999086	1.067830	1.113694	1.580874	1.661352	1.709639
5992	Florists	1	0.958308	0.958308	0.958308	0.958308	0.958308	0.958308	0.958308	0.958308	0.958308	0.958308	0.958308
5995	Optical Goods Stores	1	1.366400	1.366400	1.366400	1.366400	1.366400	1.366400	1.366400	1.366400	1.366400	1.366400	1.366400

Down-market Betas of Common Stocks by SIC Codes as of March 31, 2017

SIC Code	Description	Number of Companies	Mean	Median	1st Percentile	2.5th Percentile	5th Percentile	40th Percentile	50th Percentile	60th Percentile	95th Percentile	97.5th Percentile	99th Percentile
5999	Miscellaneous Retail Stores, Not Elsewhere Classified	11	0.911482	1.067830	-0.770125	-0.548056	-0.177942	1.009280	1.067830	1.095850	1.607700	1.674765	1.715004
	FINANCE, INSURANCE, AND REAL ESTATE												
60	DEPOSITORY INSTITUTIONS	397	1.034521	1.027380	-0.308465	-0.143984	-0.036428	0.828397	1.027380	1.276194	2.079482	2.472241	3.685749
602	COMMERCIAL BANKS	305	1.109998	1.192490	-0.305665	-0.109234	-0.018607	0.912022	1.192490	1.357310	2.154524	2.707686	3.761171
6021	National Commercial Banks	112	1.161285	1.312665	-0.559298	-0.183002	0.046683	1.005772	1.312665	1.453748	2.178707	2.334229	3.469164
6022	State Commercial Banks	166	1.007246	1.027040	-0.241183	-0.116908	-0.039369	0.770323	1.027040	1.272960	2.084135	2.347704	2.701524
6029	Commercial Banks, Not Elsewhere Classified	27	1.528990	1.263260	0.148257	0.160576	0.185501	1.160750	1.263260	1.361496	4.015351	4.144129	4.167805
603	SAVINGS INSTITUTIONS	83	0.760942	0.743732	-0.182616	-0.156188	-0.038545	0.548084	0.743732	0.908510	1.691822	1.890128	1.985456
6035	Savings Institutions, Federally Chartered	61	0.805767	0.781505	-0.205217	-0.162882	-0.052610	0.663112	0.781505	0.980477	1.691990	1.896950	1.999312
6036	Savings Institutions, Not Federally Chartered	22	0.636656	0.531621	0.007809	0.010626	0.015474	0.438354	0.531621	0.690298	1.387159	1.634333	1.790031
606	CREDIT UNIONS	1	0.519220	0.519220	0.519220	0.519220	0.519220	0.519220	0.519220	0.519220	0.519220	0.519220	0.519220
6061	Credit Unions, Federally Chartered	1	0.519220	0.519220	0.519220	0.519220	0.519220	0.519220	0.519220	0.519220	0.519220	0.519220	0.519220
609	FUNCTIONS RELATED TO DEPOSITORY BANKING	8	1.059756	1.082755	-0.267027	-0.127771	0.104324	1.058878	1.082755	1.148454	1.682941	1.703060	1.715132
6099	Functions Related To Depository Banking, Not Elsewhere Classified	8	1.059756	1.082755	-0.267027	-0.127771	0.104324	1.058878	1.082755	1.148454	1.682941	1.703060	1.715132
61	NONDEPOSITORY CREDIT INSTITUTIONS	44	1.203993	1.383095	-0.072996	-0.004450	0.035182	1.145128	1.383095	1.474894	1.998403	2.568823	2.835397
611	FEDERAL AND FEDERALLY-SPONSORED CREDIT AGENCIES	5	1.624175	1.518550	0.560338	0.614332	0.704320	1.480822	1.518550	1.571594	2.732304	2.867447	2.948533
6111	Federal And Federally-Sponsored Credit Agencies	5	1.624175	1.518550	0.560338	0.614332	0.704320	1.480822	1.518550	1.571594	2.732304	2.867447	2.948533
614	PERSONAL CREDIT INSTITUTIONS	13	1.153080	1.239130	0.039685	0.071624	0.124856	1.201762	1.239130	1.387198	1.789680	1.820370	1.838784
6141	Personal Credit Institutions	13	1.153080	1.239130	0.039685	0.071624	0.124856	1.201762	1.239130	1.387198	1.789680	1.820370	1.838784
615	BUSINESS CREDIT INSTITUTIONS	11	0.730414	0.537700	-0.111608	-0.094057	-0.064805	0.520445	0.537700	0.729367	1.614075	1.655303	1.680039
6153	Short-Term Business Credit Institutions, Except Agricultural	7	0.600049	0.520445	0.011282	0.037659	0.081619	0.480819	0.520445	0.530798	1.280619	1.338335	1.372964
6159	Miscellaneous Business Credit Institutions	4	0.958552	1.130494	-0.097729	-0.059358	0.004592	0.889818	1.130494	1.371169	1.671794	1.684162	1.691583
616	MORTGAGE BANKERS AND BROKERS	12	1.367221	1.489615	0.210274	0.330191	0.530052	1.429180	1.489615	1.521772	1.884922	1.949701	1.988568
6162	Mortgage Bankers And Loan Correspondents	9	1.413781	1.481530	0.874207	0.899872	0.942646	1.411730	1.481530	1.494466	1.732844	1.755882	1.769705
6163	Loan Brokers	3	1.227543	1.537820	0.158480	0.200705	0.271079	1.256322	1.537820	1.633152	1.966814	1.990647	2.004947
6172	FINANCE LESSORS	1	2.613770	2.613770	2.613770	2.613770	2.613770	2.613770	2.613770	2.613770	2.613770	2.613770	2.613770
6199	FINANCE SERVICES	2	1.404907	1.404907	0.912562	0.927634	0.952753	1.304428	1.404907	1.505386	1.857061	1.882180	1.897252
62	SECURITY AND COMMODITY BROKERS, DEALERS, EXCHANGES, AND SERVICES	96	1.238243	1.162460	-0.641279	-0.188915	-0.060573	0.932750	1.162460	1.529920	2.713465	2.920363	3.138619
621	SECURITY BROKERS, DEALERS, AND FLOTATION COMPANIES	35	1.318107	1.505920	-1.567587	-0.793133	-0.282243	1.130212	1.505920	1.685882	2.719746	2.926486	3.330426
6211	Security Brokers, Dealers, And Flotation Companies	35	1.318107	1.505920	-1.567587	-0.793133	-0.282243	1.130212	1.505920	1.685882	2.719746	2.926486	3.330426

Down-market Betas of Common Stocks by SIC Codes as of March 31, 2017

SIC Code	Description	Number of Companies	Mean	Median	1st Percentile	2.5th Percentile	5th Percentile	40th Percentile	50th Percentile	60th Percentile	95th Percentile	97.5th Percentile	99th Percentile
622	COMMODITY CONTRACTS BROKERS AND DEALERS	2	1.557331	1.557331	0.740972	0.765963	0.807614	1.390727	1.557331	1.723935	2.307048	2.348699	2.373690
6221	Commodity Contracts Brokers And Dealers	2	1.557331	1.557331	0.740972	0.765963	0.807614	1.390727	1.557331	1.723935	2.307048	2.348699	2.373690
623	SECURITY AND COMMODITY EXCHANGES	6	0.695558	0.647312	-0.159184	-0.109709	-0.027249	0.533321	0.647312	0.761303	1.502150	1.602380	1.662518
6231	Security And Commodity Exchanges	6	0.695558	0.647312	-0.159184	-0.109709	-0.027249	0.533321	0.647312	0.761303	1.502150	1.602380	1.662518
628	SERVICES ALLIED WITH THE EXCHANGE OF SECURITIES OR COMMODITIES	53	1.234897	1.140900	-0.029295	0.118912	0.136512	0.951887	1.140900	1.434898	2.610750	2.930372	3.039501
6282	Investment Advice	52	1.253031	1.168760	-0.032261	0.118422	0.136187	0.995239	1.168760	1.457594	2.629600	2.933709	3.040941
6289	Services Allied With The Exchange Of Securities Or Commodities	1	0.291906	0.291906	0.291906	0.291906	0.291906	0.291906	0.291906	0.291906	0.291906	0.291906	0.291906
63	INSURANCE CARRIERS	145	0.964362	0.918399	-0.292269	-0.044880	0.060864	0.813118	0.918399	0.983239	1.976734	2.593258	3.406289
631	LIFE INSURANCE	37	1.155694	1.052760	-1.042757	-0.537657	-0.168026	0.685029	1.052760	1.362886	3.180306	3.688642	3.721863
6311	Life Insurance	37	1.155694	1.052760	-1.042757	-0.537657	-0.168026	0.685029	1.052760	1.362886	3.180306	3.688642	3.721863
632	ACCIDENT AND HEALTH INSURANCE AND MEDICAL SERVICE PLANS	21	0.973944	0.905411	0.214877	0.218376	0.224207	0.720161	0.905411	0.956385	1.943510	2.087615	2.174078
6321	Accident And Health Insurance	11	1.170996	1.194670	0.213711	0.215461	0.218376	0.966360	1.194670	1.224130	2.087615	2.159668	2.202899
6324	Hospital And Medical Service Plans	10	0.757186	0.689484	0.583248	0.585222	0.588510	0.671763	0.689484	0.704026	1.069990	1.116465	1.144350
633	FIRE, MARINE, AND CASUALTY INSURANCE	69	0.812762	0.887107	-0.044244	0.019371	0.051801	0.787070	0.887107	0.932301	1.504626	1.580722	1.746623
6331	Fire, Marine, And Casualty Insurance	69	0.812762	0.887107	-0.044244	0.019371	0.051801	0.787070	0.887107	0.932301	1.504626	1.580722	1.746623
635	SURETY INSURANCE	8	1.419996	1.392345	0.856592	0.864683	0.878169	1.227272	1.392345	1.577772	1.962381	1.971366	1.976756
6351	Surety Insurance	8	1.419996	1.392345	0.856592	0.864683	0.878169	1.227272	1.392345	1.577772	1.962381	1.971366	1.976756
636	TITLE INSURANCE	7	0.875546	0.798539	0.484872	0.509271	0.549936	0.775585	0.798539	0.839289	1.363922	1.451151	1.503488
6361	Title Insurance	7	0.875546	0.798539	0.484872	0.509271	0.549936	0.775585	0.798539	0.839289	1.363922	1.451151	1.503488
637	PENSION, HEALTH, AND WELFARE FUNDS	1	1.121680	1.121680	1.121680	1.121680	1.121680	1.121680	1.121680	1.121680	1.121680	1.121680	1.121680
6371	Pension, Health, And Welfare Funds	1	1.121680	1.121680	1.121680	1.121680	1.121680	1.121680	1.121680	1.121680	1.121680	1.121680	1.121680
639	INSURANCE CARRIERS, NOT ELSEWHERE CLASSIFIED	2	0.963930	0.963930	0.948170	0.948652	0.949456	0.960714	0.963930	0.967146	0.978404	0.979208	0.979690
6399	Insurance Carriers, Not Elsewhere Classified	2	0.963930	0.963930	0.948170	0.948652	0.949456	0.960714	0.963930	0.967146	0.978404	0.979208	0.979690
64	INSURANCE AGENTS, BROKERS, AND SERVICE	15	1.239223	1.182130	0.609020	0.626728	0.656242	1.073939	1.182130	1.256654	2.114943	2.194712	2.242573
641	INSURANCE AGENTS, BROKERS, AND SERVICE	15	1.239223	1.182130	0.609020	0.626728	0.656242	1.073939	1.182130	1.256654	2.114943	2.194712	2.242573
6411	Insurance Agents, Brokers, And Service	15	1.239223	1.182130	0.609020	0.626728	0.656242	1.073939	1.182130	1.256654	2.114943	2.194712	2.242573
65	REAL ESTATE	42	1.165180	1.083965	-0.310940	-0.262363	-0.211328	0.991309	1.083965	1.297556	2.502047	2.529649	2.967506
6500	REAL ESTATE	2	0.138679	0.138679	-0.212628	-0.201874	-0.183950	0.066983	0.138679	0.210374	0.461307	0.479231	0.489985

Down-market Betas of Common Stocks by SIC Codes as of March 31, 2017

SIC Code	Description	Number of Companies	Mean	Median	1st Percentile	2.5th Percentile	5th Percentile	40th Percentile	50th Percentile	60th Percentile	95th Percentile	97.5th Percentile	99th Percentile
651	REAL ESTATE OPERATORS (EXCEPT DEVELOPERS) AND LESSORS	16	0.940246	0.991874	-0.331865	-0.313757	-0.283575	0.745882	0.991874	1.074990	1.973200	2.251705	2.418808
6512	Operators Of Nonresidential Buildings	11	1.117478	1.074990	-0.215563	-0.143727	-0.024001	0.994698	1.074990	1.215990	2.158870	2.344540	2.455942
6513	Operators Of Apartment Buildings	3	0.082199	-0.050399	-0.338067	-0.329261	-0.314584	-0.109107	-0.050399	0.087867	0.571801	0.606367	0.627107
6519	Lessors Of Real Property, Not Elsewhere Classified	2	1.252541	1.252541	0.756015	0.771215	0.796548	1.151209	1.252541	1.353873	1.708534	1.733867	1.749067
653	REAL ESTATE AGENTS AND MANAGERS	20	1.486362	1.351615	0.561667	0.646079	0.786765	1.101574	1.351615	1.531336	2.545951	2.908671	3.126302
6531	Real Estate Agents And Managers	20	1.486362	1.351615	0.561667	0.646079	0.786765	1.101574	1.351615	1.531336	2.545951	2.908671	3.126302
655	LAND SUBDIVIDERS AND DEVELOPERS	4	0.972259	1.101258	0.307550	0.335195	0.381270	0.982576	1.101258	1.219939	1.382649	1.390025	1.394450
6552	Land Subdividers And Developers, Except Cemeteries	4	0.972259	1.101258	0.307550	0.335195	0.381270	0.982576	1.101258	1.219939	1.382649	1.390025	1.394450
67	HOLDING AND OTHER INVESTMENT OFFICES	228	0.829618	0.801693	-1.059729	-0.220949	-0.023808	0.605415	0.801693	0.994833	2.027056	2.198499	2.245601
671	HOLDING OFFICES	56	0.906063	1.017105	-0.020190	0.003394	0.047643	0.718605	1.017105	1.102030	1.922968	2.008706	2.106585
6712	Offices Of Bank Holding Companies	46	0.940033	1.019630	-0.021999	-0.006902	0.037037	0.799327	1.019630	1.104800	1.950623	2.026409	2.122435
6719	Offices Of Holding Companies, Not Elsewhere Classified	10	0.749802	0.866838	0.063980	0.079231	0.104650	0.542422	0.866838	1.048942	1.440413	1.515487	1.560531
672	INVESTMENT OFFICES	28	0.648007	0.543638	-0.011587	0.042300	0.089914	0.476322	0.543638	0.619262	1.734160	2.011740	2.129700
6722	Management Investment Offices, Open-End	3	1.839957	1.917080	1.404903	1.420582	1.446713	1.812554	1.917080	1.975332	2.179214	2.193777	2.202515
6726	Unit Investment Trusts, Face-Amount Certificate Offices	25	0.504974	0.493699	-0.015578	0.032321	0.088040	0.448768	0.493699	0.580799	1.046616	1.068886	1.070196
673	TRUSTS	7	0.018961	0.160972	-2.343138	-2.123175	-1.756570	0.160949	0.160972	0.165308	1.395324	1.625012	1.762825
6733	Trusts, Except Educational, Religious, And Charitable	7	0.018961	0.160972	-2.343138	-2.123175	-1.756570	0.160949	0.160972	0.165308	1.395324	1.625012	1.762825
679	MISCELLANEOUS INVESTING	137	0.876908	0.889537	-0.994299	-0.349210	-0.061587	0.709851	0.889537	1.041428	2.075512	2.221226	2.367029
6794	Patent Owners And Lessors	12	1.212993	1.363120	-0.025884	-0.012480	0.009862	1.210458	1.363120	1.390220	2.073506	2.133038	2.168757
6798	Real Estate Investment Trusts	51	0.872723	0.790711	-0.077881	0.038352	0.119932	0.669512	0.790711	0.959258	1.840095	2.183983	2.346340
6799	Investors, Not Elsewhere Classified	74	0.825292	0.867754	-1.870186	-0.656243	-0.301792	0.614707	0.867754	1.031642	2.079624	2.219139	2.279210
	SERVICES												
70	HOTELS, ROOMING HOUSES, CAMPS, AND OTHER LODGING PLACES	29	1.276271	1.314500	-0.070644	0.070552	0.434035	1.306188	1.314500	1.423554	1.825060	1.927740	2.035848
701	HOTELS AND MOTELS	29	1.276271	1.314500	-0.070644	0.070552	0.434035	1.306188	1.314500	1.423554	1.825060	1.927740	2.035848
7011	Hotels And Motels	29	1.276271	1.314500	-0.070644	0.070552	0.434035	1.306188	1.314500	1.423554	1.825060	1.927740	2.035848
72	PERSONAL SERVICES	13	0.760831	0.898700	-0.734665	-0.689882	-0.615244	0.661044	0.898700	1.033320	2.063814	2.398197	2.598827
721	LAUNDRY, CLEANING, AND GARMENT SERVICES	3	0.762267	0.661935	0.495533	0.500627	0.509117	0.627975	0.661935	0.756094	1.085651	1.109190	1.123314
7211	Power Laundries, Family And Commercial	1	0.661935	0.661935	0.661935	0.661935	0.661935	0.661935	0.661935	0.661935	0.661935	0.661935	0.661935
7215	Coin-Operated Laundries And Drycleaning	1	0.492137	0.492137	0.492137	0.492137	0.492137	0.492137	0.492137	0.492137	0.492137	0.492137	0.492137
7218	Industrial Launderers	1	1.132730	1.132730	1.132730	1.132730	1.132730	1.132730	1.132730	1.132730	1.132730	1.132730	1.132730

Down-market Betas of Common Stocks by SIC Codes as of March 31, 2017

SIC Code	Description	Number of Companies	Mean	Median	1st Percentile	2.5th Percentile	5th Percentile	40th Percentile	50th Percentile	60th Percentile	95th Percentile	97.5th Percentile	99th Percentile
723	BEAUTY SHOPS	2	0.130920	0.130920	-0.746611	-0.719748	-0.674976	-0.048168	0.130920	0.310008	0.936816	0.981588	1.008451
7231	Beauty Shops	2	0.130920	0.130920	-0.746611	-0.719748	-0.674976	-0.048168	0.130920	0.310008	0.936816	0.981588	1.008451
726	FUNERAL SERVICE AND CREMATORIES	2	0.778091	0.778091	0.659893	0.663511	0.669542	0.753969	0.778091	0.802212	0.886639	0.892670	0.896288
7261	Funeral Service And Crematories	2	0.778091	0.778091	0.659893	0.663511	0.669542	0.753969	0.778091	0.802212	0.886639	0.892670	0.896288
729	MISCELLANEOUS PERSONAL SERVICES	6	0.964331	1.075790	-0.499961	-0.476313	-0.436899	1.061160	1.075790	1.090420	2.453928	2.593254	2.676850
7291	Tax Return Preparation Services	1	1.090420	1.090420	1.090420	1.090420	1.090420	1.090420	1.090420	1.090420	1.090420	1.090420	1.090420
7299	Miscellaneous Personal Services, Not Elsewhere Classified	5	0.939113	1.061160	-0.503114	-0.484195	-0.452664	0.556529	1.061160	1.283884	2.509658	2.621119	2.687996
73	BUSINESS SERVICES	431	1.084701	1.210260	-1.838310	-1.058205	-0.346133	1.048900	1.210260	1.329390	2.245310	2.463750	2.830029
731	ADVERTISING	20	1.018929	1.144110	-0.515981	-0.386740	-0.171338	0.868849	1.144110	1.332458	1.945156	2.029858	2.080679
7310	SERVICES-ADVERTISING	1	0.584662	0.584662	0.584662	0.584662	0.584662	0.584662	0.584662	0.584662	0.584662	0.584662	0.584662
7311	Advertising Agencies	12	0.980078	1.105905	-0.505018	-0.359331	-0.116520	0.839725	1.105905	1.309334	1.772395	1.854318	1.903471
7312	Outdoor Advertising Services	2	1.263070	1.263070	1.008701	1.016488	1.029466	1.211158	1.263070	1.314982	1.496674	1.509652	1.517439
7313	Radio, Television, And Publishers' Advertising Representatives	3	0.769749	0.343350	-0.138824	-0.124063	-0.099463	0.244947	0.343350	0.697592	1.937439	2.026000	2.079136
7319	Advertising, Not Elsewhere Classified	2	1.598800	1.598800	1.558120	1.559366	1.561441	1.590498	1.598800	1.607102	1.636159	1.638235	1.639480
732	CONSUMER CREDIT REPORTING AGENCIES, MERCANTILE REPORTING AGENCIES	10	1.455280	1.404625	1.077037	1.083347	1.093863	1.343936	1.404625	1.461098	1.961141	2.013706	2.045244
7320	SERVICES-CONSUMER CREDIT REPORTING, COLLECTION AGENCIES	1	1.497290	1.497290	1.497290	1.497290	1.497290	1.497290	1.497290	1.497290	1.497290	1.497290	1.497290
7322	Adjustment And Collection Services	3	1.457117	1.436970	1.304131	1.308198	1.314975	1.409860	1.436970	1.476168	1.613361	1.623161	1.629040
7323	Credit Reporting Services	6	1.447360	1.296420	1.075167	1.078673	1.084515	1.220560	1.296420	1.372280	2.007865	2.037068	2.054589
733	MAILING, REPRODUCTION, COMMERCIAL ART AND PHOTOGRAPHY, AND STENOGRAPHY	3	1.341260	1.406100	0.602442	0.627044	0.668047	1.242088	1.406100	1.531208	1.969086	2.000363	2.019129
7331	Direct Mail Advertising Services	2	1.308841	1.308841	0.600497	0.622181	0.658321	1.164281	1.308841	1.453400	1.959360	1.995500	2.017184
7338	Secretarial And Court Reporting Services	1	1.406100	1.406100	1.406100	1.406100	1.406100	1.406100	1.406100	1.406100	1.406100	1.406100	1.406100
734	SERVICES TO DWELLINGS AND OTHER BUILDINGS	3	0.909389	0.809062	0.702707	0.705962	0.711389	0.787357	0.809062	0.890964	1.177619	1.198095	1.210380
7342	Disinfecting And Pest Control Services	1	0.809062	0.809062	0.809062	0.809062	0.809062	0.809062	0.809062	0.809062	0.809062	0.809062	0.809062
7349	Building Cleaning And Maintenance Services, Not Elsewhere Classified	2	0.959553	0.959553	0.705716	0.713487	0.726438	0.907750	0.959553	1.011356	1.192668	1.205619	1.213390
735	MISCELLANEOUS EQUIPMENT RENTAL AND LEASING	20	1.517003	1.739455	-0.142386	-0.030943	0.154795	1.486124	1.739455	2.047076	2.642745	2.745393	2.806981
7350	SERVICES-MISCELLANEOUS EQUIPMENT RENTAL & LEASING	1	-0.216681	-0.216681	-0.216681	-0.216681	-0.216681	-0.216681	-0.216681	-0.216681	-0.216681	-0.216681	-0.216681
7353	Heavy Construction Equipment Rental And Leasing	1	1.637680	1.637680	1.637680	1.637680	1.637680	1.637680	1.637680	1.637680	1.637680	1.637680	1.637680

Down-market Betas of Common Stocks by SIC Codes as of March 31, 2017

SIC Code	Description	Number of Companies	Mean	Median	1st Percentile	2.5th Percentile	5th Percentile	40th Percentile	50th Percentile	60th Percentile	95th Percentile	97.5th Percentile	99th Percentile
7359	Equipment Rental And Leasing, Not Elsewhere Classified	18	1.606614	1.904495	0.192077	0.218673	0.263000	1.556882	1.904495	2.176698	2.664355	2.756198	2.811303
736	PERSONNEL SUPPLY SERVICES	24	1.121439	1.168695	-0.015012	-0.014119	0.001780	0.827164	1.168695	1.401482	2.265814	2.556225	2.722608
7361	Employment Agencies	4	1.282386	1.395650	0.028950	0.091903	0.196824	1.389818	1.395650	1.401482	2.209377	2.280318	2.322883
7363	Help Supply Services	20	1.089250	1.009328	0.003628	0.032483	0.080574	0.778561	1.009328	1.320288	1.834216	2.333873	2.633667
737	COMPUTER PROGRAMMING, DATA PROCESSING, AND OTHER COMPUTER RELATED	265	1.072440	1.212940	-1.911126	-1.079142	-0.517606	1.092910	1.212940	1.331334	2.211504	2.465052	2.733141
7370	SERVICES-COMPUTER PROGRAMMING, DATA PROCESSING, ETC.	1	-1.084650	-1.084650	-1.084650	-1.084650	-1.084650	-1.084650	-1.084650	-1.084650	-1.084650	-1.084650	-1.084650
7371	Computer Programming Services	58	1.185157	1.301815	-1.804084	-0.587460	0.079344	1.227158	1.301815	1.405896	2.206342	2.281024	2.389605
7372	Prepackaged Software	118	1.102089	1.215090	-1.813160	-0.982088	-0.370425	1.130260	1.215090	1.334328	2.244537	2.486211	2.598026
7373	Computer Integrated Systems Design	35	0.959312	1.195530	-1.222593	-0.766716	-0.571697	1.032161	1.195530	1.356880	1.763455	2.028432	2.578661
7374	Computer Processing And Data Preparation And Processing Services	37	0.963940	1.107650	-1.484827	-0.880263	-0.076074	0.980022	1.107650	1.222038	1.926750	1.999021	2.106540
7375	Information Retrieval Services	10	0.992893	0.854199	0.662466	0.671738	0.687191	0.804383	0.854199	0.902573	1.629237	1.704824	1.750175
7376	Computer Facilities Management Services	1	3.197470	3.197470	3.197470	3.197470	3.197470	3.197470	3.197470	3.197470	3.197470	3.197470	3.197470
7379	Computer Related Services, Not Elsewhere Classified	5	0.825531	0.958253	0.077643	0.126254	0.207273	0.917123	0.958253	1.002956	1.172986	1.185858	1.193581
738	MISCELLANEOUS BUSINESS SERVICES	86	0.981064	1.077720	-1.766794	-1.382964	-0.820866	0.969438	1.077720	1.251960	2.236480	2.391798	2.500237
7381	Detective, Guard, And Armored Car Services	1	0.211581	0.211581	0.211581	0.211581	0.211581	0.211581	0.211581	0.211581	0.211581	0.211581	0.211581
7382	Security Systems Services	3	1.461340	1.251960	1.248501	1.248607	1.248783	1.251254	1.251960	1.378294	1.820463	1.852047	1.870997
7384	Photofinishing Laboratories	1	0.814645	0.814645	0.814645	0.814645	0.814645	0.814645	0.814645	0.814645	0.814645	0.814645	0.814645
7389	Business Services, Not Elsewhere Classified	81	0.974830	1.075770	-1.781502	-1.430180	-1.014550	0.969438	1.075770	1.258780	2.250970	2.400940	2.519156
75	AUTOMOTIVE REPAIR, SERVICES, AND PARKING	6	1.431566	1.367615	0.533700	0.557795	0.597953	1.185920	1.367615	1.549310	2.443603	2.540996	2.599433
751	AUTOMOTIVE RENTAL AND LEASING, WITHOUT DRIVERS	3	1.894517	1.859240	1.199386	1.219586	1.253252	1.724576	1.859240	2.015070	2.560475	2.599433	2.622807
7513	Truck Rental And Leasing, Without Drivers	2	1.522580	1.522580	1.192653	1.202753	1.219586	1.455248	1.522580	1.589912	1.825574	1.842407	1.852507
7514	Passenger Car Rental	1	2.638390	2.638390	2.638390	2.638390	2.638390	2.638390	2.638390	2.638390	2.638390	2.638390	2.638390
753	AUTOMOTIVE REPAIR SHOPS	3	0.968615	0.838899	0.524062	0.533700	0.549763	0.774647	0.838899	0.980981	1.478269	1.513789	1.535102
7538	General Automotive Repair Shops	3	0.968615	0.838899	0.524062	0.533700	0.549763	0.774647	0.838899	0.980981	1.478269	1.513789	1.535102
76	MISCELLANEOUS REPAIR SERVICES	3	0.296120	0.135903	-0.604406	-0.581743	-0.543972	-0.015180	0.135903	0.383116	1.248363	1.310167	1.347249
762	ELECTRICAL REPAIR SHOPS	2	0.376228	0.376228	-0.599599	-0.569727	-0.519940	0.177080	0.376228	0.575376	1.272396	1.322183	1.352055
7623	Refrigeration And Air-Conditioning Service And Repair Shops	2	0.376228	0.376228	-0.599599	-0.569727	-0.519940	0.177080	0.376228	0.575376	1.272396	1.322183	1.352055
769	MISCELLANEOUS REPAIR SHOPS AND RELATED SERVICES	1	0.135903	0.135903	0.135903	0.135903	0.135903	0.135903	0.135903	0.135903	0.135903	0.135903	0.135903

Down-market Betas of Common Stocks by SIC Codes as of March 31, 2017

SIC Code	Description	Number of Companies	Mean	Median	1st Percentile	2.5th Percentile	5th Percentile	40th Percentile	50th Percentile	60th Percentile	95th Percentile	97.5th Percentile	99th Percentile
7699	Repair Shops And Related Services, Not Elsewhere Classified	1	0.135903	0.135903	0.135903	0.135903	0.135903	0.135903	0.135903	0.135903	0.135903	0.135903	0.135903
78	MOTION PICTURES	17	0.283457	0.438569	-3.585085	-2.998532	-2.020944	0.361863	0.438569	0.775946	1.377708	1.500544	1.574246
781	MOTION PICTURE PRODUCTION AND ALLIED SERVICES	11	0.101787	0.433627	-3.731723	-3.365128	-2.754135	0.314020	0.433627	0.677326	1.424940	1.524160	1.583692
7812	Motion Picture And Video Tape Production	9	0.490939	0.433627	-1.413229	-1.234848	-0.937546	0.337941	0.433627	0.867269	1.464628	1.544004	1.591630
7819	Services Allied To Motion Picture Production	2	-1.649397	-1.649397	-3.929586	-3.859784	-3.743448	-2.114742	-1.649397	-1.184052	0.444654	0.560990	0.630792
782	MOTION PICTURE DISTRIBUTION AND ALLIED SERVICES	1	-0.063447	-0.063447	-0.063447	-0.063447	-0.063447	-0.063447	-0.063447	-0.063447	-0.063447	-0.063447	-0.063447
7822	Motion Picture And Video Tape Distribution	1	-0.063447	-0.063447	-0.063447	-0.063447	-0.063447	-0.063447	-0.063447	-0.063447	-0.063447	-0.063447	-0.063447
783	MOTION PICTURE THEATERS	4	0.611570	0.640131	0.251234	0.259925	0.274409	0.519194	0.640131	0.761068	0.908744	0.914660	0.918210
7832	Motion Picture Theaters, Except Drive-In	4	0.611570	0.640131	0.251234	0.259925	0.274409	0.519194	0.640131	0.761068	0.908744	0.914660	0.918210
784	VIDEO TAPE RENTAL	1	1.316290	1.316290	1.316290	1.316290	1.316290	1.316290	1.316290	1.316290	1.316290	1.316290	1.316290
7841	Video Tape Rental	1	1.316290	1.316290	1.316290	1.316290	1.316290	1.316290	1.316290	1.316290	1.316290	1.316290	1.316290
79	AMUSEMENT AND RECREATION SERVICES	31	0.440701	0.657172	-5.763341	-5.139268	-3.096980	0.374954	0.657172	0.956596	1.836635	3.551028	6.175837
7900	SERVICES-AMUSEMENT & RECREATION SERVICES	1	-0.944246	-0.944246	-0.944246	-0.944246	-0.944246	-0.944246	-0.944246	-0.944246	-0.944246	-0.944246	-0.944246
792	THEATRICAL PRODUCERS (EXCEPT MOTION PICTURE), BANDS, ORCHESTRAS	2	-0.096615	-0.096615	-1.375304	-1.336161	-1.270922	-0.357572	-0.096615	0.164342	1.077692	1.142931	1.182074
7922	Theatrical Producers (Except Motion Picture) And Miscellaneous Theater	1	1.208170	1.208170	1.208170	1.208170	1.208170	1.208170	1.208170	1.208170	1.208170	1.208170	1.208170
7929	Bands, Orchestras, Actors, And Other Entertainers And Entertainment	1	-1.401400	-1.401400	-1.401400	-1.401400	-1.401400	-1.401400	-1.401400	-1.401400	-1.401400	-1.401400	-1.401400
793	BOWLING CENTERS	1	0.112296	0.112296	0.112296	0.112296	0.112296	0.112296	0.112296	0.112296	0.112296	0.112296	0.112296
7933	Bowling Centers	1	0.112296	0.112296	0.112296	0.112296	0.112296	0.112296	0.112296	0.112296	0.112296	0.112296	0.112296
794	COMMERCIAL SPORTS	9	0.269272	1.038030	-4.396405	-3.802172	-2.811784	0.972883	1.038030	1.050166	1.298360	1.316010	1.326600
7941	Professional Sports Clubs And Promoters	3	1.021525	1.053200	0.958528	0.961426	0.966256	1.033879	1.053200	1.053516	1.054622	1.054701	1.054748
7948	Racing, Including Track Operation	6	-0.106855	0.706492	-4.544963	-4.173568	-3.554575	0.374954	0.706492	1.038030	1.311598	1.322629	1.329248
799	MISCELLANEOUS AMUSEMENT AND RECREATION SERVICES	18	0.681304	0.619388	-5.186819	-3.697963	-1.216537	0.431729	0.619388	0.860728	2.967736	5.446723	6.934115
7993	Coin-Operated Amusement Devices	1	0.657172	0.657172	0.657172	0.657172	0.657172	0.657172	0.657172	0.657172	0.657172	0.657172	0.657172
7996	Amusement Parks	3	0.610097	0.581604	0.261515	0.271314	0.287645	0.516280	0.581604	0.664024	0.952494	0.973099	0.985462
7997	Membership Sports And Recreation Clubs	4	-0.581818	0.879660	-5.968565	-5.652328	-5.125265	0.860728	0.879660	0.898591	1.915562	2.004181	2.057352
7999	Amusement And Recreation Services, Not Elsewhere Classified	10	1.210327	0.355598	-0.320622	-0.290447	-0.240156	0.145013	0.355598	0.743141	5.070352	6.498031	7.354638
80	HEALTH SERVICES	81	1.009769	1.010870	-2.752004	-1.525230	-0.743232	0.815576	1.010870	1.239140	2.576400	3.001270	3.387756

Down-market Betas of Common Stocks by SIC Codes as of March 31, 2017

SIC Code	Description	Number of Companies	Mean	Median	1st Percentile	2.5th Percentile	5th Percentile	40th Percentile	50th Percentile	60th Percentile	95th Percentile	97.5th Percentile	99th Percentile
801	OFFICES AND CLINICS OF DOCTORS OF MEDICINE	15	1.078110	1.438310	-4.613366	-3.510186	-1.671552	1.280640	1.438310	1.582264	2.991786	3.476403	3.767173
8011	Offices And Clinics Of Doctors Of Medicine	15	1.078110	1.438310	-4.613366	-3.510186	-1.671552	1.280640	1.438310	1.582264	2.991786	3.476403	3.767173
804	OFFICES AND CLINICS OF OTHER HEALTH PRACTITIONERS	1	2.152410	2.152410	2.152410	2.152410	2.152410	2.152410	2.152410	2.152410	2.152410	2.152410	2.152410
8041	Offices And Clinics Of Chiropractors	1	2.152410	2.152410	2.152410	2.152410	2.152410	2.152410	2.152410	2.152410	2.152410	2.152410	2.152410
805	NURSING AND PERSONAL CARE FACILITIES	10	1.062672	0.960065	0.141528	0.196642	0.288499	0.827952	0.960065	1.113367	1.970009	2.028910	2.064250
8051	Skilled Nursing Care Facilities	10	1.062672	0.960065	0.141528	0.196642	0.288499	0.827952	0.960065	1.113367	1.970009	2.028910	2.064250
806	HOSPITALS	15	1.035567	1.145750	-1.444718	-1.323951	-1.122672	0.972944	1.145750	1.203368	2.384635	2.491473	2.555575
8062	General Medical And Surgical Hospitals	10	0.874021	1.000670	-1.342814	-1.069190	-0.613149	0.826622	1.000670	1.152482	1.889389	1.895865	1.899750
8069	Specialty Hospitals, Except Psychiatric	5	1.358659	1.800890	-0.870094	-0.750014	-0.549882	1.501006	1.800890	1.997758	2.537260	2.567785	2.586100
807	MEDICAL AND DENTAL LABORATORIES	17	0.686618	0.818916	-1.885269	-1.558973	-1.015146	0.811914	0.818916	0.984304	1.912748	1.932164	1.943814
8071	Medical Laboratories	17	0.686618	0.818916	-1.885269	-1.558973	-1.015146	0.811914	0.818916	0.984304	1.912748	1.932164	1.943814
808	HOME HEALTH CARE SERVICES	9	1.013381	0.760293	0.067940	0.105793	0.168881	0.756059	0.760293	1.100243	1.949998	2.049674	2.109480
8082	Home Health Care Services	9	1.013381	0.760293	0.067940	0.105793	0.168881	0.756059	0.760293	1.100243	1.949998	2.049674	2.109480
809	MISCELLANEOUS HEALTH AND ALLIED SERVICES, NOT ELSEWHERE CLASSIFIED	14	1.179577	0.811454	0.304293	0.319296	0.344301	0.717398	0.811454	0.990071	3.086380	3.165410	3.212828
8093	Specialty Outpatient Facilities, Not Elsewhere Classified	6	1.654028	1.130055	0.567603	0.591199	0.630524	1.020970	1.130055	1.239140	3.183648	3.214044	3.232282
8099	Health And Allied Services, Not Elsewhere Classified	8	0.823739	0.633394	0.299677	0.307755	0.321219	0.524962	0.633394	0.717398	1.815823	1.885061	1.926605
81	LEGAL SERVICES	1	1.052460	1.052460	1.052460	1.052460	1.052460	1.052460	1.052460	1.052460	1.052460	1.052460	1.052460
811	LEGAL SERVICES	1	1.052460	1.052460	1.052460	1.052460	1.052460	1.052460	1.052460	1.052460	1.052460	1.052460	1.052460
8111	Legal Services	1	1.052460	1.052460	1.052460	1.052460	1.052460	1.052460	1.052460	1.052460	1.052460	1.052460	1.052460
82	EDUCATIONAL SERVICES	18	1.121155	1.216395	-0.249667	-0.035203	0.322238	1.099314	1.216395	1.281918	2.084108	2.462549	2.689614
8200	SERVICES-EDUCATIONAL SERVICES	2	1.018869	1.018869	0.710756	0.720188	0.735908	0.955989	1.018869	1.081749	1.301830	1.317550	1.326982
821	ELEMENTARY AND SECONDARY SCHOOLS	6	1.280337	1.306270	0.741064	0.744852	0.751167	1.240030	1.306270	1.372510	1.860743	1.905641	1.932581
8211	Elementary And Secondary Schools	6	1.280337	1.306270	0.741064	0.744852	0.751167	1.240030	1.306270	1.372510	1.860743	1.905641	1.932581
822	COLLEGES, UNIVERSITIES, PROFESSIONAL SCHOOLS, AND JUNIOR COLLEGES	3	0.759062	1.192760	-0.360935	-0.313373	-0.234103	0.875679	1.192760	1.249622	1.448639	1.462855	1.471384
8221	Colleges, Universities, And Professional Schools	3	0.759062	1.192760	-0.360935	-0.313373	-0.234103	0.875679	1.192760	1.249622	1.448639	1.462855	1.471384
823	LIBRARIES	1	1.176880	1.176880	1.176880	1.176880	1.176880	1.176880	1.176880	1.176880	1.176880	1.176880	1.176880
8231	Libraries	1	1.176880	1.176880	1.176880	1.176880	1.176880	1.176880	1.176880	1.176880	1.176880	1.176880	1.176880
824	VOCATIONAL SCHOOLS	3	1.592414	1.316870	0.633332	0.654256	0.689131	1.177372	1.316870	1.621694	2.688578	2.764784	2.810508
8249	Vocational Schools, Not Elsewhere Classified	3	1.592414	1.316870	0.633332	0.654256	0.689131	1.177372	1.316870	1.621694	2.688578	2.764784	2.810508

Down-market Betas of Common Stocks by SIC Codes as of March 31, 2017

SIC Code	Description	Number of Companies	Mean	Median	1st Percentile	2.5th Percentile	5th Percentile	40th Percentile	50th Percentile	60th Percentile	95th Percentile	97.5th Percentile	99th Percentile
829	SCHOOLS AND EDUCATIONAL SERVICES, NOT ELSEWHERE CLASSIFIED	3	0.743243	0.508156	0.449588	0.451381	0.454369	0.496203	0.508156	0.661161	1.196678	1.234929	1.257880
8299	Schools And Educational Services, Not Elsewhere Classified	3	0.743243	0.508156	0.449588	0.451381	0.454369	0.496203	0.508156	0.661161	1.196678	1.234929	1.257880
83	SOCIAL SERVICES	3	1.233900	1.261180	0.640143	0.659155	0.690840	1.134438	1.261180	1.371554	1.757863	1.785457	1.802013
832	INDIVIDUAL AND FAMILY SOCIAL SERVICES	1	1.261180	1.261180	1.261180	1.261180	1.261180	1.261180	1.261180	1.261180	1.261180	1.261180	1.261180
8322	Individual And Family Social Services	1	1.261180	1.261180	1.261180	1.261180	1.261180	1.261180	1.261180	1.261180	1.261180	1.261180	1.261180
833	JOB TRAINING AND VOCATIONAL REHABILITATION SERVICES	1	1.813050	1.813050	1.813050	1.813050	1.813050	1.813050	1.813050	1.813050	1.813050	1.813050	1.813050
8331	Job Training And Vocational Rehabilitation Services	1	1.813050	1.813050	1.813050	1.813050	1.813050	1.813050	1.813050	1.813050	1.813050	1.813050	1.813050
835	CHILD DAY CARE SERVICES	1	0.627469	0.627469	0.627469	0.627469	0.627469	0.627469	0.627469	0.627469	0.627469	0.627469	0.627469
8351	Child Day Care Services	1	0.627469	0.627469	0.627469	0.627469	0.627469	0.627469	0.627469	0.627469	0.627469	0.627469	0.627469
86	MEMBERSHIP ORGANIZATIONS	1	1.210360	1.210360	1.210360	1.210360	1.210360	1.210360	1.210360	1.210360	1.210360	1.210360	1.210360
869	MEMBERSHIP ORGANIZATIONS, NOT ELSEWHERE CLASSIFIED	1	1.210360	1.210360	1.210360	1.210360	1.210360	1.210360	1.210360	1.210360	1.210360	1.210360	1.210360
8699	Membership Organizations, Not Elsewhere Classified	1	1.210360	1.210360	1.210360	1.210360	1.210360	1.210360	1.210360	1.210360	1.210360	1.210360	1.210360
87	ENGINEERING, ACCOUNTING, RESEARCH, MANAGEMENT, AND RELATED SERVICES	172	1.248261	1.301130	-2.645714	-0.818722	-0.569055	1.038436	1.301130	1.487730	2.889505	3.775942	5.159666
871	ENGINEERING, ARCHITECTURAL, AND SURVEYING SERVICES	20	1.320137	1.607445	-2.003317	-1.201098	0.135934	1.478420	1.607445	1.629222	2.096730	2.103660	2.107818
8711	Engineering Services	19	1.304239	1.592680	-2.031465	-1.271468	-0.004806	1.386260	1.592680	1.633574	2.097459	2.104025	2.107964
8712	Architectural Services	1	1.622210	1.622210	1.622210	1.622210	1.622210	1.622210	1.622210	1.622210	1.622210	1.622210	1.622210
872	ACCOUNTING, AUDITING, AND BOOKKEEPING SERVICES	2	1.084754	1.084754	0.547914	0.564348	0.591738	0.975195	1.084754	1.194313	1.577770	1.605160	1.621594
8721	Accounting, Auditing, And Bookkeeping Services	2	1.084754	1.084754	0.547914	0.564348	0.591738	0.975195	1.084754	1.194313	1.577770	1.605160	1.621594
873	RESEARCH, DEVELOPMENT, AND TESTING SERVICES	96	1.459532	1.418945	-1.008707	-0.679746	-0.373488	1.149130	1.418945	1.591390	3.225488	3.923489	6.062484
8731	Commercial Physical And Biological Research	83	1.445490	1.410870	-1.411873	-0.720403	-0.519930	1.146692	1.410870	1.594000	3.363278	3.928179	6.139063
8732	Commercial Economic, Sociological, And Educational Research	6	1.780886	1.809255	0.454642	0.521600	0.633196	1.492740	1.809255	2.125770	2.920378	3.042059	3.115068
8733	Noncommercial Research Organizations	5	1.568778	1.489770	0.894750	0.904229	0.920027	1.312426	1.489770	1.575706	2.512658	2.613664	2.674268
8734	Testing Laboratories	2	0.805118	0.805118	0.520552	0.529264	0.543782	0.747043	0.805118	0.863192	1.066453	1.080971	1.089683
874	MANAGEMENT AND PUBLIC RELATIONS SERVICES	54	0.852103	0.929115	-1.942904	-0.942692	-0.635809	0.796733	0.929115	1.177768	1.963670	2.351421	3.601626
8741	Management Services	14	0.914881	0.828926	-0.967737	-0.790224	-0.494367	0.605296	0.828926	0.918579	2.683115	3.743027	4.378975
8742	Management Consulting Services	34	0.772464	0.942347	-2.161916	-1.041124	-0.635809	0.796733	0.942347	1.269050	1.950910	2.066976	2.348576
8743	Public Relations Services	1	1.252880	1.252880	1.252880	1.252880	1.252880	1.252880	1.252880	1.252880	1.252880	1.252880	1.252880

Down-market Betas of Common Stocks by SIC Codes as of March 31, 2017

SIC Code	Description	Number of Companies	Mean	Median	1st Percentile	2.5th Percentile	5th Percentile	40th Percentile	50th Percentile	60th Percentile	95th Percentile	97.5th Percentile	99th Percentile
8744	Facilities Support Management Services	1	0.334407	0.334407	0.334407	0.334407	0.334407	0.334407	0.334407	0.334407	0.334407	0.334407	0.334407
8748	Business Consulting Services, Not Elsewhere Classified	4	1.338529	1.448650	0.522691	0.563977	0.632786	1.427038	1.448650	1.470262	1.890103	1.925877	1.947341
88	PRIVATE HOUSEHOLDS	1	2.035230	2.035230	2.035230	2.035230	2.035230	2.035230	2.035230	2.035230	2.035230	2.035230	2.035230
8880	AMERICAN DEPOSITARY RECEIPTS	1	2.035230	2.035230	2.035230	2.035230	2.035230	2.035230	2.035230	2.035230	2.035230	2.035230	2.035230
89	SERVICES, NOT ELSEWHERE CLASSIFIED	14	1.488551	1.296535	-0.126312	-0.072333	0.017632	1.080894	1.296535	1.474984	3.495571	4.269665	4.734122
899	SERVICES, NOT ELSEWHERE CLASSIFIED	14	1.488551	1.296535	-0.126312	-0.072333	0.017632	1.080894	1.296535	1.474984	3.495571	4.269665	4.734122
8999	Services, Not Elsewhere Classified	14	1.488551	1.296535	-0.126312	-0.072333	0.017632	1.080894	1.296535	1.474984	3.495571	4.269665	4.734122
	PUBLIC ADMINISTRATION												
94	ADMINISTRATION OF HUMAN RESOURCE PROGRAMS	1	1.048110	1.048110	1.048110	1.048110	1.048110	1.048110	1.048110	1.048110	1.048110	1.048110	1.048110
943	ADMINISTRATION OF PUBLIC HEALTH PROGRAMS	1	1.048110	1.048110	1.048110	1.048110	1.048110	1.048110	1.048110	1.048110	1.048110	1.048110	1.048110
9431	Administration Of Public Health Programs	1	1.048110	1.048110	1.048110	1.048110	1.048110	1.048110	1.048110	1.048110	1.048110	1.048110	1.048110
95	ADMINISTRATION OF ENVIRONMENTAL QUALITY AND HOUSING PROGRAMS	2	-0.584350	-0.584350	-2.271312	-2.219671	-2.133601	-0.928628	-0.584350	-0.240072	0.964901	1.050971	1.102612
951	ADMINISTRATION OF ENVIRONMENTAL QUALITY PROGRAMS	2	-0.584350	-0.584350	-2.271312	-2.219671	-2.133601	-0.928628	-0.584350	-0.240072	0.964901	1.050971	1.102612
9511	Air And Water Resource And Solid Waste Management	2	-0.584350	-0.584350	-2.271312	-2.219671	-2.133601	-0.928628	-0.584350	-0.240072	0.964901	1.050971	1.102612
96	ADMINISTRATION OF ECONOMIC PROGRAMS	2	-2.820190	-2.820190	-7.312755	-7.175228	-6.946015	-3.737040	-2.820190	-1.903340	1.305635	1.534848	1.672375
961	ADMINISTRATION OF GENERAL ECONOMIC PROGRAMS	1	1.764060	1.764060	1.764060	1.764060	1.764060	1.764060	1.764060	1.764060	1.764060	1.764060	1.764060
9611	Administration Of General Economic Programs	1	1.764060	1.764060	1.764060	1.764060	1.764060	1.764060	1.764060	1.764060	1.764060	1.764060	1.764060
963	REGULATION AND ADMINISTRATION OF COMMUNICATIONS, ELECTRIC, GAS	1	-7.404440	-7.404440	-7.404440	-7.404440	-7.404440	-7.404440	-7.404440	-7.404440	-7.404440	-7.404440	-7.404440
9631	Regulation And Administration Of Communications, Electric, Gas	1	-7.404440	-7.404440	-7.404440	-7.404440	-7.404440	-7.404440	-7.404440	-7.404440	-7.404440	-7.404440	-7.404440
	NONCLASSIFIABLE ESTABLISHMENTS												
99	NONCLASSIFIABLE ESTABLISHMENTS	61	0.999464	1.147990	-2.581854	-2.230635	-1.430130	0.724920	1.147990	1.310600	3.402150	4.472450	5.230214
999	NONCLASSIFIABLE ESTABLISHMENTS	61	0.999464	1.147990	-2.581854	-2.230635	-1.430130	0.724920	1.147990	1.310600	3.402150	4.472450	5.230214
9995	NON-OPERATING ESTABLISHMENTS	1	3.857130	3.857130	3.857130	3.857130	3.857130	3.857130	3.857130	3.857130	3.857130	3.857130	3.857130
9999	Nonclassifiable Establishments	60	0.951837	1.123285	-2.586955	-2.237995	-1.462796	0.679233	1.123285	1.296566	2.852034	4.287101	5.233775

Up-market Betas of Common Stocks by SIC Codes as of March 31, 2017

Details:
Benchmark: S&P 500 Index
Returns period and frequency: 1 year of daily returns
Risk-free rate: Federal Funds Rate

SIC Code	Description	Number of Companies	Mean	Median	1st Percentile	2.5th Percentile	5th Percentile	40th Percentile	50th Percentile	60th Percentile	95th Percentile	97.5th Percentile	99th Percentile
	AGRICULTURE, FORESTRY, AND FISHING												
01	AGRICULTURAL PRODUCTION-CROPS	7	0.885608	0.666007	-0.042571	-0.035760	-0.024408	0.363675	0.666007	0.828531	2.601277	2.882439	3.051135
011	CASH GRAINS	2	0.444884	0.444884	-0.037272	-0.022512	0.002088	0.346485	0.444884	0.543283	0.887680	0.912280	0.927040
0115	Corn	1	-0.047112	-0.047112	-0.047112	-0.047112	-0.047112	-0.047112	-0.047112	-0.047112	-0.047112	-0.047112	-0.047112
0116	Soybeans	1	0.936880	0.936880	0.936880	0.936880	0.936880	0.936880	0.936880	0.936880	0.936880	0.936880	0.936880
013	FIELD CROPS, EXCEPT CASH GRAINS	1	0.028569	0.028569	0.028569	0.028569	0.028569	0.028569	0.028569	0.028569	0.028569	0.028569	0.028569
0131	Cotton	1	0.028569	0.028569	0.028569	0.028569	0.028569	0.028569	0.028569	0.028569	0.028569	0.028569	0.028569
016	VEGETABLES AND MELONS	1	3.163600	3.163600	3.163600	3.163600	3.163600	3.163600	3.163600	3.163600	3.163600	3.163600	3.163600
0161	Vegetables And Melons	1	3.163600	3.163600	3.163600	3.163600	3.163600	3.163600	3.163600	3.163600	3.163600	3.163600	3.163600
017	FRUITS AND TREE NUTS	2	0.977599	0.977599	0.672239	0.681587	0.697166	0.915280	0.977599	1.039917	1.258031	1.273610	1.282958
0174	Citrus Fruits	2	0.977599	0.977599	0.672239	0.681587	0.697166	0.915280	0.977599	1.039917	1.258031	1.273610	1.282958
019	GENERAL FARMS, PRIMARILY CROP	1	0.162121	0.162121	0.162121	0.162121	0.162121	0.162121	0.162121	0.162121	0.162121	0.162121	0.162121
0191	General Farms, Primarily Crop	1	0.162121	0.162121	0.162121	0.162121	0.162121	0.162121	0.162121	0.162121	0.162121	0.162121	0.162121
02	AGRICULTURAL PRODUCTION-LIVESTOCK AND ANIMAL SPECIALTIES	2	0.354610	0.354610	-0.080546	-0.067225	-0.045023	0.265803	0.354610	0.443418	0.754243	0.776445	0.789766
021	LIVESTOCK, EXCEPT DAIRY AND POULTRY	1	-0.089427	-0.089427	-0.089427	-0.089427	-0.089427	-0.089427	-0.089427	-0.089427	-0.089427	-0.089427	-0.089427
0213	Hogs	1	-0.089427	-0.089427	-0.089427	-0.089427	-0.089427	-0.089427	-0.089427	-0.089427	-0.089427	-0.089427	-0.089427
025	POULTRY AND EGGS	1	0.798647	0.798647	0.798647	0.798647	0.798647	0.798647	0.798647	0.798647	0.798647	0.798647	0.798647
0252	Chicken Eggs	1	0.798647	0.798647	0.798647	0.798647	0.798647	0.798647	0.798647	0.798647	0.798647	0.798647	0.798647
07	AGRICULTURAL SERVICES	6	2.092802	1.736050	0.647260	0.661278	0.684640	1.294560	1.736050	2.177540	4.405385	4.702583	4.880901
074	VETERINARY SERVICES	2	1.501178	1.501178	0.838343	0.858634	0.892452	1.365906	1.501178	1.636450	2.109904	2.143722	2.164013
0741	Veterinary Services For Livestock	1	0.824816	0.824816	0.824816	0.824816	0.824816	0.824816	0.824816	0.824816	0.824816	0.824816	0.824816
0742	Veterinary Services For Animal Specialties	1	2.177540	2.177540	2.177540	2.177540	2.177540	2.177540	2.177540	2.177540	2.177540	2.177540	2.177540
075	ANIMAL SERVICES, EXCEPT VETERINARY	2	3.147170	3.147170	1.331612	1.387191	1.479821	2.776648	3.147170	3.517692	4.814519	4.907150	4.962728
0752	Animal Specialty Services, Except Veterinary	2	3.147170	3.147170	1.331612	1.387191	1.479821	2.776648	3.147170	3.517692	4.814519	4.907150	4.962728
076	FARM LABOR AND MANAGEMENT SERVICES	1	2.622200	2.622200	2.622200	2.622200	2.622200	2.622200	2.622200	2.622200	2.622200	2.622200	2.622200
0762	Farm Management Services	1	2.622200	2.622200	2.622200	2.622200	2.622200	2.622200	2.622200	2.622200	2.622200	2.622200	2.622200
078	LANDSCAPE AND HORTICULTURAL SERVICES	1	0.637915	0.637915	0.637915	0.637915	0.637915	0.637915	0.637915	0.637915	0.637915	0.637915	0.637915
0782	Lawn And Garden Services	1	0.637915	0.637915	0.637915	0.637915	0.637915	0.637915	0.637915	0.637915	0.637915	0.637915	0.637915
09	FISHING, HUNTING, AND TRAPPING	1	-0.879111	-0.879111	-0.879111	-0.879111	-0.879111	-0.879111	-0.879111	-0.879111	-0.879111	-0.879111	-0.879111
	MINING												
10	METAL MINING	205	0.623795	0.645840	-2.637111	-1.881654	-1.249250	0.368076	0.645840	0.885743	2.748154	3.365257	4.035101
1000	METAL MINING	2	0.541682	0.541682	-0.326244	-0.299675	-0.255393	0.364554	0.541682	0.718809	1.338756	1.383038	1.409607
101	IRON ORES	6	1.352431	1.790515	-0.969801	-0.906577	-0.801204	1.741880	1.790515	1.839150	3.344058	3.587469	3.733516
1011	Iron Ores	6	1.352431	1.790515	-0.969801	-0.906577	-0.801204	1.741880	1.790515	1.839150	3.344058	3.587469	3.733516
102	COPPER ORES	15	1.073808	0.883875	-0.383847	-0.357958	-0.314809	0.823557	0.883875	1.153893	2.666193	2.827687	2.924583
1021	Copper Ores	15	1.073808	0.883875	-0.383847	-0.357958	-0.314809	0.823557	0.883875	1.153893	2.666193	2.827687	2.924583

Up-market Betas of Common Stocks by SIC Codes as of March 31, 2017

SIC Code	Description	Number of Companies	Mean	Median	1st Percentile	2.5th Percentile	5th Percentile	40th Percentile	50th Percentile	60th Percentile	95th Percentile	97.5th Percentile	99th Percentile
103	LEAD AND ZINC ORES	2	1.756925	1.756925	1.736321	1.736951	1.738003	1.752720	1.756925	1.761130	1.775848	1.776899	1.777530
1031	Lead And Zinc Ores	2	1.756925	1.756925	1.736321	1.736951	1.738003	1.752720	1.756925	1.761130	1.775848	1.776899	1.777530
104	GOLD AND SILVER ORES	126	0.510388	0.511806	-3.073105	-1.836453	-1.245925	0.354285	0.511806	0.739242	2.117875	3.333480	3.971340
1041	Gold Ores	116	0.471750	0.476623	-3.144699	-1.973578	-1.295540	0.305902	0.476623	0.656899	2.306608	3.448236	4.000248
1044	Silver Ores	10	0.958591	1.072624	0.225794	0.281660	0.374770	0.942975	1.072624	1.199472	1.313454	1.337727	1.352291
106	FERROALLOY ORES, EXCEPT VANADIUM	4	0.770765	0.837875	-0.077056	-0.058269	-0.026958	0.531895	0.837875	1.143854	1.474533	1.485711	1.492419
1061	Ferroalloy Ores, Except Vanadium	4	0.770765	0.837875	-0.077056	-0.058269	-0.026958	0.531895	0.837875	1.143854	1.474533	1.485711	1.492419
108	METAL MINING SERVICES	26	0.565508	0.630899	-2.410748	-2.094199	-1.509991	0.392400	0.630899	0.965567	1.827453	2.273856	2.716893
1081	Metal Mining Services	26	0.565508	0.630899	-2.410748	-2.094199	-1.509991	0.392400	0.630899	0.965567	1.827453	2.273856	2.716893
109	MISCELLANEOUS METAL ORES	24	0.706828	0.974129	-2.386224	-2.008936	-1.486878	0.408458	0.974129	1.071870	2.814122	3.527517	3.984497
1094	Uranium-Radium-Vanadium Ores	13	1.049519	1.082320	-1.498334	-1.429596	-1.315032	0.994025	1.082320	1.252116	3.494402	3.891776	4.130200
1099	Miscellaneous Metal Ores, Not Elsewhere Classified	11	0.301831	0.330763	-2.457420	-2.186926	-1.736102	0.323918	0.330763	0.719239	1.907840	1.934710	1.950832
12	COAL MINING	5	1.296381	1.045730	0.385669	0.389352	0.395489	0.805274	1.045730	1.500550	2.377028	2.401309	2.415878
122	BITUMINOUS COAL AND LIGNITE MINING	4	1.509329	1.614255	0.403089	0.432903	0.482591	1.273140	1.614255	1.955370	2.389169	2.407379	2.418306
1221	Bituminous Coal And Lignite Surface Mining	4	1.509329	1.614255	0.403089	0.432903	0.482591	1.273140	1.614255	1.955370	2.389169	2.407379	2.418306
124	COAL MINING SERVICES	1	0.444591	0.444591	0.444591	0.444591	0.444591	0.444591	0.444591	0.444591	0.444591	0.444591	0.444591
1241	Coal Mining Services	1	0.444591	0.444591	0.444591	0.444591	0.444591	0.444591	0.444591	0.444591	0.444591	0.444591	0.444591
13	OIL AND GAS EXTRACTION	201	-0.591304	1.461450	-4.301630	-1.399440	-0.502817	1.296650	1.461450	1.642330	2.837790	3.581560	4.491140
131	CRUDE PETROLEUM AND NATURAL GAS	131	1.432010	1.444200	-3.511760	-1.514850	-0.430133	1.285510	1.444200	1.637240	3.327485	3.993270	4.573663
1311	Crude Petroleum And Natural Gas	131	1.432010	1.444200	-3.511760	-1.514850	-0.430133	1.285510	1.444200	1.637240	3.327485	3.993270	4.573663
132	NATURAL GAS LIQUIDS	5	1.271027	1.583830	0.463612	0.470756	0.482663	1.181465	1.583830	1.686846	1.882810	1.887990	1.891098
1321	Natural Gas Liquids	5	1.271027	1.583830	0.463612	0.470756	0.482663	1.181465	1.583830	1.686846	1.882810	1.887990	1.891098
138	OIL AND GAS FIELD SERVICES	65	-4.812317	1.473020	-145.298842	-1.230384	-0.505396	1.299248	1.473020	1.719236	2.797884	2.831178	3.105547
1381	Drilling Oil And Gas Wells	23	1.846452	1.905390	0.387116	0.399030	0.431663	1.772062	1.905390	2.036002	2.824386	3.166426	3.415506
1382	Oil And Gas Field Exploration Services	20	-19.124786	0.941618	-325.119559	-211.118898	-21.117796	0.776488	0.941618	1.161690	2.210134	2.304502	2.361123
1389	Oil And Gas Field Services, Not Elsewhere Classified	22	1.237577	1.344350	-1.218596	-0.947329	-0.530057	1.285640	1.344350	1.486892	2.743756	2.789075	2.818304
14	MINING AND QUARRYING OF NONMETALLIC MINERALS, EXCEPT FUELS	26	0.557071	0.463481	-1.477155	-1.253363	-0.961080	0.429834	0.463481	0.674419	2.609460	3.099464	3.468258
1400	MINING & QUARRYING OF NONMETALLIC MINERALS (NO FUELS)	1	0.459520	0.459520	0.459520	0.459520	0.459520	0.459520	0.459520	0.459520	0.459520	0.459520	0.459520
141	DIMENSION STONE	3	-0.557757	-0.461744	-1.603058	-1.568120	-1.509889	-0.694665	-0.461744	-0.286430	0.327167	0.370996	0.397293
1411	Dimension Stone	3	-0.557757	-0.461744	-1.603058	-1.568120	-1.509889	-0.694665	-0.461744	-0.286430	0.327167	0.370996	0.397293
142	CRUSHED AND BROKEN STONE, INCLUDING RIPRAP	2	1.872155	1.872155	1.505954	1.517164	1.535848	1.797420	1.872155	1.946890	2.208463	2.227146	2.238357
1422	Crushed And Broken Limestone	1	2.245830	2.245830	2.245830	2.245830	2.245830	2.245830	2.245830	2.245830	2.245830	2.245830	2.245830
1423	Crushed And Broken Granite	1	1.498480	1.498480	1.498480	1.498480	1.498480	1.498480	1.498480	1.498480	1.498480	1.498480	1.498480
144	SAND AND GRAVEL	3	1.579803	1.334320	0.687617	0.707414	0.740409	1.202340	1.334320	1.613590	2.591035	2.660853	2.702743

Up-market Betas of Common Stocks by SIC Codes as of March 31, 2017

SIC Code	Description	Number of Companies	Mean	Median	1st Percentile	2.5th Percentile	5th Percentile	40th Percentile	50th Percentile	60th Percentile	95th Percentile	97.5th Percentile	99th Percentile
1442	Construction Sand And Gravel	1	1.334320	1.334320	1.334320	1.334320	1.334320	1.334320	1.334320	1.334320	1.334320	1.334320	1.334320
1446	Industrial Sand	2	1.702545	1.702545	0.694982	0.725825	0.777232	1.496919	1.702545	1.908170	2.627857	2.679264	2.710107
147	CHEMICAL AND FERTILIZER MINERAL MINING	8	0.113847	0.391218	-1.003865	-0.965307	-0.901044	0.169662	0.391218	0.463095	0.912596	0.935325	0.948963
1474	Potash, Soda, And Borate Minerals	5	0.261412	0.429834	-0.974283	-0.891353	-0.753136	0.398941	0.429834	0.496355	0.885671	0.921863	0.943578
1479	Chemical And Fertilizer Mineral Mining, Not Elsewhere Classified	3	-0.132093	-0.562099	-0.660348	-0.657340	-0.652328	-0.582150	-0.562099	-0.284045	0.689145	0.758658	0.800367
148	NONMETALLIC MINERALS SERVICES, EXCEPT FUELS	3	1.597200	1.373380	-0.262514	-0.212436	-0.128972	1.039524	1.373380	1.841528	3.480046	3.597083	3.667305
1481	Nonmetallic Minerals Services, Except Fuels	3	1.597200	1.373380	-0.262514	-0.212436	-0.128972	1.039524	1.373380	1.841528	3.480046	3.597083	3.667305
149	MISCELLANEOUS NONMETALLIC MINERALS, EXCEPT FUELS	6	0.251917	0.461008	-0.738590	-0.713064	-0.670520	0.454574	0.461008	0.467442	0.952462	0.988606	1.010292
1499	Miscellaneous Nonmetallic Minerals, Except Fuels	6	0.251917	0.461008	-0.738590	-0.713064	-0.670520	0.454574	0.461008	0.467442	0.952462	0.988606	1.010292
	CONSTRUCTION												
15	CONSTRUCTION	27	1.319802	1.405940	-2.070159	-1.127917	-0.138757	1.361774	1.405940	1.480722	2.610823	2.924060	3.165224
152	GENERAL BUILDING CONTRACTORS-RESIDENTIAL BUILDINGS	3	1.770947	1.465770	1.145967	1.155757	1.172073	1.400504	1.465770	1.714142	2.583444	2.645537	2.682793
1521	General Contractors-Single-Family Houses	2	1.302605	1.302605	1.142703	1.147598	1.155757	1.269972	1.302605	1.335238	1.449454	1.457612	1.462507
1522	General Contractors-Residential Buildings, Other Than Single-Family	1	2.707630	2.707630	2.707630	2.707630	2.707630	2.707630	2.707630	2.707630	2.707630	2.707630	2.707630
153	OPERATIVE BUILDERS	19	1.359206	1.376560	-0.126366	0.107556	0.497428	1.359892	1.376560	1.456060	2.198082	2.291511	2.347568
1531	Operative Builders	19	1.359206	1.376560	-0.126366	0.107556	0.497428	1.359892	1.376560	1.456060	2.198082	2.291511	2.347568
154	GENERAL BUILDING CONTRACTORS-NONRESIDENTIAL BUILDINGS	5	0.899380	1.821940	-2.582539	-2.408867	-2.119414	1.171649	1.821940	1.833592	3.031014	3.178507	3.267003
1541	General Contractors-Industrial Buildings And Warehouses	3	0.816540	1.821940	-2.607915	-2.472307	-2.246294	0.917888	1.821940	2.122752	3.175594	3.250797	3.295919
1542	General Contractors-Nonresidential Buildings, Other Than Industrial	2	1.023641	1.023641	0.212761	0.237583	0.278955	0.858155	1.023641	1.189127	1.768327	1.809699	1.834521
16	HEAVY CONSTRUCTION OTHER THAN BUILDING CONSTRUCTION-CONTRACTORS	20	1.338382	1.579755	-0.870088	-0.743656	-0.532934	1.381224	1.579755	1.741698	2.748756	3.065163	3.255007
161	HIGHWAY AND STREET CONSTRUCTION, EXCEPT ELEVATED HIGHWAYS	3	1.149676	0.403288	-0.321048	-0.298874	-0.261918	0.255464	0.403288	0.998944	3.083742	3.232656	3.322004
1611	Highway And Street Construction, Except Elevated Highways	3	1.149676	0.403288	-0.321048	-0.298874	-0.261918	0.255464	0.403288	0.998944	3.083742	3.232656	3.322004
162	HEAVY CONSTRUCTION, EXCEPT HIGHWAY AND STREET CONSTRUCTION	17	1.371683	1.606050	-0.883397	-0.776927	-0.599478	1.502052	1.606050	1.743552	2.668690	2.692070	2.706098
1622	Bridge, Tunnel, And Elevated Highway Construction	1	1.737990	1.737990	1.737990	1.737990	1.737990	1.737990	1.737990	1.737990	1.737990	1.737990	1.737990

Up-market Betas of Common Stocks by SIC Codes as of March 31, 2017

SIC Code	Description	Number of Companies	Mean	Median	1st Percentile	2.5th Percentile	5th Percentile	40th Percentile	50th Percentile	60th Percentile	95th Percentile	97.5th Percentile	99th Percentile
1623	Water, Sewer, Pipeline, And Communications And Power Line Construction	9	0.989006	1.251390	-0.880883	-0.770641	-0.586906	0.877132	1.251390	1.493046	2.155582	2.172806	2.183140
1629	Heavy Construction, Not Elsewhere Classified	7	1.811365	1.954540	-0.392041	-0.213973	0.082807	1.830172	1.954540	2.370784	2.697915	2.706683	2.711943
17	CONSTRUCTION-SPECIAL TRADE CONTRACTORS	10	1.152545	1.338425	-0.814584	-0.615488	-0.283662	1.128436	1.338425	1.427234	2.349191	2.356441	2.360790
171	PLUMBING, HEATING AND AIR-CONDITIONING	1	0.527469	0.527469	0.527469	0.527469	0.527469	0.527469	0.527469	0.527469	0.527469	0.527469	0.527469
1711	Plumbing, Heating And Air-Conditioning	1	0.527469	0.527469	0.527469	0.527469	0.527469	0.527469	0.527469	0.527469	0.527469	0.527469	0.527469
173	ELECTRICAL WORK	5	1.080829	1.544780	-0.876257	-0.769671	-0.592027	1.258516	1.544780	1.572416	2.213726	2.288708	2.333697
1731	Electrical Work	5	1.080829	1.544780	-0.876257	-0.769671	-0.592027	1.258516	1.544780	1.572416	2.213726	2.288708	2.333697
174	MASONRY, STONEWORK, TILE SETTING, AND PLASTERING	2	1.338425	1.338425	1.328189	1.328502	1.329025	1.336336	1.338425	1.340514	1.347826	1.348348	1.348661
1742	Plastering, Drywall, Acoustical, And Insulation Work	2	1.338425	1.338425	1.328189	1.328502	1.329025	1.336336	1.338425	1.340514	1.347826	1.348348	1.348661
177	CONCRETE WORK	1	0.585515	0.585515	0.585515	0.585515	0.585515	0.585515	0.585515	0.585515	0.585515	0.585515	0.585515
1771	Concrete Work	1	0.585515	0.585515	0.585515	0.585515	0.585515	0.585515	0.585515	0.585515	0.585515	0.585515	0.585515
178	WATER WELL DRILLING	1	2.331470	2.331470	2.331470	2.331470	2.331470	2.331470	2.331470	2.331470	2.331470	2.331470	2.331470
1781	Water Well Drilling	1	2.331470	2.331470	2.331470	2.331470	2.331470	2.331470	2.331470	2.331470	2.331470	2.331470	2.331470
	MANUFACTURING												
20	FOOD AND KINDRED PRODUCTS	98	0.616438	0.684035	-2.393258	-0.834048	-0.440576	0.617834	0.684035	0.756005	1.555424	2.264355	2.527873
201	MEAT PRODUCTS	7	0.506028	0.472195	-0.444799	-0.390681	-0.300485	0.422840	0.472195	0.606038	1.307766	1.409123	1.469937
2011	Meat Packing Plants	2	1.102873	1.102873	0.703418	0.715646	0.736027	1.021352	1.102873	1.184394	1.469719	1.490100	1.502328
2013	Sausages And Other Prepared Meat Products	2	-0.180223	-0.180223	-0.474865	-0.465845	-0.450812	-0.240354	-0.180223	-0.120091	0.090367	0.105400	0.114420
2015	Poultry Slaughtering And Processing	3	0.565632	0.472195	0.391582	0.394050	0.398163	0.455743	0.472195	0.544709	0.798508	0.816637	0.827514
202	DAIRY PRODUCTS	10	0.622171	0.713779	-0.766896	-0.621814	-0.380010	0.571399	0.713779	0.798941	1.451074	1.481757	1.500167
2022	Natural, Processed, And Imitation Cheese	2	1.185426	1.185426	0.864951	0.874762	0.891112	1.120023	1.185426	1.250828	1.479739	1.496089	1.505900
2023	Dry, Condensed, And Evaporated Dairy Products	3	0.823479	0.668262	0.430947	0.438212	0.450320	0.619830	0.668262	0.809824	1.305289	1.340680	1.361914
2024	Ice Cream And Frozen Desserts	1	-0.863618	-0.863618	-0.863618	-0.863618	-0.863618	-0.863618	-0.863618	-0.863618	-0.863618	-0.863618	-0.863618
2026	Fluid Milk	4	0.561010	0.576712	0.216559	0.224797	0.238526	0.467161	0.576712	0.686262	0.861512	0.870531	0.875942
203	CANNED, FROZEN, AND PRESERVED FRUITS, VEGETABLES, AND FOOD SPECIAL	9	0.682006	0.720341	0.023577	0.048639	0.090407	0.682663	0.720341	0.763964	1.173744	1.192682	1.204045
2030	CANNED, FROZEN & PRESERVD FRUIT, VEG & FOOD SPECIALTIES	1	0.006870	0.006870	0.006870	0.006870	0.006870	0.006870	0.006870	0.006870	0.006870	0.006870	0.006870
2032	Canned Specialties	2	0.921181	0.921181	0.636551	0.645264	0.659786	0.863093	0.921181	0.979269	1.182576	1.197098	1.205811
2033	Canned Fruits, Vegetables, Preserves, Jams, And Jellies	4	0.739045	0.747606	0.674657	0.676776	0.680309	0.731247	0.747606	0.763964	0.785798	0.786762	0.787340
2034	Dried And Dehydrated Fruits, Vegetables, And Soup Mixes	1	0.215714	0.215714	0.215714	0.215714	0.215714	0.215714	0.215714	0.215714	0.215714	0.215714	0.215714
2037	Frozen Fruits, Fruit Juices, And Vegetables	1	1.116930	1.116930	1.116930	1.116930	1.116930	1.116930	1.116930	1.116930	1.116930	1.116930	1.116930

Up-market Betas of Common Stocks by SIC Codes as of March 31, 2017

SIC Code	Description	Number of Companies	Mean	Median	1st Percentile	2.5th Percentile	5th Percentile	40th Percentile	50th Percentile	60th Percentile	95th Percentile	97.5th Percentile	99th Percentile
204	GRAIN MILL PRODUCTS	8	0.623807	0.758294	-0.376215	-0.290340	-0.147217	0.717634	0.758294	0.791830	1.048408	1.080399	1.099594
2041	Flour And Other Grain Mill Products	2	0.911082	0.911082	0.892950	0.893505	0.894430	0.907382	0.911082	0.914782	0.927734	0.928659	0.929214
2043	Cereal Breakfast Foods	1	0.749945	0.749945	0.749945	0.749945	0.749945	0.749945	0.749945	0.749945	0.749945	0.749945	0.749945
2044	Rice Milling	1	-0.433464	-0.433464	-0.433464	-0.433464	-0.433464	-0.433464	-0.433464	-0.433464	-0.433464	-0.433464	-0.433464
2046	Wet Corn Milling	2	0.939517	0.939517	0.770100	0.775287	0.783930	0.904942	0.939517	0.974091	1.095103	1.103746	1.108933
2047	Dog And Cat Food	1	0.588388	0.588388	0.588388	0.588388	0.588388	0.588388	0.588388	0.588388	0.588388	0.588388	0.588388
2048	Prepared Feeds And Feed Ingredients For Animals And Fowls, Except Dog And Cat	1	0.384386	0.384386	0.384386	0.384386	0.384386	0.384386	0.384386	0.384386	0.384386	0.384386	0.384386
205	BAKERY PRODUCTS	7	0.825306	0.881368	0.314789	0.347097	0.400942	0.802598	0.881368	0.886390	1.213180	1.256635	1.282708
2051	Bread And Other Bakery Products, Except Cookies And Crackers	3	0.944560	0.881368	0.656804	0.663678	0.675136	0.835539	0.881368	0.965112	1.258218	1.279154	1.291716
2052	Cookies And Crackers	4	0.735866	0.819911	0.306956	0.327513	0.361776	0.778015	0.819911	0.861807	0.992292	1.001341	1.006770
206	SUGAR AND CONFECTIONERY PRODUCTS	4	0.821346	0.957081	-0.035184	0.006058	0.074795	0.895119	0.957081	1.019042	1.377868	1.405884	1.422694
2061	Cane Sugar, Except Refining	1	1.433900	1.433900	1.433900	1.433900	1.433900	1.433900	1.433900	1.433900	1.433900	1.433900	1.433900
2066	Chocolate And Cocoa Products	2	0.498836	0.498836	-0.051448	-0.034603	-0.006527	0.386533	0.498836	0.611139	1.004199	1.032274	1.049120
2068	Salted And Roasted Nuts And Seeds	1	0.853811	0.853811	0.853811	0.853811	0.853811	0.853811	0.853811	0.853811	0.853811	0.853811	0.853811
207	FATS AND OILS	4	0.734064	0.756070	0.024451	0.047332	0.085465	0.613018	0.756070	0.899121	1.351855	1.383388	1.402307
2075	Soybean Oil Mills	1	0.517650	0.517650	0.517650	0.517650	0.517650	0.517650	0.517650	0.517650	0.517650	0.517650	0.517650
2077	Animal And Marine Fats And Oils	2	1.204705	1.204705	0.998693	1.005000	1.015511	1.162661	1.204705	1.246748	1.393898	1.404409	1.410716
2079	Shortening, Table Oils, Margarine, And Other Edible Fats And Oils	1	0.009198	0.009198	0.009198	0.009198	0.009198	0.009198	0.009198	0.009198	0.009198	0.009198	0.009198
208	BEVERAGES	32	0.759089	0.620185	-0.579390	-0.257415	-0.085548	0.604807	0.620185	0.693119	2.435400	2.719970	3.178046
2082	Malt Beverages	4	0.987318	0.779737	0.301341	0.322542	0.357876	0.766896	0.779737	0.792578	1.907372	2.004981	2.063546
2084	Wines, Brandy, And Brandy Spirits	5	0.624129	0.600351	0.015019	0.026642	0.046013	0.440604	0.600351	0.808191	1.177662	1.184876	1.189204
2085	Distilled And Blended Liquors	5	0.602086	0.621735	0.164457	0.179087	0.203470	0.532454	0.621735	0.645176	1.060164	1.107642	1.136129
2086	Bottled And Canned Soft Drinks And Carbonated Waters	17	0.688951	0.614631	-0.683254	-0.517073	-0.240104	0.577311	0.614631	0.653028	2.603822	3.043626	3.307508
2087	Flavoring Extracts And Flavoring Syrups, Not Elsewhere Classified	1	2.498320	2.498320	2.498320	2.498320	2.498320	2.498320	2.498320	2.498320	2.498320	2.498320	2.498320
209	MISCELLANEOUS FOOD PREPARATIONS AND KINDRED PRODUCTS	17	0.189932	0.668691	-4.711972	-4.024946	-2.879902	0.615456	0.668691	0.704466	1.565776	1.682388	1.752355
2095	Roasted Coffee	4	-0.734754	0.361753	-5.015848	-4.784635	-4.399279	0.125551	0.361753	0.597954	1.394663	1.451066	1.484909
2096	Potato Chips, Corn Chips, And Similar Snacks	1	1.018500	1.018500	1.018500	1.018500	1.018500	1.018500	1.018500	1.018500	1.018500	1.018500	1.018500
2097	Manufactured Ice	1	0.668691	0.668691	0.668691	0.668691	0.668691	0.668691	0.668691	0.668691	0.668691	0.668691	0.668691
2099	Food Preparations, Not Elsewhere Classified	11	0.407333	0.624680	-2.107357	-1.807323	-1.307266	0.609306	0.624680	0.687731	1.532625	1.665813	1.745725
21	TOBACCO PRODUCTS	9	0.367202	0.491865	-0.913408	-0.760600	-0.505920	0.407912	0.491865	0.510865	0.885855	0.910017	0.924514
211	CIGARETTES	9	0.367202	0.491865	-0.913408	-0.760600	-0.505920	0.407912	0.491865	0.510865	0.885855	0.910017	0.924514
2111	Cigarettes	9	0.367202	0.491865	-0.913408	-0.760600	-0.505920	0.407912	0.491865	0.510865	0.885855	0.910017	0.924514

Up-market Betas of Common Stocks by SIC Codes as of March 31, 2017

SIC Code	Description	Number of Companies	Mean	Median	1st Percentile	2.5th Percentile	5th Percentile	40th Percentile	50th Percentile	60th Percentile	95th Percentile	97.5th Percentile	99th Percentile
22	TEXTILE MILL PRODUCTS	11	0.925693	1.001200	-0.313224	-0.155273	0.107979	0.979356	1.001200	1.160450	1.365670	1.423890	1.458822
221	BROADWOVEN FABRIC MILLS, COTTON	2	0.280416	0.280416	-0.404545	-0.383577	-0.348630	0.140628	0.280416	0.420204	0.909462	0.944409	0.965377
2211	Broadwoven Fabric Mills, Cotton	2	0.280416	0.280416	-0.404545	-0.383577	-0.348630	0.140628	0.280416	0.420204	0.909462	0.944409	0.965377
222	BROADWOVEN FABRIC MILLS, MANMADE FIBER AND SILK	2	1.058296	1.058296	0.642957	0.655672	0.676862	0.973533	1.058296	1.143058	1.439729	1.460919	1.473634
2221	Broadwoven Fabric Mills, Manmade Fiber And Silk	2	1.058296	1.058296	0.642957	0.655672	0.676862	0.973533	1.058296	1.143058	1.439729	1.460919	1.473634
225	KNITTING MILLS	3	1.086489	1.177210	0.839911	0.850236	0.867445	1.108373	1.177210	1.191614	1.242028	1.245629	1.247790
2252	Hosiery, Not Elsewhere Classified	1	1.177210	1.177210	1.177210	1.177210	1.177210	1.177210	1.177210	1.177210	1.177210	1.177210	1.177210
2253	Knit Outerwear Mills	2	1.041129	1.041129	0.837189	0.843432	0.853837	0.999508	1.041129	1.082749	1.228420	1.238825	1.245068
227	CARPETS AND RUGS	3	1.024499	1.001200	0.913633	0.916314	0.920781	0.983329	1.001200	1.033050	1.144525	1.152488	1.157265
2273	Carpets And Rugs	3	1.024499	1.001200	0.913633	0.916314	0.920781	0.983329	1.001200	1.033050	1.144525	1.152488	1.157265
228	YARN AND THREAD MILLS	1	1.172240	1.172240	1.172240	1.172240	1.172240	1.172240	1.172240	1.172240	1.172240	1.172240	1.172240
2282	Yarn Texturizing, Throwing, Twisting, And Winding Mills	1	1.172240	1.172240	1.172240	1.172240	1.172240	1.172240	1.172240	1.172240	1.172240	1.172240	1.172240
23	APPAREL AND OTHER FINISHED PRODUCTS MADE FROM FABRICS AND SIMILAR MATERIAL	19	0.960493	0.956024	-0.183550	-0.083594	0.083001	0.895201	0.956024	0.977466	1.970992	2.214316	2.360310
2300	APPAREL & OTHER FINISHD PRODS OF FABRICS & SIMILAR MATL	1	1.916920	1.916920	1.916920	1.916920	1.916920	1.916920	1.916920	1.916920	1.916920	1.916920	1.916920
232	MEN'S AND BOYS' FURNISHINGS, WORK CLOTHING, AND ALLIED GARMENTS	7	1.049638	1.054350	0.170182	0.245422	0.370823	1.009608	1.054350	1.128900	1.610599	1.671540	1.708104
2321	Men's And Boys' Shirts, Except Work Shirts	2	1.529345	1.529345	1.330273	1.336367	1.346524	1.488718	1.529345	1.569972	1.712167	1.722323	1.728417
2325	Men's And Boys' Separate Trousers And Slacks	1	1.054350	1.054350	1.054350	1.054350	1.054350	1.054350	1.054350	1.054350	1.054350	1.054350	1.054350
2326	Men's And Boys' Work Clothing	2	0.538023	0.538023	0.128382	0.140922	0.161822	0.454423	0.538023	0.621623	0.914224	0.935124	0.947664
2329	Men's And Boys' Clothing, Not Elsewhere Classified	2	1.079190	1.079190	0.981768	0.984751	0.989721	1.059308	1.079190	1.099072	1.168659	1.173630	1.176612
233	WOMEN'S, MISSES', AND JUNIORS' OUTERWEAR	7	0.835244	0.834276	-0.223413	-0.183251	-0.116314	0.716433	0.834276	0.867442	2.044798	2.251219	2.375072
2337	Women's, Misses', And Juniors' Suits, Skirts, And Coats	1	0.834276	0.834276	0.834276	0.834276	0.834276	0.834276	0.834276	0.834276	0.834276	0.834276	0.834276
2339	Women's, Misses', And Juniors' Outerwear, Not Elsewhere Classified	6	0.835406	0.763712	-0.227876	-0.194407	-0.138626	0.637871	0.763712	0.889552	2.113605	2.285623	2.388833
234	WOMEN'S, MISSES', CHILDREN'S, AND INFANTS' UNDERGARMENTS	1	0.756560	0.756560	0.756560	0.756560	0.756560	0.756560	0.756560	0.756560	0.756560	0.756560	0.756560
2341	Women's, Misses', Children's, And Infants' Underwear And Nightwear	1	0.756560	0.756560	0.756560	0.756560	0.756560	0.756560	0.756560	0.756560	0.756560	0.756560	0.756560
238	MISCELLANEOUS APPAREL AND ACCESSORIES	3	0.793905	0.917796	0.504152	0.516814	0.537919	0.833379	0.917796	0.927879	0.963168	0.965688	0.967201
2385	Waterproof Outerwear	2	0.706753	0.706753	0.499931	0.506262	0.516814	0.664544	0.706753	0.748962	0.896692	0.907244	0.913575

Up-market Betas of Common Stocks by SIC Codes as of March 31, 2017

SIC Code	Description	Number of Companies	Mean	Median	1st Percentile	2.5th Percentile	5th Percentile	40th Percentile	50th Percentile	60th Percentile	95th Percentile	97.5th Percentile	99th Percentile
2389	Apparel And Accessories, Not Elsewhere Classified	1	0.968209	0.968209	0.968209	0.968209	0.968209	0.968209	0.968209	0.968209	0.968209	0.968209	0.968209
24	LUMBER AND WOOD PRODUCTS, EXCEPT FURNITURE	13	1.109944	1.216470	-0.005665	0.146262	0.399475	1.103966	1.216470	1.251326	1.656566	1.683428	1.699545
2400	LUMBER & WOOD PRODUCTS (NO FURNITURE)	1	0.737091	0.737091	0.737091	0.737091	0.737091	0.737091	0.737091	0.737091	0.737091	0.737091	0.737091
241	LOGGING	1	0.930149	0.930149	0.930149	0.930149	0.930149	0.930149	0.930149	0.930149	0.930149	0.930149	0.930149
2411	Logging	1	0.930149	0.930149	0.930149	0.930149	0.930149	0.930149	0.930149	0.930149	0.930149	0.930149	0.930149
242	SAWMILLS AND PLANING MILLS	3	0.961333	1.370200	-0.077407	-0.033092	0.040765	1.074770	1.370200	1.420310	1.595695	1.608223	1.615739
2421	Sawmills And Planing Mills, General	3	0.961333	1.370200	-0.077407	-0.033092	0.040765	1.074770	1.370200	1.420310	1.595695	1.608223	1.615739
243	MILLWORK, VENEER, PLYWOOD, AND STRUCTURAL WOOD MEMBERS	3	1.085133	1.147420	0.896626	0.904304	0.917099	1.096238	1.147420	1.161230	1.209565	1.213018	1.215089
2431	Millwork	1	0.891508	0.891508	0.891508	0.891508	0.891508	0.891508	0.891508	0.891508	0.891508	0.891508	0.891508
2434	Wood Kitchen Cabinets	1	1.147420	1.147420	1.147420	1.147420	1.147420	1.147420	1.147420	1.147420	1.147420	1.147420	1.147420
2439	Structural Wood Members, Not Elsewhere Classified	1	1.216470	1.216470	1.216470	1.216470	1.216470	1.216470	1.216470	1.216470	1.216470	1.216470	1.216470
245	WOOD BUILDINGS AND MOBILE HOMES	2	1.172662	1.172662	0.775214	0.787381	0.807659	1.091550	1.172662	1.253773	1.537664	1.557942	1.570109
2451	Mobile Homes	2	1.172662	1.172662	0.775214	0.787381	0.807659	1.091550	1.172662	1.253773	1.537664	1.557942	1.570109
249	MISCELLANEOUS WOOD PRODUCTS	3	1.425770	1.337150	1.232016	1.235234	1.240598	1.315694	1.337150	1.411778	1.672976	1.691633	1.702827
2491	Wood Preserving	1	1.710290	1.710290	1.710290	1.710290	1.710290	1.710290	1.710290	1.710290	1.710290	1.710290	1.710290
2493	Reconstituted Wood Products	1	1.229870	1.229870	1.229870	1.229870	1.229870	1.229870	1.229870	1.229870	1.229870	1.229870	1.229870
2499	Wood Products, Not Elsewhere Classified	1	1.337150	1.337150	1.337150	1.337150	1.337150	1.337150	1.337150	1.337150	1.337150	1.337150	1.337150
25	FURNITURE AND FIXTURES	20	1.097936	1.056125	-0.584111	-0.233761	0.350155	0.954856	1.056125	1.109114	2.276515	2.487267	2.613719
251	HOUSEHOLD FURNITURE	12	1.025104	1.000314	-0.682455	-0.479621	-0.141564	0.916745	1.000314	1.081286	2.453991	2.576005	2.649214
2511	Wood Household Furniture, Except Upholstered	7	1.138415	1.031840	0.422309	0.438342	0.465064	0.994008	1.031840	1.081286	2.235000	2.466510	2.605416
2512	Wood Household Furniture, Upholstered	1	-0.817678	-0.817678	-0.817678	-0.817678	-0.817678	-0.817678	-0.817678	-0.817678	-0.817678	-0.817678	-0.817678
2515	Mattresses, Foundations, And Convertible Beds	3	0.965229	0.882050	0.865074	0.865594	0.866460	0.878586	0.882050	0.935422	1.122224	1.135567	1.143573
2519	Household Furniture, Not Elsewhere Classified	1	2.254330	2.254330	2.254330	2.254330	2.254330	2.254330	2.254330	2.254330	2.254330	2.254330	2.254330
252	OFFICE FURNITURE	6	1.344105	1.217080	0.941282	0.952265	0.970572	1.105690	1.217080	1.328470	1.881005	1.917483	1.939369
2521	Wood Office Furniture	3	1.233930	1.105690	0.937394	0.942546	0.951132	1.071344	1.105690	1.216980	1.606495	1.634318	1.651011
2522	Office Furniture, Except Wood	3	1.454280	1.328470	1.085371	1.092813	1.105216	1.278858	1.328470	1.453568	1.891411	1.922686	1.941450
253	PUBLIC BUILDING AND RELATED FURNITURE	2	0.796420	0.796420	0.774577	0.775245	0.776360	0.791962	0.796420	0.800878	0.816480	0.817595	0.818263
2531	Public Building And Related Furniture	2	0.796420	0.796420	0.774577	0.775245	0.776360	0.791962	0.796420	0.800878	0.816480	0.817595	0.818263
26	PAPER AND ALLIED PRODUCTS	25	0.770737	0.838387	-0.886993	-0.603033	-0.262903	0.661028	0.838387	0.915976	1.640466	1.813688	1.961043
261	PULP MILLS	3	0.021372	0.541380	-1.043946	-0.995416	-0.914532	0.217844	0.541380	0.552911	0.593270	0.596152	0.597882
2611	Pulp Mills	3	0.021372	0.541380	-1.043946	-0.995416	-0.914532	0.217844	0.541380	0.552911	0.593270	0.596152	0.597882
262	PAPER MILLS	9	0.807098	0.750889	-0.121856	-0.057990	0.048453	0.647714	0.750889	0.889289	1.714872	1.887076	1.990398

Up-market Betas of Common Stocks by SIC Codes as of March 31, 2017

SIC Code	Description	Number of Companies	Mean	Median	1st Percentile	2.5th Percentile	5th Percentile	40th Percentile	50th Percentile	60th Percentile	95th Percentile	97.5th Percentile	99th Percentile
2621	Paper Mills	9	0.807098	0.750889	-0.121856	-0.057990	0.048453	0.647714	0.750889	0.889289	1.714872	1.887076	1.990398
263	PAPERBOARD MILLS	4	0.854986	0.909888	0.639812	0.652303	0.673123	0.909400	0.909888	0.910375	0.959988	0.964337	0.966946
2631	Paperboard Mills	4	0.854986	0.909888	0.639812	0.652303	0.673123	0.909400	0.909888	0.910375	0.959988	0.964337	0.966946
265	PAPERBOARD CONTAINERS AND BOXES	3	1.342152	1.439300	0.993759	1.007398	1.030129	1.348373	1.439300	1.471938	1.586171	1.594331	1.599226
2655	Fiber Cans, Tubes, Drums, And Similar Products	2	1.520895	1.520895	1.440932	1.443380	1.447460	1.504576	1.520895	1.537214	1.594331	1.598410	1.600858
2657	Folding Paperboard Boxes, Including Sanitary	1	0.984666	0.984666	0.984666	0.984666	0.984666	0.984666	0.984666	0.984666	0.984666	0.984666	0.984666
267	CONVERTED PAPER AND PAPERBOARD PRODUCTS, EXCEPT CONTAINERS AND BOXES	6	0.749004	0.759556	-0.244966	-0.181134	-0.074748	0.680724	0.759556	0.838387	1.499695	1.574828	1.619907
2671	Packaging Paper And Plastics Film, Coated And Laminated	3	0.441650	0.563572	-0.270499	-0.244966	-0.202412	0.393353	0.563572	0.660638	1.000367	1.024634	1.039193
2673	Plastics, Foil, And Coated Paper Bags	1	1.649960	1.649960	1.649960	1.649960	1.649960	1.649960	1.649960	1.649960	1.649960	1.649960	1.649960
2679	Converted Paper And Paperboard Products, Not Elsewhere Classified	2	0.759556	0.759556	0.682301	0.684666	0.688607	0.743789	0.759556	0.775322	0.830504	0.834445	0.836810
27	PRINTING, PUBLISHING, AND ALLIED INDUSTRIES	41	0.919575	1.036030	-0.955198	-0.718241	-0.173048	0.882339	1.036030	1.172910	1.770570	1.856750	1.900658
271	NEWSPAPERS: PUBLISHING, OR PUBLISHING AND PRINTING	18	1.058336	1.234340	-0.001935	0.017971	0.051148	1.128217	1.234340	1.310256	1.783497	1.820124	1.842099
2711	Newspapers: Publishing, Or Publishing And Printing	18	1.058336	1.234340	-0.001935	0.017971	0.051148	1.128217	1.234340	1.310256	1.783497	1.820124	1.842099
272	PERIODICALS: PUBLISHING, OR PUBLISHING AND PRINTING	3	1.121839	1.111700	0.855946	0.863776	0.876824	1.059505	1.111700	1.169978	1.373951	1.388521	1.397262
2721	Periodicals: Publishing, Or Publishing And Printing	3	1.121839	1.111700	0.855946	0.863776	0.876824	1.059505	1.111700	1.169978	1.373951	1.388521	1.397262
273	BOOKS	4	0.871542	0.970689	0.462650	0.481833	0.513804	0.913964	0.970689	1.027414	1.090475	1.092703	1.094039
2731	Books: Publishing, Or Publishing And Printing	4	0.871542	0.970689	0.462650	0.481833	0.513804	0.913964	0.970689	1.027414	1.090475	1.092703	1.094039
274	MISCELLANEOUS PUBLISHING	4	0.325666	0.712634	-1.060600	-0.981745	-0.850319	0.668555	0.712634	0.756712	0.959895	0.975230	0.984431
2741	Miscellaneous Publishing	4	0.325666	0.712634	-1.060600	-0.981745	-0.850319	0.668555	0.712634	0.756712	0.959895	0.975230	0.984431
275	COMMERCIAL PRINTING	8	0.936271	1.013629	-0.130594	-0.066914	0.039221	0.905705	1.013629	1.070614	1.779465	1.854698	1.899837
2752	Commercial Printing, Lithographic	3	0.974897	0.991228	0.444590	0.461324	0.489213	0.879669	0.991228	1.092988	1.449150	1.474590	1.489854
2754	Commercial Printing, Gravure	3	0.773499	0.563614	-0.158315	-0.136215	-0.099382	0.416282	0.563614	0.836877	1.793298	1.861614	1.902604
2759	Commercial Printing, Not Elsewhere Classified	2	1.122490	1.122490	1.037759	1.040353	1.044676	1.105198	1.122490	1.139782	1.200304	1.204627	1.207221
276	MANIFOLD BUSINESS FORMS	1	1.517300	1.517300	1.517300	1.517300	1.517300	1.517300	1.517300	1.517300	1.517300	1.517300	1.517300
2761	Manifold Business Forms	1	1.517300	1.517300	1.517300	1.517300	1.517300	1.517300	1.517300	1.517300	1.517300	1.517300	1.517300
277	GREETING CARDS	1	0.882339	0.882339	0.882339	0.882339	0.882339	0.882339	0.882339	0.882339	0.882339	0.882339	0.882339
2771	Greeting Cards	1	0.882339	0.882339	0.882339	0.882339	0.882339	0.882339	0.882339	0.882339	0.882339	0.882339	0.882339
278	BLANKBOOKS, LOOSELEAF BINDERS, AND BOOKBINDING AND RELATED WORK	2	0.304180	0.304180	-0.697793	-0.667120	-0.615999	0.099695	0.304180	0.508664	1.224358	1.275479	1.306152

Up-market Betas of Common Stocks by SIC Codes as of March 31, 2017

SIC Code	Description	Number of Companies	Mean	Median	1st Percentile	2.5th Percentile	5th Percentile	40th Percentile	50th Percentile	60th Percentile	95th Percentile	97.5th Percentile	99th Percentile
2782	Blankbooks, Looseleaf Binders And Devices	2	0.304180	0.304180	-0.697793	-0.667120	-0.615999	0.099695	0.304180	0.508664	1.224358	1.275479	1.306152
28	CHEMICALS AND ALLIED PRODUCTS	479	1.108736	1.086030	-2.497717	-1.188834	-0.842858	0.846095	1.086030	1.335112	2.994405	3.424391	4.174912
281	INDUSTRIAL INORGANIC CHEMICALS	15	1.587958	1.762280	-0.848007	-0.660994	-0.349304	1.052412	1.762280	1.825694	3.385278	3.782899	4.021472
2812	Alkalies And Chlorine	1	2.029390	2.029390	2.029390	2.029390	2.029390	2.029390	2.029390	2.029390	2.029390	2.029390	2.029390
2813	Industrial Gases	3	0.945987	0.990375	0.788779	0.794951	0.805236	0.949233	0.990375	1.004884	1.055666	1.059293	1.061469
2816	Inorganic Pigments	4	2.020626	2.093080	1.006112	1.041822	1.101340	1.902754	2.093080	2.283406	2.838478	2.876259	2.898928
2819	Industrial Inorganic Chemicals, Not Elsewhere Classified	7	1.552788	1.762280	-0.919251	-0.839102	-0.705521	1.326902	1.762280	1.845170	3.839702	4.010111	4.112356
282	PLASTICS MATERIALS AND SYNTHETIC RESINS, SYNTHETIC RUBBER, CELLULOSIC MANMADE FIBERS	14	1.439807	1.332555	0.667020	0.740899	0.864031	1.268228	1.332555	1.464954	2.112289	2.161789	2.191490
2821	Plastics Materials, Synthetic Resins, And Nonvulcanizable Elastomers	14	1.439807	1.332555	0.667020	0.740899	0.864031	1.268228	1.332555	1.464954	2.112289	2.161789	2.191490
283	DRUGS	378	1.126132	1.110910	-2.738710	-1.547840	-0.864843	0.869372	1.110910	1.429868	3.009060	3.441616	4.259401
2833	Medicinal Chemicals And Botanical Products	15	0.493948	0.816295	-2.230081	-1.927217	-1.422444	0.186480	0.816295	0.962636	2.282791	2.336121	2.368118
2834	Pharmaceutical Preparations	281	1.104814	1.094170	-2.871318	-1.736810	-0.883754	0.827001	1.094170	1.436260	3.027190	3.478480	4.248174
2835	In Vitro And In Vivo Diagnostic Substances	21	0.776271	0.826957	-0.614955	-0.518056	-0.356557	0.717154	0.826957	1.026170	1.864770	2.010820	2.098450
2836	Biological Products, Except Diagnostic Substances	61	1.500233	1.511850	-0.927857	-0.499552	-0.042998	1.379550	1.511850	1.741050	3.075080	3.286785	3.920874
284	SOAP, DETERGENTS, AND CLEANING PREPARATIONS; PERFUMES, COSMETICS	19	0.664799	0.647292	-0.228775	-0.193499	-0.134706	0.302939	0.647292	0.678257	1.706454	2.660382	3.232739
2841	Soap And Other Detergents, Except Specialty Cleaners	5	0.640722	0.764772	0.157896	0.166114	0.179811	0.574618	0.764772	0.816448	1.061249	1.082159	1.094706
2842	Specialty Cleaning, Polishing, And Sanitation Preparations	3	0.114158	0.211784	-0.114973	-0.104970	-0.088299	0.145099	0.211784	0.219893	0.248275	0.250303	0.251519
2844	Perfumes, Cosmetics, And Other Toilet Preparations	11	0.825918	0.675147	-0.230564	-0.197971	-0.143651	0.647292	0.675147	0.679035	2.554390	3.084350	3.402326
285	PAINTS, VARNISHES, LACQUERS, ENAMELS, AND ALLIED PRODUCTS	6	0.965486	1.190490	0.226976	0.240734	0.263662	1.087740	1.190490	1.293240	1.422110	1.434940	1.442638
2851	Paints, Varnishes, Lacquers, Enamels, And Allied Products	6	0.965486	1.190490	0.226976	0.240734	0.263662	1.087740	1.190490	1.293240	1.422110	1.434940	1.442638
286	INDUSTRIAL ORGANIC CHEMICALS	21	0.993787	1.101700	-0.747348	-0.549010	-0.218446	0.935412	1.101700	1.188960	2.008830	2.145455	2.227430
2861	Gum And Wood Chemicals	2	0.947973	0.947973	0.745018	0.751231	0.761586	0.906554	0.947973	0.989392	1.134360	1.144715	1.150928
2865	Cyclic Organic Crudes And Intermediates, And Organic Dyes And Pigments	1	0.923705	0.923705	0.923705	0.923705	0.923705	0.923705	0.923705	0.923705	0.923705	0.923705	0.923705
2869	Industrial Organic Chemicals, Not Elsewhere Classified	18	1.002770	1.145330	-0.767181	-0.598594	-0.317615	0.970814	1.145330	1.191430	2.049818	2.165949	2.235628
287	AGRICULTURAL CHEMICALS	13	1.127034	0.769847	0.125614	0.167017	0.236021	0.730815	0.769847	1.352572	2.205500	2.295605	2.349668
2873	Nitrogenous Fertilizers	6	0.981799	0.751661	0.118038	0.148078	0.198144	0.733475	0.751661	0.769847	1.990410	2.037885	2.066370
2874	Phosphatic Fertilizers	2	1.539155	1.539155	1.308350	1.315416	1.327192	1.492052	1.539155	1.586258	1.751119	1.762894	1.769960

Up-market Betas of Common Stocks by SIC Codes as of March 31, 2017

SIC Code	Description	Number of Companies	Mean	Median	1st Percentile	2.5th Percentile	5th Percentile	40th Percentile	50th Percentile	60th Percentile	95th Percentile	97.5th Percentile	99th Percentile
2879	Pesticides And Agricultural Chemicals, Not Elsewhere Classified	5	1.136467	0.720175	0.342912	0.365238	0.402447	0.712155	0.720175	1.051425	2.218228	2.301969	2.352214
289	MISCELLANEOUS CHEMICAL PRODUCTS	13	0.575762	0.691009	-0.823884	-0.718405	-0.542607	0.645149	0.691009	0.824358	1.411614	1.515657	1.578083
2890	MISCELLANEOUS CHEMICAL PRODUCTS	1	-0.894203	-0.894203	-0.894203	-0.894203	-0.894203	-0.894203	-0.894203	-0.894203	-0.894203	-0.894203	-0.894203
2891	Adhesives And Sealants	2	0.385175	0.385175	-0.294342	-0.273541	-0.238872	0.246498	0.385175	0.523852	1.009222	1.043891	1.064692
2893	Printing Ink	1	0.513817	0.513817	0.513817	0.513817	0.513817	0.513817	0.513817	0.513817	0.513817	0.513817	0.513817
2895	Carbon Black	1	1.272890	1.272890	1.272890	1.272890	1.272890	1.272890	1.272890	1.272890	1.272890	1.272890	1.272890
2899	Chemicals And Chemical Preparations, Not Elsewhere Classified	8	0.727756	0.756784	-0.158297	-0.104989	-0.016142	0.688404	0.756784	0.824358	1.423532	1.521616	1.580466
29	PETROLEUM REFINING AND RELATED INDUSTRIES	22	1.436010	1.641525	0.221078	0.285708	0.407717	1.374764	1.641525	1.714664	2.138922	2.148905	2.152178
291	PETROLEUM REFINING	20	1.524870	1.704585	0.476459	0.616398	0.849630	1.549472	1.704585	1.726720	2.144490	2.149425	2.152386
2911	Petroleum Refining	20	1.524870	1.704585	0.476459	0.616398	0.849630	1.549472	1.704585	1.726720	2.144490	2.149425	2.152386
295	ASPHALT PAVING AND ROOFING MATERIALS	1	0.916819	0.916819	0.916819	0.916819	0.916819	0.916819	0.916819	0.916819	0.916819	0.916819	0.916819
2951	Asphalt Paving Mixtures And Blocks	1	0.916819	0.916819	0.916819	0.916819	0.916819	0.916819	0.916819	0.916819	0.916819	0.916819	0.916819
299	MISCELLANEOUS PRODUCTS OF PETROLEUM AND COAL	1	0.177991	0.177991	0.177991	0.177991	0.177991	0.177991	0.177991	0.177991	0.177991	0.177991	0.177991
2999	Products Of Petroleum And Coal, Not Elsewhere Classified	1	0.177991	0.177991	0.177991	0.177991	0.177991	0.177991	0.177991	0.177991	0.177991	0.177991	0.177991
30	RUBBER AND MISCELLANEOUS PLASTICS PRODUCTS	36	0.650320	0.938689	-2.917568	-2.331169	-0.996418	0.707522	0.938689	1.113390	1.805168	1.898836	2.281315
301	TIRES AND INNER TUBES	2	1.016224	1.016224	0.595808	0.608678	0.630128	0.930425	1.016224	1.102023	1.402320	1.423770	1.436640
3011	Tires And Inner Tubes	2	1.016224	1.016224	0.595808	0.608678	0.630128	0.930425	1.016224	1.102023	1.402320	1.423770	1.436640
302	RUBBER AND PLASTICS FOOTWEAR	4	1.340732	1.085592	0.661721	0.671136	0.686826	0.953029	1.085592	1.218155	2.351835	2.444067	2.499407
3021	Rubber And Plastics Footwear	4	1.340732	1.085592	0.661721	0.671136	0.686826	0.953029	1.085592	1.218155	2.351835	2.444067	2.499407
305	GASKETS, PACKING, AND SEALING DEVICES AND RUBBER AND PLASTICS HOSE	3	-0.517145	0.364666	-3.235037	-3.124842	-2.941183	-0.369967	0.364666	0.570213	1.289627	1.341013	1.371845
3052	Rubber And Plastics Hose And Belting	1	-3.308500	-3.308500	-3.308500	-3.308500	-3.308500	-3.308500	-3.308500	-3.308500	-3.308500	-3.308500	-3.308500
3053	Gaskets, Packing, And Sealing Devices	2	0.878533	0.878533	0.374943	0.390359	0.416053	0.775760	0.878533	0.981306	1.341013	1.366707	1.382123
306	FABRICATED RUBBER PRODUCTS, NOT ELSEWHERE CLASSIFIED	3	0.059226	-0.192124	-0.589922	-0.577744	-0.557448	-0.273307	-0.192124	0.039869	0.851846	0.909845	0.944644
3069	Fabricated Rubber Products, Not Elsewhere Classified	3	0.059226	-0.192124	-0.589922	-0.577744	-0.557448	-0.273307	-0.192124	0.039869	0.851846	0.909845	0.944644
308	MISCELLANEOUS PLASTICS PRODUCTS	24	0.724579	1.023145	-1.806850	-1.229800	-0.493779	0.887147	1.023145	1.165790	1.790407	1.805775	1.806972
3081	Unsupported Plastics Film And Sheet	3	0.482247	0.684540	-0.330473	-0.299402	-0.247615	0.477394	0.684540	0.770310	1.070505	1.091948	1.104813
3084	Plastics Pipe	1	1.454080	1.454080	1.454080	1.454080	1.454080	1.454080	1.454080	1.454080	1.454080	1.454080	1.454080
3086	Plastics Foam Products	3	0.990604	1.326690	-0.132862	-0.088182	-0.013715	1.028822	1.326690	1.422906	1.759662	1.783716	1.798148

Up-market Betas of Common Stocks by SIC Codes as of March 31, 2017

SIC Code	Description	Number of Companies	Mean	Median	1st Percentile	2.5th Percentile	5th Percentile	40th Percentile	50th Percentile	60th Percentile	95th Percentile	97.5th Percentile	99th Percentile
3089	Plastics Products, Not Elsewhere Classified	17	0.677486	1.008670	-1.923933	-1.522507	-0.853464	0.892744	1.008670	1.122382	1.730204	1.767252	1.789481
31	LEATHER AND LEATHER PRODUCTS	7	0.882274	1.097350	-0.032913	0.035020	0.148241	0.866179	1.097350	1.159276	1.306794	1.324062	1.334423
314	FOOTWEAR, EXCEPT RUBBER	4	1.078962	1.148955	0.689228	0.708162	0.739718	1.117992	1.148955	1.179918	1.320215	1.330772	1.337107
3142	House Slippers	1	1.097350	1.097350	1.097350	1.097350	1.097350	1.097350	1.097350	1.097350	1.097350	1.097350	1.097350
3143	Men's Footwear, Except Athletic	1	1.341330	1.341330	1.341330	1.341330	1.341330	1.341330	1.341330	1.341330	1.341330	1.341330	1.341330
3149	Footwear, Except Rubber, Not Elsewhere Classified	2	0.938583	0.938583	0.681846	0.689705	0.702804	0.886188	0.938583	0.990978	1.174362	1.187461	1.195320
317	HANDBAGS AND OTHER PERSONAL LEATHER GOODS	1	0.712065	0.712065	0.712065	0.712065	0.712065	0.712065	0.712065	0.712065	0.712065	0.712065	0.712065
3171	Women's Handbags And Purses	1	0.712065	0.712065	0.712065	0.712065	0.712065	0.712065	0.712065	0.712065	0.712065	0.712065	0.712065
319	LEATHER GOODS, NOT ELSEWHERE CLASSIFIED	2	0.574004	0.574004	-0.065157	-0.045591	-0.012981	0.443563	0.574004	0.704446	1.160989	1.193600	1.213166
3199	Leather Goods, Not Elsewhere Classified	2	0.574004	0.574004	-0.065157	-0.045591	-0.012981	0.443563	0.574004	0.704446	1.160989	1.193600	1.213166
32	STONE, CLAY, GLASS, AND CONCRETE PRODUCTS	14	0.753257	1.050944	-1.425313	-1.322268	-1.150525	0.793470	1.050944	1.408486	1.839229	1.940469	2.001214
322	GLASS AND GLASSWARE, PRESSED OR BLOWN	2	1.418315	1.418315	1.112668	1.122024	1.137619	1.355938	1.418315	1.480692	1.699012	1.714606	1.723962
3221	Glass Containers	1	1.730200	1.730200	1.730200	1.730200	1.730200	1.730200	1.730200	1.730200	1.730200	1.730200	1.730200
3229	Pressed And Blown Glass And Glassware, Not Elsewhere Classified	1	1.106430	1.106430	1.106430	1.106430	1.106430	1.106430	1.106430	1.106430	1.106430	1.106430	1.106430
323	GLASS PRODUCTS, MADE OF PURCHASED GLASS	1	1.484000	1.484000	1.484000	1.484000	1.484000	1.484000	1.484000	1.484000	1.484000	1.484000	1.484000
3231	Glass Products, Made Of Purchased Glass	1	1.484000	1.484000	1.484000	1.484000	1.484000	1.484000	1.484000	1.484000	1.484000	1.484000	1.484000
324	CEMENT, HYDRAULIC	3	1.136297	0.995457	0.748023	0.755597	0.768221	0.944960	0.995457	1.130458	1.602960	1.636710	1.656960
3241	Cement, Hydraulic	3	1.136297	0.995457	0.748023	0.755597	0.768221	0.944960	0.995457	1.130458	1.602960	1.636710	1.656960
325	STRUCTURAL CLAY PRODUCTS	1	-0.965572	-0.965572	-0.965572	-0.965572	-0.965572	-0.965572	-0.965572	-0.965572	-0.965572	-0.965572	-0.965572
3253	Ceramic Wall And Floor Tile	1	-0.965572	-0.965572	-0.965572	-0.965572	-0.965572	-0.965572	-0.965572	-0.965572	-0.965572	-0.965572	-0.965572
326	POTTERY AND RELATED PRODUCTS	1	-0.515946	-0.515946	-0.515946	-0.515946	-0.515946	-0.515946	-0.515946	-0.515946	-0.515946	-0.515946	-0.515946
3264	Porcelain Electrical Supplies	1	-0.515946	-0.515946	-0.515946	-0.515946	-0.515946	-0.515946	-0.515946	-0.515946	-0.515946	-0.515946	-0.515946
327	CONCRETE, GYPSUM, AND PLASTER PRODUCTS	6	0.716266	0.967262	-1.407200	-1.276985	-1.059959	0.442324	0.967262	1.492200	1.924578	1.983144	2.018284
3272	Concrete Products, Except Block And Brick	3	1.285695	1.573180	0.268814	0.308743	0.375293	1.306983	1.573180	1.666886	1.994857	2.018284	2.032339
3273	Ready-Mixed Concrete	1	-1.494010	-1.494010	-1.494010	-1.494010	-1.494010	-1.494010	-1.494010	-1.494010	-1.494010	-1.494010	-1.494010
3274	Lime	1	0.442324	0.442324	0.442324	0.442324	0.442324	0.442324	0.442324	0.442324	0.442324	0.442324	0.442324
3275	Gypsum Products	1	1.492200	1.492200	1.492200	1.492200	1.492200	1.492200	1.492200	1.492200	1.492200	1.492200	1.492200
33	PRIMARY METAL INDUSTRIES	39	1.483654	1.439150	0.010196	0.387634	0.521698	1.223690	1.439150	1.718684	2.453329	2.481062	2.487469
331	STEEL WORKS, BLAST FURNACES, AND ROLLING AND FINISHING MILLS	21	1.555188	1.605300	-0.086561	0.145743	0.532915	1.350960	1.605300	2.018570	2.450310	2.465405	2.474462
3312	Steel Works, Blast Furnaces (Including Coke Ovens), And Rolling Mills	15	1.677870	1.669700	0.543741	0.559980	0.587045	1.503564	1.669700	2.070158	2.459367	2.469934	2.476273

Up-market Betas of Common Stocks by SIC Codes as of March 31, 2017

SIC Code	Description	Number of Companies	Mean	Median	1st Percentile	2.5th Percentile	5th Percentile	40th Percentile	50th Percentile	60th Percentile	95th Percentile	97.5th Percentile	99th Percentile
3313	Electrometallurgical Products, Except Steel	1	2.018570	2.018570	2.018570	2.018570	2.018570	2.018570	2.018570	2.018570	2.018570	2.018570	2.018570
3315	Steel Wiredrawing And Steel Nails And Spikes	1	1.439150	1.439150	1.439150	1.439150	1.439150	1.439150	1.439150	1.439150	1.439150	1.439150	1.439150
3316	Cold-Rolled Steel Sheet, Strip, And Bars	1	1.135220	1.135220	1.135220	1.135220	1.135220	1.135220	1.135220	1.135220	1.135220	1.135220	1.135220
3317	Steel Pipe And Tubes	3	0.965986	0.780578	-0.220990	-0.190330	-0.139229	0.576176	0.780578	1.096224	2.200987	2.279898	2.327245
332	IRON AND STEEL FOUNDRIES	1	0.940938	0.940938	0.940938	0.940938	0.940938	0.940938	0.940938	0.940938	0.940938	0.940938	0.940938
3324	Steel Investment Foundries	1	0.940938	0.940938	0.940938	0.940938	0.940938	0.940938	0.940938	0.940938	0.940938	0.940938	0.940938
333	PRIMARY SMELTING AND REFINING OF NONFERROUS METALS	5	1.329217	0.956709	0.785523	0.791998	0.802790	0.929677	0.956709	1.184945	2.298852	2.395296	2.453162
3334	Primary Production Of Aluminum	2	1.690434	1.690434	0.905154	0.929193	0.969259	1.530173	1.690434	1.850695	2.411609	2.451675	2.475714
3339	Primary Smelting And Refining Of Nonferrous Metals, Except Copper	3	1.088405	0.956709	0.784716	0.789981	0.798756	0.921608	0.956709	1.070827	1.470241	1.498770	1.515888
335	ROLLING, DRAWING, AND EXTRUDING OF NONFERROUS METALS	12	1.468045	1.544325	0.464704	0.530646	0.640549	1.247452	1.544325	1.789514	2.165064	2.197877	2.217565
3351	Rolling, Drawing, And Extruding Of Copper	3	0.948742	0.870134	0.821386	0.822878	0.825365	0.860185	0.870134	0.927247	1.127143	1.141422	1.149989
3353	Aluminum Sheet, Plate, And Foil	1	1.877830	1.877830	1.877830	1.877830	1.877830	1.877830	1.877830	1.877830	1.877830	1.877830	1.877830
3356	Rolling, Drawing, And Extruding Of Nonferrous Metals, Except Copper	1	2.230690	2.230690	2.230690	2.230690	2.230690	2.230690	2.230690	2.230690	2.230690	2.230690	2.230690
3357	Drawing And Insulating Of Nonferrous Wire	7	1.523113	1.730930	0.465935	0.533723	0.646702	1.507004	1.730930	1.789514	2.089515	2.100443	2.106999
34	FABRICATED METAL PRODUCTS, EXCEPT MACHINERY AND TRANSPORTATION EQUIPMENT	42	0.760292	0.898953	-0.629512	-0.499831	-0.315139	0.773441	0.898953	0.956448	1.570303	1.900397	2.072559
341	METAL CANS AND SHIPPING CONTAINERS	5	0.943152	0.790161	0.402408	0.424045	0.460106	0.773533	0.790161	0.826221	1.703030	1.805870	1.867574
3411	Metal Cans	4	1.081944	0.835236	0.749839	0.751710	0.754827	0.808191	0.835236	0.862281	1.754450	1.831580	1.877858
3412	Metal Shipping Barrels, Drums, Kegs, And Pails	1	0.387984	0.387984	0.387984	0.387984	0.387984	0.387984	0.387984	0.387984	0.387984	0.387984	0.387984
342	CUTLERY, HANDTOOLS, AND GENERAL HARDWARE	7	0.437606	0.258119	-0.314052	-0.304274	-0.287977	0.149635	0.258119	0.668926	1.200437	1.231699	1.250455
3421	Cutlery	2	-0.266248	-0.266248	-0.319485	-0.317855	-0.315139	-0.277113	-0.266248	-0.255383	-0.217357	-0.214641	-0.213011
3423	Hand And Edge Tools, Except Machine Tools And Handsaws	1	1.262960	1.262960	1.262960	1.262960	1.262960	1.262960	1.262960	1.262960	1.262960	1.262960	1.262960
3429	Hardware, Not Elsewhere Classified	4	0.583195	0.600458	0.082737	0.090873	0.104434	0.395055	0.600458	0.805861	1.037787	1.046169	1.051197
343	HEATING EQUIPMENT, EXCEPT ELECTRIC AND WARM AIR; AND PLUMBING FIXTURES	3	0.111626	0.105288	-0.492233	-0.473941	-0.443456	-0.016655	0.105288	0.231034	0.671143	0.702580	0.721441
3433	Heating Equipment, Except Electric And Warm Air Furnaces	3	0.111626	0.105288	-0.492233	-0.473941	-0.443456	-0.016655	0.105288	0.231034	0.671143	0.702580	0.721441
344	FABRICATED STRUCTURAL METAL PRODUCTS	9	1.209019	1.114590	0.772433	0.787641	0.812987	0.995356	1.114590	1.153142	1.942320	2.064370	2.137600

Up-market Betas of Common Stocks by SIC Codes as of March 31, 2017

SIC Code	Description	Number of Companies	Mean	Median	1st Percentile	2.5th Percentile	5th Percentile	40th Percentile	50th Percentile	60th Percentile	95th Percentile	97.5th Percentile	99th Percentile
3441	Fabricated Structural Metal	2	1.431400	1.431400	1.289525	1.293869	1.301107	1.402446	1.431400	1.460354	1.561693	1.568932	1.573275
3442	Metal Doors, Sash, Frames, Molding, And Trim	3	0.930763	0.937717	0.889998	0.891459	0.893893	0.927978	0.937717	0.943283	0.962765	0.964156	0.964991
3443	Fabricated Plate Work (Boiler Shops)	2	1.474358	1.474358	0.776536	0.797898	0.833501	1.331945	1.474358	1.616770	2.115214	2.150817	2.172179
3448	Prefabricated Metal Buildings And Components	2	1.138685	1.138685	1.115072	1.115795	1.117000	1.133866	1.138685	1.143504	1.160371	1.161575	1.162298
345	SCREW MACHINE PRODUCTS, AND BOLTS, NUTS, SCREWS, RIVETS, AND WASHERS	4	-0.132977	-0.090092	-0.698294	-0.671082	-0.625727	-0.103064	-0.090092	-0.077120	0.299734	0.332222	0.351716
3451	Screw Machine Products	1	-0.111712	-0.111712	-0.111712	-0.111712	-0.111712	-0.111712	-0.111712	-0.111712	-0.111712	-0.111712	-0.111712
3452	Bolts, Nuts, Screws, Rivets, And Washers	3	-0.140066	-0.068472	-0.703477	-0.684038	-0.651640	-0.198065	-0.068472	0.018164	0.321393	0.343052	0.356047
346	METAL FORGINGS AND STAMPINGS	4	0.707799	0.825262	0.052732	0.084123	0.136441	0.767736	0.825262	0.882787	1.114710	1.131790	1.142038
3463	Nonferrous Forgings	1	1.148870	1.148870	1.148870	1.148870	1.148870	1.148870	1.148870	1.148870	1.148870	1.148870	1.148870
3465	Automotive Stampings	2	0.825262	0.825262	0.731303	0.734179	0.738973	0.806086	0.825262	0.844437	0.911550	0.916344	0.919220
3469	Metal Stampings, Not Elsewhere Classified	1	0.031804	0.031804	0.031804	0.031804	0.031804	0.031804	0.031804	0.031804	0.031804	0.031804	0.031804
347	COATING, ENGRAVING, AND ALLIED SERVICES	1	0.908881	0.908881	0.908881	0.908881	0.908881	0.908881	0.908881	0.908881	0.908881	0.908881	0.908881
3479	Coating, Engraving, And Allied Services, Not Elsewhere Classified	1	0.908881	0.908881	0.908881	0.908881	0.908881	0.908881	0.908881	0.908881	0.908881	0.908881	0.908881
348	ORDNANCE AND ACCESSORIES, EXCEPT VEHICLES AND GUIDED MISSILES	2	0.648752	0.648752	0.449695	0.455789	0.465945	0.608128	0.648752	0.689375	0.831558	0.841714	0.847808
3484	Small Arms	2	0.648752	0.648752	0.449695	0.455789	0.465945	0.608128	0.648752	0.689375	0.831558	0.841714	0.847808
349	MISCELLANEOUS FABRICATED METAL PRODUCTS	7	1.204503	1.188890	1.052686	1.054765	1.058230	1.151714	1.188890	1.202588	1.417012	1.437916	1.450458
3491	Industrial Valves	3	1.150637	1.188890	1.054052	1.058180	1.065059	1.161372	1.188890	1.193456	1.209437	1.210579	1.211263
3495	Wire Springs	1	1.319460	1.319460	1.319460	1.319460	1.319460	1.319460	1.319460	1.319460	1.319460	1.319460	1.319460
3499	Fabricated Metal Products, Not Elsewhere Classified	3	1.220050	1.126930	1.075451	1.077027	1.079653	1.116424	1.126930	1.193308	1.425631	1.442226	1.452182
35	INDUSTRIAL AND COMMERCIAL MACHINERY AND COMPUTER EQUIPMENT	176	1.062235	1.110525	-1.411420	-0.591018	-0.302786	0.995120	1.110525	1.258090	2.215345	2.541379	2.846518
351	ENGINES AND TURBINES	9	1.117588	1.114640	0.139658	0.179067	0.244748	0.898134	1.114640	1.252032	2.066508	2.124214	2.158838
3511	Steam, Gas, And Hydraulic Turbines, And Turbine Generator Set Units	5	0.908513	0.690826	0.126521	0.146226	0.179067	0.591213	0.690826	0.860352	1.968464	2.075192	2.139229
3519	Internal Combustion Engines, Not Elsewhere Classified	4	1.378932	1.389165	0.857279	0.877186	0.910364	1.327494	1.389165	1.450836	1.833174	1.863282	1.881347
352	FARM AND GARDEN MACHINERY AND EQUIPMENT	10	1.028242	0.972349	0.065969	0.128270	0.232105	0.846594	0.972349	0.989082	2.303029	2.604769	2.785814
3523	Farm Machinery And Equipment	8	0.837941	0.972349	0.056739	0.105195	0.185956	0.880105	0.972349	0.985520	1.414331	1.489886	1.535218
3524	Lawn And Garden Tractors And Home Lawn And Garden Equipment	2	1.789443	1.789443	0.694716	0.728228	0.784082	1.566029	1.789443	2.012856	2.794803	2.850657	2.884169

Up-market Betas of Common Stocks by SIC Codes as of March 31, 2017

SIC Code	Description	Number of Companies	Mean	Median	1st Percentile	2.5th Percentile	5th Percentile	40th Percentile	50th Percentile	60th Percentile	95th Percentile	97.5th Percentile	99th Percentile
353	CONSTRUCTION, MINING, AND MATERIALS HANDLING MACHINERY AND EQUIPMENT	25	1.345272	1.256610	-0.196817	0.143468	0.551517	1.193836	1.256610	1.494886	2.060134	2.117018	2.167695
3531	Construction Machinery And Equipment	6	0.879454	1.034698	-0.368924	-0.286798	-0.149922	0.822375	1.034698	1.247020	1.591448	1.647254	1.680738
3532	Mining Machinery And Equipment, Except Oil And Gas Field Machinery	4	1.324102	1.278195	0.830959	0.846744	0.873052	1.214004	1.278195	1.342386	1.839420	1.879500	1.903548
3533	Oil And Gas Field Machinery And Equipment	9	1.620497	1.521040	1.079068	1.082634	1.088578	1.486168	1.521040	1.838912	2.145172	2.173326	2.190218
3535	Conveyors And Conveying Equipment	1	1.208920	1.208920	1.208920	1.208920	1.208920	1.208920	1.208920	1.208920	1.208920	1.208920	1.208920
3536	Overhead Traveling Cranes, Hoists, And Monorail Systems	1	2.013490	2.013490	2.013490	2.013490	2.013490	2.013490	2.013490	2.013490	2.013490	2.013490	2.013490
3537	Industrial Trucks, Tractors, Trailers, And Stackers	4	1.312947	1.347002	0.529436	0.541245	0.560928	1.009197	1.347002	1.684807	2.017289	2.026754	2.032434
354	METALWORKING MACHINERY AND EQUIPMENT	9	1.200485	1.056480	0.131922	0.206978	0.332071	1.019840	1.056480	1.300224	2.102728	2.179834	2.226098
3541	Machine Tools, Metal Cutting Types	4	1.483015	1.463945	0.756506	0.770422	0.793616	1.219466	1.463945	1.708424	2.199111	2.228025	2.245374
3542	Machine Tools, Metal Forming Types	2	0.859016	0.859016	0.710384	0.714934	0.722517	0.828683	0.859016	0.889348	0.995514	1.003097	1.007647
3545	Cutting Tools, Machine Tool Accessories, And Machinists' Precision Tools	1	1.361160	1.361160	1.361160	1.361160	1.361160	1.361160	1.361160	1.361160	1.361160	1.361160	1.361160
3546	Power-Driven Handtools	1	0.081885	0.081885	0.081885	0.081885	0.081885	0.081885	0.081885	0.081885	0.081885	0.081885	0.081885
3549	Metalworking Machinery, Not Elsewhere Classified	1	1.711230	1.711230	1.711230	1.711230	1.711230	1.711230	1.711230	1.711230	1.711230	1.711230	1.711230
355	SPECIAL INDUSTRY MACHINERY, EXCEPT METALWORKING MACHINERY	21	0.928282	0.955328	-0.693998	-0.649514	-0.575373	0.902924	0.955328	1.060790	2.565660	2.696090	2.774348
3554	Paper Industries Machinery	1	0.788187	0.788187	0.788187	0.788187	0.788187	0.788187	0.788187	0.788187	0.788187	0.788187	0.788187
3555	Printing Trades Machinery And Equipment	2	1.731030	1.731030	0.657449	0.690314	0.745088	1.511931	1.731030	1.950128	2.716971	2.771745	2.804610
3556	Food Products Machinery	1	0.151627	0.151627	0.151627	0.151627	0.151627	0.151627	0.151627	0.151627	0.151627	0.151627	0.151627
3559	Special Industry Machinery, Not Elsewhere Classified	17	0.887768	0.997552	-0.699929	-0.664342	-0.605029	0.949697	0.997552	1.081730	2.050348	2.308004	2.462598
356	GENERAL INDUSTRIAL MACHINERY AND EQUIPMENT	29	1.086940	1.083660	-0.303449	-0.171553	0.010382	1.040286	1.083660	1.303938	1.918398	2.102823	2.126221
3561	Pumps And Pumping Equipment	9	1.487968	1.533620	0.994372	1.002289	1.015484	1.359044	1.533620	1.538988	2.119536	2.130678	2.137363
3562	Ball And Roller Bearings	4	1.050055	1.195711	0.165661	0.201202	0.260435	1.037335	1.195711	1.354086	1.635756	1.651293	1.660615
3564	Industrial And Commercial Fans And Blowers And Air Purification Equipment	5	0.732250	0.810153	-0.048898	-0.006232	0.064878	0.739596	0.810153	0.900728	1.213790	1.235940	1.249230
3566	Speed Changers, Industrial High-Speed Drives, And Gears	1	1.324050	1.324050	1.324050	1.324050	1.324050	1.324050	1.324050	1.324050	1.324050	1.324050	1.324050

Up-market Betas of Common Stocks by SIC Codes as of March 31, 2017

SIC Code	Description	Number of Companies	Mean	Median	1st Percentile	2.5th Percentile	5th Percentile	40th Percentile	50th Percentile	60th Percentile	95th Percentile	97.5th Percentile	99th Percentile
3568	Mechanical Power Transmission Equipment, Not Elsewhere Classified	1	1.205970	1.205970	1.205970	1.205970	1.205970	1.205970	1.205970	1.205970	1.205970	1.205970	1.205970
3569	General Industrial Machinery And Equipment, Not Elsewhere Classified	9	0.859785	0.885475	-0.321248	-0.216052	-0.040726	0.740239	0.885475	1.031847	1.542926	1.580288	1.602705
357	COMPUTER AND OFFICE EQUIPMENT	58	0.965127	1.175995	-2.495065	-1.648735	-0.439067	0.984853	1.175995	1.291866	2.398519	2.628802	2.957087
3571	Electronic Computers	12	0.971774	1.032905	-0.107088	-0.040178	0.071338	0.942439	1.032905	1.181942	1.732851	1.856900	1.931330
3572	Computer Storage Devices	8	0.821076	1.604850	-3.067201	-2.859648	-2.513725	1.477494	1.604850	1.672664	2.458749	2.479830	2.492478
3576	COMPUTER COMMUNICATIONS EQUIPMENT	9	1.234661	1.180400	0.009709	0.056736	0.135115	0.991110	1.180400	1.321112	2.767374	3.017162	3.167035
3577	Computer Peripheral Equipment, Not Elsewhere Classified	21	0.751444	0.832589	-1.627194	-1.129380	-0.299690	0.622990	0.832589	1.038670	2.320350	2.521840	2.642734
3578	Calculating And Accounting Machines, Except Electronic Computers	6	1.267932	1.331675	0.421698	0.480149	0.577568	1.318150	1.331675	1.345200	1.720658	1.731129	1.737412
3579	Office Machines, Not Elsewhere Classified	2	1.623810	1.623810	1.555288	1.557386	1.560882	1.609826	1.623810	1.637794	1.686738	1.690234	1.692332
358	REFRIGERATION AND SERVICE INDUSTRY MACHINERY	11	1.113708	1.094740	0.656192	0.678973	0.716940	1.020920	1.094740	1.155070	1.484475	1.486063	1.487015
3580	REFRIGERATION & SERVICE INDUSTRY MACHINERY	2	1.158518	1.158518	0.959605	0.965695	0.975843	1.117924	1.158518	1.199112	1.341193	1.351341	1.357431
3585	Air-Conditioning And Warm Air Heating Equipment	3	1.099258	1.094740	0.798912	0.807968	0.823062	1.034367	1.094740	1.157824	1.378618	1.394389	1.403852
3589	Service Industry Machinery, Not Elsewhere Classified	6	1.105997	1.087995	0.651457	0.667134	0.693263	1.020920	1.087995	1.155070	1.486063	1.486856	1.487333
359	MISCELLANEOUS INDUSTRIAL AND COMMERCIAL MACHINERY AND EQUIPMENT	4	0.733278	1.075348	-0.557587	-0.493359	-0.386313	0.926264	1.075348	1.224431	1.373970	1.378395	1.381050
3592	Carburetors, Pistons, Piston Rings, And Valves	1	1.323820	1.323820	1.323820	1.323820	1.323820	1.323820	1.323820	1.323820	1.323820	1.323820	1.323820
3594	Fluid Power Pumps And Motors	1	1.382820	1.382820	1.382820	1.382820	1.382820	1.382820	1.382820	1.382820	1.382820	1.382820	1.382820
3596	Scales And Balances, Except Laboratory	1	-0.600405	-0.600405	-0.600405	-0.600405	-0.600405	-0.600405	-0.600405	-0.600405	-0.600405	-0.600405	-0.600405
3599	Industrial And Commercial Machinery And Equipment, Not Elsewhere Classified	1	0.826875	0.826875	0.826875	0.826875	0.826875	0.826875	0.826875	0.826875	0.826875	0.826875	0.826875
36	ELECTRONIC AND OTHER ELECTRICAL EQUIPMENT AND COMPONENTS, EXCEPT COMPUTER	266	0.930759	0.974194	-0.924579	-0.639354	-0.425563	0.796094	0.974194	1.100560	2.114490	2.283599	3.905715
361	ELECTRIC TRANSMISSION AND DISTRIBUTION EQUIPMENT	5	0.887629	0.642652	0.558552	0.558860	0.559373	0.610981	0.642652	0.893703	1.376768	1.390079	1.398066
3612	Power, Distribution, And Specialty Transformers	3	0.588158	0.563475	0.558450	0.558603	0.558860	0.562449	0.563475	0.579310	0.634734	0.638693	0.641068
3613	Switchgear And Switchboard Apparatus	2	1.336835	1.336835	1.271611	1.273608	1.276936	1.323524	1.336835	1.350146	1.396735	1.400062	1.402059

Up-market Betas of Common Stocks by SIC Codes as of March 31, 2017

SIC Code	Description	Number of Companies	Mean	Median	1st Percentile	2.5th Percentile	5th Percentile	40th Percentile	50th Percentile	60th Percentile	95th Percentile	97.5th Percentile	99th Percentile
362	ELECTRICAL INDUSTRIAL APPARATUS	18	0.573956	0.641010	-1.839022	-1.376636	-0.605992	0.339151	0.641010	0.757512	1.868053	1.901212	1.921107
3621	Motors And Generators	11	0.727198	1.094780	-1.940226	-1.629644	-1.112009	0.692074	1.094780	1.276010	1.895360	1.914865	1.926568
3625	Relays And Industrial Controls	3	0.547980	0.589945	0.249453	0.259876	0.277248	0.520457	0.589945	0.634254	0.789336	0.800414	0.807060
3629	Electrical Industrial Apparatus, Not Elsewhere Classified	4	0.172021	0.139033	-0.325840	-0.313600	-0.293199	0.018417	0.139033	0.259648	0.683423	0.713720	0.731898
363	HOUSEHOLD APPLIANCES	5	0.874572	0.880135	0.203511	0.223556	0.256965	0.737776	0.880135	0.988625	1.531856	1.579418	1.607955
3632	Household Refrigerators And Home And Farm Freezers	1	1.626980	1.626980	1.626980	1.626980	1.626980	1.626980	1.626980	1.626980	1.626980	1.626980	1.626980
3633	Household Laundry Equipment	2	0.670754	0.670754	0.199759	0.214177	0.238208	0.574632	0.670754	0.766875	1.103299	1.127330	1.141748
3634	Electric Housewares And Fans	2	0.702186	0.702186	0.527796	0.533134	0.542032	0.666596	0.702186	0.737776	0.862340	0.871238	0.876576
364	ELECTRIC LIGHTING AND WIRING EQUIPMENT	9	0.985387	1.077280	0.172467	0.219928	0.299030	0.787586	1.077280	1.188696	1.660290	1.697300	1.719506
3640	ELECTRIC LIGHTING & WIRING EQUIPMENT	1	0.602038	0.602038	0.602038	0.602038	0.602038	0.602038	0.602038	0.602038	0.602038	0.602038	0.602038
3641	Electric Lamp Bulbs And Tubes	3	1.332911	1.549260	0.731845	0.756868	0.798573	1.382441	1.549260	1.586270	1.715805	1.725058	1.730609
3643	Current-Carrying Wiring Devices	1	1.216550	1.216550	1.216550	1.216550	1.216550	1.216550	1.216550	1.216550	1.216550	1.216550	1.216550
3645	Residential Electric Lighting Fixtures	2	0.806808	0.806808	0.541744	0.549859	0.563382	0.752713	0.806808	0.860902	1.050233	1.063756	1.071871
3646	Commercial, Industrial, And Institutional Electric Lighting Fixtures	2	0.718773	0.718773	0.152385	0.169723	0.198621	0.603184	0.718773	0.834362	1.238925	1.267823	1.285161
365	HOUSEHOLD AUDIO AND VIDEO EQUIPMENT, AND AUDIO RECORDINGS	7	0.373041	0.038103	-0.372354	-0.361357	-0.343029	-0.015083	0.038103	0.410923	1.309608	1.316274	1.320274
3651	Household Audio And Video Equipment	7	0.373041	0.038103	-0.372354	-0.361357	-0.343029	-0.015083	0.038103	0.410923	1.309608	1.316274	1.320274
366	COMMUNICATIONS EQUIPMENT	72	0.871589	0.848069	-0.588786	-0.567809	-0.458865	0.681754	0.848069	0.928377	2.180624	2.434344	3.485480
3661	Telephone And Telegraph Apparatus	19	0.882286	1.046180	-0.501143	-0.312420	0.002118	0.847814	1.046180	1.102336	1.530844	1.699612	1.800873
3663	Radio And Television Broadcasting And Communications Equipment	37	0.813004	0.800840	-0.570693	-0.566940	-0.503037	0.681754	0.800840	0.914777	2.163626	2.346603	2.725645
3669	Communications Equipment, Not Elsewhere Classified	16	0.994361	0.718622	0.042324	0.043213	0.044696	0.592268	0.718622	0.901201	2.858670	3.792885	4.353414
367	ELECTRONIC COMPONENTS AND ACCESSORIES	130	0.992341	1.067880	-0.860340	-0.748800	-0.435336	0.948220	1.067880	1.183426	2.105174	2.243949	3.124753
3671	Electron Tubes	1	-0.295740	-0.295740	-0.295740	-0.295740	-0.295740	-0.295740	-0.295740	-0.295740	-0.295740	-0.295740	-0.295740
3672	Printed Circuit Boards	14	0.889888	1.121400	-0.777530	-0.468864	0.045580	1.053432	1.121400	1.151904	1.293553	1.301867	1.306855
3674	Semiconductors And Related Devices	94	1.060915	1.102425	-0.788360	-0.699457	-0.420774	0.989526	1.102425	1.249882	2.152604	2.242024	2.575743
3675	Electronic Capacitors	1	-0.150003	-0.150003	-0.150003	-0.150003	-0.150003	-0.150003	-0.150003	-0.150003	-0.150003	-0.150003	-0.150003
3676	Electronic Resistors	1	1.123930	1.123930	1.123930	1.123930	1.123930	1.123930	1.123930	1.123930	1.123930	1.123930	1.123930
3677	Electronic Coils, Transformers, And Other Inductors	2	0.845356	0.845356	0.681026	0.686056	0.694440	0.811819	0.845356	0.878893	0.996272	1.004656	1.009686
3678	Electronic Connectors	4	0.820428	1.067872	-0.337078	-0.285309	-0.199027	0.894448	1.067872	1.241295	1.493463	1.505511	1.512741
3679	Electronic Components, Not Elsewhere Classified	13	0.859173	0.658034	-0.610014	-0.535016	-0.410019	0.413945	0.658034	0.955816	2.616374	3.039902	3.294019

Up-market Betas of Common Stocks by SIC Codes as of March 31, 2017

SIC Code	Description	Number of Companies	Mean	Median	1st Percentile	2.5th Percentile	5th Percentile	40th Percentile	50th Percentile	60th Percentile	95th Percentile	97.5th Percentile	99th Percentile
369	MISCELLANEOUS ELECTRICAL MACHINERY, EQUIPMENT, AND SUPPLIES	20	1.260056	1.128250	-0.875565	-0.520777	0.070537	0.994311	1.128250	1.250238	2.680107	3.823873	4.510133
3691	Storage Batteries	9	1.648618	1.225570	0.701875	0.737828	0.797749	1.049314	1.225570	1.431722	3.786580	4.377110	4.731428
3692	Primary Batteries, Dry And Wet	2	0.723810	0.723810	-1.075372	-1.020295	-0.928500	0.356630	0.723810	1.090990	2.376120	2.467915	2.522992
3694	Electrical Equipment For Internal Combustion Engines	1	1.225420	1.225420	1.225420	1.225420	1.225420	1.225420	1.225420	1.225420	1.225420	1.225420	1.225420
3695	Magnetic And Optical Recording Media	4	1.118659	1.131192	0.778580	0.787699	0.802897	1.037562	1.131192	1.224821	1.416874	1.428312	1.435175
3699	Electrical Machinery, Equipment, And Supplies, Not Elsewhere Classified	4	0.803970	0.874549	0.150337	0.176673	0.220566	0.780630	0.874549	0.968468	1.288562	1.311281	1.324912
37	TRANSPORTATION EQUIPMENT	100	0.939148	1.090100	-2.388855	-1.444597	-0.705915	0.936100	1.090100	1.230102	1.857173	2.120792	2.162686
371	MOTOR VEHICLES AND MOTOR VEHICLE EQUIPMENT	56	0.971791	1.228970	-2.449777	-2.091906	-0.996531	1.104970	1.228970	1.306820	1.906305	2.125981	2.153761
3711	Motor Vehicles And Passenger Car Bodies	19	0.560286	0.934680	-2.501007	-2.463623	-2.401316	0.690393	0.934680	1.122018	1.591743	1.841147	1.990789
3713	Truck And Bus Bodies	2	1.811350	1.811350	1.467978	1.478489	1.496008	1.741274	1.811350	1.881426	2.126692	2.144211	2.154722
3714	Motor Vehicle Parts And Accessories	32	1.165571	1.306880	-1.123652	-0.410179	0.213884	1.266884	1.306880	1.349338	1.801336	1.912919	2.053512
3715	Truck Trailers	1	1.029200	1.029200	1.029200	1.029200	1.029200	1.029200	1.029200	1.029200	1.029200	1.029200	1.029200
3716	Motor Homes	2	0.912354	0.912354	0.708164	0.714415	0.724833	0.870682	0.912354	0.954025	1.099874	1.110292	1.116543
372	AIRCRAFT AND PARTS	28	0.880417	0.879527	-1.108959	-0.861982	-0.379830	0.816331	0.879527	1.027416	1.940864	2.145448	2.212601
3721	Aircraft	9	0.862607	0.847506	0.274607	0.303971	0.352912	0.825009	0.847506	0.999773	1.352166	1.392818	1.417209
3724	Aircraft Engines And Engine Parts	7	1.006512	0.936091	0.548176	0.556710	0.570934	0.905373	0.936091	1.064712	1.469158	1.485649	1.495544
3728	Aircraft Parts And Auxiliary Equipment, Not Elsewhere Classified	12	0.820218	0.839136	-1.206530	-1.105910	-0.938209	0.749340	0.839136	0.964550	2.166175	2.211772	2.239131
373	SHIP AND BOAT BUILDING AND REPAIRING	4	0.977260	0.919371	0.652591	0.657382	0.665369	0.821278	0.919371	1.017464	1.370194	1.395547	1.410759
3731	Ship Building And Repairing	2	0.702639	0.702639	0.650461	0.652058	0.654720	0.691990	0.702639	0.713288	0.750558	0.753220	0.754817
3732	Boat Building And Repairing	2	1.251880	1.251880	1.086240	1.091311	1.099762	1.218076	1.251880	1.285684	1.403998	1.412449	1.417520
374	RAILROAD EQUIPMENT	5	1.496560	1.591350	1.067370	1.098194	1.149568	1.579034	1.591350	1.600166	1.659222	1.664951	1.668388
3743	Railroad Equipment	5	1.496560	1.591350	1.067370	1.098194	1.149568	1.579034	1.591350	1.600166	1.659222	1.664951	1.668388
375	MOTORCYCLES, BICYCLES, AND PARTS	2	1.036371	1.036371	0.940331	0.943271	0.948171	1.016771	1.036371	1.055970	1.124570	1.129470	1.132410
3751	Motorcycles, Bicycles, And Parts	2	1.036371	1.036371	0.940331	0.943271	0.948171	1.016771	1.036371	1.055970	1.124570	1.129470	1.132410
376	GUIDED MISSILES AND SPACE VEHICLES AND PARTS	3	-0.118039	-0.315804	-0.693486	-0.681925	-0.662655	-0.392882	-0.315804	-0.120067	0.565013	0.613947	0.643307
3761	Guided Missiles And Space Vehicles	1	0.662881	0.662881	0.662881	0.662881	0.662881	0.662881	0.662881	0.662881	0.662881	0.662881	0.662881
3764	Guided Missile And Space Vehicle Propulsion Units And Propulsion	1	-0.315804	-0.315804	-0.315804	-0.315804	-0.315804	-0.315804	-0.315804	-0.315804	-0.315804	-0.315804	-0.315804
3769	Guided Missile And Space Vehicle Parts And Auxiliary Equipment, Not Elsewhere Classified	1	-0.701194	-0.701194	-0.701194	-0.701194	-0.701194	-0.701194	-0.701194	-0.701194	-0.701194	-0.701194	-0.701194
379	MISCELLANEOUS TRANSPORTATION EQUIPMENT	2	0.866164	0.866164	0.854466	0.854824	0.855421	0.863777	0.866164	0.868551	0.876907	0.877504	0.877862

Up-market Betas of Common Stocks by SIC Codes as of March 31, 2017

SIC Code	Description	Number of Companies	Mean	Median	1st Percentile	2.5th Percentile	5th Percentile	40th Percentile	50th Percentile	60th Percentile	95th Percentile	97.5th Percentile	99th Percentile
3795	Tanks And Tank Components	1	0.854227	0.854227	0.854227	0.854227	0.854227	0.854227	0.854227	0.854227	0.854227	0.854227	0.854227
3799	Transportation Equipment, Not Elsewhere Classified	1	0.878101	0.878101	0.878101	0.878101	0.878101	0.878101	0.878101	0.878101	0.878101	0.878101	0.878101
38	MEASURING, ANALYZING, AND CONTROLLING INSTRUMENTS; PHOTOGRAPHIC, MEDICAL	259	0.720120	0.789697	-2.629160	-1.671785	-1.039753	0.652001	0.789697	0.953403	2.105857	2.438252	2.886308
381	SEARCH, DETECTION, NAVIGATION, GUIDANCE, AERONAUTICAL, AND NAUTICAL	14	0.947720	0.912122	0.501904	0.518435	0.545986	0.849200	0.912122	0.948591	1.467856	1.515553	1.544171
3812	Search, Detection, Navigation, Guidance, Aeronautical, And Nautical	14	0.947720	0.912122	0.501904	0.518435	0.545986	0.849200	0.912122	0.948591	1.467856	1.515553	1.544171
382	LABORATORY APPARATUS AND ANALYTICAL, OPTICAL, MEASURING, AND CONTROL	92	0.654214	0.757521	-2.838703	-1.671958	-1.209581	0.636714	0.757521	0.970527	1.820634	2.552096	2.974063
3821	Laboratory Apparatus And Furniture	3	0.185018	0.321284	-1.004033	-0.963462	-0.895844	0.050811	0.321284	0.509997	1.170493	1.217672	1.245979
3822	Automatic Controls For Regulating Residential And Commercial Environment	3	1.589967	1.350290	0.462028	0.489220	0.534539	1.169012	1.350290	1.675374	2.813168	2.894439	2.943202
3823	Industrial Instruments For Measurement, Display, And Control Of Processes	16	1.092081	1.112263	-0.040587	0.001096	0.070566	0.843228	1.112263	1.338290	1.931765	2.197978	2.357705
3824	Totalizing Fluid Meters And Counting Devices	1	1.067560	1.067560	1.067560	1.067560	1.067560	1.067560	1.067560	1.067560	1.067560	1.067560	1.067560
3825	Instruments For Measuring And Testing Of Electricity And Electric	22	0.337802	0.497497	-2.936119	-2.432164	-1.619028	0.263959	0.497497	0.897612	1.401827	1.541816	1.634476
3826	Laboratory Analytical Instruments	19	0.506351	0.663645	-1.381759	-0.947537	-0.223835	0.628594	0.663645	0.703109	1.118769	1.232615	1.300922
3827	Optical Instruments And Lenses	8	1.160255	1.091792	0.396309	0.410330	0.433698	0.912672	1.091792	1.259814	2.197651	2.391545	2.507882
3829	Measuring And Controlling Devices, Not Elsewhere Classified	20	0.499379	0.813982	-2.498536	-2.052579	-1.309318	0.504405	0.813982	1.050484	1.955329	2.464615	2.770186
384	SURGICAL, MEDICAL, AND DENTAL INSTRUMENTS AND SUPPLIES	143	0.715666	0.768725	-2.288783	-1.616880	-0.922132	0.612090	0.768725	0.900410	2.189341	2.403267	2.786777
3841	Surgical And Medical Instruments And Apparatus	84	0.701176	0.762594	-2.074337	-1.846210	-1.318554	0.591525	0.762594	0.895373	2.358397	2.406102	2.751533
3842	Orthopedic, Prosthetic, And Surgical Appliances And Supplies	20	0.923563	0.949897	-0.506762	-0.347651	-0.082464	0.762976	0.949897	1.178960	2.019860	2.082465	2.120028
3843	Dental Equipment And Supplies	5	1.508999	0.886809	0.542431	0.561043	0.592063	0.868174	0.886809	1.325833	3.039730	3.171650	3.250802
3844	X-Ray Apparatus And Tubes And Related Irradiation Apparatus	2	1.180067	1.180067	0.912563	0.920752	0.934400	1.125474	1.180067	1.234660	1.425734	1.439382	1.447571
3845	Electromedical And Electrotherapeutic Apparatus	32	0.470786	0.618784	-2.808572	-1.669146	-0.933103	0.527189	0.618784	0.708720	1.504079	1.710873	1.883611
385	OPHTHALMIC GOODS	2	0.776681	0.776681	0.753753	0.754455	0.755625	0.772002	0.776681	0.781360	0.797737	0.798907	0.799609
3851	Ophthalmic Goods	2	0.776681	0.776681	0.753753	0.754455	0.755625	0.772002	0.776681	0.781360	0.797737	0.798907	0.799609
386	PHOTOGRAPHIC EQUIPMENT AND SUPPLIES	6	0.971147	1.270865	0.164306	0.165231	0.166773	1.211770	1.270865	1.329960	1.534230	1.564985	1.583438

Up-market Betas of Common Stocks by SIC Codes as of March 31, 2017

SIC Code	Description	Number of Companies	Mean	Median	1st Percentile	2.5th Percentile	5th Percentile	40th Percentile	50th Percentile	60th Percentile	95th Percentile	97.5th Percentile	99th Percentile
3861	Photographic Equipment And Supplies	6	0.971147	1.270865	0.164306	0.165231	0.166773	1.211770	1.270865	1.329960	1.534230	1.564985	1.583438
387	WATCHES, CLOCKS, CLOCKWORK OPERATED DEVICES, AND PARTS	2	1.667425	1.667425	1.625437	1.626722	1.628865	1.658856	1.667425	1.675994	1.705986	1.708128	1.709413
3873	Watches, Clocks, Clockwork Operated Devices, And Parts	2	1.667425	1.667425	1.625437	1.626722	1.628865	1.658856	1.667425	1.675994	1.705986	1.708128	1.709413
39	MISCELLANEOUS MANUFACTURING INDUSTRIES	30	0.488654	0.674620	-4.516640	-2.535184	-1.188454	0.609484	0.674620	0.886810	2.755092	4.009254	4.099359
391	JEWELRY, SILVERWARE, AND PLATED WARE	2	-0.193488	-0.193488	-0.442082	-0.434472	-0.421788	-0.244221	-0.193488	-0.142754	0.034813	0.047496	0.055106
3911	Jewelry, Precious Metal	2	-0.193488	-0.193488	-0.442082	-0.434472	-0.421788	-0.244221	-0.193488	-0.142754	0.034813	0.047496	0.055106
394	DOLLS, TOYS, GAMES AND SPORTING AND ATHLETIC GOODS	21	0.629005	0.826577	-4.926596	-3.560075	-1.282540	0.669357	0.826577	1.030750	3.952290	4.055860	4.118002
3942	Dolls And Stuffed Toys	2	1.137570	1.137570	1.118078	1.118675	1.119669	1.133592	1.137570	1.141548	1.155471	1.156466	1.157062
3944	Games, Toys, And Children's Vehicles, Except Dolls And Bicycles	11	0.084505	0.602537	-5.382103	-4.698843	-3.560075	0.301744	0.602537	0.826577	2.614605	3.283448	3.684753
3949	Sporting And Athletic Goods, Not Elsewhere Classified	8	1.250550	0.787879	0.617622	0.622882	0.631648	0.677777	0.787879	0.923500	3.154265	3.656848	3.958397
399	MISCELLANEOUS MANUFACTURING INDUSTRIES	7	0.262501	0.038473	-1.025892	-0.954541	-0.835622	0.015072	0.038473	0.543849	1.198616	1.245233	1.273203
3990	MISCELLANEOUS MANUFACTURING INDUSTRIES	1	0.038473	0.038473	0.038473	0.038473	0.038473	0.038473	0.038473	0.038473	0.038473	0.038473	0.038473
3993	Signs And Advertising Specialties	1	-0.280666	-0.280666	-0.280666	-0.280666	-0.280666	-0.280666	-0.280666	-0.280666	-0.280666	-0.280666	-0.280666
3996	Linoleum, Asphalted-Felt-Base, And Other Hard Surface Floor Cover	1	0.880767	0.880767	0.880767	0.880767	0.880767	0.880767	0.880767	0.880767	0.880767	0.880767	0.880767
3999	Manufacturing Industries, Not Elsewhere Classified	4	0.299733	0.490271	-1.041272	-0.992990	-0.912520	0.195791	0.490271	0.784751	1.245233	1.268542	1.282527
	TRANSPORTATION, COMMUNICATIONS, ELECTRIC, GAS, AND SANITARY SERVICE												
40	RAILROAD TRANSPORTATION	7	1.137336	1.015800	0.863076	0.871481	0.885489	1.005572	1.015800	1.159812	1.466399	1.485205	1.496488
401	RAILROADS	7	1.137336	1.015800	0.863076	0.871481	0.885489	1.005572	1.015800	1.159812	1.466399	1.485205	1.496488
4011	Railroads, Line-Haul Operating	7	1.137336	1.015800	0.863076	0.871481	0.885489	1.005572	1.015800	1.159812	1.466399	1.485205	1.496488
41	LOCAL AND SUBURBAN TRANSIT AND INTERURBAN HIGHWAY PASSENGER TRANSPORTATION	1	0.309139	0.309139	0.309139	0.309139	0.309139	0.309139	0.309139	0.309139	0.309139	0.309139	0.309139
415	SCHOOL BUSES	1	0.309139	0.309139	0.309139	0.309139	0.309139	0.309139	0.309139	0.309139	0.309139	0.309139	0.309139
4151	School Buses	1	0.309139	0.309139	0.309139	0.309139	0.309139	0.309139	0.309139	0.309139	0.309139	0.309139	0.309139
42	MOTOR FREIGHT TRANSPORTATION AND WAREHOUSING	22	1.536119	1.480480	0.551717	0.615825	0.714960	1.350796	1.480480	1.623630	2.379336	2.409886	2.428584
421	TRUCKING AND COURIER SERVICES, EXCEPT AIR	21	1.528698	1.452880	0.549682	0.610737	0.712496	1.312760	1.452880	1.605090	2.381690	2.411370	2.429178
4213	Trucking, Except Local	21	1.528698	1.452880	0.549682	0.610737	0.712496	1.312760	1.452880	1.605090	2.381690	2.411370	2.429178
422	PUBLIC WAREHOUSING AND STORAGE	1	1.691970	1.691970	1.691970	1.691970	1.691970	1.691970	1.691970	1.691970	1.691970	1.691970	1.691970
4225	General Warehousing And Storage	1	1.691970	1.691970	1.691970	1.691970	1.691970	1.691970	1.691970	1.691970	1.691970	1.691970	1.691970
44	WATER TRANSPORTATION	46	1.283530	1.281355	-2.496452	-1.804728	-0.239039	1.089010	1.281355	1.533670	3.101655	3.439624	4.558467

Up-market Betas of Common Stocks by SIC Codes as of March 31, 2017

SIC Code	Description	Number of Companies	Mean	Median	1st Percentile	2.5th Percentile	5th Percentile	40th Percentile	50th Percentile	60th Percentile	95th Percentile	97.5th Percentile	99th Percentile
4400	WATER TRANSPORTATION	1	1.187070	1.187070	1.187070	1.187070	1.187070	1.187070	1.187070	1.187070	1.187070	1.187070	1.187070
441	DEEP SEA FOREIGN TRANSPORTATION OF FREIGHT	34	1.212185	1.281355	-2.601337	-2.168687	-0.687971	1.095794	1.281355	1.527904	2.419888	3.039530	4.489880
4412	Deep Sea Foreign Transportation Of Freight	34	1.212185	1.281355	-2.601337	-2.168687	-0.687971	1.095794	1.281355	1.527904	2.419888	3.039530	4.489880
442	DEEP SEA DOMESTIC TRANSPORTATION OF FREIGHT	1	1.575960	1.575960	1.575960	1.575960	1.575960	1.575960	1.575960	1.575960	1.575960	1.575960	1.575960
4424	Deep Sea Domestic Transportation Of Freight	1	1.575960	1.575960	1.575960	1.575960	1.575960	1.575960	1.575960	1.575960	1.575960	1.575960	1.575960
443	FREIGHT TRANSPORTATION ON THE GREAT LAKES¨ST. LAWRENCE SEAWAY	1	-0.327711	-0.327711	-0.327711	-0.327711	-0.327711	-0.327711	-0.327711	-0.327711	-0.327711	-0.327711	-0.327711
4432	Freight Transportation On The Great Lakes¨St. Lawrence Seaway	1	-0.327711	-0.327711	-0.327711	-0.327711	-0.327711	-0.327711	-0.327711	-0.327711	-0.327711	-0.327711	-0.327711
444	WATER TRANSPORTATION OF FREIGHT, NOT ELSEWHERE CLASSIFIED	1	1.089010	1.089010	1.089010	1.089010	1.089010	1.089010	1.089010	1.089010	1.089010	1.089010	1.089010
4449	Water Transportation Of Freight, Not Elsewhere Classified	1	1.089010	1.089010	1.089010	1.089010	1.089010	1.089010	1.089010	1.089010	1.089010	1.089010	1.089010
448	WATER TRANSPORTATION OF PASSENGERS	3	1.031255	0.677361	0.672453	0.672603	0.672854	0.676359	0.677361	0.890699	1.637381	1.690716	1.722716
4481	Deep Sea Transportation Of Passengers, Except By Ferry	3	1.031255	0.677361	0.672453	0.672603	0.672854	0.676359	0.677361	0.890699	1.637381	1.690716	1.722716
449	SERVICES INCIDENTAL TO WATER TRANSPORTATION	5	2.242001	2.226360	0.813202	0.852556	0.918147	1.912964	2.226360	2.653128	3.427080	3.443805	3.453840
4491	Marine Cargo Handling	1	2.226360	2.226360	2.226360	2.226360	2.226360	2.226360	2.226360	2.226360	2.226360	2.226360	2.226360
4492	Towing And Tugboat Services	1	3.460530	3.460530	3.460530	3.460530	3.460530	3.460530	3.460530	3.460530	3.460530	3.460530	3.460530
4499	Water Transportation Services, Not Elsewhere Classified	3	1.841039	1.442870	0.800084	0.819761	0.852556	1.311689	1.442870	1.812952	3.108239	3.200760	3.256272
45	TRANSPORTATION BY AIR	22	1.015564	1.189070	-1.893491	-1.214098	-0.177016	1.080836	1.189070	1.297764	1.812958	2.300666	2.621392
451	AIR TRANSPORTATION, SCHEDULED, AND AIR COURIER SERVICES	17	0.956659	1.154190	-1.961007	-1.382887	-0.419354	1.080836	1.154190	1.262212	1.751878	1.784454	1.804000
4512	Air Transportation, Scheduled	13	0.977159	1.223950	-1.979462	-1.429024	-0.511628	1.130336	1.223950	1.316782	1.768166	1.792598	1.807257
4513	Air Courier Services	4	0.890033	0.994675	0.085729	0.120704	0.178996	0.901654	0.994675	1.087696	1.454571	1.481471	1.497610
452	AIR TRANSPORTATION, NONSCHEDULED	5	1.215840	1.304460	-0.157681	-0.109777	-0.029936	1.026191	1.304460	1.390820	2.572240	2.703725	2.782616
4522	Air Transportation, Nonscheduled	5	1.215840	1.304460	-0.157681	-0.109777	-0.029936	1.026191	1.304460	1.390820	2.572240	2.703725	2.782616
46	PIPELINES, EXCEPT NATURAL GAS	11	1.212040	1.096710	0.777475	0.795076	0.824410	1.069330	1.096710	1.103250	1.983975	2.092943	2.158323
461	PIPELINES, EXCEPT NATURAL GAS	11	1.212040	1.096710	0.777475	0.795076	0.824410	1.069330	1.096710	1.103250	1.983975	2.092943	2.158323
4612	Crude Petroleum Pipelines	6	1.029241	1.064870	0.774216	0.786928	0.808115	1.033030	1.064870	1.096710	1.206923	1.224201	1.234569
4613	Refined Petroleum Pipelines	1	2.201910	2.201910	2.201910	2.201910	2.201910	2.201910	2.201910	2.201910	2.201910	2.201910	2.201910
4619	Pipelines, Not Elsewhere Classified	4	1.238770	1.152980	0.888667	0.897048	0.911017	1.102790	1.152980	1.203170	1.686629	1.726334	1.750158
47	TRANSPORTATION SERVICES	16	1.255408	1.097455	-0.106861	0.091343	0.421683	0.962039	1.097455	1.206490	2.887605	2.914163	2.930097

Up-market Betas of Common Stocks by SIC Codes as of March 31, 2017

SIC Code	Description	Number of Companies	Mean	Median	1st Percentile	2.5th Percentile	5th Percentile	40th Percentile	50th Percentile	60th Percentile	95th Percentile	97.5th Percentile	99th Percentile
472	ARRANGEMENT OF PASSENGER TRANSPORTATION	4	0.760230	1.036713	-0.203492	-0.150235	-0.061473	0.981382	1.036713	1.092043	1.194856	1.200673	1.204163
4724	Travel Agencies	1	1.206490	1.206490	1.206490	1.206490	1.206490	1.206490	1.206490	1.206490	1.206490	1.206490	1.206490
4725	Tour Operators	3	0.611476	0.944495	-0.215327	-0.179822	-0.120648	0.707797	0.944495	0.981382	1.110487	1.119708	1.125241
473	ARRANGEMENT OF TRANSPORTATION OF FREIGHT AND CARGO	10	1.471769	1.091865	0.642118	0.642430	0.642951	0.958695	1.091865	1.280794	2.908851	2.924786	2.934346
4731	Arrangement Of Transportation Of Freight And Cargo	10	1.471769	1.091865	0.642118	0.642430	0.642951	0.958695	1.091865	1.280794	2.908851	2.924786	2.934346
478	MISCELLANEOUS SERVICES INCIDENTAL TO TRANSPORTATION	2	1.163960	1.163960	1.067940	1.070879	1.075778	1.144364	1.163960	1.183556	1.252142	1.257041	1.259980
4789	Transportation Services, Not Elsewhere Classified	2	1.163960	1.163960	1.067940	1.070879	1.075778	1.144364	1.163960	1.183556	1.252142	1.257041	1.259980
48	COMMUNICATIONS	137	0.957497	0.981635	-1.438564	-0.769864	-0.205976	0.867191	0.981635	1.136596	2.422156	2.635232	2.918440
481	TELEPHONE COMMUNICATIONS	61	0.885408	1.046530	-1.966722	-1.381870	-0.727208	0.843297	1.046530	1.201800	2.000450	2.286865	2.537894
4812	Radiotelephone Communications	18	0.830752	0.881694	-0.629906	-0.483954	-0.240700	0.624934	0.881694	1.086026	2.519354	2.550872	2.569783
4813	Telephone Communications, Except Radiotelephone	43	0.908288	1.179200	-2.138789	-1.564102	-1.056161	0.947513	1.179200	1.260442	1.907430	1.996088	2.038179
482	TELEGRAPH AND OTHER MESSAGE COMMUNICATIONS	4	0.746482	0.397864	-0.780056	-0.752687	-0.707074	0.045074	0.397864	0.750654	2.688102	2.838301	2.928420
4822	Telegraph And Other Message Communications	4	0.746482	0.397864	-0.780056	-0.752687	-0.707074	0.045074	0.397864	0.750654	2.688102	2.838301	2.928420
483	RADIO AND TELEVISION BROADCASTING STATIONS	27	0.962813	0.933061	-0.209915	-0.120680	-0.002751	0.892777	0.933061	1.113738	1.954907	2.316511	2.602938
4832	Radio Broadcasting Stations	13	0.858771	0.539155	-0.025458	-0.002751	0.035094	0.399806	0.539155	0.971719	2.353232	2.573561	2.705758
4833	Television Broadcasting Stations	14	1.059423	1.038228	-0.150408	0.028089	0.325585	0.920837	1.038228	1.144532	1.683852	1.697401	1.705530
484	CABLE AND OTHER PAY TELEVISION SERVICES	24	0.898954	0.873258	0.283029	0.288682	0.316186	0.802414	0.873258	0.934765	1.575015	1.611174	1.619391
4841	Cable And Other Pay Television Services	24	0.898954	0.873258	0.283029	0.288682	0.316186	0.802414	0.873258	0.934765	1.575015	1.611174	1.619391
489	COMMUNICATIONS SERVICES, NOT ELSEWHERE CLASSIFIED	21	1.267161	1.212750	-0.297568	-0.235540	-0.132159	1.101040	1.212750	1.274410	2.670460	2.889010	3.020140
4899	Communications Services, Not Elsewhere Classified	21	1.267161	1.212750	-0.297568	-0.235540	-0.132159	1.101040	1.212750	1.274410	2.670460	2.889010	3.020140
49	ELECTRIC, GAS, AND SANITARY SERVICES	138	0.628215	0.566351	-1.658654	-1.089688	-0.322732	0.474323	0.566351	0.671609	1.774292	2.192947	2.589048
491	ELECTRIC SERVICES	53	0.578699	0.403799	-1.280872	-0.869583	-0.250615	0.358074	0.403799	0.486816	1.910944	2.199061	3.201978
4911	Electric Services	53	0.578699	0.403799	-1.280872	-0.869583	-0.250615	0.358074	0.403799	0.486816	1.910944	2.199061	3.201978
492	GAS PRODUCTION AND DISTRIBUTION	27	0.761651	0.765283	-0.857089	-0.450917	-0.032292	0.675929	0.765283	0.955118	1.414414	1.526655	1.622634
4922	Natural Gas Transmission	8	0.736216	0.876290	-1.019517	-0.856986	-0.586103	0.764850	0.876290	0.980782	1.600485	1.643553	1.669393
4923	Natural Gas Transmission And Distribution	9	0.891841	1.074380	0.125358	0.172444	0.250920	0.827102	1.074380	1.142372	1.317204	1.335352	1.346241
4924	Natural Gas Distribution	9	0.748297	0.686275	0.540710	0.546643	0.556531	0.620583	0.686275	0.724345	1.025628	1.039824	1.048342
4925	Mixed, Manufactured, Or Liquefied Petroleum Gas Production	1	-0.086403	-0.086403	-0.086403	-0.086403	-0.086403	-0.086403	-0.086403	-0.086403	-0.086403	-0.086403	-0.086403

Up-market Betas of Common Stocks by SIC Codes as of March 31, 2017

SIC Code	Description	Number of Companies	Mean	Median	1st Percentile	2.5th Percentile	5th Percentile	40th Percentile	50th Percentile	60th Percentile	95th Percentile	97.5th Percentile	99th Percentile
493	COMBINATION ELECTRIC AND GAS, AND OTHER UTILITY SERVICES	23	0.616234	0.514928	0.099959	0.115448	0.143096	0.434773	0.514928	0.526015	1.572387	2.166836	2.553556
4931	Electric And Other Services Combined	17	0.518414	0.514928	0.147013	0.162679	0.188788	0.434012	0.514928	0.517776	0.907368	1.273429	1.493066
4932	Gas And Other Services Combined	5	1.054143	0.628252	0.426020	0.426711	0.427863	0.551782	0.628252	0.764335	2.442788	2.627079	2.737654
4939	Combination Utilities, Not Elsewhere Classified	1	0.089633	0.089633	0.089633	0.089633	0.089633	0.089633	0.089633	0.089633	0.089633	0.089633	0.089633
494	WATER SUPPLY	13	0.739787	0.687197	-0.145085	-0.037625	0.141474	0.654978	0.687197	0.723849	1.426996	1.707268	1.875431
4941	Water Supply	13	0.739787	0.687197	-0.145085	-0.037625	0.141474	0.654978	0.687197	0.723849	1.426996	1.707268	1.875431
495	SANITARY SERVICES	22	0.530336	0.685410	-2.483812	-2.181654	-1.658626	0.503702	0.685410	0.932121	2.152937	2.192511	2.193884
4952	Sewerage Systems	1	-1.726020	-1.726020	-1.726020	-1.726020	-1.726020	-1.726020	-1.726020	-1.726020	-1.726020	-1.726020	-1.726020
4953	Refuse Systems	18	0.569718	0.685410	-2.293040	-1.704724	-0.724198	0.504845	0.685410	0.915506	2.191094	2.192947	2.194059
4955	HAZARDOUS WASTE MANAGEMENT	2	0.849056	0.849056	0.486805	0.497894	0.516376	0.775127	0.849056	0.922985	1.181736	1.200218	1.211307
4959	Sanitary Services, Not Elsewhere Classified	1	1.440380	1.440380	1.440380	1.440380	1.440380	1.440380	1.440380	1.440380	1.440380	1.440380	1.440380
	WHOLESALE TRADE												
50	WHOLESALE TRADE¨DURABLE GOODS	75	0.923942	0.962089	-2.172014	-1.076834	-0.213190	0.892126	0.962089	1.095886	2.191036	2.398306	3.185388
501	MOTOR VEHICLES AND MOTOR VEHICLE PARTS AND SUPPLIES	10	0.624747	0.916541	-3.461583	-2.889367	-1.935673	0.851454	0.916541	0.939374	2.061239	2.061569	2.061768
5012	Automobiles And Other Motor Vehicles	2	1.485733	1.485733	0.921089	0.938374	0.967183	1.370500	1.485733	1.600966	2.004283	2.033092	2.050377
5013	Motor Vehicle Supplies And New Parts	7	0.382224	0.923515	-3.588742	-3.207264	-2.571469	0.827978	0.923515	0.947303	1.865799	1.963115	2.021504
5015	Motor Vehicle Parts, Used	1	0.600436	0.600436	0.600436	0.600436	0.600436	0.600436	0.600436	0.600436	0.600436	0.600436	0.600436
503	LUMBER AND OTHER CONSTRUCTION MATERIALS	6	1.121497	1.099500	0.765545	0.781062	0.806923	1.072740	1.099500	1.126260	1.523573	1.582186	1.617355
5031	Lumber, Plywood, Millwork, And Wood Panels	4	1.107708	1.017415	0.761408	0.770718	0.786234	0.984219	1.017415	1.050610	1.555591	1.598196	1.623758
5033	Roofing, Siding, And Insulation Materials	1	1.126260	1.126260	1.126260	1.126260	1.126260	1.126260	1.126260	1.126260	1.126260	1.126260	1.126260
5039	Construction Materials, Not Elsewhere Classified	1	1.171890	1.171890	1.171890	1.171890	1.171890	1.171890	1.171890	1.171890	1.171890	1.171890	1.171890
504	PROFESSIONAL AND COMMERCIAL EQUIPMENT AND SUPPLIES	18	0.994395	1.028855	-0.766918	-0.436528	0.114120	0.877521	1.028855	1.085740	1.998819	2.089285	2.143564
5044	Office Equipment	1	-0.987177	-0.987177	-0.987177	-0.987177	-0.987177	-0.987177	-0.987177	-0.987177	-0.987177	-0.987177	-0.987177
5045	Computers And Computer Peripheral Equipment And Software	8	1.247360	1.094110	0.873306	0.873912	0.874923	1.078760	1.094110	1.140338	1.883832	1.925361	1.950278
5047	Medical, Dental, And Hospital Equipment And Supplies	9	0.989711	0.856570	0.313622	0.321354	0.334241	0.719820	0.856570	0.958954	1.938270	2.059010	2.131454
505	METALS AND MINERALS, EXCEPT PETROLEUM	6	1.506936	1.281305	0.351380	0.392285	0.460462	1.218730	1.281305	1.343880	2.817250	2.904530	2.956898
5051	Metals Service Centers And Offices	6	1.506936	1.281305	0.351380	0.392285	0.460462	1.218730	1.281305	1.343880	2.817250	2.904530	2.956898
506	ELECTRICAL GOODS	17	0.810106	0.908069	-0.047486	-0.034152	-0.011928	0.533532	0.908069	1.200450	1.572618	1.672914	1.733092

Up-market Betas of Common Stocks by SIC Codes as of March 31, 2017

SIC Code	Description	Number of Companies	Mean	Median	1st Percentile	2.5th Percentile	5th Percentile	40th Percentile	50th Percentile	60th Percentile	95th Percentile	97.5th Percentile	99th Percentile
5063	Electrical Apparatus And Equipment, Wiring Supplies, And Construction	5	1.087092	1.188540	0.367819	0.401585	0.457861	1.076352	1.188540	1.201256	1.662634	1.717922	1.751095
5065	Electronic Parts And Equipment, Not Elsewhere Classified	12	0.694696	0.541044	-0.050264	-0.041097	-0.025818	0.463183	0.541044	0.956474	1.367090	1.444780	1.491394
507	HARDWARE, AND PLUMBING AND HEATING EQUIPMENT AND SUPPLIES	3	0.780347	0.915059	0.482126	0.495379	0.517468	0.826705	0.915059	0.922586	0.948929	0.950810	0.951939
5074	Plumbing And Heating Equipment And Supplies (Hydronics)	2	0.712992	0.712992	0.478085	0.485276	0.497261	0.665051	0.712992	0.760932	0.928722	0.940707	0.947898
5075	Warm Air Heating And Air-Conditioning Equipment And Supplies	1	0.915059	0.915059	0.915059	0.915059	0.915059	0.915059	0.915059	0.915059	0.915059	0.915059	0.915059
508	MACHINERY, EQUIPMENT, AND SUPPLIES	8	1.476079	1.138610	0.622034	0.639592	0.668856	1.044882	1.138610	1.214858	3.204701	3.470520	3.630012
5084	Industrial Machinery And Equipment	6	1.588568	1.094911	0.618690	0.631231	0.652134	0.901092	1.094911	1.288730	3.356598	3.546469	3.660392
5085	Industrial Supplies	1	1.080830	1.080830	1.080830	1.080830	1.080830	1.080830	1.080830	1.080830	1.080830	1.080830	1.080830
5087	Service Establishment Equipment And Supplies	1	1.196390	1.196390	1.196390	1.196390	1.196390	1.196390	1.196390	1.196390	1.196390	1.196390	1.196390
509	MISCELLANEOUS DURABLE GOODS	7	0.208137	0.311138	-1.524542	-1.434020	-1.283150	0.157848	0.311138	0.701263	1.169852	1.187441	1.197994
5091	Sporting And Recreational Goods And Supplies	3	0.490008	0.961346	-0.548282	-0.502069	-0.425047	0.653259	0.961346	0.986631	1.075128	1.081449	1.085242
5094	Jewelry, Watches, Precious Stones, And Precious Metals	3	0.523941	0.311138	0.060765	0.068429	0.081204	0.260041	0.311138	0.489916	1.115641	1.160335	1.187152
5099	Durable Goods, Not Elsewhere Classified	1	-1.584890	-1.584890	-1.584890	-1.584890	-1.584890	-1.584890	-1.584890	-1.584890	-1.584890	-1.584890	-1.584890
51	WHOLESALE TRADE¨NONDURABLE GOODS	60	0.943066	0.905759	-2.293090	-1.597416	-0.451461	0.845206	0.905759	1.083486	2.339761	2.610736	3.269562
511	PAPER AND PAPER PRODUCTS	1	1.640020	1.640020	1.640020	1.640020	1.640020	1.640020	1.640020	1.640020	1.640020	1.640020	1.640020
5111	Printing And Writing Paper	1	1.640020	1.640020	1.640020	1.640020	1.640020	1.640020	1.640020	1.640020	1.640020	1.640020	1.640020
512	DRUGS, DRUG PROPRIETARIES, AND DRUGGISTS' SUNDRIES	22	0.993534	1.112150	-2.379182	-2.307816	-2.070969	0.991390	1.112150	1.211734	2.354289	2.587065	2.736192
5122	Drugs, Drug Proprietaries, And Druggists' Sundries	22	0.993534	1.112150	-2.379182	-2.307816	-2.070969	0.991390	1.112150	1.211734	2.354289	2.587065	2.736192
513	APPAREL, PIECE GOODS, AND NOTIONS	2	1.018463	1.018463	0.699622	0.709382	0.725650	0.953393	1.018463	1.083532	1.311275	1.327543	1.337303
5136	Men's And Boys' Clothing And Furnishings	1	0.693115	0.693115	0.693115	0.693115	0.693115	0.693115	0.693115	0.693115	0.693115	0.693115	0.693115
5139	Footwear	1	1.343810	1.343810	1.343810	1.343810	1.343810	1.343810	1.343810	1.343810	1.343810	1.343810	1.343810
514	GROCERIES AND RELATED PRODUCTS	15	0.719902	0.784223	-0.860485	-0.754442	-0.577703	0.706784	0.784223	0.822277	1.934828	2.914429	3.502190
5141	Groceries, General Line	10	0.308622	0.558028	-0.885734	-0.817563	-0.703945	0.337280	0.558028	0.698576	0.990184	1.042677	1.074173
5145	Confectionery	1	1.059160	1.059160	1.059160	1.059160	1.059160	1.059160	1.059160	1.059160	1.059160	1.059160	1.059160
5148	Fresh Fruits And Vegetables	1	0.795884	0.795884	0.795884	0.795884	0.795884	0.795884	0.795884	0.795884	0.795884	0.795884	0.795884
5149	Groceries And Related Products, Not Elsewhere Classified	3	1.952424	1.094130	0.873612	0.880363	0.891614	1.049126	1.094130	1.654110	3.614040	3.754035	3.838032

Up-market Betas of Common Stocks by SIC Codes as of March 31, 2017

SIC Code	Description	Number of Companies	Mean	Median	1st Percentile	2.5th Percentile	5th Percentile	40th Percentile	50th Percentile	60th Percentile	95th Percentile	97.5th Percentile	99th Percentile
515	FARM-PRODUCT RAW MATERIALS	4	1.123799	0.849627	0.468901	0.486210	0.515058	0.845051	0.849627	0.854203	2.116381	2.227481	2.294140
5153	Grain And Field Beans	2	0.649681	0.649681	0.461208	0.466978	0.476594	0.611217	0.649681	0.688145	0.822768	0.832384	0.838154
5159	Farm-Product Raw Materials, Not Elsewhere Classified	2	1.597917	1.597917	0.872067	0.894287	0.931320	1.449784	1.597917	1.746050	2.264514	2.301547	2.323767
516	CHEMICALS AND ALLIED PRODUCTS	5	1.545864	1.445380	1.061384	1.077499	1.104358	1.394920	1.445380	1.500236	2.181744	2.256647	2.301589
5162	Plastics Materials And Basic Forms And Shapes	1	2.331550	2.331550	2.331550	2.331550	2.331550	2.331550	2.331550	2.331550	2.331550	2.331550	2.331550
5169	Chemicals And Allied Products, Not Elsewhere Classified	4	1.349443	1.382305	1.058698	1.070784	1.090929	1.344460	1.382305	1.420150	1.561949	1.572235	1.578406
517	PETROLEUM AND PETROLEUM PRODUCTS	5	0.973011	0.898852	0.224012	0.251725	0.297913	0.806278	0.898852	1.064267	1.687166	1.734013	1.762121
5172	Petroleum And Petroleum Products Wholesalers, Except Bulk Station	5	0.973011	0.898852	0.224012	0.251725	0.297913	0.806278	0.898852	1.064267	1.687166	1.734013	1.762121
519	MISCELLANEOUS NONDURABLE GOODS	6	0.526865	0.461768	-0.137332	-0.113202	-0.072984	0.314295	0.461768	0.609241	1.243394	1.309402	1.349007
5191	Farm Supplies	2	0.728293	0.728293	0.611622	0.615194	0.621146	0.704482	0.728293	0.752103	0.835439	0.841391	0.844963
5192	Books, Periodicals, And Newspapers	1	0.314295	0.314295	0.314295	0.314295	0.314295	0.314295	0.314295	0.314295	0.314295	0.314295	0.314295
5199	Nondurable Goods, Not Elsewhere Classified	3	0.463437	0.168320	-0.146984	-0.137332	-0.121245	0.103972	0.168320	0.409738	1.254701	1.315056	1.351268
	RETAIL TRADE												
52	RETAIL TRADE	13	0.723013	0.797257	-0.383480	-0.372217	-0.353445	0.763401	0.797257	0.859231	1.631332	1.863946	2.003514
521	LUMBER AND OTHER BUILDING MATERIALS DEALERS	11	0.770519	0.797257	-0.384732	-0.375346	-0.359702	0.773310	0.797257	1.003500	1.708870	1.902715	2.019022
5211	Lumber And Other Building Materials Dealers	11	0.770519	0.797257	-0.384732	-0.375346	-0.359702	0.773310	0.797257	1.003500	1.708870	1.902715	2.019022
523	PAINT, GLASS, AND WALLPAPER STORES	1	0.823164	0.823164	0.823164	0.823164	0.823164	0.823164	0.823164	0.823164	0.823164	0.823164	0.823164
5231	Paint, Glass, And Wallpaper Stores	1	0.823164	0.823164	0.823164	0.823164	0.823164	0.823164	0.823164	0.823164	0.823164	0.823164	0.823164
526	RETAIL NURSERIES, LAWN AND GARDEN SUPPLY STORES	1	0.100295	0.100295	0.100295	0.100295	0.100295	0.100295	0.100295	0.100295	0.100295	0.100295	0.100295
5261	Retail Nurseries, Lawn And Garden Supply Stores	1	0.100295	0.100295	0.100295	0.100295	0.100295	0.100295	0.100295	0.100295	0.100295	0.100295	0.100295
53	GENERAL MERCHANDISE STORES	20	0.805236	0.673719	0.369824	0.391051	0.426431	0.642760	0.673719	0.721467	1.577087	1.806579	1.944273
531	DEPARTMENT STORES	10	0.838864	0.673719	0.374987	0.403960	0.452248	0.661185	0.673719	0.715451	1.646640	1.841355	1.958184
5311	Department Stores	10	0.838864	0.673719	0.374987	0.403960	0.452248	0.661185	0.673719	0.715451	1.646640	1.841355	1.958184
533	VARIETY STORES	8	0.780209	0.661990	0.437517	0.448559	0.466963	0.625592	0.661990	0.711987	1.361963	1.457447	1.514737
5331	Variety Stores	8	0.780209	0.661990	0.437517	0.448559	0.466963	0.625592	0.661990	0.711987	1.361963	1.457447	1.514737
539	MISCELLANEOUS GENERAL MERCHANDISE STORES	2	0.737203	0.737203	0.522381	0.528957	0.539918	0.693361	0.737203	0.781044	0.934487	0.945448	0.952024
5399	Miscellaneous General Merchandise Stores	2	0.737203	0.737203	0.522381	0.528957	0.539918	0.693361	0.737203	0.781044	0.934487	0.945448	0.952024
54	FOOD STORES	22	1.236082	0.870310	0.075319	0.158652	0.285039	0.695652	0.870310	0.941799	3.727406	5.903933	7.274769
541	GROCERY STORES	16	0.720156	0.706299	0.059446	0.118970	0.218176	0.533016	0.706299	0.850987	1.291348	1.470129	1.577398
5411	Grocery Stores	16	0.720156	0.706299	0.059446	0.118970	0.218176	0.533016	0.706299	0.850987	1.291348	1.470129	1.577398

Up-market Betas of Common Stocks by SIC Codes as of March 31, 2017

SIC Code	Description	Number of Companies	Mean	Median	1st Percentile	2.5th Percentile	5th Percentile	40th Percentile	50th Percentile	60th Percentile	95th Percentile	97.5th Percentile	99th Percentile
544	CANDY, NUT, AND CONFECTIONERY STORES	1	0.889632	0.889632	0.889632	0.889632	0.889632	0.889632	0.889632	0.889632	0.889632	0.889632	0.889632
5441	Candy, Nut, And Confectionery Stores	1	0.889632	0.889632	0.889632	0.889632	0.889632	0.889632	0.889632	0.889632	0.889632	0.889632	0.889632
549	MISCELLANEOUS FOOD STORES	5	2.956335	1.217320	0.437785	0.481046	0.553146	1.182372	1.217320	2.265112	7.318288	7.753474	8.014586
5499	Miscellaneous Food Stores	5	2.956335	1.217320	0.437785	0.481046	0.553146	1.182372	1.217320	2.265112	7.318288	7.753474	8.014586
55	AUTOMOTIVE DEALERS AND GASOLINE SERVICE STATIONS	20	1.065146	1.052386	-2.339412	-1.389615	0.193381	0.925778	1.052386	1.227284	2.151650	2.979100	3.475570
551	MOTOR VEHICLE DEALERS (NEW AND USED)	9	1.240424	1.197380	0.686254	0.712787	0.757007	1.140756	1.197380	1.257188	1.885228	1.936264	1.966886
5511	Motor Vehicle Dealers (New And Used)	9	1.240424	1.197380	0.686254	0.712787	0.757007	1.140756	1.197380	1.257188	1.885228	1.936264	1.966886
552	MOTOR VEHICLE DEALERS (USED ONLY)	2	2.647950	2.647950	1.512522	1.547280	1.605210	2.416230	2.647950	2.879670	3.690690	3.748620	3.783378
5521	Motor Vehicle Dealers (Used Only)	2	2.647950	2.647950	1.512522	1.547280	1.605210	2.416230	2.647950	2.879670	3.690690	3.748620	3.783378
553	AUTO AND HOME SUPPLY STORES	3	-0.297455	0.672426	-2.899709	-2.790358	-2.608106	-0.056581	0.672426	0.819505	1.334281	1.371050	1.393112
5531	Auto And Home Supply Stores	3	-0.297455	0.672426	-2.899709	-2.790358	-2.608106	-0.056581	0.672426	0.819505	1.334281	1.371050	1.393112
554	GASOLINE SERVICE STATIONS	4	1.052094	0.891907	0.374939	0.397329	0.434646	0.871304	0.891907	0.912509	1.893804	1.979177	2.030401
5541	Gasoline Service Stations	4	1.052094	0.891907	0.374939	0.397329	0.434646	0.871304	0.891907	0.912509	1.893804	1.979177	2.030401
555	BOAT DEALERS	2	0.763599	0.763599	0.553317	0.559755	0.570483	0.720684	0.763599	0.806513	0.956714	0.967442	0.973880
5551	Boat Dealers	2	0.763599	0.763599	0.553317	0.559755	0.570483	0.720684	0.763599	0.806513	0.956714	0.967442	0.973880
56	APPAREL AND ACCESSORY STORES	35	0.919039	0.898695	-0.064321	0.190980	0.318831	0.782417	0.898695	1.003057	1.859562	1.919430	1.994604
5600	RETAIL-APPAREL & ACCESSORY STORES	1	1.518570	1.518570	1.518570	1.518570	1.518570	1.518570	1.518570	1.518570	1.518570	1.518570	1.518570
561	MEN'S AND BOYS' CLOTHING AND ACCESSORY STORES	1	1.897320	1.897320	1.897320	1.897320	1.897320	1.897320	1.897320	1.897320	1.897320	1.897320	1.897320
5611	Men's And Boys' Clothing And Accessory Stores	1	1.897320	1.897320	1.897320	1.897320	1.897320	1.897320	1.897320	1.897320	1.897320	1.897320	1.897320
562	WOMEN'S CLOTHING STORES	8	0.896854	1.012775	-0.181980	-0.103168	0.028186	0.953092	1.012775	1.038526	1.607158	1.725269	1.796136
5621	Women's Clothing Stores	8	0.896854	1.012775	-0.181980	-0.103168	0.028186	0.953092	1.012775	1.038526	1.607158	1.725269	1.796136
563	WOMEN'S ACCESSORY AND SPECIALTY STORES	1	0.341443	0.341443	0.341443	0.341443	0.341443	0.341443	0.341443	0.341443	0.341443	0.341443	0.341443
5632	Women's Accessory And Specialty Stores	1	0.341443	0.341443	0.341443	0.341443	0.341443	0.341443	0.341443	0.341443	0.341443	0.341443	0.341443
565	FAMILY CLOTHING STORES	15	0.903468	0.863256	0.397195	0.417926	0.452476	0.736527	0.863256	0.978029	1.518999	1.781860	1.939576
5651	Family Clothing Stores	15	0.903468	0.863256	0.397195	0.417926	0.452476	0.736527	0.863256	0.978029	1.518999	1.781860	1.939576
566	SHOE STORES	7	0.903803	0.898695	0.293256	0.334037	0.402006	0.842846	0.898695	0.964992	1.401726	1.467573	1.507081
5661	Shoe Stores	7	0.903803	0.898695	0.293256	0.334037	0.402006	0.842846	0.898695	0.964992	1.401726	1.467573	1.507081
569	MISCELLANEOUS APPAREL AND ACCESSORY STORES	2	0.677788	0.677788	0.566869	0.570264	0.575923	0.655151	0.677788	0.700425	0.779653	0.785312	0.788707
5699	Miscellaneous Apparel And Accessory Stores	2	0.677788	0.677788	0.566869	0.570264	0.575923	0.655151	0.677788	0.700425	0.779653	0.785312	0.788707
57	HOME FURNITURE, FURNISHINGS, AND EQUIPMENT STORES	13	1.198535	1.146650	-0.217665	-0.103833	0.085886	0.966167	1.146650	1.169496	2.790806	2.966828	3.072441
571	HOME FURNITURE AND FURNISHINGS STORES	6	1.093729	1.149045	0.702335	0.723173	0.757905	1.146650	1.149045	1.151440	1.336303	1.352066	1.361525
5712	Furniture Stores	3	1.161854	1.151440	0.969996	0.975550	0.984808	1.114411	1.151440	1.194718	1.346191	1.357011	1.363502

Up-market Betas of Common Stocks by SIC Codes as of March 31, 2017

SIC Code	Description	Number of Companies	Mean	Median	1st Percentile	2.5th Percentile	5th Percentile	40th Percentile	50th Percentile	60th Percentile	95th Percentile	97.5th Percentile	99th Percentile
5713	Floor Covering Stores	1	0.688442	0.688442	0.688442	0.688442	0.688442	0.688442	0.688442	0.688442	0.688442	0.688442	0.688442
5719	Miscellaneous Homefurnishings Stores	2	1.194185	1.194185	1.147601	1.149027	1.151404	1.184678	1.194185	1.203692	1.236967	1.239343	1.240769
572	HOUSEHOLD APPLIANCE STORES	1	1.870380	1.870380	1.870380	1.870380	1.870380	1.870380	1.870380	1.870380	1.870380	1.870380	1.870380
5722	Household Appliance Stores	1	1.870380	1.870380	1.870380	1.870380	1.870380	1.870380	1.870380	1.870380	1.870380	1.870380	1.870380
573	RADIO, TELEVISION, CONSUMER ELECTRONICS, AND MUSIC STORES	6	1.191367	0.701974	-0.261933	-0.214503	-0.135453	0.438284	0.701974	0.965664	2.996165	3.069508	3.113513
5731	Radio, Television, And Consumer Electronics Stores	4	1.750868	1.760887	0.357651	0.385857	0.432869	1.283753	1.760887	2.238021	3.054839	3.098845	3.125248
5734	Computer And Computer Software Stores	1	0.438284	0.438284	0.438284	0.438284	0.438284	0.438284	0.438284	0.438284	0.438284	0.438284	0.438284
5735	Record And Prerecorded Tape Stores	1	-0.293553	-0.293553	-0.293553	-0.293553	-0.293553	-0.293553	-0.293553	-0.293553	-0.293553	-0.293553	-0.293553
58	EATING AND DRINKING PLACES	66	0.535474	0.719873	-3.326284	-1.926130	-1.260744	0.643664	0.719873	0.824901	1.261298	1.494438	1.923349
581	EATING AND DRINKING PLACES	66	0.535474	0.719873	-3.326284	-1.926130	-1.260744	0.643664	0.719873	0.824901	1.261298	1.494438	1.923349
5810	RETAIL-EATING & DRINKING PLACES	1	-1.844980	-1.844980	-1.844980	-1.844980	-1.844980	-1.844980	-1.844980	-1.844980	-1.844980	-1.844980	-1.844980
5812	Eating Places	64	0.572438	0.735172	-3.398564	-1.780970	-0.280801	0.673670	0.735172	0.860567	1.262219	1.519099	1.930243
5813	Drinking Places (Alcoholic Beverages)	1	0.550283	0.550283	0.550283	0.550283	0.550283	0.550283	0.550283	0.550283	0.550283	0.550283	0.550283
59	MISCELLANEOUS RETAIL	72	0.783551	0.844641	-5.095188	-0.630671	-0.195038	0.668478	0.844641	1.008832	2.031231	3.683473	6.566037
591	DRUG STORES AND PROPRIETARY STORES	10	1.549814	0.954400	0.267692	0.278240	0.295822	0.787004	0.954400	1.182278	4.844098	6.231664	7.064204
5912	Drug Stores And Proprietary Stores	10	1.549814	0.954400	0.267692	0.278240	0.295822	0.787004	0.954400	1.182278	4.844098	6.231664	7.064204
592	LIQUOR STORES	1	-0.286850	-0.286850	-0.286850	-0.286850	-0.286850	-0.286850	-0.286850	-0.286850	-0.286850	-0.286850	-0.286850
5921	Liquor Stores	1	-0.286850	-0.286850	-0.286850	-0.286850	-0.286850	-0.286850	-0.286850	-0.286850	-0.286850	-0.286850	-0.286850
593	USED MERCHANDISE STORES	3	1.185087	0.908010	0.506141	0.518444	0.538947	0.825996	0.908010	1.156270	2.025180	2.087245	2.124484
5932	Used Merchandise Stores	3	1.185087	0.908010	0.506141	0.518444	0.538947	0.825996	0.908010	1.156270	2.025180	2.087245	2.124484
594	MISCELLANEOUS SHOPPING GOODS STORES	16	1.034343	1.020100	-0.046271	0.034227	0.168391	0.996186	1.020100	1.046150	1.804473	1.869546	1.908591
5941	Sporting Goods Stores And Bicycle Shops	4	0.961302	0.911061	0.574756	0.584895	0.601793	0.840405	0.911061	0.981716	1.391150	1.423120	1.442302
5942	Book Stores	2	1.725385	1.725385	1.690394	1.691465	1.693251	1.718244	1.725385	1.732526	1.757520	1.759305	1.760376
5943	Stationery Stores	2	1.728840	1.728840	1.527176	1.533349	1.543638	1.687684	1.728840	1.769996	1.914042	1.924331	1.930504
5944	Jewelry Stores	3	0.624466	0.927185	-0.079394	-0.048581	0.002775	0.721761	0.927185	0.950978	1.034254	1.040202	1.043771
5945	Hobby, Toy, And Game Shops	3	0.556710	0.400916	0.260695	0.264987	0.272141	0.372299	0.400916	0.523009	0.950334	0.980857	0.999171
5947	Gift, Novelty, And Souvenir Shops	2	1.126153	1.126153	0.998785	1.002684	1.009183	1.100160	1.126153	1.152146	1.243123	1.249622	1.253521
596	NONSTORE RETAILERS	25	0.532995	0.855407	-10.240825	-5.446711	-0.100176	0.747656	0.855407	1.022058	2.754136	4.237238	5.376411
5960	RETAIL-NONSTORE RETAILERS	1	-0.119919	-0.119919	-0.119919	-0.119919	-0.119919	-0.119919	-0.119919	-0.119919	-0.119919	-0.119919	-0.119919
5961	Catalog And Mail-Order Houses	24	0.560200	0.902510	-10.351290	-5.722875	-0.002058	0.818377	0.902510	1.039106	2.808475	4.316347	5.408055
598	FUEL DEALERS	4	0.115280	0.135040	-0.024723	-0.018798	-0.008923	0.115810	0.135040	0.154270	0.211820	0.215767	0.218135
5983	Fuel Oil Dealers	4	0.115280	0.135040	-0.024723	-0.018798	-0.008923	0.115810	0.135040	0.154270	0.211820	0.215767	0.218135
599	RETAIL STORES, NOT ELSEWHERE CLASSIFIED	13	0.562584	0.681709	-1.524293	-1.278718	-0.869425	0.614429	0.681709	0.784975	1.462838	1.511609	1.540872
5992	Florists	1	0.770405	0.770405	0.770405	0.770405	0.770405	0.770405	0.770405	0.770405	0.770405	0.770405	0.770405
5995	Optical Goods Stores	1	0.843257	0.843257	0.843257	0.843257	0.843257	0.843257	0.843257	0.843257	0.843257	0.843257	0.843257

Up-market Betas of Common Stocks by SIC Codes as of March 31, 2017

SIC Code	Description	Number of Companies	Mean	Median	1st Percentile	2.5th Percentile	5th Percentile	40th Percentile	50th Percentile	60th Percentile	95th Percentile	97.5th Percentile	99th Percentile
5999	Miscellaneous Retail Stores, Not Elsewhere Classified	11	0.518175	0.659658	-1.551579	-1.346933	-1.005856	0.433514	0.659658	0.681709	1.479095	1.519738	1.544123
	FINANCE, INSURANCE, AND REAL ESTATE												
60	DEPOSITORY INSTITUTIONS	397	0.783813	0.852800	-0.609961	-0.447009	-0.269717	0.619986	0.852800	1.010192	1.735742	1.814933	2.025459
602	COMMERCIAL BANKS	305	0.848403	0.923143	-0.590769	-0.416152	-0.227578	0.748758	0.923143	1.088378	1.745258	1.868958	2.020122
6021	National Commercial Banks	112	0.895481	1.030840	-0.499285	-0.444841	-0.313871	0.828619	1.030840	1.242168	1.730692	1.783851	1.924094
6022	State Commercial Banks	166	0.794499	0.873915	-0.599281	-0.368658	-0.175830	0.661823	0.873915	0.988317	1.730338	1.810509	2.010020
6029	Commercial Banks, Not Elsewhere Classified	27	0.984521	0.895329	-0.087796	0.006484	0.117926	0.825433	0.895329	1.073850	1.996855	2.303633	2.619279
603	SAVINGS INSTITUTIONS	83	0.543384	0.453266	-0.502259	-0.445047	-0.393537	0.269114	0.453266	0.676882	1.594426	1.742422	1.829170
6035	Savings Institutions, Federally Chartered	61	0.591609	0.608328	-0.544336	-0.456607	-0.320797	0.388129	0.608328	0.741755	1.597290	1.754420	1.914664
6036	Savings Institutions, Not Federally Chartered	22	0.409667	0.259052	-0.430925	-0.419240	-0.396104	0.167503	0.259052	0.531662	1.442603	1.526333	1.573929
606	CREDIT UNIONS	1	1.770310	1.770310	1.770310	1.770310	1.770310	1.770310	1.770310	1.770310	1.770310	1.770310	1.770310
6061	Credit Unions, Federally Chartered	1	1.770310	1.770310	1.770310	1.770310	1.770310	1.770310	1.770310	1.770310	1.770310	1.770310	1.770310
609	FUNCTIONS RELATED TO DEPOSITORY BANKING	8	0.692467	0.688065	-0.574077	-0.462794	-0.277324	0.531090	0.688065	0.856220	1.508491	1.536905	1.553954
6099	Functions Related To Depository Banking, Not Elsewhere Classified	8	0.692467	0.688065	-0.574077	-0.462794	-0.277324	0.531090	0.688065	0.856220	1.508491	1.536905	1.553954
61	NONDEPOSITORY CREDIT INSTITUTIONS	44	1.190426	1.267350	-0.275542	-0.104119	0.070381	1.061574	1.267350	1.352776	2.726046	2.886406	3.079992
611	FEDERAL AND FEDERALLY-SPONSORED CREDIT AGENCIES	5	1.000415	1.275560	-0.329132	-0.231098	-0.067710	1.261096	1.275560	1.306460	1.493594	1.511192	1.521751
6111	Federal And Federally-Sponsored Credit Agencies	5	1.000415	1.275560	-0.329132	-0.231098	-0.067710	1.261096	1.275560	1.306460	1.493594	1.511192	1.521751
614	PERSONAL CREDIT INSTITUTIONS	13	1.432478	1.517550	0.184494	0.244361	0.344139	1.447918	1.517550	1.547092	2.624852	2.760116	2.841274
6141	Personal Credit Institutions	13	1.432478	1.517550	0.184494	0.244361	0.344139	1.447918	1.517550	1.547092	2.624852	2.760116	2.841274
615	BUSINESS CREDIT INSTITUTIONS	11	0.624326	0.487561	-0.096263	-0.063853	-0.009836	0.282355	0.487561	0.495029	1.511415	1.623138	1.690171
6153	Short-Term Business Credit Institutions, Except Agricultural	7	0.455687	0.282355	-0.102907	-0.080463	-0.043055	0.218758	0.282355	0.405479	1.362911	1.548885	1.660470
6159	Miscellaneous Business Credit Institutions	4	0.919445	1.145805	0.126227	0.168269	0.238339	1.077804	1.145805	1.213806	1.283646	1.285808	1.287105
616	MORTGAGE BANKERS AND BROKERS	12	1.234440	1.299790	0.071060	0.079442	0.093412	0.991227	1.299790	1.352448	2.740293	2.979776	3.123467
6162	Mortgage Bankers And Loan Correspondents	9	0.870348	0.820431	0.069536	0.075632	0.085792	0.678968	0.820431	1.162022	1.721982	1.845096	1.918964
6163	Loan Brokers	3	2.326717	2.348410	1.431199	1.459277	1.506073	2.161224	2.348410	2.522580	3.132175	3.175718	3.201843
6172	FINANCE LESSORS	1	2.775730	2.775730	2.775730	2.775730	2.775730	2.775730	2.775730	2.775730	2.775730	2.775730	2.775730
6199	FINANCE SERVICES	2	2.148925	2.148925	1.897550	1.905245	1.918071	2.097624	2.148925	2.200226	2.379780	2.392605	2.400300
62	SECURITY AND COMMODITY BROKERS, DEALERS, EXCHANGES, AND SERVICES	96	0.976617	1.027320	-0.509071	-0.305702	-0.134822	0.744538	1.027320	1.179960	2.038370	2.350293	2.571620
621	SECURITY BROKERS, DEALERS, AND FLOTATION COMPANIES	35	1.128340	1.238370	-0.298868	-0.226861	-0.053026	0.986328	1.238370	1.381946	2.368258	2.585979	2.659209
6211	Security Brokers, Dealers, And Flotation Companies	35	1.128340	1.238370	-0.298868	-0.226861	-0.053026	0.986328	1.238370	1.381946	2.368258	2.585979	2.659209

Up-market Betas of Common Stocks by SIC Codes as of March 31, 2017

SIC Code	Description	Number of Companies	Mean	Median	1st Percentile	2.5th Percentile	5th Percentile	40th Percentile	50th Percentile	60th Percentile	95th Percentile	97.5th Percentile	99th Percentile
622	COMMODITY CONTRACTS BROKERS AND DEALERS	2	1.901330	1.901330	1.422473	1.437132	1.461563	1.803604	1.901330	1.999056	2.341097	2.365529	2.380187
6221	Commodity Contracts Brokers And Dealers	2	1.901330	1.901330	1.422473	1.437132	1.461563	1.803604	1.901330	1.999056	2.341097	2.365529	2.380187
623	SECURITY AND COMMODITY EXCHANGES	6	0.824835	0.938435	0.202927	0.251391	0.332164	0.853629	0.938435	1.023240	1.047840	1.050580	1.052224
6231	Security And Commodity Exchanges	6	0.824835	0.938435	0.202927	0.251391	0.332164	0.853629	0.938435	1.023240	1.047840	1.050580	1.052224
628	SERVICES ALLIED WITH THE EXCHANGE OF SECURITIES OR COMMODITIES	53	0.858710	0.839636	-0.615953	-0.418775	-0.161555	0.684873	0.839636	1.152516	1.855204	1.909012	1.999067
6282	Investment Advice	52	0.889555	0.887492	-0.364268	-0.202466	-0.045658	0.705879	0.887492	1.153948	1.857077	1.910131	2.000664
6289	Services Allied With The Exchange Of Securities Or Commodities	1	-0.745205	-0.745205	-0.745205	-0.745205	-0.745205	-0.745205	-0.745205	-0.745205	-0.745205	-0.745205	-0.745205
63	INSURANCE CARRIERS	145	0.752867	0.809606	-0.690050	-0.261514	-0.032650	0.658275	0.809606	0.936942	1.588720	1.826808	1.955239
631	LIFE INSURANCE	37	0.825195	0.772359	-0.525218	-0.422583	-0.118727	0.505082	0.772359	1.012068	1.934694	2.028952	2.291403
6311	Life Insurance	37	0.825195	0.772359	-0.525218	-0.422583	-0.118727	0.505082	0.772359	1.012068	1.934694	2.028952	2.291403
632	ACCIDENT AND HEALTH INSURANCE AND MEDICAL SERVICE PLANS	21	0.846919	0.814699	-0.101982	-0.004745	0.157316	0.809606	0.814699	0.958774	1.416550	1.632605	1.762238
6321	Accident And Health Insurance	11	0.942207	0.958774	0.158007	0.159043	0.160770	0.845883	0.958774	1.039580	1.632605	1.740633	1.805449
6324	Hospital And Medical Service Plans	10	0.742102	0.792702	-0.111027	-0.027359	0.112088	0.700922	0.792702	0.811643	1.263453	1.273431	1.279419
633	FIRE, MARINE, AND CASUALTY INSURANCE	69	0.666009	0.672709	-0.334404	-0.077414	0.053846	0.634715	0.672709	0.863280	1.147444	1.217766	1.342184
6331	Fire, Marine, And Casualty Insurance	69	0.666009	0.672709	-0.334404	-0.077414	0.053846	0.634715	0.672709	0.863280	1.147444	1.217766	1.342184
635	SURETY INSURANCE	8	0.902025	0.915072	0.155371	0.207710	0.294940	0.814379	0.915072	1.027054	1.390626	1.402993	1.410413
6351	Surety Insurance	8	0.902025	0.915072	0.155371	0.207710	0.294940	0.814379	0.915072	1.027054	1.390626	1.402993	1.410413
636	TITLE INSURANCE	7	0.894732	0.934382	0.657231	0.658388	0.660318	0.819282	0.934382	1.000513	1.128323	1.143637	1.152825
6361	Title Insurance	7	0.894732	0.934382	0.657231	0.658388	0.660318	0.819282	0.934382	1.000513	1.128323	1.143637	1.152825
637	PENSION, HEALTH, AND WELFARE FUNDS	1	1.207560	1.207560	1.207560	1.207560	1.207560	1.207560	1.207560	1.207560	1.207560	1.207560	1.207560
6371	Pension, Health, And Welfare Funds	1	1.207560	1.207560	1.207560	1.207560	1.207560	1.207560	1.207560	1.207560	1.207560	1.207560	1.207560
639	INSURANCE CARRIERS, NOT ELSEWHERE CLASSIFIED	2	0.103398	0.103398	-0.957406	-0.924932	-0.870810	-0.113093	0.103398	0.319888	1.077605	1.131727	1.164201
6399	Insurance Carriers, Not Elsewhere Classified	2	0.103398	0.103398	-0.957406	-0.924932	-0.870810	-0.113093	0.103398	0.319888	1.077605	1.131727	1.164201
64	INSURANCE AGENTS, BROKERS, AND SERVICE	15	0.822163	0.980645	-1.355725	-1.037193	-0.506306	0.911688	0.980645	1.038744	1.522934	1.812727	1.986603
641	INSURANCE AGENTS, BROKERS, AND SERVICE	15	0.822163	0.980645	-1.355725	-1.037193	-0.506306	0.911688	0.980645	1.038744	1.522934	1.812727	1.986603
6411	Insurance Agents, Brokers, And Service	15	0.822163	0.980645	-1.355725	-1.037193	-0.506306	0.911688	0.980645	1.038744	1.522934	1.812727	1.986603
65	REAL ESTATE	42	0.863642	0.883049	-0.673769	-0.301149	-0.171391	0.640053	0.883049	1.163088	1.874877	1.925118	1.956679
6500	REAL ESTATE	2	0.590963	0.590963	0.380373	0.386819	0.397564	0.547985	0.590963	0.633941	0.784362	0.795107	0.801553

Up-market Betas of Common Stocks by SIC Codes as of March 31, 2017

SIC Code	Description	Number of Companies	Mean	Median	1st Percentile	2.5th Percentile	5th Percentile	40th Percentile	50th Percentile	60th Percentile	95th Percentile	97.5th Percentile	99th Percentile
651	REAL ESTATE OPERATORS (EXCEPT DEVELOPERS) AND LESSORS	16	0.695176	0.481064	-0.285646	-0.257739	-0.211228	0.409680	0.481064	0.931951	1.585280	1.642550	1.676912
6512	Operators Of Nonresidential Buildings	11	0.825218	0.931951	-0.248223	-0.164183	-0.024117	0.477776	0.931951	1.081680	1.623460	1.661640	1.684548
6513	Operators Of Apartment Buildings	3	0.100167	-0.003631	-0.176689	-0.171391	-0.162562	-0.038949	-0.003631	0.093966	0.435554	0.459953	0.474592
6519	Lessors Of Real Property, Not Elsewhere Classified	2	0.872455	0.872455	0.418936	0.432819	0.455958	0.779900	0.872455	0.965010	1.288953	1.312091	1.325975
653	REAL ESTATE AGENTS AND MANAGERS	20	0.986276	1.079877	-0.693040	-0.336770	0.257014	0.772307	1.079877	1.273810	1.928756	1.953318	1.968055
6531	Real Estate Agents And Managers	20	0.986276	1.079877	-0.693040	-0.336770	0.257014	0.772307	1.079877	1.273810	1.928756	1.953318	1.968055
655	LAND SUBDIVIDERS AND DEVELOPERS	4	1.060681	1.120335	0.657906	0.672493	0.696804	1.031532	1.120335	1.209138	1.341041	1.347455	1.351304
6552	Land Subdividers And Developers, Except Cemeteries	4	1.060681	1.120335	0.657906	0.672493	0.696804	1.031532	1.120335	1.209138	1.341041	1.347455	1.351304
67	HOLDING AND OTHER INVESTMENT OFFICES	228	0.642531	0.625022	-1.462384	-0.946805	-0.398526	0.492575	0.625022	0.790284	1.845270	2.092521	3.252310
671	HOLDING OFFICES	56	0.693756	0.684858	-0.508759	-0.341226	-0.214481	0.569057	0.684858	0.840374	1.638160	1.700219	1.708204
6712	Offices Of Bank Holding Companies	46	0.714949	0.734046	-0.540055	-0.359025	-0.269312	0.655391	0.734046	0.849640	1.604973	1.619885	1.667961
6719	Offices Of Holding Companies, Not Elsewhere Classified	10	0.596271	0.314017	0.049466	0.054363	0.062525	0.281872	0.314017	0.428206	1.701131	1.705745	1.708514
672	INVESTMENT OFFICES	28	0.582285	0.479045	-0.339546	-0.118063	0.072160	0.393789	0.479045	0.519430	1.957833	2.021021	2.049508
6722	Management Investment Offices, Open-End	3	1.348450	1.185090	0.868559	0.878249	0.894398	1.120492	1.185090	1.347704	1.916853	1.957507	1.981899
6726	Unit Investment Trusts, Face-Amount Certificate Offices	25	0.490345	0.442227	-0.355952	-0.159079	0.066807	0.357813	0.442227	0.490102	1.638242	1.957164	2.023966
673	TRUSTS	7	0.443174	0.048947	-0.098856	-0.091097	-0.078164	0.012021	0.048947	0.190477	1.494968	1.527614	1.547202
6733	Trusts, Except Educational, Religious, And Charitable	7	0.443174	0.048947	-0.098856	-0.091097	-0.078164	0.012021	0.048947	0.190477	1.494968	1.527614	1.547202
679	MISCELLANEOUS INVESTING	137	0.644091	0.671230	-1.523635	-1.295762	-0.874062	0.526827	0.671230	0.824037	1.985558	2.679110	3.542338
6794	Patent Owners And Lessors	12	0.645574	1.070275	-3.941564	-3.369275	-2.415460	0.827510	1.070275	1.125262	2.650852	3.215966	3.555034
6798	Real Estate Investment Trusts	51	0.594206	0.566946	-0.384846	-0.331393	-0.160311	0.462354	0.566946	0.645841	1.535935	1.715598	1.852445
6799	Investors, Not Elsewhere Classified	74	0.678231	0.788409	-1.494339	-1.440645	-1.075168	0.593750	0.788409	0.854479	2.321362	2.829400	3.493609
	SERVICES												
70	HOTELS, ROOMING HOUSES, CAMPS, AND OTHER LODGING PLACES	29	1.204549	1.161110	0.124450	0.204114	0.441793	1.126646	1.161110	1.268984	2.182242	2.544516	2.678588
701	HOTELS AND MOTELS	29	1.204549	1.161110	0.124450	0.204114	0.441793	1.126646	1.161110	1.268984	2.182242	2.544516	2.678588
7011	Hotels And Motels	29	1.204549	1.161110	0.124450	0.204114	0.441793	1.126646	1.161110	1.268984	2.182242	2.544516	2.678588
72	PERSONAL SERVICES	13	0.686083	0.773173	-2.375786	-1.901794	-1.111809	0.746323	0.773173	0.921824	2.140044	2.435007	2.611985
721	LAUNDRY, CLEANING, AND GARMENT SERVICES	3	0.727870	0.998385	-0.037357	-0.005651	0.047193	0.787009	0.998385	1.047452	1.219187	1.231453	1.238813
7211	Power Laundries, Family And Commercial	1	-0.058495	-0.058495	-0.058495	-0.058495	-0.058495	-0.058495	-0.058495	-0.058495	-0.058495	-0.058495	-0.058495
7215	Coin-Operated Laundries And Drycleaning	1	0.998385	0.998385	0.998385	0.998385	0.998385	0.998385	0.998385	0.998385	0.998385	0.998385	0.998385
7218	Industrial Launderers	1	1.243720	1.243720	1.243720	1.243720	1.243720	1.243720	1.243720	1.243720	1.243720	1.243720	1.243720

Up-market Betas of Common Stocks by SIC Codes as of March 31, 2017

SIC Code	Description	Number of Companies	Mean	Median	1st Percentile	2.5th Percentile	5th Percentile	40th Percentile	50th Percentile	60th Percentile	95th Percentile	97.5th Percentile	99th Percentile
723	BEAUTY SHOPS	2	0.516824	0.516824	0.265602	0.273292	0.286110	0.465554	0.516824	0.568094	0.747538	0.760356	0.768046
7231	Beauty Shops	2	0.516824	0.516824	0.265602	0.273292	0.286110	0.465554	0.516824	0.568094	0.747538	0.760356	0.768046
726	FUNERAL SERVICE AND CREMATORIES	2	0.819014	0.819014	0.737017	0.739528	0.743711	0.802280	0.819014	0.835748	0.894317	0.898501	0.901011
7261	Funeral Service And Crematories	2	0.819014	0.819014	0.737017	0.739528	0.743711	0.802280	0.819014	0.835748	0.894317	0.898501	0.901011
729	MISCELLANEOUS PERSONAL SERVICES	6	0.677299	1.050059	-2.548255	-2.332967	-1.974154	0.749068	1.050059	1.351050	2.484168	2.607069	2.680810
7291	Tax Return Preparation Services	1	1.351050	1.351050	1.351050	1.351050	1.351050	1.351050	1.351050	1.351050	1.351050	1.351050	1.351050
7299	Miscellaneous Personal Services, Not Elsewhere Classified	5	0.542548	0.749068	-2.576960	-2.404730	-2.117679	0.520930	0.749068	1.148145	2.533328	2.631649	2.690642
73	BUSINESS SERVICES	431	0.868455	0.975626	-2.489108	-1.441448	-0.776582	0.839431	0.975626	1.102660	2.087140	2.468895	2.777773
731	ADVERTISING	20	0.442277	0.922967	-3.751654	-2.830374	-1.294908	0.657508	0.922967	0.999378	1.415635	1.579653	1.678063
7310	SERVICES-ADVERTISING	1	1.743670	1.743670	1.743670	1.743670	1.743670	1.743670	1.743670	1.743670	1.743670	1.743670	1.743670
7311	Advertising Agencies	12	0.304603	0.922967	-3.940137	-3.301581	-2.237323	0.618843	0.922967	0.963888	1.391193	1.394781	1.396935
7312	Outdoor Advertising Services	2	1.087970	1.087970	1.054728	1.055746	1.057442	1.081186	1.087970	1.094754	1.118498	1.120194	1.121212
7313	Radio, Television, And Publishers' Advertising Representatives	3	0.458636	0.301602	0.263908	0.265062	0.266985	0.293909	0.301602	0.403515	0.760211	0.785689	0.800976
7319	Advertising, Not Elsewhere Classified	2	-0.052600	-0.052600	-1.111666	-1.079246	-1.025212	-0.268736	-0.052600	0.163536	0.920012	0.974046	1.006466
732	CONSUMER CREDIT REPORTING AGENCIES, MERCANTILE REPORTING AGENCIES	10	0.894800	1.100650	-0.018975	0.028881	0.108641	1.054777	1.100650	1.107744	1.377738	1.380834	1.382692
7320	SERVICES-CONSUMER CREDIT REPORTING, COLLECTION AGENCIES	1	1.109880	1.109880	1.109880	1.109880	1.109880	1.109880	1.109880	1.109880	1.109880	1.109880	1.109880
7322	Adjustment And Collection Services	3	0.999197	1.323810	0.324014	0.354620	0.405630	1.119770	1.323810	1.333082	1.365534	1.367852	1.369243
7323	Credit Reporting Services	6	0.806756	1.044727	-0.032750	-0.005556	0.039768	0.994473	1.044727	1.094980	1.314528	1.349229	1.370050
733	MAILING, REPRODUCTION, COMMERCIAL ART AND PHOTOGRAPHY, AND STENOGRAPHY	3	0.357177	1.127440	-1.575606	-1.492860	-1.354949	0.575798	1.127440	1.216924	1.530118	1.552489	1.565912
7331	Direct Mail Advertising Services	2	-0.251665	-0.251665	-1.603188	-1.561815	-1.492860	-0.527486	-0.251665	0.024156	0.989530	1.058485	1.099858
7338	Secretarial And Court Reporting Services	1	1.574860	1.574860	1.574860	1.574860	1.574860	1.574860	1.574860	1.574860	1.574860	1.574860	1.574860
734	SERVICES TO DWELLINGS AND OTHER BUILDINGS	3	0.716847	0.839431	0.468362	0.479721	0.498653	0.763703	0.839431	0.841609	0.849232	0.849777	0.850103
7342	Disinfecting And Pest Control Services	1	0.839431	0.839431	0.839431	0.839431	0.839431	0.839431	0.839431	0.839431	0.839431	0.839431	0.839431
7349	Building Cleaning And Maintenance Services, Not Elsewhere Classified	2	0.655555	0.655555	0.464684	0.470527	0.480266	0.616602	0.655555	0.694508	0.830844	0.840583	0.846426
735	MISCELLANEOUS EQUIPMENT RENTAL AND LEASING	20	1.458638	1.511180	-0.171010	-0.142645	-0.095368	1.331906	1.511180	1.880398	2.676716	2.716573	2.740487
7350	SERVICES-MISCELLANEOUS EQUIPMENT RENTAL & LEASING	1	-0.189921	-0.189921	-0.189921	-0.189921	-0.189921	-0.189921	-0.189921	-0.189921	-0.189921	-0.189921	-0.189921
7353	Heavy Construction Equipment Rental And Leasing	1	1.884820	1.884820	1.884820	1.884820	1.884820	1.884820	1.884820	1.884820	1.884820	1.884820	1.884820

Up-market Betas of Common Stocks by SIC Codes as of March 31, 2017

SIC Code	Description	Number of Companies	Mean	Median	1st Percentile	2.5th Percentile	5th Percentile	40th Percentile	50th Percentile	60th Percentile	95th Percentile	97.5th Percentile	99th Percentile
7359	Equipment Rental And Leasing, Not Elsewhere Classified	18	1.526548	1.511180	-0.085430	-0.077989	-0.065586	1.335708	1.511180	1.912448	2.685107	2.720768	2.742165
736	PERSONNEL SUPPLY SERVICES	24	0.955595	0.967512	-0.386337	-0.328586	-0.186195	0.799811	0.967512	1.189284	2.129621	2.170437	2.171027
7361	Employment Agencies	4	0.774346	0.625947	0.236931	0.238369	0.240766	0.411137	0.625947	0.840756	1.515686	1.562603	1.590753
7363	Help Supply Services	20	0.991845	1.057721	-0.393033	-0.345325	-0.265813	0.837573	1.057721	1.212046	2.169796	2.170608	2.171095
737	COMPUTER PROGRAMMING, DATA PROCESSING, AND OTHER COMPUTER RELATED	265	0.877338	0.975876	-2.634562	-2.123016	-0.746244	0.832349	0.975876	1.097896	2.025422	2.587022	3.080355
7370	SERVICES-COMPUTER PROGRAMMING, DATA PROCESSING, ETC.	1	0.774162	0.774162	0.774162	0.774162	0.774162	0.774162	0.774162	0.774162	0.774162	0.774162	0.774162
7371	Computer Programming Services	58	0.949640	0.981563	-1.241939	-0.807394	-0.370380	0.850361	0.981563	1.179620	1.986290	2.248092	2.350200
7372	Prepackaged Software	118	0.845534	0.909829	-2.635540	-2.145205	-0.545557	0.748131	0.909829	1.097438	2.035611	2.646322	5.639005
7373	Computer Integrated Systems Design	35	0.909998	0.999557	-1.862806	-1.488446	-0.368124	0.985176	0.999557	1.083436	1.670590	1.865237	2.300461
7374	Computer Processing And Data Preparation And Processing Services	37	0.832476	0.911932	-2.598889	-2.314757	-0.635562	0.810981	0.911932	1.030014	2.023768	2.152564	2.533178
7375	Information Retrieval Services	10	1.155676	1.063910	0.696192	0.719068	0.757195	1.024725	1.063910	1.082088	1.822634	1.832102	1.837783
7376	Computer Facilities Management Services	1	3.092630	3.092630	3.092630	3.092630	3.092630	3.092630	3.092630	3.092630	3.092630	3.092630	3.092630
7379	Computer Related Services, Not Elsewhere Classified	5	-0.086529	0.703109	-2.505684	-2.384639	-2.182899	0.194276	0.703109	0.781329	1.076484	1.098712	1.112049
738	MISCELLANEOUS BUSINESS SERVICES	86	0.798685	0.932852	-0.914397	-0.845325	-0.800065	0.836597	0.932852	1.059190	1.952550	2.210798	2.434529
7381	Detective, Guard, And Armored Car Services	1	0.360071	0.360071	0.360071	0.360071	0.360071	0.360071	0.360071	0.360071	0.360071	0.360071	0.360071
7382	Security Systems Services	3	1.578363	1.566020	1.086653	1.101328	1.125785	1.468190	1.566020	1.671256	2.039582	2.065891	2.081676
7384	Photofinishing Laboratories	1	0.734850	0.734850	0.734850	0.734850	0.734850	0.734850	0.734850	0.734850	0.734850	0.734850	0.734850
7389	Business Services, Not Elsewhere Classified	81	0.776011	0.930900	-0.935073	-0.850001	-0.812552	0.836597	0.930900	1.051840	1.855890	2.227740	2.436128
75	AUTOMOTIVE REPAIR, SERVICES, AND PARKING	6	0.839850	1.302500	-2.983509	-2.683672	-2.183945	1.023020	1.302500	1.581980	2.576520	2.664010	2.716504
751	AUTOMOTIVE RENTAL AND LEASING, WITHOUT DRIVERS	3	1.552193	1.581980	1.034199	1.050968	1.078916	1.470188	1.581980	1.675900	2.004620	2.028100	2.042188
7513	Truck Rental And Leasing, Without Drivers	2	1.302500	1.302500	1.028610	1.036994	1.050968	1.246604	1.302500	1.358396	1.554032	1.568006	1.576390
7514	Passenger Car Rental	1	2.051580	2.051580	2.051580	2.051580	2.051580	2.051580	2.051580	2.051580	2.051580	2.051580	2.051580
753	AUTOMOTIVE REPAIR SHOPS	3	0.127507	0.814421	-3.103444	-2.983509	-2.783618	0.014857	0.814421	1.201837	2.557792	2.654646	2.712758
7538	General Automotive Repair Shops	3	0.127507	0.814421	-3.103444	-2.983509	-2.783618	0.014857	0.814421	1.201837	2.557792	2.654646	2.712758
76	MISCELLANEOUS REPAIR SERVICES	3	0.356014	-0.094600	-0.222018	-0.218117	-0.211616	-0.120603	-0.094600	0.201772	1.239074	1.313167	1.357623
762	ELECTRICAL REPAIR SHOPS	2	0.581321	0.581321	-0.208499	-0.184321	-0.144024	0.420133	0.581321	0.742509	1.306666	1.346963	1.371141
7623	Refrigeration And Air-Conditioning Service And Repair Shops	2	0.581321	0.581321	-0.208499	-0.184321	-0.144024	0.420133	0.581321	0.742509	1.306666	1.346963	1.371141
769	MISCELLANEOUS REPAIR SHOPS AND RELATED SERVICES	1	-0.094600	-0.094600	-0.094600	-0.094600	-0.094600	-0.094600	-0.094600	-0.094600	-0.094600	-0.094600	-0.094600

Up-market Betas of Common Stocks by SIC Codes as of March 31, 2017

SIC Code	Description	Number of Companies	Mean	Median	1st Percentile	2.5th Percentile	5th Percentile	40th Percentile	50th Percentile	60th Percentile	95th Percentile	97.5th Percentile	99th Percentile
7699	Repair Shops And Related Services, Not Elsewhere Classified	1	-0.094600	-0.094600	-0.094600	-0.094600	-0.094600	-0.094600	-0.094600	-0.094600	-0.094600	-0.094600	-0.094600
78	MOTION PICTURES	17	0.708771	0.858762	-0.876049	-0.767899	-0.587649	0.725672	0.858762	0.953238	1.594818	2.137594	2.463260
781	MOTION PICTURE PRODUCTION AND ALLIED SERVICES	11	0.599480	0.655071	-0.903087	-0.835493	-0.722837	0.493835	0.655071	0.858762	2.001900	2.341135	2.544676
7812	Motion Picture And Video Tape Production	9	0.893329	0.858762	-0.263762	-0.206890	-0.112103	0.695809	0.858762	0.929088	2.137594	2.408982	2.571815
7819	Services Allied To Motion Picture Production	2	-0.722837	-0.722837	-0.943643	-0.936883	-0.925618	-0.767899	-0.722837	-0.677774	-0.520055	-0.508790	-0.502030
782	MOTION PICTURE DISTRIBUTION AND ALLIED SERVICES	1	0.957616	0.957616	0.957616	0.957616	0.957616	0.957616	0.957616	0.957616	0.957616	0.957616	0.957616
7822	Motion Picture And Video Tape Distribution	1	0.957616	0.957616	0.957616	0.957616	0.957616	0.957616	0.957616	0.957616	0.957616	0.957616	0.957616
783	MOTION PICTURE THEATERS	4	0.802915	0.913012	0.350367	0.372691	0.409897	0.864149	0.913012	0.961875	1.041795	1.045973	1.048479
7832	Motion Picture Theaters, Except Drive-In	4	0.802915	0.913012	0.350367	0.372691	0.409897	0.864149	0.913012	0.961875	1.041795	1.045973	1.048479
784	VIDEO TAPE RENTAL	1	1.285550	1.285550	1.285550	1.285550	1.285550	1.285550	1.285550	1.285550	1.285550	1.285550	1.285550
7841	Video Tape Rental	1	1.285550	1.285550	1.285550	1.285550	1.285550	1.285550	1.285550	1.285550	1.285550	1.285550	1.285550
79	AMUSEMENT AND RECREATION SERVICES	31	-0.163859	0.253116	-12.627119	-6.830098	-2.463910	0.018128	0.253116	0.546852	2.202780	3.135535	3.835654
7900	SERVICES-AMUSEMENT & RECREATION SERVICES	1	-0.781301	-0.781301	-0.781301	-0.781301	-0.781301	-0.781301	-0.781301	-0.781301	-0.781301	-0.781301	-0.781301
792	THEATRICAL PRODUCERS (EXCEPT MOTION PICTURE), BANDS, ORCHESTRAS	2	0.267582	0.267582	-0.585790	-0.559667	-0.516127	0.093424	0.267582	0.441740	1.051291	1.094831	1.120954
7922	Theatrical Producers (Except Motion Picture) And Miscellaneous Theater	1	1.138370	1.138370	1.138370	1.138370	1.138370	1.138370	1.138370	1.138370	1.138370	1.138370	1.138370
7929	Bands, Orchestras, Actors, And Other Entertainers And Entertainment	1	-0.603206	-0.603206	-0.603206	-0.603206	-0.603206	-0.603206	-0.603206	-0.603206	-0.603206	-0.603206	-0.603206
793	BOWLING CENTERS	1	0.344486	0.344486	0.344486	0.344486	0.344486	0.344486	0.344486	0.344486	0.344486	0.344486	0.344486
7933	Bowling Centers	1	0.344486	0.344486	0.344486	0.344486	0.344486	0.344486	0.344486	0.344486	0.344486	0.344486	0.344486
794	COMMERCIAL SPORTS	9	0.782494	0.546852	-0.594263	-0.515892	-0.385274	0.443325	0.546852	1.023306	2.311540	2.529060	2.659572
7941	Professional Sports Clubs And Promoters	3	0.839171	0.417443	-0.625231	-0.593312	-0.540115	0.204652	0.417443	0.883270	2.513666	2.630123	2.699997
7948	Racing, Including Track Operation	6	0.754155	0.844636	0.007158	0.008024	0.009468	0.546852	0.844636	1.142420	1.532228	1.595604	1.633630
799	MISCELLANEOUS AMUSEMENT AND RECREATION SERVICES	18	-0.678911	0.157609	-14.301814	-11.016835	-5.541871	-0.037109	0.157609	0.342238	1.899697	3.101048	3.821859
7993	Coin-Operated Amusement Devices	1	0.001545	0.001545	0.001545	0.001545	0.001545	0.001545	0.001545	0.001545	0.001545	0.001545	0.001545
7996	Amusement Parks	3	0.696776	0.698724	0.252382	0.266046	0.288818	0.607634	0.698724	0.788645	1.103369	1.125850	1.139338
7997	Membership Sports And Recreation Clubs	4	-3.724413	0.059230	-16.036595	-15.353787	-14.215774	-0.767282	0.059230	0.885742	1.469849	1.472770	1.474522
7999	Amusement And Recreation Services, Not Elsewhere Classified	10	0.058537	-0.059891	-3.402661	-3.092356	-2.575183	-0.270107	-0.059891	0.144413	2.917134	3.609767	4.025347
80	HEALTH SERVICES	81	0.748994	0.821262	-2.910110	-2.674670	-1.293320	0.720478	0.821262	0.899609	2.301780	2.486810	3.280126

Up-market Betas of Common Stocks by SIC Codes as of March 31, 2017

SIC Code	Description	Number of Companies	Mean	Median	1st Percentile	2.5th Percentile	5th Percentile	40th Percentile	50th Percentile	60th Percentile	95th Percentile	97.5th Percentile	99th Percentile
801	OFFICES AND CLINICS OF DOCTORS OF MEDICINE	15	1.122618	0.878892	0.184659	0.233160	0.313996	0.831145	0.878892	0.946121	2.377353	2.809467	3.068735
8011	Offices And Clinics Of Doctors Of Medicine	15	1.122618	0.878892	0.184659	0.233160	0.313996	0.831145	0.878892	0.946121	2.377353	2.809467	3.068735
804	OFFICES AND CLINICS OF OTHER HEALTH PRACTITIONERS	1	0.098112	0.098112	0.098112	0.098112	0.098112	0.098112	0.098112	0.098112	0.098112	0.098112	0.098112
8041	Offices And Clinics Of Chiropractors	1	0.098112	0.098112	0.098112	0.098112	0.098112	0.098112	0.098112	0.098112	0.098112	0.098112	0.098112
805	NURSING AND PERSONAL CARE FACILITIES	10	0.903888	0.898765	-0.098492	-0.094859	-0.088804	0.839799	0.898765	1.003923	1.870995	1.915433	1.942095
8051	Skilled Nursing Care Facilities	10	0.903888	0.898765	-0.098492	-0.094859	-0.088804	0.839799	0.898765	1.003923	1.870995	1.915433	1.942095
806	HOSPITALS	15	0.630470	0.764354	-2.629332	-2.182186	-1.436941	0.465246	0.764354	0.795707	2.641539	3.037925	3.275756
8062	General Medical And Surgical Hospitals	10	0.172446	0.430092	-2.735796	-2.448344	-1.969259	0.249329	0.430092	0.669261	1.396509	1.412499	1.422094
8069	Specialty Hospitals, Except Psychiatric	5	1.546519	1.202160	-0.008440	0.044466	0.132643	1.056518	1.202160	1.642008	3.207804	3.321057	3.389009
807	MEDICAL AND DENTAL LABORATORIES	17	0.451398	0.597648	-2.501644	-2.242106	-1.809542	0.562800	0.597648	0.743324	2.100226	2.293518	2.409493
8071	Medical Laboratories	17	0.451398	0.597648	-2.501644	-2.242106	-1.809542	0.562800	0.597648	0.743324	2.100226	2.293518	2.409493
808	HOME HEALTH CARE SERVICES	9	0.802500	0.809024	0.222505	0.246717	0.287070	0.738187	0.809024	0.844052	1.374384	1.497702	1.571693
8082	Home Health Care Services	9	0.802500	0.809024	0.222505	0.246717	0.287070	0.738187	0.809024	0.844052	1.374384	1.497702	1.571693
809	MISCELLANEOUS HEALTH AND ALLIED SERVICES, NOT ELSEWHERE CLASSIFIED	14	0.738497	0.997734	-2.592041	-2.121432	-1.337084	0.853759	0.997734	1.061928	2.048237	2.239149	2.353695
8093	Specialty Outpatient Facilities, Not Elsewhere Classified	6	0.048963	0.273539	-2.785111	-2.604108	-2.302436	0.268153	0.273539	0.278924	1.707540	1.775090	1.815620
8099	Health And Allied Services, Not Elsewhere Classified	8	1.255649	1.043100	0.568969	0.597454	0.644928	1.006125	1.043100	1.149738	2.182649	2.306354	2.380578
81	LEGAL SERVICES	1	0.878627	0.878627	0.878627	0.878627	0.878627	0.878627	0.878627	0.878627	0.878627	0.878627	0.878627
811	LEGAL SERVICES	1	0.878627	0.878627	0.878627	0.878627	0.878627	0.878627	0.878627	0.878627	0.878627	0.878627	0.878627
8111	Legal Services	1	0.878627	0.878627	0.878627	0.878627	0.878627	0.878627	0.878627	0.878627	0.878627	0.878627	0.878627
82	EDUCATIONAL SERVICES	18	1.029570	0.944382	-0.296439	-0.214911	-0.079031	0.818722	0.944382	1.211794	2.025427	2.436108	2.682517
8200	SERVICES-EDUCATIONAL SERVICES	2	1.883717	1.883717	0.939905	0.968798	1.016951	1.691102	1.883717	2.076332	2.750483	2.798636	2.827529
821	ELEMENTARY AND SECONDARY SCHOOLS	6	1.162028	1.356395	-0.001711	0.042333	0.115738	1.232410	1.356395	1.480380	1.873810	1.877145	1.879146
8211	Elementary And Secondary Schools	6	1.162028	1.356395	-0.001711	0.042333	0.115738	1.232410	1.356395	1.480380	1.873810	1.877145	1.879146
822	COLLEGES, UNIVERSITIES, PROFESSIONAL SCHOOLS, AND JUNIOR COLLEGES	3	0.637743	0.756130	-0.328653	-0.295445	-0.240099	0.534746	0.756130	0.906482	1.432714	1.470302	1.492855
8221	Colleges, Universities, And Professional Schools	3	0.637743	0.756130	-0.328653	-0.295445	-0.240099	0.534746	0.756130	0.906482	1.432714	1.470302	1.492855
823	LIBRARIES	1	1.536000	1.536000	1.536000	1.536000	1.536000	1.536000	1.536000	1.536000	1.536000	1.536000	1.536000
8231	Libraries	1	1.536000	1.536000	1.536000	1.536000	1.536000	1.536000	1.536000	1.536000	1.536000	1.536000	1.536000
824	VOCATIONAL SCHOOLS	3	0.604217	0.503697	0.344092	0.348978	0.357121	0.471125	0.503697	0.596581	0.921677	0.944898	0.958831
8249	Vocational Schools, Not Elsewhere Classified	3	0.604217	0.503697	0.344092	0.348978	0.357121	0.471125	0.503697	0.596581	0.921677	0.944898	0.958831

Up-market Betas of Common Stocks by SIC Codes as of March 31, 2017

SIC Code	Description	Number of Companies	Mean	Median	1st Percentile	2.5th Percentile	5th Percentile	40th Percentile	50th Percentile	60th Percentile	95th Percentile	97.5th Percentile	99th Percentile
829	SCHOOLS AND EDUCATIONAL SERVICES, NOT ELSEWHERE CLASSIFIED	3	0.843593	0.834370	0.496662	0.507000	0.524230	0.765450	0.834370	0.908824	1.169413	1.188027	1.199195
8299	Schools And Educational Services, Not Elsewhere Classified	3	0.843593	0.834370	0.496662	0.507000	0.524230	0.765450	0.834370	0.908824	1.169413	1.188027	1.199195
83	SOCIAL SERVICES	3	1.414051	1.522920	0.636590	0.663723	0.708944	1.342036	1.522920	1.638482	2.042949	2.071840	2.089174
832	INDIVIDUAL AND FAMILY SOCIAL SERVICES	1	2.100730	2.100730	2.100730	2.100730	2.100730	2.100730	2.100730	2.100730	2.100730	2.100730	2.100730
8322	Individual And Family Social Services	1	2.100730	2.100730	2.100730	2.100730	2.100730	2.100730	2.100730	2.100730	2.100730	2.100730	2.100730
833	JOB TRAINING AND VOCATIONAL REHABILITATION SERVICES	1	1.522920	1.522920	1.522920	1.522920	1.522920	1.522920	1.522920	1.522920	1.522920	1.522920	1.522920
8331	Job Training And Vocational Rehabilitation Services	1	1.522920	1.522920	1.522920	1.522920	1.522920	1.522920	1.522920	1.522920	1.522920	1.522920	1.522920
835	CHILD DAY CARE SERVICES	1	0.618502	0.618502	0.618502	0.618502	0.618502	0.618502	0.618502	0.618502	0.618502	0.618502	0.618502
8351	Child Day Care Services	1	0.618502	0.618502	0.618502	0.618502	0.618502	0.618502	0.618502	0.618502	0.618502	0.618502	0.618502
86	MEMBERSHIP ORGANIZATIONS	1	1.212140	1.212140	1.212140	1.212140	1.212140	1.212140	1.212140	1.212140	1.212140	1.212140	1.212140
869	MEMBERSHIP ORGANIZATIONS, NOT ELSEWHERE CLASSIFIED	1	1.212140	1.212140	1.212140	1.212140	1.212140	1.212140	1.212140	1.212140	1.212140	1.212140	1.212140
8699	Membership Organizations, Not Elsewhere Classified	1	1.212140	1.212140	1.212140	1.212140	1.212140	1.212140	1.212140	1.212140	1.212140	1.212140	1.212140
87	ENGINEERING, ACCOUNTING, RESEARCH, MANAGEMENT, AND RELATED SERVICES	172	0.812672	0.956190	-6.397238	-2.235661	-1.345108	0.773393	0.956190	1.134680	2.567751	3.451380	5.011479
871	ENGINEERING, ARCHITECTURAL, AND SURVEYING SERVICES	20	1.676056	1.331990	-0.277497	0.003492	0.471807	1.220318	1.331990	1.507466	2.738102	5.954061	7.883636
8711	Engineering Services	19	1.702140	1.383060	-0.287356	-0.021156	0.422510	1.253696	1.383060	1.566262	3.076624	6.123322	7.951341
8712	Architectural Services	1	1.180460	1.180460	1.180460	1.180460	1.180460	1.180460	1.180460	1.180460	1.180460	1.180460	1.180460
872	ACCOUNTING, AUDITING, AND BOOKKEEPING SERVICES	2	0.989658	0.989658	0.142092	0.168038	0.211281	0.816685	0.989658	1.162630	1.768034	1.811277	1.837223
8721	Accounting, Auditing, And Bookkeeping Services	2	0.989658	0.989658	0.142092	0.168038	0.211281	0.816685	0.989658	1.162630	1.768034	1.811277	1.837223
873	RESEARCH, DEVELOPMENT, AND TESTING SERVICES	96	0.709691	0.918729	-8.893970	-2.782025	-1.676333	0.782062	0.918729	1.178860	2.652483	3.085514	3.698275
8731	Commercial Physical And Biological Research	83	0.762928	0.932899	-4.558060	-2.292148	-1.513205	0.786512	0.932899	1.212414	2.575171	3.162361	3.743006
8732	Commercial Economic, Sociological, And Educational Research	6	-0.638621	0.542934	-8.324953	-7.664868	-6.564727	0.336742	0.542934	0.749126	2.419133	2.675877	2.829923
8733	Noncommercial Research Organizations	5	1.233234	1.048890	0.213141	0.245785	0.300192	0.923514	1.048890	1.328738	2.303254	2.372597	2.414203
8734	Testing Laboratories	2	1.236445	1.236445	1.107276	1.111230	1.117821	1.210084	1.236445	1.262806	1.355070	1.361660	1.365614
874	MANAGEMENT AND PUBLIC RELATIONS SERVICES	54	0.669423	0.781409	-3.637835	-1.898297	-1.173698	0.548523	0.781409	0.947772	1.837056	3.067834	5.374683
8741	Management Services	14	0.903966	0.433576	-0.348566	-0.290997	-0.195047	0.254660	0.433576	0.485659	3.375850	5.401055	6.616178
8742	Management Consulting Services	34	0.464527	0.875705	-4.314169	-2.640242	-1.748144	0.682550	0.875705	0.960678	1.624213	1.722912	1.922333
8743	Public Relations Services	1	3.555360	3.555360	3.555360	3.555360	3.555360	3.555360	3.555360	3.555360	3.555360	3.555360	3.555360

Up-market Betas of Common Stocks by SIC Codes as of March 31, 2017

SIC Code	Description	Number of Companies	Mean	Median	1st Percentile	2.5th Percentile	5th Percentile	40th Percentile	50th Percentile	60th Percentile	95th Percentile	97.5th Percentile	99th Percentile
8744	Facilities Support Management Services	1	1.033030	1.033030	1.033030	1.033030	1.033030	1.033030	1.033030	1.033030	1.033030	1.033030	1.033030
8748	Business Consulting Services, Not Elsewhere Classified	4	0.777753	0.695006	0.017255	0.040961	0.080471	0.594952	0.695006	0.795060	1.590882	1.655216	1.693816
88	PRIVATE HOUSEHOLDS	1	0.763788	0.763788	0.763788	0.763788	0.763788	0.763788	0.763788	0.763788	0.763788	0.763788	0.763788
8880	AMERICAN DEPOSITARY RECEIPTS	1	0.763788	0.763788	0.763788	0.763788	0.763788	0.763788	0.763788	0.763788	0.763788	0.763788	0.763788
89	SERVICES, NOT ELSEWHERE CLASSIFIED	14	1.048889	1.049770	-1.843687	-1.540353	-1.034795	0.959327	1.049770	1.098692	3.688549	5.110524	5.963710
899	SERVICES, NOT ELSEWHERE CLASSIFIED	14	1.048889	1.049770	-1.843687	-1.540353	-1.034795	0.959327	1.049770	1.098692	3.688549	5.110524	5.963710
8999	Services, Not Elsewhere Classified	14	1.048889	1.049770	-1.843687	-1.540353	-1.034795	0.959327	1.049770	1.098692	3.688549	5.110524	5.963710
	PUBLIC ADMINISTRATION												
94	ADMINISTRATION OF HUMAN RESOURCE PROGRAMS	1	0.728108	0.728108	0.728108	0.728108	0.728108	0.728108	0.728108	0.728108	0.728108	0.728108	0.728108
943	ADMINISTRATION OF PUBLIC HEALTH PROGRAMS	1	0.728108	0.728108	0.728108	0.728108	0.728108	0.728108	0.728108	0.728108	0.728108	0.728108	0.728108
9431	Administration Of Public Health Programs	1	0.728108	0.728108	0.728108	0.728108	0.728108	0.728108	0.728108	0.728108	0.728108	0.728108	0.728108
95	ADMINISTRATION OF ENVIRONMENTAL QUALITY AND HOUSING PROGRAMS	2	3.299700	3.299700	1.259222	1.321686	1.425792	2.883276	3.299700	3.716124	5.173608	5.277714	5.340178
951	ADMINISTRATION OF ENVIRONMENTAL QUALITY PROGRAMS	2	3.299700	3.299700	1.259222	1.321686	1.425792	2.883276	3.299700	3.716124	5.173608	5.277714	5.340178
9511	Air And Water Resource And Solid Waste Management	2	3.299700	3.299700	1.259222	1.321686	1.425792	2.883276	3.299700	3.716124	5.173608	5.277714	5.340178
96	ADMINISTRATION OF ECONOMIC PROGRAMS	2	2.974930	2.974930	1.676430	1.716180	1.782430	2.709930	2.974930	3.239930	4.167430	4.233680	4.273430
961	ADMINISTRATION OF GENERAL ECONOMIC PROGRAMS	1	1.649930	1.649930	1.649930	1.649930	1.649930	1.649930	1.649930	1.649930	1.649930	1.649930	1.649930
9611	Administration Of General Economic Programs	1	1.649930	1.649930	1.649930	1.649930	1.649930	1.649930	1.649930	1.649930	1.649930	1.649930	1.649930
963	REGULATION AND ADMINISTRATION OF COMMUNICATIONS, ELECTRIC, GAS	1	4.299930	4.299930	4.299930	4.299930	4.299930	4.299930	4.299930	4.299930	4.299930	4.299930	4.299930
9631	Regulation And Administration Of Communications, Electric, Gas	1	4.299930	4.299930	4.299930	4.299930	4.299930	4.299930	4.299930	4.299930	4.299930	4.299930	4.299930
	NONCLASSIFIABLE ESTABLISHMENTS												
99	NONCLASSIFIABLE ESTABLISHMENTS	61	0.486854	0.630259	-3.922212	-3.336030	-2.749470	0.432166	0.630259	0.737412	1.980720	3.492670	5.983232
999	NONCLASSIFIABLE ESTABLISHMENTS	61	0.486854	0.630259	-3.922212	-3.336030	-2.749470	0.432166	0.630259	0.737412	1.980720	3.492670	5.983232
9995	NON-OPERATING ESTABLISHMENTS	1	1.149560	1.149560	1.149560	1.149560	1.149560	1.149560	1.149560	1.149560	1.149560	1.149560	1.149560
9999	Nonclassifiable Establishments	60	0.475809	0.618352	-3.928001	-3.353762	-2.761067	0.315982	0.618352	0.722267	2.048020	3.500968	6.041347

Preferred Stocks by SIC Codes

Betas of Preferred Stocks by SIC Codes as of March 31, 2017

Details:
Benchmark: S&P 500 Index
Returns period and frequency: 1 year of daily returns
Risk-free rate: Federal Funds Rate

SIC Code	Description	Number of Companies	Mean	Median	1st Percentile	2.5th Percentile	5th Percentile	40th Percentile	50th Percentile	60th Percentile	95th Percentile	97.5th Percentile	99th Percentile
	MINING												
13	OIL AND GAS EXTRACTION	12	1.285140	1.507125	-0.028035	0.012687	0.080557	1.335894	1.507125	1.696296	1.991163	1.994172	1.995977
131	CRUDE PETROLEUM AND NATURAL GAS	11	1.406988	1.596960	0.228239	0.283172	0.374728	1.417290	1.596960	1.762520	1.991710	1.994445	1.996086
1311	Crude Petroleum And Natural Gas	11	1.406988	1.596960	0.228239	0.283172	0.374728	1.417290	1.596960	1.762520	1.991710	1.994445	1.996086
132	NATURAL GAS LIQUIDS	1	-0.055183	-0.055183	-0.055183	-0.055183	-0.055183	-0.055183	-0.055183	-0.055183	-0.055183	-0.055183	-0.055183
1321	Natural Gas Liquids	1	-0.055183	-0.055183	-0.055183	-0.055183	-0.055183	-0.055183	-0.055183	-0.055183	-0.055183	-0.055183	-0.055183
	CONSTRUCTION												
15	CONSTRUCTION	2	0.872527	0.872527	-0.018874	0.008414	0.053894	0.690609	0.872527	1.054446	1.691161	1.736640	1.763928
153	OPERATIVE BUILDERS	2	0.872527	0.872527	-0.018874	0.008414	0.053894	0.690609	0.872527	1.054446	1.691161	1.736640	1.763928
1531	Operative Builders	2	0.872527	0.872527	-0.018874	0.008414	0.053894	0.690609	0.872527	1.054446	1.691161	1.736640	1.763928
	MANUFACTURING												
20	FOOD AND KINDRED PRODUCTS	1	0.516668	0.516668	0.516668	0.516668	0.516668	0.516668	0.516668	0.516668	0.516668	0.516668	0.516668
207	FATS AND OILS	1	0.516668	0.516668	0.516668	0.516668	0.516668	0.516668	0.516668	0.516668	0.516668	0.516668	0.516668
2075	Soybean Oil Mills	1	0.516668	0.516668	0.516668	0.516668	0.516668	0.516668	0.516668	0.516668	0.516668	0.516668	0.516668
28	CHEMICALS AND ALLIED PRODUCTS	6	0.528867	0.476200	-0.133634	-0.125933	-0.113096	0.203881	0.476200	0.748518	1.382352	1.474616	1.529974
282	PLASTICS MATERIALS AND SYNTHETIC RESINS, SYNTHETIC RUBBER, CELLULOSIC MANMADE FIBERS	1	1.566880	1.566880	1.566880	1.566880	1.566880	1.566880	1.566880	1.566880	1.566880	1.566880	1.566880
2821	Plastics Materials, Synthetic Resins, And Nonvulcanizable Elastomers	1	1.566880	1.566880	1.566880	1.566880	1.566880	1.566880	1.566880	1.566880	1.566880	1.566880	1.566880
283	DRUGS	3	0.593722	0.748518	0.214774	0.231113	0.258345	0.639591	0.748518	0.764568	0.820742	0.824755	0.827162
2834	Pharmaceutical Preparations	2	0.788643	0.788643	0.749320	0.750524	0.752530	0.780618	0.788643	0.796667	0.824755	0.826761	0.827965
2835	In Vitro And In Vivo Diagnostic Substances	1	0.203881	0.203881	0.203881	0.203881	0.203881	0.203881	0.203881	0.203881	0.203881	0.203881	0.203881
287	AGRICULTURAL CHEMICALS	2	-0.087423	-0.087423	-0.137742	-0.136202	-0.133634	-0.097692	-0.087423	-0.077154	-0.041212	-0.038644	-0.037104
2879	Pesticides And Agricultural Chemicals, Not Elsewhere Classified	2	-0.087423	-0.087423	-0.137742	-0.136202	-0.133634	-0.097692	-0.087423	-0.077154	-0.041212	-0.038644	-0.037104
29	PETROLEUM REFINING AND RELATED INDUSTRIES	1	1.528010	1.528010	1.528010	1.528010	1.528010	1.528010	1.528010	1.528010	1.528010	1.528010	1.528010
291	PETROLEUM REFINING	1	1.528010	1.528010	1.528010	1.528010	1.528010	1.528010	1.528010	1.528010	1.528010	1.528010	1.528010
2911	Petroleum Refining	1	1.528010	1.528010	1.528010	1.528010	1.528010	1.528010	1.528010	1.528010	1.528010	1.528010	1.528010
33	PRIMARY METAL INDUSTRIES	2	0.653656	0.653656	0.041288	0.060034	0.091278	0.528683	0.653656	0.778628	1.216034	1.247277	1.266023
331	STEEL WORKS, BLAST FURNACES, AND ROLLING AND FINISHING MILLS	1	1.278520	1.278520	1.278520	1.278520	1.278520	1.278520	1.278520	1.278520	1.278520	1.278520	1.278520

Betas of Preferred Stocks by SIC Codes as of March 31, 2017

SIC Code	Description	Number of Companies	Mean	Median	1st Percentile	2.5th Percentile	5th Percentile	40th Percentile	50th Percentile	60th Percentile	95th Percentile	97.5th Percentile	99th Percentile
3312	Steel Works, Blast Furnaces (Including Coke Ovens), And Rolling Mills	1	1.278520	1.278520	1.278520	1.278520	1.278520	1.278520	1.278520	1.278520	1.278520	1.278520	1.278520
333	PRIMARY SMELTING AND REFINING OF NONFERROUS METALS	1	0.028791	0.028791	0.028791	0.028791	0.028791	0.028791	0.028791	0.028791	0.028791	0.028791	0.028791
3334	Primary Production Of Aluminum	1	0.028791	0.028791	0.028791	0.028791	0.028791	0.028791	0.028791	0.028791	0.028791	0.028791	0.028791
34	FABRICATED METAL PRODUCTS, EXCEPT MACHINERY AND TRANSPORTATION EQUIPMENT	1	0.077830	0.077830	0.077830	0.077830	0.077830	0.077830	0.077830	0.077830	0.077830	0.077830	0.077830
341	METAL CANS AND SHIPPING CONTAINERS	1	0.077830	0.077830	0.077830	0.077830	0.077830	0.077830	0.077830	0.077830	0.077830	0.077830	0.077830
3412	Metal Shipping Barrels, Drums, Kegs, And Pails	1	0.077830	0.077830	0.077830	0.077830	0.077830	0.077830	0.077830	0.077830	0.077830	0.077830	0.077830
35	INDUSTRIAL AND COMMERCIAL MACHINERY AND COMPUTER EQUIPMENT	1	0.098569	0.098569	0.098569	0.098569	0.098569	0.098569	0.098569	0.098569	0.098569	0.098569	0.098569
358	REFRIGERATION AND SERVICE INDUSTRY MACHINERY	1	0.098569	0.098569	0.098569	0.098569	0.098569	0.098569	0.098569	0.098569	0.098569	0.098569	0.098569
3581	Automatic Vending Machines	1	0.098569	0.098569	0.098569	0.098569	0.098569	0.098569	0.098569	0.098569	0.098569	0.098569	0.098569
37	TRANSPORTATION EQUIPMENT	1	1.485380	1.485380	1.485380	1.485380	1.485380	1.485380	1.485380	1.485380	1.485380	1.485380	1.485380
371	MOTOR VEHICLES AND MOTOR VEHICLE EQUIPMENT	1	1.485380	1.485380	1.485380	1.485380	1.485380	1.485380	1.485380	1.485380	1.485380	1.485380	1.485380
3711	Motor Vehicles And Passenger Car Bodies	1	1.485380	1.485380	1.485380	1.485380	1.485380	1.485380	1.485380	1.485380	1.485380	1.485380	1.485380
	TRANSPORTATION, COMMUNICATIONS, ELECTRIC, GAS, AND SANITARY SERVICE												
40	RAILROAD TRANSPORTATION	1	0.160986	0.160986	0.160986	0.160986	0.160986	0.160986	0.160986	0.160986	0.160986	0.160986	0.160986
401	RAILROADS	1	0.160986	0.160986	0.160986	0.160986	0.160986	0.160986	0.160986	0.160986	0.160986	0.160986	0.160986
4011	Railroads, Line-Haul Operating	1	0.160986	0.160986	0.160986	0.160986	0.160986	0.160986	0.160986	0.160986	0.160986	0.160986	0.160986
44	WATER TRANSPORTATION	14	0.398267	0.270263	0.126670	0.128604	0.131827	0.239076	0.270263	0.368412	0.923963	0.985156	1.021873
441	DEEP SEA FOREIGN TRANSPORTATION OF FREIGHT	13	0.388050	0.255909	0.126571	0.128356	0.131331	0.225367	0.255909	0.305566	0.933377	0.989864	1.023755
4412	Deep Sea Foreign Transportation Of Freight	13	0.388050	0.255909	0.126571	0.128356	0.131331	0.225367	0.255909	0.305566	0.933377	0.989864	1.023755
449	SERVICES INCIDENTAL TO WATER TRANSPORTATION	1	0.531083	0.531083	0.531083	0.531083	0.531083	0.531083	0.531083	0.531083	0.531083	0.531083	0.531083
4499	Water Transportation Services, Not Elsewhere Classified	1	0.531083	0.531083	0.531083	0.531083	0.531083	0.531083	0.531083	0.531083	0.531083	0.531083	0.531083
45	TRANSPORTATION BY AIR	1	1.353420	1.353420	1.353420	1.353420	1.353420	1.353420	1.353420	1.353420	1.353420	1.353420	1.353420
451	AIR TRANSPORTATION, SCHEDULED, AND AIR COURIER SERVICES	1	1.353420	1.353420	1.353420	1.353420	1.353420	1.353420	1.353420	1.353420	1.353420	1.353420	1.353420
4512	Air Transportation, Scheduled	1	1.353420	1.353420	1.353420	1.353420	1.353420	1.353420	1.353420	1.353420	1.353420	1.353420	1.353420
47	TRANSPORTATION SERVICES	1	-0.003455	-0.003455	-0.003455	-0.003455	-0.003455	-0.003455	-0.003455	-0.003455	-0.003455	-0.003455	-0.003455
473	ARRANGEMENT OF TRANSPORTATION OF FREIGHT AND CARGO	1	-0.003455	-0.003455	-0.003455	-0.003455	-0.003455	-0.003455	-0.003455	-0.003455	-0.003455	-0.003455	-0.003455
4731	Arrangement Of Transportation Of Freight And Cargo	1	-0.003455	-0.003455	-0.003455	-0.003455	-0.003455	-0.003455	-0.003455	-0.003455	-0.003455	-0.003455	-0.003455

Betas of Preferred Stocks by SIC Codes as of March 31, 2017

SIC Code	Description	Number of Companies	Mean	Median	1st Percentile	2.5th Percentile	5th Percentile	40th Percentile	50th Percentile	60th Percentile	95th Percentile	97.5th Percentile	99th Percentile
48	COMMUNICATIONS	3	0.805638	1.029330	0.080007	0.109068	0.157503	0.835591	1.029330	1.088854	1.297188	1.312069	1.320998
481	TELEPHONE COMMUNICATIONS	3	0.805638	1.029330	0.080007	0.109068	0.157503	0.835591	1.029330	1.088854	1.297188	1.312069	1.320998
4812	Radiotelephone Communications	1	1.029330	1.029330	1.029330	1.029330	1.029330	1.029330	1.029330	1.029330	1.029330	1.029330	1.029330
4813	Telephone Communications, Except Radiotelephone	2	0.693792	0.693792	0.073297	0.092291	0.123949	0.567160	0.693792	0.820423	1.263634	1.295292	1.314287
49	ELECTRIC, GAS, AND SANITARY SERVICES	22	0.264428	0.116032	-0.169648	-0.163647	-0.153769	0.100140	0.116032	0.138034	1.556896	1.895966	2.091130
491	ELECTRIC SERVICES	11	0.208294	0.107331	-0.141476	-0.121793	-0.088986	0.095346	0.107331	0.110870	0.887947	1.244809	1.458925
4911	Electric Services	11	0.208294	0.107331	-0.141476	-0.121793	-0.088986	0.095346	0.107331	0.110870	0.887947	1.244809	1.458925
492	GAS PRODUCTION AND DISTRIBUTION	2	0.266271	0.266271	-0.164850	-0.151652	-0.129656	0.178287	0.266271	0.354255	0.662198	0.684194	0.697392
4923	Natural Gas Transmission And Distribution	1	0.706190	0.706190	0.706190	0.706190	0.706190	0.706190	0.706190	0.706190	0.706190	0.706190	0.706190
4924	Natural Gas Distribution	1	-0.173648	-0.173648	-0.173648	-0.173648	-0.173648	-0.173648	-0.173648	-0.173648	-0.173648	-0.173648	-0.173648
493	COMBINATION ELECTRIC AND GAS, AND OTHER UTILITY SERVICES	9	0.332626	0.196754	-0.130816	-0.120054	-0.102118	0.136306	0.196754	0.200689	1.432466	1.826853	2.063485
4931	Electric And Other Services Combined	9	0.332626	0.196754	-0.130816	-0.120054	-0.102118	0.136306	0.196754	0.200689	1.432466	1.826853	2.063485
	WHOLESALE TRADE												
50	WHOLESALE TRADE¨DURABLE GOODS	1	0.057264	0.057264	0.057264	0.057264	0.057264	0.057264	0.057264	0.057264	0.057264	0.057264	0.057264
507	HARDWARE, AND PLUMBING AND HEATING EQUIPMENT AND SUPPLIES	1	0.057264	0.057264	0.057264	0.057264	0.057264	0.057264	0.057264	0.057264	0.057264	0.057264	0.057264
5072	Hardware	1	0.057264	0.057264	0.057264	0.057264	0.057264	0.057264	0.057264	0.057264	0.057264	0.057264	0.057264
59	MISCELLANEOUS RETAIL	1	0.145238	0.145238	0.145238	0.145238	0.145238	0.145238	0.145238	0.145238	0.145238	0.145238	0.145238
598	FUEL DEALERS	1	0.145238	0.145238	0.145238	0.145238	0.145238	0.145238	0.145238	0.145238	0.145238	0.145238	0.145238
5983	Fuel Oil Dealers	1	0.145238	0.145238	0.145238	0.145238	0.145238	0.145238	0.145238	0.145238	0.145238	0.145238	0.145238
	FINANCE, INSURANCE, AND REAL ESTATE												
60	DEPOSITORY INSTITUTIONS	88	0.188216	0.177964	-0.042859	-0.026876	-0.013045	0.156414	0.177964	0.193530	0.309744	0.370250	1.080337
602	COMMERCIAL BANKS	85	0.191645	0.179948	-0.035475	-0.021365	-0.008868	0.156891	0.179948	0.194659	0.311461	0.372999	1.108507
6021	National Commercial Banks	57	0.163884	0.179948	-0.015086	-0.003485	0.012640	0.163927	0.179948	0.191477	0.287531	0.304967	0.341432
6022	State Commercial Banks	19	0.224544	0.141302	-0.066753	-0.053957	-0.032631	0.128814	0.141302	0.180257	0.461805	1.179548	1.610193
6029	Commercial Banks, Not Elsewhere Classified	9	0.298011	0.257734	0.006816	0.026021	0.058029	0.257666	0.257734	0.270605	0.710962	0.834612	0.908803
603	SAVINGS INSTITUTIONS	3	0.091056	0.138172	-0.034491	-0.029205	-0.020396	0.102935	0.138172	0.145140	0.169526	0.171268	0.172313
6035	Savings Institutions, Federally Chartered	3	0.091056	0.138172	-0.034491	-0.029205	-0.020396	0.102935	0.138172	0.145140	0.169526	0.171268	0.172313
61	NONDEPOSITORY CREDIT INSTITUTIONS	31	0.688138	0.694996	0.027563	0.041539	0.053859	0.647081	0.694996	0.819393	1.409325	1.577840	1.671188
611	FEDERAL AND FEDERALLY-SPONSORED CREDIT AGENCIES	28	0.747994	0.748977	0.051764	0.055454	0.087536	0.678065	0.748977	0.824051	1.444322	1.593398	1.677411
6111	Federal And Federally-Sponsored Credit Agencies	28	0.747994	0.748977	0.051764	0.055454	0.087536	0.678065	0.748977	0.824051	1.444322	1.593398	1.677411
614	PERSONAL CREDIT INSTITUTIONS	2	0.115377	0.115377	0.020188	0.023102	0.027959	0.095951	0.115377	0.134803	0.202795	0.207651	0.210565
6141	Personal Credit Institutions	2	0.115377	0.115377	0.020188	0.023102	0.027959	0.095951	0.115377	0.134803	0.202795	0.207651	0.210565
6199	FINANCE SERVICES	1	0.157697	0.157697	0.157697	0.157697	0.157697	0.157697	0.157697	0.157697	0.157697	0.157697	0.157697

Betas of Preferred Stocks by SIC Codes as of March 31, 2017

SIC Code	Description	Number of Companies	Mean	Median	1st Percentile	2.5th Percentile	5th Percentile	40th Percentile	50th Percentile	60th Percentile	95th Percentile	97.5th Percentile	99th Percentile
62	SECURITY AND COMMODITY BROKERS, DEALERS, EXCHANGES, AND SERVICES	25	0.104137	0.160146	-1.004731	-0.518763	0.028723	0.142406	0.160146	0.174666	0.272424	0.288819	0.297039
621	SECURITY BROKERS, DEALERS, AND FLOTATION COMPANIES	19	0.096936	0.166969	-1.074332	-0.692764	-0.056818	0.146625	0.166969	0.189653	0.281970	0.292244	0.298408
6211	Security Brokers, Dealers, And Flotation Companies	19	0.096936	0.166969	-1.074332	-0.692764	-0.056818	0.146625	0.166969	0.189653	0.281970	0.292244	0.298408
628	SERVICES ALLIED WITH THE EXCHANGE OF SECURITIES OR COMMODITIES	6	0.126941	0.141571	0.023082	0.025902	0.030603	0.132496	0.141571	0.150645	0.210425	0.216013	0.219366
6282	Investment Advice	6	0.126941	0.141571	0.023082	0.025902	0.030603	0.132496	0.141571	0.150645	0.210425	0.216013	0.219366
63	INSURANCE CARRIERS	21	0.137076	0.126133	0.010358	0.028375	0.058403	0.121045	0.126133	0.138979	0.240028	0.251720	0.258735
631	LIFE INSURANCE	1	0.108427	0.108427	0.108427	0.108427	0.108427	0.108427	0.108427	0.108427	0.108427	0.108427	0.108427
6311	Life Insurance	1	0.108427	0.108427	0.108427	0.108427	0.108427	0.108427	0.108427	0.108427	0.108427	0.108427	0.108427
632	ACCIDENT AND HEALTH INSURANCE AND MEDICAL SERVICE PLANS	1	0.169904	0.169904	0.169904	0.169904	0.169904	0.169904	0.169904	0.169904	0.169904	0.169904	0.169904
6321	Accident And Health Insurance	1	0.169904	0.169904	0.169904	0.169904	0.169904	0.169904	0.169904	0.169904	0.169904	0.169904	0.169904
633	FIRE, MARINE, AND CASUALTY INSURANCE	19	0.136856	0.126133	0.009157	0.025372	0.052397	0.121987	0.126133	0.137052	0.242366	0.252889	0.259203
6331	Fire, Marine, And Casualty Insurance	19	0.136856	0.126133	0.009157	0.025372	0.052397	0.121987	0.126133	0.137052	0.242366	0.252889	0.259203
64	INSURANCE AGENTS, BROKERS, AND SERVICE	1	0.040955	0.040955	0.040955	0.040955	0.040955	0.040955	0.040955	0.040955	0.040955	0.040955	0.040955
641	INSURANCE AGENTS, BROKERS, AND SERVICE	1	0.040955	0.040955	0.040955	0.040955	0.040955	0.040955	0.040955	0.040955	0.040955	0.040955	0.040955
6411	Insurance Agents, Brokers, And Service	1	0.040955	0.040955	0.040955	0.040955	0.040955	0.040955	0.040955	0.040955	0.040955	0.040955	0.040955
65	REAL ESTATE	2	0.021719	0.021719	-0.061792	-0.059236	-0.054975	0.004676	0.021719	0.038762	0.098412	0.102673	0.105230
653	REAL ESTATE AGENTS AND MANAGERS	2	0.021719	0.021719	-0.061792	-0.059236	-0.054975	0.004676	0.021719	0.038762	0.098412	0.102673	0.105230
6531	Real Estate Agents And Managers	2	0.021719	0.021719	-0.061792	-0.059236	-0.054975	0.004676	0.021719	0.038762	0.098412	0.102673	0.105230
67	HOLDING AND OTHER INVESTMENT OFFICES	146	0.091307	0.086623	-0.105058	-0.093692	-0.081560	0.068594	0.086623	0.113413	0.296288	0.402083	0.435444
671	HOLDING OFFICES	3	0.054755	0.113413	-0.090230	-0.083996	-0.073606	0.071853	0.113413	0.119778	0.142056	0.143647	0.144602
6712	Offices Of Bank Holding Companies	3	0.054755	0.113413	-0.090230	-0.083996	-0.073606	0.071853	0.113413	0.119778	0.142056	0.143647	0.144602
672	INVESTMENT OFFICES	19	-0.031028	-0.013688	-0.266262	-0.213588	-0.125800	-0.031500	-0.013688	0.000308	0.052134	0.066177	0.074602
6726	Unit Investment Trusts, Face-Amount Certificate Offices	19	-0.031028	-0.013688	-0.266262	-0.213588	-0.125800	-0.031500	-0.013688	0.000308	0.052134	0.066177	0.074602
673	TRUSTS	3	0.079455	0.081990	0.041661	0.042895	0.044953	0.073760	0.081990	0.088699	0.112181	0.113859	0.114865
6733	Trusts, Except Educational, Religious, And Charitable	3	0.079455	0.081990	0.041661	0.042895	0.044953	0.073760	0.081990	0.088699	0.112181	0.113859	0.114865
679	MISCELLANEOUS INVESTING	121	0.111717	0.104668	-0.092631	-0.077923	-0.058832	0.081767	0.104668	0.128568	0.309676	0.403156	0.436779
6798	Real Estate Investment Trusts	120	0.112031	0.105858	-0.092664	-0.078226	-0.058928	0.083821	0.105858	0.128901	0.312089	0.403890	0.436833
6799	Investors, Not Elsewhere Classified	1	0.074029	0.074029	0.074029	0.074029	0.074029	0.074029	0.074029	0.074029	0.074029	0.074029	0.074029
	SERVICES												

Betas of Preferred Stocks by SIC Codes as of March 31, 2017

SIC Code	Description	Number of Companies	Mean	Median	1st Percentile	2.5th Percentile	5th Percentile	40th Percentile	50th Percentile	60th Percentile	95th Percentile	97.5th Percentile	99th Percentile
70	HOTELS, ROOMING HOUSES, CAMPS, AND OTHER LODGING PLACES	1	0.085486	0.085486	0.085486	0.085486	0.085486	0.085486	0.085486	0.085486	0.085486	0.085486	0.085486
701	HOTELS AND MOTELS	1	0.085486	0.085486	0.085486	0.085486	0.085486	0.085486	0.085486	0.085486	0.085486	0.085486	0.085486
7011	Hotels And Motels	1	0.085486	0.085486	0.085486	0.085486	0.085486	0.085486	0.085486	0.085486	0.085486	0.085486	0.085486
73	BUSINESS SERVICES	1	-0.088571	-0.088571	-0.088571	-0.088571	-0.088571	-0.088571	-0.088571	-0.088571	-0.088571	-0.088571	-0.088571
736	PERSONNEL SUPPLY SERVICES	1	-0.088571	-0.088571	-0.088571	-0.088571	-0.088571	-0.088571	-0.088571	-0.088571	-0.088571	-0.088571	-0.088571
7363	Help Supply Services	1	-0.088571	-0.088571	-0.088571	-0.088571	-0.088571	-0.088571	-0.088571	-0.088571	-0.088571	-0.088571	-0.088571
80	HEALTH SERVICES	1	0.204791	0.204791	0.204791	0.204791	0.204791	0.204791	0.204791	0.204791	0.204791	0.204791	0.204791
805	NURSING AND PERSONAL CARE FACILITIES	1	0.204791	0.204791	0.204791	0.204791	0.204791	0.204791	0.204791	0.204791	0.204791	0.204791	0.204791
8051	Skilled Nursing Care Facilities	1	0.204791	0.204791	0.204791	0.204791	0.204791	0.204791	0.204791	0.204791	0.204791	0.204791	0.204791

Down-market Betas of Preferred Stocks by SIC Codes as of March 31, 2017

Details:
Benchmark: S&P 500 Index
Returns period and frequency: 1 year of daily returns
Risk-free rate: Federal Funds Rate

SIC Code	Description	Number of Companies	Mean	Median	1st Percentile	2.5th Percentile	5th Percentile	40th Percentile	50th Percentile	60th Percentile	95th Percentile	97.5th Percentile	99th Percentile
	MINING												
13	OIL AND GAS EXTRACTION	12	1.097092	1.031922	-0.915697	-0.887490	-0.840479	0.350619	1.031922	1.764348	3.549722	3.758106	3.883136
131	CRUDE PETROLEUM AND NATURAL GAS	11	1.266241	1.629540	-0.904019	-0.858295	-0.782087	0.434303	1.629540	1.854220	3.587610	3.777050	3.890714
1311	Crude Petroleum And Natural Gas	11	1.266241	1.629540	-0.904019	-0.858295	-0.782087	0.434303	1.629540	1.854220	3.587610	3.777050	3.890714
132	NATURAL GAS LIQUIDS	1	-0.763551	-0.763551	-0.763551	-0.763551	-0.763551	-0.763551	-0.763551	-0.763551	-0.763551	-0.763551	-0.763551
1321	Natural Gas Liquids	1	-0.763551	-0.763551	-0.763551	-0.763551	-0.763551	-0.763551	-0.763551	-0.763551	-0.763551	-0.763551	-0.763551
	CONSTRUCTION												
15	CONSTRUCTION	2	1.090645	1.090645	0.028526	0.061040	0.115229	0.873886	1.090645	1.307404	2.066060	2.120250	2.152764
153	OPERATIVE BUILDERS	2	1.090645	1.090645	0.028526	0.061040	0.115229	0.873886	1.090645	1.307404	2.066060	2.120250	2.152764
1531	Operative Builders	2	1.090645	1.090645	0.028526	0.061040	0.115229	0.873886	1.090645	1.307404	2.066060	2.120250	2.152764
	MANUFACTURING												
20	FOOD AND KINDRED PRODUCTS	1	0.419663	0.419663	0.419663	0.419663	0.419663	0.419663	0.419663	0.419663	0.419663	0.419663	0.419663
207	FATS AND OILS	1	0.419663	0.419663	0.419663	0.419663	0.419663	0.419663	0.419663	0.419663	0.419663	0.419663	0.419663
2075	Soybean Oil Mills	1	0.419663	0.419663	0.419663	0.419663	0.419663	0.419663	0.419663	0.419663	0.419663	0.419663	0.419663
28	CHEMICALS AND ALLIED PRODUCTS	6	0.389630	0.267625	-0.327558	-0.323397	-0.316463	-0.213801	0.267625	0.749051	1.352474	1.426782	1.471367
282	PLASTICS MATERIALS AND SYNTHETIC RESINS, SYNTHETIC RUBBER, CELLULOSIC MANMADE FIBERS	1	1.501090	1.501090	1.501090	1.501090	1.501090	1.501090	1.501090	1.501090	1.501090	1.501090	1.501090
2821	Plastics Materials, Synthetic Resins, And Nonvulcanizable Elastomers	1	1.501090	1.501090	1.501090	1.501090	1.501090	1.501090	1.501090	1.501090	1.501090	1.501090	1.501090
283	DRUGS	3	0.441781	0.749051	-0.308744	-0.276363	-0.222394	0.533174	0.749051	0.780566	0.890868	0.898746	0.903474
2834	Pharmaceutical Preparations	2	0.827838	0.827838	0.750627	0.752990	0.756930	0.812081	0.827838	0.843595	0.898746	0.902686	0.905049
2835	In Vitro And In Vivo Diagnostic Substances	1	-0.330332	-0.330332	-0.330332	-0.330332	-0.330332	-0.330332	-0.330332	-0.330332	-0.330332	-0.330332	-0.330332
287	AGRICULTURAL CHEMICALS	2	-0.244328	-0.244328	-0.274243	-0.273328	-0.271801	-0.250433	-0.244328	-0.238222	-0.216854	-0.215327	-0.214412
2879	Pesticides And Agricultural Chemicals, Not Elsewhere Classified	2	-0.244328	-0.244328	-0.274243	-0.273328	-0.271801	-0.250433	-0.244328	-0.238222	-0.216854	-0.215327	-0.214412
29	PETROLEUM REFINING AND RELATED INDUSTRIES	1	1.195250	1.195250	1.195250	1.195250	1.195250	1.195250	1.195250	1.195250	1.195250	1.195250	1.195250
291	PETROLEUM REFINING	1	1.195250	1.195250	1.195250	1.195250	1.195250	1.195250	1.195250	1.195250	1.195250	1.195250	1.195250
2911	Petroleum Refining	1	1.195250	1.195250	1.195250	1.195250	1.195250	1.195250	1.195250	1.195250	1.195250	1.195250	1.195250
33	PRIMARY METAL INDUSTRIES	2	1.109885	1.109885	-0.095628	-0.058724	0.002782	0.863862	1.109885	1.355908	2.216989	2.278494	2.315398
331	STEEL WORKS, BLAST FURNACES, AND ROLLING AND FINISHING MILLS	1	2.340000	2.340000	2.340000	2.340000	2.340000	2.340000	2.340000	2.340000	2.340000	2.340000	2.340000

Down-market Betas of Preferred Stocks by SIC Codes as of March 31, 2017

SIC Code	Description	Number of Companies	Mean	Median	1st Percentile	2.5th Percentile	5th Percentile	40th Percentile	50th Percentile	60th Percentile	95th Percentile	97.5th Percentile	99th Percentile
3312	Steel Works, Blast Furnaces (Including Coke Ovens), And Rolling Mills	1	2.340000	2.340000	2.340000	2.340000	2.340000	2.340000	2.340000	2.340000	2.340000	2.340000	2.340000
333	PRIMARY SMELTING AND REFINING OF NONFERROUS METALS	1	-0.120230	-0.120230	-0.120230	-0.120230	-0.120230	-0.120230	-0.120230	-0.120230	-0.120230	-0.120230	-0.120230
3334	Primary Production Of Aluminum	1	-0.120230	-0.120230	-0.120230	-0.120230	-0.120230	-0.120230	-0.120230	-0.120230	-0.120230	-0.120230	-0.120230
34	FABRICATED METAL PRODUCTS, EXCEPT MACHINERY AND TRANSPORTATION EQUIPMENT	1	0.080897	0.080897	0.080897	0.080897	0.080897	0.080897	0.080897	0.080897	0.080897	0.080897	0.080897
341	METAL CANS AND SHIPPING CONTAINERS	1	0.080897	0.080897	0.080897	0.080897	0.080897	0.080897	0.080897	0.080897	0.080897	0.080897	0.080897
3412	Metal Shipping Barrels, Drums, Kegs, And Pails	1	0.080897	0.080897	0.080897	0.080897	0.080897	0.080897	0.080897	0.080897	0.080897	0.080897	0.080897
35	INDUSTRIAL AND COMMERCIAL MACHINERY AND COMPUTER EQUIPMENT	1	0.167880	0.167880	0.167880	0.167880	0.167880	0.167880	0.167880	0.167880	0.167880	0.167880	0.167880
358	REFRIGERATION AND SERVICE INDUSTRY MACHINERY	1	0.167880	0.167880	0.167880	0.167880	0.167880	0.167880	0.167880	0.167880	0.167880	0.167880	0.167880
3581	Automatic Vending Machines	1	0.167880	0.167880	0.167880	0.167880	0.167880	0.167880	0.167880	0.167880	0.167880	0.167880	0.167880
37	TRANSPORTATION EQUIPMENT	1	2.059000	2.059000	2.059000	2.059000	2.059000	2.059000	2.059000	2.059000	2.059000	2.059000	2.059000
371	MOTOR VEHICLES AND MOTOR VEHICLE EQUIPMENT	1	2.059000	2.059000	2.059000	2.059000	2.059000	2.059000	2.059000	2.059000	2.059000	2.059000	2.059000
3711	Motor Vehicles And Passenger Car Bodies	1	2.059000	2.059000	2.059000	2.059000	2.059000	2.059000	2.059000	2.059000	2.059000	2.059000	2.059000
	TRANSPORTATION, COMMUNICATIONS, ELECTRIC, GAS, AND SANITARY SERVICE												
40	RAILROAD TRANSPORTATION	1	-0.066404	-0.066404	-0.066404	-0.066404	-0.066404	-0.066404	-0.066404	-0.066404	-0.066404	-0.066404	-0.066404
401	RAILROADS	1	-0.066404	-0.066404	-0.066404	-0.066404	-0.066404	-0.066404	-0.066404	-0.066404	-0.066404	-0.066404	-0.066404
4011	Railroads, Line-Haul Operating	1	-0.066404	-0.066404	-0.066404	-0.066404	-0.066404	-0.066404	-0.066404	-0.066404	-0.066404	-0.066404	-0.066404
44	WATER TRANSPORTATION	14	0.324443	0.317490	-0.333965	-0.225034	-0.043481	0.290712	0.317490	0.407653	0.656866	0.750787	0.807139
441	DEEP SEA FOREIGN TRANSPORTATION OF FREIGHT	13	0.284423	0.307213	-0.339551	-0.238999	-0.071412	0.277885	0.307213	0.347738	0.542257	0.548989	0.553028
4412	Deep Sea Foreign Transportation Of Freight	13	0.284423	0.307213	-0.339551	-0.238999	-0.071412	0.277885	0.307213	0.347738	0.542257	0.548989	0.553028
449	SERVICES INCIDENTAL TO WATER TRANSPORTATION	1	0.844707	0.844707	0.844707	0.844707	0.844707	0.844707	0.844707	0.844707	0.844707	0.844707	0.844707
4499	Water Transportation Services, Not Elsewhere Classified	1	0.844707	0.844707	0.844707	0.844707	0.844707	0.844707	0.844707	0.844707	0.844707	0.844707	0.844707
45	TRANSPORTATION BY AIR	1	1.708780	1.708780	1.708780	1.708780	1.708780	1.708780	1.708780	1.708780	1.708780	1.708780	1.708780
451	AIR TRANSPORTATION, SCHEDULED, AND AIR COURIER SERVICES	1	1.708780	1.708780	1.708780	1.708780	1.708780	1.708780	1.708780	1.708780	1.708780	1.708780	1.708780
4512	Air Transportation, Scheduled	1	1.708780	1.708780	1.708780	1.708780	1.708780	1.708780	1.708780	1.708780	1.708780	1.708780	1.708780
47	TRANSPORTATION SERVICES	1	0.113137	0.113137	0.113137	0.113137	0.113137	0.113137	0.113137	0.113137	0.113137	0.113137	0.113137
473	ARRANGEMENT OF TRANSPORTATION OF FREIGHT AND CARGO	1	0.113137	0.113137	0.113137	0.113137	0.113137	0.113137	0.113137	0.113137	0.113137	0.113137	0.113137

Down-market Betas of Preferred Stocks by SIC Codes as of March 31, 2017

SIC Code	Description	Number of Companies	Mean	Median	1st Percentile	2.5th Percentile	5th Percentile	40th Percentile	50th Percentile	60th Percentile	95th Percentile	97.5th Percentile	99th Percentile
4731	Arrangement Of Transportation Of Freight And Cargo	1	0.113137	0.113137	0.113137	0.113137	0.113137	0.113137	0.113137	0.113137	0.113137	0.113137	0.113137
48	COMMUNICATIONS	3	0.922021	1.163380	0.243975	0.272120	0.319029	0.975746	1.163380	1.206198	1.356061	1.366766	1.373188
481	TELEPHONE COMMUNICATIONS	3	0.922021	1.163380	0.243975	0.272120	0.319029	0.975746	1.163380	1.206198	1.356061	1.366766	1.373188
4812	Radiotelephone Communications	1	1.163380	1.163380	1.163380	1.163380	1.163380	1.163380	1.163380	1.163380	1.163380	1.163380	1.163380
4813	Telephone Communications, Except Radiotelephone	2	0.801341	0.801341	0.236735	0.254018	0.282825	0.686115	0.801341	0.916567	1.319857	1.348664	1.365947
49	ELECTRIC, GAS, AND SANITARY SERVICES	22	0.252729	0.113263	-0.450115	-0.359329	-0.220905	0.069526	0.113263	0.161509	1.623021	2.131650	2.434368
491	ELECTRIC SERVICES	11	0.222153	0.087160	-0.174490	-0.164942	-0.149030	0.075971	0.087160	0.139366	1.001583	1.338376	1.540453
4911	Electric Services	11	0.222153	0.087160	-0.174490	-0.164942	-0.149030	0.075971	0.087160	0.139366	1.001583	1.338376	1.540453
492	GAS PRODUCTION AND DISTRIBUTION	2	0.271981	0.271981	-0.081031	-0.070225	-0.052214	0.199938	0.271981	0.344025	0.596176	0.614187	0.624994
4923	Natural Gas Transmission And Distribution	1	0.632198	0.632198	0.632198	0.632198	0.632198	0.632198	0.632198	0.632198	0.632198	0.632198	0.632198
4924	Natural Gas Distribution	1	-0.088236	-0.088236	-0.088236	-0.088236	-0.088236	-0.088236	-0.088236	-0.088236	-0.088236	-0.088236	-0.088236
493	COMBINATION ELECTRIC AND GAS, AND OTHER UTILITY SERVICES	9	0.285823	0.168389	-0.487581	-0.452997	-0.395355	-0.092882	0.168389	0.223164	1.724034	2.180107	2.453751
4931	Electric And Other Services Combined	9	0.285823	0.168389	-0.487581	-0.452997	-0.395355	-0.092882	0.168389	0.223164	1.724034	2.180107	2.453751
	WHOLESALE TRADE												
50	WHOLESALE TRADE¨DURABLE GOODS	1	0.063532	0.063532	0.063532	0.063532	0.063532	0.063532	0.063532	0.063532	0.063532	0.063532	0.063532
507	HARDWARE, AND PLUMBING AND HEATING EQUIPMENT AND SUPPLIES	1	0.063532	0.063532	0.063532	0.063532	0.063532	0.063532	0.063532	0.063532	0.063532	0.063532	0.063532
5072	Hardware	1	0.063532	0.063532	0.063532	0.063532	0.063532	0.063532	0.063532	0.063532	0.063532	0.063532	0.063532
59	MISCELLANEOUS RETAIL	1	0.260135	0.260135	0.260135	0.260135	0.260135	0.260135	0.260135	0.260135	0.260135	0.260135	0.260135
598	FUEL DEALERS	1	0.260135	0.260135	0.260135	0.260135	0.260135	0.260135	0.260135	0.260135	0.260135	0.260135	0.260135
5983	Fuel Oil Dealers	1	0.260135	0.260135	0.260135	0.260135	0.260135	0.260135	0.260135	0.260135	0.260135	0.260135	0.260135
	FINANCE, INSURANCE, AND REAL ESTATE												
60	DEPOSITORY INSTITUTIONS	88	0.239363	0.237732	-0.182378	-0.140795	-0.058553	0.210322	0.237732	0.269136	0.492255	0.545636	1.192168
602	COMMERCIAL BANKS	85	0.242628	0.242166	-0.190007	-0.144439	-0.062831	0.215848	0.242166	0.270341	0.493494	0.548304	1.214173
6021	National Commercial Banks	57	0.203197	0.242166	-0.261207	-0.129876	-0.074970	0.216575	0.242166	0.269639	0.370160	0.392396	0.441688
6022	State Commercial Banks	19	0.287431	0.235564	-0.129627	-0.100121	-0.050943	0.204189	0.235564	0.251859	0.579012	1.204671	1.580066
6029	Commercial Banks, Not Elsewhere Classified	9	0.397776	0.450697	0.019067	0.029592	0.047133	0.273803	0.450697	0.479649	0.878831	0.987820	1.053214
603	SAVINGS INSTITUTIONS	3	0.146839	0.181024	0.074276	0.077544	0.082990	0.159239	0.181024	0.182298	0.186758	0.187076	0.187268
6035	Savings Institutions, Federally Chartered	3	0.146839	0.181024	0.074276	0.077544	0.082990	0.159239	0.181024	0.182298	0.186758	0.187076	0.187268
61	NONDEPOSITORY CREDIT INSTITUTIONS	31	1.003172	0.959555	-0.178831	-0.171306	-0.028194	0.617937	0.959555	1.056490	2.199680	2.564690	2.968844
611	FEDERAL AND FEDERALLY-SPONSORED CREDIT AGENCIES	28	1.097206	1.028800	-0.104310	0.014997	0.211433	0.784119	1.028800	1.243084	2.241824	2.632049	2.995788
6111	Federal And Federally-Sponsored Credit Agencies	28	1.097206	1.028800	-0.104310	0.014997	0.211433	0.784119	1.028800	1.243084	2.241824	2.632049	2.995788
614	PERSONAL CREDIT INSTITUTIONS	2	0.063807	0.063807	-0.162506	-0.155578	-0.144032	0.017621	0.063807	0.109993	0.271646	0.283192	0.290120

Down-market Betas of Preferred Stocks by SIC Codes as of March 31, 2017

SIC Code	Description	Number of Companies	Mean	Median	1st Percentile	2.5th Percentile	5th Percentile	40th Percentile	50th Percentile	60th Percentile	95th Percentile	97.5th Percentile	99th Percentile
6141	Personal Credit Institutions	2	0.063807	0.063807	-0.162506	-0.155578	-0.144032	0.017621	0.063807	0.109993	0.271646	0.283192	0.290120
6199	FINANCE SERVICES	1	0.248945	0.248945	0.248945	0.248945	0.248945	0.248945	0.248945	0.248945	0.248945	0.248945	0.248945
62	SECURITY AND COMMODITY BROKERS, DEALERS, EXCHANGES, AND SERVICES	25	-0.005078	0.227714	-4.214996	-2.230414	-0.011012	0.214659	0.227714	0.240241	0.376439	0.397070	0.408175
621	SECURITY BROKERS, DEALERS, AND FLOTATION COMPANIES	19	-0.048637	0.229375	-4.523194	-3.000910	-0.463770	0.227927	0.229375	0.258458	0.387816	0.401697	0.410026
6211	Security Brokers, Dealers, And Flotation Companies	19	-0.048637	0.229375	-4.523194	-3.000910	-0.463770	0.227927	0.229375	0.258458	0.387816	0.401697	0.410026
628	SERVICES ALLIED WITH THE EXCHANGE OF SECURITIES OR COMMODITIES	6	0.132861	0.156620	-0.021746	-0.016379	-0.007434	0.117903	0.156620	0.195337	0.247211	0.255064	0.259776
6282	Investment Advice	6	0.132861	0.156620	-0.021746	-0.016379	-0.007434	0.117903	0.156620	0.195337	0.247211	0.255064	0.259776
63	INSURANCE CARRIERS	21	0.230518	0.258518	-0.019981	-0.004661	0.020872	0.188683	0.258518	0.276704	0.395427	0.411032	0.420395
631	LIFE INSURANCE	1	0.314876	0.314876	0.314876	0.314876	0.314876	0.314876	0.314876	0.314876	0.314876	0.314876	0.314876
6311	Life Insurance	1	0.314876	0.314876	0.314876	0.314876	0.314876	0.314876	0.314876	0.314876	0.314876	0.314876	0.314876
632	ACCIDENT AND HEALTH INSURANCE AND MEDICAL SERVICE PLANS	1	0.188683	0.188683	0.188683	0.188683	0.188683	0.188683	0.188683	0.188683	0.188683	0.188683	0.188683
6321	Accident And Health Insurance	1	0.188683	0.188683	0.188683	0.188683	0.188683	0.188683	0.188683	0.188683	0.188683	0.188683	0.188683
633	FIRE, MARINE, AND CASUALTY INSURANCE	19	0.228280	0.258518	-0.021002	-0.007215	0.015765	0.167307	0.258518	0.275175	0.398548	0.412593	0.421019
6331	Fire, Marine, And Casualty Insurance	19	0.228280	0.258518	-0.021002	-0.007215	0.015765	0.167307	0.258518	0.275175	0.398548	0.412593	0.421019
64	INSURANCE AGENTS, BROKERS, AND SERVICE	1	0.142904	0.142904	0.142904	0.142904	0.142904	0.142904	0.142904	0.142904	0.142904	0.142904	0.142904
641	INSURANCE AGENTS, BROKERS, AND SERVICE	1	0.142904	0.142904	0.142904	0.142904	0.142904	0.142904	0.142904	0.142904	0.142904	0.142904	0.142904
6411	Insurance Agents, Brokers, And Service	1	0.142904	0.142904	0.142904	0.142904	0.142904	0.142904	0.142904	0.142904	0.142904	0.142904	0.142904
65	REAL ESTATE	2	0.173466	0.173466	0.029740	0.034139	0.041472	0.144134	0.173466	0.202798	0.305459	0.312792	0.317192
653	REAL ESTATE AGENTS AND MANAGERS	2	0.173466	0.173466	0.029740	0.034139	0.041472	0.144134	0.173466	0.202798	0.305459	0.312792	0.317192
6531	Real Estate Agents And Managers	2	0.173466	0.173466	0.029740	0.034139	0.041472	0.144134	0.173466	0.202798	0.305459	0.312792	0.317192
67	HOLDING AND OTHER INVESTMENT OFFICES	146	0.113202	0.116333	-0.372916	-0.296898	-0.181451	0.083318	0.116333	0.162785	0.401252	0.496424	0.637688
671	HOLDING OFFICES	3	0.020943	0.186056	-0.368951	-0.351961	-0.323645	0.072789	0.186056	0.200255	0.249952	0.253502	0.255632
6712	Offices Of Bank Holding Companies	3	0.020943	0.186056	-0.368951	-0.351961	-0.323645	0.072789	0.186056	0.200255	0.249952	0.253502	0.255632
672	INVESTMENT OFFICES	19	-0.034253	-0.038299	-0.312794	-0.270275	-0.199410	-0.051129	-0.038299	0.004527	0.116332	0.135667	0.147269
6726	Unit Investment Trusts, Face-Amount Certificate Offices	19	-0.034253	-0.038299	-0.312794	-0.270275	-0.199410	-0.051129	-0.038299	0.004527	0.116332	0.135667	0.147269
673	TRUSTS	3	0.141067	0.164510	0.027939	0.032120	0.039088	0.136638	0.164510	0.178316	0.226636	0.230088	0.232158
6733	Trusts, Except Educational, Religious, And Charitable	3	0.141067	0.164510	0.027939	0.032120	0.039088	0.136638	0.164510	0.178316	0.226636	0.230088	0.232158
679	MISCELLANEOUS INVESTING	121	0.137953	0.146653	-0.345205	-0.202281	-0.156626	0.104043	0.146653	0.171003	0.408692	0.600031	0.638138
6798	Real Estate Investment Trusts	120	0.139022	0.147159	-0.346140	-0.203983	-0.157536	0.107074	0.147159	0.171664	0.408861	0.600948	0.638156

Down-market Betas of Preferred Stocks by SIC Codes as of March 31, 2017

SIC Code	Description	Number of Companies	Mean	Median	1st Percentile	2.5th Percentile	5th Percentile	40th Percentile	50th Percentile	60th Percentile	95th Percentile	97.5th Percentile	99th Percentile
6799	Investors, Not Elsewhere Classified	1	0.009679	0.009679	0.009679	0.009679	0.009679	0.009679	0.009679	0.009679	0.009679	0.009679	0.009679
	SERVICES												
70	HOTELS, ROOMING HOUSES, CAMPS, AND OTHER LODGING PLACES	1	0.206238	0.206238	0.206238	0.206238	0.206238	0.206238	0.206238	0.206238	0.206238	0.206238	0.206238
701	HOTELS AND MOTELS	1	0.206238	0.206238	0.206238	0.206238	0.206238	0.206238	0.206238	0.206238	0.206238	0.206238	0.206238
7011	Hotels And Motels	1	0.206238	0.206238	0.206238	0.206238	0.206238	0.206238	0.206238	0.206238	0.206238	0.206238	0.206238
73	BUSINESS SERVICES	1	0.265148	0.265148	0.265148	0.265148	0.265148	0.265148	0.265148	0.265148	0.265148	0.265148	0.265148
736	PERSONNEL SUPPLY SERVICES	1	0.265148	0.265148	0.265148	0.265148	0.265148	0.265148	0.265148	0.265148	0.265148	0.265148	0.265148
7363	Help Supply Services	1	0.265148	0.265148	0.265148	0.265148	0.265148	0.265148	0.265148	0.265148	0.265148	0.265148	0.265148
80	HEALTH SERVICES	1	0.082681	0.082681	0.082681	0.082681	0.082681	0.082681	0.082681	0.082681	0.082681	0.082681	0.082681
805	NURSING AND PERSONAL CARE FACILITIES	1	0.082681	0.082681	0.082681	0.082681	0.082681	0.082681	0.082681	0.082681	0.082681	0.082681	0.082681
8051	Skilled Nursing Care Facilities	1	0.082681	0.082681	0.082681	0.082681	0.082681	0.082681	0.082681	0.082681	0.082681	0.082681	0.082681

Up-market Betas of Preferred Stocks by SIC Codes as of March 31, 2017

Details:

Benchmark: S&P 500 Index

Returns period and frequency: 1 year of daily returns

Risk-free rate: Federal Funds Rate

SIC Code	Description	Number of Companies	Mean	Median	1st Percentile	2.5th Percentile	5th Percentile	40th Percentile	50th Percentile	60th Percentile	95th Percentile	97.5th Percentile	99th Percentile
	MINING												
13	OIL AND GAS EXTRACTION	12	0.857144	0.813686	-0.620291	-0.524584	-0.365073	0.540316	0.813686	1.252854	1.899048	1.927439	1.944474
131	CRUDE PETROLEUM AND NATURAL GAS	11	0.893767	0.958020	-0.626091	-0.539085	-0.394075	0.669352	0.958020	1.449410	1.904210	1.930020	1.945506
1311	Crude Petroleum And Natural Gas	11	0.893767	0.958020	-0.626091	-0.539085	-0.394075	0.669352	0.958020	1.449410	1.904210	1.930020	1.945506
132	NATURAL GAS LIQUIDS	1	0.454292	0.454292	0.454292	0.454292	0.454292	0.454292	0.454292	0.454292	0.454292	0.454292	0.454292
1321	Natural Gas Liquids	1	0.454292	0.454292	0.454292	0.454292	0.454292	0.454292	0.454292	0.454292	0.454292	0.454292	0.454292
	CONSTRUCTION												
15	CONSTRUCTION	2	0.950218	0.950218	-0.002746	0.026427	0.075047	0.755736	0.950218	1.144700	1.825389	1.874009	1.903182
153	OPERATIVE BUILDERS	2	0.950218	0.950218	-0.002746	0.026427	0.075047	0.755736	0.950218	1.144700	1.825389	1.874009	1.903182
1531	Operative Builders	2	0.950218	0.950218	-0.002746	0.026427	0.075047	0.755736	0.950218	1.144700	1.825389	1.874009	1.903182
	MANUFACTURING												
20	FOOD AND KINDRED PRODUCTS	1	0.734540	0.734540	0.734540	0.734540	0.734540	0.734540	0.734540	0.734540	0.734540	0.734540	0.734540
207	FATS AND OILS	1	0.734540	0.734540	0.734540	0.734540	0.734540	0.734540	0.734540	0.734540	0.734540	0.734540	0.734540
2075	Soybean Oil Mills	1	0.734540	0.734540	0.734540	0.734540	0.734540	0.734540	0.734540	0.734540	0.734540	0.734540	0.734540
28	CHEMICALS AND ALLIED PRODUCTS	6	0.570484	0.491596	-0.039600	-0.018884	0.015641	0.300725	0.491596	0.682466	1.242221	1.295751	1.327868
282	PLASTICS MATERIALS AND SYNTHETIC RESINS, SYNTHETIC RUBBER, CELLULOSIC MANMADE FIBERS	1	1.349280	1.349280	1.349280	1.349280	1.349280	1.349280	1.349280	1.349280	1.349280	1.349280	1.349280
2821	Plastics Materials, Synthetic Resins, And Nonvulcanizable Elastomers	1	1.349280	1.349280	1.349280	1.349280	1.349280	1.349280	1.349280	1.349280	1.349280	1.349280	1.349280
283	DRUGS	3	0.608769	0.682466	0.231989	0.245780	0.268763	0.590532	0.682466	0.730182	0.897187	0.909116	0.916273
2834	Pharmaceutical Preparations	2	0.801756	0.801756	0.684852	0.688430	0.694395	0.777898	0.801756	0.825613	0.909116	0.915081	0.918659
2835	In Vitro And In Vivo Diagnostic Substances	1	0.222796	0.222796	0.222796	0.222796	0.222796	0.222796	0.222796	0.222796	0.222796	0.222796	0.222796
287	AGRICULTURAL CHEMICALS	2	0.123657	0.123657	-0.049869	-0.044557	-0.035703	0.088244	0.123657	0.159071	0.283018	0.291872	0.297184
2879	Pesticides And Agricultural Chemicals, Not Elsewhere Classified	2	0.123657	0.123657	-0.049869	-0.044557	-0.035703	0.088244	0.123657	0.159071	0.283018	0.291872	0.297184
29	PETROLEUM REFINING AND RELATED INDUSTRIES	1	1.401030	1.401030	1.401030	1.401030	1.401030	1.401030	1.401030	1.401030	1.401030	1.401030	1.401030
291	PETROLEUM REFINING	1	1.401030	1.401030	1.401030	1.401030	1.401030	1.401030	1.401030	1.401030	1.401030	1.401030	1.401030
2911	Petroleum Refining	1	1.401030	1.401030	1.401030	1.401030	1.401030	1.401030	1.401030	1.401030	1.401030	1.401030	1.401030
33	PRIMARY METAL INDUSTRIES	2	0.059529	0.059529	-0.431226	-0.416203	-0.391164	-0.040625	0.059529	0.159683	0.510222	0.535261	0.550284
331	STEEL WORKS, BLAST FURNACES, AND ROLLING AND FINISHING MILLS	1	0.560299	0.560299	0.560299	0.560299	0.560299	0.560299	0.560299	0.560299	0.560299	0.560299	0.560299

Up-market Betas of Preferred Stocks by SIC Codes as of March 31, 2017

SIC Code	Description	Number of Companies	Mean	Median	1st Percentile	2.5th Percentile	5th Percentile	40th Percentile	50th Percentile	60th Percentile	95th Percentile	97.5th Percentile	99th Percentile
3312	Steel Works, Blast Furnaces (Including Coke Ovens), And Rolling Mills	1	0.560299	0.560299	0.560299	0.560299	0.560299	0.560299	0.560299	0.560299	0.560299	0.560299	0.560299
333	PRIMARY SMELTING AND REFINING OF NONFERROUS METALS	1	-0.441241	-0.441241	-0.441241	-0.441241	-0.441241	-0.441241	-0.441241	-0.441241	-0.441241	-0.441241	-0.441241
3334	Primary Production Of Aluminum	1	-0.441241	-0.441241	-0.441241	-0.441241	-0.441241	-0.441241	-0.441241	-0.441241	-0.441241	-0.441241	-0.441241
34	FABRICATED METAL PRODUCTS, EXCEPT MACHINERY AND TRANSPORTATION EQUIPMENT	1	-0.018386	-0.018386	-0.018386	-0.018386	-0.018386	-0.018386	-0.018386	-0.018386	-0.018386	-0.018386	-0.018386
341	METAL CANS AND SHIPPING CONTAINERS	1	-0.018386	-0.018386	-0.018386	-0.018386	-0.018386	-0.018386	-0.018386	-0.018386	-0.018386	-0.018386	-0.018386
3412	Metal Shipping Barrels, Drums, Kegs, And Pails	1	-0.018386	-0.018386	-0.018386	-0.018386	-0.018386	-0.018386	-0.018386	-0.018386	-0.018386	-0.018386	-0.018386
35	INDUSTRIAL AND COMMERCIAL MACHINERY AND COMPUTER EQUIPMENT	1	0.026272	0.026272	0.026272	0.026272	0.026272	0.026272	0.026272	0.026272	0.026272	0.026272	0.026272
358	REFRIGERATION AND SERVICE INDUSTRY MACHINERY	1	0.026272	0.026272	0.026272	0.026272	0.026272	0.026272	0.026272	0.026272	0.026272	0.026272	0.026272
3581	Automatic Vending Machines	1	0.026272	0.026272	0.026272	0.026272	0.026272	0.026272	0.026272	0.026272	0.026272	0.026272	0.026272
37	TRANSPORTATION EQUIPMENT	1	0.832713	0.832713	0.832713	0.832713	0.832713	0.832713	0.832713	0.832713	0.832713	0.832713	0.832713
371	MOTOR VEHICLES AND MOTOR VEHICLE EQUIPMENT	1	0.832713	0.832713	0.832713	0.832713	0.832713	0.832713	0.832713	0.832713	0.832713	0.832713	0.832713
3711	Motor Vehicles And Passenger Car Bodies	1	0.832713	0.832713	0.832713	0.832713	0.832713	0.832713	0.832713	0.832713	0.832713	0.832713	0.832713
	TRANSPORTATION, COMMUNICATIONS, ELECTRIC, GAS, AND SANITARY SERVICE												
40	RAILROAD TRANSPORTATION	1	0.349609	0.349609	0.349609	0.349609	0.349609	0.349609	0.349609	0.349609	0.349609	0.349609	0.349609
401	RAILROADS	1	0.349609	0.349609	0.349609	0.349609	0.349609	0.349609	0.349609	0.349609	0.349609	0.349609	0.349609
4011	Railroads, Line-Haul Operating	1	0.349609	0.349609	0.349609	0.349609	0.349609	0.349609	0.349609	0.349609	0.349609	0.349609	0.349609
44	WATER TRANSPORTATION	14	0.497343	0.336340	-0.046234	-0.044542	-0.041722	0.262434	0.336340	0.415462	1.493464	1.647322	1.739637
441	DEEP SEA FOREIGN TRANSPORTATION OF FREIGHT	13	0.497579	0.265392	-0.046321	-0.044759	-0.042156	0.243866	0.265392	0.409332	1.517134	1.659157	1.744371
4412	Deep Sea Foreign Transportation Of Freight	13	0.497579	0.265392	-0.046321	-0.044759	-0.042156	0.243866	0.265392	0.409332	1.517134	1.659157	1.744371
449	SERVICES INCIDENTAL TO WATER TRANSPORTATION	1	0.494274	0.494274	0.494274	0.494274	0.494274	0.494274	0.494274	0.494274	0.494274	0.494274	0.494274
4499	Water Transportation Services, Not Elsewhere Classified	1	0.494274	0.494274	0.494274	0.494274	0.494274	0.494274	0.494274	0.494274	0.494274	0.494274	0.494274
45	TRANSPORTATION BY AIR	1	1.355940	1.355940	1.355940	1.355940	1.355940	1.355940	1.355940	1.355940	1.355940	1.355940	1.355940
451	AIR TRANSPORTATION, SCHEDULED, AND AIR COURIER SERVICES	1	1.355940	1.355940	1.355940	1.355940	1.355940	1.355940	1.355940	1.355940	1.355940	1.355940	1.355940
4512	Air Transportation, Scheduled	1	1.355940	1.355940	1.355940	1.355940	1.355940	1.355940	1.355940	1.355940	1.355940	1.355940	1.355940
47	TRANSPORTATION SERVICES	1	-0.083737	-0.083737	-0.083737	-0.083737	-0.083737	-0.083737	-0.083737	-0.083737	-0.083737	-0.083737	-0.083737
473	ARRANGEMENT OF TRANSPORTATION OF FREIGHT AND CARGO	1	-0.083737	-0.083737	-0.083737	-0.083737	-0.083737	-0.083737	-0.083737	-0.083737	-0.083737	-0.083737	-0.083737

Up-market Betas of Preferred Stocks by SIC Codes as of March 31, 2017

SIC Code	Description	Number of Companies	Mean	Median	1st Percentile	2.5th Percentile	5th Percentile	40th Percentile	50th Percentile	60th Percentile	95th Percentile	97.5th Percentile	99th Percentile
4731	Arrangement Of Transportation Of Freight And Cargo	1	-0.083737	-0.083737	-0.083737	-0.083737	-0.083737	-0.083737	-0.083737	-0.083737	-0.083737	-0.083737	-0.083737
48	COMMUNICATIONS	3	0.757586	0.940694	0.045876	0.073269	0.118923	0.758078	0.940694	1.013445	1.268074	1.286262	1.297175
481	TELEPHONE COMMUNICATIONS	3	0.757586	0.940694	0.045876	0.073269	0.118923	0.758078	0.940694	1.013445	1.268074	1.286262	1.297175
4812	Radiotelephone Communications	1	1.304450	1.304450	1.304450	1.304450	1.304450	1.304450	1.304450	1.304450	1.304450	1.304450	1.304450
4813	Telephone Communications, Except Radiotelephone	2	0.484154	0.484154	0.036746	0.050442	0.073269	0.392847	0.484154	0.575462	0.895040	0.917867	0.931563
49	ELECTRIC, GAS, AND SANITARY SERVICES	22	0.266468	0.017782	-0.150686	-0.141561	-0.126785	-0.051661	0.017782	0.135128	1.610951	2.023523	2.267739
491	ELECTRIC SERVICES	11	0.133464	-0.053637	-0.153872	-0.149527	-0.142285	-0.057319	-0.053637	-0.044456	0.912564	1.283912	1.506721
4911	Electric Services	11	0.133464	-0.053637	-0.153872	-0.149527	-0.142285	-0.057319	-0.053637	-0.044456	0.912564	1.283912	1.506721
492	GAS PRODUCTION AND DISTRIBUTION	2	0.250874	0.250874	-0.086462	-0.076135	-0.058924	0.182030	0.250874	0.319718	0.560672	0.577883	0.588210
4923	Natural Gas Transmission And Distribution	1	0.595094	0.595094	0.595094	0.595094	0.595094	0.595094	0.595094	0.595094	0.595094	0.595094	0.595094
4924	Natural Gas Distribution	1	-0.093346	-0.093346	-0.093346	-0.093346	-0.093346	-0.093346	-0.093346	-0.093346	-0.093346	-0.093346	-0.093346
493	COMBINATION ELECTRIC AND GAS, AND OTHER UTILITY SERVICES	9	0.432495	0.244782	-0.106727	-0.105582	-0.103673	0.112973	0.244782	0.251278	1.765958	2.098254	2.297632
4931	Electric And Other Services Combined	9	0.432495	0.244782	-0.106727	-0.105582	-0.103673	0.112973	0.244782	0.251278	1.765958	2.098254	2.297632
	WHOLESALE TRADE												
50	WHOLESALE TRADE¨DURABLE GOODS	1	-0.054326	-0.054326	-0.054326	-0.054326	-0.054326	-0.054326	-0.054326	-0.054326	-0.054326	-0.054326	-0.054326
507	HARDWARE, AND PLUMBING AND HEATING EQUIPMENT AND SUPPLIES	1	-0.054326	-0.054326	-0.054326	-0.054326	-0.054326	-0.054326	-0.054326	-0.054326	-0.054326	-0.054326	-0.054326
5072	Hardware	1	-0.054326	-0.054326	-0.054326	-0.054326	-0.054326	-0.054326	-0.054326	-0.054326	-0.054326	-0.054326	-0.054326
59	MISCELLANEOUS RETAIL	1	0.193623	0.193623	0.193623	0.193623	0.193623	0.193623	0.193623	0.193623	0.193623	0.193623	0.193623
598	FUEL DEALERS	1	0.193623	0.193623	0.193623	0.193623	0.193623	0.193623	0.193623	0.193623	0.193623	0.193623	0.193623
5983	Fuel Oil Dealers	1	0.193623	0.193623	0.193623	0.193623	0.193623	0.193623	0.193623	0.193623	0.193623	0.193623	0.193623
	FINANCE, INSURANCE, AND REAL ESTATE												
60	DEPOSITORY INSTITUTIONS	88	0.169127	0.150490	-0.197327	-0.141061	-0.109371	0.120456	0.150490	0.178389	0.394052	0.476020	0.791877
602	COMMERCIAL BANKS	85	0.172516	0.153112	-0.201412	-0.141895	-0.112924	0.119729	0.153112	0.179347	0.396744	0.477193	0.830174
6021	National Commercial Banks	57	0.159207	0.165523	-0.078498	-0.014271	0.021568	0.124537	0.165523	0.178746	0.312076	0.356562	0.424789
6022	State Commercial Banks	19	0.171940	0.088446	-0.291282	-0.254517	-0.193242	0.061698	0.088446	0.145999	0.550549	1.226514	1.632094
6029	Commercial Banks, Not Elsewhere Classified	9	0.258020	0.207104	0.014851	0.030687	0.057082	0.171721	0.207104	0.242064	0.560805	0.593365	0.612901
603	SAVINGS INSTITUTIONS	3	0.073100	0.133864	-0.064720	-0.058641	-0.048509	0.093337	0.133864	0.137933	0.152174	0.153191	0.153801
6035	Savings Institutions, Federally Chartered	3	0.073100	0.133864	-0.064720	-0.058641	-0.048509	0.093337	0.133864	0.137933	0.152174	0.153191	0.153801
61	NONDEPOSITORY CREDIT INSTITUTIONS	31	0.862773	0.887353	-0.337416	-0.123617	0.010696	0.720274	0.887353	1.036370	1.862150	1.986635	1.987058
611	FEDERAL AND FEDERALLY-SPONSORED CREDIT AGENCIES	28	0.934005	0.900588	-0.351669	-0.159250	0.006035	0.825134	0.900588	1.162194	1.899425	1.986706	1.987086
6111	Federal And Federally-Sponsored Credit Agencies	28	0.934005	0.900588	-0.351669	-0.159250	0.006035	0.825134	0.900588	1.162194	1.899425	1.986706	1.987086
614	PERSONAL CREDIT INSTITUTIONS	2	0.232350	0.232350	0.221941	0.222260	0.222791	0.230225	0.232350	0.234474	0.241908	0.242439	0.242758

Up-market Betas of Preferred Stocks by SIC Codes as of March 31, 2017

SIC Code	Description	Number of Companies	Mean	Median	1st Percentile	2.5th Percentile	5th Percentile	40th Percentile	50th Percentile	60th Percentile	95th Percentile	97.5th Percentile	99th Percentile
6141	Personal Credit Institutions	2	0.232350	0.232350	0.221941	0.222260	0.222791	0.230225	0.232350	0.234474	0.241908	0.242439	0.242758
6199	FINANCE SERVICES	1	0.129120	0.129120	0.129120	0.129120	0.129120	0.129120	0.129120	0.129120	0.129120	0.129120	0.129120
62	SECURITY AND COMMODITY BROKERS, DEALERS, EXCHANGES, AND SERVICES	25	0.289693	0.101434	-0.065648	-0.059520	-0.049176	0.081356	0.101434	0.128543	0.263994	2.212633	3.960131
621	SECURITY BROKERS, DEALERS, AND FLOTATION COMPANIES	19	0.374967	0.128368	-0.032528	-0.028765	-0.022493	0.095011	0.128368	0.136132	0.756385	2.940758	4.251381
6211	Security Brokers, Dealers, And Flotation Companies	19	0.374967	0.128368	-0.032528	-0.028765	-0.022493	0.095011	0.128368	0.136132	0.756385	2.940758	4.251381
628	SERVICES ALLIED WITH THE EXCHANGE OF SECURITIES OR COMMODITIES	6	0.019660	-0.007608	-0.068883	-0.067606	-0.065478	-0.013892	-0.007608	-0.001323	0.140998	0.147592	0.151548
6282	Investment Advice	6	0.019660	-0.007608	-0.068883	-0.067606	-0.065478	-0.013892	-0.007608	-0.001323	0.140998	0.147592	0.151548
63	INSURANCE CARRIERS	21	0.125134	0.106606	-0.002302	-0.001266	0.000462	0.094004	0.106606	0.137613	0.266893	0.313991	0.342250
631	LIFE INSURANCE	1	0.020405	0.020405	0.020405	0.020405	0.020405	0.020405	0.020405	0.020405	0.020405	0.020405	0.020405
6311	Life Insurance	1	0.020405	0.020405	0.020405	0.020405	0.020405	0.020405	0.020405	0.020405	0.020405	0.020405	0.020405
632	ACCIDENT AND HEALTH INSURANCE AND MEDICAL SERVICE PLANS	1	0.143544	0.143544	0.143544	0.143544	0.143544	0.143544	0.143544	0.143544	0.143544	0.143544	0.143544
6321	Accident And Health Insurance	1	0.143544	0.143544	0.143544	0.143544	0.143544	0.143544	0.143544	0.143544	0.143544	0.143544	0.143544
633	FIRE, MARINE, AND CASUALTY INSURANCE	19	0.129677	0.106606	-0.002371	-0.001438	0.000117	0.096348	0.106606	0.134601	0.276313	0.318701	0.344134
6331	Fire, Marine, And Casualty Insurance	19	0.129677	0.106606	-0.002371	-0.001438	0.000117	0.096348	0.106606	0.134601	0.276313	0.318701	0.344134
64	INSURANCE AGENTS, BROKERS, AND SERVICE	1	0.118931	0.118931	0.118931	0.118931	0.118931	0.118931	0.118931	0.118931	0.118931	0.118931	0.118931
641	INSURANCE AGENTS, BROKERS, AND SERVICE	1	0.118931	0.118931	0.118931	0.118931	0.118931	0.118931	0.118931	0.118931	0.118931	0.118931	0.118931
6411	Insurance Agents, Brokers, And Service	1	0.118931	0.118931	0.118931	0.118931	0.118931	0.118931	0.118931	0.118931	0.118931	0.118931	0.118931
65	REAL ESTATE	2	-0.054360	-0.054360	-0.176686	-0.172941	-0.166700	-0.079324	-0.054360	-0.029395	0.057981	0.064222	0.067967
653	REAL ESTATE AGENTS AND MANAGERS	2	-0.054360	-0.054360	-0.176686	-0.172941	-0.166700	-0.079324	-0.054360	-0.029395	0.057981	0.064222	0.067967
6531	Real Estate Agents And Managers	2	-0.054360	-0.054360	-0.176686	-0.172941	-0.166700	-0.079324	-0.054360	-0.029395	0.057981	0.064222	0.067967
67	HOLDING AND OTHER INVESTMENT OFFICES	146	0.071102	0.063918	-0.228953	-0.195415	-0.148500	0.031822	0.063918	0.107501	0.294871	0.368378	0.515733
671	HOLDING OFFICES	3	-0.045144	0.025080	-0.189049	-0.182494	-0.171569	-0.018620	0.025080	0.026646	0.032126	0.032517	0.032752
6712	Offices Of Bank Holding Companies	3	-0.045144	0.025080	-0.189049	-0.182494	-0.171569	-0.018620	0.025080	0.026646	0.032126	0.032517	0.032752
672	INVESTMENT OFFICES	19	-0.004819	-0.013306	-0.209594	-0.183885	-0.141038	-0.035534	-0.013306	-0.006779	0.165547	0.215950	0.246193
6726	Unit Investment Trusts, Face-Amount Certificate Offices	19	-0.004819	-0.013306	-0.209594	-0.183885	-0.141038	-0.035534	-0.013306	-0.006779	0.165547	0.215950	0.246193
673	TRUSTS	3	0.076964	0.040504	0.016937	0.017658	0.018861	0.035694	0.040504	0.067189	0.160588	0.167260	0.171262
6733	Trusts, Except Educational, Religious, And Charitable	3	0.076964	0.040504	0.016937	0.017658	0.018861	0.035694	0.040504	0.067189	0.160588	0.167260	0.171262
679	MISCELLANEOUS INVESTING	121	0.085760	0.091640	-0.224364	-0.174100	-0.146893	0.046474	0.091640	0.126054	0.314945	0.380412	0.542820
6798	Real Estate Investment Trusts	120	0.085918	0.092314	-0.224684	-0.174716	-0.147000	0.044652	0.092314	0.126305	0.315406	0.382305	0.543904

Up-market Betas of Preferred Stocks by SIC Codes as of March 31, 2017

SIC Code	Description	Number of Companies	Mean	Median	1st Percentile	2.5th Percentile	5th Percentile	40th Percentile	50th Percentile	60th Percentile	95th Percentile	97.5th Percentile	99th Percentile
6799	Investors, Not Elsewhere Classified	1	0.066801	0.066801	0.066801	0.066801	0.066801	0.066801	0.066801	0.066801	0.066801	0.066801	0.066801
	SERVICES												
70	HOTELS, ROOMING HOUSES, CAMPS, AND OTHER LODGING PLACES	1	-0.046219	-0.046219	-0.046219	-0.046219	-0.046219	-0.046219	-0.046219	-0.046219	-0.046219	-0.046219	-0.046219
701	HOTELS AND MOTELS	1	-0.046219	-0.046219	-0.046219	-0.046219	-0.046219	-0.046219	-0.046219	-0.046219	-0.046219	-0.046219	-0.046219
7011	Hotels And Motels	1	-0.046219	-0.046219	-0.046219	-0.046219	-0.046219	-0.046219	-0.046219	-0.046219	-0.046219	-0.046219	-0.046219
73	BUSINESS SERVICES	1	-0.384912	-0.384912	-0.384912	-0.384912	-0.384912	-0.384912	-0.384912	-0.384912	-0.384912	-0.384912	-0.384912
736	PERSONNEL SUPPLY SERVICES	1	-0.384912	-0.384912	-0.384912	-0.384912	-0.384912	-0.384912	-0.384912	-0.384912	-0.384912	-0.384912	-0.384912
7363	Help Supply Services	1	-0.384912	-0.384912	-0.384912	-0.384912	-0.384912	-0.384912	-0.384912	-0.384912	-0.384912	-0.384912	-0.384912
80	HEALTH SERVICES	1	-0.048326	-0.048326	-0.048326	-0.048326	-0.048326	-0.048326	-0.048326	-0.048326	-0.048326	-0.048326	-0.048326
805	NURSING AND PERSONAL CARE FACILITIES	1	-0.048326	-0.048326	-0.048326	-0.048326	-0.048326	-0.048326	-0.048326	-0.048326	-0.048326	-0.048326	-0.048326
8051	Skilled Nursing Care Facilities	1	-0.048326	-0.048326	-0.048326	-0.048326	-0.048326	-0.048326	-0.048326	-0.048326	-0.048326	-0.048326	-0.048326

Mutual Funds by Peer Groups

Betas of Mutual Funds by Peer Groups as of March 31, 2017

Details:
Benchmark: S&P 500 Index
Returns period and frequency: 1 year of daily returns
Risk-free rate: Federal Funds Rate

Peer Group	Number of Mutual Funds	Mean	Median	1st Percentile	2.5th Percentile	5th Percentile	40th Percentile	50th Percentile	60th Percentile	95th Percentile	97.5th Percentile	99th Percentile
Allocation--15% to 30% Equity	188	0.235342	0.243554	0.005514	0.057026	0.081439	0.208924	0.243554	0.266210	0.365514	0.405929	0.422808
Allocation--30% to 50% Equity	479	0.399026	0.404213	0.163070	0.187367	0.266143	0.374259	0.404213	0.424155	0.555951	0.581116	0.611733
Allocation--50% to 70% Equity	735	0.621070	0.621260	0.301786	0.416430	0.490916	0.604416	0.621260	0.634570	0.784828	0.827185	0.840536
Allocation--70% to 85% Equity	352	0.801437	0.814108	0.422675	0.531711	0.572477	0.799302	0.814108	0.853107	0.941035	1.001513	1.035972
Allocation--85%+ Equity	134	0.993535	0.996964	0.670521	0.793117	0.867403	0.977710	0.996964	1.028076	1.087950	1.137252	1.138221
Bank Loan	37	0.061728	0.058259	0.030274	0.030689	0.030960	0.057613	0.058259	0.061613	0.098038	0.101927	0.103031
Bear Market	60	-1.745980	-1.589115	-3.418527	-3.103274	-2.739542	-1.998510	-1.589115	-1.283706	-0.907051	-0.774863	-0.773143
China Region	60	0.812812	0.881450	0.324031	0.328483	0.335434	0.752981	0.881450	0.943351	1.037593	1.044640	1.046613
Commodities Broad Basket	117	0.427621	0.422708	0.024067	0.221628	0.261578	0.406398	0.422708	0.434167	0.682047	0.697237	0.707044
Commodities Precious Metals	1	-0.407928	-0.407928	-0.407928	-0.407928	-0.407928	-0.407928	-0.407928	-0.407928	-0.407928	-0.407928	-0.407928
Communications	27	0.970380	0.979184	0.856297	0.856635	0.857328	0.973175	0.979184	0.980260	1.062781	1.063232	1.063591
Consumer Cyclical	24	0.921169	0.938101	0.588575	0.588777	0.589199	0.934782	0.938101	0.941819	1.037327	1.192348	1.314671
Consumer Defensive	18	0.790411	0.734700	0.480758	0.484936	0.491899	0.675051	0.734700	0.734957	1.048781	1.049436	1.049828
Convertibles	85	0.617174	0.640912	0.112934	0.131087	0.397788	0.629086	0.640912	0.652298	0.804012	0.805546	0.808025
Corporate Bond	146	-0.048999	-0.052009	-0.171873	-0.168553	-0.151336	-0.060347	-0.052009	-0.046765	0.015106	0.044620	0.213548
Diversified Emerging Mkts	730	0.851127	0.894815	0.321473	0.402278	0.488232	0.868587	0.894815	0.916613	1.068262	1.115548	1.135877
Diversified Pacific/Asia	34	0.733407	0.704997	0.412472	0.442475	0.453302	0.695084	0.704997	0.816332	0.945752	0.949726	0.949757
Emerging Markets Bond	252	0.157270	0.144694	-0.018242	-0.008976	0.032548	0.127356	0.144694	0.162589	0.325238	0.336813	0.363649
Emerging-Markets Local-Currency Bond	85	0.439602	0.458694	0.162955	0.185133	0.348176	0.448765	0.458694	0.464566	0.503345	0.550633	0.553177
Energy Limited Partnership	99	1.066330	1.075940	0.692452	0.698346	0.711347	1.051926	1.075940	1.111138	1.408772	1.574777	1.714003
Equity Energy	88	1.429293	1.439800	1.108099	1.142738	1.180583	1.382836	1.439800	1.476862	1.788384	1.789483	2.067271
Equity Precious Metals	57	0.173862	0.137542	0.041490	0.044944	0.081646	0.118713	0.137542	0.184378	0.359693	0.370449	0.417722
Europe Stock	91	1.192517	1.209850	0.602248	0.603937	0.870439	1.153040	1.209850	1.302050	1.419210	1.423420	1.500849
Financial	74	1.267061	1.276885	0.613425	0.616361	0.897360	1.252816	1.276885	1.328940	1.601462	1.628933	1.629402
Foreign Large Blend	720	1.099918	1.123050	0.607033	0.734436	0.841675	1.098926	1.123050	1.152960	1.269129	1.296005	1.347674
Foreign Large Growth	300	1.047502	1.059865	0.835053	0.840416	0.871496	1.027140	1.059865	1.093632	1.215795	1.231391	1.241625
Foreign Large Value	299	1.148737	1.164890	0.518904	0.646427	0.832474	1.142968	1.164890	1.223516	1.378704	1.441472	1.448297
Foreign Small/Mid Blend	88	0.866139	0.940720	0.314937	0.359455	0.563443	0.927544	0.940720	0.954235	1.046318	1.052304	1.058393
Foreign Small/Mid Growth	120	0.906866	0.920452	0.434552	0.588573	0.666020	0.911373	0.920452	0.956099	1.083842	1.097025	1.098838
Foreign Small/Mid Value	57	0.880762	0.938212	0.410351	0.563975	0.591253	0.903018	0.938212	0.949845	1.057430	1.101256	1.131002
Global Real Estate	219	0.742644	0.749634	0.500726	0.542387	0.594460	0.725616	0.749634	0.771261	0.887901	0.906939	0.916300
Health	106	1.173353	1.130570	0.950673	0.963190	0.979721	1.073430	1.130570	1.152180	1.582040	1.724528	1.726355
High Yield Bond	596	0.184869	0.187288	0.066308	0.079804	0.088594	0.176197	0.187288	0.198872	0.261566	0.314617	0.388027
High Yield Muni	125	-0.041028	-0.039527	-0.072140	-0.066229	-0.064239	-0.043651	-0.039527	-0.037282	-0.018633	-0.016291	-0.013737
India Equity	14	0.542992	0.555242	0.390210	0.390365	0.390625	0.509710	0.555242	0.610537	0.618263	0.618604	0.618809
Industrials	23	1.130965	1.156430	0.891730	0.891780	0.891924	1.134556	1.156430	1.158668	1.368984	1.369089	1.369162
Inflation-Protected Bond	215	-0.000114	-0.020081	-0.077239	-0.053628	-0.042513	-0.024928	-0.020081	-0.008305	0.175176	0.179137	0.231873
Infrastructure	67	0.787229	0.811248	0.460089	0.464898	0.468618	0.779292	0.811248	0.827942	0.943973	0.946466	0.955011
Intermediate Government	259	-0.064279	-0.066614	-0.131256	-0.127530	-0.120021	-0.073363	-0.066614	-0.048620	-0.023387	-0.016534	-0.011876
Intermediate-Term Bond	890	-0.053333	-0.061111	-0.109238	-0.099593	-0.094817	-0.065803	-0.061111	-0.055218	-0.003447	0.048735	0.147036
Japan Stock	30	0.776629	0.784534	0.444786	0.497035	0.533558	0.778321	0.784534	0.807923	1.072002	1.074710	1.077542
Large Blend	1303	1.009869	1.004190	0.684435	0.753843	0.831381	0.996073	1.004190	1.029582	1.184961	1.233378	1.281143
Large Growth	1291	1.029853	1.030490	0.828236	0.859020	0.901055	1.014080	1.030490	1.048450	1.177255	1.212678	1.262884

Betas of Mutual Funds by Peer Groups as of March 31, 2017

Peer Group	Number of Mutual Funds	Mean	Median	1st Percentile	2.5th Percentile	5th Percentile	40th Percentile	50th Percentile	60th Percentile	95th Percentile	97.5th Percentile	99th Percentile
Large Value	1141	1.046138	1.063440	0.623379	0.719722	0.795725	1.029820	1.063440	1.094440	1.307370	1.399185	1.461962
Latin America Stock	20	1.358549	1.332975	1.198291	1.200363	1.203817	1.330004	1.332975	1.340856	1.547312	1.547326	1.547334
Long Government	26	-0.315405	-0.325082	-0.475439	-0.475048	-0.464669	-0.327876	-0.325082	-0.306856	-0.159575	-0.126016	-0.092923
Long-Short Credit	58	0.077121	0.068487	-0.048319	-0.043106	-0.028795	0.039243	0.068487	0.075847	0.184982	0.290825	0.294402
Long-Short Equity	276	0.539707	0.533936	-0.095296	0.061627	0.148414	0.512283	0.533936	0.596484	0.901256	1.029939	1.097438
Long-Term Bond	29	-0.169532	-0.191787	-0.317046	-0.316124	-0.307839	-0.214635	-0.191787	-0.162861	-0.009453	-0.005762	-0.001406
Managed Futures	132	0.092254	0.106452	-0.507456	-0.221313	-0.146031	0.083848	0.106452	0.138836	0.342749	0.350714	0.417495
Market Neutral	143	0.085130	0.074233	-0.192847	-0.111717	-0.059668	0.049892	0.074233	0.089241	0.325580	0.349565	0.364994
Mid-Cap Blend	354	1.127686	1.145660	0.560545	0.673884	0.903201	1.123078	1.145660	1.169698	1.314631	1.383187	1.879026
Mid-Cap Growth	585	1.151878	1.139260	0.903253	0.933657	0.986359	1.119446	1.139260	1.167638	1.306504	1.385368	1.484586
Mid-Cap Value	383	1.160239	1.161060	0.782251	0.852730	0.902812	1.147100	1.161060	1.179382	1.338424	1.421510	1.494136
Miscellaneous Region	29	0.922909	0.885251	0.517933	0.580019	0.624658	0.869942	0.885251	0.920919	1.446716	1.475690	1.509500
Miscellaneous Sector	6	1.364495	1.358395	1.305827	1.306003	1.306295	1.309970	1.358395	1.406820	1.433630	1.436340	1.437966
Multialternative	391	0.260567	0.218685	-0.246487	-0.055085	-0.012403	0.194128	0.218685	0.259231	0.684674	0.942253	1.047237
Multicurrency	52	0.182053	0.213855	-0.202695	-0.191106	-0.163023	0.074062	0.213855	0.363030	0.392329	0.393848	0.396721
Multisector Bond	259	0.104338	0.085800	-0.104600	-0.081945	-0.077030	0.068423	0.085800	0.094458	0.376449	0.389799	0.400844
Muni California Intermediate	61	-0.041910	-0.046042	-0.066872	-0.066244	-0.063949	-0.047602	-0.046042	-0.042755	0.013251	0.015034	0.017747
Muni California Long	88	-0.049918	-0.050772	-0.064143	-0.063187	-0.060717	-0.054068	-0.050772	-0.047057	-0.037177	-0.035999	-0.032906
Muni Massachusetts	51	-0.045704	-0.048420	-0.062056	-0.060468	-0.059291	-0.049321	-0.048420	-0.046906	-0.020123	-0.017837	-0.017138
Muni Minnesota	44	-0.043169	-0.042565	-0.058318	-0.057763	-0.055275	-0.045451	-0.042565	-0.040158	-0.031101	-0.028784	-0.028430
Muni National Interm	240	-0.041632	-0.046335	-0.077131	-0.068076	-0.063136	-0.049088	-0.046335	-0.044120	0.008999	0.034379	0.042127
Muni National Long	140	-0.047877	-0.046531	-0.082444	-0.074463	-0.070486	-0.049134	-0.046531	-0.044168	-0.027656	-0.024890	-0.020238
Muni National Short	29	-0.006644	-0.028116	-0.040458	-0.039337	-0.038423	-0.031979	-0.028116	-0.027946	0.049290	0.049514	0.049696
Muni New Jersey	45	-0.047733	-0.048473	-0.060550	-0.059444	-0.058505	-0.049757	-0.048473	-0.046414	-0.027556	-0.025512	-0.023629
Muni New York Intermediate	45	-0.042099	-0.047314	-0.058531	-0.058188	-0.055189	-0.048882	-0.047314	-0.044899	0.002685	0.005842	0.006416
Muni New York Long	69	-0.043549	-0.044848	-0.059847	-0.058721	-0.056356	-0.046238	-0.044848	-0.042829	-0.015958	0.000457	0.002833
Muni Ohio	40	-0.048236	-0.047610	-0.067383	-0.066485	-0.063397	-0.048677	-0.047610	-0.046888	-0.032420	-0.030888	-0.030233
Muni Pennsylvania	54	-0.040940	-0.042939	-0.057445	-0.056002	-0.055457	-0.045030	-0.042939	-0.037576	-0.016622	-0.015550	-0.013733
Muni Single State Interm	146	-0.048036	-0.048875	-0.063106	-0.059904	-0.057917	-0.049884	-0.048875	-0.047466	-0.037203	-0.033502	-0.023268
Muni Single State Long	223	-0.041400	-0.042882	-0.066099	-0.062197	-0.057869	-0.045230	-0.042882	-0.040613	-0.013715	0.000092	0.009795
Muni Single State Short	12	-0.036140	-0.036818	-0.042702	-0.042447	-0.042022	-0.037867	-0.036818	-0.035426	-0.029290	-0.028066	-0.027331
Natural Resources	103	1.262620	1.252630	0.606406	0.930726	0.963704	1.237190	1.252630	1.320642	1.523955	1.607379	1.609006
Nontraditional Bond	272	0.095116	0.074615	-0.114239	-0.083073	-0.006419	0.049891	0.074615	0.105013	0.274217	0.360830	0.395684
Option Writing	97	0.536870	0.558801	0.104126	0.139890	0.189534	0.515465	0.558801	0.578510	0.855086	0.873767	0.879804
Pacific/Asia ex-Japan Stk	78	0.710141	0.708404	0.239883	0.463828	0.495117	0.689898	0.708404	0.746540	0.976193	0.986663	0.988561
Preferred Stock	44	0.132468	0.099618	0.057825	0.059825	0.060445	0.084383	0.099618	0.108519	0.333275	0.333978	0.334561
Real Estate	236	0.654344	0.659980	0.226692	0.250005	0.475283	0.653445	0.659980	0.663076	0.764022	0.821403	1.098738
Short Government	41	-0.046905	-0.044955	-0.093539	-0.092674	-0.066775	-0.047756	-0.044955	-0.040099	-0.027386	-0.026480	-0.023467
Short-Term Bond	155	-0.014726	-0.031283	-0.075811	-0.069052	-0.056516	-0.036153	-0.031283	-0.027730	0.139535	0.158995	0.175609
Small Blend	696	1.266386	1.289650	0.907096	1.037063	1.064128	1.256280	1.289650	1.307280	1.400828	1.432736	1.452302
Small Growth	621	1.294548	1.300540	0.999576	1.112400	1.130050	1.279130	1.300540	1.324630	1.442870	1.462670	1.482546
Small Value	386	1.262858	1.288770	0.675820	0.848952	1.030178	1.257060	1.288770	1.308700	1.489475	1.616976	1.666800
Tactical Allocation	268	0.564464	0.559417	-0.050969	0.115563	0.203780	0.474444	0.559417	0.642041	0.956635	1.096365	1.227391
Target-Date 2000-2010	111	0.393753	0.409386	0.118833	0.122228	0.172779	0.398740	0.409386	0.418521	0.487634	0.496932	0.499742
Target-Date 2015	138	0.435475	0.481126	0.109119	0.113121	0.165720	0.443497	0.481126	0.490123	0.576866	0.590521	0.594581
Target-Date 2020	219	0.505360	0.533631	0.190300	0.192073	0.261066	0.520770	0.533631	0.556788	0.656680	0.660828	0.667660
Target-Date 2025	193	0.625323	0.658727	0.336360	0.403066	0.413621	0.617518	0.658727	0.666488	0.764024	0.770218	0.786365

Betas of Mutual Funds by Peer Groups as of March 31, 2017

Peer Group	Number of Mutual Funds	Mean	Median	1st Percentile	2.5th Percentile	5th Percentile	40th Percentile	50th Percentile	60th Percentile	95th Percentile	97.5th Percentile	99th Percentile
Target-Date 2030	219	0.720144	0.755712	0.257963	0.262614	0.534858	0.730972	0.755712	0.763326	0.866768	0.879662	0.891116
Target-Date 2035	191	0.828390	0.841967	0.476161	0.624782	0.682625	0.834396	0.841967	0.853905	0.954949	0.993763	0.998723
Target-Date 2040	218	0.874885	0.911552	0.304630	0.309158	0.719865	0.886011	0.911552	0.931257	0.994811	0.999597	1.002210
Target-Date 2045	191	0.926337	0.936105	0.612856	0.745079	0.813312	0.920225	0.936105	0.949139	1.007105	1.036795	1.040570
Target-Date 2050	210	0.920262	0.943022	0.348526	0.356603	0.771942	0.930539	0.943022	0.970751	1.030320	1.048823	1.051183
Target-Date 2055	195	0.944352	0.941416	0.665761	0.771120	0.802415	0.928950	0.941416	0.975377	1.057688	1.062213	1.065442
Target-Date 2060+	124	0.970303	0.977052	0.883804	0.888985	0.891653	0.967142	0.977052	0.995853	1.060600	1.065824	1.068579
Target-Date Retirement	164	0.312360	0.329063	0.109371	0.111895	0.146989	0.285991	0.329063	0.349685	0.440908	0.481766	0.484223
Technology	165	1.157761	1.112970	0.745331	1.005299	1.012242	1.105336	1.112970	1.153666	1.363896	1.365842	1.380485
Trading--Inverse Commodities	4	-0.675484	-0.675138	-1.212377	-1.212312	-1.212204	-0.996643	-0.675138	-0.353633	-0.139249	-0.139245	-0.139243
Trading--Inverse Debt	15	0.121585	0.341637	-0.358195	-0.357031	-0.355089	0.199543	0.341637	0.373643	0.469541	0.474047	0.476751
Trading--Inverse Equity	7	-2.059937	-1.857480	-2.539980	-2.538945	-2.537220	-2.234262	-1.857480	-1.851378	-1.472868	-1.392714	-1.344622
Trading--Leveraged Debt	9	-0.325844	-0.458971	-0.459429	-0.459428	-0.459428	-0.459077	-0.458971	-0.454502	0.203481	0.381359	0.488087
Trading--Leveraged Equity	82	1.901558	1.934055	0.164037	0.633332	0.958631	1.821828	1.934055	2.075994	2.723960	2.773018	3.417049
Trading--Miscellaneous	5	-0.385484	-0.182455	-0.692137	-0.692120	-0.692090	-0.386215	-0.182455	-0.181982	-0.180006	-0.179847	-0.179752
Ultrashort Bond	1	-0.005324	-0.005324	-0.005324	-0.005324	-0.005324	-0.005324	-0.005324	-0.005324	-0.005324	-0.005324	-0.005324
Utilities	50	0.620931	0.618187	0.445545	0.446519	0.449032	0.559694	0.618187	0.657747	0.809880	0.809918	0.810567
Volatility	4	-1.535335	-2.261845	-2.345500	-2.345500	-2.345500	-2.312038	-2.261845	-2.211652	0.291943	0.509896	0.640668
World Allocation	488	0.609707	0.600188	0.207823	0.230875	0.308344	0.582712	0.600188	0.619220	0.917619	0.924280	0.962735
World Bond	275	0.076162	0.039217	-0.077059	-0.068848	-0.054629	0.009124	0.039217	0.057064	0.385862	0.510434	0.512457
World Stock	957	1.021964	1.041670	0.604441	0.685336	0.738176	1.015716	1.041670	1.069422	1.236046	1.251486	1.349209

Down-market Betas of Mutual Funds by Peer Groups as of March 31, 2017

Details:
Benchmark: S&P 500 Index
Returns period and frequency: 1 year of daily returns
Risk-free rate: Federal Funds Rate

Peer Group	Number of Mutual Funds	Mean	Median	1st Percentile	2.5th Percentile	5th Percentile	40th Percentile	50th Percentile	60th Percentile	95th Percentile	97.5th Percentile	99th Percentile
Allocation--15% to 30% Equity	188	0.269509	0.275240	0.028897	0.047139	0.065474	0.260786	0.275240	0.303039	0.389251	0.430561	0.458959
Allocation--30% to 50% Equity	479	0.451613	0.450612	0.159654	0.197968	0.295846	0.422333	0.450612	0.481766	0.621183	0.642182	0.669750
Allocation--50% to 70% Equity	735	0.678418	0.681582	0.305161	0.428176	0.517298	0.651143	0.681582	0.708998	0.848895	0.886805	0.985201
Allocation--70% to 85% Equity	352	0.892414	0.932458	0.393439	0.557235	0.592580	0.908421	0.932458	0.963276	1.056105	1.087641	1.141901
Allocation--85%+ Equity	134	1.116072	1.124955	0.750963	0.882590	0.902617	1.118642	1.124955	1.160302	1.249594	1.291854	1.294640
Bank Loan	37	0.115042	0.116458	0.058228	0.067601	0.072081	0.112603	0.116458	0.120361	0.145276	0.145831	0.146082
Bear Market	60	-1.810446	-1.572580	-3.274078	-3.266978	-3.247952	-1.998894	-1.572580	-1.371376	-0.953487	-0.848021	-0.843388
China Region	60	0.944669	0.958817	0.560368	0.562274	0.631429	0.927184	0.958817	0.988657	1.126073	1.132653	1.172080
Commodities Broad Basket	117	0.303823	0.290756	0.033801	0.058827	0.074190	0.273850	0.290756	0.309803	0.585433	0.590173	0.595578
Commodities Precious Metals	1	-0.629594	-0.629594	-0.629594	-0.629594	-0.629594	-0.629594	-0.629594	-0.629594	-0.629594	-0.629594	-0.629594
Communications	27	1.114581	1.112260	0.897098	0.948712	0.995321	1.094684	1.112260	1.149430	1.234437	1.235709	1.235751
Consumer Cyclical	24	0.980964	1.011330	0.601756	0.602355	0.603101	0.964844	1.011330	1.018012	1.082335	1.357190	1.580246
Consumer Defensive	18	0.885608	0.746374	0.451583	0.455115	0.461001	0.721387	0.746374	0.746938	1.295066	1.295508	1.295773
Convertibles	85	0.650591	0.675834	0.116977	0.137831	0.399119	0.655683	0.675834	0.688480	0.824407	0.832371	0.834907
Corporate Bond	146	-0.015988	-0.023710	-0.131743	-0.102302	-0.093388	-0.033052	-0.023710	-0.017042	0.069555	0.075183	0.206717
Diversified Emerging Mkts	730	1.085796	1.124600	0.400241	0.563467	0.727495	1.084766	1.124600	1.164138	1.334437	1.356876	1.388724
Diversified Pacific/Asia	34	0.880189	0.917991	0.648730	0.663502	0.668904	0.816473	0.917991	0.935860	1.112897	1.113784	1.115210
Emerging Markets Bond	252	0.183132	0.149196	-0.040054	-0.018796	0.023624	0.130323	0.149196	0.169199	0.423119	0.466486	0.531363
Emerging-Markets Local-Currency Bond	85	0.609148	0.640473	0.191992	0.204116	0.508778	0.627523	0.640473	0.653735	0.700661	0.733169	0.737341
Energy Limited Partnership	99	1.011151	1.041460	0.679789	0.709580	0.712954	1.011892	1.041460	1.054706	1.439386	1.508882	1.565206
Equity Energy	88	1.268933	1.267925	1.036128	1.044241	1.047210	1.255608	1.267925	1.285102	1.545822	1.560217	1.691390
Equity Precious Metals	57	0.032535	0.013074	-0.214756	-0.210940	-0.133133	-0.013091	0.013074	0.057415	0.312186	0.314817	0.355168
Europe Stock	91	1.749647	1.802380	1.082112	1.182765	1.184110	1.727040	1.802380	1.964450	2.065195	2.066265	2.123690
Financial	74	1.419959	1.329960	0.687897	0.689375	0.940406	1.300428	1.329960	1.400894	2.014747	2.025276	2.036254
Foreign Large Blend	720	1.528396	1.571260	0.935295	1.001381	1.162606	1.527940	1.571260	1.597414	1.781011	1.806356	1.907903
Foreign Large Growth	300	1.432883	1.425840	1.111200	1.151954	1.171994	1.394632	1.425840	1.483324	1.666292	1.767618	1.774986
Foreign Large Value	299	1.616995	1.635150	0.783294	0.942673	1.145199	1.597254	1.635150	1.695272	1.932572	1.953810	1.976288
Foreign Small/Mid Blend	88	1.414684	1.487045	0.494097	0.567817	0.900920	1.366434	1.487045	1.547450	1.773207	1.807180	1.809503
Foreign Small/Mid Growth	120	1.399282	1.440070	0.735815	0.958507	0.990776	1.431602	1.440070	1.464566	1.638152	1.655239	1.663137
Foreign Small/Mid Value	57	1.375514	1.428490	0.535023	0.633618	0.892475	1.363436	1.428490	1.503250	1.593386	1.595238	1.652109
Global Real Estate	219	1.131584	1.118930	0.718254	0.770591	0.901915	1.092428	1.118930	1.156366	1.412593	1.424558	1.515944
Health	106	1.185706	1.121550	0.868787	0.873342	0.940876	1.096560	1.121550	1.150060	1.703655	1.753758	1.756841
High Yield Bond	596	0.219155	0.221512	0.076695	0.094622	0.126146	0.208383	0.221512	0.231277	0.305240	0.341362	0.423307
High Yield Muni	125	-0.088453	-0.086932	-0.143120	-0.138766	-0.130205	-0.089897	-0.086932	-0.082907	-0.054089	-0.048700	-0.024973
India Equity	14	0.735647	0.727439	0.614049	0.614916	0.616362	0.725762	0.727439	0.766390	0.849959	0.851057	0.851716
Industrials	23	1.208617	1.197020	0.990329	0.993736	0.998531	1.195374	1.197020	1.207292	1.462875	1.463116	1.463274
Inflation-Protected Bond	215	0.014091	-0.007114	-0.066367	-0.040689	-0.037697	-0.012828	-0.007114	-0.000550	0.217499	0.229103	0.240982
Infrastructure	67	0.975476	1.007120	0.622594	0.623326	0.625384	0.969019	1.007120	1.039502	1.121930	1.141663	1.178109
Intermediate Government	259	-0.046054	-0.047081	-0.131904	-0.124491	-0.114926	-0.059156	-0.047081	-0.027935	0.007594	0.012137	0.017926
Intermediate-Term Bond	890	-0.030288	-0.037908	-0.103349	-0.092868	-0.085322	-0.045450	-0.037908	-0.029817	0.038531	0.084443	0.197931
Japan Stock	30	0.927278	0.882483	0.514671	0.626492	0.697804	0.836688	0.882483	0.922340	1.399148	1.406083	1.410533
Large Blend	1303	1.026297	1.009210	0.701568	0.749317	0.833774	0.996832	1.009210	1.046590	1.241115	1.276318	1.349420
Large Growth	1291	1.053974	1.051680	0.780554	0.853482	0.885082	1.031460	1.051680	1.074730	1.240605	1.300393	1.325373

Down-market Betas of Mutual Funds by Peer Groups as of March 31, 2017

Peer Group	Number of Mutual Funds	Mean	Median	1st Percentile	2.5th Percentile	5th Percentile	40th Percentile	50th Percentile	60th Percentile	95th Percentile	97.5th Percentile	99th Percentile
Large Value	1141	1.111356	1.067970	0.659939	0.739985	0.799684	1.039880	1.067970	1.103350	1.337350	1.443980	1.544254
Latin America Stock	20	1.367038	1.364510	1.186065	1.186883	1.188247	1.325796	1.364510	1.368290	1.558065	1.558677	1.559045
Long Government	26	-0.287315	-0.288730	-0.417706	-0.417609	-0.417376	-0.299409	-0.288730	-0.284355	-0.159160	-0.121744	-0.084701
Long-Short Credit	58	0.093144	0.086952	-0.097173	-0.095454	-0.087684	0.079769	0.086952	0.113024	0.243839	0.316654	0.317609
Long-Short Equity	276	0.572488	0.595518	-0.184564	-0.093683	0.035608	0.525274	0.595518	0.657061	0.958132	1.119276	1.263225
Long-Term Bond	29	-0.127755	-0.134875	-0.277018	-0.271575	-0.267350	-0.137630	-0.134875	-0.119422	0.042845	0.050668	0.051075
Managed Futures	132	-0.205301	-0.199644	-0.915205	-0.851550	-0.790436	-0.266095	-0.199644	-0.108444	0.172926	0.389220	0.433658
Market Neutral	143	0.087801	0.080702	-0.243046	-0.170196	-0.125590	0.064345	0.080702	0.113096	0.261969	0.409517	0.436744
Mid-Cap Blend	354	1.194969	1.219895	0.652439	0.676424	0.903173	1.183940	1.219895	1.252088	1.419431	1.486701	1.921886
Mid-Cap Growth	585	1.211619	1.199520	0.927807	0.969350	1.010668	1.174858	1.199520	1.227690	1.389410	1.474218	1.565212
Mid-Cap Value	383	1.239744	1.245270	0.786855	0.887211	0.966296	1.217002	1.245270	1.276312	1.466045	1.517892	1.625381
Miscellaneous Region	29	1.192603	1.015650	0.812621	0.815894	0.818274	1.006518	1.015650	1.058184	2.124848	2.340884	2.626686
Miscellaneous Sector	6	1.369168	1.357940	1.271065	1.271281	1.271643	1.277160	1.357940	1.438720	1.484500	1.488150	1.490340
Multialternative	391	0.251628	0.218055	-0.282425	-0.171826	-0.125982	0.193745	0.218055	0.252027	0.684578	0.813133	1.140702
Multicurrency	52	0.226029	0.370370	-1.058594	-0.865757	-0.375668	0.305911	0.370370	0.479587	0.559648	0.561890	0.565002
Multisector Bond	259	0.138090	0.108317	-0.110542	-0.071577	-0.063995	0.090403	0.108317	0.133878	0.426012	0.465584	0.481230
Muni California Intermediate	61	-0.084980	-0.086408	-0.116887	-0.113886	-0.112586	-0.090298	-0.086408	-0.083536	-0.050559	-0.047828	-0.046333
Muni California Long	88	-0.095498	-0.097238	-0.133577	-0.126475	-0.119767	-0.100116	-0.097238	-0.093049	-0.064801	-0.060964	-0.059488
Muni Massachusetts	51	-0.083934	-0.085184	-0.112350	-0.111280	-0.108880	-0.086551	-0.085184	-0.082187	-0.056969	-0.049558	-0.045351
Muni Minnesota	44	-0.077752	-0.078857	-0.110321	-0.106115	-0.103431	-0.080692	-0.078857	-0.076359	-0.044911	-0.040978	-0.040699
Muni National Interm	240	-0.080549	-0.084339	-0.142762	-0.128646	-0.118184	-0.087246	-0.084339	-0.080121	-0.023237	0.008280	0.017392
Muni National Long	140	-0.089178	-0.087100	-0.142814	-0.137901	-0.123103	-0.089604	-0.087100	-0.081827	-0.061843	-0.058531	-0.054535
Muni National Short	29	-0.038160	-0.046333	-0.072674	-0.071865	-0.071240	-0.059148	-0.046333	-0.043485	0.009990	0.012829	0.014295
Muni New Jersey	45	-0.082597	-0.079750	-0.110496	-0.109287	-0.107953	-0.082162	-0.079750	-0.077694	-0.064990	-0.063228	-0.056082
Muni New York Intermediate	45	-0.084027	-0.082760	-0.117331	-0.115851	-0.109934	-0.086790	-0.082760	-0.079901	-0.052629	-0.049153	-0.045864
Muni New York Long	69	-0.082122	-0.082094	-0.108266	-0.104740	-0.101597	-0.084968	-0.082094	-0.078352	-0.058733	-0.051196	-0.045943
Muni Ohio	40	-0.088549	-0.090052	-0.113279	-0.113187	-0.111958	-0.093581	-0.090052	-0.087985	-0.062921	-0.058854	-0.055518
Muni Pennsylvania	54	-0.075423	-0.077584	-0.115214	-0.108263	-0.099213	-0.079219	-0.077584	-0.073924	-0.044445	-0.038158	-0.033730
Muni Single State Interm	146	-0.083356	-0.083424	-0.118092	-0.107993	-0.100699	-0.085651	-0.083424	-0.080897	-0.064602	-0.052936	-0.040025
Muni Single State Long	223	-0.073588	-0.074344	-0.110520	-0.105766	-0.100499	-0.077763	-0.074344	-0.069829	-0.044525	-0.033495	-0.026665
Muni Single State Short	12	-0.068172	-0.071029	-0.079557	-0.079015	-0.078110	-0.071580	-0.071029	-0.068787	-0.053967	-0.051300	-0.049701
Natural Resources	103	1.241357	1.254080	0.524583	0.770479	1.091441	1.191642	1.254080	1.273084	1.503607	1.521549	1.553506
Nontraditional Bond	272	0.120164	0.115713	-0.157658	-0.124730	-0.017797	0.072679	0.115713	0.138490	0.371236	0.408503	0.414293
Option Writing	97	0.600061	0.626994	0.183400	0.188872	0.231648	0.586741	0.626994	0.661844	0.998983	1.012536	1.039422
Pacific/Asia ex-Japan Stk	78	0.946034	1.005765	0.270432	0.565150	0.640829	0.966576	1.005765	1.023726	1.185002	1.221056	1.227052
Preferred Stock	44	0.211039	0.179963	0.102074	0.103464	0.105638	0.171312	0.179963	0.190294	0.431080	0.432173	0.432440
Real Estate	236	0.859315	0.867066	0.337064	0.417979	0.594003	0.858184	0.867066	0.881353	0.997022	1.076034	1.296608
Short Government	41	-0.040748	-0.037521	-0.092380	-0.089730	-0.065420	-0.045701	-0.037521	-0.036149	-0.012726	-0.012547	-0.007032
Short-Term Bond	155	-0.003100	-0.019999	-0.067061	-0.056881	-0.051311	-0.026827	-0.019999	-0.013632	0.164049	0.174226	0.197685
Small Blend	696	1.296398	1.316400	0.961583	1.030760	1.088025	1.294740	1.316400	1.333240	1.456510	1.476224	1.497265
Small Growth	621	1.332255	1.334760	1.063110	1.103130	1.151230	1.313070	1.334760	1.369900	1.492800	1.537510	1.554504
Small Value	386	1.284242	1.305265	0.701042	0.842781	0.971995	1.286600	1.305265	1.325970	1.485988	1.551414	1.746632
Tactical Allocation	268	0.586860	0.594414	-0.222908	-0.020949	0.137458	0.493975	0.594414	0.697511	1.024775	1.272059	1.409697
Target-Date 2000-2010	111	0.464063	0.475496	0.170515	0.172266	0.222308	0.470926	0.475496	0.483624	0.572644	0.575836	0.578762
Target-Date 2015	138	0.511385	0.554303	0.117104	0.124726	0.230240	0.510281	0.554303	0.572788	0.680431	0.684579	0.689190
Target-Date 2020	219	0.584498	0.613569	0.143319	0.150747	0.307870	0.596901	0.613569	0.655732	0.766512	0.780313	0.783161
Target-Date 2025	193	0.725313	0.739994	0.471509	0.491181	0.502553	0.714882	0.739994	0.774278	0.886975	0.900023	0.904504

Down-market Betas of Mutual Funds by Peer Groups as of March 31, 2017

Peer Group	Number of Mutual Funds	Mean	Median	1st Percentile	2.5th Percentile	5th Percentile	40th Percentile	50th Percentile	60th Percentile	95th Percentile	97.5th Percentile	99th Percentile
Target-Date 2030	219	0.824648	0.874216	0.197174	0.205124	0.602711	0.859334	0.874216	0.883986	1.000840	1.005967	1.011862
Target-Date 2035	191	0.953966	0.969317	0.708884	0.744556	0.758750	0.953904	0.969317	0.987981	1.062250	1.122800	1.127861
Target-Date 2040	218	0.997912	1.044885	0.227582	0.235838	0.812086	1.024090	1.044885	1.062922	1.129951	1.141342	1.151895
Target-Date 2045	191	1.066293	1.079930	0.855097	0.891020	0.947943	1.060230	1.079930	1.094460	1.175335	1.183408	1.189729
Target-Date 2050	210	1.048571	1.095150	0.264472	0.276988	0.863281	1.080354	1.095150	1.103072	1.188676	1.200991	1.211011
Target-Date 2055	195	1.086423	1.095650	0.862254	0.914905	0.976043	1.079634	1.095650	1.106482	1.201334	1.210751	1.236945
Target-Date 2060+	124	1.110069	1.118015	1.007059	1.007548	1.012609	1.093364	1.118015	1.131138	1.203374	1.211120	1.213955
Target-Date Retirement	164	0.362728	0.379415	0.112255	0.116556	0.128978	0.346995	0.379415	0.396510	0.518008	0.544390	0.552433
Technology	165	1.274935	1.224660	1.000278	1.069260	1.087628	1.206128	1.224660	1.254680	1.538794	1.543208	1.563317
Trading--Inverse Commodities	4	-0.495432	-0.495264	-0.946669	-0.946473	-0.946146	-0.763568	-0.495264	-0.226959	-0.044954	-0.044677	-0.044511
Trading--Inverse Debt	15	0.125432	0.325761	-0.304486	-0.303759	-0.302549	0.201408	0.325761	0.332198	0.455639	0.466057	0.472307
Trading--Inverse Equity	7	-2.187929	-1.860730	-2.838620	-2.837886	-2.836662	-2.390788	-1.860730	-1.850110	-1.501312	-1.428226	-1.384374
Trading--Leveraged Debt	9	-0.289982	-0.400913	-0.408307	-0.408159	-0.407912	-0.404760	-0.400913	-0.400454	0.168260	0.339322	0.441958
Trading--Leveraged Equity	82	1.968096	2.021965	-0.016622	0.714539	0.904560	1.832380	2.021965	2.129470	3.084356	3.239959	3.268644
Trading--Miscellaneous	5	-0.838728	-0.816504	-0.876245	-0.875980	-0.875537	-0.838702	-0.816504	-0.816292	-0.813387	-0.813063	-0.812869
Ultrashort Bond	1	-0.006683	-0.006683	-0.006683	-0.006683	-0.006683	-0.006683	-0.006683	-0.006683	-0.006683	-0.006683	-0.006683
Utilities	50	0.710531	0.691005	0.472231	0.478832	0.492746	0.583336	0.691005	0.742077	0.965118	0.966054	0.966315
Volatility	4	-1.823244	-2.581445	-2.856090	-2.856090	-2.856090	-2.746232	-2.581445	-2.416658	0.271084	0.498545	0.635021
World Allocation	488	0.721938	0.719704	0.174954	0.277940	0.321159	0.689319	0.719704	0.774263	1.065662	1.133380	1.149618
World Bond	275	0.152514	0.130920	-0.071594	-0.063680	-0.048535	0.110122	0.130920	0.145253	0.487385	0.561650	0.609022
World Stock	957	1.227470	1.239100	0.725813	0.823388	0.859593	1.203266	1.239100	1.272316	1.530378	1.561870	1.702042

Up-market Betas of Mutual Funds by Peer Groups as of March 31, 2017

Details:
Benchmark: S&P 500 Index
Returns period and frequency: 1 year of daily returns
Risk-free rate: Federal Funds Rate

Peer Group	Number of Mutual Funds	Mean	Median	1st Percentile	2.5th Percentile	5th Percentile	40th Percentile	50th Percentile	60th Percentile	95th Percentile	97.5th Percentile	99th Percentile
Allocation--15% to 30% Equity	188	0.218524	0.221431	0.012270	0.055370	0.077539	0.187297	0.221431	0.243537	0.364625	0.369198	0.381214
Allocation--30% to 50% Equity	479	0.369084	0.372665	0.148791	0.157041	0.231590	0.346229	0.372665	0.388477	0.523755	0.543923	0.588898
Allocation--50% to 70% Equity	735	0.576763	0.582477	0.305260	0.363659	0.446005	0.567579	0.582477	0.593707	0.726653	0.773351	0.783170
Allocation--70% to 85% Equity	352	0.735965	0.750508	0.373597	0.482276	0.531310	0.734409	0.750508	0.775679	0.888815	0.939855	0.986604
Allocation--85%+ Equity	134	0.901759	0.899669	0.542539	0.723331	0.814346	0.893605	0.899669	0.907994	1.006294	1.023373	1.028068
Bank Loan	37	0.058686	0.050646	0.025982	0.027422	0.029656	0.045518	0.050646	0.059704	0.110623	0.114951	0.115762
Bear Market	60	-1.667794	-1.573540	-3.293560	-2.963375	-2.599657	-1.997000	-1.573540	-1.199464	-0.836459	-0.731358	-0.728009
China Region	60	0.818625	0.857771	0.295227	0.331715	0.339332	0.821493	0.857771	0.870441	1.095894	1.096469	1.098039
Commodities Broad Basket	117	0.401852	0.401141	0.146184	0.156336	0.227613	0.394764	0.401141	0.413790	0.612050	0.618554	0.647958
Commodities Precious Metals	1	-0.216025	-0.216025	-0.216025	-0.216025	-0.216025	-0.216025	-0.216025	-0.216025	-0.216025	-0.216025	-0.216025
Communications	27	0.896666	0.880176	0.769305	0.770441	0.771811	0.877111	0.880176	0.916968	0.992489	0.996004	0.999914
Consumer Cyclical	24	0.872694	0.915791	0.540283	0.540613	0.541555	0.891057	0.915791	0.918961	0.987566	1.042144	1.084555
Consumer Defensive	18	0.756553	0.755924	0.535884	0.536872	0.538519	0.695275	0.755924	0.757182	0.913551	0.913699	0.913787
Convertibles	85	0.528979	0.568020	0.044936	0.064579	0.340137	0.548041	0.568020	0.574270	0.680482	0.682751	0.701197
Corporate Bond	146	-0.043252	-0.044162	-0.185399	-0.184288	-0.160197	-0.052635	-0.044162	-0.037060	0.033819	0.056573	0.186904
Diversified Emerging Mkts	730	0.769100	0.814670	0.235715	0.310837	0.419633	0.761761	0.814670	0.848517	1.008125	1.040296	1.059321
Diversified Pacific/Asia	34	0.645139	0.638517	0.333640	0.341507	0.345501	0.631948	0.638517	0.702098	0.816519	0.824643	0.828186
Emerging Markets Bond	252	0.166570	0.167232	-0.026411	-0.001437	0.021569	0.147270	0.167232	0.180195	0.316907	0.347984	0.351630
Emerging-Markets Local-Currency Bond	85	0.405373	0.423970	0.143220	0.176184	0.286486	0.415248	0.423970	0.434416	0.473846	0.535516	0.539924
Energy Limited Partnership	99	1.014457	1.022560	0.630189	0.634652	0.642041	1.007550	1.022560	1.046034	1.331554	1.503279	1.674046
Equity Energy	88	1.336450	1.341880	0.947952	0.973299	1.027605	1.294280	1.341880	1.372020	1.694868	1.698042	2.082716
Equity Precious Metals	57	0.542348	0.527624	0.223504	0.351107	0.412992	0.498441	0.527624	0.576941	0.762682	0.764577	0.783349
Europe Stock	91	0.956310	1.034980	0.369530	0.381072	0.702635	0.918064	1.034980	1.052490	1.122800	1.153440	1.287607
Financial	74	1.093481	1.117615	0.538000	0.542250	0.756891	1.090692	1.117615	1.131566	1.397114	1.399474	1.399892
Foreign Large Blend	720	0.897743	0.922569	0.500127	0.554282	0.648342	0.897341	0.922569	0.938170	1.043245	1.064040	1.088947
Foreign Large Growth	300	0.889786	0.906694	0.698223	0.728133	0.737046	0.876797	0.906694	0.915420	1.046399	1.061020	1.069271
Foreign Large Value	299	0.937185	0.936430	0.298841	0.638863	0.671571	0.914984	0.936430	0.980163	1.141904	1.166075	1.183613
Foreign Small/Mid Blend	88	0.659465	0.699806	0.265699	0.297095	0.446226	0.632340	0.699806	0.719467	0.800791	0.805648	0.811492
Foreign Small/Mid Growth	120	0.736649	0.732993	0.474841	0.524794	0.564152	0.704944	0.732993	0.741458	0.918574	0.927993	0.941612
Foreign Small/Mid Value	57	0.673743	0.711292	0.244326	0.291572	0.393680	0.676063	0.711292	0.721965	0.850552	0.878573	0.889326
Global Real Estate	219	0.566334	0.572116	0.309560	0.329315	0.387949	0.561391	0.572116	0.580558	0.653735	0.674941	0.717437
Health	106	1.176836	1.099355	0.831981	0.917118	0.936277	1.079070	1.099355	1.112160	1.649560	1.689348	1.692613
High Yield Bond	596	0.199810	0.204589	0.053322	0.067980	0.087611	0.188653	0.204589	0.221250	0.279742	0.317159	0.402660
High Yield Muni	125	-0.015348	-0.013267	-0.055350	-0.053610	-0.045595	-0.016951	-0.013267	-0.009967	0.009087	0.011405	0.020432
India Equity	14	0.334922	0.337120	0.234814	0.235518	0.236690	0.318184	0.337120	0.353563	0.421522	0.422353	0.422852
Industrials	23	1.014049	1.079740	0.779805	0.780587	0.781770	1.024560	1.079740	1.106008	1.148998	1.150623	1.151725
Inflation-Protected Bond	215	0.001335	-0.014138	-0.102997	-0.053131	-0.045348	-0.021024	-0.014138	-0.005630	0.170811	0.182960	0.228167
Infrastructure	67	0.698086	0.705392	0.437364	0.439002	0.442797	0.696365	0.705392	0.718507	0.827026	0.832683	0.865545
Intermediate Government	259	-0.052337	-0.050229	-0.138327	-0.113163	-0.104525	-0.062283	-0.050229	-0.042612	-0.009595	-0.000864	0.005525
Intermediate-Term Bond	890	-0.043988	-0.049035	-0.107690	-0.089331	-0.084055	-0.055064	-0.049035	-0.043656	0.008969	0.039636	0.136277
Japan Stock	30	0.666641	0.670602	0.389507	0.441661	0.479497	0.661405	0.670602	0.688734	0.849638	0.934822	0.936343
Large Blend	1303	0.981758	0.996891	0.615817	0.729345	0.808830	0.980199	0.996891	1.004374	1.124006	1.166828	1.209072
Large Growth	1291	0.997002	0.996348	0.773226	0.837257	0.872478	0.981320	0.996348	1.012530	1.125160	1.168005	1.242101

Up-market Betas of Mutual Funds by Peer Groups as of March 31, 2017

Peer Group	Number of Mutual Funds	Mean	Median	1st Percentile	2.5th Percentile	5th Percentile	40th Percentile	50th Percentile	60th Percentile	95th Percentile	97.5th Percentile	99th Percentile
Large Value	1141	1.008668	1.018140	0.580164	0.700636	0.769900	0.993905	1.018140	1.042600	1.218710	1.328605	1.382654
Latin America Stock	20	1.389111	1.391210	1.266104	1.266666	1.267602	1.368062	1.391210	1.395626	1.531604	1.531737	1.531817
Long Government	26	-0.295151	-0.312854	-0.468113	-0.468064	-0.452450	-0.317372	-0.312854	-0.293819	-0.131506	-0.098979	-0.066571
Long-Short Credit	58	0.070936	0.054499	-0.024221	-0.017016	-0.008962	0.046328	0.054499	0.058670	0.169906	0.292545	0.293340
Long-Short Equity	276	0.481503	0.490190	-0.175605	0.041019	0.136508	0.449190	0.490190	0.505883	0.849187	0.925178	0.957577
Long-Term Bond	29	-0.158494	-0.197779	-0.291741	-0.290765	-0.286642	-0.208579	-0.197779	-0.160527	0.012296	0.016723	0.017085
Managed Futures	132	0.117150	0.128220	-0.311655	-0.115235	-0.100962	0.105586	0.128220	0.148599	0.352614	0.373558	0.599599
Market Neutral	143	0.067706	0.068271	-0.183848	-0.104413	-0.102087	0.025877	0.068271	0.084890	0.276444	0.330439	0.363127
Mid-Cap Blend	354	0.986315	0.994753	0.497470	0.599125	0.769827	0.984816	0.994753	1.015634	1.157625	1.284840	1.618512
Mid-Cap Growth	585	1.006259	0.992640	0.773380	0.808060	0.879106	0.975628	0.992640	1.010586	1.177020	1.213120	1.310768
Mid-Cap Value	383	1.022921	1.019030	0.742916	0.787659	0.834473	1.004676	1.019030	1.041820	1.168886	1.262423	1.313840
Miscellaneous Region	29	0.776359	0.795018	0.279515	0.282631	0.361181	0.791222	0.795018	0.803175	1.211642	1.237917	1.267523
Miscellaneous Sector	6	1.566987	1.568135	1.396261	1.397011	1.398263	1.420730	1.568135	1.715540	1.732605	1.732878	1.733041
Multialternative	391	0.235331	0.203590	-0.221251	-0.030786	0.006455	0.171006	0.203590	0.235589	0.642633	0.782749	0.889742
Multicurrency	52	0.171984	0.240658	-0.116222	-0.114347	-0.106268	0.162254	0.240658	0.252658	0.355134	0.364064	0.365085
Multisector Bond	259	0.103764	0.084466	-0.086215	-0.081724	-0.075359	0.077179	0.084466	0.106180	0.324877	0.348980	0.352295
Muni California Intermediate	61	-0.017930	-0.023287	-0.046408	-0.039244	-0.035928	-0.025461	-0.023287	-0.019721	0.043644	0.045568	0.046248
Muni California Long	88	-0.021986	-0.022787	-0.046382	-0.043756	-0.041495	-0.025517	-0.022787	-0.020079	-0.004199	-0.002495	0.000163
Muni Massachusetts	51	-0.020201	-0.020388	-0.042526	-0.039088	-0.038235	-0.021623	-0.020388	-0.018273	-0.003037	-0.001692	0.000094
Muni Minnesota	44	-0.024084	-0.023224	-0.049997	-0.047495	-0.043182	-0.024895	-0.023224	-0.021027	-0.009922	-0.004632	-0.003968
Muni National Interm	240	-0.020822	-0.026006	-0.053233	-0.049624	-0.045928	-0.028452	-0.026006	-0.024274	0.030316	0.058661	0.066027
Muni National Long	140	-0.021221	-0.021707	-0.047286	-0.044156	-0.039857	-0.024708	-0.021707	-0.018393	0.001716	0.011713	0.013824
Muni National Short	29	0.008071	-0.019647	-0.036312	-0.035528	-0.033888	-0.020357	-0.019647	-0.017452	0.075996	0.076258	0.076614
Muni New Jersey	45	-0.021649	-0.022350	-0.045602	-0.040865	-0.039382	-0.025116	-0.022350	-0.018395	-0.005938	-0.004207	-0.003022
Muni New York Intermediate	45	-0.014192	-0.016847	-0.041704	-0.039727	-0.035800	-0.022822	-0.016847	-0.015037	0.038808	0.042923	0.044619
Muni New York Long	69	-0.017490	-0.018357	-0.043413	-0.042898	-0.042275	-0.020087	-0.018357	-0.016293	0.015270	0.030316	0.032345
Muni Ohio	40	-0.027052	-0.024570	-0.054778	-0.049159	-0.044716	-0.027370	-0.024570	-0.022138	-0.013426	-0.010843	-0.010518
Muni Pennsylvania	54	-0.020135	-0.021682	-0.040342	-0.038419	-0.035961	-0.023279	-0.021682	-0.018376	-0.006435	-0.001448	0.001530
Muni Single State Interm	146	-0.024749	-0.024735	-0.047152	-0.043985	-0.041500	-0.026700	-0.024735	-0.022640	-0.008613	-0.006334	-0.001944
Muni Single State Long	223	-0.017926	-0.018440	-0.067626	-0.056964	-0.038452	-0.020716	-0.018440	-0.015586	0.002625	0.008627	0.062511
Muni Single State Short	12	-0.024852	-0.024999	-0.039991	-0.038552	-0.036152	-0.026984	-0.024999	-0.021007	-0.015336	-0.014832	-0.014530
Natural Resources	103	1.165030	1.196920	0.465435	0.783842	0.791060	1.170320	1.196920	1.253870	1.386953	1.478553	1.481885
Nontraditional Bond	272	0.093199	0.079892	-0.069410	-0.025495	-0.009483	0.062757	0.079892	0.096513	0.303125	0.331294	0.349204
Option Writing	97	0.525396	0.524754	0.168899	0.199109	0.202684	0.494386	0.524754	0.598874	0.804088	0.832205	0.838814
Pacific/Asia ex-Japan Stk	78	0.634129	0.651758	0.223841	0.371647	0.418858	0.573641	0.651758	0.694334	0.871881	0.878698	0.882319
Preferred Stock	44	0.087488	0.065993	0.021828	0.022824	0.023727	0.047979	0.065993	0.070220	0.259666	0.260200	0.261504
Real Estate	236	0.567126	0.580451	0.147300	0.155846	0.376926	0.572434	0.580451	0.590634	0.661202	0.772488	0.922993
Short Government	41	-0.039968	-0.034556	-0.080508	-0.079202	-0.078757	-0.036017	-0.034556	-0.030372	-0.019987	-0.018697	-0.018627
Short-Term Bond	155	-0.007095	-0.022927	-0.060663	-0.054302	-0.049429	-0.027013	-0.022927	-0.017688	0.151272	0.179236	0.191966
Small Blend	696	1.089111	1.102060	0.726103	0.818291	0.908625	1.077960	1.102060	1.124330	1.208635	1.225888	1.295874
Small Growth	621	1.120067	1.129350	0.872479	0.918926	0.943082	1.107990	1.129350	1.156690	1.270350	1.298570	1.305828
Small Value	386	1.080288	1.085435	0.579526	0.701108	0.858335	1.060220	1.085435	1.126100	1.250840	1.380229	1.417251
Tactical Allocation	268	0.509563	0.504368	-0.091832	0.116487	0.158507	0.432842	0.504368	0.570534	0.885716	1.043697	1.082422
Target-Date 2000-2010	111	0.360807	0.377570	0.097259	0.101685	0.155324	0.372865	0.377570	0.385729	0.444280	0.458527	0.463129
Target-Date 2015	138	0.396105	0.432831	0.107893	0.116909	0.144575	0.425240	0.432831	0.444539	0.520615	0.538200	0.543648
Target-Date 2020	219	0.457569	0.493490	0.196389	0.201797	0.226444	0.476500	0.493490	0.503982	0.607993	0.611694	0.614193
Target-Date 2025	193	0.563041	0.597537	0.228638	0.311775	0.363101	0.576503	0.597537	0.609931	0.688049	0.701069	0.728155

Up-market Betas of Mutual Funds by Peer Groups as of March 31, 2017

Peer Group	Number of Mutual Funds	Mean	Median	1st Percentile	2.5th Percentile	5th Percentile	40th Percentile	50th Percentile	60th Percentile	95th Percentile	97.5th Percentile	99th Percentile
Target-Date 2030	219	0.652803	0.686796	0.270952	0.276596	0.391023	0.657726	0.686796	0.698313	0.796456	0.816314	0.825471
Target-Date 2035	191	0.748376	0.768228	0.307653	0.445648	0.571966	0.747393	0.768228	0.783574	0.880089	0.914910	0.920401
Target-Date 2040	218	0.794661	0.830721	0.326900	0.336617	0.537445	0.816938	0.830721	0.840648	0.912796	0.921054	0.925592
Target-Date 2045	191	0.835573	0.850880	0.409746	0.535443	0.701813	0.839588	0.850880	0.869732	0.923275	0.931128	0.937783
Target-Date 2050	210	0.835773	0.862649	0.373544	0.377406	0.573108	0.842240	0.862649	0.883088	0.936632	0.939989	0.954235
Target-Date 2055	195	0.852425	0.865013	0.463298	0.577036	0.708947	0.849261	0.865013	0.889289	0.934027	0.958480	0.970828
Target-Date 2060+	124	0.880650	0.892781	0.776070	0.777956	0.809202	0.878405	0.892781	0.901284	0.941202	0.957450	0.963222
Target-Date Retirement	164	0.282988	0.303181	0.089585	0.098085	0.147359	0.264459	0.303181	0.319762	0.392521	0.439137	0.446789
Technology	165	1.078432	1.076860	0.706605	0.971907	1.002358	1.068932	1.076860	1.087566	1.223792	1.231106	1.231750
Trading--Inverse Commodities	4	-0.915697	-0.914272	-1.222364	-1.221695	-1.220580	-1.090473	-0.914272	-0.738070	-0.612811	-0.612124	-0.611711
Trading--Inverse Debt	15	0.096893	0.295110	-0.407221	-0.405668	-0.403080	0.170840	0.295110	0.384074	0.433534	0.435608	0.436852
Trading--Inverse Equity	7	-2.047014	-1.914830	-2.436672	-2.436225	-2.435479	-2.196668	-1.914830	-1.908392	-1.519560	-1.437990	-1.389048
Trading--Leveraged Debt	9	-0.321227	-0.455368	-0.474946	-0.474817	-0.474602	-0.456686	-0.455368	-0.451838	0.244546	0.421859	0.528247
Trading--Leveraged Equity	82	1.857961	1.825205	0.641448	0.929404	0.937167	1.702290	1.825205	2.029804	2.581172	2.657964	3.292048
Trading--Miscellaneous	5	-0.272823	-0.031483	-0.637698	-0.637617	-0.637482	-0.273450	-0.031483	-0.031455	-0.027936	-0.027501	-0.027240
Ultrashort Bond	1	-0.005871	-0.005871	-0.005871	-0.005871	-0.005871	-0.005871	-0.005871	-0.005871	-0.005871	-0.005871	-0.005871
Utilities	50	0.564220	0.547403	0.442813	0.443059	0.443434	0.528701	0.547403	0.553084	0.705893	0.707223	0.707603
Volatility	4	-1.220082	-1.828865	-1.833390	-1.833390	-1.833390	-1.831580	-1.828865	-1.826150	0.245522	0.428157	0.537738
World Allocation	488	0.543321	0.541515	0.173472	0.217914	0.248152	0.504032	0.541515	0.572741	0.818662	0.832433	0.848874
World Bond	275	0.051311	0.012415	-0.097886	-0.091480	-0.074742	-0.004375	0.012415	0.027648	0.300643	0.445475	0.460524
World Stock	957	0.918756	0.936334	0.531540	0.593319	0.660469	0.901464	0.936334	0.964297	1.106108	1.125880	1.164693

The paper printed in the following section, "Measuring Risk for Cost of Capital: The Downside Beta Approach" by James Chong and G. Michael Phillips, was first published in the *Journal of Corporate Treasury Management,* 4(4), on pages 344-352, and has been re-published in *Beta Estimates for Valuation & Cost of Capital* with the permission of Henry Stewart Publications http://www.henrystewartpublications.com/.

Measuring risk for cost of capital: The downside beta approach

Received (in revised form): 14th December, 2011

James Chong
is an associate professor and Associate Director of the Center for Financial Planning and Investment at California State University, Northridge. He also serves as the Research Economist for MacroRisk Analytics. James received his MS in financial mathematics from the University of Chicago and his PhD in finance from the ICMA Centre at the University of Reading.

G. Michael Phillips
is the Director of the Center for Financial Planning and Investment, and a professor of Finance, Real Estate, and Insurance at California State University, Northridge. He also serves as Chief Scientist for MacroRisk Analytics. Michael received his BS in mathematics and economics from Illinois State University and his PhD from the University of California, San Diego, with specialisations in econometrics and applied economics.

James Chong, Department of Finance, Real Estate, & Insurance, California State University, Northridge, 18111 Nordhoff Street, Northridge, CA 91330-8379, USA
Tel: +1 (818) 677-2459; E-mail: jchong@macrorisk.com.
G. Michael Phillips, Department of Finance, Real Estate, & Insurance, California State University, Northridge, 18111 Nordhoff Street, Northridge, CA 91330-8379, USA
Tel: +1 (818) 677-2459; E-mail: mphillips@macrorisk.com.

Abstract The cost of capital is partly determined by a cost of equity which centres on the concepts of the 'capital asset pricing model' (CAPM) and, ultimately, beta. Beta traditionally assumes that risks are linear, but according to findings from behavioural finance, they are not; especially downside risks which are not reflected correctly in the traditional CAPM beta. In this paper, the authors discuss the down-market beta and its growing importance as an alternative to the traditional CAPM beta in computing cost of capital and making capital budgeting and valuation decisions. In addition, they demonstrate that equity rates based on CAPM betas can be quite different from those based on down-market beta, leading to significantly different value estimates. In their sample computations, valuations based on CAPM betas would lead to excessive value when there was greater downside risk and lower values when there was less downside risk.

KEYWORDS: valuation, downside risk, WACC, capital budgeting, dual beta

INTRODUCTION

By and large, behavioural finance studies have consistently found that economic decision-makers try to avoid 'pain', including that of disastrous economic loss. Business valuation analysts, corporate decision-makers, and investors try to include measures of risk in their calculations to help account for the possibility that a project might fail, a loan might not be repaid, or that an investment could lose value. On the other hand, these same analysts, investors, and decision-makers hope that their projects succeed beyond their expectations, that all their loans are repaid on schedule, and that various investments produce spectacular profits.

In a sense, both unexpectedly low profits and unexpectedly high profits are 'risk'. But the risk of losing money is generally a bad thing, while the risk of making extra profits is generally a good thing.

The Capital Asset Pricing Model (CAPM) estimate of beta, often used as a component of investment risk, is based on assumptions of symmetry such that the risk of losing money or the risk of making extra profits are viewed as equivalent.

This paper discusses the dual-beta model, which separately accounts for these two types of risk and provides an empirical analysis of how confusing the two types of risk can generate markedly different estimates of required return and, for the business valuation analyst, quite different computations of value.

The authors begin with a discussion of the importance of beta in computing the cost of capital and making capital budgeting and valuation decisions, and then discuss historically significant, but often forgotten, research that highlights the importance of separately assessing the risk of profits and losses. They then discuss the growing importance of the dual-beta model as an alternative. In the empirical section of this paper, the authors compute the equity component of the cost of capital using traditional beta and also a down-market beta estimated using a dual-beta model. They find that traditional beta underestimates equity risk about half the time, compared with the dual-beta estimate and that this can translate into large differences in present value computations. The paper concludes with several suggestions for practitioners.

CONTEXT AND LITERATURE

Investors, business valuation analysts, and corporate decision-makers are frequently faced with the problem of placing a current value on a future payment stream. Investors may be concerned with valuing a stock or mutual fund, corporate decision-makers may be concerned with evaluating a potential acquisition or new product line, and business valuation analysts focus on the current value of an ownership interest in businesses which may range from small personal service firms to large multinationals. In each case, however, there is usually a reduction of expected cash flows to present value.

CAPM in corporate finance

The challenge of forecasting cash flows is not the topic of this paper; rather, it focuses on the discount rate used to compute the present value of equity. In typical corporate finance and investment textbooks, the determination of this discount rate begins with the CAPM equation:

$$(r_j - r_f)_t = \alpha_j + \beta_j(r_m - r_f)_t + \varepsilon_t \qquad (1)$$

in which the excess return (the risk premium) for stock j is linearly related to the excess return (the risk premium) of the market index. The slope of this line, β_j, or simply beta, is perhaps the most commonly used measure of equity risk. The intercept, α_j, is known as 'Treynor's alpha' and represents the sustained economic profit, if any, associated with the investment. In most cases, α_j is assumed to be zero.

With slight modification to (1), the more common equation for the equity discount rate is obtained:

$$r_{jt} = r_{ft} + \beta_j(r_m - r_f)_t + \varepsilon_t. \qquad (2)$$

The riskless rate has added to it a systematic risk component, obtained by multiplying an equity risk premium by an estimate of beta. If there is any sustained economic profit, then one could add an estimate of additional alpha (α_j), if any. In such a case, the resulting equation would be:

$$r_{jt} = r_{ft} + \alpha_j + \beta_j(r_m - r_f)_t + \varepsilon_t. \quad (2')$$

The CAPM has been found to be widely used in business settings for establishing a cost of capital for discounting purposes. Graham and Harvey[1] found that 73.5 per cent of financial executives they surveyed 'always or almost always use the CAPM' for estimating the cost of capital. Bruner *et al.*[2] found that 80 per cent of financial advisers they surveyed rely on the CAPM; they also found that at least 85 per cent of corporate representatives, and at least 90 per cent of financial planners they surveyed, view the α term as not a part of the CAPM calculation.

Adjustments to the CAPM

With a few exceptions, business valuation texts tend to disagree with the above consensus and routinely discuss firm-specific risk premiums and other added factors that are analogous to the term. Pratt *et al.*[3] are typical in that they present the simple CAPM and then identify a number of additional risk factors, premiums, and discounts that are used to manually adjust the CAPM estimate to obtain discount rates. Hitchner[4] discusses various general premiums to be added to the CAPM and states 'the final component of the discount rate is the risk specific to the company being valued and/or the industry in which it operates'. McKinsey & Company[5] proceeds straight from the CAPM to the weighted average cost of capital (WACC) estimate without other premiums, discounts, or firm-specific adjustments. At the other extreme, Trugman[6] discusses the 'build up method', essentially adding risk premiums to a version of the CAPM in which β_j is assumed to equal 1, as well as the CAPM with estimated coefficients and no additional terms. He then discusses (2) as 'CAPM for the closely held business' in which α_j is identified as unsystematic risk, a specific company risk adjustment, or perhaps a size adjustment.

However, whether one is looking at college texts or professional valuation references, the preponderance that were reviewed are planted firmly on a behavioural theory in which rational economic agents have preferences over the expected outcomes of their investments and also the variance of those outcomes. This is the standard 'modern portfolio theory' approach closely associated with Markowitz[7,8] and Sharpe[9].

Downside risk approach

At about the same time that Markowitz was developing mean-variance theory, an alternative was being developed, which has been termed 'safety first'. Rather than on the entire distribution of possible returns, focus was placed on the probability of disaster or downside loss. First modelled by Roy,[10,11] the 'safety first' criterion has led to an alternative approach to viewing risk and return and, consequently, discount rates and capital budgeting.[12] This alternative approach is the 'mean-semivariance' or 'downside risk' approach, which defines risk in terms of the distribution of possible unfavourable outcomes, instead of all possible outcomes. Semi-variance is the variance determined by the lower portion of a statistical distribution; in the 'safety first' paradigm, it is a measure of the spread of outcomes below a critical value. The square root of the semi-variance is the semideviation, just as the standard deviation is the square root of variance. Curiously, Markowitz also discussed a mean-semivariance approach, but chose to use mean-variance for computational reasons even though he grants that 'semi-variance is the more plausible measure of risk'.[13]

In 1970, focus groups of executives in eight industries exploring their definitions of risk found 'the executives' emphasis on downside risk indicates that their concept of risk is better described by semi-variance than by ordinary variance'.[14] In a companion paper Mao analysed a framework for making capital budgeting decisions based on specific probabilities of outcomes, but concludes that in practical applications 'to work out such a distribution will be very difficult indeed'.[15]

Soon after, a theoretical analysis of capital market values by Hogan and Warren[16] demonstrated that 'the fundamental structure of the "capital-asset pricing model is retained when standard semideviation is substituted for standard deviation to measure portfolio risk."' This suggested that the computationally simpler CAPM type models could be revised to focus on downside risk rather than both upside and downside as measured by the variance. Presumably such revised models would better reflect the view of risk actually held by people.

Non-normal distribution

Development of capital budgeting, based on downside risk measures, slowed down following the 1979 demonstration by Nantell and Price: when the forecasted cash flows of the asset being valued and the returns from the overall market are related, following a bivariate normal distribution, then the equilibrium rates of return (discount rates) computed from the traditional CAPM or from the form using semideviation are equal and therefore there is little need to use semideviation methods.[17]

Intuitively, the normal distributions have a strong symmetry, so that if one knows the left-hand shape of the statistical distribution, one also knows the right-hand shape; the lower semideviation would be half the standard deviation and optimal behaviour with respect to one would be the same as the other. Unfortunately, asset returns series are not normally distributed but follow more complicated statistical distributions such that the probability of loss is not symmetric with the probability of gain.[18]

The investment performance literature actively discussed the impact of non-normality and downside risk, as in Sortino and Price;[19] and, in a series of papers, Estrada[20–22] developed applications of the downside CAPM (D-CAPM) and showed how that measure provides superior estimates of the cost of equity for purposes of present value computations of cash flows in developing markets.

Equity rates reflecting downside risk have also been tested using data from developed countries. An application to US stocks was performed by Post and Van Vliet,[23] who found that the model 'strongly outperforms the traditional ...

CAPM in terms of its ability to explain the cross-section of US stock returns.' The D-CAPM model was successfully applied to stocks on the London Stock Exchange and the Paris Stock Exchange in Artavanis *et al.*[24]

There is a conundrum. A wide range of academic research has confirmed that while the CAPM treats positive surprises (windfalls) and negative surprises (disasters) as equivalent risks, investors and business owners do not. The various measurements of alternative asset pricing models, based on downside risk, have generally proven superior to the symmetric CAPM in terms of their ability to explain the differences in equity returns across assets.[25] Theoretically the downside models provide a 'more plausible' approach to risk.[26] Statistically, they explain the differences in stock returns better than the traditional CAPM. But does it really matter to a business valuation analyst, corporate decision-maker, or investor which model provides the estimated beta, so long as one is provided? The authors provide an initial answer in the next section of this paper, focusing exclusively on down-market beta, in line with business owners' concern over downside risk.

THE DUAL-BETA MODEL AND THE DATA

The version of dual-beta model addressed in this paper is more precisely an 'up-market/down-market' model in which separate model parameters are estimated for times when the market benchmark goes up and for when it goes down, as shown in equation (3).

$$(r_j - r_f)_t = \alpha_j^+ D + \beta_j^+ (r_m^+ - r_f)_t D + \alpha_j^- (1 - D) + \beta_j^- (r_m^- - r_f)_t (1 - D) + \varepsilon_t. \quad (3)$$

In this equation, the dependent variable is the asset return in excess of the riskless rate, the two intercepts are α_j^+ and α_j^-, for the 'up-market' and 'down-market' regime respectively, and $\beta_j^+(r_m^+ - r_f)_t$ is the product of the 'up-market beta' and the up-market excess return, and similarly $\beta_j^-(r_m^- - r_f)_t$ is the product of the 'down-market beta' and the down-market excess return. D is a dummy variable, which takes the value of 1 when the market index daily return is non-negative, and zero otherwise. The final term, ε_t, reflects the idiosyncratic information not proportional to either the up-market or down-market excess returns. For this paper, 'down-market' days are when the market went down and 'up-market' days are the others. Parameter estimates for β_j, β_j^+, and β_j^- were provided by MacroRisk Analytics, a commercial provider of these estimates, from their database as of 29th October, 2010 for 4,500 common stocks traded on the NYSE, NASDAQ, and AMEX. A graph showing average up-market and down-market beta values per unit of average CAPM beta, by 2-digit SIC code, is provided in Figure 1 — this is to illustrate that seldom would up- and down-market betas equal CAPM beta. Indeed, the authors found that they were lower than those based on the down-market beta about 48 per cent of the time. The down-market equity rates are an average of 7.4 per cent higher than the CAPM equity rates. For those cases where the down-market beta is greater than the CAPM beta, the down-market equity rates are an average of 23.9 per cent higher.

The next exercise is to actually construct 'equity rates' for each of the 4,500 observations as a user might in

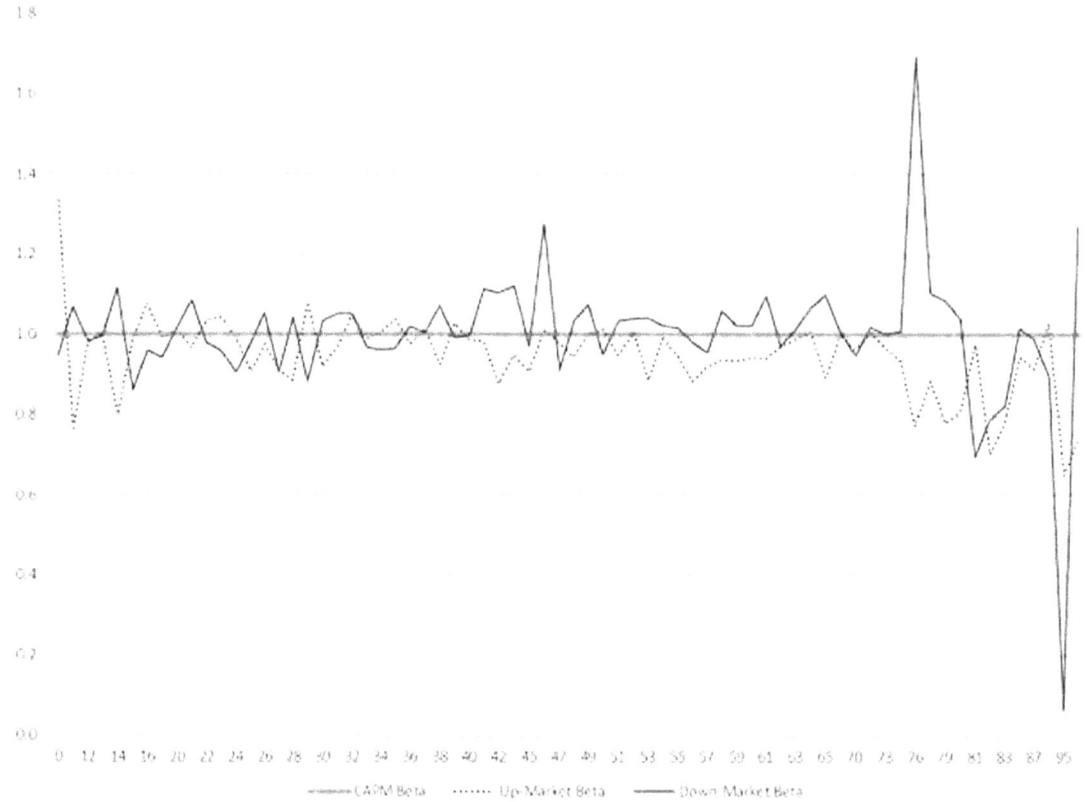

Source: MacroRisk Analytics, data as of 29/10/2010

Figure 1: Average up-market and down-market betas per unit of average CAPM beta, by industry (2-digit SIC)

practice by taking a measure of the riskless rate and adding to it the equity risk premium scaled by the estimated beta. Certainly there are differences regarding the selection of these inputs (see, for example, Fama and French[27]). For this computation, the authors use 3.41 per cent as the riskless rate, based on the forecast values of the 10-year Treasury bond from the third quarter 2010 Survey of Professional Forecasters from the Philadelphia Federal Reserve, and 6.2 per cent as a representative expected equity premium. For each of the approximately 4,500 observed companies the authors compute

$$k_{js} = 0.341 + \beta_{js} * (0.0620) \quad (4)$$

where 's' refers to the style of beta being used (CAPM, up-market, down-market) and k_{js} is the estimated equity discount rate.

In Table 1, the authors show the average present values of a hypothetical earnings stream of US$100,000 per year for 10 years. The table gives the average results separately for those times when the down-market beta is no greater than the CAPM beta, when the down-market beta exceeds the CAPM beta, and overall without regard to which beta estimate is larger.

On average, using the CAPM beta or the down-market beta produced present values that were fairly close (US$629,817 for the average result using

Table 1: Sample impact of different betas on present value computations

	Present value of US$100,000 per year for 10 years		
	CAPM Beta (US$)	Down-market Beta (US$)	Up-market Beta (US$)
Down-market beta ≤ CAPM beta	609,229.20	646,446.19	609,196.34
Down-market beta > CAPM beta	651,884.44	608,914.08	680,220.75
Overall average	629,816.81	628,331.27	643,476.36

CAPM beta and US$628,331 for the down-market beta). However, that average is based on over-estimated values about half of the time and under-estimated values for the other half. When the CAPM beta exceeds the down-market beta, it is being 'pulled up' by higher upside volatility; the relatively higher chance of profits is being misinterpreted as risk, resulting in too high a discount rate and consequently too low an estimated value. The average value was US$609,229.20 when using the CAPM beta, but would have been estimated as US$646,446.19 if only the down-market beta, reflecting downside risk rather than profit potential, had been used. Similarly, when the CAPM beta is lower than the down-market beta, there is a situation where the downside risk exceeds the upside profit volatility. Using the CAPM beta would have resulted in an overestimated average value of US$651,884.44 compared with the average of US$608,914.08 obtained using the downside beta. In those rare instances when the down-market beta and CAPM beta were practically the same, which the authors did not separately report, the estimated values would be essentially the same using any of the beta estimates. However, as graphically represented in Figure 1, this would be a rare event.

Table 1 reflects that about half the time a financial analyst using CAPM betas for estimating cost of capital would be overstating value and about half the time understating value; while overall 4,500 companies might cancel those errors, they certainly would not for any given analyst. In the Table 1 example, an average financial analyst using CAPM betas would be making approximately a 7 per cent error, but would not know in advance whether that was an error causing an overestimate or an underestimate of value. That error is readily corrected by using downside betas when computing cost of capital.

CONCLUSIONS

"Come to the downside ... we have cookies."

— paraphrase of a bumpersticker, *circa* 2010

That investors, analysts, and decision-makers do not value financial disasters and windfalls as equivalent risks seems a matter of common sense and has been confirmed repeatedly in the financial literature. A long tradition of considering 'safety first' and focusing on the risk of having losses, or having returns below some designated target, points to the use of downside risk measures. Commercial banks, with value-at-risk, and pensions and hedge funds, with return to semideviation ratios ('Sortino ratios'), have begun focusing on downside risk measures as part of their standard analytical practice.

For corporate treasurers, business owners, business valuation analysts, and investors without the resources of a large investment bank, the difference in estimated value caused by using CAPM betas, instead of downside betas, has not been widely understood.

This paper has demonstrated that equity rates based on traditional CAPM betas can be quite different from those based on down-market betas and can lead to significantly different value estimates. In the sample computations, valuations based on traditional betas would lead to excessive value when there was greater downside risk and lower values when there was less downside risk.

The authors do not believe this is the final word on the use of downside risk measures in business valuation. Much additional research remains to be done. The empirical work in this paper, while employing a broad sample of companies, reflects only one point in time. It is not yet known how these values change with the business cycle or credit conditions, or how alternative specifications such as the Fama-French three-factor model would work in a dual-beta formulation.[28] Even so, whether one uses commercially provided values, as used here, or one computes one's own with spreadsheet or regression software, down-market estimates of beta are readily available and can be used at least to provide an alternative calculation of value as part of model 'stress-testing'and perhaps to avoid substantial mispricing of businesses, projects, and investment assets.

Acknowledgments

The authors thank an anonymous reviewer for helpful suggestions, MacroRisk Analytics for providing data used in this paper, and Robert Neff, Sean Chasworth, and Nhat Ho for assistance and comments throughout this project.

References

1 Graham, J.R. and Harvey, C.R. (2001) 'The theory and practice of corporate finance: Evidence from the field', *Journal of Financial Economics*, Vol. 60, No. 2, pp. 187–243.

2 Bruner, R.F., Eades, K.M., Harris, R.S. and Higgins, R.C. (1998) 'Best practices in estimating the cost of capital: Survey and synthesis', *Financial Practice and Education*, Spring/Summer, pp. 13–28.

3 Pratt, S.P., Reilly, R.F. and Schweihs, R.P. (2000) 'Valuing a Business: The analysis and appraisal of closely held companies (4e)', McGraw-Hill, New York, NY.

4 Hitchner, J. R. (2006) 'Financial Valuation: Applications and Models (2e)', John Wiley & Sons, Hoboken, NJ.

5 McKinsey & Company (2011) 'Valuation workbook: Step-by-step exercises and tests to help you master valuation', John Wiley & Sons, Hoboken, NJ.

6 Trugman, G.R. (2008) 'Understanding business valuation: A practical guide to valuing small to medium-sized businesses', AICPA, New York, NY.

7 Markowitz, H. (1952) 'The utility of wealth', *Journal of Political Economy*, Vol. 60, No. 2, pp. 151–158.

8 Markowitz, H. (1991) 'Portfolio selection: Efficient diversification of investment (2e)', Blackwell Publishers Inc., Malden, MA.

9 Sharpe, W.F. (1964) 'Capital asset prices: A theory of market equilibrium under conditions of risk', *Journal of Finance*,

Vol. 19, No. 3, pp. 425–442.
10 Roy, A.D. (1952) 'Safety first and the holding of assets', *Econometrica*, Vol. 20, No. 3, pp. 431–449.
11 Roy, A.D. (1956) 'Risk and rank or safety first generalised', *Economica*, Vol. 23, No. 91, pp. 214–228.
12 Thompson, J.R., Williams, E.E., and Findlay, M.C. (2003) 'Models for investors in real world Markets', John Wiley & Sons, Hoboken, NJ.
13 Markowitz, ref. 8 above.
14 Mao, J.C.T. (1970) 'Survey of capital budgeting: Theory and practice', *Journal of Finance*, Vol. 25, No. 2, pp. 349–360.
15 Mao, J.C.T. (1970) 'Models of capital budgeting, E-V vs E-S', *Journal of Financial and Quantitative Analysis*, Vol. 4, No. 5, pp. 657–675.
16 Hogan, W.W. and Warren, J.M. (1974) 'Toward the development of an equilibrium capital-market model based on semivariance', *Journal of Financial and Quantitative Analysis*, Vol. 9, No. 1, pp. 1–11.
17 Nantell, T.J., and Price, B. (1979), 'An analytical comparison of variance and semivariance capital market theories', *Journal of Financial and Quantitative Analysis*, Vol. 14, No. 2, pp. 221–242.
18 Mandelbrot, B. (1963) 'The variation of certain speculative prices', *Journal of Business*, Vol. 36, No. 4, pp. 394–419.
19 Sortino, F.A., and Price, L.N. (1994) 'Performance measurement in a downside risk framework', *Journal of Investing*, Vol. 3, No. 3, pp. 59–64.
20 Estrada, J. (2000) 'The cost of equity in emerging markets: A downside risk approach', *Emerging Markets Quarterly*, Fall, pp.19–30.
21 Estrada, J. (2002), 'Systematic risk in emerging markets: The D-CAPM', *Emerging Markets Review*, Vol. 3, No. 4, pp. 365–379.
22 Estrada, J. (2007) 'Mean-semivariance behavior: Downside risk and capital asset pricing', *International Review of Economics and Finance*, Vol. 16, No. 2, pp. 169–185.
23 Post, T. and Van Vliet, P. (2004) 'Conditional downside risk and the CAPM', ERIM Report Series, available at: http://papers.ssrn.com/sol3/papers.cfm?abstract_id=797286 (accessed 20th December, 2011).
24 Artavanis, N., Diacogiannis, G. and Mylonakis, J. (2010) 'The D-CAPM: The case of Great Britain and France', *International Journal of Economics and Finance*, Vol. 2, No. 3, pp. 25–38.
25 Chong, J., Pfeiffer, S. and Phillips, G.M. (2011) 'Can dual beta filtering improve investor performance?' *Journal of Personal Finance*, Vol. 10, No. 1, pp. 63–86.
26 Chong, J. and Phillips, G. M. (2011) 'Beta measures market risk except when it doesn't: Regime-switching alpha and errors in beta', *Journal of Wealth Management*, Vol. 14, No. 3, pp. 67–72.
27 Fama, E. F. and French, K. R. (2002) 'The equity premium', *Journal of Finance*, Vol. 57, No. 2, pp. 637–659.
28 Fama, E. F. and French, K. R. (1993) 'Common risk factors in the returns on stocks and bonds', *Journal of Financial Economics*, Vol. 33, No. 1, pp. 3–56.

The paper printed in the following section, "The Entrepreneur's Cost of Capital: Incorporating Downside Risk" by James T. Chong, Yanbo Jin, and G. Michael Phillips, was first published in *Business Valuation Review,* 33(3), on pages 81-91, and has been re-published in *Beta Estimates for Valuation & Cost of Capital* with the permission of the American Society of Appraisers.

Business Valuation Review
Volume 33 • Number 3

The Entrepreneur's Cost of Capital: Incorporating Downside Risk

James T. Chong, PhD, Yanbo Jin, PhD, and G. Michael Phillips, PhD

The capital asset pricing model (CAPM) suggests that an investor's cost of equity capital is determined by beta, a measure of systematic risk based on how returns co-move with the overall market. We propose to replace beta with downside beta, a measure more consistent with investors' perception of risk. Recent empirical evidence suggests that downside beta better captures the risk-return relationship in both emerging markets and developed markets. Grouping companies into industries by two-digit Standard Industrial Classification (SIC) code, we show that the average downside beta can be very different from traditional beta. We discuss the implications of using downside beta on valuation and provide a simple example to illustrate the application in valuation for both diversified and undiversified investors.

Introduction

Investors are risk-averse. That is, they try to avoid losses and would not mind if their investments produced higher than expected returns. However, modern portfolio theory measures risk in terms of standard deviation of asset returns, which treats both positive and negative deviations from expected returns as risk. The positive deviations can be labeled ''upside risk,'' and negative deviations can be labeled ''downside risk.'' The upside risk is not necessarily undesirable. For example, if a project provided better than expected cash flows, or a stock had higher than average return, such outcome from ''upside risk'' would certainly be welcome by investors. On the other hand, investors would avoid downside risk. This asymmetric view on upside risk and downside risk is certainly not reflected by standard deviation.

The concept of beta in the capital asset pricing model (CAPM) faces a similar problem. Beta is a measure of systematic risk. By definition, it measures how an investment co-moves with the market, whether the market is going up (leading to profits), or going down (leading to losses). It is then plugged into an equation for the required return of an investment. This means that if an investment provided large positive returns when the market went up, and limited losses when the market went down, it would still have a high beta, and thus investors should require a higher rate of return for bearing this ''risk.'' However, this is not consistent with how investors view risk.

This paper discusses downside risk and downside beta, and the way in which downside beta can be incorporated in cost of equity capital estimation. We begin by reviewing the CAPM, followed by a discussion of problems with risk measurement in modern portfolio theory. We then discuss the theoretical background on downside risk and recent empirical evidence on downside beta. Empirically, we compute both downside beta and standard beta for US companies and group them into industries by two-digit Standard Industrial Classification (SIC) code. We show that two-thirds of the time, at the industry-average level, standard beta would underestimate downside beta, which would lead to value overestimation, and for the other one-third of the time, standard beta would overestimate downside beta, leading

James T. Chong, PhD, is a Professor of Finance and Associate Director of the Center for Financial Planning and Investment at California State University, Northridge. He also serves as a Research Economist at MacroRisk Analytics. He received his PhD in Finance from the ICMA Centre, The University of Reading.

Yanbo Jin, PhD (corresponding author), is an Associate Professor of Finance and Director of the Center for China Finance and Business Research at California State University, Northridge. She received her PhD in Finance from University of California, Irvine.

G. Michael Phillips, PhD, is the Director of the Center for Financial Planning and Investment and a Professor of Finance, Financial Planning, and Insurance at California State University, Northridge. He also serves as Chief Scientist for MacroRisk Analytics. He received his PhD from the University of California, San Diego, with specializations in econometrics and applied economics.

to value underestimation. Finally, we use a simple example to illustrate how an entrepreneur can incorporate downside beta in the cost of equity estimation.

The CAPM

For investors in large, publicly traded firms, the cost of equity capital can be measured by CAPM, which shows that for an investor with a well-diversified portfolio, the required return on a security can be measured by the following equation:

$$E(R_i) = R_f + \beta * RP_m \qquad (1)$$

where:

$E(R_i)$ = required return on security i,
R_f = risk-free rate, and
RP_m = general market risk premium,

and where β measures the systematic risk, or the sensitivity of a security's excess return (over the risk-free rate) to the excess return on the overall market, such as the New York Stock Exchange (NYSE) Composite Index or S&P 500 Index.

CAPM is widely used in large publicly traded corporations in estimating the cost of equity capital. For example, Graham and Harvey (2001)[1] found that 73.5% of financial executives surveyed "always or almost always use the CAPM" for estimating the cost of equity capital. Bruner et al. (1998)[2] also found that CAPM is the dominant model for estimating cost of equity capital: It is used by 80% of the corporations and 81% of the financial advisors surveyed.

Admittedly, for privately held firms, beta cannot be directly measured, since the market price of equity is unobservable. However, one can estimate a proxy beta using comparable firms operating in the same industry. As suggested by Pratt and Grabowski (2010),[3] an average or median industry beta can be estimated using publicly traded firms, which is then adjusted by leverage. The leverage-adjusted beta, via Equation (1), is then employed to compute the estimated cost of equity capital.

There is evidence showing that business appraisers also use CAPM in cost of equity capital estimation. Dukes et al. (1996)[4] surveyed members of the American Society of Appraisers (ASA) and the Institute of Business Appraisers (IBA) on the valuation practice of closely held firms. They found that when estimating the discount rate, the first choice for practitioners was to use the risk-free rate plus a risk premium. Furthermore, the most popular method to estimate the risk premium was to multiply a market risk premium by the beta of the firm, where beta is derived from a group of publicly traded comparable firms.

Additionally, CAPM can be augmented to incorporate size premium and specific risk. This is particularly important for investors in privately held firms who often do not hold a well-diversified portfolio. The resulting equation can be presented as:

$$E(R_i) = R_f + \beta * RP_m + RP_s \ +/- \ RP_u{}^{5} \qquad (2)$$

where:

RP_s = risk premium for small size, and
RP_u = risk premium due to company-specific risk factor.[6]

Modern Portfolio Theory: Problems

Modern portfolio theory considers risk of an asset in two different settings: If an asset is held in isolation, then the *total risk* measured by *standard deviation* is the relevant measure of risk; if an asset is part of a well-diversified portfolio, then the *systematic risk* is the relevant measure of risk, which is measured by *beta*.

Standard deviation measures how returns deviate from their mean. Both positive and negative deviation will contribute equally to the magnitude of standard deviation. However, as discussed previously, investors would treat upside risk differently from downside risk.

Similarly, the measure of systematic risk (beta) faces the same problem. Beta measures how an asset return co-moves with the market. Consider two hypothetical stocks: U and L. Suppose the returns on U, L, and the market follow the probability distribution in Table 1.

The distribution from Table 1 shows that, when the market goes down, U goes down half as much as the market while L goes down twice as much as the market, and when the market goes up, U goes up twice as much as the market, while L goes up only half as much as the market. Most investors would probably agree L is riskier than U, and therefore require a higher return to hold L.

---

[1] J. R. Graham and C. R. Harvey, "The theory and practice of corporate finance: Evidence from the field," *Journal of Financial Economics* 60(2) (2001):187–243.

[2] R. F. Bruner, K. M. Eades, R. S. Harris, and R. C. Higgins, "Best practices in estimating the cost of capital: Survey and synthesis," *Financial Practice and Education* Spring/Summer (1998):13–28.

[3] S. P. Pratt and R. J. Grabowski, *Cost of Capital: Applications and Examples*, 4th ed. (New York: Wiley Finance, 2010), chap. 11.

[4] W. P. Dukes, O. D. Bowlin, and C. K. Ma, "Valuation of closely-held firms: A survey," *Journal of Business Finance and Accounting* 23(3) (1996):419–438.

[5] S. P. Pratt and R. J. Grabowski, *Cost of Capital: Applications and Examples*, 4th ed. (New York: Wiley Finance, 2010), 110.

[6] Examples include industry risk factor, country risk factor, or other "specific risk" factors for investors who do not hold a perfectly diversified portfolio.

Table 1
Returns on the Market and Stocks U and L

Probability	Market	U	L
0.25	−20%	−10%	−40%
0.25	−10%	−5%	−20%
0.25	10%	20%	5%
0.25	20%	40%	10%

However, according to CAPM, U and L would have the same beta, and thus investors would require the same rate of return.

This example highlights the important difference between investor's perception of risk and the measure of beta. Investors focus on the downside risk, while beta measures both upside and downside risk. Next, we discuss the measure of downside risk, its theoretical background, and recent empirical evidence.

Downside Risk

The measure of downside risk was developed at about the same time that Markowitz developed the mean-variance theory.[7] Roy (1952)[8] was the first to formally model downside risk. In his model, an investor would prefer safety of principal first, and the resulting technique is termed the ''safety-first'' technique. The measure focuses on the downside loss, rather than on the entire distribution of returns.

Downside risk of a single asset

Generally speaking, downside risk for a single asset can be measured relative to the mean, or to any benchmark return. The resulting statistic is known as semivariance, for which the square root is termed semideviation.

Denote semideviation with respect to a benchmark B as $\sum_B$, we have:

$$\sum_{B} = \sqrt{\left(\frac{1}{T}\right) * \sum_{t=1}^{T} [\min(R_t - B), 0]^2} \qquad (3)$$

When B is the mean return, semideviation measures the spread of outcomes below the mean. However, semideviation can also be measured relative to any benchmark returns, thus making it an effective tool in risk analysis. In fact, this measure of downside risk has been widely used in the investment community to evaluate fund performance.[9]

As can be seen from the formula, only returns below a certain threshold would be considered in semideviation. Thus, the focus is on the downside of asset returns. This is consistent with investors' perception of risk. In fact, Markowitz himself admitted that ''semi-variance is the more plausible measure of risk.''[10] However, he chose to use the mean-variance framework for computational reasons.

Another reason for using the downside risk measure is that security distributions may not be normal or symmetrical. Markowitz (1959)[11] shows that when distributions are normal, both the semivariance and the variance measure are equivalent. Intuitively, since the normal distribution is symmetrical, the upper-tail and lower-tail would provide the same information. Thus, semivariance would simply be one-half of variance. However, empirical research has shown that security distributions are non-normal, and nonsymmetrical.[12] Therefore, focusing on the part of the distribution below the threshold value gives a more accurate portrait of downside risk.

Empirically, researchers have shown that this measure of downside risk is more consistent with investors' perception of risk. For example, in a survey of business executives in medium and large companies, when asked what they understood by the term ''investment risk,'' the typical answers were:

> *''Risk is the prospect of not meeting the target rate of return. That is the risk, isn't it? If you are one hundred percent sure of making the target return, then it is a zero risk proposition.''*
>
> *''...I never worry about the project return going above the target return. Risk is what might happen when the return is going to be less.''*[13]

[7] H. Markowitz, ''The utility of wealth,'' *Journal of Political Economy* 60(2) (1952):151–158; H. Markowitz, ''Portfolio selection,'' *Journal of Finance* 7(1) (1952):77–91.

[8] A. D. Roy, ''Safety first and the holding of assets,'' *Econometrica* 20(3) (1952):431–449.

[9] See, for example, F. A. Sortino and R. V. Meer, ''Downside risk,'' *Journal of Portfolio Management* 17(4) (1991):27–31; F. A. Sortino, and L. N. Price, ''Performance measurement in a downside risk framework,'' *Journal of Investing* 3(3) (1994):59–64; C. Mamoghli and S. Daboussi, ''Performance measurement of hedge fund portfolios in a downside risk framework,'' *Journal of Wealth Management* 12(2) (2007):101–112.

[10] H. Markowitz, *Portfolio Selection: Efficient Diversification of Investment*, 2nd ed. (Malden, MA: Blackwell Publishers Inc., 1991).

[11] H. Markowitz, *Portfolio Selection*, 1st ed. (New York: John Wiley & Sons, 1959).

[12] B. Mandelbrot, ''The variation of certain speculative prices,'' *Journal of Business* 36(4) (1963):394–419; G. Bekaert, C. Erb, C. Harvey, and T. Viskanta, ''Distributional characteristics of emerging market returns, and asset allocation,'' *Journal of Portfolio Management* 24(1998):102–116; F. Aparicio and J. Estrada, ''Empirical distributions of stock returns: European securities markets, 1990–95,'' *European Journal of Finance* 7(2001):1–21.

[13] J. C. T. Mao, ''Survey of capital budgeting: Theory and practice,'' *Journal of Finance* 25(2) (1970):349–360.

These statements clearly show that investors view risk as the probability of loss. Consistent with this view, investors would require higher return to hold assets with higher downside risk.

Downside beta

According to CAPM, when an asset is held in a portfolio, asset risk can be measured by its risk contribution to the market portfolio, also known as market beta. Extending the notion of downside risk to modern portfolio theory, one can measure the downside risk of an asset by downside beta.

In fact, Hogan and Warren (1974)[14] showed that CAPM can be revised with semi–standard deviation in place of standard deviation to measure portfolio risk. Bawa and Lindenberg (1977)[15] demonstrated that CAPM can be naturally extended to incorporate the measure of downside beta as:

$$\beta^{-} = \frac{cov(r_i, r_m | r_m < u_m)}{var(r_m | r_m < u_m)} \tag{4}$$

where r_i and r_m are the excess returns to security i and market m, and u_m is the average market excess return.

Similarly, an upside beta can be measured as follows:

$$\beta^{+} = \frac{cov(r_i, r_m | r_m > u_m)}{var(r_m | r_m > u_m)} \tag{5}$$

Therefore, β^- and β^+ can be estimated with a regression of excess return of security i on excess return of the market, conditional on excess market return being below the mean (downside beta) and above the mean (upside beta).

Recent empirical studies have shown increasing support for using downside beta. In the US market, Ang et al. (2006)[16] showed that investors are rewarded with higher returns for bearing downside risks. The authors estimated that the cross section of stock returns exhibits a downside risk premium of about 6% annually. More importantly, they showed that the reward for bearing downside risk cannot be explained by standard market beta, size, or value, nor can it be explained by liquidity risk or momentum characteristics. They also illustrated that individual stocks with higher downside betas have higher average returns over the same period. More recently, Botshekan et al. (2012)[17] further confirmed that downside risk is priced consistently across different samples, periods, and decomposition methods, using individual US stocks over the period 1963–2008. They also found that downside risks carry higher risk premiums compared to other risk measures.

In addition, downside beta has been shown to explain the cross-section returns better than standard beta among other developed markets.[18] In emerging markets, Alles and Murray (2013)[19] studied eight Asian markets[20] and found that downside beta is priced by investors.

A series of studies by Estrada[21] supported the use of downside beta in both emerging markets and developed markets. In a comprehensive study,[22] he computed standard betas and downside betas for stocks across twenty-three developed markets and twenty-seven emerging markets included in the Morgan Stanley Capital Indices (MSCI). He found that downside beta outperformed standard beta in explaining the variations of cross-section returns in both types of markets. In particular, across emerging market companies, downside beta alone explained 55% of the variability in mean returns.

Estrada also showed that standard beta and downside beta could differ significantly, especially in emerging markets, where stock returns are more skewed than those in developed markets. For example, average standard beta for Brazilian firms is 1.44, while downside beta is 2.16; Indian firms' average standard beta is 0.54, while downside beta is 1.10.

Furthermore, Estrada computed the required return on equity based on both measures of beta. Using downside beta, the mean required annual return[23] of firms across developed markets is 74 basis points higher than that measured by standard beta. However, in emerging markets, required return based on downside beta is 254 basis points higher than the standard beta counterpart. Such a big difference will no doubt affect the valuation of

---

[14] W. W. Hogan and J. M. Warren, "Toward the development of an equilibrium capital-market model based on semi-variance," *Journal of Financial and Quantitative Analysis* 9(1) (1974):1–11.

[15] V. Bawa and E. Lindenberg, "Capital market equilibrium in a mean-lower partial moment framework," *Journal of Financial Economics* 5 (1977):189–200.

[16] A. Ang, J. Chen, and Y. Xing, "Downside risk." *Review of Financial Studies* 19(4) (2006):1191–1239.

[17] M. Botshekan, R. Kraeussl, and A. Lucas, "Cash flow and discount rate risk in up and down markets: What is actually priced?" *Journal of Financial and Quantitative Analysis* 47(6) (2012):1279–1301.

[18] For an analysis on UK individual stocks, see: C. Pedersen and S. Huang, "Does downside beta matter in asset pricing?" *Applied Financial Economics* 17(2007):961–978. For an application on stocks listed on the London Stock Exchange and Paris Stock Exchange, see: N. Artavanis, G. Diacogiannis, and J. Mylonakis, "The D-CAPM: The case of Great Britain and France," *International Journal of Economics and Finance* 2(3) (2010):25–38.

[19] L. Alles and L. Murray, "Rewards for downside risk in Asian markets," *Journal of Banking and Finance* 37(7) (2013):2501–2509.

[20] The eight Asian markets are: China, India, Indonesia, Korea, Malaysia, Pakistan, Taiwan and Thailand.

[21] J. Estrada, "The cost of equity in emerging markets: A downside risk approach," *Emerging Markets Quarterly* Fall (2000):19–30; J. Estrada, "Systematic risk in emerging markets: The D-CAPM," *Emerging Markets Review* 3(4) (2002):365–379; and J. Estrada, "Mean-semivariance behavior: Downside risk and capital asset pricing," *International Review of Economics and Finance* 16 (2007):169–185.

[22] J. Estrada, "Mean-semivariance behavior: Downside risk and capital asset pricing," *International Review of Economics and Finance* 16 (2007):169–185.

[23] The author used a risk-free rate of 5.03% and market risk premium of 5.5%.

companies significantly, private or public. As the author argued in the paper, "Differences of this magnitude are simply too large for practitioners to ignore" (Estrada 2007, 184).

In fact, Pratt and Grabowski (2010) also discussed downside risk as one of the risk measures beyond beta.[24] The authors noted that downside risk measures such as semivariance are more consistent with the common concept of risk. In addition to reviewing the literature, they also computed standard betas and downside betas for five industries as of December 2008. Interestingly, it appears that downside betas are almost always higher than standard betas during this time period, possibly due to investors' sentiment at the time of the financial crisis.

More recently, Chong and Phillips (2012)[25] discussed implications of using downside beta on corporate valuation. They showed that even at the industry level, the average downside beta can be quite different from that of the standard beta. About half of the time, the average downside beta is higher than the standard beta. Under these occasions, a financial analyst using CAPM betas would underestimate the cost of capital and overestimate the project or corporate value.

Other measures of downside risk

In addition to downside beta, researchers have also looked at skewness as a measure of downside risk. As discussed before, asset return distributions are rarely symmetrical. When an asset return has negative skewness, the asset will tend to have more downside returns than upside gains. In a portfolio setting, risk-averse investors will prefer to hold securities that have positive co-skewness with the market, and they will require higher returns to hold securities with negative co-skewness with the market.

Harvey and Siddique (2000)[26] examined an extended CAPM that incorporates conditional skewness. They show that systematic skewness is economically important and requires an average annual risk premium of 3.6%. They also show that systematic skewness helps explain the cross-section variation of expected returns beyond factors like size and book-to-market.

Galagedera and Brooks (2007)[27] used downside co-skewness as an alternative measure of downside risk to examine the explanatory power of this measure to cross-section returns in emerging markets. They found evidence that downside co-skewness is a better explanatory variable of emerging market monthly returns than downside beta.

Both downside beta and downside co-skewness measure the downside risk consistent with investors' perception of risk. However, so far, there seems to be much more empirical evidence supporting the use of downside beta, across both developed markets and emerging markets.

In the next section, we use a simple model to illustrate the application of downside beta and to compare the valuation difference between standard beta and downside beta.

The Dual-beta Model and the Data

To illustrate the difference in standard beta and downside beta, we follow the model used in Chong and Phillips (2012). We estimate the following regression using daily stock returns:

$$\begin{aligned}(r_j - r_f)_t = \alpha_j^+ D + \beta_j^+ \left(r_m^+ - r_f\right)_t D + \alpha_j^- (1-D) \\ + \beta_j^- \left(r_m^- - r_f\right)_t (1-D) + \varepsilon_t\end{aligned} \tag{6}$$

In this equation, D is a dummy variable that takes a value of 1 when the daily market return is non-negative. Thus, two sets of intercept and beta are estimated separately: α_j^- and β_j^- during market downturns (when market return is negative), and α_j^+ and β_j^+ when the market goes up. We label β_j^- as "down-market beta" and β_j^+ as "up-market beta," to be precise.[28]

We computed down-market and up-market beta for 4,500 stocks traded on NYSE, NASDAQ, and AMEX, using daily returns over the past year. We also computed the standard beta using the same data.[29] We then grouped the companies into industries by two-digit SIC code and computed the average and median standard beta and downside beta by industry.

Table 2 presents the results. As shown from the calculated difference, the down-market beta seldom equals the standard beta at the industry level. Roughly two-thirds of the time, the down-market beta is higher than the standard beta. In some cases, the difference can

[24] S. P. Pratt, and R. J. Grabowski, *Cost of Capital: Applications and Examples*, 4th ed. (New York: Wiley Finance, 2010), 222–225.

[25] J. Chong, and G. M. Phillips, "Measuring risk for cost of capital: The downside beta approach," *Journal of Corporate Treasury Management* 4(4) (2012):344–352.

[26] C. Harvey and A. Siddique, "Conditional skewness in asset pricing," *Journal of Finance* 65(3) (2000):1263–1295.

[27] D. Galagedera and R. Brooks, "Is co-skewness a better measure of risk in a downside than downside beta? Evidence in emerging market data," *Journal of Multinational Financial Management* 17 (2007):214–230.

[28] Notice here that the down-market and up-market betas are slightly different from those estimated in Equations (4) and (5). The downside beta in Equation (4) is estimated conditional on when the market excess return is lower than the mean excess return. Similarly, the upside beta in Equation (5) is conditional on when the market excess return is above the mean excess return.

[29] Parameter estimates were provided by MacroRisk Analytics, a commercial provider of these estimates, from their database as of February 22, 2013.

Table 2
Standard Beta and Downside Beta by Two-Digit SIC Code

Two-Digit SIC	Label	Standard Beta (Mean)	Down-market Beta (Mean)	Difference (Mean)	Standard Beta (Median)	Down-market Beta (Median)	Difference (Median)
1	Agricultural production—crops	0.873	0.692	0.181	1.000	0.686	0.315
2	Agricultural production—livestock and animal specialties	0.386	1.002	−0.617	0.476	0.618	−0.142
7	Agricultural services	0.830	1.039	−0.210	0.830	1.039	−0.210
8	Forestry	0.450	0.479	−0.029	0.450	0.479	−0.029
10	Metal mining	1.263	0.485	0.778	1.232	0.293	0.940
12	Coal mining	1.464	1.500	−0.036	1.549	1.419	0.130
13	Oil and gas extraction	1.439	1.371	0.068	1.467	1.387	0.080
14	Mining and quarrying of nonmetallic minerals, except fuels	1.284	0.856	0.428	1.321	0.807	0.513
15	Building construction—general contractors & operative builders	1.430	1.417	0.013	1.599	1.524	0.075
16	Heavy construction, except building construction—contractors	1.243	1.364	−0.121	1.341	1.449	−0.108
17	Construction—special trade contractors	1.281	1.356	−0.075	1.100	1.173	−0.072
20	Food and kindred products	0.743	0.747	−0.003	0.689	0.704	−0.015
21	Tobacco products	0.751	0.874	−0.123	0.547	0.604	−0.057
22	Textile mill products	0.976	1.005	−0.029	1.108	1.075	0.033
23	Apparel, finished products from fabrics & similar materials	1.097	1.288	−0.191	1.150	1.335	−0.185
24	Lumber and wood products, except furniture	1.691	1.569	0.121	1.546	1.458	0.088
25	Furniture and fixtures	1.009	1.189	−0.180	1.157	1.284	−0.127
26	Paper and allied products	1.083	1.100	−0.018	1.047	1.172	−0.126
27	Printing, publishing, and allied industries	0.956	0.987	−0.030	1.028	1.006	0.022
28	Chemicals and allied products	0.960	1.088	−0.128	1.009	1.103	−0.094
29	Petroleum refining and related industries	1.368	1.359	0.009	1.188	1.133	0.055
30	Rubber and miscellaneous plastic products	1.006	0.999	0.007	1.045	1.139	−0.093
31	Leather and leather products	0.946	1.099	−0.153	1.101	1.068	0.033
32	Stone, clay, glass, and concrete products	1.322	1.218	0.104	1.518	1.214	0.304
33	Primary metal industries	1.380	1.200	0.179	1.488	1.338	0.150
34	Fabricated metal products, except machinery & transport equipment	1.026	1.138	−0.112	1.192	1.165	0.027
35	Industrial and commercial machinery and computer equipment	1.220	1.180	0.039	1.300	1.232	0.068
36	Electronic, electrical equipment & components, except computer equipment	1.138	1.049	0.089	1.195	1.053	0.142
37	Transportation equipment	1.370	1.333	0.037	1.362	1.235	0.127
38	Mesr/anlyz/cntrl instruments; photo/med/opt gds; watches/clocks	0.917	1.040	−0.123	0.973	1.060	−0.087
39	Miscellaneous manufacturing industries	0.879	0.976	−0.097	0.907	0.974	−0.067
40	Railroad transportation	0.927	0.907	0.020	1.100	0.880	0.220
41	Local, suburban transit & interurban highway passenger transport	0.429	0.994	−0.564	0.429	0.994	−0.564
42	Motor freight transportation	1.160	1.270	−0.110	1.060	1.210	−0.150
44	Water transportation	1.061	0.990	0.071	1.080	0.986	0.094
45	Transportation by air	0.954	1.021	−0.068	0.859	0.957	−0.098
46	Pipelines, except natural gas	0.572	0.596	−0.024	0.589	0.485	0.105
47	Transportation services	0.937	0.951	−0.013	0.909	0.811	0.099
48	Communications	0.878	1.021	−0.143	0.875	1.075	−0.201
49	Electric, gas, and sanitary services	0.523	0.629	−0.106	0.526	0.593	−0.067
50	Wholesale trade—durable goods	0.957	0.906	0.051	1.006	1.032	−0.025
51	Wholesale trade—nondurable goods	0.898	0.916	−0.018	0.848	0.915	−0.067
52	Building materials, hardware, garden supply & mobile home dealers	1.116	1.197	−0.081	1.016	1.213	−0.196
53	General merchandise stores	0.903	0.955	−0.053	0.896	0.880	0.016
54	Food stores	0.967	0.895	0.072	0.917	0.931	−0.014

Table 2
Continued

Two-Digit SIC	Label	Standard Beta (Mean)	Down-market Beta (Mean)	Difference (Mean)	Standard Beta (Median)	Down-market Beta (Median)	Difference (Median)
55	Automotive dealers and gasoline service stations	0.988	0.972	0.017	1.217	1.524	−0.307
56	Apparel and accessory stores	1.065	1.045	0.021	1.105	1.156	−0.051
57	Home furniture, furnishings and equipment stores	0.978	0.875	0.103	1.048	0.975	0.073
58	Eating and drinking places	0.834	0.931	−0.097	0.924	0.893	0.032
59	Miscellaneous retail	0.909	0.941	−0.032	0.953	1.037	−0.084
60	Depository institutions	0.620	0.719	−0.099	0.498	0.701	−0.203
61	Nondepository credit institutions	0.627	0.722	−0.095	0.575	0.631	−0.056
62	Security & commodity brokers, dealers, exchanges & services	0.630	0.666	−0.035	0.757	0.835	−0.078
63	Insurance carriers	0.792	0.877	−0.085	0.724	0.783	−0.059
64	Insurance agents, brokers and service	0.834	0.740	0.094	0.741	0.785	−0.044
65	Real estate	0.806	0.968	−0.161	0.775	0.978	−0.203
67	Holding and other investment offices	0.602	0.649	−0.047	0.744	0.839	−0.095
70	Hotels, rooming houses, camps, and other lodging places	1.132	1.189	−0.057	1.291	1.278	0.013
72	Personal services	1.013	1.057	−0.043	0.971	1.110	−0.140
73	Business services	1.003	1.025	−0.022	1.036	1.043	−0.007
75	Automotive repair, services and parking	1.294	1.407	−0.114	1.319	1.301	0.018
76	Miscellaneous repair services	0.981	2.324	−1.343	0.981	2.324	−1.343
78	Motion pictures	0.821	0.835	−0.015	0.873	0.870	0.002
79	Amusement and recreation services	0.735	0.718	0.017	0.827	0.857	−0.030
80	Health services	0.947	1.010	−0.063	0.976	1.118	−0.142
81	Legal services	1.023	1.335	−0.312	1.023	1.335	−0.312
82	Educational services	0.861	1.103	−0.243	0.845	1.126	−0.280
83	Social services	0.806	−0.381	1.187	0.806	0.505	0.301
86	Membership organizations	1.389	1.253	0.135	1.389	1.253	0.135
87	Engineering, accounting, research, management & related services	0.866	1.037	−0.171	0.834	0.890	−0.056
89	Services, not elsewhere classified	1.136	1.118	0.018	1.215	1.074	0.141
95	Administration of environmental quality and housing programs	1.161	2.721	−1.560	1.161	2.721	−1.560
96	Administration of economic programs	1.210	1.540	−0.330	1.210	1.540	−0.330
99	Nonclassifiable establishments	0.773	0.817	−0.045	0.900	0.924	−0.023

be quite significant. Take for example, the "agricultural production—livestock and animal specialties" industry (SIC = 2): The average standard beta is 0.386, while the downside beta is 1.002, i.e., more than twice the estimate of standard beta. In the cases when down-market beta is higher than the standard beta, the down-market beta is higher by about 21.3% on average.

We also computed equity rates using both down-market and standard beta. We used a risk-free rate of 2%, which is close to the ten-year US Treasury note yield as of the end of February 2013, and equity risk premium of 6%, as suggested in Ang et al. (2006). Thus, the equity rates are computed using:

$$k_{is} = 2\% + \beta_{is} * 6\% \qquad (7)$$

where i stands for the industry, and s refers to the style of beta used (down-market or standard beta).

The equity rates are presented in Table 3. In addition, assuming a hypothetical annual perpetual cash flow of $100,000, we computed the value of the cash flows using both equity rates. PV(std) shows the present value of cash flows using equity rates with standard beta, while PV(down) shows the value using equity rates with down-market beta. The last column shows the value difference. Since about two-thirds of the time the standard beta is lower than the down-market beta, using equity rates based on standard beta would overestimate the value of the cash flows about two-thirds of the time. The average overvaluation is about 14%. For the other one-third of the time, standard beta is higher than down-market beta. This leads to value underestimation by 7.3% on average.

Next, we use a simple example to illustrate the valuation impact to an entrepreneur. For simplification,

Table 3
Equity Rates and Present Value of Cash Flows Based on Standard Beta and Down-market Beta

Equity Risk Premium	6%
Riskless Rate	2%
Annual Cash Flow	$ 100,000

Two-Digit SIC	Label	Standard Beta (Mean)	Base Rate (Standard Beta)	Down-market Beta (Mean)	Base Rate (Down Beta)	PV (Std)	PV (Down)	(PV[Std] − PV[Down])	As % of Std
1	Agricultural production—crops	0.873	7.2%	0.692	6.2%	$ 1,381,802	$ 1,625,062	$ (243,260)	−17.60%
2	Agricultural production—livestock and animal specialties	0.386	4.3%	1.002	8.0%	$ 2,317,940	$ 1,247,894	$ 1,070,046	46.16%
7	Agricultural services	0.830	7.0%	1.039	8.2%	$ 1,433,244	$ 1,214,413	$ 218,831	15.27%
8	Forestry	0.450	4.7%	0.479	4.9%	$ 2,127,345	$ 2,051,690	$ 75,654	3.56%
10	Metal mining	1.263	9.6%	0.485	4.9%	$ 1,044,148	$ 2,036,063	$ (991,915)	−95.00%
12	Coal mining	1.464	10.8%	1.500	11.0%	$ 927,207	$ 909,233	$ 17,974	1.94%
13	Oil and gas extraction	1.439	10.6%	1.371	10.2%	$ 940,378	$ 977,916	$ (37,538)	−3.99%
14	Mining and quarrying of nonmetallic minerals, except fuels	1.284	9.7%	0.856	7.1%	$ 1,030,499	$ 1,401,812	$ (371,313)	−36.03%
15	Building construction—general contractors & operative builders	1.430	10.6%	1.417	10.5%	$ 945,070	$ 952,144	$ (7,074)	−0.75%
16	Heavy construction, except building construction—contractors	1.243	9.5%	1.364	10.2%	$ 1,057,105	$ 982,010	$ 75,095	7.10%
17	Construction—special trade contractors	1.281	9.7%	1.356	10.1%	$ 1,032,657	$ 986,846	$ 45,812	4.44%
20	Food and kindred products	0.743	6.5%	0.747	6.5%	$ 1,548,045	$ 1,543,053	$ 4,992	0.32%
21	Tobacco products	0.751	6.5%	0.874	7.2%	$ 1,536,729	$ 1,380,446	$ 156,283	10.17%
22	Textile mill products	0.976	7.9%	1.005	8.0%	$ 1,272,792	$ 1,245,607	$ 27,185	2.14%
23	Apparel, finished products from fabrics & similar materials	1.097	8.6%	1.288	9.7%	$ 1,165,366	$ 1,027,970	$ 137,395	11.79%
24	Lumber and wood products, except furniture	1.691	12.1%	1.569	11.4%	$ 823,450	$ 875,920	$ (52,471)	−6.37%
25	Furniture and fixtures	1.009	8.1%	1.189	9.1%	$ 1,241,776	$ 1,094,704	$ 147,072	11.84%
26	Paper and allied products	1.083	8.5%	1.100	8.6%	$ 1,176,978	$ 1,162,573	$ 14,404	1.22%
27	Printing, publishing and allied industries,	0.956	7.7%	0.987	7.9%	$ 1,292,576	$ 1,262,717	$ 29,860	2.31%
28	Chemicals and allied products	0.960	7.8%	1.088	8.5%	$ 1,288,427	$ 1,172,573	$ 115,854	8.99%
29	Petroleum refining and related industries	1.368	10.2%	1.359	10.2%	$ 979,462	$ 984,840	$ (5,378)	−0.55%
30	Rubber and miscellaneous plastic products	1.006	8.0%	0.999	8.0%	$ 1,244,356	$ 1,250,604	$ (6,249)	−0.50%
31	Leather and leather products	0.946	7.7%	1.099	8.6%	$ 1,302,577	$ 1,163,756	$ 138,820	10.66%
32	Stone, clay, glass, and concrete products	1.322	9.9%	1.218	9.3%	$ 1,007,065	$ 1,074,342	$ (67,277)	−6.68%
33	Primary metal industries	1.380	10.3%	1.200	9.2%	$ 972,862	$ 1,086,709	$ (113,848)	−11.70%
34	Fabricated metal products, except machinery & transport equipment	1.026	8.2%	1.138	8.8%	$ 1,226,432	$ 1,132,974	$ 93,457	7.62%

Table 3
Continued

Two-Digit SIC	Label	Standard Beta (Mean)	Base Rate (Standard Beta)	Down-market Beta (Mean)	Base Rate (Down Beta)	PV (Std)	PV (Down)	(PV[Std] − PV[Down])	As % of Std
35	Industrial and commercial machinery and computer equipment	1.220	9.3%	1.180	9.1%	$ 1,073,285	$ 1,101,246	$ (27,961)	−2.61%
36	Electronic, electrical equipment & components, except computer equipment	1.138	8.8%	1.049	8.3%	$ 1,132,839	$ 1,205,575	$ (72,736)	−6.42%
37	Transportation equipment	1.370	10.2%	1.333	10.0%	$ 978,461	$ 1,000,370	$ (21,909)	−2.24%
38	Mesr/anlyz/cntrl instruments; photo/med/opt gds; watches/clocks	0.917	7.5%	1.040	8.2%	$ 1,333,118	$ 1,213,593	$ 119,524	8.97%
39	Miscellaneous manufacturing industries	0.879	7.3%	0.976	7.9%	$ 1,374,484	$ 1,272,984	$ 101,500	7.38%
40	Railroad transportation	0.927	7.6%	0.907	7.4%	$ 1,322,213	$ 1,343,712	$ (21,499)	−1.63%
41	Local, suburban transit & interurban highway passenger transport	0.429	4.6%	0.994	8.0%	$ 2,185,376	$ 1,255,994	$ 929,382	42.53%
42	Motor freight transportation	1.160	9.0%	1.270	9.6%	$ 1,116,175	$ 1,039,822	$ 76,353	6.84%
44	Water transportation	1.061	8.4%	0.990	7.9%	$ 1,195,613	$ 1,259,540	$ (63,927)	−5.35%
45	Transportation by air	0.954	7.7%	1.021	8.1%	$ 1,294,867	$ 1,230,278	$ 64,589	4.99%
46	Pipelines, except natural gas	0.572	5.4%	0.596	5.6%	$ 1,840,985	$ 1,792,958	$ 48,027	2.61%
47	Transportation services	0.937	0.076	0.951	0.077	$ 1,311,559	$ 1,298,055	$ 13,504	1.03%
48	Communications	0.878	0.073	1.021	0.081	$ 1,375,891	$ 1,230,688	$ 145,203	10.55%
49	Electric, gas and sanitary services	0.523	0.051	0.629	0.058	$ 1,946,198	$ 1,731,549	$ 214,648	11.03%
50	Wholesale trade—durable goods	0.957	0.077	0.906	0.074	$ 1,292,067	$ 1,345,090	$ (53,024)	−4.10%
51	Wholesale trade—nondurable goods	0.898	0.074	0.916	0.075	$ 1,352,997	$ 1,333,582	$ 19,415	1.43%
52	Building materials, hardware, garden supply & mobile home dealers	1.116	0.087	1.197	0.092	$ 1,150,202	$ 1,089,120	$ 61,082	5.31%
53	General merchandise stores	0.903	0.074	0.955	0.077	$ 1,348,331	$ 1,293,372	$ 54,959	4.08%
54	Food stores	0.967	0.078	0.895	0.074	$ 1,281,851	$ 1,356,711	$ (74,860)	−5.84%
55	Automotive dealers and gasoline service stations	0.988	0.079	0.972	0.078	$ 1,261,054	$ 1,277,161	$ (16,107)	−1.28%
56	Apparel and accessory stores	1.065	0.084	1.045	0.083	$ 1,191,688	$ 1,209,458	$ (17,771)	−1.49%
57	Home furniture, furnishings and equipment stores	0.978	0.079	0.875	0.073	$ 1,271,051	$ 1,379,006	$ (107,955)	−8.49%
58	Eating and drinking places	0.834	0.070	0.931	0.076	$ 1,428,257	$ 1,318,356	$ 109,901	7.69%
59	Miscellaneous retail	0.909	0.075	0.941	0.076	$ 1,341,547	$ 1,308,369	$ 33,178	2.47%
60	Depository institutions	0.620	0.057	0.719	0.063	$ 1,748,077	$ 1,584,223	$ 163,855	9.37%
61	Nondepository credit institutions	0.627	0.058	0.722	0.063	$ 1,735,717	$ 1,578,887	$ 156,830	9.04%
62	Security & commodity brokers, dealers, exchanges & services	0.630	0.058	0.666	0.060	$ 1,729,787	$ 1,668,390	$ 61,397	3.55%
63	Insurance carriers	0.792	0.068	0.877	0.073	$ 1,481,042	$ 1,377,551	$ 103,491	6.99%
64	Insurance agents, brokers and service	0.834	0.070	0.740	0.064	$ 1,427,276	$ 1,552,399	$ (125,124)	−8.77%
65	Real estate	0.806	0.068	0.968	0.078	$ 1,462,278	$ 1,281,165	$ 181,113	12.39%

Table 3
Continued

Two-Digit SIC	Label	Standard Beta (Mean)	Base Rate (Standard Beta)	Down-market Beta (Mean)	Base Rate (Down Beta)	PV (Std)	PV (Down)	(PV[Std] − PV[Down])	As % of Std
67	Holding and other investment offices	0.602	0.056	0.649	0.059	$ 1,781,693	$ 1,697,051	$ 84,642	4.75%
70	Hotels, rooming houses, camps, and other lodging places	1.132	0.088	1.189	0.091	$ 1,137,444	$ 1,094,716	$ 42,728	3.76%
72	Personal services	1.013	0.081	1.057	0.083	$ 1,237,498	$ 1,199,005	$ 38,493	3.11%
73	Business services	1.003	0.080	1.025	0.081	$ 1,247,487	$ 1,227,027	$ 20,460	1.64%
75	Automotive repair, services and parking	1.294	0.098	1.407	0.104	$ 1,024,412	$ 957,513	$ 66,899	6.53%
76	Miscellaneous repair services	0.981	0.079	2.324	0.159	$ 1,268,101	$ 627,200	$ 640,901	50.54%
78	Motion pictures	0.821	0.069	0.835	0.070	$ 1,444,394	$ 1,425,975	$ 18,419	1.28%
79	Amusement and recreation services	0.735	0.064	0.718	0.063	$ 1,559,968	$ 1,584,869	$ (24,901)	−1.60%
80	Health services	0.947	0.077	1.010	0.081	$ 1,302,047	$ 1,240,797	$ 61,250	4.70%
81	Legal services	1.023	0.081	1.335	0.100	$ 1,229,111	$ 999,211	$ 229,901	18.70%
82	Educational services	0.861	0.072	1.103	0.086	$ 1,395,811	$ 1,160,094	$ 235,717	16.89%
83	Social services	0.806	0.068	−0.381	−0.003	$ 1,462,779	$ (34,838,593)	$ 36,301,372	2481.67%
86	Membership organizations	1.389	0.103	1.253	0.095	$ 967,809	$ 1,050,316	$ (82,508)	−8.53%
87	Engineering, accounting, research, management & related services	0.866	0.072	1.037	0.082	$ 1,389,458	$ 1,216,283	$ 173,175	12.46%
89	Services, not elsewhere classified	1.136	0.088	1.118	0.087	$ 1,134,405	$ 1,148,598	$ (14,193)	−1.25%
95	Administration of environmental quality and housing programs	1.161	0.090	2.721	0.183	$ 1,115,683	$ 545,716	$ 569,967	51.09%
96	Administration of economic programs	1.210	0.093	1.540	0.112	$ 1,079,599	$ 889,594	$ 190,005	17.60%
99	Nonclassifiable establishments	0.773	0.066	0.817	0.069	$ 1,507,031	$ 1,448,662	$ 58,369	3.87%

we assume the entrepreneur does not have any debt, and the annual projected cash flow is $100,000 for ten years. The entrepreneur uses the CAPM model to estimate the cost of capital. The comparable industry is the *miscellaneous repair service* with SIC = 76. We chose this industry because it gives an example where downside beta is significantly higher than the standard beta.

Table 4 shows the cost of equity capital and present value calculation. We assume the size premium is 6.36%.[30] For a diversified investor, we assume there is no additional risk premium ($RP_u = 0$ in Equation [2]). Based on downside beta, the estimated present value is $388,480. If the entrepreneur used the standard beta instead, he would have estimated the present value to be $516,642, leading to an overestimation of $128,162, or about a 33% value overestimation.

If the entrepreneur is undiversified, the required return would be higher to reflect the investor's lack of diversification.[31] For illustration purposes, we add a risk premium of 5% for the owner's lack of diversification. The cost of equity capital based on downside beta and standard beta is 27.3% and 19.25%, respectively. The present value based on downside beta is $333,486, while that based on standard beta is $430,212. Again, using standard beta would overestimate value by about 30%.

This example illustrates how downside beta can improve the accuracy of cost of capital estimation, compared to standard beta. It is important to note that downside beta applies to both diversified and undiversified investors, as long as the investors are risk averse. However, for undiversified investors, it is important to add additional

[30] Ibbotson SSBI 2011 Valuation Yearbook, Decile 10.

[31] For a more detailed discussion on cost of capital adjustment to reflect investors' lack of diversification, see: D. McConaughy and V. Covrig, "Owner's lack of diversification and the cost of equity capital for a closely-held firm," *Business Valuation Review* 26(4) (2007):115–120.

Table 4
Sample Impact of Downside and Standard Beta on Valuation

Build-Up Model (Assuming Comparable Industry SIC = 76)		
Risk-Free Rate	2%	
Equity Risk Premium	6%	
Size Premium*	6.36%	
Lack-of-Diversification Premium**	5%	
Annual Cash Flow (for 10 Years)	$100,000	
Downside Beta	2.324	
Standard Beta	0.981	
Diversified Investor	**Downside Beta**	**Standard Beta**
Cost of Equity	22.30%	14.25%
Present Value	$388,480	$516,642
Value Difference (Standard-Down)	$128,162	
Undiversified Investor	**Downside Beta**	**Standard Beta**
Cost of Equity	27.30%	19.25%
Present Value	$333,486	$430,212
Value Difference (Standard-Down)	$96,726	

* Size premium, group 10, last page of SBBI Valuation Edition 2011.
** For a more detailed discussion on diversification discount, see McConaughy and Covrig (2007).[31]

risk premium to compensate for the investor's lack of diversification.

Admittedly, not all industries experience such a big difference between standard beta and downside beta. However, for most of the industries, the difference is still quite significant. Thus, using downside beta could potentially lead to more accurate valuation estimation. Besides, the estimation procedure on downside beta requires no additional information beyond that required by standard beta. At a minimum, it would provide an alternative, and arguably better, valuation measure than those derived from standard beta.

Conclusion

There is now increasing evidence showing that downside risk is priced by investors. Downside risk focuses on the risk of losses, instead of the entire distribution of investment returns. Theoretically, this measure is more consistent with investors' perception of risk. Empirically, studies have shown that investment with higher downside risk is rewarded with higher returns, both in emerging markets and in developed markets. The reward for bearing downside risk is significant and cannot be explained by the standard beta.

This paper reviewed the theoretical and empirical literature on downside beta. More importantly, using daily returns of about 4,500 stocks over February 2012–February 2013, we showed that downside beta can be quite different from standard beta, even at the industry-average level. More specifically, we find that around two-thirds of the time, standard beta would underestimate the downside risk. Under these scenarios, valuation based on standard beta would lead to overestimation.

Using a simple example, we illustrated how an entrepreneur could incorporate downside beta in the cost of equity capital estimation, and how using standard beta would lead to significant value overestimation when downside beta is much higher than standard beta.

Downside beta is readily available through commercial data providers or by using a spreadsheet.[32] At a minimum, valuation based on downside beta would provide an alternative measure to the entrepreneur, perhaps leading to a more accurate valuation of the business.

[32] See, for example, Pratt, S.P. and Grabowski, R.J. (2010) *The Cost of Capital: Applications and Examples 4th ed. Workbook and Technical Supplement*, Chapter 4, which contains an example of computing downside beta.

The paper printed in the following section, "Why Downside Beta is Better: An Educational Example" by James T. Chong, William P. Jennings, and G. Michael Phillips, was first published in the *American Journal of Business Education,* 6(3), on pages 371-374, and has been re-published in *Beta Estimates for Valuation & Cost of Capital* with the permission of the authors and The Clute Institute.

American Journal Of Business Education – May/June 2013 Volume 6, Number 3

Why Downside Beta Is Better: An Educational Example

James T. Chong, California State University, USA
William P. Jennings, California State University, USA
G. Michael Phillips, California State University, USA

ABSTRACT

An educational example is presented that is an effective teaching illustration to help students understand the difference between traditional CAPM beta and downside (or down-market) beta and why downside beta is a superior measure for use in personal financial planning investment policy statements.

Keywords: CAPM; Downside Beta; Investment Policy Statements; Teaching Illustration

INTRODUCTION

Beta is ubiquitous in investment planning as a measure of the relative riskiness of an asset or portfolio compared to the overall market risk. Beta is often used as a limit on acceptable investments in investment policy statements. Beta is provided as a statistic in numerous printed and electronic databases and is widely used to summarize portfolio risk characteristics.

This paper proposes that downside beta - a beta estimated just from those data points of the asset or portfolio return when the benchmark return is negative - is a superior measure. This is because traditional beta includes any observations when the asset or portfolio outperforms the benchmark. If there is any asymmetry in the returns process, this could result in a misstatement of beta and lead to the incorrect exclusion of assets from consideration.

THE BASIC EXAMPLE

Consider the follow simple example: Suppose you have an investment policy statement in which a client specifies that she only wants assets with beta less than or equal to 1. That is, she only wants assets that are no riskier than the market portfolio.

Now, suppose that there are two assets to consider. Mutual fund A is identical to the market portfolio and has a beta of 1 regardless of whether the market is rising or falling. Mutual fund B is identical to the market portfolio on days that the market goes down, but goes up twice as much as the benchmark on up-days in the market. Figure 1 shows a comparison of these two investments in returns space, with the market index return as the horizontal axis. Note that P1SIM1 and P1SPX are essentially identical in returns.

Figure 1: Returns For Two Simulated Series (Y-axis) Against Returns For S&P Index (X-axis)

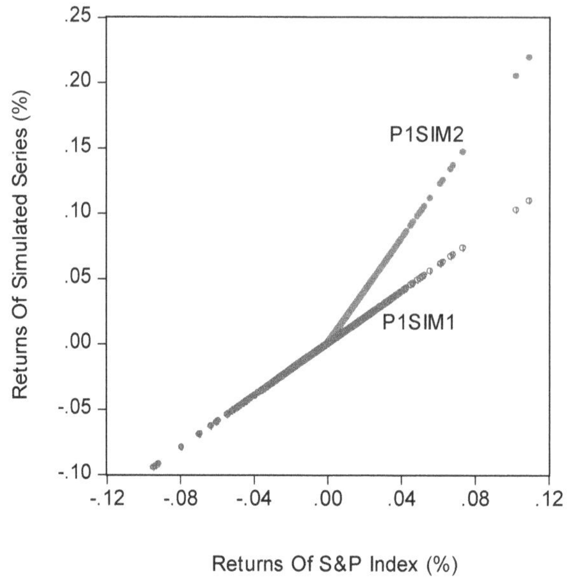

When the two returns series are plotted against each other, the difference between the two simulated portfolios becomes more apparent (Figure 2).

Figure 2: Comparison Of Two Simulated Series (Same Downside Beta, Series 1 With Lower Upside Beta, Series 2 With Higher Upside Beta)

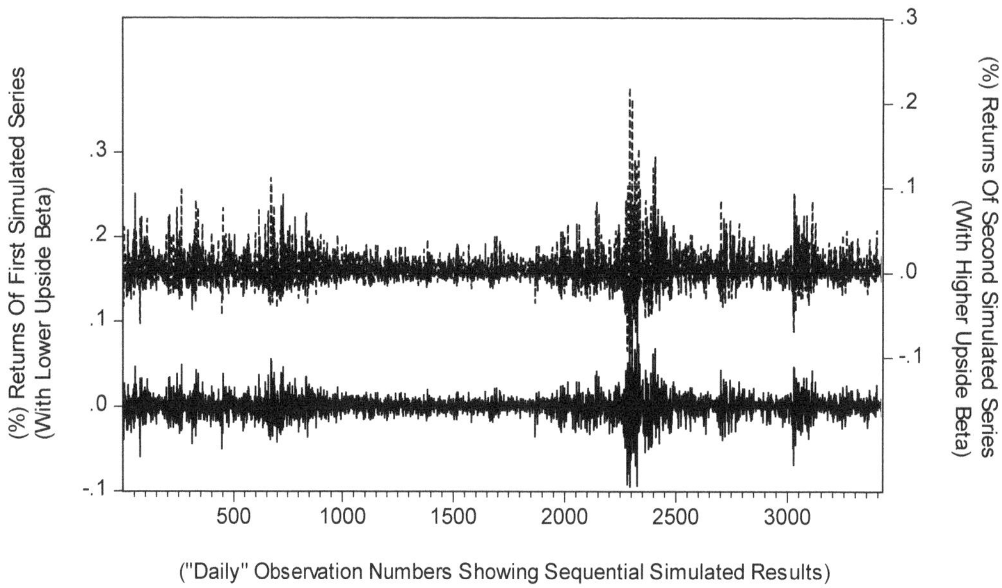

One can see that the P1SIM2 line, the second simulation, exceeds the first but is never less.

When converting from returns space into price space, the real difference in these portfolios is apparent (Figure 3).

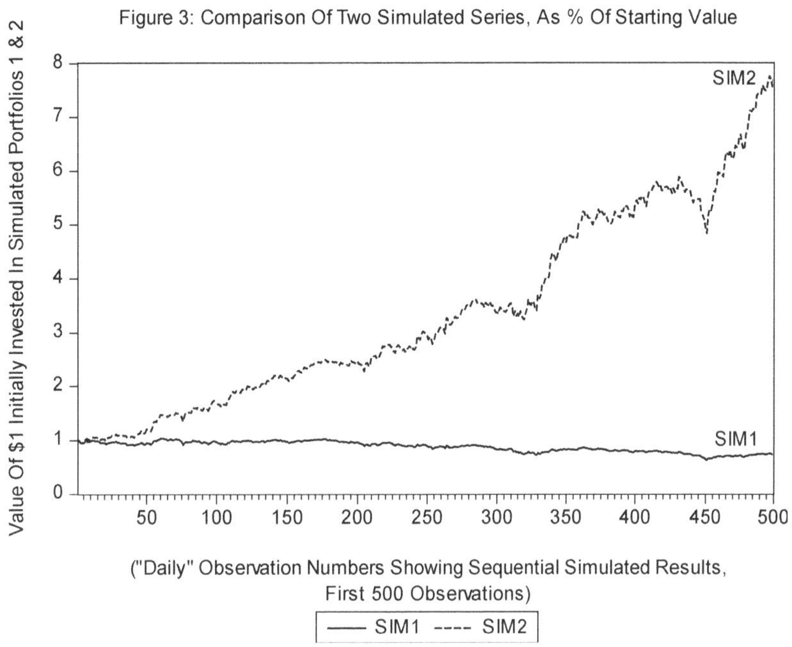

Now, one asks the students which portfolio is preferred: The dashed one (PISIM2) or the solid one (P1SIM1)? Virtually everybody would prefer the dashed-line since the two portfolios have the same downside movement, but the dashed-line portfolio shows substantially greater gain.

Running a basic market model equation against each of the two simulated portfolios verifies that the estimated beta for P1SIM1 is 1 and the estimated beta for P1SIM2 is 1.489.

According to the investment policy statement's guidelines, the dominant portfolio would not be acceptable because the beta exceeds the market.

If instead a downside beta measure was used, finding the beta using just those days when the market return was negative, then both investments would have the same downside beta, 1. At that point, other criteria such as upside beta (1 for P1SIM1 and 2 for P1SIM2) could be used to determine which investment is most appropriate.

CONCLUSION

Downside beta is not a hard concept, but it is unfamiliar to many financial professionals and students and is seldom discussed in textbooks. For purposes of investment policy statements, it is superior to traditional beta because it does not confuse positive return—profits—with loss.

This simple, yet effective, example quickly illustrates these differences and the problem with an investment policy statement designed to use beta limits.

Additional information on downside beta is available in Chong, Halcoussis, and Phillips (2012), Chong, Pfeiffer, and Phillips (2011), and Chong and Phillips (2011).

AUTHOR INFORMATION

James T. Chong, Ph.D., is a Professor and Associate Director of the Center for Financial Planning and Investment at California State University, Northridge. He also serves as a Research Economist at MacroRisk Analytics. He received his Ph.D. in Finance from the ICMA Centre, The University of Reading. E-mail: jchong@csun.edu

William P. Jennings, Ph.D., is Professor of Finance and Emeritus Dean of Business at California State University, Northridge, where he currently serves as Interim Vice President of University Advancement. He received his Ph.D. from the University of California, Los Angeles. E-mail: william.jennings@csun.edu

G. Michael Phillips, Ph.D., is the Director of the Center for Financial Planning and Investment and a Professor of Finance, Real Estate, and Insurance at California State University, Northridge. He also serves as Chief Scientist for MacroRisk Analytics. He received his Ph.D. from the University of California, San Diego, with specializations in econometrics and applied economics. E-mail: mphillips@csun.edu (Corresponding author)

REFERENCES

1. Chong, James, Dennis Halcoussis, and G. Michael Phillips. (2012). Misleading Betas: An Educational Example. *American Journal of Business Education, 5*(5), 617-622.
2. Chong, James, Shawn Pfeiffer, and G. Michael Phillips. (2011). Can Dual Beta Filtering Improve Investor Performance? *Journal of Personal Finance, 10*(1), 63-86.
3. Chong, James, and G. Michael Phillips. (2011). Beta Measures Market Risk Except When It Doesn't: Regime-Switching Alpha and Errors in Beta. *The Journal of Wealth Management*, *14*(3), 67-72.

The paper printed in the following section, "Misleading Betas: An Educational Example" by James Chong, Dennis Halcoussis, and G. Michael Phillips, was first published in the *American Journal of Business Education,* 5(5), on pages 617-622, and has been re-published in *Beta Estimates for Valuation & Cost of Capital* with the permission of the authors and The Clute Institute.

American Journal Of Business Education – September/October 2012 Volume 5, Number 5

Misleading Betas: An Educational Example

James Chong, California State University-Northridge, USA
Dennis Halcoussis, California State University-Northridge, USA
G. Michael Phillips, California State University-Northridge, USA

ABSTRACT

The dual-beta model is a generalization of the CAPM model. In the dual-beta model, separate beta estimates are provided for up-market and down-market days. This paper uses the historical "Anscombe quartet" results which illustrated how very different datasets can produce the same regression coefficients to motivate a discussion of the dual-beta model. Using data from 39 mutual funds, it is shown how very different dual-beta models can lead to the same CAPM beta estimates, much like the Anscombe quartet scenarios.

Keywords: CAPM; Beta; Dual-Beta; Anscombe

INTRODUCTION

The use of the standard Capital Asset Pricing Model (CAPM) beta to measure risk is well known and widely discussed in the finance literature (see, for example, Scholes and Williams, 1977; Todorov and Bollerslev, 2010). Lesser known is the concept of using asymmetric betas—estimating one value for an upswing in the market and another different value for downswings in the market (Chong, Pfeiffer, and Phillips, 2011). In fact, there is no reason to believe that one value for beta will accurately capture market risk for both an up- and down-market. The prevalent use of one estimate of a beta per stock or mutual fund for both up- and downturns in the market can lead investors to oversimplify the risk characteristics of the investment.

The misleading impression given to investors by the use of a single beta estimate for both up- and down-markets is analogous to Anscombe's quartet, four very different data sets that produce the same set of regression results (Anscombe, 1973). In fact, the comparison of the two problems is more than analogous. The concept of dual-betas exploits the fact that data used to estimate a single overall beta can be divided into two separate, distinct subsets. One subset is from the up-market and another from the down-market, giving two different beta estimates that capture different levels of market risk for the stock or fund. Ignoring these differences in the data by estimating a single beta gives a misleading portrait of asset risk in the same way that different data sets can lead to the same regression results (as demonstrated by Anscombe's quartet).

STANDARD CAPM MODEL

Beta has been shown by Fama and French (1992) to be an imperfect measure of investment risk. However, the standard CAPM model, which originally developed the idea of beta, is still popular among investment professionals and can be expressed as:

$$(r_j - r_f)_t = \alpha_j + \beta_j (r_m - r_f)_t + \varepsilon_t, \tag{1}$$

where r_f is the risk-free rate (the overnight U.S. Federal funds rate is used as proxy), r_j is the return on asset j, $(r_j - r_f)_t$ is the observed excess return on asset j, α_j is the estimated regression intercept, called alpha, $(r_m - r_f)_t$ is the estimated excess return on the market index (here, the S&P 500 Index), and ε_t is the unexplained portion of the model.

DUAL-BETA MODEL

As an extension of the standard CAPM model, the dual-beta model estimates separately the parameters for up-market when the daily return for the market index is non-negative and down-market when the daily return for the market index is negative. The dual-beta model can thus be expressed as:

$$\left(r_j - r_f\right)_t = \alpha_j^+ D + \beta_j^+ (r_m^+ - r_f)_t D + \alpha_j^- (1 - D) + \beta_j^- (r_m^- - r_f)_t (1 - D) + \varepsilon_t, \quad (2)$$

where α_j^+, β_j^+, α_j^-, and β_j^- are the estimated parameters for up-market and down-market days, respectively; $r_m^+ = r_m$ on days the market index did not decline and $r_m^- = r_m$ on days it did; *D* is a dummy variable, which takes the value of 1 when the market index daily return is non-negative and zero otherwise. If there is no asymmetry in beta, then the dual-beta model is identical to the standard CAPM model. In this study, the standard CAPM beta, up-market beta, and down-market beta are estimated using one-year daily returns as of September 16, 2011.

Chong, Pfeiffer, and Phillips (2011) had explored the dual-beta model's efficacy in containing risk during stock market downturns and found it superior to the standard CAPM beta, while Chong and Phillips (2011) provided the theoretical basis for the relevance of the dual-beta model.

ANSCOMBE'S QUARTET

Anscombe (1973) gives four different data sets which all produce the same regression results. Figures 1 through 4 show the four different data sets for Anscombe's quartet. All four data sets give the following results:

$$Y = 3 + 0.5X \quad (3)$$

Figure 1: Anscombe (1973) Data Set 1

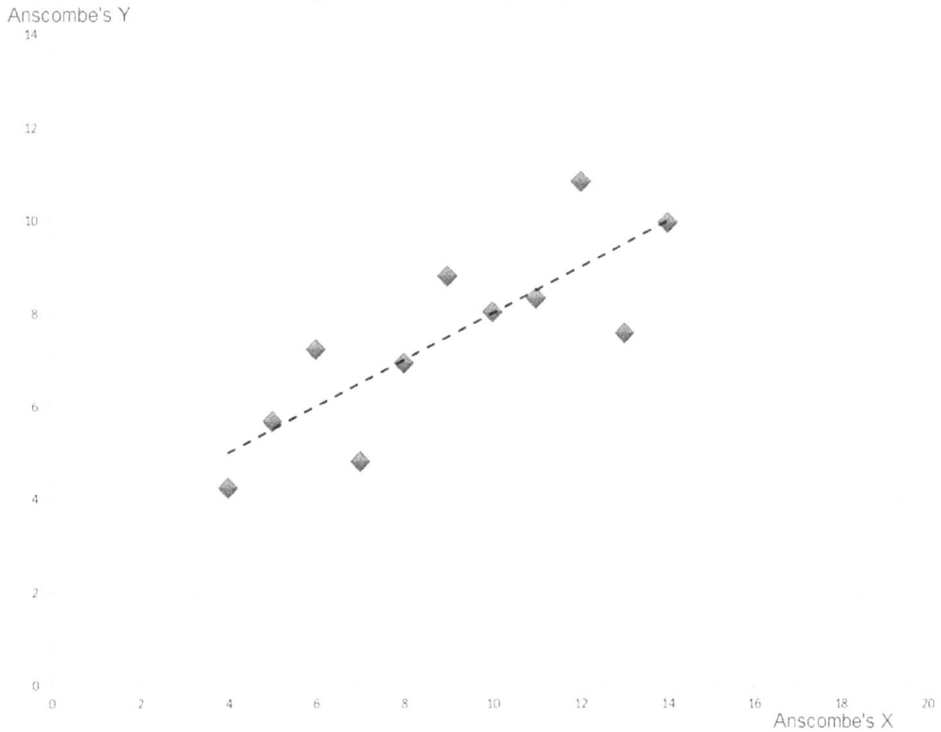

Clearly, Equation (3) does not adequately describe the data displayed in Figures 2 to 4, even though the results are accurate for all four figures. The data in Figure 2 would be better described by a non-linear equation than a simple linear regression model. If you take away the outlier in Figure 3, it looks like the intercept would be higher than 3 and the slope lower than 0.5. In Figure 4, most of the data points have the same X value and form a vertical line. Like Figure 3, only one point or outlier forces the regression to have the same outcome as the others. Only Figure 1 displays data that one would typically imagine after seeing Equation (3). Anscombe's point is that just looking at regression results without a data plot or more information can mislead the reader.

Figure 2: Anscombe (1973) Data Set 2

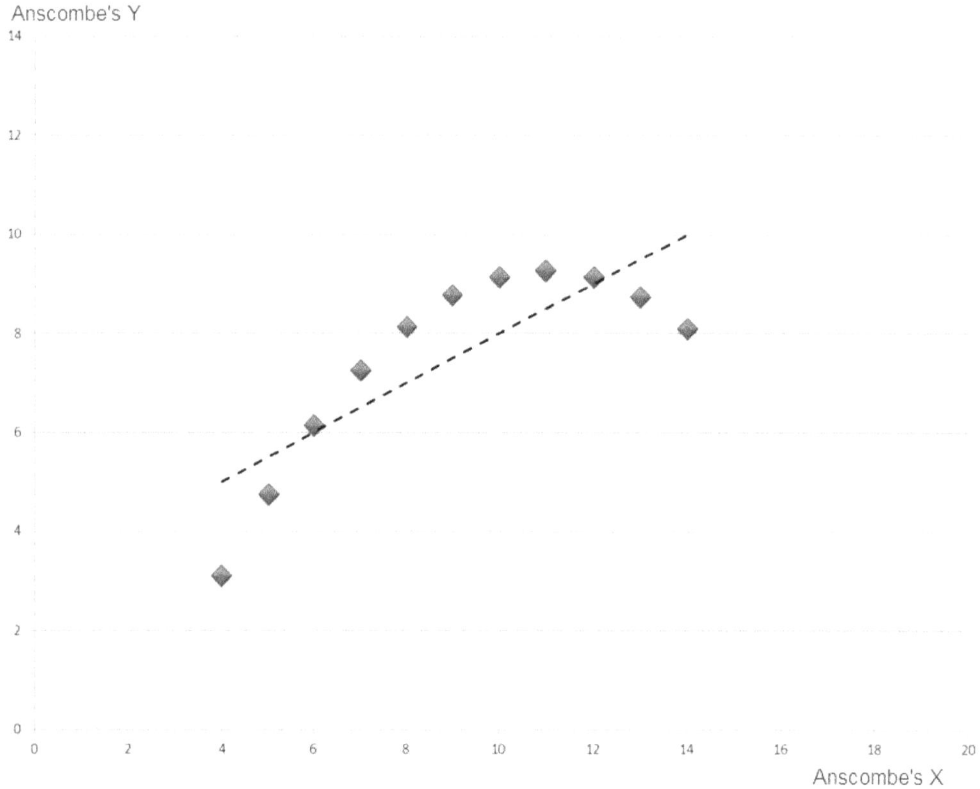

Figure 3: Anscombe (1973) Data Set 3

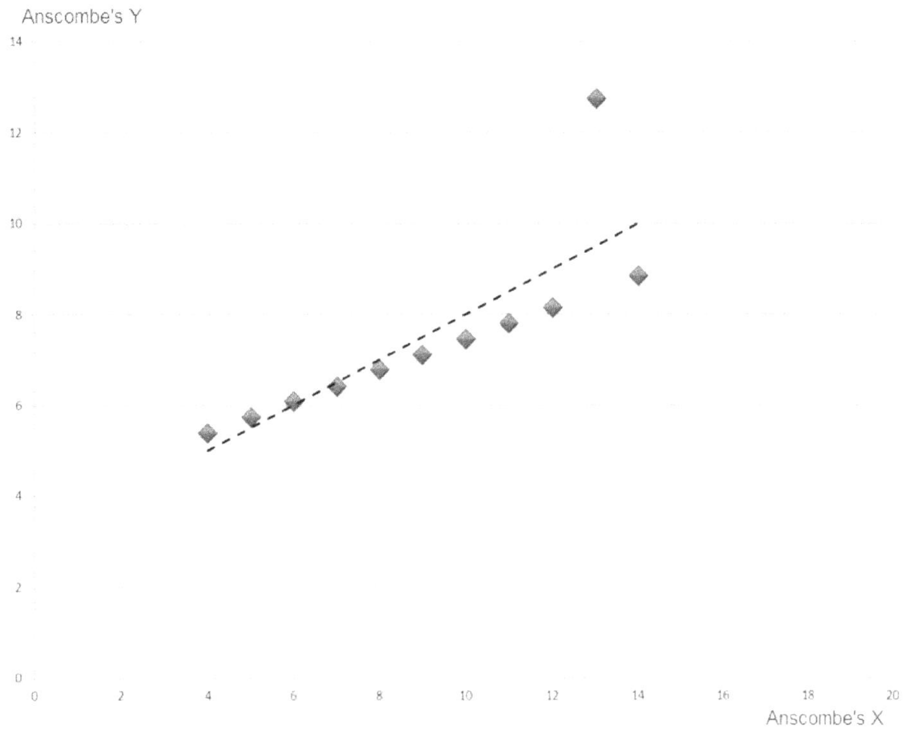

Figure 4: Anscombe (1973) Data Set 4

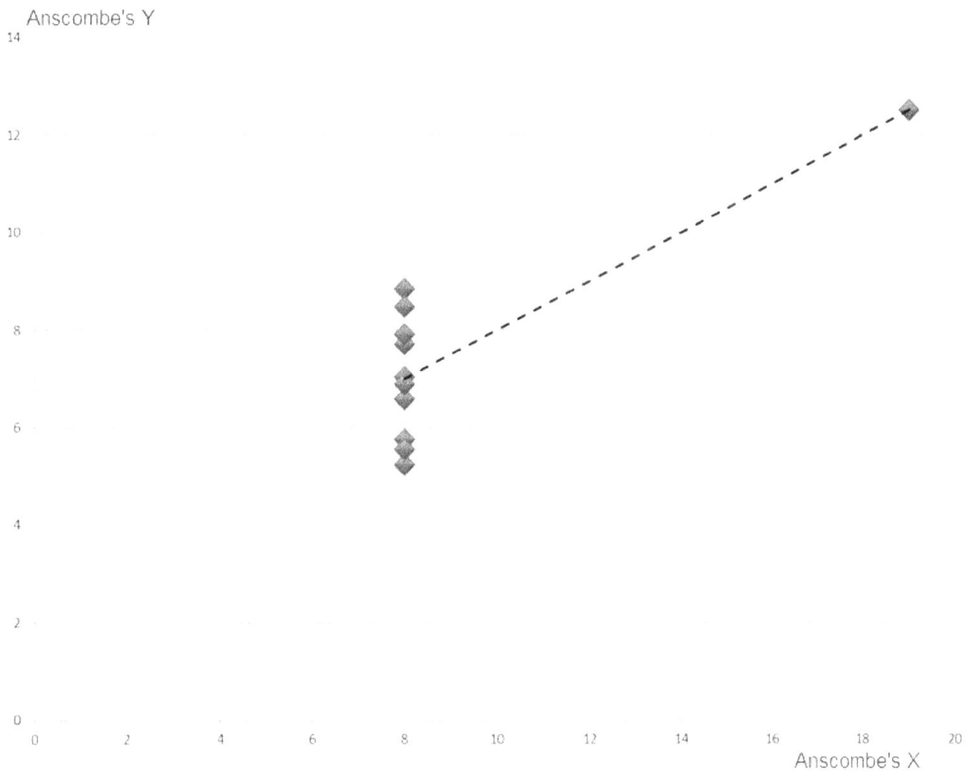

Figure 5 shows the up-market and down-market betas for 39 mutual funds. All 39 funds have an overall standard CAPM beta of 1.1. Figure 5 shows the great variety of up- and down-market betas that can result in a traditional beta with the same value. As discussed above, similar to Anscombe's quartet, investors considering a stock or mutual fund can be misled by examining one value for beta for both up- and downturns in the economy. Consider two mutual funds - MCVIX (MFS Mid Cap Value Fund) and SSMAX (SEI Institutional Investment Trust-Small/Mid Cap Equity Fund). MCVIX and SSMAX are observations 8 and 9 in Figure 5, respectively. Both these mutual funds have an estimated beta of 1.1. Both funds have the same alphas - 0.02. MCVIX has both an up-market beta and down-market beta of 1.1, so, in this case, the overall beta estimate of 1.1 gives an accurate picture for both up- and down-markets. SSMAX has an up-market beta of 1.28 and a down-market beta of 0.086. An investor who just looked at the typical beta estimate for each fund would think they are the same in terms of risk. MCVIX exhibits the same risk whether it is an up- or down-market with a beta of 1.1, but SSMAX is a very different investment, even though it also has a standard CAPM beta of 1.1. Note that the differences in betas here are relatively conservative since mutual funds rather than stocks are being used.

Figure 5: CAPM Beta, Up-Market Beta, and Down-Market Beta for 39 Mutual Funds

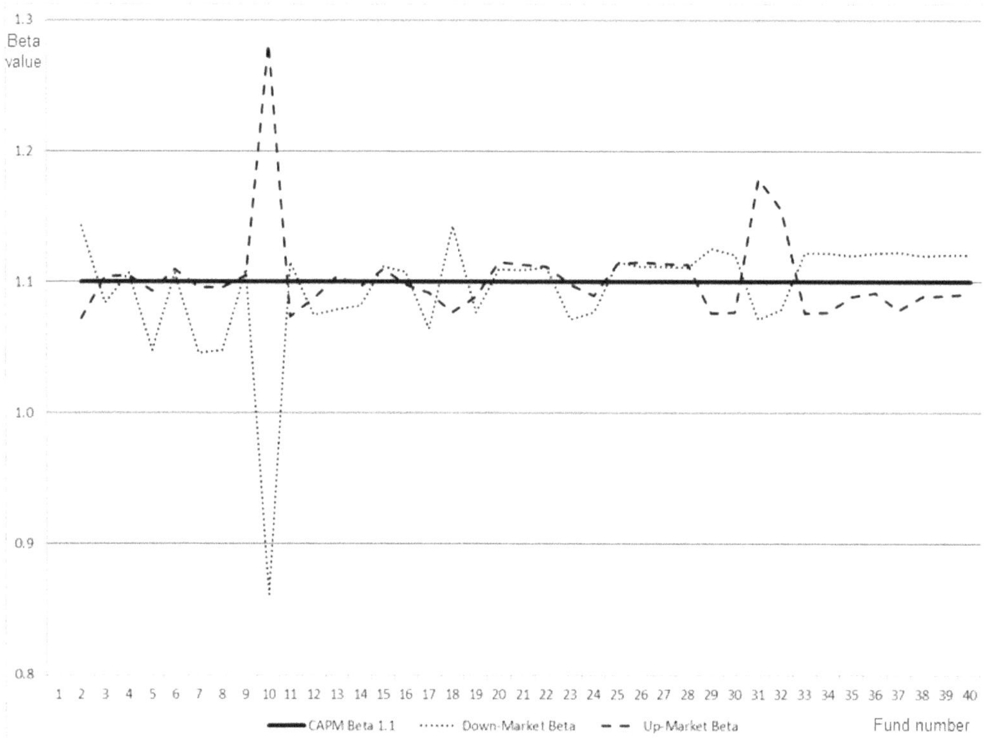

CONCLUSION

In finance, the use of beta as a measure of risk is well-known. Not as well-known is the use of separate beta estimates for up- and down-markets. Using one beta estimate to measure risk, rather than looking at both an up-market beta estimate and a down-market beta estimate, can mislead investors. We provide mutual fund examples showing how the possible confusion arises and how this problem is analogous to the problem explored in Anscombe (1973) that very different data sets can lead to the exact same regression results.

Using these examples, investment professors may be able to better motivate the discussion of dual-beta models while reinforcing better data analysis practices, such as looking at data charts rather than simply numerical summaries.

AUTHOR INFORMATION

James Chong, Ph.D., is a Professor and Associate Director of the Center for Financial Planning and Investment at California State University, Northridge. He also serves as a Research Economist at MacroRisk Analytics. He received his Ph.D. in Finance from the ICMA Centre, The University of Reading. E-mail: jchong@csun.edu

Dennis Halcoussis, Ph.D., is Professor of Economics at California State University, Northridge, where he teaches courses in econometrics and data analysis. He is the author of the popular textbook "*Understanding Econometrics*" and is the author of numerous papers applying econometric methods to diverse economic topics. He received his Ph.D. from the University of Pennsylvania in 1992. E-mail: dhalcoussis@csu.edu

G. Michael Phillips, Ph.D., is the Director of the Center for Financial Planning and Investment and a Professor of Finance, Real Estate, and Insurance at California State University, Northridge. He also serves as Chief Scientist for MacroRisk Analytics. He received his Ph.D. from the University of California, San Diego, with specializations in econometrics and applied economics. E-mail: mphillips@csun.edu (Corresponding author)

REFERENCES

1. Anscombe, Francis J. 1973. "Graphs in Statistical Analysis", *The American Statistician* 27(1), 17-21.
2. Chong, James, Shawn Pfeiffer, and G. Michael Phillips. 2011. "Can Dual Beta Filtering Improve Investor Performance?" *Journal of Personal Finance* 10 (1), 63-86.
3. Chong, James, and G. Michael Phillips. 2011. "Beta Measures Market Risk Except When It Doesn't: Regime-Switching Alpha and Errors in Beta", *Journal of Wealth Management* 14(3), 67-72.
4. Fama, Eugene F., and Kenneth French. 1992. "The Cross-Section of Expected Stock Returns", *Journal of Finance* 47(2), 427-465.
5. Scholes, Myron, and Joseph Williams. 1977. "Estimating Betas from Nonsynchronous Data", *Journal of Financial Economics* 5(3), 309-327.
6. Todorov, Viktor, and Tim Bollerslev. 2010. "Jumps and Betas: A New Framework for Disentangling and Estimating Systematic Risks", *Journal of Econometrics* 157(2), 220-235.

Walnut Oak Press Valuation Reference Series

Financial Data Estimates

Beta Estimates for Valuation and Cost of Capital: CAPM, Down-Market, and Up-Market Betas by Industry is a series of books published quarterly that provides betas, up-market betas and down-market betas of common stocks, preferred stocks, and mutual funds. The data for common stocks and preferred stocks are grouped by SIC codes. The data for mutual funds are provided by peer groups. Unlike other reference books that usually include only the average or median betas, these books also include different percentiles to provide the reader with additional information to value companies. Valuation analysts would find these books helpful when conducting valuation of companies in different industries.

(Volumes are available with quarterly updates beginning with End of 4th Quarter, 2016.)

Beta Estimates for Valuation and Cost of Capital: CAPM, Down-Market, and Up-Market Betas by Industry (G. Michael Phillips, William P. Jennings, James Chong, George Arzumanyan)

Book sections available as separate eBook purchases include tables for

Common Stocks
Preferred Stocks
Mutual Funds

Sample Size Illustrations, Confidence Intervals, & Margins of Error

The *Sample Size Illustrations, Confidence Intervals, & Margins of Error* volumes provide sample size illustrations with corresponding confidence intervals and margins of error at the 80, 85, 90, 95, and 99 percent confidence levels. These books will help you determine the sample size, for a particular population size, which would not result in the margin of error exceeding your prespecified margin of error. For instance, what sample size should be taken from a population of 100 so that the sample results do not exceed 10 percent margin of error at the 80 percent confidence level?

The tables are calculated using the "population adjusted hypergeometric distribution" (sometimes called "hypergeometric distribution"). The calculations are performed using a variation of the Clopper-Pearson exact method to calculate confidence intervals.

Population sizes in these books range from one to 500. All integer population sizes are included between one to 250 after which the population size increases by 10 up to 500.

Tables for 80, 85, 90, 95 and 99 percent confidence levels can be purchased as separate volumes from Walnut Oak Press.

Sample Size Illustrations, Confidence Intervals, & Margins of Error: Hypergeometric Distributions Tables for Attorneys & Experts (George Arzumanyan, Dennis Halcoussis, G. Michael Phillips)

Walnut Oak Press Valuation Reference Series

Mortality Adjusted Valuation Factors

This series of reference works specializes in probabilities and factors which forensic economists, valuation experts, and attorneys will frequently find useful. Encompassing everything from age-based conditional probabilities of death and cumulative survival probabilities to factors made specifically for calculating the present values of remainder perpetuities and life annuities, this series provides professionals with estimators which cannot be found elsewhere.

(Volumes are currently available based on 2012 and 2013 life table data. The underlying data were published in 2016 and 2017.)

Mortality Factors for Valuation: Age-Based Cumulative Probabilities of Survival
(G. Michael Phillips, David Fractor, Dennis Halcoussis, Edward T. Garcia, Laurel J. Fish)

Mortality Factors for Valuation: Age-Based Conditional Probabilities of Death
(G. Michael Phillips, David Fractor, Dennis Halcoussis, Edward T. Garcia, Laurel J. Fish)

Mortality Factors for Valuation: Life Expectancy Based Remainder Perpetuity Present Value Factors
(G. Michael Phillips, David Fractor, Dennis Halcoussis, Edward T. Garcia, Laurel J. Fish)

Mortality Factors for Valuation: Probability Adjusted Remainder Perpetuity Present Value Factors
(G. Michael Phillips, David Fractor, Dennis Halcoussis, Edward T. Garcia, Laurel J. Fish)

Mortality Factors for Valuation: Single Life Annuity Present Value Factors
(G. Michael Phillips, David Fractor, Dennis Halcoussis, Edward T. Garcia, Laurel J. Fish)

For each Mortality Adjusted Valuation Factor series, sections available for separate eBook purchases include

United States Total Population
United States Male Population
United States Female Population
United States White Population
United States White Male Population
United States White Female Population
United States Black Population
United States Black Male Population
United States Black Female Population
United States Hispanic Population
United States Hispanic Male Population
United States Hispanic Female Population
United States Non-Hispanic White Population
United States Non-Hispanic White Male Population
United States Non-Hispanic White Female Population
United States Non-Hispanic Black Population
United States Non-Hispanic Black Male Population
United States Non-Hispanic Black Female Population

www.ingramcontent.com/pod-product-compliance
Ingram Content Group UK Ltd.
Pitfield, Milton Keynes, MK11 3LW, UK
UKHW051508290926
15471UKWH00008B/1502

9 780998 907796